THE HOLY GRAIL

WORKS ON *THE SECRET TRADITION* By Arthur Edward Waite

THE PICTORIAL KEY TO THE TAROT. Being fragments of a secret tradition under the veil of
divination. With 78 plates in full color, illustrating
the Greater and Lesser Arcana, from designs by
Pamela Colman Smith.

SEVENTY-EIGHT TAROT CARDS IN FULL COLOR.
Created by Pamela Colman Smith and Arthur
Edward Waite.

THE HOLY KABBALAH. With an introduction by Kenneth Rexroth. A study of the secret tradition in
Israel as unfolded by Sons of the Doctrine for the
benefit and consolation of the Elect dispersed
through the lands and ages of The Greater Exile.

THE BOOK OF CEREMONIAL MAGIC. Complete
Grimoire. Part I, the Literature of Ceremonial
Magic, provides the key passages from the principal
texts of the 14th, 15th and 16th centuries. Part II
contains the complete Grimoire. Nine plates and 94
line illustrations.

THE BROTHERHOOD OF THE ROSY CROSS. Being
Records of the House of the Holy Spirit in its Inward and Outward History.

By ARTHUR EDWARD WAITE

The
HOLY
GRAIL

The Galahad Quest in the

Arthurian Literature

UNIVERSITY BOOKS, *New Hyde Park, New York*

Copyright new matter © 1961 by University Books Inc.

Library of Congress Catalog Card Number: 61-17178

Manufactured in the United States of America

INTRODUCTION by JOHN C. WILSON

Twelfth-century France produced the great bulk of the Arthurian literature, England and Wales came next, and then it spread to the rest of Europe. For nearly five hundred years, until well into the Sixteenth Century, the cycle of stories of the rise and fall of King Arthur's Round Table was popular in Europe. A glimpse of the popularity of this literature at its height (before printing, of course) is given by the fact that there survive a hundred manuscripts of one prose version, the Prose LANCELOT, written about the year 1215. When printing began, seven printed editions of it appeared in Paris between 1488 and 1533. It was toward the end of this original popularity, in 1485, that Caxton printed Sir Thomas Malory's version, MORTE D'ARTHUR. The new world of the arquebus and cannon overwhelmed the spear and sword of knighthood and the tales of chivalry were forgotten until a great new vogue began at the beginning of the Nineteenth Century, when the poet-laureate Robert Southey brought out a new edition of Malory, and the stories were told again by Wagner, Tennyson, Swinburne, Matthew Arnold. Today every schoolboy knows the stories of the Round Table and the continued interest of his elders is indicated by the fact that T. H. White's THE ONCE AND FUTURE KING became a best seller when it was published in 1958. White's book, in turn, provided the libretto for the enormously successful musical, *Camelot*.

It would seem from this account that the place of Arthurian romance is secure. But if we look a little more closely, the facts are not at all pleasant. It was inevitable, of course, that the original Arthurian literature written in the Middle Ages should no longer be read except by scholars and students. Even in translation most of it is no longer readable. But Malory's version, in modern spelling, remains intensely readable. Yet today you will no longer find in print an unexpurgated Malory in an attractively printed form (only the little volumes of the Everyman edition). What you find are numerous bowdlerized versions, spinsterishly edited for children.

Two things seem to have happened. One already began in Victorian times, the editing out of Malory of the two great stories of adultery which are everywhere interlaced in his tales, the liaisons of Lancelot and Guinevere, of Tristan and Isolt. The editing out, too, of the pre-marital and extra-marital amours of knights and ladies, also integral to Malory. Romantic love, in the days of chivalry was, almost by definition, outside marriage. This bowdlerization for sexual reasons has continued into our time, which remains Victorian enough in its attitude toward what school children may be allowed to read. Now, however, a second bowdlerization has been added which at first sight seems quite incomprehensible. Some case might be made out for keeping away from the children the fact that King Arthur was conceived in adultery, that he as well as his Queen was unfaithful to marriage vows, and that it was in incest with his sister that he became the father of the Sir Mordred who became his nemesis. I suppose the same criteria make it impossible to let our children know how Merlin was fathered by a demon but was saved for good by the fact that his mother did not know it was happening. But why should it be kept from the children that Lancelot was reared by the Lady of the Lake in a miraculous, inhuman land under waves? Or that the Grail King lies wounded in the thighs? Or that (like the candidate for the priesthood who slays his predecessor in Frazer's GOLDEN BOUGH) the Knight with the Lion weds the Lady of the Fountain as soon as he kills her husband? One can multiply these instances, and you can do this for yourself by opening any children's encyclopedia and see how it emasculates the Arthurian stories.

This second kind of bowdlerization is, I believe, usually not as conscious as the sexual bowdlerization. Ostensibly concerned with making the Arthurian stories more readable for children, it removes from them a great deal of both the pre-Christian magic and enchantments and the Christian mysticism connected with the quest for the Holy Grail. Usually all this emasculation is committed without explanation or apology. We are indebted to one editor for telling us why he did it. You will find his version in well-nigh every school and library, as you will not find Malory's. This editor says:

> Here, then, is MORTE D'ARTHUR as I hazard Malory might have edited it ...

In one phase only has the context of MORTE D'ARTHUR been altered. I have eliminated from the text the incidents in the search of the Holy Grail itself, and have retained as little as possible of the interrelated Joseph of Arimathea legend. I believe this unorthodox treatment is fully justifiable from a literary point of view.

Malory's tale is predominantly historical and factual in feeling; the story of the quest is predominantly allegorical. For this reason the quest itself, lacking the realism and earthy quality which stamp the far larger portion of MORTE D'ARTHUR, suffers greatly in comparison. Furthermore, these episodes, which must have had their source in monkish interpolation in earlier folk-lore, introduce monastic ideas of sin, chastity and penance entirely foreign to all other parts of the tale.

Malory's characters are dissolute, worldly, noble, ambitious, cruel and brave; his ladies quite amorous. The characters of the quest, however, are rarely human; rather are they religious abstractions . . . This, I feel, has given rise to a generally false impression of the tale and of the character of Arthur and his knights.

The quest is so foreign in its feeling that it is interesting, in the light of contrary popular impression, to note the attitude of Arthur towards it. He is "greatly displeased" at the departure of his knights and in sorrow says to Gawain, "ye have nigh slain me with the avow and promise that ye have made"; and then later, with tears in his eyes, he turns to Lancelot for counsel, "for I would that this quest were undone, as it might be."

This abridged edition, then, seeks to bring the original and to my mind the infinitely more amusing, interesting and adult MORTE D'ARTHUR within the scope of popular reading.*

This particular "editor" of Malory is, no doubt, more impudent and brazen than is typical. But what is typical is his denuding of Malory of all the mystical elements. His justification, of course, is beneath argument.

Why this flight from the magic and mysticism of the Arthurian stories? Be it understood, it is not the potential readers who

*Foreword from ARTHUR PENDRAGON OF BRITAIN, by John W. Donaldson. G. P. Putnam's Sons, New York, 1943.

are fleeing. T. H. White's THE ONCE AND FUTURE KING is steeped in the original spirit and has won and continues to win an ever growing audience. The non-existence of unbowdlerized Malorys may well mean that book publishers are passing up a good thing at this time. But the existence of bowdlerized Malorys, for which in large part educational authorities are responsible, does indicate the flight of these educational people and "authority" in general. Some of their reasons are clear. Roman Catholicism never had any enthusiasm for the Arthurian romances, even though on the surface they are full of respect for the church: the art of courtly love was once too powerful to be challenged by the church, but the church never countenanced it; likewise the pre-Christian magic and enchantment which pervade the stories—Merlin, as one student has well said, although the founder of the Round Table and the organizer of the quest for the Holy Grail, has no proper place in a Christian court, rather he is comparable to the *guru* as the house priest and master of the initiation ceremonies in India, or to the medicine man as the oracle and spiritual leader of the tribe. To put it quite bluntly, Merlin is the master of the entire cycle, but there is nothing Christian about him. Even the quest of the Holy Grail, which appears to be a tribute to Christianity, never won the good will of the church, and we shall see why before we are through. As for the Protestants, fleeing from relics and transubstantiation, they are quite likely to misunderstand the Holy Grail as a mystery of transubstantiation and the magic as superstition of the Middle Ages. Thus Christians of neither persuasion feel at home in the quest for the Holy Grail. Today it takes a polymorphist, one who can delve empathically in all the great religions, to understand the Holy Grail, to explain it to us, and inspire us to understand the present value of the quest.

Arthur Edward Waite is such a polymorphist. He would not protest our so naming him, even though he calls himself a Christian mystic. As he makes very clear in his book, he is utterly unsympathetic to the militancy of the Protestant sects. On the other hand, he knows very well that in the days when the church had the power he would have been slaughtered with the Albigensians and the Catharists. He considers as nothing less than anti-Christ the Pope who established the doctrine of transubstantiation and followed it up by proclaiming the Crusade against the

Albigensians. There is nothing literal in his Christianity, it is quite clear that like the Gnostics (he would have written about them next had he lived long enough) his Christ was not first born in Galilee but is eternal. What interests him in the Holy Grail is what interests him in Rosicrucian literature, in the Kabbalah, in Alchemy, in all the secret traditions. What interests him is the journey of the soul, by whatever name it is called. It is the ecstasy of the mystic.

Now the ecstasy of the mystic is not for all. It is, in fact, for the very few. The secret is there for all who can and will seek it but very few can and will. The many settle for the established church or churches, or make new ones, and look askance at the mystics who do not oppose them but who also do not agree with them. Closest to A. E. Waite's heart, I think, are those mystics who managed to be themselves and carried out their meditation without coming into conflict with the church into which they were born, whatever that church was. This attitude arises not from prudence but from the deepest conviction that nothing doctrinal or theological matters literally.

What draws A. E. Waite to the Holy Grail is that, beneath its pious surface, it is as subversive as is all true mysticism. In the face of the Latin rite, "the Grail is an early recognition that doctrinal teachings are symbols which are no more meant for literal acceptance than any express fables." The same thing is meant when he says: "The quest is not pursued with horses or clothed in outward armor, but in the spirit." Christ's blood in the Grail Cup is there and it is not there. "It is like the Cup of the Elixir and the Stone of Transmutation in Alchemy—described in numberless ways and seldom after the same manner; yet it seems to be one thing under its various veils, and blessed are those who find it."

Interlaced in the Arthurian romances are assertions and stories which, had they been uttered in the name of religious doctrine, would have won the speaker a martyr's death. Such is the claim that Christ passed on to Joseph of Arimathea (apocryphal uncle of Mary) certain words of power, Secret Words, and that these have been passed on ever since. This would mean, of course, words of power outside the church. Such is the claim that Joseph's son was invested by Christ as the first Bishop. Such is the claim that Joseph and/or his son brought the Holy Grail to

England and that a line of Grail Kings or Grail Keepers continued in its possession. This would mean a super-apostolical
succession independent of the church. Such is the claim that the
Holy Grail was taken up to heaven, for how can there be such
holy doings without the church? All this expresses an undertone
of dissent from Rome, but what draws Waite's interest is that
the dissent does not take the form of sectarian literalness but
the mystic road of symbolic expression. For this is the road of
mysticism at its highest.

A. E. Waite says all this better than I can and more profoundly, but his method of exposition may cause difficulties to
the unaccustomed reader. That is why I want to provide the
reader with this quick description of Waite's own view, as a
touchstone with which it may be easier to make one's way into
his book. For Waite is a great polemicist, who in all his books
develops his position by counterposing it to all other views. Since,
by and large, he is generally in the right, and his opponents quite
wrong-headed, and since he does not suffer fools gladly, there
is a good deal of fur and sparks in the air. It is characteristic of
all of Waite's books that at least some of the most important
matters to be divulged are saved for the very last chapter. In
this case, too, this is so, for the last chapter is quite correctly
called "The Secret of the Holy Grail." What is more, among the
appendices, and again, characteristically, among the very last of
the appendices, is a very important note showing quite convincingly that the four Hallows of the Holy Grail are identical with
the four suits of the Tarot cards. The unaccustomed reader will
not be cheating, nor will he spoil the book for himself, if he reads
the last chapter and the appendices first. I am confident they will
send him back to the beginning of the book, quite eager to read
the rest.

It will help the reader, also, to know clearly against whom
Waite's polemics are directed. Those aimed at unscholarly and
wishful-thinking occultists are, I think, quite clear, and require
little explanation. It is quite well known that he was the scourge
of all fake Rosicrucians and other secret societies making fraudulent claims to antiquity. It was against such mountebanks that
most of his books are directed.

In this book, too, he gives them hard blows, but here his main
polemics are aimed at the class of scholars who professionally

devote themselves to the Arthurian literature of the Middle Ages. What do they do with this literature? In Waite's eyes, they search for its antecedents as if these antecedents are sufficient in themselves to account for the literature. Everything antecedent is equally important. One endless consequence of this procedure is to attribute everything in the literature to pre-Christian origins. Behind the decorum of the archeologist and the philologist there is often the gleeful snicker of the village atheist. More often, however, the search for an infinite regression of antecedents produces a potpourri of folklore material, some of which may be useful, some interesting but irrelevant, and a good deal of it neither interesting nor relevant.

It is important to understand Waite's legitimate objections to this kind of scholarship. I shall cite two philological examples from the work of Roger Sherman Loomis, the reigning scholar in this field.* Loomis seeks antecedents for GAWAIN AND THE GREEN KNIGHT, and finds them in early Irish epics in which the giant is not green but black; he concludes that the color green came into the legend through the fault of a mistranslation of the Irish word *glas,* which can mean either "gray" or "green." The great Sanscrit scholar, Heinrich Zimmer, whose spirit is akin to A. E. Waite, gently suggests to Loomis that even if this were so, the green color is appropriate to the character of the giant and "It must have been regarded as such by both the narrator and his audience." For who is this giant Green Knight? In this story it is safe to assume that he is Death. Zimmer adduces examples of the use of pale green in Buddhist art to denote death, but the main point is, to repeat, "the color is appropriate to the original character" and "It must have been regarded as such by both the narrator and his audience," or it would not have been told for hundreds of years? Another Loomis example is the very heart of the question of the Holy Grail. In this book Waite deals very fully with a complicated series of instances in which the Holy Grail at times serves as a horn of plenty, feeding in one case the whole Round Table, other instances in which it is no horn of plenty but does appear to feed materially the Fisher

*The latest work from his hand, which brings together his own work, the work of his peers, Frappier of the Sorbonne and Vinaver of Manchester, plus all their disciples, is: ARTHURIAN LITERATURE IN THE MIDDLE AGES, A Collaborative History, Edited by Roger Sherman Loomis, Oxford University Press. 1959.

King's father and, finally, instances in which there is no idea of material feeding but only of spiritual food. Waite makes plain his preference for the latter instances as the significant aspects of the Legend of the Holy Grail. This is not an arbitrary choice by him; what he is saying is that the horn of plenty is part of pagan lore and provides no clue to the development of spiritual life, whereas the instances in which the Holy Grail appears in a purely spiritual role, while they may well exemplify the Christianizing of pagan tales, are precisely what is *new*, vital and pregnant of meaning. Otherwise the final ecstasy of Sir Galahad can never be understood in any terms. Is not all this self-evident? Yet Loomis in his latest book once again offers the explanation that the transition from the drinking horn of plenty to the Holy Grail can be explained philologically by the fact that the ancient Welsh and Old French word for horn (*cors*) is the same as the word for body (*cors*). Any summary of Loomis' position must sound like a burlesque, the reader would have to read Loomis' own pages to assure himself that I am not making fun of him.* Loomis thinks of everything except what is important: he does not deal with Joseph's Secret Words, nor the super-apostolic succession established by Joseph II, nor any of the other implications of the sense of new wonders which Waite shows to be central to an understanding of the legend of the Holy Grail.

It is Loomis' kind of reduction of the Christian symbols to their antecedents that Waite is fighting against. Waite puts it cogently and most soundly in the following words: "I know that every literature has its antecedents in some other literature, and that every religion owes something to a religion that preceded it. Sometimes the consanguinity is close and sometimes it is very far away. Only those who affirm that the one accounts for the other, and this simply and only, seem to be a little unwise. Christianity rose with Judaism and doctrinally out of Judaism, but this fact only brings their generic difference into greater relief. So also the Grail literature rose up in the Celtic Church; its

---

* "Thus we see that three of the queerest, most puzzling features of the sanctified Grail legend—the use of a dish, large enough to hold a salmon, as the receptacle for the Corpus Christi; the setting of a eucharistic feast, not in a church but in the hall of a castle named Corbenic or Cambenoyt; the identification of Joseph of Arimathea with the Fisher King—can be most satisfactorily explained by the confusion of *cors*, 'horn,' with *cors*, 'body,' by the substitution of the body of Christ, either in a literal or a sacramental sense, for a horn of plenty."—ARTHURIAN LITERATURE IN THE MIDDLE AGES. p. 289

analogies may be found therein; there may be many in folk-
lore; but there are also as many ways in which the one, as we
know it, does not account for the other, as we have it actually."
(Page 364)

So far we have been on the side of Waite. It is these views of
his which make this book so valuable. Before we close, however,
we must separate ourselves from Waite when he is manifestly
wrong.

We have already referred to the strange and unique role of
Merlin. He is Arthur's teacher, founder of the Round Table,
organizer of the quest for the Holy Grail, and his magic is
everywhere apparent. Waite never calls him magician, all his
references are always to "the Prophet and Magician." Waite
uses the biblical word "prophet," no doubt quite unconsciously,
to soften the word "magician." Waite treats of the end of Arthur
and the Round Table, but is silent about the end of Merlin.
The wizard has sent the knights off to the quest, but he gives
himself up to his fairy mistress, giving her his magic lore. And,
as Zimmer says: ". . . And all that she can think of to do with
it is to bewitch the master of magic himself. Thus the lord of
the enchanted forest is made spellbound, wittingly and willingly,
in his own domain, and by an enchanting fairy child who is the
incarnation of the magic depths of the forest itself."*

Here we see the arbitrary weakness of Waite's method. He is
as silent as he can be about Merlin because he knows very well
that by no stretch can Merlin be made to belong to the world of
Christianity, or higher mysticism of any kind. Merlin's magic
is a difficult problem for Waite, and it is not a new problem for
him. The close ties existing between religion and magic in every
time and place remain an insuperable problem for Waite. He
grapples with it without success in a number of his books. He is
unalterably opposed to magic in all its manifestations. The
subject fascinated him so that he wrote THE BOOK OF CERE-
MONIAL MAGIC, which remains the most complete grimoire ever
published, but he condemned the magic that he wrote about.
In THE HOLY KABBALAH, he vainly tried to separate Kabbalistic
wisdom from all magical elements. In THE PICTORIAL KEY TO
THE TAROT there is his equally vain attempt to separate the

---

*THE KING AND THE CORPSE by Heinrich Zimmer, p. 197.

Tarot cards as a repository of mystic initiation from the cards as a method of divination. The inextricable intertwining of magic and religion defeated him. It was his one fixed idea, or one might say it was the one point where he grew mistakenly literal, considering all magic as relics of a pagan and evil past.

That is why he steers clear not only of Merlin, but a great deal else in the Arthurian literature, limiting himself as well as he can only to matters connected to the Holy Grail. The rich results of his spiritual interest in the Holy Grail are spread out in this book and will be a memorable experience for the reader. The rich results of Waite's method could, however, apply also to the magical side of Arthurian literature. Unfortunately, those who professionally devote themselves to the Arthurian literature make very little contribution to this kind of study. In sharp contrast to their method is that of Heinrich Zimmer, the Sanscrit scholar whom we have already cited, who shares Arthur Edward Waite's spiritual interest. Arthurian literature is not his chosen field of endeavor, but he has shown what can be done with it in one long essay from which I have already borrowed his gentle rebuke to Loomis on the green giant and his characterization of Merlin. While Waite teaches us, and very well, that the quest of the Holy Grail seeks fresh mystic powers elsewhere than Rome and out of weariness with the Vatican, Heinrich Zimmer can put this in the same spiritual path but more broadly:

The growth of the heathen religions of northern Europe was nipped in the bud when the peoples who had practiced them came within the sphere of Christian influence. The church did more than Roman culture to deprive the mythology of the Celts, the Teutons, and the pre-Celtic primitive population of the British Isles of the old creed in which it lived, moved, and had its being. Nevertheless it survived, without foundation or foothold, no longer a cult, and shorn of its ancient ritual. As elsewhere under similar circumstances, mythology became transformed into poetry and saga, became secularized, and lost its binding power; and since in this form there was nothing about it that the church could attack, it continued to develop through the Middle Ages, supplying a rich nourishment for the soul, when the church with its theology of salvation had nothing comparable to offer. Medieval man dreamed out his broken youth in the images and figures of Celtic and pre-Celtic myths and sagas; and it was these, in the form of the Grail and other romances of the Arthurian cycle, that became the popular novels of the knightly and courtly circles of the whole of Europe.*

In the same essay, strangely enough, there is the following interpretation of the Major Arcana of the Tarot cards:

One of these, *The Fool,* bore no number; it was, apparently, the forerunner of the present-day Joker. The other twenty-one were numbered to denote an increasing series. Now it is my belief that the pictorial script of these face cards represented the degrees of an esoteric order of initiation, employing largely Christian signs, but masking the formulae of the heretical Gnostic teaching that was so widespread in Southern France up to the fifteenth century. The initiate, passing through twenty degrees of gradually amplifying enlightenment and beset by as many characteristic temptations, at last arrived at the stage of a mystical union with the Holy Trinity, and this is what was symbolized in the culminating image of the series, *The Dancing Hermaphrodite.* The Soul was the bride of the Lord; in the figure of the Hermaphrodite the two were one. The figure is immediately suggestive of the Dancing Shiva; Shiva unites in himself the female and the male.**

"The above seems not have been hit upon before," says Zimmer. The reader of Waite's PICTORIAL KEY TO THE TAROT and the appendix of the present book can correct Zimmer on this point. Waite was never quite free to tell us everything he knew about the Tarot cards, but it is quite clear that the Major Arcana represents the degrees of a secret society's initiation. Zimmer dismisses *The Fool* as of no moment but Waite calls it "the most speaking of all the symbols" and writes on it at length. And in Waite, too, the final climactic card is not a hermaphrodite but a beautiful female, *The World.*

All Waite's books belong under the heading of a study of the Secret Tradition in Christian Times. There are certainly times and places in which the Secret Tradition was actually embodied in an esoteric order and a system of initiations and written records. It is indubitable that the Tarot was among the appurte-

*THE KING AND THE CORPSE by Heinrich Zimmer, p. 181.   **Ibid, page 178

nances of such an order (I am not referring to the Order of the Golden Dawn to which Waite and the poet Yeats belonged, but to something much earlier.) Waite makes very clear, I think, that such an order, initiation and records are not necessarily in each case part of a secret tradition. Certainly he claims no evidence that such appurtenances were connected with the Secret Tradition of the Holy Grail. His book on the Rosicrucians offers no evidence of an actual order having been in existence at any time. He is at special pains to insist that the values of these Secret Traditions are not lessened by our failure to find them carried on for any time by an esoteric order, let alone one existing continuously over the centuries. Nor are the values of each of these Secret Traditions lessened by the plain fact that neither their ideas, literature or creators were necessarily connected with each other at any time nor continued each other's work. Nor should we mistakenly assume that the Secret Traditions necessarily result from the fact that inquisitors of Church and State were ready to rend limb from limb anyone calling himself an Alchemist, a Kabbalist or a Rosicrucian. Rather, in the end, the Secret Tradition is that which goes beyond the ken of the literal-minded many. Completed in 1933, THE HOLY GRAIL was Waite's last new contribution to the Secret Tradition. He died in 1940, at the age of 73.

PREFACE

I AM about to set forth after a new manner the nature of the Mystery which is imbedded in the old Romance-Literature of the Holy Grail. As a literature it can be approached from several standpoints ; and as it is needful on the ground of sincerity to establish my own view, even from the beginning, I have found that it has a direct consanguinity with other Mysteries, which belong to the more secret life of the soul. I propose to give a very full account of all the considerations involved and of the criticism which has arisen therefrom in various schools of thought. It comes about in this manner that there will be included the imperfect speculations of some who have preceded me and whose interest at a far distance is not utterly dissimilar to my own, though their equipment has been all too slight. The task will serve, among several objects, two which may be put on record at the moment : on the one hand and quite obviously, to illustrate the deeper suggestions of the Grail Legends and, on the other, certain collateral intimations which lie behind the teachings of the great Churches and are, in the official sense, as if beyond their ken. I should add that the undertaking has been imposed, in part if not entirely, through familiarity with analogical fields of symbolism, the correspondence of which must be unknown almost of necessity to students who have not passed beyond the normal fields of qualified speculation into those of more hidden research.

After adequate and sympathetic study of every hypothesis adopted or hazarded on the origin of the Grail Legend, its purpose and its term, there remain over various features of the Romances as things outside the general horizon of inquiry, and they are of the last and most real importance. For example, a scheme of criticism which fails to account for an almost *ab origine* claim on a concealed and super-valid mode of Eucharistic Consecration and, later on, for a Super-Apostolical Succession accounts for very little that matters finally.

It is indubitable that some slight acquaintance with the Legends of the Holy Grail can be presupposed in my readers ; but in many it will be so unsubstantial that I have concluded to assume nothing, save only that I am addressing those who, in some wise at least, are concerned with the Great Quest in one of its departments, if not indeed dedicated thereunto. I have returned from explorations of my own with a synopsis of the results obtained to shew them that the literature of the Grail is of kinship with our common purpose and that this also is ours.

In order to simplify the issues, all the essential materials have been so grouped that those for whom the bulk of the original texts is, by one or another reason, either partially or wholly sealed, may attain, in the first place, an accurate and sufficing knowledge of that which the writers of the several great Cycles understood by the Grail itself, and that also which was involved in the Quests thereof, according to the mind of each successive expositor. I have sought, in the second place, to furnish a reasonable conversance with the intention, whether manifest or concealed, which has been attributed to the makers of the Romances by various students of these in different countries and times. In the third place, there is presented the mystical side of the Legends as that only in which the Grail literature can repay pursuit. All great subjects bring us back to the one subject which alone is great ; all High Quests end in the Spiritual City ; scholarly criticism, primeval folk-lore and learned researches are little less than useless if they fall short of directing us to our true end. It is on such an understanding, and so only, that either authorised scholar or graduating pupil can reach those things which will recompense knowledge concerning the Vision and the End in Grail literature, as it remains to us in the forms that survive—in which forms the Mystery of the Holy Cup has been passed through the mind of Romance and has been deflected sometimes like a staff in a pool.

Let it be joined to this that the high spirit of the Quest of old may be with us as much in the contemplation of the literature of the Quest as if we were adventuring forth ourselves in search of the Grail Castle, the Chalice, the Lance and the Sword. Herein is the consecrating motive which moves through the whole investigation. So also the Mystery of Quest does not differ in its root-matter, or considerably in its external form, wherever we meet it : there are always certain signs by which we can recognise it and may know also its consanguinities and its lineage.

Essentially speaking, the long story of critical research has left the foundation problems of the Cycles not only unsolved but untouched. That research has subsided now so far as England is concerned, the star which rules it having moved Westward and having reached perhaps its zenith in the United States. It would seem an opportune moment to look back upon the subject at large, to ascertain where we stand therein and to indicate the direction in which we should look for further light, it may be, even the term of a long protracted inquest.

The talismans of the solar hypothesis which once explained everything have melted in the hands of those who held them up. For not a few among us the knell of Vegetation Gods has sounded some time since : it is realised now that the Rites of Adonis cannot explain a Mystery which knows nothing of a Dead or Risen God. Eleusis also throws no light thereon, because the rapture and restoration of Persephone are foreign to a Cycle of Romance in which no Goddess figures. Finally, a story without a Grail cannot explain a Grail story, whatever the age which we may assign provisionally thereto.

As scholarship, from time immemorial—that which remains authentic and that which has been exploded long ago—has been in search of a meaning behind folk-lore, custom, myth and Instituted Mystery ; and as, however baffled and discounted, the feeling that it all means something has persisted ; so when I met first (1) with an admittedly ancient Metrical Romance of the Holy Grail, telling of Secret Words handed down from Christ Himself, and (2) at a subsequent date, with another text affirming a Priesthood Consecrated by Him, from Him alone perpetuated and not through Church channels, I could do no otherwise than look for a meaning behind such strange clouds of intimation. I turned in all directions and produced an earlier record of Quests and Findings. The time has arrived to make a final and more methodical survey ; for it may be that my day is far spent, that it is vain to hope for a life of research prolonged and that I can plan only for a space in which to revise, offer summaries in fine and deliver the last messages. The Secret Tradition in Christian Times has been the chief study of my literary life, and I have collected so far into their ultimate forms the records of exploration through the years into the Alchemical Tradition, Jewish Kabbalistic Theosophy and the LEGENDA AUREA of the Rosy Cross. Here now is my final construction and interpretation of the Grail Mythos, that which lies behind it included and whatever is connected therewith. As in the other cases, so here, it embodies in reconstructed form all that I have written on this subject, so far as I have proposed to preserve it. The Tradition in Emblematic Freemasonry, authentic or putative, is the next path before me and is one of peculiar difficulty because of its manufactured nature. The other Schools were things of natural growth, but this is very curious invention superimposed upon a slight basis of Operative Myth.

There is one thing further which it may be proper to add in concluding these prefatory words. I have adhered to the old orthography of Sir Thomas Malory and his beloved printer Caxton in respect of certain Knightly names, because it has been consecrated and made familiar by the use and wont of generations and even centuries. Tristram, Bors and Kay, Balyn and Balan, a dozen other Companions of the Round Table, are familiar in this spelling as household words and not under the variants of the original French texts. The orthography of MSS. especially was a chaos at that remote period ; but there is a fashion pursued in these matters, to conform with which, for the benefit of all concerned, the salient distinctions are given throughout in the index.

CONTENTS

BOOK V

THE VULGATE CYCLE OF THE HOLY GRAIL

BOOK VI

OTHER AND LATER TEXTS OF THE GRAIL LEGEND

BOOK VII

THE GERMAN CYCLE OF THE HOLY GRAIL

BOOK VIII

WELSH AND ENGLISH TEXTS

BOOK IX

CRITICAL APPARATUS IN RESPECT OF THE GRAIL CYCLES: CELTIC HYPOTHESIS

Book X

FURTHER CRITICAL APPARATUS: THE SCHOOLS, THE CHURCHES, AND THE SECTS

Book XI

FURTHER CRITICAL APPARATUS: THE RITUAL HYPOTHESIS

Book XII

THE SECRET OF THE HOLY GRAIL

APPENDICES

BOOK I

THE HOLY VESSEL AND ITS LITERATURE

THE ARGUMENT

I. SOME ASPECTS OF THE GRAIL LEGEND.—The Word which came forth out of Galilee—The Sacramental Vessel—Its History and the Quests thereof —The Grail in the Books of Chivalry—The Grail in modern poetry—The composite elements of the Legend—The Grail as a Reliquary. II. EPOCHS OF THE LEGEND.—The Higher Understanding of the Quest—The Outlook of Romanticism—The Attitude of Poetry—The Direction of Archæology— The prospect which is called Spiritual—The consideration of the present thesis—The Hidden Motives of the Literature—Concerning the Interpretation of Books. III. THE LITERATURE OF THE CYCLES.—Its various Modes of Classification and that Mode which is most proper to the present Inquiry—The Places of the Grail Legends—The Welsh Peredur and the English Sir Percyvelle—The Conte del Graal—The Lesser Chronicles of the Holy Grail—The Vulgate Cycle of the Holy Grail—The German Cycle—The question which is posed for consideration. IV. FURTHER CONSIDERATIONS RESPECTING THE SEVERAL GROUPS OF TEXTS.—The first consideration concerning a Concealed Sense of the Literature The Secret Words of Consecration and what follows therefrom, namely, that a true Mass has never been said in the world since the Grail was taken away—The Super-Apostolical Succession, the peculiar Divine Warrants and Ecclesiastical Pre-Eminence claimed for the Grail Keepers—That these claims must be distinguished from errors of doctrinal confusion and theological ignorance, of which there is evidence otherwise—That any concealed sense must be held to co-exist with manifest insufficiency, even within its own province, and more especially regarding the Eucharist—The Lesser Implicits of the Literature.

THE HOLY GRAIL

BOOK I

THE HOLY VESSEL AND ITS LITERATURE

I

SOME ASPECTS OF THE GRAIL LEGEND

THERE are a few Legends which may be said to stand forth among the innumerable Traditions of humanity, wearing the external signs and characters of some inward Secret or Mystery which belongs rather to eternity than to time. They are in no sense connected one with another—unless, indeed, by certain roots which are scarcely in time and place—and yet by a suggestion which is deeper than any message of the senses each seems appealing to each, one bearing testimony to another, and all recalling all. They kindle strange lights, they awaken dim memories in the antecedence of an immemorial past.[1] There are also other Legends— strange, melancholy and long haunting—which seem to have issued from the depths of aboriginal humanity, below all horizons of history, pointing, as we might think, to terrible periods of a past which was of the body only, not of a soul in man. To the latter class belongs part of what remains to us from the folk-lore of cave-dwellers, the Traditions of pre-Aryan races of Europe, as well as those Crafts and Arts which pass under the conventional but incorrect name of super- stition,[2] the records of Savage Sorcery and Diabolical Magic. To the former class, among many others, belongs the Grail Legend, which in all its higher aspects is to be grouped among the Legends of the Soul.

The Mystery of the Grail is, *ex hypothesi*, a word which came forth out

---

[1] The meaning is that these roots are not discovered by research and do not belong to history : they are recognised by authentic intuitions of the soul ; and because this kind of clairvoyance lies at the poles asunder from the common substitutes of professional psychism, those who possess the gift do not bear witness concerning it or parade its fruits.

[2] It has been pointed out truly that superstition connotes a survival of the sign when the thing signified has passed from all living memory. The practices to which I refer do not answer to this valid use of the word. They were acts of vital faith and their efficacy was unquestioned.

of Galilee. The literature which enshrines this Mystery, setting forth the circumstances under which it was from time to time discovered and, in fine, its imputed removal, with all involved thereby, is one of such considerable dimensions that it may be described accurately as large. This notwithstanding, there is no difficulty in presenting its broad outlines, as they are found in the texts which remain, with such reasonable simplicity that if there be anyone who is new to the subject, he can be instructed sufficiently for my purpose even from the beginning. It is to be understood therefore that the Holy Grail is represented invariably, excepting in one German version of the Legend, as that Vessel in which Christ either celebrated the Last Supper or consecrated for the first time the Elements of the Eucharist. It is therefore a Passover or Sacramental Vessel,[1] and, according to the Legend, its next use was to receive the Blood from the Wounds of Christ when His body was taken down from the Cross or, alternatively, from the side which was pierced by the Lance of Longinus. The Grail is a permanent Christian Reliquary from either point of view. Under circumstances which are recounted variously, the Vessel, its content included, was carried Westward in safe guardianship—coming, in fine, to Britain and there remaining, either in the hands of successive Keepers or in those of a single Warden, whose life was prolonged through the centuries. In the days of King Arthur the Prophet and Magician Merlin assumed the responsibility of carrying the Legend to its term, with which object he brought about the Institution of the Round Table ; and the flower of Arthurian Chivalry —Perceval, Lancelot, Gawain, Bors, Galahad, among many others— set out to find the Sacred Vessel. In two of the Quests which followed, the Knighthood depicted in the greater Romances became a Mystery of Ideality, and nothing save its feeble reflection could have been found on earth. The Quests were to some extent preconceived in the mind of the Legend ; but a few of them only were successful ; and that which followed thereafter was the removal or deeper concealment of the Holy Grail. The Companions of the Quest asked, as one may say, for Bread and to those who were unworthy there was given the stone of their proper offence, but to a few others the Spiritual Meat which passes all understanding. That this account instructs the uninitiated person most imperfectly will be obvious to anyone who is acquainted with the great body of the literature ; but, within the limits to which it is restricted, I do not know that if it were put differently it would prove to be more in harmony with the general sense of the Romances.

It might appear at first sight almost a superfluous precaution,

---

[1] The point of fact in both cases is that—figuratively speaking—the Last Supper fulfilled at once and abrogated the Old Law. The Passover dissolved into the Eucharist. And as regards the Grail Vessel, if it was the Dish of the Old Law it was transformed significantly into a Reliquary of the New ; while if it was the Cup of the New and Eternal Testament it was the Living Sign of the Presence in the World of Legend, which was also a World of Faith at the Grail epoch.

even in an introductory sketch, to reply so fully as I have done to the assumed question : What then was the Holy Grail ? Those who are unacquainted with its literature in the old Books of Chivalry, through which it entered first into the Romance of Europe, will know it by the IDYLLS OF THE KING. But it is not so superfluous as it seems, more especially with the class which I am addressing, since this has other concerns, like folk-lore scholarship ; and many answers to the question—based on the evidence of variant texts—would differ from that which is given by the Knight Perceval to his fellow-monk in the poem of Tennyson :—

> " What is it ?
> The phantom of a Cup which comes and goes ?—
> Nay, monk ! What phantom ? answered Perceval.
> The Cup, the Cup itself, from which our Lord
> Drank at the last sad supper with his own.
> This, from the blessed land of Aromat. . . .
> Arimathæan Joseph, journeying brought
> To Glastonbury. . . .
> And there awhile it bode ; and if a man
> Could touch or see it, he was heal'd at once,
> By faith, of all his ills. But then the times
> Grew to such evil that the Holy Cup
> Was caught away to Heaven and disappear'd." [1]

This is the answer with which, in one or another of its forms, chivalrous or poetic, everybody is expected to be familiar, or he must be counted as too unlettered for consideration, even in these introductory words. But it is so little the only answer, and it is so little full or exhaustive, that no person acquainted with the archaic literature would accept it otherwise than as one of its many aspects ; and even the enchanting gift of Tennyson's poetic faculty leaves something to be desired in Perceval's reply to the direct question of Ambrosius. Something of the quintessential spirit has evaporated in an obscure manner. There is a strange allusiveness, a pregnancy, a suggestion about the old Legend in its highest forms—as it is found, for example, in the longer prose chronicle of Perceval le Gallois, but yet more fully in the Quest *par excellence*, which is of Galahad, the *haut prince*.[2] A touch of it is found later in Tennyson's own poem, when Perceval's sister, the nun of " utter whiteness ", describes her vision :—

> " I heard a sound
> As of a silver horn from o'er the hills. . . .
> The slender sound
> As from a distance beyond distance grew
> Coming upon me. . . .
> And then
> Stream'd thro' my cell a cold and silver beam,
> And down the long beam stole the Holy Grail,
> Rose-red with beatings in it."

---

[1] THE HOLY GRAIL, edition of 1870.

[2] It is to be observed that this title is ascribed to him by Malory. See MORTE D'ARTHUR, *Lib*. XIII, *cap*. 4. The words are written on the Siege Perilous, where Galahad takes his place.

And again :—

> " I saw the spiritual city and all her spires
> And gateways in a glory like one pearl. . . .
> Strike from the sea ; and from the star there shot
> A rose-red sparkle to the city, and there
> Dwelt, and I knew it was the Holy Grail."[1]

So also in the Books of Chivalry the Legend is treated with an aloofness, and yet with a directness of circumstance and a manifoldness of detail, awakening a sense of reality amidst enchantment which is scarcely heightened when the makers of the chronicles testify to the truth of their story. The explanation is, according to one version, that it was written by Christ Himself after the Resurrection,[2] and that there is no clerk, however hardy, who will dare to suggest that any later scripture is referable to the same hand. Sir Thomas Malory, the last and greatest compiler of the Arthurian Legend, suppresses this hazardous ascription, and in the colophon of the seventeenth book his immortal printer, Caxton, is contented with adding that it is " a story chronicled for one of the truest and the holiest that is in this world ".

There is ample evidence no further afield than Malory's own work, the MORTE D'ARTHUR, that the Grail Legend was derived into his glorious codification from various sources and that some elements entered therein which are excluded by the description of Sir Perceval in the IDYLLS or by the colophon of Malory's twelfth book, which reads : " And here followeth the noble tale of the Sangraal, that called is the Holy Vessel and the signification of the Blessed Blood of our Lord Jesus Christ, blessed mote it be, the which was brought into this land by Joseph of Armathye : therefore on all sinful souls, Blessed Lord, have Thou mercy."

As an equipoise to the religious and devotional side of the Legend, it has been affirmed, as we shall see in its place, that more than one of the Grail Cycles took over something from Irish and Welsh folk-lore of the pagan period concerning a mysterious and magical vessel full of miraculous food. This is illustrated by the MORTE D'ARTHUR, in the memorable episode of the High Festival held by the King at Pentecost : in the midst of the supper " there entered into the Hall the Holy Grail, covered with white samite ; but there was none might see it nor who bare it. And there was all the Hall fulfilled with good odours, and every knight had such meats and drinks as he loved best in this world." That is a state of the Legend which offers little connection with the Mystical Vessel carried out of Palestine, whether by Joseph or another ; but either the simple-minded chroniclers of the past did not observe the anachronism, if they married a Christian Mystery

---

[1] As I am dealing at the moment with the question of atmosphere and of intimation " high erected ", it signifies nothing that this lovely episode had no authority in the old texts.

[2] This claim appears in the Prologue to a Romance usually entitled the GRAND SAINT GRAAL.

to a cycle of antecedent fable, or there is an explanation of a deeper kind, in which case we may meet with it at a later stage of these studies.

We shall make acquaintance meanwhile successively with various entanglements which render the Grail Legend perhaps the most embedded of all Romance Cycles. I have said that the Sacred Vessel is sacramental in a high degree, at least in the later developments : it connects intimately with the Eucharist ; it is the most precious of all Relics in the eyes of all Christendom indifferently ; for, supposing that it were manifested at this day, I doubt whether the most rigid of Protestant Sects could do otherwise than bow down before it. And if at the same time the roots of it lie deep in folk-lore of the pre-Christian period, in this sense it is a Dish of Plenty, with abundance for an eternal festival, like that which the Blessed Bran provided for his heroic followers. So also from another point of view, it is not a Cup but a Stone ; and it came to this earth owing to the Fall of the Angels. In either case, it is brought to the West ; it is carried to the East again ; it is assumed into Heaven ; for all that we know to the contrary, it is at this day in Northumbria ; it is in the Secret Temple of a Knightly Company among the High Pyrenees ; and it is in the land of Presbyter Johannes. It is like the Cup of the Elixir and the Stone of Transmutation in Alchemy—described in numberless ways and seldom after the same manner ; yet it seems to be one thing only under its various veils ; and blessed are those who find it.

II

EPOCHS OF THE LEGEND

A MINUTE inquiry into the materials and their sources of a moving and stately Legend is opposed to the purposes and interests of the general reader, for whom the Grail has two epochs only in literature, so far as England is concerned : they are those of Sir Thomas Malory and the IDYLLS OF THE KING. As Tennyson was indebted mainly to Malory, except for things of his own invention, so it is through his gracious poems that many people have been sent back to the old Book of Chivalry from which he reproduced his motives and sometimes derived his words. But without entering into the domain of archæology, even some ordinary persons, and certainly the literate reader, will know well enough that there are branches of the Legend, both old and new, outside these two palmary names, and that some of them are close enough to their hands. They may be familiar with the Cornish poet, Robert Stephen Hawker, whose QUEST OF THE SAN GRAAL[1] has, as Madame de Stael

[1] POETICAL WORKS OF ROBERT STEPHEN HAWKER, Vicar of Morwenstow, Cornwall. Original edition, 1879.

once said of Saint-Martin, " some sublime gleams ". They will have realised that the old French Romance of Perceval le Gallois, as translated into English of an archaic kind, ever beautiful and stately, by the late Dr. Sebastian Evans, is a gorgeous chronicle, full of richly painted pictures and endless pageants.[1] They will know also more dimly that there is a German Cycle of Grail Tradition—that Titurel, Parzival, Lohengrin, to whom a strange and wonderful life beyond all common teachings of Nature, all common conventions of Art, has been given by Wagner, are also legendary heroes of the Holy Grail. In their transmuted presence something may have hinted to the heart that the Quest is not pursued with horses or clothed in outward armour, but in the spirit along a *via mystica*.

There are therefore, broadly speaking, three points of view, outside all expert evidence, as regards the whole subject, and these are :—

(1) The Romantic, and the reversion of literary sentiment at the present day towards Romanticism will make it unnecessary to mention that this is now a very strong point. It is exemplified by moderately serviceable editions of the MORTE D'ARTHUR intended for general reading ; by others produced for students ;[2] by illustrated editions which are works of art ; nor less indeed by those which have been modified in the interests of youth, and in which a large space is given always to the Grail Legend. They follow one another, even to this day, a shadowy masque, not excepting, at a far distance, some obscure and illiterate versions in dim byways of periodical literature.[3]

(2) The Poetic, and having regard to what has been said previously, I need only affirm that it has done much to exalt and spiritualise the Legend without removing the romantic element ; but I speak here of modern invention. In the case of Tennyson it added that elevated emotion which belongs essentially to the Spirit of Romance, and this saved English literature during the second half of the nineteenth century. But taking the work at its highest, it may still be that the Grail Legend must wait to receive its treatment more fully by some poet who is to come. The literary form assumed by the Grail IDYLL OF THE KING—a tale within a tale twice-told—leaves something to be desired.

(3) The Archæological, and this includes naturally a number of branches, each of which has the character of a learned inquiry calling for special knowledge, and it is only of limited interest beyond the field of scholarship.

---

[1] THE HIGH HISTORY OF THE HOLY GRAAL, 1898 and 1903, the second or octavo edition being much better and adorned with pictures in the spirit of the story.

[2] There should be mentioned in this connection Dr. Oskar Sommer's magnificent edition of Vulgate Arthurian Texts prepared under the auspices of the Carnegie Institute.

[3] It is not always illiterate : there is the ever-memorable and desirable YOUNG FOLKS' BUDGET, in which William Sharp once had a hand, when Fiona Macleod was immanent as yet in his consciousness. And there Roland Quiz—who was Quittenton —wrote about a transfigured Jack and the Beanstalk, who became JACK THE VALIANT and an Arthurian Knight. There also in a long sequel Tor of the Round Table was Companion to Jack the Valiant. And Proctor drew the great page pictures from issue to issue through many moons of dream.

Outside these admitted aspects which lie, so to speak, upon the surface of current literature, there is a fourth point of view which has been in course of emerging for some years past, though scarcely into public view : it is only in an accidental and sporadic fashion that it has entered as yet into the written word. For want of a better term it must be called spiritual : it cares little for the archæology of the subject, little for its romantic aspects, and possibly rather less than little for the poetic side. It would know scarcely of Hawker's QUEST— not that it signifies vitally—and would be disposed to contemplate the Grail exclusively as one of the Legends of the Soul : I might have said, as a Sacramental Legend ; but this point of view is not usual, nor is it found to an appreciable extent among those who hold extreme or any Eucharistic views. In other words, it is not specially a High Anglican or a Latin interest : it characterises rather those who regard Religious Doctrine, Institute and Ritual as things typical or analogical, without realising that they may rank as such among Channels of Grace. So far as their conception has been put clearly to themselves, they look upon the Grail as an early recognition that doctrinal teachings are symbols which are no more meant for literal acceptance than any express fables. It includes also a hazardous inquiry into obscure Migrations of Doctrine from East to West, outside the Christian aspects of Grail literature.[1] This view appreciates perhaps only in an ordinary degree the evidence of history, nor can history be said to endorse it in existing forms of presentation. At the same time it is much too loose and indeterminate to be classed as a metaphysical construction of certain facts manifested in the life of a literature. It is a consideration of several serious but not fully equipped minds, and in some cases it has been impeded by sentimental aspects ; but the reference made here enables me to add that it might have reached a better term in stronger and surer hands. No one can read the available Romances without seeing that the Legend has its spiritual side, though it may have that also which connects with folk-lore. No further afield than the MORTE D'ARTHUR—where it embodies the Quest of Galahad—the theme is treated openly as an allegory, where episodes have a supernatural meaning, which is explained sometimes in rather a tiresome manner.

Superfluities and misinterpretations notwithstanding, it is directly or indirectly from the fact of this spiritual side, thus designated tentatively, that the present thesis emerges as its development and final term. The literature carries, moreover, on its surface the proof rather than the mere suggestion of a hidden motive as well as a hidden meaning, and three sources of evidence can be cited on the authority of the texts : (1) Confessed allegory ; but this is occasional only, being

---

[1] LE VASE SACRÉ ET CE QU'IL CONTIENT, by Emile Burnouf, is a French case in point ; the late Mrs. Cooper-Oakley's MYSTICAL TRADITIONS is a typical English example ; and those who care to go in quest of a German instance may consult : CHRISTLICHE, THEOLOGIE, COSMOSOFIE NACH DEM ZEICHEN DES HEILIGEN GRAAL, under the pseudonym of Intermediarius, 1914, privately printed at Stuttgart.

confined to two branches. (2) Ideological metathesis, the presence of which is not to be confused with allegory. (3) Certain traces and certain express claims which tend to set the Custodians of the Holy Grail in a position superior to that of the Official Church, though the Cycles are not otherwise manifestly hostile to that Church.[1] On the contrary, its own language is spoken and its own doctrines are enforced apparently.

It must be understood otherwise that the critical difficulties of Grail literature are grave within their own lines and that authorities thereon have been in conflict over issues which, from their own standpoint, are occasionally not less than vital. This notwithstanding, the elements of the problem lie actually within a comparatively small compass, though scattered through a literature which is not readily available, while it is, for the most part, in languages very far from familiar to readers of modern French and German. It has been so far mainly in the hands of those who, whatever their claims, have no horizon outside the issues of folk-lore, and who, like other specialists, have been a little disposed to create, on the basis of their common agreement, a certain autocracy among themselves, recognising nothing beyond their particular canons of criticism and the circle of their actual views. To these views there is no reason that we ourselves should take exception : they are excellent in their way, but from time to time they may not happen to signify, unless antecedently or provisionally, for those higher consequences with which we shall be concerned here. The sincerity of scholarship imputes to it a certain sanctity, but in respect of these consequences most scholarship has its eyes bandaged.

III

THE LITERATURE OF THE CYCLES

SOME of my readers may remember the " heap of letters " which, according to Matthew Arnold, was put into the hand of man and out of which he was left to make what word he might and would. He produced many combinations, but ever was haunted by a feeling that the right and true word had not come out of the medley. The Cycle of the Holy Grail seems put into our own hands like counters which can be arranged after more than one manner : it came about therefore that through recent generations scholarship has been turning them over and over, while some who stand and watch have wondered whether they have found their true meaning.[2] It happens also, having regard to the complications of Grail literature, that what may obtain reasonably for a specific purpose will

---

[1] They are the very opposite, as we shall see, throughout.

[2] It is not, however, the only kind of watch which can be pictured in the Grail subject ; for scholarship may have watched—and perhaps rather disdainfully—the esoteric interpretations which have been offered from time to time of the past in England,

not conform of necessity to a given chronological order which on other considerations may be recommended to archæological research and maintained keenly till—as ever and continually—the makers of such research find cause to change their views. It will be pertinent therefore to say a few words about the classification adopted for these studies. In the first place, it should be indicated that my arrangement depends solely from the indubitable sequence of texts, as they stand now, and secondly, by an exercise of faith, from several palmary findings of scholarship itself. It follows that the disposition of the literature adopted for my own purpose is, on the evidence before us, a legitimate way in which to treat that literature. There are certain texts which arise out of one another, and it is a matter of logic to group them under their proper sections. It has been affirmed at its value that comparatively few documents of the general Cycle have reached us in their original form, even subsequently to that period at which several old Legends are thought to have been taken over in Christian interest, while others have been unified and harmonised so that they could be placed together in a series. It is the relation which has been thus instituted that I have sought to preserve, because among the questions posed for our consideration there is that of the motive which prompted various writers to create texts in succession, designed to follow from one another—although often of distinct authorship ; as also to re-edit earlier inventions ; and adjust works to one another with the object of presenting in a series of connected narratives the Mystery of the Holy Grail manifested in Britain. The bulk of the texts as they stand represents the acquisition completed and certain intentions exhibited to their highest degree. Hence an arrangement which shews this most plainly is for my object the reasonable grouping of all, that object depending from almost the last state of the literature and differing to this extent from ordinary textual criticism, to which the first state may be not only important but vital.

The Grail Cycle, as it is understood and as it will be set forth in these pages, belongs chiefly to France and Germany. Within these limits of place and language there is also a limit of time, for textual criticism has assigned, under specific reserves, the production of the chief works to a period of *circa* fifty years intervening between 1170 and 1220. As regards the reserves, I need mention only that the Romance-Histories of Merlin subsequent to the coronation of Arthur have not been regarded so far by scholarship as an integral part of Grail literature,[1] while one important German text has been ignored

France and Germany for the elucidation of the literature and that which lies behind it : it happens that too many of these could not have been proffered, had their writers any real knowledge. And there is more even than this ; for I think that some of us who have dwelt through the years in figurative Houses of the Grail, who know them in one sense as if from roof to basement, may be most of all disposed to feel that there is another door to open, leading to a more Secret Sanctuary, if only they could discover where it is.

[1] We shall see that Robert de Borron, who may be called the first historian of the Grail, wrote a poem on Merlin which had no other object than to indicate his intimate connection with the Holy Grail and its manifestation in Arthurian days. His story was retold in prose and long sequels were added thereto, actuated by the same motive.

practically in England. Seeing that within the stated period and perhaps later many of the texts were subjected, as just indicated, to editing and even to re-editing, it seems to follow that approximate dates of composition would be the most precarious of arrangements for my special design. As regards that course which I have chosen, the chief French Romances fall into three divisions and cannot be classified otherwise. The elaborate analyses of contents prefixed to these divisions will of themselves convey the general scheme ; but I speak of it more expressly in the present place because of the implicits with which we shall be concerned shortly.

It can be assumed as indubitably correct that the earliest Romances of the Holy Grail—certain speculative versions which have been supposed in the interests of folk-lore being set apart for obvious reasons —are the first portion of the CONTE DEL GRAAL, written by Chrétien de Troyes, and the metrical JOSEPH OF ARIMATHÆA by Robert de Borron, as the text now stands.[1] In the earlier records of criticism the preference was given to the latter in respect of date, but it is exercised now in favour of the former text. Ignoring the non-Christian Legends of Peredur, of Syr Percyvelle and a Bowl of Plenty—which will be considered in their proper place—there was another class of Traditions taken over in the interests of the Holy Grail. That the Arthurian Legend had pre-existed in a different form is shewn not only by incorporations of early chronicles, by Nennius and pre-Nennius, by William of Malmesbury, Layamon and Geoffrey of Monmouth, but by the early metrical literature of Northern and Southern France and possibly by a few late and isolated English texts, such as the fourteenth-century MORTE D'ARTHUR, which suggest older prototypes that are not now extant.[2] It is shewn otherwise by certain Welsh MABINOGION which represent indigenous, if not early Traditions, irrespective of others which derive from French sources. The Northern French Romances were reconstructed in the interest of Grail sub-surface design, whatever that may be held to have been. The most notable example in another sense is perhaps the Merlin Cycle, which took over floating Traditions concerning the Prophet and Enchanter, creating two divergent Romances, each having the object of connecting Merlin with the Grail. The general process was something after the manner following : (1) Lays innumerable, originally oral but drifting into the written form ; (2) the same Lays re-edited in an Arthurian interest ; (3) the Grail Mystery, at first independent of Arthurian Legend, or such at least is the recurring inference concerning it ; (4) the Grail Legend married to Arthurian Romance, the connection being at first incidental ; Arthurian Tradition after it had been assumed entirely in the interests of the Holy Grail.[3]

[1] The proposition brought forward by Hucher, its first and only editor, that a prose version of the JOSEPH is earlier than the metrical, has found practically no acceptance.

[2] It will be remembered that Layamon paraphrased LE ROMAN DE BRUT of Wace. There are two MORTE D'ARTHURS, an alliterative and a stanzaic, both of the fourteenth century.

[3] It has been so assumed in the great so-called Vulgate Arthurian Cycle, analysed in Book V of the present work.

I recur therefore to my original thesis, that there is one aspect at least in which for my purpose a superior importance resides not in the primordial elements of the literature—real or alleged—but in their latest and unified form. As a typical example, it is customary to recognise that there was an early state of the GRAND SAINT GRAAL which is not now extant. The text, as we have it, is later than most of the Cycle to which it belongs,[1] yet it poses as an introduction thereto. When a day came for the major branches of the literature to be brought together and harmonised, there is a sense in which the historical text was and remains entitled to the priority which it claimed ; but such priority is of course in respect of its place in a series and not in respect of time.

The reconstruction of Romances in the Grail interest must be distinguished, however, from innumerable alterations made otherwise by inventive scribes, but to which no ulterior motive can be attributed. There is further no difficulty in assuming (1) that the passage of folk-lore into Christian symbolical literature—if indeed it ever took place— may have followed a fixed plan ; (2) that when late editing exhibits throughout a number of texts some defined scheme of instituted correlation, there may have been again a design in view, and the actuality of such design is obviously one concern of our research.

The places of Grail Legend, its reflections and its rumours are France, Germany, England and Wales, Holland, Italy, Spain and Portugal. In matters of literature France and England were united during the Anglo-Norman period, and when this period was over England produced nothing but reflections of French texts and one immortal compilation therefrom.[2] Germany had an independent version of the Legend, derived by its own evidence from a French source which is now unknown, if it is not a matter of invention. The German Cycle differs therefore in important respects from the extant French Cycles : the central figure is a characteristic hero in each ; but the central Sacred Object is different, the subsidiary *dramatis personæ* are different in certain cases—or have at least undergone transformation —and, within limits, the purpose is apparently diverse. The Dutch version is comparatively an old compilation from French sources, some of which either cannot be identified or, in the hands of the poet who translated them, they have passed out of recognition. The Italian Cycle has not been regarded as of consequence to any issue of the literature, either directly or otherwise, and has been almost ignored by students until quite recently. Its consideration is deferred and so also is that of Spanish and Portuguese contributions to the subject-matter of the Grail. As regards Wales there are difficult questions involved, and they will demand full inquiry at a later stage. Of the Grail, as we know of it in France, there is no indigenous Welsh

---

[1] But late or early, it is a pseudo-historicity text, leading up to Arthurian times and all the Romance thereof.

[2] The reference—as need hardly be said—is to the MORTE D'ARTHUR of Sir Thomas Malory.

literature, but there are certain bardic remanents and traditional tales which were held once to be fundamental elements of the subject at large, while more than one of the Questing Knights are found among MABINOGION heroes. In the thirteenth century and later some French texts were carried across the Marches and are represented by translations.

For the purpose of the classification which follows there must be set aside, for the time being, whatsoever may be found, in any and all quarters, concerning Quests, Missions and so forth, in connection with which the central object known as the Holy Grail does not appear. We shall deal with them fully when we come to the study of the textual apparatus at large. The remaining works may be grouped into Cycles, according either to affinities of intention or to the seat of their origin, and among these the chief Northern French texts fall —as we have seen—into three divisions, the distribution of two being, within their own lines, a strictly chronological arrangement.

I. The CONTE DEL GRAAL. Let me say, in the first place, that our problems are not the authorship of an individual prose or metrical Romance, nor yet the comparative dates of certain documents as they stand actually, but whether those among us who have come to know the significance and value of the Hidden Life of Doctrine, can determine by research the extent to which the intimations of such Doctrine found in the Grail literature are true or false lights. Now, I suppose that there is no question as to the literary greatness of Chrétien de Troyes, while the sequels and alternatives added to his unfinished poem are not altogether unworthy to rank after his own work ; the collection, however, as a whole, offers very little to our purpose. So far as Chrétien himself carried the story, we are not only unable to gather clearly what he intended by the Grail, but why he had adventured so far from his normal path as to plan and even to begin such a story. If he had gone further, we might have found that the Sacred Vessel, Telesma or Wonder-Working Palladium carried with it the same Legend as it carried for some other writers ; but we do not know and it matters less than little, for the CONTE DEL GRAAL at its best is Nature in the pronaos of the Temple testifying that she is properly prepared. If we grant this claim, we know that in Chrétien at least, however she may have been prepared conventionally, she has not been sanctified. An alternative termination of Gerbert carries the story up to a higher level, moving it in the direction of Wolfram's PARZIVAL, yet not attaining that level. So far as any spiritual term is concerned, the great CONTE is rather after the manner of a hindrance which calls to be taken out of the way : it is useless for the higher issues, and even for the business of scholarship it seems of late days to have lapsed from its first importance.[1]

The chief *additamentum* of this Cycle is the unprinted metrical

[1] Cf. Miss J. L. Weston : FROM RITUAL TO ROMANCE, p. 3.

PERCEVAL, which is preserved in the library at Berne.[1] The desire of
the eyes of students is a lost or supposed Provençal poem, connected
by the hypothesis with Perceval, as to which we shall hear more fully
when we come to the German Cycle of the Holy Grail.

The Chrétien portion of the CONTE DEL GRAAL was written not
later than 1189, but the most recent speculations are disposed to
place it between 1175 and 1180. The Chrétien story was left unfinished
because the death of the poet intervened, and his story was continued
by an anonymous writer who passes as pseudo-Wauchier, by allusion
to Wauchier de Denain, who took up the theme in turn, not earlier
than 1189 and probably between that year and the end of the twelfth
century. Manessier and Gerbert are believed to have produced their
independent conclusions between 1211 and 1244. As regards Chrétien,
it has been recognised and may be called obvious that his work
" presupposes an Early History ".[2] This being so, it may not be
unreasonable to infer tentatively that such History was (1) a
problematical first draft of Borron's poem, on which scholarship has
dwelt ; (2) the extant poem itself ; or (3) that it corresponded to the
book from which Borron claimed to draw and of which he is possibly
at this day the only representative. To cite Borron's alleged source
is virtually to cite Borron himself, and it is still a moot question
whether his metrical JOSEPH may not have been in existence when
Chrétien opened his CONTE. On the other hand, if the particular
Quest does not draw directly or indirectly from the particular History,
then my own view is that in the question of date but little can be held
to depend from the priority of Chrétien's poem—which is a Quest—or
that of Borron—which is a History. There is hence no call to indicate
a special persuasion, more especially as exact chronological arrangement in so tinkered a cycle of literature as that of the Holy Grail is
scarcely possible anywhere, nor is it my concern exactly.

II. The Cycle of Robert de Borron, being that which is connected
more especially and accurately with his name ; and therein is comprised : (1) The Metrical Romance of Joseph of Arimathæa, in which
we learn the Origin, Early History and Migration of the Grail Westward, though it does not shew that the Sacred Vessel came actually
into Britain. (2) The Lesser Holy Grail, called usually LE PETIT
SAINT GRAAL. We have here a prose version of the poem by Robert
de Borron, which accounts for its missing portions ; but the two
documents are not entirely coincident : for example, the later text
brings Joseph of Arimathæa into Britain, with the Palladium, though
he is left behind in the Metrical Romance. (3) The EARLY HISTORY
OF MERLIN, and this represents in prose another Metrical Romance of
the same authorship, of which the first five hundred lines are alone
extant. (4) The Didot-Modena Perceval ; but this text is almost
unquestionably a much later composition, though it seems to contain

---

[1] See Appendix I, being Additional Notes and Extensions, Note 1.
[2] Not, it should be observed, an earlier version or root-matter of his adventurous
story, though he appeals to a *Conte* which it was his task to put into rhyme.

some primitive elements of the Perceval Quest-motive. Its designation is explained by the facts that (*a*) the Didot codex was at one time in the possession of M. Firmin Didot, a well-known Parisian bookseller ;[1] while (*b*) a second and superior text, discovered long after, is preserved at Modena.[2] This Romance has been regarded generally as the prose version of yet another lost poem by Robert de Borron : the very serious difficulties which impede this view will be discussed later.

These documents constitute what may be termed the Lesser Histories or Chronicles of the Holy Grail. Their characteristics in common, by which they may be grouped into a Cycle, are (1) the idea that certain Secret and possibly Sacramental Words were transmitted from Apostolic Times and were taken from East to West ; (2) the succession of a certain Brons as Keeper of the Holy Grail immediately after Joseph of Arimathæa. The Metrical JOSEPH may have been written soon after 1170 ; but the balance of opinion favours the last years of the twelfth century. Some criticism has supposed that there were two drafts, of which only the second is extant. It was succeeded in either case by the Early MERLIN. As regards the DIDOT-MODENA PERCEVAL, the first codex is dated 1301, meaning, of course, the date of the MS. and not of its composition. The Modena version is referable to *circa* 1230 and is the work of a scribe towards the end of the thirteenth century.

III. The Vulgate Cycle of the Holy Grail and the Great Quest, comprising : (1) L'ESTOIRE DEL SAINT GRAAL, that is, THE BOOK OF THE HOLY GRAIL, or JOSEPH OF ARIMATHÆA, called also the FIRST BRANCH OF THE ROMANCES OF THE ROUND TABLE and the GRAND SAINT GRAAL. The last designation is due perhaps to its dimensions ; but it may be held to deserve the title on higher considerations, as the most important development of the Legend in its pseudo-historical aspects, apart from the heroes who followed the various Quests. The work—in common with the whole Vulgate Cycle—has been imputed in the past to Walter Map, some time Archdeacon of Oxford and Chaplain to Henry II of England. It is, however, of unknown authorship, like the rest of the Cycle, though the ascription of certain texts to Map was not regarded untenderly by past scholarship.[3] Unfortunately several of the Vulgate Romances seem generically distinct in respect of style, and from this point of view only their attribution to a single hand is to be set aside decisively. The GRAND SAINT GRAAL was intended to create a complete sequence and harmony between those parts of the Cycle with which it was concerned and the Galahad Quest, as well as to provide an Early History in plenary form. (2) The VULGATE MERLIN, which in certain respects is an attempt to reconcile the Borron Early History with that of the GRAND SAINT GRAAL.

---

[1] It is now in the BIBLIOTHÈQUE NATIONALE, and the press-reference is given by J. D. Bruce as No. 4166 of the NOUVELLES ACQUISITIONS. THE EVOLUTION OF ARTHURIAN ROMANCE, Vol. II, p. 104.

[2] BIBLIOTHECA ESTENSI, Bruce's press-reference being MS. 2 E. 49.

[3] See Appendix I, Note 2.

The History of Merlin is taken to his final enchantment in the Forest of Broceliande, and in particular to that point when Monseigneur Gawain hears the last utterance of the Prophet.[1]   An analogous term is reached by the HUTH MERLIN—another and alternative text—in respect of Bademagus, through a long series of entirely distinct episodes.   It should be stated that the references to the Holy Grail are comparatively few ; but they seem pregnant with meaning.   As an addendum to these Branches, there is a late work called THE PROPHECIES OF MERLIN, which I know chiefly by the printed edition of Rouen.   It has wide variations from the texts mentioned previously, in so far as it covers their ground, but it has also Grail references. It has been regarded as a continuation of the Early Prose MERLIN, and in this sense it would be alternative to the Vulgate and the Huth texts.   (3) The great prose LANCELOT, which in spite of its subject matter is in its proper understanding a book of high purpose, or it lies at least on the fringe of this description and passes towards the close therein.   (4) THE QUEST OF THE HOLY GRAIL, called also THE LAST BOOK OF THE ROUND TABLE, containing the term of the Mystery as given in the Chronicle concerning Galahad, the *haut prince*, and this is the Quest *par excellence*, the head and crown of the Grail Legend. I know that this statement would have been challenged once in certain high quarters of research in England, but the protagonists of alternative views have passed away some time since and another spirit of criticism has entered the lists.   It must be added that all which is understood commonly by human interest, all that has been regarded as ethically characterising the chief German text is excluded by the Great Prose Quest.   We have in place thereof a Spiritual Romance, setting forth under this guise a Mystery of the Soul in its progress. Hereof is the Galahad Quest.

These four Romances constitute what is termed the Vulgate Cycle, otherwise the Greater Chronicles of the Holy Grail.   They are followed in this Cycle by the MORTE ARTHUR, as a fifth Branch, recounting the last great battle of the West, the breaking up of the Round Table, and the end of all its Chivalry.   There are no Grail references, for the Grail has gone away.   The characteristics of this Cycle are (1) the succession of Joseph II as Keeper of the Holy Grail immediately after his father and during the latter's lifetime, this dignity not being conferred upon Brons, either then or later ; (2) the substitution of a claim in respect of Apostolical Succession—which placed the Grail Keepers in a superior position to any Priesthood holding from the Apostles—for that of a Secret Verbal Formula, sometimes connected with the Eucharist.

The dates of the texts which are included in the Vulgate Cycle differ widely, and the canon of the Grail literature was not closed in reality till the end of the thirteenth century.   As to lost and alleged antecedent documents it is obvious that no dates can be assigned,

[1] See Sommer's VULGATE VERSION OF THE ARTHURIAN ROMANCES, Vol. II, LESTOIRE DE MERLIN, pp. 461, 462.

however speculative. It has been suggested, for example, that a proposed prototype of the GRAND SAINT GRAAL and the QUEST OF GALAHAD preceded the Wauchier continuation of Chrétien.

The *additamenta* of this Cycle are the Quests of the Holy Grail in Italian, Spanish and Portuguese versions, and one rendering into Welsh, but these will be dealt with in their place. There is, moreover, material of importance in a draft of the Great Quest printed at Rouen in 1488 together with the LANCELOT and the MORTE D'ARTHUR, as also in a Paris edition of 1533. Finally, the English Metrical Chronicle of Hardyng contains a version of the Galahad Legend which differs in express particulars from anything with which we are acquainted in the chief Romance texts.[1]

IV. The pseudo-Robert de Borron Cycle, regarded as a derivative or alternate version of the Vulgate Cycle and presupposing therefore the GRAND SAINT GRAAL, less or more as it stands, but possibly in a shortened form. The specific claim on authorship stultifies itself and has been set aside long since. The Northern French originals of this collection are represented only by the HUTH MERLIN, which pretends to derive from Secret Archives of the Grail. It takes the Prophet's story up to the same point as the Vulgate text, with Bademagus as witness in place of Gawain, and through a long series of stirring and romantic episodes. It has been referred to 1225 or 1230 and is represented by an unique manuscript, itself belonging to the last quarter of the thirteenth century. A final part which is now wanting in French contained a version of the Galahad Quest. When Gaston Paris issued the text under notice in 1886 he indicated for the first time the existence of a pseudo-Robert de Borron Cycle. The subject attracted scholarship and has passed through various developments, the probable branches of the Cycle being tabulated after more than one manner. We need be concerned only with that of Bruce, which happens to be last and may be set forth as follows : (1) The GRAND SAINT GRAAL, most likely with few variants. It is to be noted, however, that the scribe of the HUTH MERLIN prefixed the LESSER HOLY GRAIL to his Merlin text, with which it is manifestly out of touch. (2) The EARLY PROSE MERLIN. (3) The HUTH MERLIN continuation, but this is alleged to have existed in a more expanded form. (4) The VULGATE LANCELOT, which is not supposed to have been recast and is thought to have been implied or taken for granted. (5) A Quest of Galahad, represented now by a Portuguese translation which is held to be fairly close. (6) The MORT D'ARTUS in the abbreviated form of an epilogue. It will be seen that the HUTH MERLIN corresponds roughly to this Cycle, with a substituted first branch. As the VULGATE MERLIN also lays claim on the authorship of Robert de Borron, the critical position of this supposed Cycle is not on very sure ground. It seems quite possible that in its speculative original form, as in the HUTH MERLIN, it began with the LESSER HOLY GRAIL and proceeded thence to the

[1] Appendix I, Note 3.

EARLY PROSE MERLIN, subsequently presupposing the GRAND SAINT GRAAL in its MERLIN continuation, as it does manifestly in the Huth text. Obviously also it presupposed a form of the LANCELOT or at least an excerpt therefrom giving account of the birth of Galahad.[1]

V. The German Cycle, comprising three texts, which, like the CONTE DEL GRAAL, except in its latest sequels and then by chance allusions or derivations at a far distance, has nothing to tell us of Secret Words, Eucharistic or otherwise, and no hint of any Super-Apostolical Succession. The Legend is in fact revolutionised, and (1) the PARZIVAL Quest of Wolfram von Eschenbach, though it follows some broad lines of other Percevals, has suffered I know not what greatness of alteration. It was composed not later than 1210. (2) The TITUREL of Albrecht, which deserves a notice that it has never received in England, is of considerable importance to the German Cycle, but is of all texts the latest, being referable at its earliest to the year 1250. In fine, to dispose of this Cycle, there is (3) the Metrical Romance of DIU CRÔNE—*circa* 1220—by Heinrich von dem Turlin, in which Ghosts or the Dead-Alive are Custodians of the Mysteries, a fact which will lead us to estimate later on the value of those views which have sought to connect the Grail Quests with Legends of the Other World.

It must be said in respect of the above tabulation that while the Grail literature is divisible into several Cycles there are three only which belong to our most particular concern. The classification which I have made may prove serviceable therefore in yet another way, by enabling us not only to set apart that which is ultimately *nihil ad rem nostram catholicam et sanctam*, but also to come into our own.

It should be added that one text has been omitted from this classification, namely, the *Longer Prose Perceval*, called also the *Perlesvaus*, because it stands utterly alone. In one sense and one only it has an unacknowledged debt to the *Grand Saint Graal ;* but this isolated fact exhibits the more clearly how the story, from beginning to end, stands far apart therefrom. The *Perlesvaus* is otherwise most important for the Cycle-General of the Holy Grail.

IV

FURTHER CONSIDERATIONS RESPECTING THE SEVERAL GROUPS OF TEXTS

THERE are several literatures which exhibit with various degrees of plainness the presence of that sub-surface meaning to which I have referred in respect of the Grail Legend. This additional sense may underlie the body-general of a literature, speaking one language without and another within, as in the

---

[1] The HUTH MERLIN was utilised largely by Malory in the MORTE D'ARTHUR for events leading up to the Galahad Quest. As regards the Quest itself in the pseudo-Robert Cycle, see my Book VI, Sections 6 and 7.

case of Alchemy ; it may answer to some concealed intention, which
can be glimpsed there and here, as in the case of many parables ; or
it may be a claim put forward evasively and yet with sufficient clearness
to indicate that a wide field of significance extends behind. The sub-
surface import of Grail literature belongs mainly to the third class. It
is from this point of view that my departure is made here ; and if
it proves a warrantable assumption some portion at least of the
literature will be found, explicitly or otherwise, to contain these
elements in no uncertain manner. As a matter of fact, we shall
find them, sometimes as things expressed apart from comment or
development, sometimes as things which are implied, or which follow
as inferences ; but they may not be for such reason less decisive
or demonstrable. The implicits of the Grail literature are the
more unexpected and more pregnant in suggestion because of
their peculiar vehicle, which is that of Romance, derived—as we
shall find—in respect of its root-matter from an Apocryphal
Gospel.[1]

The most important of the Grail implicits are those from which
my study depends ; but there are others, and in the present place
they need only be specified as to the point of fact, since they belong
more properly to considerations of individual texts. There is, in
fine, one implicit which is reserved for the end, because it is that in
which the debate culminates.

The implicit-in-chief of that Cycle which passes under the name of
Robert de Borron and which I have termed the Lesser Histories or
Chronicles of the Holy Grail, follows from the affirmed fact that
certain Secret Words, with an affirmed application to the Most Holy
Sacrament of the Altar, were communicated to Joseph of Arimathæa
by Christ Himself, and that these remained in reserve, being committed
from Keeper to Keeper by a secret method only. It must be noted,
moreover, that the Secret Words are represented in the poem of
Robert de Borron as Words of Counsel on the external plane, that is
to say, outside any efficacy which they may have been assumed to
possess in Consecrating the Elements at the Mass. They are " sweet,
precious and holy words " It is these qualities which stand out more
strongly in the Metrical Romance than any Eucharistic side of the
formula ; and there seems consequently a certain doubt as to Borron's
chief intention respecting their office. But in a later prose version of
the Metrical Romance, usually known as the LITTLE or LESSER HOLY
GRAIL, this chief implicit passes into actual expression, and it becomes
more clear in consequence that the Secret Words were those used
ex hypothesi by the Wardens of the Holy Grail in the Sacred Work
of the Eucharist. We shall see, however, that they were not so used
in fact, on the open evidence of the texts.

Let it be understood that I am not seeking at present to press any
inference but am stating a case only. If the references to Secret Words

See Book IX, Sect. 2.

in the metrical JOSEPH do not offer a sacramental connection with full clearness—because they are also talismanic and protective—their operation in the latter respects must be regarded either as subsidiary and apart from the real concern of the Holy Grail or we are in the presence of another implied claim, which at the moment lies wholly *perdu* in sources that are concealed utterly. It is to be noted further that any Eucharistic Mystery has nothing to do with Transubstantiation, of which there is no trace in the Lesser Chronicles. Lastly, the sole Custodian of the Sacred Vessel lives in utter seclusion through a period of many centuries, and after the Words were at length imparted to his only lawful successor, Brons was removed for ever through the Gates of Death. The message of the Lesser Chronicles seems to be that something was brought into Britain which it was intended to manifest; but no manifestation took place.[1]

When the GRAND SAINT GRAAL was produced as an imputed branch of Arthurian literature there is no need to say that the Roman Pontiff was then as now, at least in respect of his claim, the first Bishop of Christendom, and he derived *ex hypothesi* from St. Peter, who was *episcopus primus et pontifex primordialis*. The life of the Papal Pontificate, through long centuries, was a life of warfare in the aggressive and unremitting prosecution of this claim, with all that attached thereto and all that arose therefrom.[2] Now, the Romance in question attributes the same title to a son of Joseph of Arimathæa, who may be called the Second Joseph; and here is the first suggestion. The GRAND SAINT GRAAL and the Metrical Romance of Borron are the historical texts in chief of their particular Cycles; but it does not follow that their several continuations or derivatives are planned extensions throughout of the implicits which I have mentioned. In the second case, the Early Prose MERLIN has an implied motive of its own which need not detain us at the moment, while the DIDOT-MODENA PERCEVAL is of more than dubious authenticity as a sequel and does not as such represent fully the mind of the earlier texts, though—as suggested already—it has also an importance of its own and also its own implicits. On the other hand, in the Vulgate Arthurian Cycle, or Greater Chronicles of the Holy Grail, there is, if possible, a more complete divergence in respect of its Quest codex; and I can explain it best by saying that could we suppose for a moment that the GRAND SAINT GRAAL was produced in the interests of a pan-Britannic Church, or alternatively of some Secret School of Religion, then the Great Prose Quest or Chronicle of Galahad might represent an interposition on the part of the Official Church to take over the literature. At the same time, the several parts of each Cycle

---

[1] This is one reason why the DIDOT-MODENA PERCEVAL is not an authentic *terminus ad quem* of the Borron texts.

[2] As, for example, the iniquitous Albigensian Crusade and the Holy Inquisition, which came to birth in its later days.

under consideration belong thereto and cannot be located other-wise.[1]

The further divisions under which I have scheduled the body-general of the literature, and especially the German Cycle, will be considered at length in their proper places, when their explicit and implied motives will emerge : for the present it must be sufficient to say that the German poems do not put forward the claims with which I am dealing now, namely, the Secret Formula in respect of the Borron Cycle and a Super-Apostolical Succession in respect of the GRAND SAINT GRAAL, and of that which is classed therewith.

We do not know that Wolfram had prototypes to follow outside those to which he confesses himself. As to these, he rejected one of them—at least by word of mouth—and it is only by inference that we can ascertain what he derived from the other, assuming, for a moment only, that this other is not his own invention. It will seem certain, however, for many that his acknowledged exemplar could not have originated the numerous generic distinctions which characterise the German PARZIVAL, and the fact of what Wolfram borrowed—if any-thing outside a single text with which we are acquainted—throws perhaps into clearer light all that which he created.

As regards both the claims with which I am concerned more especially at the present moment, we must remember that although we are dealing with a department of romantic literature, their content does not belong to Romance. The faculty of invention in stories is one thing, and it is indubitable that modern criticism has made insufficient allowance for its spontaneity ; yet through all the Tales of Chivalry it worked within certain lines. It would not devise Secret Eucharistic Words or put forward strange claims which almost make void the Christian Apostolate in favour of some unheard-of succession communicated directly from Christ after Pentecost. We know absolutely that this kind of machinery belongs to another order. If it does not, then the Apocryphal Gospels were imbued with the romantic spirit and the explanation of Manichean Heresy may be sought in a flight of verse. In particular, the higher understanding of Secret Consecration is not a question of literature but of the com-munication to the human soul of the Divine Nature. It lies behind the Eucharistic Doctrine of the Latin Church ; but on the external side that Doctrine communicates, by the hypothesis of Transub-stantiation, the Divine Humanity rather than the Eternal and Divine Substance.[2]

I suppose that what follows from the claims has not entered into the consciousness of official scholarship ; but it may have entered

[1] In so far as they are of independent authorship, those of the Vulgate Cycle were casually harmonised with the GRAND SAINT GRAIL, especially the GALAHAD QUEST. On the other hand, the DIDOT-MODENA PERCEVAL sees that the Secret Words are com-municated officially to the third Custodian of the Holy Grail.

[2] The affirmation is requisite at this point because of the research before us, and it is put as if dogmatically : its evidential examination belongs to our final stage.

already into the thought of some among my readers whose pre-occupations are similar to my own, and it can be stated in summary form.   As the Sacred Palladium, which uttered its guiding Oracles from within the Holy Grail, was the Voice of Christ and the Voice of the Holy Spirit, its removal would mean that direct Divine Inspiration was taken away from the world : it depended henceforward at best on a *consensus sanctorum*, assumed to be *sensus Spiritus Sancti*. As alternatively Secret Words of Consecration, Extra-Efficacious Words which must be pronounced over Sacramental Elements, so that they may be converted into an Arch-Natural Eucharist, have never been expressed in writing, or have been enshrined only in a lost book, from which Robert de Borron claims to derive, it follows that since the Grail was withdrawn from the world, together with its Wardens, the Christian Church has had to be content with what it has, namely, a substituted Sacrament.   And as the Super-Apostolical Succession, also by the hypothesis, must have ceased from the world when the last Keeper of the Grail went before his Vessel into Heaven, the Christian Church has been reduced to the ministry of some other and apparently lesser Ordination.   It follows that the Grail literature is not only a Cycle of Romance originating from many Traditions but is also, in respect of those claims, a marked departure from Tradition.

In conclusion as to the greater implicits, seeing that the import of the Secret Words in the Cycle of Robert de Borron has eluded critical analysis, while that of the Extra-Apostolical Succession was appreciated by Paulin Paris[1] now many years ago and has occasioned scarcely any notice, there is one thing at least obvious, namely, that the second is written more largely on the surface of particular texts than the first, and when we come to consider in their order the Romances comprised in the Cycle of Lesser Chronicles, we shall find that there are several difficulties.   It is only after their grave and full evaluation that it will be possible to put forward the possession of certain Secret Words, whether in relation to an infallible Guiding Voice or to the Eucharistic Office as being one of two sovereign implicits of the Grail literature.

The lesser implicits may, for purposes of convenience, be tabulated simply as follows : (1) The Implicits of Moses and Simeon.   (2) The Implicits of the Merlin Legend.   (3) The Implicits of the Grail Keepers. (4) The Implicits of the several Quests and the distinctions belonging thereto.

I recognise that the general subject of these and the other sub-surface meanings is at this stage beyond the scope of a reader who is new to the whole problem.   For this reason those that are major have been sketched only in outline, while those that are minor have been limited to a simple enumeration.   It has been necessary to

---

[1] See LES ROMANS DE LA TABLE RONDE, 1865, Vol. I, pp. 96 *et seq.*

tabulate all, so that the scope of the literature may be indicated even from the beginning in respect of our proper concern. When they have been studied in the light of the texts themselves, the greater task will follow, which is to establish, if this be possible, their motive and their term.

BOOK II

THE HOLY GRAIL IN ITS MANIFESTATION AND REMOVAL

THE ARGUMENT

I. THE KEYNOTES OF GRAIL HISTORIES AND QUESTS.—Quest Versions and Versions of Early History—The Suppressed Word of the Perceval Quests—The Suppressed Sacramental Formula—The Secret School of Ordination—The Passing of the Sacraments—The Hallows in Britain—An Alternative Division of the Cycles. II. THE INSTITUTION OF THE HALLOWS.—Texts of the Sacramental Claims—Implied Mystery of the Hallows—The Four Hallows-in-Chief. III. THE VARIATIONS OF THE CUP LEGEND.—The Holy Vessel in the Legend of Joseph of Arimathæa—Sources and Authority of the Texts—Certain Apocryphal Gospels and certain Chronicles of Britain—Variations of the Conte del Graal—The Cup in the Metrical Romance of Robert de Borron—Its Eucharistic Character—Philology of the word GRAAL—The Cup in the Lesser Holy Grail—In the Early Prose Merlin—In the Didot-Modena Perceval—The Cup in the Grand Saint Graal—The Chalice and the Paschal Dish—References in the Later Prose Merlins—The Grail in the Longer Prose Perceval—The Doctrine of Transubstantiation —The Grail in the Quest of Galahad—The Hallow in the German Cycle—Possible Hypotheses regarding the Most Precious Vessel—The Conclusion of this matter. IV.—THE GRAIL VESSEL CONSIDERED AS A BOWL OF PLENTY.—Testimony of the Conte del Graal—The Tradition in the Vulgate Chronicles—In the Poem of Robert de Borron—Concerning Spiritual Refreshment—The Grand Saint Graal as a Legend of the Feeding Dish—The Great Prose Lancelot—The Dish of Plenty in the Quest of Galahad—Two Aspects of Magical Feeding in the German Cycle. V. THE LESSER HALLOWS OF THE LEGEND.—The Summary of these matters—The Legends of the Sacred Lance—The Broken Sword—The Dish or Salver. VI. THE CASTLE OF THE HOLY GRAIL.—Abode of the Sacred Vessel—The House of the Rich King Fisherman—The Castle in the Valley—The Building of the Holy House—Corbenic as the Treasury of the Holy Vessel—The Sanctuary of the Quest—The Castle of Souls—The Feudal Fortress of the German Parzival—The Palace of Dead Men. VII. THE KEEPERS OF THE HALLOWS.—Variations of Tradition in respect of the Grail and its Guardians —How the Life of Brons was prolonged throughout the Centuries—Hereditary Stewardships—The Keepers in the Vulgate Chronicles—Of Titurel, Amfortas and Parzival—The Mystery of Succession in the Longer Prose Perceval. VIII. THE PAGEANTS IN THE QUESTS.—Order of the Ceremonial Procession in the Conte del Graal—The Pageant in the Romance of Lancelot —In the Quest of Galahad—In the Longer Prose Perceval—In the German Cycle. IX. THE ENCHANTMENTS OF BRITAIN, THE TIMES CALLED ADVENTUROUS AND THE WOUNDING OF THE KING.—The Cloud upon the Sanctuary —The Suspension of Nature—Times of Peril and Distress—The Sickness of the King—Of Sin entering the Sanctuary—Of Help coming only from

41

BOOK II

THE HOLY GRAIL IN ITS MANIFESTATION AND REMOVAL

I

THE KEYNOTES OF GRAIL HISTORIES AND QUESTS

IT is a very curious heaven which stands about the infancy of Romance Literature, and more than one warrant is required to constitute any valid title for the interpretation of those strange signs and portents which are seen in some of its zones. The academies of official learning are consecrated places, and those who have graduated in other schools must be among the first to recognise and respect the unsleeping vigilance and patience of students who are their colleagues and brothers in a different sphere. The external history of texts and the criticisms belonging thereto are in the hands of these unincorporated colleges, whose authority at the best is final : yet the inward spirit of the literature is sometimes an essence which escapes academical processes. At the same time, any department of criticism which should decide that certain Books of the Holy Grail do not put forward extraordinary claims of an evasive kind, and do not so far contain the suggestion of an inward purpose, must be held to have failed even within its own province.[1]

Having indicated after what manner the literature at large with which we are dealing falls readily into several groups for the purpose of particular classification, we are called now to regard it a little differently, though without prejudice to the schedule-in-chief of my proper choice. The distinction between Quest-versions and versions of Early History is known to students, and though it is not absolutely definite in itself, so far as the intention of criticism is concerned solely, it is important from another point of view. The reason is that both classes have their particular Mystery, which is not without its antecedents in distinct schools of symbolism. The keynotes of the historical series—to make use of the expression in a sense which is not usually or so concisely attached to it—are those which have been considered as the implicits-in-chief of the literature. They are two in number,

---

[1] I am concerned at the moment with the question of fact only. It does not follow that the recognition of such purpose will lead anywhere : its attempted investigation may be baffled or may issue in wild hypotheses alone.

and they are embodied in two palmary historical texts, from which they were carried forward through intermediate documents which answer, broadly speaking, to the same description, and thence through certain Quest-versions by which the literature is taken to its term. I am speaking, however, only of those Cycles which have been classified in the previous section as the Lesser and Vulgate Chronicles of the Holy Grail ; but it should be understood that the same or analogous early histories are presupposed by later sequels to the poem of Chrétien de Troyes. On the other hand, the German Cycle, as represented by Wolfram von Eschenbach and the TITUREL of Albrecht, has an early history which differs from all existing French sources, though the Quest of Parzival is in close correspondence as such with the Perceval Quests current in Northern France, so far as the early story of the hero is concerned.

We have seen, concerning the keynotes of the Early Histories, that they are :—

I. The suppression or concealment of a potent formula, in the absence of which—if it was sacramental in character—the Office of the Christian Ministry is not indeed abrogated but is foreshortened or has become substituted, so that there seems to be something of a vital character wanting to all the Sanctuaries. Whatever therefore the elements which entered into the composition of the Grail conception, several versions of the Legend unite in relating it to the Mystery and Power of certain High Consecrations or of certain unmanifested and withheld forms of speech. Those who can acquire and retain the words may exercise at will a strange power and mastery over all about them and shall possess great credit in the sight of God. They need never fear the deprivation of their proper rights, sufferings from evil judgments or conquest in battle, so long as their cause is just.[1] It is, however, as I have intimated, either (1) impossible to communicate these words in writing or (2) they are recorded in one place only—that is to say, in unknown archives or in a Hidden Book of the Grail. They are too precious and holy for common utterance and, moreover, they are the Secret of the Grail itself.[2]

II. The removal, cessation or assumption of a certain School of Ordination, which held from Heaven the highest warrants, which was perpetuated from generation to generation in one line of descent, which had the custody of Sacred Mysteries, which in fine ordained no one outside its own circle ; and the perpetuation, concurrently and thereafter, of an alternative form of succession which did not produce the evidence of things unseen made spiritually and materially manifest as the term of faith. To this extent did the powers of an alleged Secret Sanctuary differ by the hypothesis concerning it from the powers of Holy Church manifested in the world. In the Prologue or Preamble to the GRAND SAINT GRAAL, the Hermit who receives

---

[1] LE ROMAN DU SAINT GRAAL, edited by Francisque Michel, 1841, pp. 39, 40.
[2] Ib., pp. 40, 140.

the revelations and the custody of the Mysterious Book of its Legend testifies that the Greatest Secret of the World has been confided to him, and the communication took place amidst inexpressible experiences, as if in that third heaven to which St. Paul was translated.[1] The description of his ecstasy is written in fervent language, but in place of an Indicible Formula there is a great mystery attributed to the entire text of that cryptic record which, although it is said to be translated, yet remains seemingly unknown. The form wherein we have it seems like a concession to human disqualification and even to the frailty of external Nature. It is as if we had only a substitute. On the other hand, the keynotes of the French Quests are also of two kinds, by which—if it were possible otherwise—they might be divided into two Cycles. That of the several Percevals is the Suppression of a certain Word, Question, or formula, which suppression, on the surface side of things, causes dire misery and postpones the advancement of the elect hero ; though in the end it makes for his further recognition and ensures his more perfect calling, so that he is crowned in fine as he might not have been crowned at first. If at his initial opportunity he had asked in the Grail Castle that simple Question which covers the whole adventure with so dense a cloud of Mystery, he would not have been perfected in suffering, sorrow and exile ; some of the Quests would have terminated almost at their inception ; and one vital text could not have existed at all.

The Withheld Word of the Perceval Quests takes, as I have indicated, the form of a simple Question—a Question, that is to say, which should have been asked but was not : as such it is, so to speak, the reverse side or antithesis of the old classical Legend of the Sphinx. The Sphinx asked questions and devoured those who did not reply or whose answers blundered. Perceval kept silence when he should have urged his inquiries, sometimes through false modesty, sometimes because he had been cautioned against idle curiosity ; but in both cases, by the working of some apparently blind destiny, the omission carried with it the long series of its disastrous consequences. There came, however, a time of joy and deliverance, and it followed a belated utterance of the Word : thereby great enchantments were determined, great wrongs were redressed, and the wounds and sufferings endured through many years were healed and annulled. It follows that there is a twofold Mystery of Words connected by certain texts with the Quest of Perceval. Its higher sense is that of a Sacramental Formula, and this was interned with Perceval according to the Lesser Chronicles. But the Word alternative—that which could be reserved or uttered—had performed in the meantime, and was still fulfilling, a certain office of amelioration, so that it is not by a merely vain observance that, in a sense, it is replaced by the Quests for that unknown formula which was reserved as the Last Mystery of a Hidden Sanctuary. In contradistinction to this,

---

[1] See Lestoire del Saint Graal—otherwise Grand Saint Graal—in Sommer's Vulgate Version of the Arthurian Romances, I, pp. 1–8.

there is one Quest—and it is to be noted that it is one only—which depends entirely from the second alternative of the historical implicits —namely, the Super-Apostolical Succession. This is the Galahad Quest, which stands apart from all Mysteries of asking, all joy of answer, as if these were of the Lesser Enigmas, while it is uplifted into a world of sanctity wherein is reflected only the shadow or similitude of secret claims—doctrinal or ecclesiastical. The heroism of human life is received into the Divine Rapture, so that the last formulary of the search after and finding of the Holy Grail is in all truth that which is expressed by the Admirable Doctor Ruysbroeck—*in vastissimum divinitatis pelagus navigare*. Of such is the Grail Legend, and those who are acquainted with it in the most elect of its early forms will agree not only that many portions of it are of talismanic attraction, but that it is indeed

> " A part
> Of the hunger and thirst of the heart."

It is also on the external side a very melancholy Legend ; it is the passing of a Great Procession and a Great Sacrament, which, owing to the imputed stress and terror of the time, is destined never to return in the same form : it is a portion of the loss of humanity on one side of its manhood ; and it is no matter for surprise that in these late days, which are so full of the " hunger and thirst ", several persons have attempted to read into it the particular significance which appeals to them. This has been in various cases anything but that which could have been intended consciously by any maker of chronicles ; and the Question of Perceval abides therefore among us, but now in the reverse sense, seeing that it is asked, and this often, yet it remains unanswered to this day, unless in those Holy Places, beyond the external voices, of which this world as such knows not anything.

II

THE INSTITUTION OF THE HALLOWS

HAVING thus indicated after what manner the Grail Legend and its literature is tinged with Mystery and Symbolism *a parte ante et a parte post*, the next matter of our inquiry is concerned with the Institution of the Hallows. In all its forms indifferently, the Legend of the Holy Grail depends upon postulated values attaching to certain Sacred Objects. Those texts which it has become customary to term the Early Histories, equally with those which present the various versions of the Quest, revolve about these Hallows, shewing how they arose, how they came into Britain, in whose care they were placed at first, to whom they were transmitted successively, why and by whom they were sought and what, in fine, became of them.

Among the general characteristics of the French Cycles we shall find that there is the transit of these Hallows from East to West. They are in hereditary keeping, and in the end they are taken into uttermost seclusion or ascend to Heaven. There are, however, numerous phases of the Legend, important variations in the Hallows, while claims which are manifest in certain texts are non-existent in others. The Cycle in Germany took over the Legend of the Swan Knight and imported a suggestion of Templar interest : on the other hand, the introduction of certain ascetic elements seems characterised by the coming of Galahad into the Grail Quest. The peculiar ecclesiastical claims which are the sub-surface warrant of the Northern French Cycles were never put forward ostensibly in any Quest whatever ; and in the Galahad Legend there remains only the shadow of those earlier designs which might be constructed as in dissonance with the Latin Rite.

The Quest of the Holy Grail and of the other Hallows which are from time to time connected therewith is followed by many knightly heroes as the Quest-motive evolves, and most of these are unsuccessful : the preliminary conditions of attainment are purity and sanctity in the latest versions ; but there is nothing to shew that these were sufficient in themselves ; and as there were other qualifications, so in some signal instances a partial success was not impossible in the absence, or at least comparatively, of those warrants which in given places were claimed as essential. Once more therefore, the Cycle of Northern France may be regarded as falling into four divisions : (1) The Institution of the Hallows, and more especially that which concerns the origin of the Sacred Vessel. (2) The circumstances under which the Hallows were carried into Britain, or alternatively were found therein, and the later circumstances of their partial manifestation. (3) The details of the search for the Hallows, and other things within and without which led to their removal or recession. (4) The occasion of their final departure.

The texts purport to provide therefore the complete History of the Grail, including whence it came, where it abode for a while, and whither it has gone. This is not to say that there are express books treating of each section only. The Metrical Romance of Borron does stand, however, simply for the first part, and the same applies to its prose rendering in the LESSER HOLY GRAIL. The second part is found in the GRAND SAINT GRAAL, and the third in the DIDOT-MODENA PERCEVAL, the CONTE DEL GRAAL, the PARZIVAL of Wolfram, the LONGER PROSE PERCEVAL and the QUEST OF GALAHAD. The German PARZIVAL excepted, all these stories of research give an account of the withdrawal—some at considerable length, and some briefly.

Again, the later Romances may be divided into two sections : (1) those which speak of an Enchantment fallen on Britain, and (2) those which are concerned with the termination of certain Adventurous Times. If the literature follows any set purpose, a definable importance must be attributed to the meaning of that Enchantment and those Adventures. In this manner, the chief questions may be summarised alternatively as follows :—

(1) The Secret Verbal Formula and its connections, so far as these appear in any Quest.
(2) The qualifications for the Quest.
(3) The Hereditary Keepers of the Grail.
(4) The King's Wounding and the King's Healing.
(5) The Enchantments of Britain in connection with the Wounded Keeper.
(6) The removal of the Grail and the close of those times which certain texts term Adventurous, since when there has been silence on earth in respect of the Holy Grail.

The Verbal Formula is introduced in, among other documents' (1) the De Borron poem ; (2) the LESSER HOLY GRAIL ; while its shadow is projected as a secret which cannot be told in (3) the Proem to the CONTE DEL GRAAL. It seems to be found by a vague and remote inference in the LONGER PROSE PERCEVAL, while it may be identified by brief allusions in the early prose MERLIN. There is no trace of it in the Great Quest, while it is outside the Tradition as represented by Wolfram. The Quest qualifications are doubtful in Chrétien, and so also in his successors. They are what might be termed ethical in the PARZIVAL, which presents the Marriage of its hero. The so-called ascetic element appears fully, as we have seen, in the GRAND SAINT GRAAL, in the PERLESVAUS and in the QUEST OF GALAHAD. The King's Wounding is accounted for differently in every Romance ; the withdrawal of the Grail also is told differently : sometimes it passes simply into deeper concealment ; sometimes it is taken away utterly ; in one version there is another Keeper appointed, but of the Realm apart from the Hallows ; it is carried to the far East in another ; and in two texts it remains apparently where it was.

If there is a secret intention permeating the bulk of the literature, again it must reside partly in those epochs into which the literature falls : their consideration should manifest it and should enable us to deal, at the close of the whole research, with the final problem, being that which is signified by the departure of the Sacred Vessel.

Each of the Hallows has its implied enigma, besides that which appears openly in its expressed nature ; and as there are some which are met with only from time to time, so there are suggestions and inferences concerning others which never come into view. That which was always in evidence is that to which the distinctive name of Grail is applied in every text ; but enough has been said concerning it till we come to its exhaustive consideration in the next section. The second and third Hallows are the Lance and the Sword. The Lance is that which was used by the Roman soldier Longinus to pierce the side of Christ at the Crucifixion, or it is this at least according to the more general Tradition. Of the Sword there are various stories, and it is this which in some cases serves to inflict the wound from which the Enchantments of Britain follow. It is (1) that which was used to behead St. John the Baptist, in which connection we can understand its position as a Sacred Object ; (2) that of the King and Prophet David, committed by Solomon to a mythical ship, which went voyaging, voyaging throughout the ages till it should be seen by Galahad, the last scion of the Royal House of Israel ; or (3) it is simply an instrument preserved as a token belonging to a Legend of Vengeance, in which relation it is nothing to the real purpose of the Grail.

The Dish, which is the fourth and final object included among the authorised Hallows, is more difficult to specify, because its almost invariable appearance in the Pageant of certain High Processions is accompanied by no intelligible explanation respecting it ; and although it has also its antecedents in folk-lore, its mystic explanation need not be sought very far away. Its sacramental analogy is in the Paten of the Catholic Mass. Like the rest of the Hallows, it is described with many variations in the different books. It may be a salver of gold and precious stones, set on a silver cloth and carried by two Maidens ; it may be a goodly plate of silver, or a little golden vessel, and this simply, except in the LONGER PROSE PERCEVAL, which as it multiplies the Hallows so it divides their ministry ; but here, as elsewhere, the Dish does not embody those feeding properties which are one aspect of the Mystery and would seem at first sight as if introduced to stultify.

In summary therefore : subject to characteristic variations which are peculiar to each text, it will be found that the several Romances follow or forecast one general process, exhibiting a general secret intention, manifested though not declared ; and it is for this intention that my study seeks to account.

III

VARIATIONS OF THE CUP LEGEND

WE have seen that the Secret of the Grail, signifying the super-substantial nourishment of man and (or) the Guiding Voice of a certain Holy Assembly, was communicated by Christ to His chosen disciple Joseph of Arimathæa, who, by preserving the body of his Master after the Crucifixion, became an instrument of the Resurrection. He laid it in the Sepulchre, and thus sowed the seed whence issued an arch-natural body. On Ascension Day this was removed from the world ; but there remained the Holy Vessel, into which the Blood of the natural Body had been received by Joseph. Strangely endued with virtues of the risen Christ and the power of the Holy Ghost, it sustained him spiritually, and by a kind of reflection physically, during forty years of imprisonment, through which period he was in that condition of ecstasy which is said by Christian Masters of Contemplation to last for half an hour—being that time when there is silence in Heaven. We find accordingly that Joseph had no sense of duration in respect of the years : he was already in that Mystery of God into which the ages pass. After his release the Holy Vessel became a sign of saving grace, instruction and all wonder to a certain baptised Company which he was elected to take Westward. He committed it in fine to another Keeper, by whom it was brought into Britain ; and there, or otherwhere, certain lesser Hallows were added to the Hallow-in-Chief, and were held with it in the places of concealment. Those which are met with most frequently, as we have seen, are four in number ; but the Mystery is really one, since it is all assumed into that Vessel which is known for the most part as the Cup of Legend.

The Four Hallows are therefore the Cup, the Lance, the Sword and the Dish, Paten or Patella—these four and the greatest of these is the Cup. As regards this Hallow-in-Chief, of two things one : either the Grail Vessel contained the most sacred of all Relics in Christendom— living and also speaking—or it contained also a Secret Mystery of the Eucharist. Now, the first question which arises is whether the general description that obtains concerning it reposes on the authority of texts outside its own Cycles, as well as within. Here also will be found our first difficulty. There are three available sources of information concerning the Sacred Vessel : (1) The Myth of Joseph, being Apocryphal Legends respecting Joseph of Arimathæa. (2) The Early English Chronicles which recite the conversion of Britain. (3) The Romances themselves, which are the chief bases of our knowledge, but on the understanding that there is no criterion for the distinction between that which is embodied Tradition and that which is pure invention.

As regards the evangelisation of Britain by Joseph of Arimathæa there is no authentic record in any Chronicle till about the end of the twelfth century,[1] onward from which period the sources of information utilised to expand the Glastonbury stories of William of Malmesbury are the Grail Romances themselves. These also were known and used by John of Glastonbury. The Pious Legends which connect Joseph with the cultus of the Precious Blood are late, and they lie under the suspicion of having been devised in the interests of Glastonbury, or through Glastonbury of ecclesiastical pretensions on the part of the British Church at or about the period of Henry II. Above these as a substratum of solid fact—I refer to the fact of the inventions— there has been superposed the dream of an alleged pan-Britannic Church, which belongs, however, more particularly to the Romance of History. The Chivalrous Romances have so overlaid the Grail object with decorations and wonder elements that the object itself

[1] J. Armitage Robinson : Two Glastonbury Legends, 1926, p. 50.

has been obscured, and in some cases its nature can be scarcely extricated.

We come therefore to the putative Historical Romances and the Poems and Tales of Chivalry which contain the developed Legend of the Grail. The CONTE DEL GRAAL, which is the first text for our consideration, has many embroidered descriptions of the Sacred Vessel ; but they present certain difficulties in the successive sections, as will be exhibited by their simple recitation in summary. (1) It was covered with the most precious stones that are found in the world, while it gave forth so great a light that the candles on the table were eclipsed, even as are the stars of heaven in the glory of the sun and moon (Chrétien de Troyes).[1] (2) It passed to and fro quickly amidst the lights ; but no hand appeared to hold it (pseudo-Wauchier).[2] (3) It was borne uplifted by a beautiful Maiden, who was discounselled and weeping (Montpellier MS.).[3] (4) It was carried to and fro before the table by a Maiden more lovely than flowers in April (account of Wauchier de Denain,[4] with which compare a similar recital of Gerbert).[5] (5) It was exalted amidst great light by an Angel, to heal Perceval (Manessier).[6] (6) It was supported in the Pageant by a Maiden through the Castle Chamber (ibid.).[7] (7) It was manifested in full view at the Coronation of Perceval, also in the hands of a maiden (ibid.).[8] (8) It was in fine ravished with the soul of Perceval and has never since been seen so openly :

" Ne ja mais nus hommes qui soit nes
Nel vera si apiertement."[9]

What follows from these citations will have occurred to the reader : that the CONTE DEL GRAAL has no intelligible description of the Sacred Object ; that the poets of the various sections knew of it as if at a far distance only ; that some of their references might indicate a brilliant lamp rather than a Chalice. When those who followed Chrétien allocated it to Christian Symbolism, they seemed to have wavered in their understanding between the notion of the Paschal Dish and the Cup in which Christ Consecrated the Wine of the first Eucharist ; but we cannot tell. I should add that the Prologue,[10] which is the work of another hand, and embodies some curious material, mentions very briefly the Pageant of the Grail Procession, saying that the Vessel appears at the Castle without sergeant or seneschal, but again there is no description.[11] In conclusion of this account, the alternative ending of Gerbert retells with variations part of the story of Joseph, and although there is once again no intimation as to

---

[1] See Perceval le Gallois, ou le CONTE DEL GRAAL, edited by C. Potvin, 1866–1871, Vol. II, pp. 147, 148, lines 4398–4417.
[2] Op. cit., III, pp. 367, 368, ll. 20114–20132. [3] Ib., p. 369.
[4] Ib., V, pp. 143, 144, ll. 34738–34768. [5] Ib., VI, p. 257.
[6] Ib., pp. 119, 120, ll. 44275–44315. [7] Ib., pp. 132–133, ll. 44680–44719.
[8] Op. cit., VI, p. 151, ll. 45234–45236. [9] Ib., p. 155, ll. 45352–45362.
[10] Otherwise, the ÉLUCIDATION DE L'HYSTOIRE DU GRAAL, as it is termed in the prose version of 1530.
[11] Potvin, Op. cit., II, p. 11, ll. 303, 304.

the form of the Grail, an account of the service performed at an Altar over " the holy, spiritual thing "—the Vessel more beautiful than eye of man has seen—is there recounted, while it leaves no doubt in the mind that this service was a Mass of the Graal, though it is not so termed. It is the only suggestion of the kind which is afforded by the vast poem, though Gerbert's origin and early history of the Sacred Object is in accordance with received Tradition.

The fuller memorials of this Tradition are embodied, as we have seen, in two Cycles of the literature ; but the text which is first in time and chief in importance is the metrical ROMANCE OF THE GRAAL, OR JOSEPH OF ARIMATHÆA, by Robert de Borron. A French and a German critic have said that this is the earliest text of the Grail literature proper, and an English writer—among others—has concluded, on the contrary, that it is not : *mais que m'importe ?* I will not even ask for the benefit of the doubt, so far as enumeration is concerned. The metrical JOSEPH says that the Grail was a passing fair Vessel, wherein did Christ make His sacrament.[1] This is vague admittedly and, assuming a certain confusion in the mind of the writer, it might have been that Dish in which the Paschal Lamb was eaten by Christ and His disciples. In place of the words *mout gent*, which are given by the original French editor of the only text, Paulin Paris, following I know not what authority, or imagining a variant reading, substituted the words *mout grant*, which might well apply to the Paschal Dish. But Robert de Borron certifies to his own meaning when he recites an utterance of Christ in His discourse to Joseph, for it is there said that the Vessel which has served as a Reliquary shall be called henceforth a Chalice :

> " Cist vaisseau ou men sanc meis,
> Quant de men cors le requeillis,
> Calices apelez sera."

It is difficult to read the later verses in which the Eucharistic Chalice is compared with the Sepulchre of Christ, the Mass Corporal with the grave-clothes, and the Paten with the stone at the mouth of the tomb, without concluding that by the Grail there was intended the first Eucharistic Vessel ; and the presence of this symbolism in the mind of Robert de Borron suggests a figurative intention on his part throughout the Legend which he presented. If it be objected that his idea of a Chalice does not correspond to a Vessel the content of which is Sacramental Wine, it should be remembered that a Reliquary which by the hypothesis contained the Precious Blood was obviously in Sacramental correspondence with Eucharistic Wine. We shall see, however, at a later stage that we are placed in many

---

[1] *Op. cit.*, ed. Michel, p. 17, l. 396. Paulin Paris proposed reading *lavement* instead of *sacrement*, in which case the Grail would be the Vessel in which Christ washed the feet of the Apostles, the excuse being that Borron gives account of this observance but does not mention the First Eucharist. But Christ Himself describes it to Joseph in the Tower where the latter is imprisoned. See *ib.*, p. 38, ll. 893–900. The substitution is therefore arbitrary.

difficulties by the description thus allocated incautiously to a Divine Source.[1]

Be it added for the moment that the idea of the devotional poet, supposing it to have been as purely mystical as he was himself deeply religious, might have embodied an attempt to shadow forth in the perpetuation of the most precious of all Reliquaries the Sacramental Mystery of the Real Presence.

It seems certain, in any case, that when Robert de Borron speaks of the Grail as that Vessel in which Christ made His Sacrament, this ought not to be understood as referring to the Paschal Dish, though one probable derivation of the word Grail would support the latter view. In the dialect of Languedoc, *Grazal* signified a large vessel, usually of clay ; in that of Provence *Grasal* was a bowl or platter ; in Anglo-Norman, *Graal* was a dish made of some costly material for the purpose of great feasts, which, it may be said, is the description of Helinandus. With all this some of the later romancers were dissatisfied and, following Robert de Borron, they exalted the Vessel into a Chalice, so that they might bring it into line with the Eucharistic side of the Legend. The material of such a Chalice in the days of Robert de Borron must be left an open question, and still more that of a Wine Cup in the House of Simon of Jerusalem. It follows from Tertullian that in Rome at the beginning of the third century they used Glass Chalices ; so did the Bishop of Toulouse at the end of the fourth century ; and about A.D. 550 the same custom prevailed, as appears by the life of Cesarius, Bishop of Arles. A Council of Rheims in the days of Charlemagne is said to have forbidden Glass Chalices because they were brittle. The use of precious metals would grow from more to more as time went on and the wealth of the Church increased.

The LESSER HOLY GRAIL places its own construction on the Secret Words, which are applied decisively to the Consecration of the Eucharist. Where the poem says that there is a Great Book in which has been written the Great Secret called the Grail,[2] the LESSER HOLY GRAIL says : " This is the Secret uttered at the Great Sacrament performed over the Grail—that is to say, over the Chalice."[3] The Vessel is described otherwise as the one in which Christ " sacrificed " at the First Mass, and from an Eucharistic standpoint this seems much stronger than the corresponding *feisoit son sacrement*, which are the words of Robert de Borron. The repetition of the experience at the Sacred Table which is enjoined on Joseph in both texts is in both termed the Service of the Grail ; but in the prose version alone is it adjudged to the hour of Tierce, as if a Mass of the Grail were celebrated.

[1] One of them may be mentioned at the moment and is occasioned by the fact that there is only a single Hallow in the Metrical Romance of Borron. Obviously Christ did not " make His Sacrament " in a single Vessel : there must have been a Dish or Paten for the Bread and a Cup for the Wine. I cannot remember that this inevitable *lieu commun* of the subject has ever occurred to any critic of the text.

[2] Michel, *Op. cit.*, p. 40, ll. 929–936.

[3] See E. Hucher : LE SAINT GRAAL, Vol. I, p. 227.

The EARLY MERLIN and the DIDOT-MODENA PERCEVAL neither reduce nor increase the evidence.

In the EARLY MERLIN there is no allusion to the Office of Secret Words and no Grail Hallows are mentioned, excepting the Cup, as it is obvious that we cannot include the Sword of Merlin—sometimes identified with Excalibur—through which Arthur was chosen to be King. It does not appear that this weapon had any antecedent history. In the DIDOT-MODENA PERCEVAL the rumour and the wonder of the Grail moves pageant-like through all the pages ; but it is more shorn of descriptive allusions than anything that has preceded in the Cycle to which it belongs. When the Predestined Knight visits the Castle, Tower or Hold in which the Hallow has been preserved through so many centuries, he sees it plainly enough at the supper-table, along which it passes, carried with no ostentation by a mere Page of the Chamber ; but he is said only to hold a Vessel wherein the Blood of our Saviour reposed.[1] This is at the first visit, and at the second, when Perceval is initiated into the whole Mystery and becomes Lord of the Grail, this description is repeated, as if it were a counsel of perfection to maintain and even to increase in the third text of a supposed trilogy whatsoever could be called vague and dubious in the first.

The GRAND SAINT GRAAL, even when it reproduces with several variations the prose version of Robert de Borron's poem, gives in some of its codices an explanation of the Sacred Vessel which is the antithesis of his own. It is described as that Dish in which the Son of God partook of the Last Supper before He gave to the disciples His own Flesh and Blood.[2] It was therefore the Paschal Dish, in reality a preposterous suggestion, seeing that there are no circumstances under which it could serve as a Reliquary. Certain manuscripts differ, however, so widely that it is difficult to determine the original state of the text. Another codex follows the account of the LESSER HOLY GRAIL. According to a third codex, it was the content and not the vessel which was called the Holy Grail ; but, speaking generally most versions concur in describing it as the Holy Dish. The connection with the Eucharist is otherwise sufficiently close, for he who is elected to say the First Mass and to Consecrate the Unspotted Elements is he also to whom by Divine Instruction Joseph surrenders the Vessel, being that which belonged to him in virtue of his High Office. But the Blessed Reliquary of the GRAND SAINT GRAAL would seem to have been rather the outward witness to the Presence within those Elements. For example, in the first unveiled vision of the Holy Grail which is granted to anyone outside Joseph himself, we hear of an Altar, on one side of which were the Nails used for the

---

[1] It was a Reliquary pure and simple, and the shapes of these are manifold.

[2] Cf. Sommer's text in VULGATE VERSION OF THE ARTHURIAN ROMANCES, Vol. I, p. 13. In the house used for the Last Supper, *le jor de paskes*,—that is, on the day of the Passover—Joseph found *lescuele en le quele li fiex dieu avoit mangiet*—the Vessel in which the Son of God had eaten. It is the antithesis of Borron's account.

Crucifixion, together with the Hallowed Lance ; on the other side was the Dish ; and in the centre there was an exceeding Rich Vessel of gold in the semblance of a Goblet—obviously the Chalice of Consecration : it had a lid after the manner of a *ciborium*.[1] More astonishing still, the Cup of the Eucharist is placed within the Grail during a ceremony which corresponds to the Mass.[2] In a Romance so overcharged with decoration and so lavish in episodes of wonder, we should expect, and shall not be disappointed, that many pageants and ornaments would collect about the Holy Vessel, and that it should work many marvels. The Sacrament consecrated within it reveals the Mysteries of Christ openly to chosen eyes ; but thereon can no man look until he is cleansed from sin. It gives also on occasion the vision of an Eternal Eucharist and a Great Company sitting at a High Table in the Paradise which is above. So far as concerns the authority of the text itself, it would appear that the Mass of the Grail is not like that of the Church without but an Arch-Natural Sacrifice, at which the Incarnate Christ figures as the sensible oblation and subsequently as the Melchisedech of the Rite, communicating Himself to the witnesses,[3] while a thousand voices about him give thanks to God amidst a great beating of birds' wings, and

> " Young men whom no one knew went in and out
> With a far look in their eternal eyes."

The texts of the later MERLIN have several references to the Grail, and it is the chief purpose which moves through the two Romances, leading up as they do obviously to a Quest of the Sacred Vessel. But what is understood thereby must be gathered chiefly from its reflections of the Joseph Legends. We shall see that in certain codices the account differs from that of Robert de Borron. The VULGATE MERLIN has one very remarkable passage, which tells how the tidings of the Holy Grail spread through the realm of King Arthur, and how the Grail was that Vessel in which Joseph of Arimathæa received the Blood from the side of Jesus Christ when He hung upon the Cross.[4] It represents therefore a tradition which is familiar enough, not only in the literature of Romance but in that of Religious Legend, though it is the antithesis of the account given in the Lesser Chronicles, wherein we are told that the Blood was drawn into the Vessel after Joseph and Nicodemus had taken down the Body of the Lord.[5] Secondly, the Grail was that Holy Vessel which came from Heaven above into the City of Sarras, a notable suggestion, recalling the Grail Stone of the German Cycle and Wolfram's supposititious source in Kyot de Provence. Thirdly, and to us most important, the Grail was that Vessel in which Christ first Sacrificed His Blessed Body and His Blood by the mediation

---

[1] Cf. Furnivall's edition of Lovelich's HOLY GRAIL, p. 79.
[2] *Ib.*, p. 91. The Chalice is so placed by an Angel.
[3] Cf. the corresponding Vision which took place at Corbenic in the Galahad Romance when the term of Quest was finished.
[4] See Sommer's text, *Op. cit.*, II, pp. 334, 335.
[5] Michel, *Op. cit.*, pp. 24, 25, ll. 551–574.

of His Bishop, the Second Joseph, whom He Ordained with His own hands.[1] According to the HUTH MERLIN the Grail was that Vessel in which Jesus and His Apostles ate the Last Supper.[2] It was again therefore the Paschal Dish.

The LONGER PROSE PERCEVAL has many descriptions of the Vessel, all of which are designed, directly or otherwise, to connect it with the Chalice, but they are highly enigmatic in their nature. As one of the most express attempts to relate the Grail with the Eucharist, it must be regarded as important for the subject of the Hallow-in-Chief. This Romance and the great QUEST OF GALAHAD are both texts of Transubstantiation, and they must rank also among later documents of the literature. The Lesser Chronicles, even in the prose version of Borron's poem, offer no suggestion concerning this doctrine, the Grail Vessel being simply a Hallow containing a Precious Relic, as we have seen previously. About the period of the QUEST and the PERLESVAUS, the tide of ecclesiastical feeling, which long previously had set towards the definition of the dogma, must have permeated the mind of the laity, prepared as it also was by the desire of things sensible and tangible in matters of religion. It was, this notwithstanding, still long to the establishment of the high, symbolical Festival of Corpus Christi, which provided an external epilogue to the closed canon of the Grail, as if by a final substitution that which was taken away, or at least *ex hypothesi*, was to be in perpetuity memorialised about the precincts of the gate by the Wardens thereof. In connection with Transubstantiation, it may be remarked that the Religious Office of Knighthood was above all things to hear Mass and, next, to confess sins. There are few records in the Grail Romances that the Chivalry of Logres communicated, except in the QUEST OF GALAHAD, and then only in the case of Elect Knights. All high festivals were observed, all penances fulfilled ; but to participate in the Eucharistic Mystery seemed apart from the life of the world and withdrawn into the sphere of sanctity. However this may be, the LONGER PROSE PERCEVAL has two cryptic descriptions of the Grail Vessel, which, on account of their complexity, I must present as they stand in the story. (1) It is said concerning Monseigneur Gawain, when he looked at the Grail in his wonder, that it seemed to him a Chalice was therein, " albeit there was none at this time."[3] Was it therefore an Ark or a Tabernacle which was designed to contain a Cup, but when the latter was removed it held the shadow or semblance thereof ? (2) In the course of the same episode a change was performed in the aspect of the external object, and it appeared to be " all in flesh," meaning that it was transformed into a vision of Christ crucified.[4] Towards the close of the story, when a certain Queen Jandree relates her visions to Perceval, she sees, in one of these, an

---

[1] Sommer, *Op. cit.*, I, pp. 40, 41.
[2] See Gaston Paris : MERLIN, ROMAN EN PROSE, etc., I, p. 95.
[3] Potvin, *Op. cit.*, I, p. 88 ; HIGH HISTORY OF THE HOLY GRAIL, translated by Sebastian Evans, Branch VI, Title 18,
[4] *Ib.*, p. 89 ; Title 20,

image of the crucifixion from which people collect the Blood into a most Holy Vessel, elevated for that object by one of them. There are no names mentioned, but for purposes of simplicity it may be assumed that they were Joseph and Nicodemus. In the Castle of King Fisherman the Office of the Cup was to receive the Blood which fell from the point of the Sacred Lance. The Priest who officiated at the Grail Service is said to begin his Sacrament, with which expression we may compare the words *feisoit son sacrement*, which are those of Robert de Borron.[1] There is indubitable reference to the Eucharist in both cases. Speaking generally, the historical account of the Cup follows the GRAND SAINT GRAAL rather than Borron's poem ; for the Blood which flowed from the wounds of Christ when He was set upon the Cross is said to have been received into the Sacred Vessel. There is no ministry in respect of material sustenance attributed to the Grail in this Spiritual Romance.

It is therefore in one sense the antithesis of the QUEST OF GALAHAD, which dwells with equal fullness on the food-giving properties of the Vessel and on its connection with the Mystery of such a Mass and such an Office of the Eucharist as never before or after was or would be said in the wide world, apart from this sacred text. When the Holy Grail enters the Court of King Arthur and into the banqueting-hall it is clothed in white samite ; but neither the Vessel nor its Bearer is visible to human eyes.[2] On a later occasion it manifests as a Holy Vessel on a table of silver in an old chapel.[3] Elsewhere it is observed that the Flesh and Blood of God are present in the Grail.[4] When it appears to Lancelot in the Castle of Corbenic it is still upon a table of silver ; but this time the object is covered with red in place of white samite, and it is surrounded by Angels.[5] In the course of the Ceremony Lancelot sees three men, who represent the Trinity, exalted above the head of the Officiating Priest. Two of them place the youngest between the hands of the Priest, by whom He is uplifted.[6] On another occasion a Child enters visibly into the substance of the Mass-Bread. A Man also is elevated, bearing the signs of the Passion, and this Personage issues out of the Vessel, coming subsequently among the Knights present and causing them to communicate sacramentally.[7] It is after this episode that the Grail is removed to the Spiritual City of Sarras. There Christ appears to Galahad and his Companions, and this is the last manifestation in connection with the Sacred Vessel. It is the *viaticum* of the *haut prince*, who thereafter exercises the high option which has been granted previously and demands that he should be taken away.

As the chief Hallow in the PARZIVAL of Wolfram differs from all the other Romances, it will be left for more full consideration in dealing

---

[1] *Ante*, pp.52, 53.   [2] Sommer, *Op. cit.*, Vol. VI, p. 13.   [3] *Ib.*, pp. 42, 43.
[4] It is also (1) the Heavenly Food which sustains both soul and body—*Op. cit.*, p. 117 ; (2) a Treasury of " Great Secrets " —*ib.*, p. 96 ; (3) " good pasture " and " food of sweetness "—*ib.*, p. 113 ; (4) Grace of the Holy Spirit—*ib.*, p. 114.
[5] *Op. cit.*, p. 180.   [6] *Ib.*   [7] *Ib.*, p. 190.

with the German Cycle ; but seeing that in this Cycle there are correspondences, outside Wolfram, with the Northern French accounts, one
of these may be placed here so as to illustrate the Germanic allusions
to the Sacred Vessel in the general understanding thereof. DIU CRÔNE,
the poem of Heinrich, says that it was borne on a cloth of samite and
had a base of red gold, on which a Reliquary of gold and gems was
superposed. It ·was carried by a Crowned Maiden. There is here,
however, a fresh departure from the Grail in Christian symbolism,
for as, on the one hand, it is the Quest of a different hero, so, on the
other, the content ascribed to the Reliquary is not the true content.
It holds the semblance of Bread, as if that of the Divine Body ; but
the Wine or Royal Blood, which corresponds to the Second
Element of the Eucharist, is distilled from the Lance of the
Legend.

We are approaching now the term of the inquiry allocated to this
section, and it will be seen on reflection that we have three possible
hypotheses regarding the Precious Vessel : (1) that it was a cruet or phial,
wherein the Blood of Christ was reserved permanently—in which case
we can understand the Legend on the score of comparative possibility ;
(2) that it was an open Platter or Bowl, which, it is obvious, could
have held no permanent content, much less the Precious or indeed any
other Blood ; (3) that it corresponded to the notion of a Chalice but
probably with a cover, after the manner of a *Ciborium*. It is in late
texts that the Vessel appears most indubitably in connection with the
Sacrifice of the Mass : it was and could be only that which was recognised by DIU CRÔNE of Heinrich, namely, a Reliquary ; but the
mystical side of the Legend, reflecting in the minds of the romancers
many conflicting issues, took it over to the Eucharist, influenced by
the irresistible connection between the Sacramental Blood and the
sang réal poured out at the Crucifixion. There is evidence that this
view is almost coincident with the marriage of the Legend to Romance.
The mind of Romance connected the Vessel and its Office with Secret
Words of Consecration and a wonderful Grade of Priesthood.

In conclusion as to this matter, the Holy Grail, according to the
Greater Chronicles, was not the only Hallow which was brought into
Britain by those whose mission was to preach first the gospel therein ;
but it was more especially the exotic of the Legend, as this was
developed in Northern France. In several cases the other Hallows,
as we shall see, were either present in Britain or arrived some centuries
later. As regards the Lesser Chronicles, it may prove warrantable
to decide that, in the mind of Robert de Borron, the Sacred Vessel
was a covered Chalice, and that in some manner which is not declared
clearly it was connected with a·Sacramental Service performed in great
seclusion. As regards the Vulgate Cycle, it was originally a Dish, and
that Dish in which the Paschal Lamb was eaten at the Last Supper ;
but from the very beginning of this ascription the notion of a Cup was
essential to the Eucharistic Office which resided also in the Vessel. In

one codex at least of the GRAND SAINT GRAAL we have seen that a Cup is inserted therein ; but in later texts of the Cycle the Dish sometimes undergoes transmutation and reappears as a Chalice.

IV

THE GRAIL VESSEL CONSIDERED AS A BOWL OF PLENTY

THE incidental allusions which have been made already to certain physical properties which are ascribed to the Holy Grail in several branches of the literature seem to call at this point for some further explanation, without anticipating what will be said at the close as to any higher aspects of this Tradition or exhausting specifically its connections with folk-lore, which remain to be examined separately. The conception itself seems so repugnant to all that we attach to the Grail that it is at least desirable to ascertain its scope in the texts. As it appears to embody a transcript from old non-Christian fable, we should expect it to be most prominent in those texts which are nearest to a postulated transitional stage, and more especially in the Chrétien portion of the CONTE DEL GRAAL. It should be understood in the first place—as indeed it follows sufficiently from previous sections—that in the Perceval Quests—one sequel of the CONTE excepted—and in more than one of the Gawain Quests the visit to the Grail Castle is followed by a banquet or supper, at which the Questing Knight is treated for the most part as an honoured guest. The exception as regards Perceval is in the longer prose Romance or PERLESVAUS, the action of which is subsequent to the first visit of the hero, and he does not enter it a second time till he has taken it by force of arms out of the hands of God's enemy and the enemy of Holy Church.[1] In other cases, where the ceremonial meal is described—sometimes at considerable length—it is nearly always at the table, and before or in the midst of the festival, that the Grail and the other Hallows make their processional appearance ; and there are certain texts which say that the Sacred Vessel serves the High Company—sometimes with rarest meats, sometimes also with wine. In these specific instances the manifestation is that which occurs first after they are seated at table. It was to be expected, as I have said, that we should hear of this material efficacy in Chrétien ; but though the courses of the banquet are described fully, and are rare and precious enough, it is only a high reverence in a lordly castle of this world, and it is precisely from this text that it proves wanting. The wonder resides in the Hallows ; but they dispense nothing to the body. It follows that a certain anonymous poet who continued the work of

---

[1] It is not a Quest, and Perceval is not seeking to repair his original failure.

Chrétien prior to Wauchier had no precedent in his precursor, and it was therefore from other antecedents that he derived his notion of a Feeding Dish and from yet others his knowledge of early Grail history which does not appear in Chrétien. When he brings Gawain to the Grail Castle, he says that the Sacred Vessel served various courses ; but the wine was served by the butlers.[1] His idea of the Sacred Vessel must have corresponded therefore rather to the Paschal Dish than to a Reliquary of the Precious Blood. On the other hand, Wauchier's account of Perceval's second visit contains no allusion to this side of the festival. Manessier, in continuation of the same visit, offers no suggestion ; but when the time comes for him to tell the story of Perceval's third arrival, the Hallows appear in their order and all are filled at the table.[2] At the fourth and final visit, and the Coronation of the Questing Knight, Manessier recounts how the Grail sustains the whole Company with costliest meats and wines.[3] On the other hand, Gerbert, preoccupied by far other matters, gives no indication of the kind.

Except in so far as the EARLY HISTORY OF MERLIN reproduces one episode from the LESSER HOLY GRAIL, it has no allusion to the properties under consideration, and they are absent also in the DIDOT-MODENA PERCEVAL. On the other hand, the Greater Chronicles or Vulgate Cycle, represented by the GRAND SAINT GRAAL and the QUEST OF GALAHAD, embody a marked development of this particular Tradition. Between them there is the later MERLIN without any reference whatever ; the prose LANCELOT, in which the Grail provides all manners of meats and drinks when Sir Bors visits Corbenic ; and the LONGER PROSE PERCEVAL, into the consciousness of whose author it has not entered once, and by whom assuredly it would have been repudiated. Its recurrence on a single occasion in the presence of Galahad, and in connection with his Quest, may seem unsearchable, having regard to the claims which inhere in this Romance ; but in the order of texts it is explained by antecedents in the first form of the first document of the Cycle. We must recur therefore to the root-matter of the Early Histories.

The poem of Robert de Borron narrates that among those who accompanied Joseph on the journey Westward a certain number departed from Grace, through the sin of luxury ; but the spiritual mind of the minstrel has spared us all particulars. The result was famine in the Company : it does not appear that it fell upon all without exception, for the fact of want among the people was brought to the notice of the leaders ; but, these apart, good and bad seem to have suffered indifferently. An appeal was made to Brons that he should take counsel with his kinsman Joseph, which was done accordingly, and Joseph invoked the Son of God on his knees in the presence of the Grail, reciting the petition of his people, who were in need of

---

[1] CONTE DEL GRAAL, edited by C. Potvin, III, p. 367.
[2] *Ib.*, VI, p. 132.   [3] *Ib.*, p. 151.

bread and meat. He was told in reply to expose the Sacred Vessel openly in the presence of the Brethren on a Table similar to that of His own Last Supper, by which means the sinners would be discovered speedily.[1] It is the Holy Spirit Who was speaking, and He ordained further that Brons should repair to a certain water and there angle for a Fish. The first which he caught must be brought straightway to Joseph who, on his part, should place it upon the Grail Table over against the Sacred Vessel.

The people were then to be summoned and informed that if they were true believers, who had kept the commandments and followed out the teachings of Christ, as given through Joseph, so that they had trespassed in nothing, they would be welcome to sit down at the Table. These instructions were followed, with the result that a part only of the Company accepted this invitation.[2] The Table was arranged duly, and whosoever was seated thereat had the accomplishment of his heart's desire, and that entirely. Petrus, who was one of the recipients, asked the crowd that stood about whether they did not experience anything of the good which penetrated those at the Table, and they answered that they felt nothing. Thereupon Petrus denounced them as guilty of a vile, dolorous sin, and they went forth out of the house of Joseph covered with shame. The poem says :—

> " La taule toute pleinne estoit,
> Fors le liu qui pleins ne pooit
> Estre ; "

but the experience of the sitters, thus collected together, seems to indicate that they were fed from within rather than from without.[3] It will be seen and we must remember always that the chief necessity and often the chief privation of early Quests and Ventures in the Voyages of Romance was that of food in season ; but in this case what I have called the spiritual mind of the poet could not connect the idea of physical refreshment with the Divine Powers of the Relic. As regards the elect who were present, when the Service was finished each of them rose up and went out among the rest, Joseph commanding that they should return day by day to partake of the grace administered. Thus was the Vessel, says the poem, proved for the first time. In the speech of Petrus to the people who were rejected there is further evidence that the sustenance was more especially of the spiritual order, and it is important to establish this point from the earliest of the Grail Histories. He speaks of the great delight experienced in what is called the Grace and of the inexpressible joy with which the communicants were penetrated. They were filled as the Psalmist was filled and she who sang the Magnificat : *Esurientes implevit bonis.* What was filled was the heart of man and what was

---

[1] ROMAN DU SAINT-GRAAL, edited by Francisque Michel, pp. 104 *et seq.*
[2] " Dou pueple assist une partie,
   Li autre ne s'assistrent mie ". p. 108.
[3] The statement is that they experienced the fulfilment of their hearts' desire. *Ib.*

refected was the entire soul. My contention is therefore that—whether or not Robert de Borron had the idea of the so-called Feeding Dish present to his mind when he made the scarcity of food for his company an opportunity for the discriminating test of the second great Table of Refection—in place of bodily meat and bread, symbolised by the single Fish, as something placed intentionally out of all reasonable proportion, he administered *extasis*. That question of Petrus to the unworthy crowd about him : do you experience nothing ? is so evidently impossible, in their case, as a reference to eating and drinking that there is no need to dwell thereon. It left no opening to the prose editors whose versions complete the trilogy, and they lose all touch with the subject. Presumably the Grace of the Grail preserved the animal body from corruption.

As regards the Fish, by which there is brought to remembrance an early and pregnant form of Christian symbolism, the text offers a comparison which, although a little cryptic, seems also significant. It says that in the sight of the Grail, in its presence and the service thereof, true believers experience as much satisfaction as a fish, which, having been taken by a man in his hand has contrived to escape therefrom and again go swimming in the sea. The specific Fish of the story was placed before the Sacred Vessel, as instructed, and was covered with a cloth. There is no suggestion that it was eaten, and it appears to have remained as a kind of fixed dish whenever the Service was celebrated.[1]

It follows by inevitable inference that the Company partook of no physical sustenance, while all processes of language seem enlisted by Robert de Borron to shew that they were sustained spiritually. Apart from this the palmary miracle accomplished by the Vessel on this first occasion was one of discrimination between the good and evil among the people : for such judgment the Table of Joseph was set up and the goats were separated from the sheep. Presumably there was no question in the poet's mind that what could nourish the soul, which is vital, could refresh at need the body, which is accessory only. It is small wonder therefore that when the fountain text says so little the records which derive therefrom and belong thereto as its sequels are content to leave it thereat, and they add, as I have said, nothing. For Joseph and his brethren it remained that the Lord was the part of their Chalice, as if in the last understanding that famine which fell upon the Companions was a scarcity of Grace in the soul rather than of food in the stomach.

On the other hand, the GRAND SAINT GRAAL is in one sense a Legend of the Feeding Dish consecrated and exalted ; while seeing that as the texts stand it is that from which the greatest of all Quests is made to derive *ex hypothesi*, it is essential that we should understand its position clearly, and I will tabulate the references as follows :—

(1) The people on their way to Britain are fed marvellously with all

---

[1] We have seen that this was daily, like Daily Mass. ROMAN, p. 109.

manner of viands, both meat and drink, as, for example, at Houses by the way and at Lordly Castles. (2) In this primary allusion the Grail is not said to feed them. (3) They receive nourishment from the Table of the Grail ; but this is the Eucharist, and it is stated expressly that the Company had nothing else on that day.[1] (4) At a later stage, a second instance is given of this Super-Substantial Refreshment. (5) It is not till we are approaching comparatively the close of the Chronicle that we reach something more definite. The Company are already in Britain, and through the persecution of their heathen enemies they are hungry. Twelve loaves are obtained ; they are broken by Joseph, in the presence of the Grail, and they feed 500 people, more than the twelve loaves being left subsequently.[2] (6) It does not prove food of spiritual life, for those who were filthy before are filthy still. (7) At yet a later stage, the heathens test the feeding powers of the Vessel by the imprisonment of the Christians. In Wales the Vessel again furnishes all manner of viands, and one fish is a super-abundant provision for the whole company. After a similar manner, they are nourished with all possible delicacies in Scotland.

Passing over the later Merlin Romances, which are neither exactly Grail Histories nor Quests, and offer nothing to our purpose, we find that the shadow of the Quest is projected into the prose LANCELOT, though there is no questing intention ; and the visit of Gawain to the Grail Castle is the one example of indignity offered to a guest therein.[3] The responsibility, however, does not rest with the royal and saintly host, whose " high-erected thought " is " seated in a heart of courtesy." There is the flight of the mystical dove from casement to Inmost Shrine, as if the bird went to renew the virtues of the Holy Grail ; there is the apparition of the unattended Damosel, bearing that which itself bore the likeness of a Chalice ; there is the genuflection of all knees before the Holy Vessel; and there are sweet odours with all delicacies lavished upon the great table. But in the feast which follows, the peer of the Round Table alone has an empty plate. It was the discrimination and forejudgment of the Hallow in respect of that Knight who, in the days of Galahad was prompted to propose the Quest but did not persevere therein.

In the LONGER PROSE PERCEVAL, after the restitution of all things, there is abundance everywhere in the Castle, " insomuch that there is nought wanting that is needful for the bodies of noble folk," even as for noble souls.[4] But the source of all this plenty is in a river which comes from the Earthly Paradise and not in the Holy Grail. On the occasion of Gawain's visit the Table is garnished richly ; but it is with game of the forest and other meats of this world. It is the same on the arrival of Lancelot ; and then even the earthly food does not vary.

[1] Sommer, *Op. cit.*, I, p. 41.   [2] *Ib.*, pp. 216, 217.
[3] *Ib.*, *s.v.* LE LIVRE DE LANCELOT DEL LAC, Part II, vol. 4, pp. 343 *et seq*.
[4] Potvin, *Op. cit.*, I, p. 249 ; HIGH HISTORY, Branch XXII, Title 1.

In the QUEST OF GALAHAD the manifestations of the Grail are these : (1) In the banqueting-hall of King Arthur, and here is the only record of its appearance in any Castle of the external world, the reason being that the Grail is " going about ". On this occasion— yes, even in the presence of Galahad—" every knight had such meats and drinks as he best loved in this world ". The Table having been dight for the Festival, it seems to follow that what had been provided otherwise underwent transformation, probably in the minds of the participants. (2) At the Stone Cross in the forest and in the waste land, where stood the old Chapel and where in the presence of Lancelot a sick Knight was made whole by the Precious Vessel. (3) To Lancelot in the Grail Castle, where there was, firstly, a Mass of the Grail and, secondly, a banquet at which all were fed by the Vessel, but under such circumstances and after such an experience that whether they were nourished in or out of the body—that is to say, in the soul— there is no criterion for distinction. (4) To Galahad and his Elect Companions at the Consummation of the Quest ; but the sweet meats were those of the Eucharistic exalted to an arch-natural degree. (5) In Sarras at the close of all, " when the deadly flesh began to behold the spiritual things ", and Christ's transcendence was manifested in Christ's immanence. Of these five changes in the Exposition of the Holy Grail, the first only and the lowest was in the guise of earthly food : it was communicated, as if by a special indulgence in the Palace of a Lord of the World as an encouragement to the Quest of Heaven.[1]

If we turn to the German Cycle, we shall find that the feeding qualities are before all things obvious in Wolfram. At the first visit of Parzival, what is taken from the Grail is bread, but other dishes stand full before it in great plenty, both rare and common.[2] Some say that there are no such riches on earth, but to the poet this is a word of foolishness, since the Grail is the crown of all. The wine also was the gift of the precious object, and the cups on the table were filled by the power thereof. In the great and high festival, when the Questing Knight was crowned as King and Warden of the Mystery, even the ordinary fowl of the forest were taken from the Grail. I am afraid that such ministry in the PARZIVAL is comparable to the Proces- sion therein, somewhat indiscriminate in method and " like a tale of little meaning, though the words are strong." In the curious Chronicle of Heinrich, the service of the Table is after the manner born of this world ; but the host does not partake till he is served from the Sacred Reliquary with something which, by its description, bears the external semblance of the Symbolical Bread of Heaven. The poem, however, has otherwise no sacramental connections, nor has the Vessel, strictly speaking, what is understood here by feeding properties.

It remains now to sum up and to ask—though an authentic answer is remote in our quest—what is the meaning of all this disconcerting

---

[1] Sommer, *Op. cit.*, VI, LA QUESTE DEL SAINT GRAAL, p. 13 ; *ib.*, pp. 42, 43 ; *ib.*, pp. 179, 180, 182, 183 ; *ib.*, pp. 189–191 ; *ib.*, p. 197.　　　[2] See Book VII, sect. 1.

medley, which out of the Holy Grail, as an issue in time and place, brings now the voice of an oracle, like the classical Bætylus ; now a certain βάσανος or touchstone, a criterion of judgment which separates the good from the evil ; now a suspended viaticum, which keeps the sick alive and the dead in a false life, but offers no relief in suffering for those who belong thereto ; now manifests corporeal changes in the growth of the Divine Body ; now shews Christ crucified ; and now out of all reason—like a coarse Talmudic Allegory—provides the game of the forest, all commonest and rarest meats ; yet in the Northern French Cycles is (1) a Repository of the Voice of Christ ; (2) the Mystery of the Eucharist ; and (3) a simple Reliquary containing *ex hypothesi* the Precious Blood of the Redeemer. At the moment let us note further that two out of the three texts of Transubstantiation are texts of the Feeding Dish ; but the third in the series has spiritualised all its Houses and acknowledges not the flesh or its ministry except in the Eucharist. In the Chrétien portion of the CONTE DEL GRAAL there speaks no Voice of the Spirit, yet regarding the Service of the Sacred Vessel it bears better testimony than the GRAND SAINT GRAAL or the Great Quest itself in respect of the material side, when this is taken literally. But those who continued and one who finished the CONTE are fitful in their introduction of the feeding element and reflect anterior texts.

I think in conclusion that the intention of the Vulgate Cycle concerning the Feeding Dish is to be taken in another sense of the QUEST OF GALAHAD, which says of Lancelot : " If ye would ask how he lived, He that fed the people of Israel with manna in the desert, so was he fed. For every day when he had said his prayers, he was sustained with the Grace of the Holy Ghost ". And, as the Welsh version has it, " So that he thought himself to be full of the best meats ". It seems to me that in these pregnant words there lies a way of understanding the meats and drinks even at King Arthur's Court. From this suggested interpretation it is obvious that the poem of Wolfram stands apart.

V

THE LESSER HALLOWS OF THE LEGEND

A.—THE SUMMARY OF THESE MATTERS

THE Hallows of the Grail Legend are the beginning of its wonders and of its meanings only ; but, as I have intimated already, there is a sense in which the greater includes the lesser, and that which is of all the highest has assumed from the beginning in its symbolism the things by which it is encompassed. As it is in the light of man's higher part that we are able to interpret the lower, as the body is explained by the soul, so even the Castle of the

Grail and the Great Temple, with all their allusions and all their sacred intimations, are resolved into the Mystery of the Cup, because there is a cloud of witnesses but one authentic voice serving as the spokesman of all. It is unnecessary therefore to lay stress upon the subsidiary Hallows as if they were an integral portion of the Holy Grail, regarded symbolically. They are of the accidents only, and as such they are not vital. The Lance is important to the Legends, but not otherwise than from the legendary standpoint; the Sword is also important, but not in a sacramental sense; the Dish has no settled significance and no traditional story is attached thereto.[1] It is to be understood that the French literature of the Holy Grail, in its form as now extant, has on the external side its roots in Traditions and Memorials connected with the Passion of Christ. The different Cycles of the literature develop their account of these memorials with motives that vary; but they combine therewith certain implied Sacred Objects derived from other sources and not belonging logically to the scheme.

Speaking generally of the Lesser Hallows, the following points are clear. The German Cycle, as represented by Wolfram, derived its idea of the Lance from a source in folk-lore apart from the Grail Legend, as we know it in Northern French. The Northern French literature is clear as to those Hallows connecting with the Passion of Christ; these are the Cup, otherwise the Paschal Dish, and the Lance. It is dubious and variable about the Sword and Dish or Platter, for which there are no real antecedents in the Passion. Several texts have carried over some of the Hallows without modification from folk-lore, even when great Christian Relics were ready to their hands. For example, the Sword used by Peter at Gethsemane did not occur to them, though it would have been more to their purpose, the reason being that there was no Official Tradition concerning it in the external life of the Church. The Dish—on the surface of the stories—is in the same position of unmodified folk-lore; the platter on which the head of St. John the Baptist was served to Herodias is a chance missed even by the LONGER PROSE PERCEVAL, despite its allocation of the Sword to the instrument of the Precursor's martyrdom. Other subsidiary Hallows, mentioned therein, which are by way of after-thought, increase without exhausting the possible Relics of the Passion: one of them is the Crown of Thorns;[2] another the Cloth with which Christ was covered when He was laid in the sepulchre;[3] and yet another the Sacred Nails used at the Crucifixion. I do not think that the Scourge occurs save in the GRAND SAINT GRAAL. The Crown of Thorns was called the Golden Circle, having been set in precious metal and jewels by the Queen of a certain Castle where it was preserved. We have also the Pincers wherewith the Nails were drawn

---

[1] It is obvious that when the Grail itself is represented as the Paschal Dish in which Christ and His Apostles " ate the Lamb on Sher-Thursday ", such Dish has a vital traditional story. When, however, a Dish which is not the Grail appears among the Hallows in the Northern French Cycle, it follows that the Grail is the Wine-Cup of the First Eucharist.

[2] Potvin, *Op. cit.*, I, p. 156; HIGH HISTORY, Branch XIV, Title 2.

[3] *Ib.*, p. 173; HIGH HISTORY, Branch XV, Title 12.

from the limbs of Christ when He was taken down from the Crcss.[1]
Finally, the Shield of Judas Maccabæus is met with in this Romance,
being won in battle by Gawain. The Sword has been referred also
to the same Prince in Israel.

I suppose that the Legend of the Face-Cloth, which is part of the
Veronica Legend, is the earliest of the Passion Relics ; and among
the Evangelisation Traditions that of Lazarus and his Companions
coming to the South of France, carrying the Face-Cloth with them,
has the palm of antiquity in the West. But this Relic, though it
occupies an important position in the Early History of the Grail, is
not included anywhere among the Hallows of the Grail Castle.

The Metrical Romance of Robert de Borron has one Hallow only, and
this is the first extant Grail History. The first extant Quest is that
portion of the CONTE DEL GRAAL which we owe to Chrétien. So far
as his work is concerned there are four Hallows, the Vessel called the
Grail, the Lance, the Sword and the Dish.[2] They are not in any
case connected with the Passion. The Lance has been called his
particular introduction : he is responsible in this manner for the
Blood which flows therefrom in his own and later texts. The DIDOT-
MODENA PERCEVAL, which owes something, it is thought, to Chrétien,
introduces the Lance without any explanation concerning it. The
Chrétien sequels, the PERLESVAUS and the Galahad QUEST lay stress
upon the Sacred Sword, which is usually broken, and the task of the
elect hero is to resolder the weapon. In all texts the Lance ranks
next to the Cup in importance, and when the one is removed to Heaven
at the close of the Galahad Quest it is accompanied by the other.
The PERLESVAUS is a very late Quest, and it has Hallows innumerable.
The GRAND SAINT GRAAL, at least in its present form, is a very late
History, and it lays stress on the Nails of the Passion : it gives also an
invented and artificial allegory to account for the Sword.

I have said that the Sword and the Dish seem but little to the
purpose of the Grail, and those who took over these objects from
antecedent Legends were not of one mind concerning them, more
especially in respect of the Dish, which remains on the surface a
superfluity in the Pageant, though at a later stage we may be enabled
to ascertain its meaning. The Sword in several cases is important,
especially—as I have said also—to the plot of the particular story ;
but it has no reason in the symbolism.

B.—LEGENDS OF THE SACRED LANCE

In the pseudo-Wauchier section of the CONTE DEL GRAAL and in
the description of Monseigneur Gawain's visit to the Grail Castle, he sees
among the Sacred Objects a Lance, which bleeds into a Silver Cup ;
but it is not the Cup of the Grail. The Lance is that weapon which
pierced the side of Christ, and it is said that it will bleed till Doomsday.

[1] Potvin, *Op. cit.*, I, p. 179 ; HIGH HISTORY, Branch XV, Title 24.
[2] *Ib.*, II, pp. 146 *et seq.*

The body of the Lance was of wood ; the blade was white as snow ; and the weapon was fixed at the head of the master dais, with two tapers burning before it. The stream of blood issued from the point of the Lance and ran down the shaft into the vessel, from which it poured into a channel of gold and passed without the Hall.[1] This extravagant description is substituted for a much simpler account in Chrétien's portion of the poem : there only a single drop of blood trickles down to the hand of a Squire who bears the weapon in the Pageant. The fuller historical story is found in Manessier's section, which says that the Lance is that of the Roman soldier who pierced the side of Christ. According to a Montpellier Manuscript, Joseph of Arimathæa was present at the foot of the Cross and seeing, as the spear was withdrawn, how the blood ran down, he collected it in the Holy Vessel, turning black as he did so with sorrow. The DIDOT-MODENA PERCEVAL says only that a Squire in the Grail Castle carried a Lance in his two hands ; that it was that of Longinus ; and that a drop of blood flowed from the sacred point. I believe that this Romance reflects a primitive state of the Quest though it is regarded as late in its actual form, my reason being that the Hallows of the Passion are the only wonder-objects which belong properly to the Quest. The wider field of vision offered in the Vulgate Cycle and the multiplication of Relics in the PERLESVAUS are indubitable signs of lateness. In the GRAND SAINT GRAAL the Hallows which are seen in the vision preceding the Ordina-tion of the younger Joseph are a great ensanguined Cross, three Nails from which blood seems to flow, a Lance—of which the iron point is stained also with blood—an ensanguined Cincture and a Scourge or Rod dyed in the same manner.[2] It will be seen that the writer of this Romance knew well enough that with the Grail itself he could connect only the things thereto belonging—namely, the other Relics of the Passion—and realising this fact in later branches of his Chronicle, while he perpetuates other objects through centuries of hidden life, he is careful not to locate them in the Grail Castle. The HUTH MERLIN is the only Legend of the Prophet which knows of another Hallow than the Sacred Vessel ; and this is the Lance ; but the circumstances under which it is introduced and the account which is given concerning it belong to a later stage of our research. I may say, however, that it was an instrument of mystical vengeance, and as such it reappears in the great prose LANCELOT. It is seen therein by Gawain, who is smitten by its blade of fire, but afterwards is healed by the Grail. It is seen also by Sir Bors when he visits Corbenic : an old man carries it in one hand, while he swings a censer with the other. In the Romance of Galahad, as we know it, the Lance manifests twice, and this is at the end of the Quest, when it is borne in one hand by an Angel, who holds in the other a box to receive the blood from its point. The *ipsissima verba* of the LONGER PROSE PERCEVAL are that of the Hallows there

---

[1] Potvin, *Op. cit.*, III, p. 369, an extract from the Montpellier MS.
[2] Sommer, *Op. cit.*, I, p. 33. Cf. Furnivall's text of Lovelick.

was " right great plenty." Perceval's shield had in the boss thereof some of the Blood of our Lord and a piece of His garment : they were placed therein by Joseph of Arimathæa. As regards the Lance itself, the point bleeds into the Holy Grail, and here also the weapon is one of vengeance, or rather of doom ; for he who is elected to the Quest has something to perform in respect of it, and he fails therein. This notwithstanding, the Hallow in the Romance under notice serves little purpose because it does nothing. For the sake of completeness the Lesser Hallows of the German Cycle may be mentioned with great brevity in this section, though their history and import must be held over for a long time to come. In the PARZIVAL of Wolfram the ensanguined head of a Lance is carried round a certain chamber : it has no connection with the Passion, but once more it is a memorial of vengeance, of fatality which is long and grievous.[1] In Heinrich's DIU CRÔNE, the Lance is held by two Young Men, and it sheds three great drops of blood, which are received in a salver.[2] I should observe in conclusion, for the time being, as to this Hallow that the French Cycle may be classified in three sections, of which the first does not mention the Lance, the second mentions but does not explain its antecedents, while the third affirms that it is the Lance of Longinus used at the Crucifixion. Late or early, there is no other history concerning it.

C.—THE BROKEN SWORD

The Grail Cup was not so much connected with the Passion as originated therefrom, because it is clear in history that, before ever Robert de Borron spoke of Secret Words, the meaning of Mass Chalices and the transit of a Great Hallow from East to West, the Precious Blood had been brought already within the wonder-world of Relics.[3] So also the Sacred Lance had received its justification in Tradition before it was exalted in Romance.[4] The allocation of other objects within the same sphere of devotion was so natural that it was not likely to be resisted ; but it must be observed that the attributions were inherited and not invented by the makers of Books of Chivalry. Face-Cloth and Loin-Cloth, Nails and Crown of Thorns had been long included among objects provided for veneration before the GRAND SAINT GRAIL or the LONGER PROSE PERCEVAL had dreamed of register-ing some among the Hallows of the Graal Ark, or otherwhere in their Holy and Marvellous Shrines. That Romance was capable of inventing Hallows is shewn by the history of the Sacred Sword, and such things had their imputed antecedents in Scripture ; but those of the Passion of Christ were too sacred for their interference, and they were left in the hands of the Church. The Church perhaps was not idle, and the Church did not scruple perhaps ; but minstrels and weavers of stories knew their proper limits and abode therein. Their respect in the case

[1] See Book VII, § 1. [2] *Ib.*, § 3. [3] See Book IX, pp. 332-336. [4] *Ib.*, § 2.

under notice guarantees it in yet another, for which reason I hold it as
certain that never did Robert de Borron tamper with Eucharistic
formulæ, or, in other words, that, whether from far or near, he inherited
and did not invent the Secret Words of the Mystery.[1]

The Sword of the Grail is considerable under two aspects—firstly,
as a derivative from folk-lore, which passes, as we have seen, through
certain branches of the literature without suffering an especial change
in its nature ; secondly, as a hallowed object having an imputed
derivation from the History of the Church of God under one of its
two covenants. In the second case, we must be prepared to find—
and this is natural also—that certain reflections from folk-lore, as
from an earlier state of the object, are to be found in its consecrated
form. In the Chrétien portion of the CONTE DEL GRAAL the Sword
is suspended from the neck of a Page or Squire and is brought to the
Master of the House as a present from his Niece, with leave to bestow
it apparently howsoever he will, so only that it shall be well used. An
inscription upon it says that it will never break except in one peril,
which is known only to the smith who forged it.[2] In his time as a
craftsman he made three such weapons, and no others will follow. As
regards this particular example, the belt was worth a treasure, the
crosspiece was of fine gold, and the sheath was of Venetian smith's
work. It is given to Perceval by the King of the Grail Castle as something to him predestined. But it is only at a later stage that he learns
under what circumstances it will fly in pieces and how it may be
repaired—namely, by plunging it in a certain lake which is hard by the
smithy of him who wrought it.[3] The continuation of pseudo-Wauchier
ignores these facts and reproduces the Sword at the Castle, where it is
carried by a Crowned Knight : it is broken already and Gawain is asked
to resolder it, in which task he fails. Perceval succeeds, on the occasion
of his second visit, except for a slight crevice, thus proving that, at
least in a certain measure, he is a lover of God, a true Knight, and one
who loves also the Church, which is the Spouse of God. The conclusion
of Manessier furnishes the history of the Hallow in full, though it
has been the subject of allusion previously : (a) one stroke was given
therewith ; it destroyed the realm of Logres and the country adjacent
thereto ; (b) this stroke was inflicted on the King's Brother, in the
course of a battle ; (c) when the King himself took up the fragments
unwarily, he was pierced through the thigh, and the wound will be
healed only when his Brother's death has been avenged. In Chrétien,
on the contrary, the wound of the Grail King is caused by a Spear which
passes through his two thighs. The alternative conclusion of Gerbert
sends Perceval again into exile, because certain imperfections in his life
account for the fact that—paceWauchier—he cannot resolder the Sword,
and the Quest must be fulfilled better. The Hallow remains in the Castle,
but another Sword is introduced and serves to indicate that behind the

---

[1] It is being assumed that the Mystery centred in the Eucharist and not in a Religious
Oracle.   [2] It is not therefore a Sword of Legend.   [3] See Book III, § 2.

strange memorial of this unknown poet there were sources of Legend which, if we could now recover them, might place yet another construction upon the root-matter of the Grail Myth. In Gerbert the Sword under notice is broken, not in a conflict which calls for a conventional vengeance, after the familiar motives of folk-lore, but in an attempt to enforce an entrance into the Earthly Paradise.[1]

Passing over the Lesser Chronicles which—although in the DIDOT-MODENA PERCEVAL it is hinted on one occasion that there were many worthy Relics—make no reference to the Sword, and coming to the Vulgate Cycle we find that in the GRAND SAINT GRAAL there is a Hallow of this kind, and it is important not only from the standpoint of the Romance itself but for the Quest which follows therefrom. It was the Sword of David the King, and it was placed, as we have seen, by Solomon in a Mysterious Ship, destined to sail the seas for centuries as a testimony to Galahad that his ancestor was aware of his coming at the end of the times of the Grail. During the course of its history more than one wound is inflicted therewith, while the circumstances under which it is broken are told variously. In the GRAND SAINT GRAAL there are actually two Swords : to that of David the particular virtue ascribed is that no one can draw it—before the predestined hero in the days of Quest—without being visited heavily for his rashness. The doom works automatically, even to the infliction of death. It is only by a kind of accident that this Sword is broken, and then it is rejoined instantly, according to one of the codices. In another there is a distinct account, which does not say how or whether the Sword was resoldered in fine. As regards the Second Sword, it is merely an ordinary weapon with which Joseph II is smitten by a certain seneschal when he is endeavouring to convert the Prince in some part of Great Britain. The Sword breaks when it pierces him, and the point remains in the wound. After various miracles, which result in the general conversion of the people, the sufferer places his hand on the point of the Sword, which is protruding apparently from his side. It comes out of the wound, and the place heals up immediately. Joseph then takes the two portions of the Broken Sword and says : " God grant that this good weapon shall never be soldered except by him who is destined to accomplish the Adventure of the Siege Perilous at the Round Table, in the time of King Arthur ; and God grant also that the point shall not cease to exude blood until the two portions are so soldered."[2]

It is reasonable to expect that these Hallows should prove a source of confusion as to their duplication and their purpose. I do not conceive that the Sword which is brought out of Fairyland in the HUTH MERLIN, which is claimed by Balan, which brings about the Dolorous Stroke—though this is inflicted actually by another instrument—which in fine involves two Brothers in mutual destruction, can be

---

[1] See Book III, § 5. At the end of Gerbert's narrative Perceval returns to the Castle of the Fisher King and makes the more authentic Sword perfect.

[2] Sommer, Op. cit., I, pp. 253-256.

connected with either of the weapons with which we have been just dealing.[1] The alternative later MERLIN has no Mystery of Swords which can be identified with the Hallow of the Grail, and the prose LANCELOT knows nothing of that of David. It speaks, however, of a knight named Eliezer, who carries two Swords ; one of them is enclosed in a priceless sheath, and is said to be that which pierced the loins of Joseph of Arimathæa and was broken therein,[2] thereafter repeating at full length the story recounted in the GRAND SAINT GRAAL. In the Great Quest the Sword by which Joseph was wounded is presented to Galahad for soldering ; and when the Elect Knight has performed the task, it is given into the charge of Bors, because he was a Good Knight and a worthy man.[3] After the soldering " it arose grete and marvellous, and was full of grete hete that many men felle for drede." It seems to follow that it was brought back to Logres on the return of Sir Bors from Sarras. The Sword of David was carried to Sarras, as we may infer, by Galahad, but it was not taken to Heaven with the Grail and Lance, the reason being doubtless that it was not a Symbol of the Passion. In the LONGER PROSE PERCEVAL the Sword, as we know, is that with which St. John the Baptist was beheaded, and though there is, firstly, no attempt to account for the presence of this Hallow in England, nor, secondly, any reference to it in the earlier literature, the identification helps us to understand better its place among the Hallows, as some other Swords met with in the texts have scarcely a title to be included among sacred objects. The office of Gawain, before he can know anything about Grail Mysteries, is to obtain this Sword from its wrongful keepers, and herein he succeeds. The scabbard is loaded with precious stones and the mountings are of silk, with buttons of gold. The hilt is also gemmed, while the pommel is a holy and sacred stone set in it by a certain Roman Emperor. When the Sword came forth from the scabbard it was covered with blood, and this seems to have been the case invariably at the hour of noon, which was the time of the Saint's Martyrdom. When noon has passed it becomes clear and green like an emerald. Its length is like that of a normal sword, but when sheathed neither weapon nor scabbard seems to be of two spans' length. It is said on the testimony of pseudo-Josephus that the Old Law was destroyed beyond recovery by a stroke of this Sword and that to effect such destruction our Lord Himself suffered to be smitten in the side with a Spear. These things are not to be understood on the open sense of the text.[4]

The Vulgate Chronicles of the Grail may be, as they are indeed, upon God's side ; but the judgment concerning this sub-section of the Lesser Hallows must be that the Sword is an impediment before the face of the symbolism and little better than an idle wonder which we could wish to be taken out of the way. We could wish also—or I

---

[1] Gaston Paris : MERLIN, I, pp. 215–221 ; II, pp. 24–30.
[2] Sommer, *Op. cit.*, IV, pp. 323–328.　　　[3] *Ib.*, VI, pp. 187, 188.
[4] Potvin, *Op. cit.*, I, pp. 74, 75 ; HIGH HISTORY, Branch VI, Titles 4 and 6.

personally at least—that something of the Mystery behind the ascription of Gerbert might come at this day into our hands. In the PARZIVAL of Wolfram the hero of that Great Quest is refreshed by fruits brought from the Earthly Paradise on the occasion of his first visit to the Temple of the Holy Grail. We know not how or why, but this is another reflection, possibly from the source of Gerbert, and one which takes us no further, except that from time to time, by dim hints and allusions, we see that the Legend of the Grail is not so far apart from the Legend of Eden. In this manner we recur to the German Cycle, and there we find that there is a Sword of note in the PARZIVAL : it is that which was given to the hero by Anfortas, the Grail King. Now that this, amidst any variations, is the same story as that which is told by Chrétien is rather evident than likely. Another Sword broke when Parzival was fighting with his unknown Brother Feirfeis, because it would not drink the blood of his kinship ; and this is the far antithesis of some of the French stories. In Heinrich's DIU CRÔNE, a Fair Youth of exalted mien carries a fair broad Sword, which he lays before the King of the Castle, and this Sword is given by the King to Gawain after he has asked the Question which we know to be all important. It has no later history.

In conclusion as to this matter, the Hallow of the Sword is not unlike a corresponding weapon in some of the Grades of Masonic Chivalry : in the same way as the Reverend Knights therein are not, in many cases, qualified to use the symbolic arm, so in the Grail literature the poets and romancers have accepted the custody of something which is so little to their purpose that they know scarcely what they shall do therewith. Had they only thought less of their folk-lore and vengeance-complex, they might have told a better—aye, even a truer—story from the standpoint of their own symbolism.

D.—THE DISH

The Sacred Dish being also, as we have seen, rather an unmeaning mystery, and as although it recurs frequently the descriptions are brief and the office which it holds is doubtful, it will be desirable only to distinguish those texts in which it is found. Subject to one possibility, and this is of the speculative order, it is, as we have seen, an unmodified survival from folk-lore ; we should have expected it to appear therefore in the Chrétien portion of the CONTE DEL GRAAL, and this is the case actually ; but it serves therein a very practical and mundane purpose, being used by the King and his Guests to wash their hands. It is a silver plate and is carried by a Damosel. It reappears in one codex of the continuation by Wauchier. The conclusion by Manessier describes it after a similar manner, but its purpose is not delineated : Perceval asks all the necessary questions regarding the Grail and Lance ; he asks also concerning the Dish, but there is apparently nothing to tell, or at least he hears nothing. At the same time it may have had a higher significance for this poet than for all the others, since he causes the Holy Dish to follow Perceval with the other Hallows when he accompanies a Hermit into the wilderness where he serves the Lord for ten years. Finally, Manessier states in his last words that the Dish was doubtless assumed into Heaven with the other Sacred Objects, namely, the Lance and the Sword. According to Gerbert, a Lady named Philosofine, who here, as in another Romance, figures as the Mother of Perceval, came over with Joseph of Arimathæa bearing a certain Plate ; another lady carried an ever-bleeding Lance ; while Joseph himself bore a fairer Vessel than eye had ever beheld. In the Lesser Chronicles there is only a single reference, which occurs in the DIDOT-MODENA PERCEVAL. When the Grail and the other Hallows are manifested first to Perceval, it is said that the Damosel bears two silver plates, adorned with draperies. In the GRAND SAINT GRAAL, and on the occasion when Joseph II is raised to the High Pontificate, the Paschal Dish is seen on the Altar, and in the middle place thereof is an exceedingly Rich Vessel of gold and precious stones. Here the reference is probably to the Sacramental Cup, but the account is confused ; and elsewhere the complex Romance, in one of its codices, presents a new aspect of folk-lore, for there is pictured an Angel, bearing a Great and Glorious Head, about which we have no explanation and of which we hear nothing subsequently, either in the text itself or in later documents of the Cycle.[1] The Dish also passes out of the horizon, not only in the prose LANCELOT but in the QUEST OF GALAHAD. The German Cycle speaks of a Golden Salver, jewelled with precious stones and carried upon a silken cloth. It is used in the poem of Heinrich to receive the Blood which issues from the Lance.

It seems possible that there was an early tendency on the part of Christian romancers to distinguish between the Chalice, being the Cup " in which Christ made His Sacrament ", and the Dish, being the Vessel in which He and His disciples ate the Paschal Lamb. They are confused to some extent in the GRAND SAINT GRAAL, while the prose LANCELOT knows of a single Vessel only, which is the Eucharistic Cup.[2] If such an implication were present to the mind of Manessier, we could understand why he says that the Dish was assumed into Heaven. It would have also a logical place among the Relics of the Passion ; and if the Grail were a Mass Chalice, the Dish would be the Paten:

---

[1] It is found in the text edited by Dr. Furnivall for the Roxburghe Club, *anno* 1861, but not in the Vulgate Version of Sommer. See *Op. cit.*, I, p. 80, and the second manifestation of Angels recited therein.

[2] *Si estoit fait en semblance de calice.*—Sommer, *Op. cit.*, Vol. V, LE LIVRE DE LANCELOT DEL LAC, Part 3, p. 10 8. English readers may compare Miss L. A. Paton's SIR LANCELOT OF THE LAKE, based on a manuscript in the *Bibliothèque Nationale*, p. 311. The words are identical: " and it was fashioned in semblance of a Chalice."

VI

THE CASTLE OF THE HOLY GRAIL

THE Custodians of the Holy Grail, which was a Mystery of all Secrecy, "there where no sinner can be", abode sometimes in the uttermost seclusion, despite the kingly titles to them ascribed. Let us seek in the first instance to realise the nature and alternative places of that Castle or Temple which, according to the Legend, was for a period of centuries the Sanctuary of the Sacred Vessel and of the other Hallowed Objects connected therewith. Whether or not in the several locations of the Hallows we may come at a later time into fuller understanding of their Offices and of the meanings which abide behind them, they are not to be regarded exactly as a part of the Mystery belonging to the Castle itself ; but at least this is more than a casket, while between the container and the things contained, distinct though their significance may be, there are points of correlation, so that the one throws light on the other.

We have seen that the Vessel itself was brought from Salem to Britain, and it follows from the historical texts that the transit had a special purpose, one explanation of which will be found ready to our hands when the time comes for its consideration. The Castle is described after several manners, the later Romances being naturally the more specific, and we get in fine a geographical settlement and boundary. In the Chrétien portion of the CONTE DEL GRAAL, Perceval discovers the Castle in a valley, wherein it is well and beautifully situated, having a four-square tower, with a principal hall and a bridge leading up to the chief entrance.[1] In some of the other Legends the Asylum is so withdrawn that it is neither named nor described. The EARLY HISTORY OF MERLIN speaks of it simply and shortly as the place where they had the Holy Vessel in keeping. According to the DIDOT-MODENA PERCEVAL, it is the House of the Rich King Fisherman : this also is situated in a valley ; it has a tower and is approached by a bridge. It might be a tower merely, for the description is not less vague than are many accounts of the Cup. One of the later Merlin texts says only that the Holy Vessel is in the West—that is, in the Land of Vortigern—or that it abides in Northumbria. Another certifies that the Castle is Corbenic ; but though we hear much concerning it there is no description whatever.

That section of the CONTE DEL GRAAL which is referable to Wauchier de Denain says that it is situated on a causeway tormented by the sea. The building is of vast extent and is inhabited by a great folk. We hear of a ceiling emblazoned with gold and embroidered with silver stars ; of tables of precious metal ; of images and of rich gems which enlighten it.[2] In a word, we are already in the region of imaginative

---

[1] Potvin, II, 142, ll. 4228–42.   [2] Potvin, V, pp. 139, 140, ll. 34628–44.

development and adornment ; but it is all mere decoration which carries with it no meaning, beyond the heavy tokens of splendour. Manessier furnishes no special account, while Gerbert, who has other affairs at heart than solicitude about a supposed material building or desire to exalt it into allegory, leaves it unsketched entirely.

The GRAND SAINT GRAAL is the only French text which describes in a methodical manner the building of the Holy House. The first Wardens have passed from the Land of the Living, and Alain le Gros is the Keeper of the Blessed Vessel. The actual builder is a certain converted King of *Terre Foraine*,[1] and there is a covenant between him and Alain, one condition of which is that the Grail shall remain in his kingdom. The Castle on its completion is given the mystical name of Corbenic, in obedience to an inscription which is found blazoned on one of the entrance gates. The name is said to signify the Most Holy Vessel. The Grail is placed in a fair Chamber of the Castle, as if on an Altar of Repose ; but all his munificence notwithstanding and all the sacramental visions which he sees in the Holy Place—beating of birds' wings and chanting of innumerable voices—the King is visited speedily for his mere presence and receives his death wound at the very Altar.[2] It is the judgment of the Sanctuary on those who desecrate the Sanctuary by carrying, however unwittingly, an unhallowed past therein ; and it recalls the traditional conclusion of certain Cabiric Mysteries, wherein the Candidate was destroyed by the Gods. Setting aside an analogy on which I am by no means insisting, the event was the beginning of those wonders which earned for Castle Corbenic the name of the Palace Adventurous, because no one could enter therein, and no one could sleep, its lawful dwellers excepted, without death overtaking them, or some other grievous penalty.

The prose LANCELOT is in near correspondence with Chrétien, representing the Castle as situated at the far end of a great valley, with water encircling it.[3] On another occasion it is named rather than described, and visited but not expounded, though we learn that it is situated in a town which has many dwellers therein. In the QUEST OF GALAHAD it is a rich and fair building, with a postern opening towards the sea ; and this was guarded by lions, between which a man might pass only if he carried the arms of faith, since the sword availed nothing and there was no protection in harness.[4] For the visitor who was expected or tolerated, it would seem that all doors stood open, except the door of the Sanctuary. But this would unclose of itself ; the light would issue from within ; the silver table would be seen ; and thereon the Holy Vessel, covered with drapery of samite. There also on a day might be celebrated, with reverence of high worship, the Great Mass

---

[1] He was named Kalafes and became Alphasem in Baptism. The Castle is described as *fort et bon et bien seant*. It would seem that the subsequent visitation on the builder was quite arbitrary. He had slept in the Castle on a certain night and witnessed the Service of the Holy Grail, for which he was smitten with a spear between the thighs by a " fiery man " and died ten days later. It is to be noted that he was ignoring no prohibition and no caution. [2] Sommer, *Op. cit.*, I, pp. 288, 289.
[3] *Ib.*, V, p. 105. [4] *Ib.*, VI, pp. 178–180.

of the Supersanctified, and this even in the presence of those who were not clean in their past, so only that they had put away their sin when they entered on the Quest, or during the course thereof. It was beheld thus by Lancelot, though he lay as one dead afterwards, because of his intrusion.[1] So also the welcome guest had reason to know that the Court of King Pelles held a great fellowship in the town of Corbenic. But there were other visitors at times and seasons who saw little of all this royalty, like Hector de Marys, who—brother as he was to my Lord Sir Lancelot—found the doors barred against him and no Ostiarius to open, long as he hailed thereat.[2]

The most decorative of all the French accounts is, however, in the LONGER PROSE PERCEVAL, where the Castle is reached by means of three Bridges, which are horrible to cross. Three great waters run below them, the first bridge being a bow-shot in length and not more than a foot in width. This is the Bridge of the Eel ; but it proves wide and a fair thorough-way in the act of crossing. The second Bridge is of ice, feeble and thin, and it is arched high above the water. It is transformed on passing into the richest and strangest ever seen, and its abutments are full of images. The third and last Bridge stands on columns of marble. Beyond it there is a sculptured gate, giving upon a flight of steps, which leads to a spacious hall painted with figures in gold.[3] When Perceval visited the Castle a second time he found it encompassed by a river, which came from the Earthly Paradise and proceeded through the forest beyond as far as the hold of a hermit, where it " found peace in the earth."[4] To the Castle itself there were three names attributed : the Castle of Eden, the Castle of Joy and the Castle of Souls. In conclusion as to this matter, the location, in fine, is Corbenic—not as an unvaried name, but as that which may be called the accepted, representing the Temple at its highest, and corresponding in French Romance to Montsalvatch in German—which our extant redaction of the GRAND SAINT GRAAL mentions specifically and which, all doubtful clouds of occult adventure notwithstanding, looms almost as a landmark in the LANCELOT and the QUEST OF GALAHAD.

I must speak very lightly of the German Cycle, because, through all these branches, it is understood that I shall recur of necessity, there and here, to the subject matter of the present section. In the PARZIVAL of Wolfram the Temple is so decorated that it has ceased almost to be a house made with human hands, though the descriptions on the external side may be called almost severe in their simplicity. On that side it has the strength of a feudal fortress, turret above turret rising. But on the inward side and in the master-hall of the Palace there is a wealth of oriental splendour—carpets and couches and cushions, marble hearths burning strange fragrant woods, and a great blazing

---

[1] *Op. cit.*, VI, pp. 180, 181.   [2] *Ib.*, pp. 182, 183.
[3] Potvin, *Op. cit.*, I, pp. 83–85 ; HIGH HISTORY, Branch VI, Titles 14, 15.
[4] *Ib.*, p. 249 ; Branch XXII, Titles 1, 2.

of lights. So far the PARZIVAL of Wolfram ; but we must turn to a later text for the building of the Temple—which is after another manner than anything told of Corbenic in the Northern French Cycle.[1] That building was the work of Titurel, the first King of the Grail ; and in answer to his prayers the High Artificers of Heaven prepared the ground-plan of the Holy Place and furnished the raw material. Over the construction itself the earthly craftsmen toiled by day and the Powers of Heaven by night. The floor was of pure onyx ; at the summit of the tower there was a ruby surmounted by a Cross of crystal, and carbuncles shone at the meeting-points of the great arches within. The roof was of sapphire, and a pictured starry heaven moved there in true order.

We are on a different level when we have recourse to the poem of Heinrich, which presents several anomalies in respect of the literature as a whole. The road leading to the Grail Castle was one of harsh and hazardous enterprise—world without end. But it brought the questing hero at some far point into a Plenteous and Gracious Land, where rose the Palace of Desire, looking beautiful exceedingly, with a meadow before it which was set apart for joust and tournament. A great concourse of Knights and Gentlewomen abode in the burg, and for the Castle itself we are told that there was none so fair. Though it will be seen that there is nothing distinctive in this account, as it is reduced here into summary, the design is among many things strange, for if it is not the Castle of Souls it is that of a Living Tomb, as the story concerning it will shew at the proper time.

So did the place of the Mysteries, from a dim and vague allusion, become

> " A wilderness of building, sinking far
> And self-withdrawn into a wondrous depth,
> Far sinking into splendour."

We can scarcely say whether that which had begun on earth was assumed into the Spiritual Place, or whether the powers and virtues from above descended to brood thereon and even abide therein.

I have left over from this consideration all reference to another " spiritual place," in Sarras on the confines of Egypt, where the Grail, upon its outward journey, dwelt for a period, and whither, after generations and centuries, it returned also for a period. As this was not the point of its origin, so it was not that of its rest : it was a stage in the passage from Salem and a stage in the transit to Heaven. What was meant by this infidel city, which was yet consecrated so strangely, is hard to determine ; but its meaning—if any—belongs to a later stage. It is too early again to ask what are the implicits of the PERLESVAUS when it identifies the Castle of the Grail with the Earthly Paradise and the Place of Souls ; but we may note it as a sign of intention, and we shall meet with it in another connection where no one has thought to look for it.[2]

[1] Appendix I, Note 4.   [2] *Ib:*, Note 5.

VII

THE KEEPERS OF THE HALLOWS

SUCH was the abode of the Hallows ; and those who dwelt therein, the succession of Grail Keepers, belonged to that order which we should expect in such precincts. It should be noted that in the poem of Chrétien the Keeper is called the Fisher King,[1] but his other name and his lineage are not disclosed. It is, however, the beginning only of a very long story, and though it is difficult to say how the first poet would have carried his theme to its term, personally I do not question that he might have borne no different witness to the rest of the Grail Cycle in Northern French. By this, without exception, Joseph of Arimathæa is the first Guardian of the Sacred Vessel ; but either he passes from the scene before it has found a Sanctuary or he assumes a secondary position in his Son's favour. According to the Metrical Romance of Borron and the Borron Cycle generally, he was succeeded by his son-in-law, Brons ; but according to the Vulgate Chronicles he was succeeded by his own Son, the Second Joseph, who is unknown to the other Cycle. The Lesser Chronicles bridge the centuries between that generation which saw the Ascension of Christ and that which was to behold the Flower of Chivalry in Arthur, by means of a single Keeper, who was to remain on earth until he had seen his Grandson, Perceval, and had remitted into his hands the Secrets and Hallows of which he had been in charge so long. Perceval is the third who counts in the line of election to complete the human trinity of Grail Guardians, reflecting, after their own vaguely mystical manner, those Three who bear witness in Heaven, namely, the Divine Trinity. To accomplish the hero's geniture, Alain, the Son of Brons, although he had accepted celibacy, married in some undeclared manner ; and it was as his issue that Perceval was born in the fullness of Enchanted Times. For the EARLY HISTORY OF MERLIN the Keepers are those—not otherwise described or specified— who had the Holy Vessel, and the reticence in this case may seem like that of Chrétien : this, however, is not so actually, because the prose Romance of Merlin follows directly from the Metrical Romance of Joseph. We are told further that the promise of union with the Keepers is like *la joie perdurable*.

Pseudo-Wauchier's continuation of the CONTE DEL GRAAL offers no materials for the identification of the Fisher King, nor is even this name applied to him. But the variants or interpolated passages in the Montpellier MS. follow the Borron Cycle, representing him as the Father of Alain le Gros who married Enigea, the Sister of Joseph.[2] Manessier and Gerbert, on the other hand, would appear to reflect the

---

[1] *Le rice roi Pescéour.* See the CONTE DEL GRAAL, edited by Potvin, l. 4673, Vol. II, p. 156.   [2] Potvin, *Op. cit.*, IV, pp. 343 *et seq.*

Vulgate Cycle, though as regards the GRAND SAINT GRAAL they know nothing concerning a younger Joseph.

From one point of view, the succession, as it is found in the Vulgate texts, involves fewer difficulties, because it exhibits a rudimentary sense of symbolical chronology and develops in consequence a long line of successive Custodians. They are, however, quite shadowy, and exist only to bridge the gulf of time in the order following : (1) Joseph of Arimathæa and Joseph II ; (2) Alain, the Son of Brons ; (3) Eminadap, the Son of Joshua, who was himself a Brother of Alain ; (4) Carceloys ; (5) Manuiel ; (6) Lambor : the last four were Kings, holding from Calafas of *Terre Foraine*, called Alphasan or Alphisem in baptism ; (7) the King Pelles.[1]

So far as regards the GRAND SAINT GRAAL, and it is difficult to say what version or prototype of this text was before the authors of the VULGATE and HUTH MERLIN ; but whatever it was they seem to have drawn from the same source. The Grail Castle, as we have seen, is Corbenic, situated in the realm of Listenoys, and the Keeper is King Pelles. As much and no more may be said concerning the prose LANCELOT. Enumerations of this kind serve very little purpose, and I will speak therefore only of the alternative Keepers who were in evidence during the days of Quest. On the one side, there is Brons, to whom succeeded Perceval at the close of a life of search ;[2] on the other, there is King Pelles, of the Castle Corbenic, whose Daughter, Elaine, gave Galahad as issue to Lancelot, himself the lineal descendant of the King reigning at Sarras in the days of Joseph of Arimathæa and the first flight of the Grail. Galahad was the last Keeper recognised by this Cycle, and he seems to have been appointed only for the purpose of removing the Vessel. It was : *Ite, missa est*, and *est consummatum*, when he died and rose to the stars.[3] As the PERLESVAUS is extra-lineal and thus stands by itself, I will say of it only in the present place that the King's title is that adopted by Chrétien, namely, the King Fisherman, and that his name is not declared otherwise.[4] His successor is Perceval ; but he enters into the Secret Royalty after an interregnum only, and his Stewardship also is with a view to the withdrawal of the Mystery. As regards the German Cycle, which will be dealt with elsewhere, the succession of Grail Keepers is Titurel, Frimutel and Anfortas, to whom succeeds Parzival. Titurel at the beginning was a saintlike hero of Earthly Chivalry, to whom a Divine Voice brought the strange tidings that he had been elected to guard the Holy Grail on Mont Salvatch. His progenitor was a man of Cappadocia who was attached to the Emperor Vespasian, and received for his services a grant of land in Southern France.[5]

The Hereditary Stewardship of the Holy Grail was the Most Secret

---

[1] Sommer's VULGATE VERSION OF ARTHURIAN ROMANCES, I, p. 289.
[2] See *post*, Book IV, § 4, *s.v.* DIDOT-MODENA PERCEVAL.
[3] Sommer : *Op. cit.*, VI, *passim*.
[4] Potvin, *Op. cit.*, I, LE ROMAN EN PROSE, p. 130 and elsewhere.
[5] See *post*, Book VII, § 1.

of all Mysteries, and never initiated anyone outside the predestined family. There is seclusion in all cases, but that of the Brons Keepership is greater beyond comparison than that of Alain and his successors in the GRAND SAINT GRAAL. One explanation of this may be sought speculatively in the simple fact that, as regards the first case, several intermediate texts are wanting and may have been planned in part, if indeed they were never finished. This is admissible *per se ;* but in the most proximate pre-Arthurian period, and in the time of the King, we find still the same concealment, though it is not quite so unvaried in the records of the CONTE DEL GRAAL as it is in the EARLY HISTORY OF MERLIN and in the DIDOT-MODENA PERCEVAL. The comparative position seems as another line of demarcation between the Lesser and Vulgate Chronicles ; but the distinctions between the two branches will be appreciated most clearly by a comparison between the EARLY HISTORY OF MERLIN[1] and the later VULGATE[2] and HUTH texts.[3] The Sanctuary is shrouded in the EARLY HISTORY, and we know only that those who have the Sacred Vessel are somewhere in Northumbria. In the Vulgate, the Keeper, King Pelles, is in continual evidence. He is also a King in warfare, and it is by no means certain that he is always on the side of the Over-Lord Arthur. In the HUTH MERLIN the Grail Castle is so accessible that King Pellinor can be maimed by a strange Knight.

It would be easy to extend this section very much further than I purpose doing, in view of all that is to follow. My intention here is a schedule, or this mainly ; and the specific summary is as follows. There are two Early History versions, and they are represented, firstly, by Borron's Metrical Romance, which is much earlier than any other historical account : they are represented, secondly, by the GRAND SAINT GRAAL, allowance—at its value—being made in both cases for the hypothetical possibility of those earlier drafts which were dear to the heart of scholarship, now somewhat far in the past. About the extant work in the second case there are two points certain : (1) that it is very much later than any first recension or transcript of the alleged book which had come into the hands of Robert de Borron ; (2) that it is later also than the QUEST OF GALAHAD as we know it, which involves also an antecedence in some form of the prose LANCELOT and the later histories of Merlin. We are left therefore with two claims which appear to be at the root of the Mystery of the Holy Grail, as it is manifested in French literature of the twelfth and thirteenth centuries : these are the claim of an Eucharistic formula, the validity and efficacy of which transcended the Words of Institution known by the Official Church, and the claim of a Priesthood which did not draw from the Official Apostolate, though it did not question its authority. These two are likely to be one in their essence, and it is out of these respectively that we may come to understand why Perceval

---

[1] Sommer, *Op. cit.*, II, pp. 19, 27.   [2] *Ib.*
[3] MERLIN : ROMAN EN PROSE, edited by Gaston Paris and Jacob Ulrich.

is withdrawn into the innermost seclusion by the Lesser Chronicles, and why in the Vulgate Cycle Galahad is assumed into Heaven—both carrying their warrants.

VIII

THE PAGEANTS IN THE QUESTS

THE presence of the Holy Vessel signified the Divine Presence. The Life of Life had remained in the Precious Blood. The Voice of the Angel of Great Counsel, the Voice of the Son and the Voice of the Holy Spirit abode therein, or spoke as if from behind it. The Presence was sacramental, but the Presence was also real, and through the soul it was one which sustained the body itself at need. So far as regards the Lesser Chronicles and in those which may be called Greater—otherwise, the Vulgate Cycle—there was a Reservation which continued through centuries, an Arch-Natural Mass—*ex hypothesi* a Daily Celebration according to its Rule of Institution, and in any case—an unfailing ministry to body and soul alike. In a word, the Last Supper was maintained for ever and ever. It was a sacramental side of the eternal Festival of the followers of Bran,[1] and those who say that the roots of the Mystery are in folk-lore say only the most negligible part of the truth concerning it ; for if I accomplish by a secret science the transmutation of lead into gold, it will be useless for any scholarship of science to depose that the important fact is the lead. The latter is the antecedent, and as such is, of course, indispensable, but the great fact is the conversion ; and I say the same of the Grail literature.

On this and all other considerations, it will be understood that the Mystic Castle was a place of the highest reverence, and that all things concerning the Sacred Vessel were done with ceremonial solemnity, following a prescribed order. In this way it comes about that the Quests present the Pageant of the Grail on its manifestation within the Hall and Shrine of the Castle. There are instances in which it is exceedingly simple, and others in which it is ornate. It is the former in the Lesser Chronicles, and demands scarcely the express name of a Pageant ; in the Vulgate Cycle it is decorative, and this term will apply to some of the manifestations which are described in the CONTE DEL GRAAL. The section which is referable to Chrétien offers, however, nothing to detain us. The Procession enters the hall in single file, and consists in succession of a Page, or Squire, who carries the mysterious Sword which will break in one danger only ; of another Squire who bears the Sacred Lance from which the blood issues ; and then of two Squires together, each supporting a ten-branched candle-stick. Between these there walks the gentle and beautiful Maiden who

---

[1] That is, the Blessed Bran of Celtic lore.

lifts up the Holy Grail in her two hands : she is followed by another
Maiden, who carries the Silver Dish.   The Procession passes twice
before the couch on which the King of the Castle reclines, and it is to
be noticed that whatever efficacy and wonder may reside in the objects
which are manifested thus, the office of the Bearers is as purely ceremonial as that of the Acolytes and Thurifers at any High Mass in the
world.[1]   When the Questing Knight pays his first visit in the DIDOT-
MODENA PERCEVAL, the Offices are transposed partially and the
Sword is missing from the Pageant.[2]   He who upraises the Lance
enters in the prescribed manner ; but he carries it with both hands
and is followed by a Maiden with two silver plates and a napkin on
her arm ;   while the Vessel containing the Precious Blood of our
Saviour, as if it were a Phial or Reliquary, is in the charge of a second
Squire.   On the occasion of the later visit, it is said, still more tersely,
that the Grail and the other Venerable Relics come out from a chamber
beyond ;   but we do not learn who carries them.[3]   It is a characteristic
of all the versions that, even in telling the same story, this is done with
respect to a certain genius of difference and of variants intervening in
the text.   The pseudo-Wauchier text recounts in two versions the visit
of Monseigneur Gawain to the Grail Castle, in the more important case
under circumstances of unexplained Mystery, for no one was less on
the Quest.   This is comparable to the Reception, in some Mystery-
House, of a Neophyte who is neither introduced nor prepared, but is
mistaken at first for another.   The Pageant is dismembered also, for
the Dish does not appear, while the Hallow of the Broken Sword is
placed upon the breast of a dead body, which lies on a rich bier.[4]   As
if it were a subsidiary Hallow, a Stately Clerk carries an enormous Cross
of jewelled silver, and the only Procession described is that of Canons
in silken copes, who celebrate an Office of the Dead amidst thuribles
and golden candlesticks.   The Grail itself does not appear till the supper
is served in the hall, when it is held by no visible hand and no other
Sacred Object is seen in connection therewith.   At a later stage of the
episode, the Lance manifests and the Blood which distils from its point
is received, as we have seen, in a Silver Cup.   The Broken Sword, in fine,
reappears at the close :   it is a very curious and piecemeal Pageant.
When Perceval revisits the Castle, the account of Wauchier de Denain
is in better conformity with what may be termed the conventional or
authorised ceremonial type.

Passing to this point at the close of the continuation by Wauchier,
there is again a very simple Pageant, in which the Grail comes first—
a Holy and Glorious Vessel—under the charge of a Maiden, who issues
from the Secret Chamber and passes before the Royal Table, carrying
the Hallow exalted.[5]   There follows a second Maiden, than whom none
is fairer, clothed in white drapery, and bearing the Lance from

[1] Potvin, *Op. cit.*, II, pp. 146–148.   [2] Hucher, *Op. cit.*, I, p. 465.
[3] *Ib.*, I, p. 482.
[4] Potvin, *Op. cit.*, III, pp. 363–368.   [5] *Op. cit.*, V, pp. 143–150.

which flows the Mysterious Blood. In fine, there enters the Squire exposing a naked Sword, broken in the middle thereof. It is at this point that, abruptly enough, the continuation reaches its term and is taken up by Manessier,[1] who causes the Grail and Lance to pass for a second time before the King and his Guest, together with a noble Silver Dish, which is carried by a third Maiden—a Procession of Vestals only, seeing that the work of the Sword—which has been resoldered partly by Perceval—has no longer its place in the Pageant. When the questing hero pays his third visit to the Grail Castle, under the auspices of the same poet, the Lance and Grail are carried by two Maidens ; but a Squire holds the Silver Dish, enveloped in his rich amice of red samite.[2] The Sacred Objects pass three times, and return whence they issued, into the Secret Chamber, the Mystery of which is never disclosed fully by the makers of this Romance. In fine, when Perceval is crowned—and this is his fourth visit—a gentle Maiden exalts the Holy Vessel, the Lance is borne by a Squire, while another Maiden holds the Silver Dish.[3] It will be seen that on each occasion there is some variation in the Offices, as if these were determined by accident. The alternative of Gerbert—which should have intervened before the partial resoldering of the Sword by Perceval in the Wauchier version—some few verbal modifications notwithstanding—gives the same account of the Grail Procession.

In the prose LANCELOT, which prefaces the great and glorious QUEST, the Pageant has this characteristic—that it is preceded invariably by a Dove, which enters through a window bearing a golden censer in its beak, and the Palace fills thereupon with the eternal sweetness of the Paradise which is above. The bird passes through the Hall and out of sight into a Chamber beyond. From that Chamber —as if at a concerted signal—or almost as if the Dove had suffered transformation—there issues the Maiden of the Grail, carrying the Precious Vessel. The Grail manifestation in the LANCELOT is at first on the occasion of Monseigneur Gawain's visit, and he sees nothing of the other Hallows till the Lance, at a later stage, issues from the Chamber beyond and smites him between the shoulders. In the middle of the night of terror which follows this event, he beholds another Pageant preceded by a choir of voices. Once more the Maiden issues from the Hidden Chamber carrying the Sacred Vessel, with lights and thuribles before her ; and the Service of the Grail is performed on a silver table in the middle place of the Hall ; but there are no other Hallows.[4] When Lancelot comes to the Castle—from which visit follows the conception of Galahad—the manifestation of the Grail is identical ; but because of that which must be consummated he suffers no infliction and does not behold therefore the avenging Lance. It can be said scarcely that there is a Pageant : the Dove enters and vanishes ; it passes within the Secret Chamber, that the Maiden in charge of the

[1] Potvin, Op cit., V, pp. 150 et seq.   [2] Ib., VI, pp. 132 et seq.   [3] Ib., pp. 151, 152.
[4] Sommer : VULGATE ARTHURIAN ROMANCES, IV, pp. 342–347.

Vessel may come out therefrom : she appears accordingly, bearing the Holy Palladium, a Vessel of Gold, " the richest thing that any man hath living ". Having issued from the Secret Chamber, she returns again therein, but not before Lancelot—also for that which was to follow—is dazzled by her surpassing beauty.[1]

In the time of the Great Quest there are, strictly speaking, no Pageants in the sense of the other Romances, for the Grail is going about. Its apparition at the Court of King Arthur is heralded by a sunbeam only, and it is borne by no visible hand.[2] In Corbenic, when all things draw to the holy marvel of their close, there is a solemn Procession of Angels to the Secret Shrine of the Grail, two of them bearing wax lights, the third a cloth, and the last the Sacred Lance, because Heaven has come down at the removal of that which is meant for earth no more.[3] In Sarras, at the last scene of all, which ends the strange, eventful Mystery, there is a Great Cohort of Angels ; but this is the Choir Above descending to witness that which must be done in fine below.[4] There is no passing between intermediate spaces.

In the PERLESVAUS two Damosels issue together from a Chapel which is attached to the banqueting-hall, one of them carrying the most Holy Grail and the other the Lance, the point of which distils its blood therein.[5] It is suggested also, but as if by a dream within a dream, that there are two Angels, bearing two candlesticks of gold filled with wax lights. The Damosels move through the hall and pass into another Chapel. Again they come forth, and it seems then that there are three Maidens, with the figure of a Child in the midst of the Holy Grail. They pass for a third time, and then above the Vessel there is a Vision of the Crucified King.

In the PARZIVAL of Wolfram a Squire enters hurriedly, bearing the Lance, which bleeds profusely into his sleeve—an uncouth and ill-begotten symbol.[6] Two gracious Maidens, wearing chaplets on their heads, follow with flowing hair : they are holding Golden Candlesticks. Two other Women, of whom one is described as a Duchess, carry two stools of ivory, which they place before the King. Next in order are four Maidens having as many tapers, and four other Maidens who sustain between them an oblong slab of jacinth. There are then two Princesses carrying knives of silver, and these also are preceded by four Maidens. The Princesses are followed by six additional Maidens, bearing tall glasses filled with rare perfumes. There is, in fine, the Queen of all, with the Grail in the hands of her, and behind is the Squire who carries the Sword of Legend. When we come at the proper time to see how much and how little on the surface sense of things follows from this cumbrous display, we shall turn with the more relief to versions which are less decorative, though we can understand and excuse also the influence of the oriental mind, if this be

---

[1] *Ib.*, V, p. 108. [2] *Ib.*, VI, p. 13.
[3] Sommer, *Op. cit.*, VI, p. 189. [4] *Ib.*, p. 197.
[5] Potvin, *Op. cit.*, I, pp. 88, 89 ; HIGH HISTORY, Branch VI, Titles 19, 20.
[6] See Book VII, sect. 7.

reflected in the PARZIVAL, whether from the alleged prototype of Kyot de Provence or from Arabian sources, through Southern France as a channel. Relief at the moment may come also from the poem of Heinrich, though it is the idlest of all the Quests. Here the Procession is in two parts. In the first there is a beautiful youth of highest mien, upholding the Sword and followed by Cup-Bearers who serve wine at the Feast. When this is over there enter two Maidens, carrying golden candlesticks ; behind them come two Youths, who bear the Lance between them ; they are followed by other two Maidens, in whose charge is a Salver of jewelled gold, reposing on a silken cloth. Behind these there walks the Fairest of Women, dowered with the Precious Reliquary of the Grail, and after her comes the last Maiden of all, whose hands are empty, whose Office is weeping only—a variation which will be found also in the Montpellier codex of the CONTE DEL GRAAL.

IX

THE ENCHANTMENTS OF BRITAIN, THE TIMES CALLED ADVENTUROUS AND THE WOUNDING OF THE KING

THE PERLESVAUS or LONGER PROSE PERCEVAL says that the Secret Sanctuary gives upon the Earthly Paradise, even as the visible world may be said to give upon the world unseen. We have now to consider how a Horror fell upon the Secret House of God and a subtle work of Sorcery on the world which encompassed it. All texts indifferently of the Northern French Cycles say that, as a consequence of certain events connected with the Castle of the Grail, there came an interdiction upon Logres. In the LESSER CHRONICLES it is termed an Enchantment, while in the Vulgate Cycle it is characterised as Adventurous Times ; but the distinctions dissolve into one another : there is not less Adventure, nor is it less hazardous, in the Texts of Enchantment, while in the Adventurous Texts the graces and terrors of Sorcery abound on every side. We can consider them therefore together, being aspects of the same subject which are scarcely so much as alternative, and, in fact, on a study of the documents, it will be found that the Adventurous Times are almost too vague by themselves to admit of being specified separately. As regards the Enchantments, they are a consequence which works outward from within—that is to say, directly or indirectly, something which has transpired within is responsible for the inhibition without. The Enchantments are the result of an evil which has fallen on the Keeper for the time being of the Holy Grail. They are the exteriorised sorrow of the King and his Holy House. The action is however, reciprocal, for in some instances that sorrow has reached him by an intrusion of the external order, though in certain other cases it has arisen in his own Palace or in his own person. It remains that as Enchantment fell upon

Merlin, so also it has fallen about the Secret House and has entered into the Holy of Holies. Now, the places of Enchantment are also places of sadness, and the nature of the horror within, abiding as a certain cloud upon the Sanctuary, is described after several manners. In one story, the flesh, which at no time profits anything, has smitten deeply into the life of the Keeper, who has been a victim of earthly passion. In another, he is unable to die till he has seen the last scion of his House, and because of the protraction of the centuries, he is suffering, in the meantime, the heavy burden of his great age, the mill-stone of many centuries about his neck. He has received alternatively a dolorous stroke, or as a final explanation he is afflicted by the failure of a Knight to ask a conventional Question, which is at once vital and mystic. These things are reflected upon the order without, sometimes, as it would seem, only in the immediate neighbourhood of the Castle ; more generally through the whole of Logres ; while in rare instances the world itself is involved, at least by imputation.

The Perceval Quests turn entirely on the asking of that Question which I have specified in the previous enumeration, and the pivot of the Question itself is the failure to perform what is expected in this respect—namely, to ask and to receive. In the Chrétien section of the CONTE DEL GRAAL the explanation of the King's sickness is that he was wounded by a spear in battle, and hence is carried by four sergeants because he has no strength in his bones.[1] In the DIDOT-MODENA PERCEVAL, Brons, the Rich Fisherman, is said to be in great infirmity, an old man and full of maladies, nor will his health be restored until the Office of the Question has been fulfilled in all perfection.[2] But this is not ordinary old age ; rather—as I have just intimated—it is the oppression of many centuries. It is clear, however, that Brons was not suffering from any curse or enchantment : he cannot depart from this life until he has communicated to Perceval the Secret Words pronounced at the Sacrament of the Grail, which he learned himself from Joseph. This and the instruction which will follow the Question asked by the hero shall put a period to the Enchantments of Britain. There is a failure in the first instance, as in the poem of Chrétien. The Quest in the CONTE DEL GRAAL is to some extent assumed by Gawain, who visits the Grail Castle in the continuation of pseudo-Wauchier. He does ask, and thereupon the King promises him that, subject to one other condition, he shall hear the great story of the Broken Sword and of the woe which it brought upon the Kingdom of Logres. But Gawain fails and falls asleep.[3] The failure of Perceval has worked the destruction of kingdoms, which may mean certain petty principalities of Britain passing under this name—otherwise they cannot have been of this world, as the alleged visitation does not come to pass herein. On the occasion of Perceval's second visit, the King is seated on a couch as before, and the discourse is not

[1] Potvin, *Op. cit.*, II, pp. 144, 151.   [2] Hucher, *Op. cit.*, I, pp. 418, 419.
[3] Potvin, *Op. cit.*, III, pp. 84, 364-368 ; IV, 1-6 ; III, 369-372.

closed in the section of Wauchier.[1] The conclusion of Manessier recounts how the Broken Sword dealt that stroke which, prior to the voided Question, has destroyed the Realm of Logres and all the surrounding country. The unfinished inquiry of Gawain, before he fell into slumber, restored verdure to the land about the Grail Castle, and the waters found their course. It was not, however, the Keeper but his ˚Brother who received the Dolorous Stroke, being slain treacherously in a battle. The Sword, which broke in the act, was placed upon the bier when the body was brought to the Castle ; it was taken up incautiously by the King and in some undeclared manner it wounded him in both thighs—a wound which could not be healed till the death of his Brother was avenged.[2] For these events the late Prologue to the Conte del Graal substitutes a desolation which fell upon Logres prior to the coming of King Arthur. There were certain Maidens who kept the wells and ministered refreshment to travellers out of golden cups. So admirable as was this custom, an Evil King despoiled the Maidens and scattered them, after which the service ceased. The elements of the Prologue stand apart from the rest of the literature, like an allegory in another tongue ; and though it is very curious in itself, it connects with nothing which follows in the texts that it is supposed to introduce.

The Grand Saint Graal, like the Metrical Romance of Borron, antecedes the period alike of Enchantments and Quests; but as it is later in fact than the Chronicles which it is supposed to precede, so, as a part of its warrants, it forestalls many of their characteristics by a kind of spurious prophecy. It tells how the younger Joseph, the Second Keeper of the Grail, was smitten in the thighs by an Angel for aiding certain people who did not embrace Christianity ; and it testifies that the Avenging Spear with which the wounds were inflicted will be heard of again at the beginning of those marvels that shall occur in the Land of Britain. In this manner it appears to foreshadow the particular Dolorous Stroke of which we have a full account in the Huth Merlin, with all the Sorrowful Adventures that follow thereon. They are destined to continue for twenty-two years, corresponding to the twenty-two days during which the head of the Lance was imbedded in the flesh of Joseph.[3]

The Vulgate Merlin has nothing to say concerning Enchantments of Britain : on the contrary the Prophet's skill and discretion were gifts vouchsafed by God so that he might accomplish the Adventures of the Holy Grail. That it was the rumour of the Sacred Vessel which inaugurated the Times of Adventure is clear from this text, as it is also from the Huth Merlin, which speaks of a prophecy written by the

---

[1] Potvin, *Op. cit.*, V, p. 140–150.　　[2] *Ib.*, pp. 159–162, ll. 35187–35290.
[3] There is no question that the Lance or Spear which ranks as second only in importance to the Hallow-in-Chief of the Grail Castle is always and only that Lance of Longinus which pierced the side of Christ, or that the Blood which flows therefrom represents the Precious Blood. Whether carried as now by an Angel or as later by the Knight Balyn, one would have thought that an object so utterly sacred would not have been in what must be called promiscuous use. I refer only to the Northern French Cycle.

Enchanter on parchment and concerned with those wonders which would characterise the Quest, encompassing in fine the destruction of the marvellous Lion, that is to say, the overthrow of King Arthur. The implicits of this statement are one crux of the Merlin Cycle. It is also, as I have intimated, to the HUTH MERLIN that we owe our first acquaintance with the beautiful story of Balyn and Balan, the two brethren born in Northumberland, who were good Knights, according to Malory. Balyn was destined to inflict the Dolorous Stroke, which during the allotted period of twenty-two years would cause dire distress throughout three kingdoms ; for by this Stroke he would pierce the most holy man in the world and inaugurate the Marvels of the Grail in Great Britain.[1]

There can be no doubt that the Warden of the Sacred Vessel is here the intended victim, and that the stroke is actually given in the Grail Castle, with the Hallowed Lance of the Legend. Balyn himself nearly loses his life in the cataclysm which follows, and is informed by Merlin that he has deserved the hatred of the whole world, the obvious reason being that he has desecrated a Great Sanctuary. The recipient of the wound is said, however, to be King Pellehan, who is the Brother of King Pelles the Keeper. In any chronological tabulation this event would most likely precede the sole visit of Gawain—in the Vulgate Cycle—to the Grail Castle and indubitably to the first arrival of Lancelot therein. These occurrences are related in the prose LANCELOT ; but in this Romance the Keeper of the Sacred Vessel is, as I have said, King Pelles, and he is not wounded. Pellehan reappears in the QUEST OF GALAHAD not only as the Maimed King, but as he who bears the title of Rich Fisher, which is reserved to the Royalty of the Grail Wardens. It will be seen therefore that a certain confusion has arisen, owing doubtless to continuous editing ; and it may follow that there was originally but one King in the Castle, that his name was Pelles, that he was wounded by the Dolorous Stroke, and was destined to be healed by Galahad at the term of the Quest.[2] As it is, there is actually a dual healing—that of the King Pellehan and that of another personage whose sin dates back to the first times of the Legend, being one of unprepared intrusion into the Most Secret Mysteries of the Grail. In the QUEST OF GALAHAD the confusion which I have noticed is made greater by the story of Perceval's Sister concerning the maiming of King Pelles, who found the Ship of Solomon towards the coast of Ireland. He entered therein and drew the Sword of David about half-way from its scabbard. In punishment of this rashness a spear smote him through both thighs, and never since might he be healed, says she, " to fore we come to hym ".[3] None of this takes place actually, but it goes to shew

---

[1] The Marvels do not emerge, except as the occasional and rather fitful manifestation of the Sacred Vessel, and the fact that its Temple was thrown open to rare visitors, awaiting the time when he would appear at last who should heal the Maimed King.

[2] It may be thought alternatively that the complete disability of Pellehan brought to pass the succession of Pelles—a speculative possibility about which we cannot rule.

[3] Sommer, *Op. cit.*, VI, p. 150.

that the original intention of the story was the intention of the Perceval Quests—namely, to wound the Keeper of the Grail, or insure otherwise (1) his prolonged suffering and (2) his ultimate healing by the heir to come. Speaking otherwise of this great Romance, the whole process of the Quest is lifted into a high spiritual region, the implicits of which may provide us at a later stage with one key of the Mystery.

In the LONGER PROSE PERCEVAL or PERLESVAUS it is said that there shall be no rest in the land till the Grail has been achieved. But here the Horror of the House was the failure of Perceval to ask that Question, the simplicity of which is the seal of the whole enigma. As a consequence, the shepherd has been smitten and the sheep have been scattered. Those who ministered in the Castle were sent out by the general fatality beyond the Sacred Precincts, for no other reason apparently than to act as witnesses of the woe abroad before the face of the world ; and so therefore in place of Ceremonial Pageants within there are strange Processions without.[1]

In the German Cycle, the adequate consideration of which must be referred as before to a later stage,[2] the PARZIVAL of Wolfram makes a blot on the scutcheon by shewing that sin entered the Sanctuary ; and in this, as in other respects, the story is set apart from all else in the general scheme of the literature. On the other hand, the poem of Heinrich, though its root-matter is almost out of knowledge, conforms, as it does usually, to the more normal Tradition in points of detail, saying that the Doom of the King was the outcome of war between Brothers. With this, in other connections and a far other sense, we have some analogy in the LONGER PROSE PERCEVAL

It may be that the implicits of the Grail Keepers rank among the most important of those which at once challenge and elude explanation. While they are connected more especially with the Headship in the persons of successive Wardens, there are also subsidiary matters emerging therefrom or belonging otherwise thereto. Woe has fallen on the Wardens, though, speaking symbolically, they abide in the place of life. Not only is the Hereditary Custodian of the Secrets that person in most of the Romances on whom comes the symbolic grief, but he is dependent peculiarly on help expected from without, and although his sustenance is within his healing is beyond the Sanctuary. Even the unqualified Monseigneur Gawain can bring him a partial consolation. He receives a nondescript savage like Perceval, as he is depicted in the more primitive stories, within the fold of election, for doing something after a clownish failure which any child might have been expected to perform at once. All this is so out of reason on the surface that a meaning in concealment seems inevitable. Its investigation stands over of necessity ; but as something consistent with the subject, down the first vistas of which we are looking only, it may be said, as the characteristic of every Initiation, that the Candidate does not ask

---

[1] Potvin, Op. cit., I, p. 2 ; HIGH HISTORY, Branch I, Title I.
[2] See Book VII, § I.

questions : it is he who is catechised and must answer. One key from one point of view might again be the counsel : Ask, and ye shall receive. But the Grail Quester is to bestow before he receives. It has been proposed that we are dealing with a Rite which follows a defined procedure ; but—if so—it is one which works rather the reverse way, so far as normal Instituted Mysteries are concerned. That Rite has been going on for generations, inviting and accepting no Candidate, for it is perpetuated by hereditary transmission, though its treasury has been a heritage of woe. There is no symbolical object in all the lore of Mysteries to compare with the Secret Guardianship, whether the Keeper is wounded for his own, or another's, and even for our transgressions ; whether also the consideration of his Mystery arises from the texts themselves or from suggestions belonging thereto and admitted from a very high standpoint. No one could find the Castle, or come into the presence of the King, except by a special warrant and almost invariably by a congenital election. The Castle was hidden from the world, like the analogous House of the Holy Ghost in the Rosicrucian Mystery, and he who entered therein had somehow to awaken the Oracle. The Hidden Life of the Keepers passed in the Castle, but not in the visionary rapture of those who go into Avalon and other Isles of the Blessed.[1] Now, there are two palmary Mysteries connected with two divisions of the Chronicles of Quest—one is the silence of Perceval and the other is the conception of Galahad. By the way of anticipation, something more will be said of the first in the next section.

X

THE SUPPRESSED WORD AND THE MYSTIC QUESTION

IT is agreed that the essential and predominant characteristic of the Perceval literature is the asking and answering of a Question which bears on its surface every aspect of triviality, but is yet the pivot on which the whole circle of these Romances may be said to revolve. On the other hand, the Question is absent from the Galahad story, and in place of it we have a stately Pageant of Chivalry moving through the World of Logres to find the High Mystery of Sanctity. But that finding is destined only to dismember the Arthurian Empire and to pass, in fine, leaving no trace behind it, except the sporadic vision of a rejected Knight, which is mentioned but not described, and occurs under circumstances that justify grave doubts as to its existence in any original text.

Now, the entire critical literature of the Grail may be searched in vain for a serious explanation as to the actuating motive, in or out of folk-lore, concerning the Grail Question. On the part of folk-lore

---

[1] This offers therefore a useful distinction between the Quest of the Holy Grail and that of Other World Islands in records of folk-lore.

authorities there have been attempts to find something antecedent within the scope of their subject ; but the analogies have been no analogies, and as much extravagance has resulted as we have yet heard of in the connection which some scholars have vaguely termed Mysticism. The symbolical and sacramental value of the Grail Quest, outside all issues in folk-lore, is from my standpoint paramount, as it is this indeed without any reference to opinions which are founded in folk-lore or to speculations arising therefrom. For the rest, it is impossible to survey the Cycle of Perceval Quests without seeing that the Question of the Grail is second in importance only to the Grail itself and that the one is a key to the other, as it is also a title to the know-ledge of those Secret Words which should uncover the whole Mystery. If ever a Rite of Initiation was veiled in myth it is assuredly in the Perceval Cycle, which bears the seeming marks and seals by which those who are Initiates themselves can recognise the presence of a Mystery. At the same time, Initiation, like folk-lore, knows many offices of silence but few of asking ; and after many researches I conclude—at least tentatively—that in this respect the Grail Romances stand practically alone.[1]

In the CONTE DEL GRAAL of Chrétien, the law and order of the Quest is that Perceval shall ask the meaning of those wonders which he beholds in the Pageant at the Castle of the Quest. The references are many in the poem, but they are merely repetitions. Perceval did not ask (1) how such things came to pass ; (2) nor anything whatso-ever ; (3) he did not dare to ask about the Grail, *qui on en servoit*, because his teacher in Chivalry had cautioned him against idle curiosity and such impertinence ; (4) for which reason he reserved his speech.[2] It is understood—and we have seen—that through the oppression of the centuries the Keeper of the Holy Grail is, according to the DIDOT-MODENA PERCEVAL, in a state of distress, longing for his delayed release. Before he can go in peace he must pass on the Divine Tradition of the Secret Words ; but before he can so transmit them he must be asked a Question. That Question is : *De quoi li Graus sert*. It will perform a two-fold office, firstly, to heal the King and, secondly, to liberate his speech. Perceval reaches the Castle ; but notwithstanding that the voice of One who was invisible had announced at the Court of King Arthur, in Perceval's presence and in that of all the Knights, both the nature and effect of the Question, he inquires nothing for fear of offending his host. Hence he departs in disgrace, and the King remains unhealed.[3]

---

[1] It was suggested, now long ago, by Birch-Hirschfeld that the Question of the Grail was an invention of Borron and devoid of real significance. See DIE SAGE VOM GRAL, in which it is held not only that the DIDOT-MODENA PERCEVAL was the work of Robert de Borron but that his trilogy anteceded Chrétien and was used by him in the CONTE.

[2] Potvin, *Op. cit.*, II, ll. 4380–4390, p. 147 ; ll. 4420–4431, p. 148. Cf. *ib.*, ll. 4744–4782, pp. 159, 160, containing the denunciation of Perceval's silence by his cousin on the morning following his first visit to the Grail Castle. Cf. also the malediction pronounced on him by the Messenger of the Grail at the Court of King Arthur, *ib.*, ll. 6024–6061, pp. 201–203.   [3] Hucher, *Op. cit.*, I, pp. 464–466.

Within the limits of the pseudo-Wauchier section of the CONTE DEL GRAAL there are not less than three versions of the visit of Monseigneur Gawain to the Grail Castle, representing specific variations of different manuscripts. Without exercising any discrimination between them, but rather by a harmony of all, it may be said that he does ask concerning the Lance and Grail; but as he cannot resolder the Sword, he can learn nothing regarding the Sacred Vessel, or, if there is a sign of willingness to communicate on the part of the Keeper, Gawain goes to sleep and so escapes most of the story.[1] The result is that the Enchantment is in part only removed from the land. When Wauchier himself recounts the second visit of Perceval, that Knight on beholding the Hallows does not know where to begin, but at length prays that he may hear the whole truth concerning the Grail, the Sword and the Lance. The condition of the answer, as in the case of Gawain, is that he shall resolder the Sword, and we have seen already that in this task Perceval is successful partly; but the king's healing does not happen to be effected, though the path thereof is open : so the knight has not yet achieved the Quest.[2] The result on external Nature is not stated by Manessier.

At the beginning of the PERLESVAUS it is said that the reticence of the Questing Knight at the Grail Castle caused such mischances in Greater Britain that all the lands and islands fell into sorrow. There appeared to be war everywhere, no knight meeting another in the forest without running on him and slaying him, if he could. The King Fisherman himself passed into languishment. The Question which ought to have been asked was : " Unto whom one serveth of the Grail."[3] Many penances will be ended, it is said, when he who visits the Castle demands unto whom it is served ; but this event never comes to pass in the story. The desire to ask questions seems to have been rare therein, for Gawain when conversing with a wandering damsel, who was formerly the Bearer of the Grail, fails to inquire why she carries her arm slung from her neck in a golden stole, or concerning the rich pillow whereon her arm reposes. He is told that he will give no greater heed at the Court of King Fisherman.[4] The King himself dwells always on the misfortune which overtook him through the failure of Perceval. When Gawain reaches the mystic Castle, he sees the Grail and the Lance ; but he is lost in a joy of contemplation and he utters no word.[5]

It has been said that there is a Question in the Romance of Galahad, and it might have been added that there is one in the prose LANCELOT : the second illustrates the first, and we shall find that they are both mere traces and survivals, as the Prologue to the CONTE DEL GRAAL has the shadow of the Secret Words, peculiar to the Cycle of Borron,

---

[1] Potvin, Op. cit., IV, pp. 5, 6. See ante, p. 87.
[2] Ib., V, pp. 148, 149, ll. 34890–34899.
[3] Ib., I, pp. 26, 27 ; HIGH HISTORY, Branch II, Title 1.
[4] Ib., I, pp. 34, 35 ; HIGH HISTORY, Branch II, Title 4.
[5] Ib., pp. 86–91 ; ib., Branch VI, Titles 17–23.

when it affirms that the Grail Secret must be never disclosed.[1] I do not think that, as regards the later instance, I should be justified in assuming that he who wrote this Prologue was in touch direct with the implicit of the Borron Cycle, and I do think alternatively that if people were disposed to lay stress on such remanents of the Question as I am citing here, they are likely to find that it will work rather in a reverse direction. The fact remains that Lancelot saw the Grail according to the text of Malory ; that he asked the Question which is so important in some other Romances ; that he asked it quite naturally—as who would have failed to do ?—that he was answered also naturally, and that nothing depended therefrom. He cried in his wonder : " O Jesu ! what does this mean ? " He was told : " This is the richest thing in the world."[2] In the Galahad Romance, when he beheld, by the Stone Cross in the wild, a sudden passage of the Grail and the healing of a certain Knight, it is said to be hinted by some texts that he ought to have asked something ; but he was so far right on the fact that his imputed omission carried no visible consequence.[3]

The hindrance to the question in the PARZIVAL is the same as we have found in Chrétien : at all that he saw the Knight of the Quest was agaze with wonder ; he thought also that if he refrained from asking he would be told eventually. That which followed herefrom was sorrow to the host, with continued suffering, and woe also to the guest. For this silence he is represented always in the Romances as earning reproach and contumely from persons outside the Castle ; but in the German poem there is no suggestion of an external Enchantment. It is to be noted further that Parzival has not received a prefatory warning regarding the Question, as he has in the CONTE DEL GRAAL and the DIDOT-MODENA PERCEVAL.

In DIU CRÔNE by Heinrich, when the Questing Knight has beheld the Reliquary and the Spear, he does the opposite exactly. He can no longer contain himself, and so asks his host, for the sake of God, to tell him what the marvels mean and who also are the great Company whom he beholds. Even as he speaks, all present spring from their seats with a loud cry and the sound of great rejoicing. The host tells them to sit down again, and then he explains to the Knight that he has seen the Holy Vessel, of which he may say nothing,[4] except that joy and consolation supervene upon his saving Question. Many are liberated from the bondage which they have endured so long, having little hope of a quittance. There was a time when they trusted in Percéval, as in one predestined to enter into the knowledge of the Grail, as if through everlasting portals ; but he fell away like a Knight

---

[1] Potvin, *Op. cit.*, II, p. 1, ll. 4, 5.

[2] MORTE DARTHUR, Book XI, *cap.* 2. Not in the corresponding account of the Vulgate LANCELOT.

[3] For the episode in question, see *ib.*, VI, pp. 41–45, but it does not contain the suggestion, nor have I met with it in any printed edition : the reference is therefore to unspecified MSS. It would seem that Lancelot on the Quest of the Grail had far other cares than those of interrogations and responsions.

[4] It may be said therefore that the Vessel reserves its speech—in truth a voided Quest.

of no spirit who dared and demanded nothing. Had he done otherwise, he would have released many from their toil who remain in the semblance of life and are yet dead. The woe came about through the strife of kinsmen, " when one Brother smote[1] the other for his land." For this disloyalty the judgment of God descended upon him and his consanguinities, so that doom overtook them all. The living were expatriated and the dead, under greater disaster, remained in the shadow of life. To end their woe it was necessary that a man of their race should seek an explanation of these sad, long-enduring prodigies. It does not emerge that either Grail or Spear has any connection with the Passion of Christ, and there is no Secret communicated, for the History of the Sacred Vessel is not recounted.

From the consideration of this subject we may come away therefore, confirmed in our reasonable certainty that the Question with which we have been dealing is unlike anything in literature. We shall see ultimately how it has been accounted for by expert knowledge of folk-lore—connected or otherwise with Quests and Vengeance Missions in Welsh or English literature.

XI

THE HEALING OF THE KING

IT came about therefore at the end of the Quest that the Suppressed Word was at last spoken, that the Question was asked and answered. There are certain texts in which such asking and answering are all that was required by the hypothesis, and then it was well in the Secret House of the Wardens. There is another text in which the King's healing depended upon a dual office, of which the first part was the Question itself as a kind of interlocutory discourse, and then upon a Mission of Vengeance. It was fulfilled in either case. The Head of the Blessed Bran does not appear in the symbolism of these branches ; but the Head as the sign of the accomplished sacrifice is essential to the Quest completed ; and this is the characteristic-in-chief of the CONTE DEL GRAAL.[2] As a Rite of the Observance with Mercy, the Question and its answer were held to be all-sufficient in the Lesser Chronicles, because the curse on the Keeper is like that on the Wandering Jew—it is the ages continued henceforward ; and he comes at length to his rest.[3] The Vulgate Chronicles offer another Pageant of the Quest, the particulars of which are as follows : (1) The Building of a Ship of the Secret Faith, that at the end of a certain time it might carry into the far distance the most valid and efficacious symbols of the Mystery of Christ ; (2) the healing of a King of the East who is not to be confused with the Keeper him-

---

[1] As when Simon de Montfort smote his brother in Christ, Raymond of Toulouse, for his fiefs in Southern France and the faith of Rome.

[2] Potvin, Op. cit., VI, p. 130.   [3] Hucher, Op. cit., I, p. 484.

self, but he dates *ab initio symboli* and is doubtless the Witness-in-chief
of the Mystery even to the times of the Quest : concerning him it may
be said that he tried to take the Mystery of faith by violence, outside
which his existence is parallel to that of the Keeper Brons, having been
prolonged through the centuries from the first times of the Legend ;
(3) the redemption of the Cain of the Legend who slew his brethren ;
(4) an intercalatory and voided wonder concerning the maiming of the
Grail King when he drew the Sword of David.[1]

The Particulars in all branches may be collected shortly as follows :
In the CONTE DEL GRAAL pseudo-Wauchier presents a certain lifting
of the heavy veil of enchantment, so that the desert becomes the sown,
and we are enabled to compare how it was in the dry tree with that
which it is in the green. Winter has passed, so to speak, and the voice
of the turtle is heard again in the land.[2] In Manessier, the Keeper,
who has suffered from that illogical maiming occasioned by the death
of his Brother, is healed at the sight of his head who committed the
original act of violence. The whole business is foolish, and so unutter-
ably. It was necessary, for some reason that derived probably its roots
from folk-lore, for the King to be smitten in his thighs ; the event
comes to pass under circumstances that are quite and frankly impossible ; and there is also no reason why the wound which was self-
inflicted unconsciously should not have been healed at once, unless
death intervened as the term.[3] Assuming that Gerbert knew nothing
of Manessier's conclusion and that he regarded the last words of
Wauchier—in which the Rich Fisher hails Perceval as the Lord of his
House—as the term, in fine, of the story, his own intercalation was
intended to account for the closing along better lines, and he did not
concern himself with any explanation of the King's wounding. On the
contrary, his intention was to shew that the proper demand and reply
exercised their proper office, and that the one thing which remained to
complete the whole was for Perceval to redeem his past. The poem
does not offer a termination which follows from the text, while that of
Manessier, from any explanatory standpoint, is so much idle baggage.
The CONTE DEL GRAAL, considered as a Grail story, is therefore at once
imperfect and piecemeal. The DIDOT-MODENA PERCEVAL may not be
satisfactory as a completion of Borron's trilogy, but in the simple term
of a Quest which is exceedingly simple, it leaves nothing undone. The
Keeper of the Grail, as we have seen, must communicate his Mystery
before he departs hence. The mode of communication presupposes the
arbitrary Question which is a pretext for unveiling the Mysteries, and
the issue, which is clear from the beginning, is not clouded subsequently
by extraneous matters. The King is healed—that is to say, he is
relieved of the long burden of the centuries, and he is enabled to pass
in peace.[4] In the GREAT PROSE QUEST it is the hands of Galahad which

---

[1] Sommer, *Op. cit.*, VI, pp. 144–163 ; 184, 185 ; 185, 186 ; 146, 147.
[2] Potvin, *Op. cit.*, IV, pp. 7, 8.   [3] Potvin, *Op. cit.*, VI, p. 130.
[4] Hucher, *Op. cit.*, I, pp. 482–484.

prove to be hands of healing. The Hallow of the ensanguined Lance inflicted the wound from which the unknown King Pellehan suffered through the whole period during which the Quest was prepared and achieved.[1] The restoration was accomplished by Galahad with the blood from the same weapon : therewith he anointed the King.[2] It is after this or another manner that the remedial elements are found in the House of the Grail ; but they must be administered by one who comes from external places. It may be admitted that, at least on the surface, both wounding and healing in the Galahad Quest are a burden to the logical understanding. For what it is worth—which is little—in other respects, there is on this point a certain consistence in the CONTE DEL GRAAL. At the beginning it carries the implicits of a Vengeance Legend, and though something is forgotten in the antecedents by Wauchier and something else by Manessier, as if they had not read their precursors fully, that is explicated in fine which was implied at first. The PERLESVAUS has a root-difficulty, because there is no attempt to explain either why the Question was necessary when all was well with the King, or why—whether necessary or not—the failure of Perceval should have caused the Keeper of the Holy Grail to fall into such languishment that ultimately he died unhealed. For these are the distinctions, among many, between this High History and all other Perceval Quests, namely, that it begins about the middle point of the story and that the Keeper perishes. Among the correspondences in the reverse order of these differences is the Quest of Monseigneur Gawain, according to DIU CRÔNE, where the King indeed dies coincidently with his release ; but this is his desired liberation from the condition of death in life.[3] Speaking generally, the death of the Wounded Keeper serves to make room for his successor. In the DIDOT-MODENA PERCEVAL he is released according to his yearning, and that almost at once ; in the CONTE DEL GRAAL Perceval, far from the Castle, awaits the Keeper's demise, which occurs in the natural course. In the PARZIVAL of Wolfram there is a kind of abdication by Anfortas in favour of the Questing Knight ; but the two abide together and, as in the DIDOT-MODENA PERCEVAL, there is in fact a trinity of Keepers. In the QUEST OF GALAHAD that glorious and saintly Knight is scarcely to be called a Keeper : if I may be pardoned the expression, he and his Companions act as the transport agents of the Sacred Vessel, to the term of all at Sarras ; though we may elect to regard Galahad as the Keeper in Heaven. We are not concerned with the healing of King Pellehan, because he is not a Keeper of the Grail, as the text stands, though we feel that some editor has blundered.

[1] Gaston Paris, HUTH MERLIN, II, pp. 32, 43.
[2] Sommer, *Op. cit.*, VI, p. 191.   [3] See Book VII, § 3.

XII

THE REMOVAL OF THE HALLOWS

WE have seen that the Rich Fisherman, King and Warden of the Grajl, was healed as the consequence of the Quest, or that, this failing, a provision was made for his successor after some other manner. Now, this is the penultimate stage of the Mystery regarded as a whole, and the one question which still remains to be answered is—What became of the Grail ? Subject to characteristic variations which are particular to each text, it will be found—as I have said—that the several Romances follow or forecast one general process, suggesting a prevailing secret intention, and it is for this intention that my study will have to account. At the moment the external answer to the problem above propounded, resting on the evidence of the documents, is an example of variation—which tends, however, to one term : this term is that either the Holy Grail and the other Hallows of the Passion were removed altogether or they were taken into deeper concealment. The specific testimonies follow. After the death of King Fisher, Perceval inherits his kingdom—in the CONTE DEL GRAAL—and he reigns for seven years. He appoints his successor, who does not become a Warden of the Hallows, and he passes himself into the seclusion of a Hermitage, where he remains for ten years, having been Ordained a Priest. The Grail follows him, and he is at length assumed into the joy of Paradise, since which time the Sacred Vessel and the other precious objects have never been beheld so openly.[1] As a rider to this, it is added that no doubt they were taken to Heaven, which is an argument from the unworthiness of the world. In the DIDOT-MODENA PERCEVAL the Knight of the Quest and a certain Hermit, who is a character of importance in the Lesser Chronicles, become the Guardians of the Grail, while the Prophet Merlin also abides with them. Merlin, in fine, goes away, seeking a deeper seclusion, and neither he nor the Grail is heard of subsequently.[2] The inference is that the Grail remains in the Asylum of the Holy House, under the charge of its Wardens. Alternatively, it may have followed Merlin. The LONGER PROSE PERCIVAL, after a fiathful picture of the Questing Knight in loneliness and rapture, surviving all his kindred, says that a secret voice commanded him to divide the Hallows—not including the Grail, which had gone before— among a certain Company of Hermits, after which a mystical ship anchored by the Castle, and Perceval, taking his leave of those who still remained about him, entered that vessel and was carried far over the sea, " nor never thereafter did no earthly man know what

---

[1] See the Conclusion of Manessier in Potvin, *Op. cit.*, VI, ll. 45271–45362, pp. 152–155.
[2] For the DIDOT PERCEVAL, see Hucher, *Op. cit.*, I, pp. 415–505, and for the Modena text Miss Weston's LEGEND OF SIR PERCEVAL, Vol. II.

became of him, nor doth the history speak of him more."[1] In the
GREAT PROSE QUEST the most holy Companions—Galahad, Perceval
and Bors—are conveyed in the Ship of Solomon to a place in the East,
named Sarras : the Hallows with which they are charged are the
Sacred Vessel and the Lance, together with the Sword of David,
wherewith Galahad is girded. For a certain allotted period of days
that are sad, consecrated and strange, the Companions watch over
the Hallows in the City of Sarras ; and then the call comes to Galahad.
" There with he kneeled down to fore the Table, and made his prayers ;
and then suddenly his soul departed to Jesu Christ, and a great multitude of Angels bore his soul up to Heaven, that the two fellows might
well behold it. Also the two fellows saw come from Heaven a hand ;
but they saw not the body. And then it came right to the Vessel, and
took it and the Spear, and so bore it up to Heaven. Since then was
there never man so hardy to say that he had seen the Sangrail ".[2] In
the German Cycle, the PARZIVAL of Wolfram leaves the Grail where
it was always, since its first manifestation ; but the TITUREL of
Albrecht—a text which is so late that it is excluded generally from the
modern canon of the literature—narrates the rise and growth of an evil
time, wherein, for its better protection, Parzival and the Chivalry of the
Grail, bearing the Blessed Palladium, go forth from Mont Salvatch into
the far East, where is the Kingdom of Prester John ; and there it may
remain to this day—most surely in another Kingdom which is not of
this world. After these high memorials it is almost unnecessary to
speak of the Quest in Heinrich, at the term of which the Grail and its
Ghostly Company dissolve before the eyes of the Questing Knight, and
thenceforth the tongue of man cannot shew forth the Mysteries.

Seeing now that the Great Sacraments do not pass away, it must
follow that in the removal of the Holy Grail, as it is narrated in the
texts, we are in the presence of another Mystery of Intention which
appears the most obscure of all. The cloud that dwelt on the Sanctuary,
the inhibition which was on the world without, the hurt almost past
healing which overtook the Hereditary Keeper, are ample evidence in
themselves that evil had entered into the Holy place, despite all the
warrants which it held and all the Graces and Hallows which dwelt
therein. With one curious exception, the Keeper was, in fine, healed ;
the Enchantment also was removed ; and the achievement of the last
Warden, at least in some instances, must have been designed, after
a certain manner and within a certain measure, to substitute a greater
glory for the cloud on the Secret Sanctuary. All this notwithstanding,
the end of the great Quests, the term of the whole Mystery, was simply
the removal thereof. It occurs in each Romance under different
circumstances, and it was not, as we shall learn more fully, always of
an absolute kind. In the CONTE DEL GRAAL it is said—and we have

[1] Potvin, Op. cit., I, p. 347, and Evans, HIGH HISTORY, Branch XXXV, Title 27.
[2] See Sommer's VULGATE VERSION OF ARTHURIAN ROMANCES, VI, pp. 197, 198 ;
and Caxton's BIRTH, LIFE AND ACTS OF KING ARTHUR, in the Southey edition, II, p. 314.
Cf. Sommer's reprint, p. 723.

seen previously—that it was taken away, possibly to Heaven.   In the DIDOT-MODENA PERCEVAL it was seen no more.   In the LONGER PROSE PERCEVAL or PERLESVAUS those who had higher warrants than any Warden in the manifest world removed it into a realm unknown. Perceval was called thereto and assumed therein another Office of Kinghood.   In Wolfram the whole question is left open in perpetuity, for at the close of the poem the Keeper remains alive.   In the TITUREL of Albrecht the Vessel was carried Eastward into the dubious realm of Prester John, and there apparently it remains.   In the Quest of Galahad it is assumed by Heaven itself, and the last Keeper followed ; but, in spite of this, a lost recension, represented faithfully or otherwise, by the Welsh Quest, says that though it was not seen so openly, it was seen once by Sir Gawain, the least prepared and least warranted of all the Grail seekers, whose Quest, moreover, was abandoned in the particular text, soon after it was undertaken.

Of such are the Mysteries of the Grail, considered in their manifestation and considered also in their removal.   I have passed through many Houses of Initiation in Hidden Life and in literature ; but I know of nothing in suggestion and allusion to compare with the House of the Grail.

BOOK III

THE CONTE DEL GRAAL

THE ARGUMENT

I. Preliminary to the whole Subject.—Epochs of the Grail Quest in Northern France—Concerning the Poetic Romance of Chrétien de Troyes —The Conte del Graal as the Work of a Nature-Born Poet who has heard Strange Tidings—Its Connections with the Mystical Side of the Legend—The Conte as a Product of Successive Generations. II. The Poem of Chrétien de Troyes.—His Account of the Grail and the Problems raised thereby—Other Hallows of the Story—The Secret Chamber of the Grail—The Quest in Chrétien presupposes an Early History—The Story of Perceval—His Quest of Knighthood—His Visit to the Court of King Arthur —Episode of the Red Knight—His Instruction by an Old Knight—The Castle of Beau-Repaire—The Fair Maid Blanchefleur—He does Battle in her Cause—He sets forth subsequently in search for his Mother—He Reaches the Grail Castle—His Silence in the Presence of the Grail—A Maid in Lamentation who condemns his Silence at the Castle—She is his Cousin and knows the Story of the Grail as well as his own Story—She tells the death of Perceval's Mother, owing to his desertion—Arthur and his Knights go forth in search of Perceval—He returns with the Court to Caerleon—Because of the Grail and Lance, he is denounced by a Laidly Maiden—He sets forth to learn the Mysteries—The years of Hard Adventure—A Good Friday Episode—What Perceval learned of the Grail and other matters in a Hermit's Hold—The Covenant of a Secret Prayer. III. The Extension of Wauchier.—And firstly of the Anonymous Poet who succeeded Chrétien— Perceval pursues his Quest—The Castle of the Chess-Board—The Mission of the Stag and Basset—A Second Visit to Beau-Repaire—Perceval returns unexpectedly to his home in the Waste Forest—He finds his Sister—They visit a Hermit Uncle—The Chess-Board Venture is Accomplished and Perceval receives his Dues—A Castle of Maidens in Faërie—The Light of the Grail—A Maiden describes the Vessel—A Mount Dolorous Episode—The Tree of a Thousand Candles—Perceval reaches the Court of King Fisher—He asks the Question of the House—His mending of a Broken Sword—He is hailed as Lord of the House. IV. The Conclusion of Manessier.—Intervention of a Vengeance Legend—The new Mission of Perceval—Miscellaneous Digressions— A Messenger from Blanchefleur—A Third Visit to Beau-Repaire—Perceval and Hector are Healed by the Grail—The Vengeance Mission Accomplished —Third Visit to the Grail Castle—The Healing of the Grail King—Perceval returns to Court—Vacancy of the Royal Office in the House of the Grail— King Arthur and the Chivalry of the Round Table escort the Heir of the House to the Grail Castle—The Coronation of Perceval—His Reign of Seven Years—He becomes a Hermit and is Ordained Priest—He is fed only by the Holy Grail—The death of Perceval and the Assumption of the Great Palladium. V. The Alternative Sequel of Gerbert.—Its Enchantments and Spiritual Meaning—The Dual Failure of Perceval—The Atonement which he has cause to make in respect of Blanchefleur—The Expiation

BOOK III

THE CONTE DEL GRAAL

I

PRELIMINARY TO THE WHOLE SUBJECT

IT may be said that there are three epochs of the Grail Quest in Northern France :—

(1) The epoch of Chrétien de Troyes, all continuations included, and of the DIDOT-MODENA PERCEVAL, considered as a derivative of Robert de Borron, one of growth and development after its own manner.

(2) The epoch of the Great Prose LANCELOT and the QUEST OF GALAHAD.

(3) The epoch of the PERLESVAUS, as head and crown of the composite Perceval Myths.

It is understood that I am using the term epoch to characterise aspects of purpose and mind rather than succession in time, and, secondly, that the German Cycle of the Holy Grail remains over for consideration.

The agreement of scholarship is not perhaps *concensus omnium sanctorum ;* but after much fluctuation of opinion, and notwithstanding a dissentient voice heard there and here in the precincts, it has been resolved—as we have seen—that the first Romance dedicated to the Grail and its Mystery is that of Chrétien,[1] who opened the CONTE DEL GRAAL at an undetermined date between 1168 and 1190, there being a certain conditional but reasonably strong disposition towards 1180 for a *terminus* on the hither side—as we have seen also previously. A bolder hypothesis, which happens to be most recent of all, has ventured to suggest the specific alternative years 1174 or 1175.[2] The question may be left at this point, because the only possible other claimant to rank

---

[1] There is a strong feeling on my own part that something lay behind him, so to speak. It is put on record here in a note because there is no tangible evidence to offer for the expansion of intimations in my text above. I think that there was something of which Chrétien had heard or read ; but it did not connect with the folk-lore Feeding-Dish or he would have loved to provide a material feast of good things for the refection of his errant Knight. It seems to me that he was the least likely poet of his period to invent a service-flagon or a serving-dish, which was after all a *Ciborium*, containing Sacred Hosts, and was certainly misdescribed under the title of Grail. The MEILLEUR CONTE on which he lays claim as source may have explained, at its beginning or end, and must be surely presupposed.

[2] J. D. Bruce, *Op. cit.*, Vol. I, pp. 220, 223. It is to be observed that he affirms a persuasion or predilection only and offers no evidential argument to sustain his view. I am not aware that it has enlisted any approval or attracted any notice, so little no doubt attaching to the question of a year less or more when the one possible competitor has been ruled definitely out.

as the first Grail poet is Robert de Borron, between whom and Chrétien there is only one vestige of correspondence, namely, that the Warden of the Grail in both is called the Fisher King. Independently of all dates, Borron remains the first historian of the Sacred Vessel, while Chrétien also is author not only of the first Quest thereof but is the first to present Perceval le Gallois as the Questing Knight. He is therefore the fountain source of all the French Quests, even the GALAHAD, in which Perceval is one of the twelve attaining heroes, with the son of Lancelot as first among peers.

The elements of Chrétien's poem are perhaps the most simple that it has entered into the heart to conceive. The narrative is beautiful, or perhaps I should say that it is charming, after the manner of Nature : it is like a morning in the Spring. It has something more than the touch of Nature which takes us at once into its kinship ; there are moments when it seems Nature speaking ; and so much of the Grail Mystery as can be said to enter within its own dimensions is this Mystery expressed in the terms of the outside world. But if Chrétien's work is that of a Nature-born poet, he has heard at a great distance, as it were, strange tidings which are not of the natural order, and he opens the story about them, as if at a venture and apart from any certain evidence on that which he has to tell. The poem, taken as a whole, has few religious elements, and it is on comparatively rare occasions only that we can recognise one touch of Grace therein. What is termed the interpolation of Gerbert must be excepted, however, from this description : in comparison with the rest, it is like a Masonic Tracing-Board Lecture compared with an essay of Goldsmith. This analogy is instituted to shew that in the widest construction Gerbert has moments and Gerbert has also allusions which sound and may be pregnant ; but he does not reach a goal.

The CONTE is a product of successive generations, but this granted it is the work of a single epoch, in the previous sense of this term. If it be approached from the poetic standpoint, there is much to repay the reader who is not deterred by the difficulties of extremely archaic French verse. But of the *odor suavitatis* of the Temple, of that which criticism has agreed to describe as the mystical element, being that element which I and those whom I represent desire and look for, there is so little that it can be said barely to exist. Many who know and appreciate the Sacramental Mystery which attaches in certain parts to the Grail Quest of the Malory *Magnum Opus* and to the Longer Prose PERCEVAL, which has been termed THE HIGH HISTORY OF THE HOLY GRAAL, by Dr. Evans, its translator, will recognise this contrast and will understand that in Chrétien above all there is little of the Secret once delivered to the Saints of any Sanctuary, though he made use of materials which carried the suggestion with them. He is described by his earliest editor as the poet of love and as the poet who created the poetry of sentiment.[1] He is singularly fresh and direct,

---

[1] Potvin, *Op. cit.*, Vol. VI, *Introduction*, pp. lxi, lxii.

while he carried his intention plainly on the surface in respect of his presentation of the story, so far as he is known to have taken it. In brief expression, anything that seems recondite in its significance is auto-suggested to an instructed reader by that which is typical of the entire Cycle, while that which is obvious is of the poet.

II

THE POEM OF CHRÉTIEN DE TROYES

AFTER certain preliminary matters which are curious but late in comparison and dubious,[1] the CONTE DEL GRAAL was opened in ample form by a master-singer of his period. We have seen already that, in his long section of the great poem which is set for our consideration, there is no trace of that Bowl of Plenty which obtrudes continually in several later texts, though Chrétien is supposed to have heralded and inaugurated everything which belongs to the seeking part of the Grail literature. Evidently therefore it was not from this source in folk-lore that he derived his knowledge of the mysterious object which he calls a Grail and from which was diffused so great a light, according to the graphic account, though nowhere in his long contribution does he term it the Holy Grail.[2] It was carried by the Maid who had charge of it in both hands, from which it might follow either that it was a heavy object, as would be a large Dish, or something exceedingly sacred—to be exalted with reverence—for example, an Eucharistic Chalice or a Most Holy Reliquary. That it was certainly not the first is made evident by the fact that a Dish was carried separately in the Pageant at the Grail Castle. We know further, from the brief description given, that it was a jewelled Vessel :

> " Pières pressieuses avoit
> El graal, de maintes manières,
> Des plus rices et des plus cières
> Qui el mont u en tière soient ;
> Tote autre pières pasoient
> Celes dou grèal, sans dotance."[3]

That it connects after some manner with the second or third in my enumeration of possible objects is shewn at a much later stage to Perceval in the narrative of his uncle the Hermit, who tells how a Hidden King of the Grail is sustained and comforted by a Sacred Host therein. Whencesoever the German poet Heinrich drew his materials, we shall see that he and Chrétien speak of the same Vessel and rather of a *Ciborium* than a Reliquary. The essence of a Reliquary is that it should contain an invariable sacred deposit, as, for example, the

---

[1] Appendix I, Note 6.
[2] This being elsewhere its almost invariable and, so to speak, official designation. We shall see, however, that in one place Chrétien finds occasion to call it a *sainte chose*.
[3] Ch. Potvin : PERCEVAL LE GALLOIS, OU LE CONTE DU GRAAL, Vol. II, p. 148, ll. 4412–4417.

Precious Blood of our Saviour or the liquefying blood of St. Januarius. The essence of a *Ciborium* is that it should contain Consecrated Hosts. We are therefore at once in the region of traditional wonders. The Legends of Sanctity had borne witness already in far other texts to certain cases in which the Supersensual Bread of Life had served for the Saints as their only daily nourishment. This is therefore the manner in which Chrétien de Troyes understood—had he indeed heard of them—the " feeding properties " of the Grail. It follows—and we shall see duly—that three poets—Chrétien, Wolfram and Heinrich— who are at the poles sometimes in variance over matters of symbolism, do yet tell the same story in the most important of their concerns. And we who know better than ever they could have known all that is involved in the root-matter of their testimony, can say in our hearts, hearing these dim echoes which are far from the term of Quest :

> " Tu qui cuncta scis et vales,
> Qui nos pascis hic mortales,
> Tuos ibi commensales,
> Cohæredes et sodales
> Fac sanctorum civium."

We have no doubt as to the service or the table, and can bear witness on our own part that " many men, both of high and low condition, in these last years past," have to our knowledge seen the Mystery of all Sacredness and Sweetness unveiled before their spiritual eyes.[1] It follows that, even if there are many antecedents, the Grail is still one, and that even at the epoch of Chrétien the true nature and authentic office of the Sacred Vessel had been settled in the mind of those who wrote concerning it. Of himself the poet knew nothing ; but in some book or rumour which he followed there must have been strange materials, as already suggested. One of the keynotes may be that Hugh, Bishop of Lincoln, investigated about 1140 a case of miraculous sustenance by the Eucharist.[2]

As regards the source of his story the poet himself gives us an exceedingly simple explanation. He says that he wrote by command of a certain Count—that is to say, Count Philip of Flanders. The order was :—

> " A rimoir le mellor conte
> Qui soit contes en court roial."

The materials therefore were written materials, at least *ex hypothesi*, namely, *li contes del Gréal*, as to which *li Quens li bailla le livre*. Such was the source of the earliest Quest-matter ; and the earliest extant History-matter depends, also *ex hypothesi*, from a great book, wherein great clerks wrote " the great secrets which are called the Grail " :—

> " Ge n'ose conter ne retreire,
> Ne ge ne le pourroie feire,
> Neis, se je feire le voloie,
> Se je le grant livre n'avoie

---

[1] Cf. LA QUESTE DEL SAINT GRAAL, pp. 62, 63, in Sommer's VULGATE ARTHURIAN ROMANCES, Vol. VI.

[2] This incident is cited at second hand, and I have failed to trace its source ; but the alleged cases of such sustenance are numerous.

Où les estoires sunt escrites,
Par les granz clers feites et dites :
La sunt li grant secré escrit
Qu'en nvmme le Graal et dit.''

Whereas therefore his patron communicated to Chrétien, it was Robert de Borron who communicated to Walter Montbéliard, in whose service he was. We observe in this manner that the first poet of the CONTE DEL GRAAL claimed antecedent authority which was not of the oral kind : by one stage the question of source raised here has been moved back, and there must be left for the present.

It will be seen in the Welsh Perceval that there was a Sword which broke and was rejoined, but in the stress of the last trial it was shattered beyond recovery. The episode in Chrétien which corresponds hereto is represented sufficiently for my purpose by the details already given when considering the Hallows of the Legend. It may be added only that while certain codices make no attempt to account for the return of the Broken Sword to the Grail Castle, there are others which illustrate the foreknowledge of the King by his despatch, for example, of a messenger to follow Perceval in his travels till the mischance of the promised peril overtakes him.[1] In yet others the fragments of the weapon seem to have been spirited away. We shall find in the Welsh Perceval that there is nothing to connect the maiming of the Lord of the Castle with the gigantic Lance which is carried about therein. The connection remains naturally a reasonable inference, but we cannot tell, while the Sword serves no purpose save that of a trial of strength. In Chrétien it appears, on the other hand, almost as a part of the plot, and the scheme is carried out by the sequels in accordance with so much as may be called manifest in the intention of the first poet.

Turning from the Hallows of the story, it happens to be after the manner of Chrétien to furnish his most important elucidations with the least suggestion of design. I have spoken of the Mystery of that Chamber wherein the Grail enters or returns after its manifestation in the Pageant, or into which alternatively the Dove flies in one Quest of the Vulgate Chronicles, before the Sacred Vessel is displayed. It is Chrétien only who discloses the secret of the Hidden Place, or at least manifests up to what point he understands it himself, when he says of the dweller therein, whom I interpret as sometime King of the Grail :

" . XX . ans i a estet ensi.
Que fors de la cambre n'issi
U le Greal veis entrer.''[2]

It was the bedchamber of that Warden of the Hallows who was far more concealed than he who is called or miscalled the Rich Fisher in

---

[1] In the Mons MS. King Fisher bids a youth follow the Knight who slept in the Castle and bring back the pieces if the Sword has broken. The lad finds Perceval fighting with Orguellous de la Lande, otherwise the Proud Knight, and manages to abstract the pieces unwatched by the combatants. He takes them back to his Lord but cannot tell him who had the better of the fray.—CONTE, 5169–5295, Potvin, II, pp. 175–177.   [2] *Op. cit.*, ll. 7803–7805, p. 261.

the same text. The further question which arises for our consideration concerns therefore this nameless being who is the father of the King in evidence. The allusions to him are so brief and so vague that those who continued the story thought it best to ignore them, though I hold it as certain that Wauchier had the elements of an explanation in his hands. Without forestalling the little to be said on this point at the end of this section, I will refer back to an earlier part of our inquiry, when it was noted that the Quest in Chrétien presupposes an Early History and—notwithstanding certain confusions, as for example, regarding the origin of the title King Fisherman—that this History may have corresponded, in respect of its essence, to a supposed first draft of the Metrical Romance by Robert de Borron, or alternatively to the source from which the latter drew, and in which it may be hazarded that there seem to have been several Histories. It is of course idle to speculate whether the text or texts claimed to have been in the possession of the pious minstrel included the single story which the Count of Flanders placed in the hands of Chrétien ; but there may have been a general prototype.[1] Apart from the LONGER PROSE PERCEVAL, which is extra-lineal in most details of its Tradition, there are three persons connected immediately with the Grail in the various Quests. In the PARZIVAL OF WOLFRAM there are (1) Titurel—precisely in the position of the Mysterious King in Chrétien, and like him abdicated ; (2) the Reigning King Anfortas, who is fed by the Grail ; and (3) Parzival, the King who is to come. In the QUEST OF GALAHAD there are (1) the Maimed King, Pellehan ; (2) the Reigning King, Pelles ; and (3) Galahad, the King who is to come. In the DIDOT-MODENA PERCEVAL there are (1) Brons, who is sick of the centuries, but still the Grail King ; (2) his son Alain, but in this case he dies, without it being possible for us to assign his special place in the Mystery; and (3) Perceval, grandson of Brons, as a coming King who is in the warfare of his training. Now, this notion of a triple guardianship was first put forward in the Metrical Romance of Robert de Borron and is evidently one of the root-ideas of the historical branches: if in a certain sense it is broken in the GRAND SAINT GRAAL to establish some phantom of a chronological succession, the Quest which follows therefrom recurs, as we shall see, thereto. I should add that the Royal Family of the Holy Grail in the story of Chrétien and its sequels has no names in most of the codices till Perceval comes into his own ; but there is a variant or interpolation in a Berne manuscript which follows the Keepership in Robert de Borron.

We must set apart from the poem of Chrétien not merely the Prologue, which is by another hand, but an introductory part, also of uncertain authorship. In the latter we hear of Bliocadrans, the Father of Perceval, as one of twelve brothers in Wales who all practised

---

[1] We should remember, however, that the alleged " best story " is likely to have been fairly well known in Courts and otherwhere, and that there may have been more than one copy of the *livre* in which it was contained.

Chivalry, for ever seeking tournaments or joustings. It came about that the brothers died in arms ; but Bliocadrans, being overpersuaded because of these tragedies, settled down with his wife for two years, apart from his wonted activities. There are two sons in the course of growing up, probably the fruit of a previous marriage, and the time comes for them to go forth into the world. They are commissioned to the Courts of two Kings, where they are both knighted on the same day and, though widely separated, both are also slain. Towards the end of the two years the wife mentioned in the poem and described as childless has conceived to their great joy and expects to be delivered, when her husband is called to a tournament convoked by the King of Wales and Cornwall.[1] There he performs prodigies but only to be slain in the end. The news of his death reaches the wife in due course, she meanwhile having brought forth Perceval during the father's absence. She proposes a pilgrimage to St. Brandan in Scotland, taking the babe with her ; but in reality she seeks refuge in a Waste Forest, where she rears him after a semi-savage fashion, apart from all knowledge of Courts and Chivalries and giving him, as he grows to boyhood, a solemn warning that men clothed in armour are in reality devils.

There came, however, a day in the Spring when Perceval met with five knights riding through the wood in all their glittering harness. He who was most splendidly accoutred was taken by Perceval for God and the others for Angels.[2] Time and again the leader asked him whether he had seen certain other knights and three damsels, who had passed on their way before ; but his only answer was to put his own questions about their lances, shields, halberts and so forth. He learned in this manner that they belonged to King Arthur's Court and that to him they owed their arms and appointments. In fine he heard that Arthur was then at Carduel. He returned to his mother, who was overwhelmed at the news of his encounter and above all at his resolve to visit the King and demand Knighthood. It shewed that all her schemes had failed and that she would never keep him at her side, to be her stay and comfort when age began to overtake her. She recounted to no purpose the fate of his brothers and his father's mournful death. In the end she prepared him for the journey as best she could, with the help of a shirt of hemp and a leathern jerkin, made in Welsh fashion. She gave him also her counsels, some of which were quaint enough. He was not only to frequent Churches and pray to God therein, not only to help ladies and damsels, to act as a loyal Knight when he became such, but he should take a kiss from a damsel, she being willing, and accept a ring if offered the gift of one. Leaving the grief-stricken lady, he started at length on his palfrey, armed with a single javelin. He

---

[1] No previous marriage is mentioned in the poem, and nothing is heard of the two brothers till Perceval has reached the age of fourteen years and is told of their fate by his mother. The 1530 prose version of the CONTE gives a variant account, which serves to harmonise matters. It is the maiming of Perceval's father which takes the family into the woods, where he ultimately dies of grief on learning the death of his sons.

[2] Potvin : *Op. cit.*, II, pp. 43 *et seq.*, beginning at l. 1283.

spent one night in the forest and next morning came to a handsome
pavilion where he found a damsel sleeping, who awoke at the clatter
of his entrance and of whom he required a kiss in accordance with his
mother's instructions.[1] Being refused, it was taken by force, as well as
a ring from her hand, though he was told that it would endanger her
life. Being hungry also, he devoured a pasty and drank wine in the
pavilion, after which he took his leave. As he drew to the Court of King
Arthur he met and talked with a Knight in red armour, carrying a
Golden Cup, of which he had deprived the King when in the act of
drinking and had spilt the wine on the Queen. It appears that Arthur's
best Knights were at that time out on adventure. Perceval heard these
things from the lips of the King himself and replied by demanding
Knighthood, but refused to come down from his palfrey, the dejected
and discounselled monarch, who had undertaken to grant his wish,
seeming scarcely in his view one fitted to make Knights. He demanded
further the arms and armour of him who had taken the Cup ; whereat
Kay the Seneschal told him to go and take them. A very fair maiden
listened, saluted Perceval and smiled for the first time in ten years,
foretelling that if he lived there would be no more valiant or better
chevalier in the whole world. This enraged Kay, who struck her to
the ground and afterwards flung a fool into the fire because he had been
accustomed to say that the damsel would never smile till the advent
of him who should prove Master of all Chivalry.[2] We shall be in a
position to compare the plight of King Arthur's Court on this visit of
Perceval with that described in the PERLESVAUS when its story opens,
and shall find that the latter compares favourably, all its desolation
notwithstanding.

Perceval heard in silence the feeble protest of the King when
Kay jeered at the youth : he witnessed also in silence the maltreat-
ment of maid and dwarf ; but the sequel shews that he remembered to
some purpose, in her case at least. Meanwhile he returned to the Red
Knight, who awaited further adventure, if any should come, and also a
message from the King by the mouth of Perecval. The youth, however,
demanded on his part that the Red Knight should lay aside arms and
armour as the King had transferred them to himself. To this broad
comedy the Knight replied with his lance, but only to be slain forthwith by Perceval's javelin, which passed through eye to brain. An
attempt thereafter to strip the body of its mail proved more than he
could manage till he was helped by a Squire of the Court, to whom he
delivered the Cup, that it might be restored to Arthur. Perceval
sent also salutations and his promise to the maid that the injury
offered her by the Seneschal should be avenged unfailingly. Being
armed at length in the likeness of the Red Knight and having mounted
his horse, Perceval rode through a forest and came ere night to a
Castle.[3] There he was received by an old warrior and vavassour, who

---

[1] Potvin, II, pp. 62–67, ll. 1829–1972.   [2] *Op. cit.*, pp. 75, 76, ll. 2226–2254.
[3] *Op. cit.*, pp. 84–97, ll. 2498–2890.

soon discovered his visitors raw youth and inexperience. He taught
him how to carry his arms, lance and shield included. On the next
morning Perceval received from his instructor the High Order of
Chivalry and departed thereupon, the bearer of final counsels in the
following terms : (1) to spare a vanquished enemy who prayed for life ;
(2) to keep a still tongue ; (3) to give advice when asked ; and (4) to
make his prayers in Churches that God would bless his arms and keep
him ever in the way of a Christian life.

Perceval left his Sire in Knighthood with an expressed resolve to
visit his Mother, if he could find the way, and learn how she fared in
his absence ; but he arrived instead at another Castle, that of Beau-
Repaire and the fair maid Blanchefleur. She proved to be his Instructor's Niece, now in dereliction and besieged by Clamadieu, King of
the Isles of the Sea. Her it would seem that he desired beyond all
isles and kingships, but she would have death rather ; and he sought to
overcome her reluctance by force of arms till her walled town was
wasted, her host reduced and the remnant nearly starved.[1] In such an
hour Perceval came over moat and bridge, demanding and receiving
harbour. He beheld the waste without but apparently no besiegers,
nor did Blanchefleur speak openly, on couch in hall or at table. She
came to him rather at night, when her tears aroused him, since an end
must come on the morrow, town and tower being yielded. A knife in her
casket would close her own days before she fell into the hands of the
besieging King. Perceval gave her such fair assurance that the dark
hours were spent in each other's arms. On the morrow he called for his
mail, for sword and lance and shield : a gate was opened ; he thundered
forth thereby, to do battle with the King's seneschal, who had charge
of the siege that day. Him he overcame, him also he sent to King
Arthur's Court, to place himself at the mercy of that Damsel whom
Kay had smitten, saying that she should be yet avenged. On the next
morning he fought and overcame Clamadieu, whom he sent to Court in
like manner, with the self-same greeting and pledge. So was Beau-
Repaire delivered and Blanchefleur, the Queen thereof. The Kingship
was his for the claiming and the Queen as Bride ; but still on the
quest of his Mother in the Waste Land, he dared not and would not
tarry. Did he find her alive and well, she could be brought to the
Castle : if otherwise, he would return alone.

He remembered bitterly, it will be seen, that he left her at parting
in a swoon of grief, and he sought now to repair his fault. The stars
ordained that he should be diverted again from his penitent quest ;
and having travelled the livelong day without meeting anyone, he drew
up by a deep river, where he found no means of crossing and no
harbourage where he could abide in sight. There were, however, two
men in a skiff, one of whom was fishing. He appealed to these and the
Fisher offered to lodge him in his own hostel.

---

[1] The story of Beau-Repaire begins at line 2898 and ends for the time being at 4149.
See *Op. cit.*, II, pp. 98–139.

H

The way of the Grail is the way of the Quest thereof, for those who are called and chosen. There was no one less on that mission than the lad—still in his 'teens presumably—who was called Perceval. The thought of his Mother filled his heart as he drew to the deep river and spoke with those in the little craft thereon. A prayer for her weal broke forth on his lips some few moments before he arrived at the water's brink ; but he followed directions which brought him to a third Castle, and this was the Keep of the Grail, while he who had sent him thither was called the Rich Fisher, its Warden and its King. The youth was admitted and disarmed by squires, was clothed with a scarlet mantle and presented to the Lord of the place, who had somehow returned before him, appearing now as an ancient man who could not rise to welcome him because of his maimed limbs. Perceval was seated beside him on a rich couch, and when a few words had passed between them the observances of the Castle began. A Sword which would break in a single peril only was presented to the visitor under circumstances which have been described previously.[1] Amidst a great splendour of torches and candles, a Knight issued from another chamber bearing the Bleeding Lance and at the head of the Grail Procession. The tables were laid meanwhile, the meats were served and eaten, the wine was poured, with the Grail passing up and down, till in fine the Office ended and the Hallows went back as they came. Perceval longed to ask about Grail and Lance, but remembered his instructor's counsel on the gift of silence and therefore postponed questions until the morrow at least. The hour for retiring was signalled, and his sleep was unbroken through all the night ; but no one appeared in the morning to help him vest and arm. When he emerged from his own room all doors were locked against him, so he went alone to the stables, where he found his horse saddled. He mounted and crossed the drawbridge, but this was drawn up so quickly that beast and man almost fell into the moat.[2] In vain he sought for someone to whom he could put his questions concerning Grail and Lance, for no living creature appeared about the precincts. He entered therefore the forest, as one who after good hostel has suffered rough treatment for some cause unknown. He met presently a maid in lamentation over the body of her slain lover and remained in communion with her, till not only did she discover where he had spent the night but he on his part learned with whom he had lodged. She addressed to him also two tests of merit, being whether he had asked what caused the Lance to bleed and what the Grail signified. She called him caitiff for his pains when his answers proved negative and then resumed her lamentations, saying that the Rich Fisher would have recovered his health, as well as his lands, had those questions been put. The Grail King had been pierced through both thighs in a battle no long time since, but under circumstances which were not disclosed and with which she may have been unacquainted. He was

---

[1] See *ante*, p. 70.
[2] Perceval reaches the Grail Castle at l. 4228, and the drawbridge rises at l. 4590. *Op. cit.*, II, pp. 142–154.

unable to mount a horse and was now carried in a litter to the waterside and put in a small skiff, that he might enjoy fishing as his only available relaxation. It was he who had built the Castle, prior presumably to the warfare in which he was maimed. The failure of Perceval was a sin as well as an offence against his bounteous host and would bring sorrow to himself as to others. As regards Perceval's Mother, she had died of grief when he deserted her. The maid who testified had been present at her burial, for though Perceval did not know her she knew him, being his cousin-german, who was brought up with him in his infancy. She warned him further that the Sword which had been given him at the Grail Castle would break at the first encounter in which he should attempt to use it. There was but one smith in the world by whom it could be reforged, namely, he who made it, and his smithy was by a certain lake. Perceval prayed the maiden to cast in her lot with his, but she refused decisively, as she would not move from the spot till he whom she had loved was buried.[1]

He departed therefore, and his next encounter was with the Lady of the Pavilion, her whom he had kissed by force and ravished of a ring which she held apparently in trust on account of her lord. He found her riding a starved palfrey, she herself being clothed in very tatters. As he learned from her lips the cause of her woeful plight and his own hand therein, he who was her husband, the Proud Knight of the Plain, rode out of a wood and challenged, repeating to him his own story and vowing that the ill-starred damsel should never change a garment till he, the Proud Knight, should master him who had constrained her. Perceval declared himself, the attack began, but the youth conquered in the end and admitted his foe to mercy on these sole conditions : (1) that the Lady should be taken to his best manor and there restored to health ; whereafter (2) the Proud Knight should lead her in rich attire to King Arthur's Court, put himself at the Monarch's command and (3) testify to the Damsel whom Kay had smitten that he, Perceval, would never return to Court till he had avenged that insult. It was so done accordingly, with such results that the King and his Knights, the Queen and her train of Ladies left Caerleon to go forth in search of Perceval.[2]

It came about that they encamped in a meadow where snow fell in the night, and that in the early morning after Perceval drew rein thereby, to mark how a falcon swooping attacked a flying bird, which contrived, however, to escape but left three drops of blood on the driven snow. He paused and leaned upon his lance, thinking of the red and white on the face of Blanchefleur. The hours passed over in such reverie, even from dawn to noon, when the dreaming Knight was observed by certain squires, who reported to Arthur that there was one asleep on his steed. Sagramour the Unruled was directed to awaken and bring the stranger to Court, which was attempted roughly and with the result that Perceval, aroused unduly, dealt

---

[1] *Op. cit.*, pp. 154–163, ll. 4609–4864.   [2] *Op. cit.*, pp. 163–185, ll. 4865–5532.

Sagramour a buffet with his lance and stretched him on the ground, after which he resumed his reverie. Sir Kay jeered when Sagramour returned with his own spear broken, whereupon the King bade him fare better if he could. Kay swore that he would do so, with or without the stranger's will. Going forth accordingly, he accosted Perceval with a threat, and the result of this second disturbance was another mellay, in which the Seneschal earned a broken leg and a broken arm. He was carried back swooning and Perceval returned to dream. The task of awaking the dreamer was now assumed by Gawain, and it happened that as he approached Perceval the sun was melting the blood drops, whence the sleeper had begun to awaken of his own accord. There were fair words exchanged, and with his heart of courtesy the King's nephew invited the young Knight, on the King's part, to come into the presence of the King. Perceval remembered his vow and asked whether Kay was there, in which manner he learned to his soul's content that now at last the insult offered to the maid had been well and truly avenged. His words of satisfaction revealed to Gawain that this indeed was he whom the Court had gone aseeking, while great was the joy of Perceval when he embraced one of whom he had heard so often. Sir Gawain clothed him in a coat and mantle chosen from his own store, and together they greeted the King. But Perceval greeted also the Damsel who once had smiled upon him and wished her joy and honour as the best of ladies and the fairest, according to the prose version of 1530, and as her faithful Knight, according to the poem.[1]

The Court returned to Caerleon, Perceval being carried in its train. There was feasting at evening and feasting till noon followed, when a Damsel on a tawny mule, and beyond all words for hideousness,[2] saluted the King and his Chivalry, Perceval alone excepted. Him she denounced and him also she cursed for the business of Grail and Lance ; for the word unspoken and the woe that followed thereon ; for wounds which were not healed ; for land now lost for ever ; for dames deprived of husbands ; for maids discounselled ; for knights destroyed and widows and orphans left. She turned thereafter to the King, telling of a Proud Castle where Knights of fame abide and none repairing thither shall want for joust and battle. She told also of greater glory yet which awaited him who on a height above Mont Esclaire should liberate a besieged maiden. The Sword of Strange Hangings would be

---

[1] Potvin, *Op. cit.*, II, pp. 185–200, ll. 5538–5980.

[2] *Ib.*, pp. 200, 201, ll. 5992–6015. The description includes eyes like those of a rat, the proboscis of a monkey, lips of an ass or an ox, the beard of a goat, and a humped back. I am almost disposed to think that this description would not have occurred to Chrétien as befitting a Messenger of the Holy House, and that something coming down from the past is indicated. If I am right herein and in my previous suggestion respecting the term Grail, it may be thought that the primeval Quest or History corresponded more nearly to the wild, fantastic Prologue of the CONTE than to any other extant text. A Grail Warden who, owing to his skill in Sorcery, could change his semblance perpetually might have sent out the kind of emissary depicted above and reproduced faithfully by Wolfram. She would serve also as a courier of the Venusberg in the last stages of the decaying Mythos, about which we shall hear later.

his to wear henceforth. The accuser went thereafter on her way, while Sir Gawain vowed that he would seek to succour the maid, and Girflet, son of Do, that he would visit the Proud Castle. As for Perceval he resolved never to lie for two nights in the same hold till he learned who was served of the Grail and why the Lance was bleeding.

There followed five years of hard adventure in Quest and Errantry, during which the poem represents him as sending sixty conquered Knights to place themselves at the King's mercy and become at need his prisoners. But he knew so little of Grail and Lance that during all this period he heard no Mass and remembered nothing of God.[1] At the close of the faithless time he was riding, all armed as usual, through a wild country, when he met with a company of Lords and Dames, going barefoot on pilgrimage in penitential garb, and was reproached for faring in guise of war on the day of the Passion of Christ. He learned in this manner that it was Good Friday, to his great surprise and dismay, and later that the Company had confessed their sins to a Hermit who dwelt hard by in the forest. Perceval, recalled to himself and full of sorrow, sought out the good man's hold and made his own confession, more especially concerning the failure in respect of Grail and Lance. He heard on his part (1) that the sin of his Mother's death, brought about by his desertion, had sealed his lips at the Castle of the Rich Fisher; (2) that one unseen who was served with the Grail therein was the Hermit's Brother; (3) that their Sister was Perceval's Mother; (4) that the Hermit was therefore his Uncle and the Rich Fisher his Cousin; (5) that the Hidden King had dwelt for twenty years in the Secret Chamber from which Grail and Lance came forth; and (6) that during all this period the ancient man had been nourished only by a Host brought in the Grail.[2] Henceforth, in the name of his penitence, Perceval was to lose no opportunity of hearing Mass, of honouring God and the Priesthood, giving aid to widows and orphans, helping all in distress and ever relieving the poor. The penitent Knight pledged himself to these observances, and this was the conversion of Perceval. He remained with the Hermit till Easter Day and then received the Eucharist, with great reverence and worship. Such is the story of Perceval le Gallois according to Chrétien de Troyes, who began and left unfinished the CONTE DEL GRAAL. It is interrupted by long digressions recounting adventures of Gawain: these, however, will be considered in a later section.

I have said that Chrétien is a poet—born of his period under the ministry of Nature; but for a last word concerning him I have left over to this point the Hermit's final instruction to his kneeling nephew. After the latter had made his solemn promise, the Uncle taught him

---

[1] Op. cit., p. 254, ll. 7591–7611. The episode of the pilgrims ends at p. 257, l. 7704.

[2] D'une sole oiste li sains hom
 Quant en ce Gréal li aporte,
 Sa vie sostient et conforte,
 Tant sainte cose est li Graaus.—ll. 7796–7799.
Whether administered (1) daily, (2) from time to time, or (3) once and for all only, does not appear in the story.

a Prayer in whispered words, repeating it over and over till the youth knew it by heart. He was covenanted, moreover, to recite it only when the danger of death was upon him. Whether it was to serve as a viaticum or as a defending formula we do not know, for it is described simply as an Orison containing certain Names of Christ too potent for human lips to utter, except in mortal peril. The brief account is as follows :

> " Et li ermites li conselle
> Une orison dedens s'orelle,
> Si l'afrema tant qu'il le sot ;
> Et en cele orison si ot
> Assés des noms Notre Signor,
> Car il i furent li gregnor
> Que nomer doie boce d'ome
> Se por paor de mort nes nome.
> Quant l'orison li ot aprise
> Deffendi lui qu'en nule guise
> Ne le déist sans grant péril.
> ' Non ferai-je, sire,' fait-il."[1]

I cannot remember that this notable incident has attracted the attention of criticism. Those who would follow its strange intimations must go back through the Christian centuries to the days of that veiled theosophist who wrote on Divine Names under the title of Dionysius the Areopagite, and behind him they may be carried further still.[2] Chrétien must have puzzled the later contributors to the CONTE DEL GRAAL, for they do not provide an occasion when Perceval might have used the Prayer. On the other hand, the puzzle for us is how the Minstrel commissioned by Philip of Flanders came to hear—at however far a distance—of secret, potent and super-sacred Names which were also titles of Christ, and what imagined event to come in the later story of Perceval was to justify the introduction of such an incident at an early epoch of the Quest.

III

THE EXTENSION OF WAUCHIER

AN anonymous poet succeeded Chrétien and is known— awkwardly enough—as pseudo-Wauchier, because in the opinion of certain scholars of the past his contribution was held to be the work of Wauchier de Denain, who took up the thread of the narrative where the nameless successor left off.[3] This identification has lapsed, but the qualified name clings, like an

---

[1] Potvin, Op. cit., II, pp. 262, 263, ll. 7855–7866.

[2] For an aperçu on the field which opens to the exploration of words and names of power, see F. Lenormant : LA MAGIE EN CHALDÉE.

[3] According to Bruce—I, p. 229—Chrétien's poem breaks off at l. 9198, in the middle of a sentence. Nutt fixed the break at l. 10601, also in the middle of a sentence. See Potvin, II, p. 1 and II, p. 47. A note at the latter point may have influenced Nutt and others.

undesigned stigma. The question does not concern us at this point, seeing that his section of the CONTE is devoted solely to Monseigneur Gawain, whose place in the poem, and generally as a Knight of God on the Quest of the Holy Grail, will be discussed at a later stage.

It has been advanced that Wauchier had antecedent texts to go upon outside the work of his predecessors, and that one at least of these is not to be identified with purely folk-lore materials. It has been held, on the other hand, that the Metrical Romance of Borron was not among these documents ; and on the hypothesis of a primordial non-Grail Quest, presumably in Northern French, it might follow that he had seen this. So also might the authors of a certain Welsh MABINOGI and an archaic English poem to which we shall come later and to which I have referred already. Now, there are traces in the MABINOGI of an intention which could have led up to the Marriage of Perceval and Blanchefleur, if his enchantment by an Empress had not extended over a period which put such a possibility out of the question. In the English metrical story the Marriage is a natural conclusion, and it takes place accordingly. In Chrétien there are the same traces, and they reappear more strongly in Wauchier, but the term of his design is unmanifest because he failed to conclude. The general consent of scholarship might be disposed to hold that the prototype—if any— of both poets celebrated a Bridal at its end. It would contain also the widely diffused story of the stag and basset, and, in one or another form, the curious episode of a self-moving Chess-Board. But, fully developed as these are in the extension of Wauchier, they are after all of his accidents only, while—*pace* Dr. Bruce—of his essence is the Grail Quest, which overrules all things else in his sheaf of inventions—or his ingarnering of diverse memorials.

The story of Perceval is resumed by Wauchier[1] at that point when the hero has departed from the Hermitage of his Uncle, who had brought him into a tolerable state of repentance, purging him by the Offices of the Church, and in a sense had communicated the first Mysteries of the Grail, being those of his own genealogy, that of Perceval and their relation to the Wardens of the Hallows. Perceval had been denounced previously for an omission which he had almost covenanted to make, and no hope had been extended that he should yet act as repairer in fine, so that from initial point to term, as he could then perceive it, some blind and implacable fatality appeared to have been at work alone. Now, on the other hand, and if not all too plainly, it looked as if there followed by inference that a high hope of achievement was held out to him by his Uncle's words. Once again, therefore, he resolved that he would not return to King Arthur's Court till he had revisited the Fisher King's Castle and inquired concerning the Grail. But all without that secret fastness was not only beset by

---

[1] That is to say, at l. 21917, *Op. cit.*, IV, p. 59. Pseudo-Wauchier had reached a definite point in his long story of Monseigneur Gawain, and Wauchier's first sentence is : "*Or revenrons à Perceval.*"

perils and hard encounters, but it turned in a glass of strange vision
and great deception. Once more, I am not concerned in summarising
the story to take in all its details, because, as usual, several of its
episodes are idle and extrinsic in respect of our proper purpose.[1] The
Castle of all Desire moved near or far upon the confused horizon
of adventure, and at a certain point Perceval reached a river, beyond
which he was assured that the bourne rose up grandly, in a rich and
peopled land. But he could find no means of crossing. The day passed
from noon to vespers, and still on the farther side he came to a vacant
palace, beautiful exceedingly in situation, *moult bien séant*, but now
standing drearily in ruins. There he found a Maiden who was prepared
to shew him a place of crossing and mounted her mule for the purpose ; but her intention was only to drown him.[2] I find nothing herein
except an unmeaning hindrance, and the same may be said of an
episode which occurs hereabouts in certain manuscripts, being the
meeting between Perceval and a huntsman who reproached him for the
fatality of the Unasked Question at the Grail Castle. It shews only
that the rumour of the ill-starred visit had gone about the district,
which was acquainted otherwise, and too well, with the sorrows of the
Holy House and their effects beyond the precincts. As regards the
Maiden and the mule, I would note further that in the CONTE DEL GRAAL
there is a curse on Logres which occupies a middle term between Times
of Adventure and Times of Enchantment, an irresponsible spirit of
revenge, which might be now that of a Water-Fairy, belonging to the
Kelpie type, or the malice of an earthly maiden. The brief occurrence in
the present case may be due perhaps to the former, in the imagination of
Wauchier. However this may be, the Knight, having been better counselled, learned of a ford and so entered presumably on the direct road
which led, by the hypothesis, to the desired House of Great Hallows. Yet
he was still far from his term, and many adventures in the vicinity intervened without him reaching the goal. First among these was a visit to
another deserted Castle—such desolation being perhaps a part of the curse
—and therein he found that self-moving Chess-Board of which we have
heard previously and which managed to mate Perceval several times
when he sat down to play.[3] A maid of great beauty rose from the midst
of the lake into which Perceval proposed in his fury to cast the board
and pieces. The fact that she came into the Castle and that her
reproaches held his hands substituted another Quest, as if it were
in place of the Grail. A white stag ranged in the park of the Castle, and
if he would receive those favours which her beauty led him to demand
he must—for no assignable reason—bring her the head of this animal,
to facilitate which she lent him a basset, with express injunctions to
return it. I do not propose to follow the adventures that arose out of
this undertaking. The favours involved by his covenant had been
granted to Perceval in the case of Blanchefleur, though not perhaps

[1] Appendix I, Note 7.   [2] Potvin, *Op. cit.*, Vol IV, pp. 73–76, ll. 22291–22392.
[3] *Op. cit.*, ll. 22393 *et seq*.

when her distress, at the time of their first meeting, had brought her to his bedside and into his arms afterwards, through the whole night.[1] Her true love was to follow her liberation by him from the violence of an undesired suitor. But it was granted indubitably in the plenary sense when he reached her Castle—still in the course of his stag and basset quest—for the second time unexpectedly. Still it was under circumstances which are not apt to occur in these Romances of Chivalry unless the consummation of Marriage is intended at the close of all. That she was a bride-elect is clear enough in the poem, and in yielding, it was to her future husband that she yielded, which makes one later episode in Perceval's story the more inexcusable for this reason. That Perceval, his inconstancy notwithstanding, was self-devoted to Blanchefleur follows from the episode of the love-trance ; but his inclinations are variable in the CONTE, as they are in that Welsh story to which I have referred already and possibly out of due time. For the love of the Lady of the Chess-Board he goes through long-enduring toils, which so end that at length he attains his desires—as will be found shortly. In all this there are only two points which concern us—firstly, that the attainment involves the desertion of Blanchefleur under circumstances that for the Knight are disgraceful ; and, secondly, that the prolongation of the adventures which follow the slaying of the stag are due to a Daughter of the Fisher King, or at least in part, and are designed —out of all reason—to punish Perceval for not having asked the Question.[2]

I have said that the locality of the Grail Castle is as if it were a place in flux : there is nothing in the opening of the story to lend colour to the supposition that the Sacred Vessel, its Mystery and the House of these were close to the manorial residence and rural retreat wherein Perceval passed his childhood. Hence it is because peradventure the Castle was here to-day and gone to-morrow that they are brought suddenly into comparative proximity. Perceval was still in the course of his stag-adventures and still seeking the prize which was to follow their completion ; still also he was hearing casually concerning the Grail, or at least was in occasional speculation regarding its whereabouts ; when he found himself, without expectation and without intention, at the door of his old home, for the first time only in ten years. There he entered, there he tarried but too briefly, and there he met with his Sister—of whom Chrétien knows nothing, even as Wauchier elects to ignore entirely the cousin-german introduced by the earlier poet. He may, however, have been following—by bare possibility—some earlier stage of the Legend, to which the LONGER PROSE PERCEVAL and the Great Quest also conform ; and in that last and glorious text the personality of the Sister is exalted to a high grade of sanctity, of which we find nothing but the first traces—for the first

---

[1] Dr. J. D. Bruce differs decisively on this point and sees no evidence for any alternative view. So also did Nutt before him.

[2] It is obvious that she delays thereby her Father's desired healing.

traces are present—in the account of Wauchier. Herein she is a spirit
of recollection and a meditative recluse—

> " Une moult très cointe pucièle,
> Blanc com flours en may novele."

But she is clothed richly withal and encompassed by a fair retinue, so
living sad and unfriended in the woodland, lamenting the loss of her
Brother, of whose fate she had heard nothing. When Perceval declared
himself there was great joy between them, and of her he learned the
particulars of their Mother's death, through the love and the loss of him.
Together they visited a Hermit Uncle who is not to be identified with the
former, being on the Father's side. To him Perceval made his confession
—though of all prayers he knew only the *Pater Noster*—was present
when a Mass of the Holy Ghost was celebrated, knelt at the tomb of
their Mother, and of his Uncle prayed piteously that he might learn
concerning the Grail and the other Hallows. But this Uncle would tell
him nothing at the time, though he gave him instruction regarding
Holy Mysteries of Religion. That the heart of Perceval was not reached,
his reverence notwithstanding, was too soon made evident by the fact
that he bequeathed his Sister to renewed isolation, with a mere promise
to return which is never fulfilled ; and soon or some time afterwards he
was in a position—as we shall see—to claim and receive his dues from
the Lady of the Chess-Board.[1]

Neither sin of concupiscence nor sin of desertion has disqualified
him for the Quest of the Grail in the opinion of Wauchier ; and he was
still less or more on that Quest when he came to a Castle of Maidens,
who were reputed to have raised the beautiful edifice with their own
hands—

> " Ains le fisent . IIII . pucièles,
> Moult avenans et moult très bièles."

Of these he heard the story, though he was weary and looked rather
for rest. So was he delivered to his slumber ; but the place was all
work of faërie, and he reposed that night in enchantment. Faërie
Houses are, however, like faërie gold—dead leaves and dry in the
morning, or luminous shadow and rainbow semblance which dissolve
in the Eastern Light.[2] So Perceval woke in a meadow with an oak
murmuring above him. From all this there follows nothing ; but it is
designed that the next adventure should take him a further step in the
direction of his term. It seems that in the neighbourhood of the Grail
Castle there was always a river to cross, and as on the first occasion he
met with a Lady and a mule, from whom followed his destruction
almost, so now there was another Maiden with a similar beast in her
charge, thus creating a kind of equilibrium between false and true
assistance. The story is very long, and much of it is outside the object,
but it may be reduced under three heads : (1) Perceval was riding with

---

[1] For Perceval's visit to his old house, see *Op. cit.*, IV, pp. 187–209, ll. 25758–26448.
[2] *Op. cit.*, IV., 210–227, ll. 26471–27003.

the Lady, whom he lost at night in the forest. Alone and also lost, he beheld a great light—very clear and very resplendent—but it was followed by tempest. (2) In the morning he recovered the Damosel, who said that it was the light of the Grail, which the Rich King Fisher was accustomed to carry in the forest, so that no infernal temptation should have power over him. In the CONTE therefore, as in the QUEST OF GALAHAD, the Grail goes about ; but it is not for the same reason. (3) The Maiden described the Vessel as that which contained the Glorious Blood of the King of Kings, which was received therein as He hung upon the Cross.[1] This is rather the account of the VULGATE MERLIN than of Robert de Borron ; but the distinction is one of detail, and it follows that the Early History which was known to Wauchier was that of a Relic of the Passion. (4) More than this the Lady would not reveal, because it was a thing too secret for Dame or Damosel to recount : it was also a tale of terror, though a man of holy life might express the marvels. (5) That which she might and could she would do, however—namely, lend him her white mule—the beast which another Romance declares to be on God's side—and she would lend him also her ring, by which the mule was governed. Thus assisted, he would be able to cross a certain bridge of glass, over which he might travel direct to the King's Castle. Thereafter the mule would return of itself. He was not destined all the same to continue his journey far beyond the waterside. He was riding the mule, and leading his horse by the bridle, when he encountered a Knight who gave him news of a tourney about to be held by King Arthur, and—ignoring his original resolve—he turned aside from the straight path to attend it. The digression delayed his achievement ; but it left him the Best Knight of the World, and this was a condition of the achievement. It did not meet, however, the views of the Damosel who was owner of the mule and the ring ; for she reappeared and demanded their return, on ascertaining that his Quest was not achieved. They were both delivered, and thereafter —without salutation or farewell—he was left to shift as he might on the way, now all unknown, to the Holy House. It was at this time, as if once more without God in the world, that his road took him back to the Castle of the Chess-Board, for during all these scenes and times he was burdened by the stag's head and the dog of the damosel.[2] The term of this foolish business should have increased the difficulties of his Quest, but—on the contrary—the Lady was to a certain extent his conductress in place of the Maiden of the mule ; for she it was who took him again to the waterside and to a great boat there at hand which carried him—horse and all—to the opposite shore, beyond which stretched that broad way which led to the Court of King Fisher.[3]

The subsequent occurrences are intended to connect intimately with his arrival thereat and with the Rite of Questioning which is his prime object ; but they are fantastic rather than important—which

[1] Ib., pp. 250, ll. 27711 et seq.   [2] Op. cit., IV, p. 321, ll. 29900 et seq.
[3] Ib., V, pp. 1, 2, ll. 30499–30520.

appears also on their surface. He found a child of apparently five years old, clothed in rich vestments and seated on a branch of a tree higher than any lance could reach.[1] Of him Perceval, now full of his mission, inquired concerning the Fisher King, but was told only that if he would learn news which might prove good and pleasant he must go to Mount Dolorous, after which the speaker put a period to further questioning by ascending higher in the tree and thence in fine vanishing. Perceval reached the Mountain and met with a Maid coming down on a palfrey who counselled him against the adventure ; but he began the ascent and at the summit found fifteen crosses, of which five were white, five red and five blue. These encircled a pillar, to which he must fasten his steed. To fail was to lose reason. The achievement seems childish ; but it was a proof of valour devised of old by Merlin in order that the flower of Chivalry should alone serve King Arthur ; and the Maid who told this story was Merlin's Daughter, of whom we find nothing otherwise in the canonical Romances of the Grail. Seeing that very few Knights of the Round Table ever heard of Mount Dolorous and much less of the testing, the account seems an idle invention ; but it was once regarded as important for early Arthurian history. Perceval being still on his journey, at the conclusion of this adventure, and having received some further directions from the Maid in question, came next to a great tree which was illuminated by innumerable candles, like a High Altar at the Exposition of the Most Holy Sacrament.[2] It was the spectacle of a moment only, for the lights vanished on his approach, and he found himself at a wonderful Chapel, where a dead Knight lay in repose on the Altar and a black hand, appearing behind the Altar, extinguished one great light thereon. The significance—such as it is—of this episode appears in the sequel. In fine, Perceval arrived at the Grail Castle. Therein he found the King and told him of his latest adventures, namely, those on his way to the Castle. The Hallows appeared, and for the first time in the poem the expression *Saint Greal* is used in connection with the actual vision of the object. When the Procession had passed and repassed, Perceval asked, as we know, the required Questions ; whereat the King told him that these were great matters, and in the first place he recounted the meaning of the child seated on the branch of that tree which the Knight passed on his way thither. Perceval did not learn what he wanted, because of his sins, and the episode as a whole indicated that the thought of man should be raised towards his Creator—an allegorical trifle which is after the manner of Masonic Teaching, as this appears on the surface, or much ado about little. Before he could hear further Perceval was invited to piece the Broken Sword together, which he did, apparently by the power of his magnetism as the Best Knight in the World. He left only a slight crevice at the point of junction, which I should account for as signifying those other points in time at which the sorcery of sense

---

[1] Potvin, *Op. cit.*, V, pp. 109–112, ll. 33755–33839.
[2] *Ib.*, p. 132, ll. 34410–34429.

entered into his life. But this is without prejudice to the explanation provided in one of the sequels which stand over for consideration. Th partial success led the Keeper of the Hallows to embrace and hail Perceval as one of the Lords of the House, though it was obvious that the Quest was yet unfinished.[1] In other words, the Keeper is not healed. The next teller of the story will be found, however, to import still another element, which so far may have been an implicit of the poem but has not been explicated. For the rest, Wauchier explains nothing concerning that withdrawn and abdicated King, of whom we hear vaguely in Chrétien, nor does he make more than the one reference, which I have cited, to the Daughter of the Rich Fisher: to all appearance, however, she continued her Office as Bearer of the Holy Grail.

IV

THE CONCLUSION OF MANESSIER

THERE is a disposition to think that the extension of Wauchier broke off in the middle of a sentence, which was brought by the poet who followed him to its due point, and the narrative continues thereafter, in his hands remaining to the very end. This poet was Manessier.[2] We have to remember, however, that at or about the alleged break there intervened another singer, who intended, almost certainly, to furnish an alternative or independent conclusion, not a prolonged interpolation leading up to a further and already existing sequel. As the text is found in the extant MSS., it opens by completing the broken sentence of Wauchier's version, or just after the Fisher King calls Perceval to enter within the fold of the house—

> " Sires soiés de ma maison,
> Je vos met tout en abandon
> Quan que jou ai, sans nul dangier ;
> À tous jours vos arai plus cier
> Que nul homme qui jà mais soit."[3]

It explains to Perceval, on the part of the Fisher King, that he has failed in the Sword trial because of his Mother's death and cannot know as yet the Secret of the Grail.[4] Perceval is plunged in desolation by this judgment, whereas in the Manessier version he is filled with joy, for there is no further question respecting the Sword. The two

---

[1] The story of Perceval's second visit to the Grail Castle is found in *Op. cit.*, V, pp. 139–150, between ll. 34611 and 34934. It looks as if Wauchier stultifies Chrétien by the fact that the Question is asked, but the Keeper is not healed.

[2] Manessier belongs to the thirteenth century and wrote at the instance of Countess Jeanne of Flanders, whose rule extended from 1206 to 1244—or 1214–1227, according to Nutt. So also did Wauchier de Denain, though his work has been ascribed to the end of the thirteenth century.

[3] Potvin, *Op. cit.*, V, p. 150, ll. 34925–34929.

[4] The codex referred to by Potvin is described as *le manuscrit de Paris*, No. 12576, in what is now the BIBLIOTHÈQUE NATIONALE and had just ceased to be the BIBLIOTHÈQUE IMPÉRIALE, when Potvin published his sixth volume, where the reference will be found on p. 161. There is, however, a second MS. in the same Library.

poets are, however, of one mind as to the unfinished state of the Quest, though Manessier—on taking up the thread of the narrative, holds evidently that Perceval has accomplished enough to deserve as much information concerning the Grail and Lance as he intends to provide under any circumstances,[1] together with so exhaustive a history of the Broken Sword that the hero shall be equipped fully for the undertaking which remains to be fulfilled.[2] It would seem that Wauchier was concerned especially with the repair of this weapon, and it is out of the same Talisman that Manessier obtains his keynote, or that which concerns himself in the palmary sense, namely, the Vengeance Legend. It was the Sword which inflicted a certain Dolorous Stroke and by fraud encompassed the destruction of the Grail King's Brother —breaking, however, in the act. It was the Broken Sword which wounded the King himself, by a chance in which lurked a fatality, and his healing depended—as we know—on the visitation of tardy wrath and delayed justice upon him who used and misused the weapon. With Manessier's explanation of Grail and Lance we are acquainted also : it is that with which Longinus " pierced the side of God " when the Divine Majesty hung upon the Cross at Calvary. The Grail is that Holy Vessel which received the Precious Blood.[3] The historical account which follows not only differs from the Romance of Robert de Borron but has variants also from the GRAND SAINT GRAAL, on which it depends mainly. It knows nothing of a Second Joseph, that Son of Joseph of Arimathæa to whom such prominence is given in the later text ; but in opposition to Borron, it was the elder or, for the early version, the only Joseph of the Grail who brought the Hallows into Britain, who erected the Manor or Castle in which the King was now speaking to Perceval, and the speaker was of his own lineage.[4]

On the great night of his visit to the House of Hallows, Perceval heard other wonders than those connected with supposed Relics of the Passion or with the Sword of Wrath and Vengeance. He learned that the Maiden who carried the Holy Grail was of Royal Descent, and so also was she who bore the Salver ; but the former was the King's Daughter,[5] while the latter was his Niece, Daughter of Goon Desert, who was a King also and the Grail Keeper's Brother. He learned, moreover, that the Illuminated Tree, which he had passed recently on his journey, was a Tree of Enchantment, where the Fairies assemble ;[6] for the powers of the height and the powers of the deep and the powers of the intermediate world seem to have encompassed the Grail Castle, that the Times of Enchantment, Times of Adventure and Times of Wonder might be illustrated by abundant Pageants. He heard in fine of the Chapel and the Mystery of the Black Hand, to which I have alluded as

[1] Potvin, *Op. cit.*, V, pp. 152, 153, ll. 34990–35030.
[2] *Ib.*, pp. 159–164, ll. 35184–35334.
[3] The inter-relation between the two Hallows is drawn closer in a Montpellier MS. than it is in the Mons version. As the Sacred Spear penetrated the side of Christ, the Grail was raised up to receive the outpouring Blood, and Joseph turned black from sorrow.   [4] *Op. cit.*, V, pp. 154–157, ll. 35031–35138.
[5] *Ib.*, p. 158, ll. 35159–35174.   [6] *Ib.*, p. 165, ll. 3566–3587.

a tale of little meaning, wherein the Grail has no part, and there is no need to dwell on the explanation here.[1]

After these narratives, Perceval covenanted to visit the death of the King's Brother on the person who accomplished it. On the morning following he took his leave, commending his Host to God and refusing all invitations to tarry. Perhaps Manessier did not know what to do in order to retard, for the purpose of storytelling, the accomplishment of his Vengeance Quest. Alternatively, perhaps he regarded it as a point of honour to follow his precursors by giving an inordinate space to the adventures of Gawain, with whom he couples those of Sagramour, another Knight of Fame in Arthurian Romance. In any case, there are various digressions at this point which account for one-half of his sequel. When the story returns ultimately to Perceval he was again in the Chapel which he had visited previously—that of the Black Hand, the extinguished candle and the corpse on the Altar.[2] He did battle with and expelled a demon, purified the place and slept therein. The next day he assisted three hermits to bury the body of the last person whom the Black Hand had slain. All this notwithstanding—indeed, perhaps because of it—for a considerable part of his mission the powers of the deep attacked him. On one occasion the Accuser, in the form of a horse, endeavoured to carry him to hell; but he was saved by the Sign of the Cross.[3] Later on he arrived at that river which he had crossed originally; and there the demon sought once more to deceive him, assuming the guise of Blanchefleur coming to him in a wherry. But at the right moment another vessel appeared, with sails of samite, bearing a holy man; and Perceval took refuge therein.[4]

It is evident that the story has reached a point when its proper term is on the threshold rather than merely in sight; and the various delays which intervene can be dealt with in a few words, if we omit miscellaneous episodes which serve no important object, as they are nothing to do with the Grail.[5] The most purposeful of all was the arrival of a messenger from Blanchefleur, who was again in peril; and so Perceval paid his third visit to Beau-Repaire, which he delivered duly and departed again from the Lady, this time, however, in all purity and reserve.[6] She who had declared to him her love, now in the far past, she who expected to wed him, was destined to see him no more.

[1] *Op. cit.*, V, pp. 166, 167, ll. 35395-35448. It is sufficient to say that Brangemore, Queen of Cornwall, was murdered in the Chapel by her son, King Pinogrés, from which time forward every Knight who came therein was slain by a Black Hand.

[2] *Ib.*, pp. 304-320, ll. 39786-40288.   [3] *Ib.*, VI, pp. 1, 2, ll. 40473-40522.

[4] *Ib.*, pp. 4-11, ll. 40564-40768.

[5] It is to be noted, however, that Perceval reaches a smithy attached to a Castle carrying a Broken Sword, when on his way to Blanchefleur, and that it is made whole by Tribuet—otherwise doubtless Trebuchet—who had forged it originally, and who bids him guard it well, as no King had ever a better one. I find nothing in the text to explain how Perceval came by the damaged weapon, nor do we hear further concerning it. Far back in Manessier's story Perceval's Sword breaks in a combat which he and Sagremors waged against ten Knights, for the delivery of a Damsel, with whom Perceval stays for a month and is healed of his wounds. For the Tribuet incident see *Op. cit.*, VI, pp. 34-37, ll. 41477-41582, and for the previous combat and the episode of the Broken Sword see V, p. 181, ll. 35861 *et seq.*

[6] *Op. cit.*, VI, p. 45, ll. 41819 *et seq.*

The next most important episode was Perceval's stormy encounter with Hector of the Round Table, as a result of which both were destroyed nearly.[1] But in the dark of the midnight there shone a great light about them, being that of the Grail carried by an Angel, and thereby they were again made whole. It follows, once more, that here, as in the QUEST OF GALAHAD, the Grail was going about, at least on occasion, and we have had an instance previously in connection with the wanderings of the Fisher King. Like all Hallows the efficacy of which is transcendent, there was no active ministry on the part thereof, while nothing was done by the Angel. He moved simply about them, holding the Precious Vessel, and their wounds, with the pains, left them. Doubtless after such manner was the Company of the Blessed Joseph sustained and fed in the wilderness.

After this miraculous healing, Perceval, departing from Hector, as those who after great experiences have quenched all hatred in their heart, continued his way, as we may suppose, concerned now only with the accomplishment of his mission. And so in the fullness of time he reached a Castle wherein there dwelt the Knight who slew the Brother of the Fisher King. Sorrow and outrage had that evil Master of Chivalry brought to his intended victim, and more even than that to the Keeper of the Sacred Vessel. Why it had entailed such consequences nobody knows—perhaps also no one would care to speculate. The Grail had healed Perceval, and it had healed even Hector, in the absence of any desert on his own part, for he was the unworthy step-brother of Lancelot ; but its own custodian it could not cure of the wound which a seeming accident had inflicted.[2] After a long encounter, Perceval despatched the worker of this mischief and started on his return journey to the Grail Castle, carrying the head of the destroyer with him.[3] His mission once accomplished, all the hard and doubtful roads ran behind the hoofs of Perceval's horse : all the hindrances were taken out of the way. Of that way he knew nothing probably, and there was no need that he should. To the right he went and the left, with a certain sense of questing ; the moons of the magical summer waxed and waned above ; and all suddenly the Castle rose up before him.[4] A herald on the walls without beheld his approach and hurried to the Master of the House, not so much with the news of his coming as of that which he bore slung from the front of his saddle ; whereupon the Fisher King rose up healed—with a great cry. Perceval presented his terrible gift, and it was fixed on the summit of the tower belonging to that Castle which so far was a place of vengeance rather than of mercy. Thus finished the last and crowning adventure. Whether it was the implicit of Chrétien that the Question properly put would have restored all things within and without the Castle we cannot say : perhaps it would have led only to a Vengeance Quest, but again we cannot say. There is nothing in Chrétien to make us infer that Quest,

[1] Potvin, Op. cit., pp. 113–121, ll. 44107–44348.   [2] Ib., V, p. 162, ll. 35278–35286.
[3] Ib., VI, p. 122, ll. 44355 et seq.   [4] Ib., p. 130, ll. 44605 et seq.

and in the DIDOT-MODENA PERCEVAL—the Prose Romance which corresponds in the French Cycle most nearly to the first portion of the CONTE DEL GRAAL—the whole mission is one of asking and receiving a true answer. The relationship between the King and the Knight was declared now for the first time by one to another : the King appointed his lands to the hero, promising to make him King in succession at Pentecost—as one who devises to an heir, or perhaps as if he also were a Priest having power to consecrate. To this, however, Perceval would not accede so long as his Uncle was alive, and he was also under covenant to visit the Court of King Arthur, which he departed to fulfil accordingly. He was still there when a Maiden arrived with the news that the Fisher King was dead, and that there was a vacancy of the Royal Office in the House of the Grail.[1]

King Arthur accompanied Perceval to the Castle with all the Chivalry of the Round Table—remaining a full month and being served daily by the Sacred Vessel. It does not appear who consecrated and crowned Perceval, whether this was effected, in the ordinary way, by a Prelate of the Church, or whether the Office itself carried with it its own anointing and enthroning. The text says only that he was crowned at the Feast of All Saints,[2] and thereafter followed a high festival at which all were fed by the Grail, as with Manna sent down from Heaven. After seven long years of reign in peace Perceval bequeathed the lands in turn, and the official part of his royalty, to the King of Maronne, who had married the daughter of King Fisher ; but the Hallows he did not bequeath. He retired into a hermitage, whither the Grail followed him. By a departure from Tradition, he was consecrated Acolyte, Sub-Deacon, Deacon, and, in five years, he was ordained Priest and sang Mass. Thereafter so did he serve God and so love Him that he was called at length from this world into the joy of Paradise. During the last period of his earthly life one codex says that he was fed only by the Holy Grail—that is to say, by the Eucharist. It is supposed, but not affirmed dogmatically, that Grail and Lance and Dish were assumed with his soul into Heaven. In any case, no man has seen them since Perceval left this life.

V

THE ALTERNATIVE SEQUEL OF GERBERT

IT will be seen that in his wonderful kingdom Perceval had neglected Blanchefleur, who is no longer even mentioned : he went unto his own, and his own seem to have received him with no interrogation of the past. Had his sins been scarlet, the fulfilment of the Vengeance Mission and the consequent healing of

---

[1] Potvin, *Op. cit.*, VI, pp. 149, 150, ll. 45183–45217.

[2] According to the 1530 prose version, King Arthur certifies his intention to crown Perceval, and this is why the Royal and Illustrious Company escort him to the Grail Castle. It is said also that fourteen Kings in all assisted at the Great Ceremony.

the King would have made them white as snow, so far as we can follow Manessier ; and yet in some obscure manner the poet knew that the things which he dealt in were sealed with holiness and that the Office of the Warden, if it did not begin with Priesthood, and all its sanctity, must end therein. The sense of poetical justice might have suggested another conclusion, and so did, but this was not to the mind of Manessier. There is, as we are aware, a prolonged alternative sequel by another writer which interpenetrates the last lines of Wauchier, and —as it stands in the two MSS. by which it is known—leads up in over 17,000 lines to Manessier's conclusion. It is a Romance truly which is not without enchantments and vestiges of spiritual meaning. It has been summarised very fully indeed by the first editor of the CONTE DEL GRAAL ; and recently is in course of being printed in full, as it demands and deserves.[1] My own impression is that Gerbert completed the CONTE DEL GRAAL, either ignoring or unacquainted with Manessier. The scribes, however, of the two extant texts had the CONTE complete before them, as well as Gerbert's sequel and intercalated his text, less the concluding part, to the confusion of himself and Manessier.

I do not know what Gerbert de Montreuil thought of the Chess-Board episode and that which followed thereafter as the term of its whole adventure. He seems to have isolated it from his mind and thus contrived to ignore it. Certainly a subsequent action, or a denial, as I should say rather, which he attributes to his hero, seems to assume tacitly the previous continence of his life. Putting aside this question of an implicit, there are three express preoccupations to which the poem confesses : (1) that the desertion of Perceval's Mother was an offence which called for expiation ; (2) that the neglect of his Sister must be overglossed by due solicitude in the future ; and (3) that the rest of his life must atone for all his previous deficiences in respect of Blanchefleur, who—as I do not doubt that he determined in his secret mind—must be united through him with the Grail. Of such was his programme, and after what manner he fulfilled it can be told shortly.

Perceval had reason to say in his heart : *mea culpa, mea culpa, mea maxima culpa*—for three offences, and of these one was the greatest. His task for the time being was to be one of expiation, and he was to be treated, meanwhile, precisely as we shall find that Wauchier presents the treatment of Gawain over his particular failure : he was not to know the truth concerning the Grail—the Mystery, that is to say, of all Sanctity. A state less remote from perfection was to deserve so high a prize. The King, who pronounced the judgment, consoled him, and him counselled, after which Perceval was left to his repose in the Hallowed and Glorious Castle. The night of sleep was a night also which was intended to recall him to the sense of his first duty. The clear strokes of a clock, proclaiming the hour of midnight, awoke him : he saw a great light and he heard sweet singing, after which came the voice of one who was unseen, warning him concerning his Sister,

---

[1] Appendix I, Note 8.

who was encompassed by great danger in the Manorial House of their Mother. He passed again into deep wells of slumber, and again—but now in the morning—he awoke, as others had awakened previously, to find himself lying on greensward, since the Castle had passed for the time being beyond the witness of the senses. He mounted his horse, which stood caparisoned and ready ; he went forward, and soon—as it might seem, suddenly—a wonder of great wonders awaited him. It took the form of crystal walls, within which he heard all manner of instruments making joyful music. A door in the hither wall being fastened closely, he smote it three times with increasing vehemence, on the last occasion using his Sword for the purpose. It should be noted that this weapon neither was nor could have been the Grail Hallow or Talisman ; but it broke with a great clatter. Thereupon the door moved back, and a Warder who was in white and shining appeared and challenged. For Perceval there was a rebuff to come in more senses than he could understand at the moment : albeit he entreated earnestly, not only was he denied entrance, but was told by one who knew all his failure and success at the Grail Castle, that this his business with the Sword must cost him another seven years of Quest and Exile, before he returned to the Hidden House of Hallows. Apparently for the King's sake and the relief of him, he had striven in the first place, though the measure of his intention was small : now it was his own purification that was to be the chief work in hand. So he knocked and he did not enter, even as in the youth and inexperience of his brave spirit he saw the Pageant and the Hallows, but asked nothing concerning them. On both occasions, it was accounted to him as if he had sinned with knowledge. The truth is that the counsels of prudence do not obtain in the presence of the Mysteries, nor do the high conventions of good conduct, at least utterly. This was in the earlier case, and in the present one, while it is true that the Kingdom of Heaven is taken by violence, no one can enter unwarranted into the Secret Sanctuaries that have been instituted on earth to guard the memorials of the Kingdom which as yet is not upon earth, though with harp and viol and lute, and with all manner of music and psaltery, we pray that it may come quickly.

What, it will be asked, was this enclosure—within walls as the luminous shadow of the Jerusalem which is above ? What manner of Castle was this which resounded with the hallowings and enchantments of melody ? Was it not, indeed, the Grail Castle, to which he had returned unwittingly by a devious way ? According to the answer which the text furnishes, it was the Earthly Paradise ; but another and very different text tells us that among the added names of the Grail Shrine there was to be included the Castle of Eden, that it was the Castle of Joy also—as of music for ever sounding—and that behind it there was the Earthly Paradise, one of the rivers of which encircled the sacred enclosure.[1] Therefore I leave those who will to draw the

---

[1] See the " Romance in Prose " of PERCEVAL LE GALLOIS, called also the PERLESVAUS and LONGER PROSE PERCEVAL, in Potvin's CONTE DEL GRAAL, Vol. I, p. 249. See also Dr. Sebastian Evans' translation in THE HIGH HISTORY OF THE HOLY GRAAL, edition of 1903, p. 267.

conclusion which pleases them, knowing, as at least I do, that places of this unquestionable order may be now on the crown of a causeway which the sea lashes, and again

" . I . clos de mur fait a crestiax."[1]

Perceval retired discounselled ; but had he been advanced further in the knowledge of secret things, he might have recognised perhaps that there was encouragement and high hope which he could put to his heart because he had not been met by Swords of Fire, keeping the way of the Tree of Life, but by one in his own likeness, exalted gloriously, who had said to him : Not yet ! Moreover, at the end of the terse inter-locutory discourse, he was given what is termed in the poem a Brief, Charter or Warranty, which—so long as he bore it—would insure that through all his subsequent exile he should suffer no grievous harm, for thereby was he rendered invincible and thereby would his wounds be healed. We see in this manner that all kinds of miracle in medicine and every form of palladium were available there and here for Knights of Quest and Pilgrimage ; that they seemed to be reflections or radia-tions from the central star of the Holy Grail ; and hence that when he who was served thereby and maintained thereof could find not even a palliative in its Vision and Mystery, the explanation can be only that his sickness was not of this world. It was rather of the emblematic order, enacted in a world of parable, with a meaning reserved to those who could put an authentic question, which was also figurative.

Thus equipped, Perceval resumed his pilgrimage, much as the Novice in some Temple of Instituted Mysteries circumambulates the Hall of Reception under the guidance of its Wardens, having only a vague notion of what is the intention and the term, but still progressing thereto. Again the road was strewn with wonders before him, but to his exaltation on this occasion. The world itself had assumed an aspect of May-time on a morning of Fairyland ; and hold and keep and city poured out their garlanded trains, as with bells and banners and thuribles, to honour and acclaim him. Of the reason no one knew less than Perceval, or divined as little ; but he had asked the Question at the Castle, and although it had not been answered, although he had learned nothing of Grail and Lance, and was therefore less instructed than Monseigneur Gawain, the interdict had been lifted from Nature ; the winter was over and done, and all the cushats and turtles in all green places of the land—and all the ballad voices—broke into joy and melody, as if a Rite of Marriage had been celebrated between Heaven and Earth. He was clothed at castles in rich vestments, and from high-born maiden to simple peasant all hearts were his and all welcomes.

It must be said at this point that we know little, and so little, of Gerbert that it may be reasonably a matter for speculation whether the place at which his sequel is introduced by the scribes of certain codices

[1] Potvin, *Op. cit.*, VI, p. 163.

corresponds or not to his intention.   There are some respects in which
it could be allocated better if it were possible to suppose that it was part
only of a Grail poem which was meant to follow immediately from the
section of Chrétien.   A pertinent case in favour of this view is the
palmary fact that Gerbert seems to assume, as we have seen, the
virginity of Perceval up to and, as we shall see, after his marriage night,
which supposition is doubly impossible in view of the Wauchier section.
It must be noted further that in one remarkable reference to CRESTIENS
DE TROIE, he speaks of himself as the poet who resumed the task,
following the true history :—

> " Si com li livres li aprent,
>   Où la matière en est escripte."[1]

I feel that in making this suggestion I am exceeding my proper province,
which is not that of textual criticism, and I recognise that it has its
difficulties, assuming, as it does, that the Gerbert sequel must have
existed in a much more extended form, because at the opening Perceval
is at the Grail Castle for a second time, which is either pursuant to the
account of Wauchier or to some unknown portion of his own narrative.
If, however, he followed Wauchier, then he chose to forget or ignore
him at several crucial moments.   Sometimes he seems to forget
Chrétien himself, for except on this hypothesis it is difficult to understand his introduction of another Broken Sword, being that which
was shattered on the door of the Earthly Paradise.   Now we have,
in all respects, to remember that the putative Hallow which causes
this confusion is in the position that we should expect it to occupy,
seeing that it has no true place in the Legend of the Holy Grail.
Not only does its history differ in every Quest, but within the limits
of the CONTE DEL GRAAL it is contradictory under circumstances
which exclude one another.   Almost at the poem's very inception the
weapon is adjudged to Perceval, and he carries it away.   In certain
codices the only farther reference made to the Hallow by Chrétien is
found in the warning which the Questing Knight receives from his
cousin-german, immediately after his departure from the Castle ; in
others we hear how the Sword splinters in the hands of Perceval, and
thereafter how it is restored to the Castle.   It is there, in any case,
not only on the hero's revisit but long previously—in connection with
the arrival of Gawain.   Manessier tells a story concerning it from which
it follows that in breaking it occasioned the wounding of the King at a
period which was antecedent to all the Quests.   Therefore it could not
have been at any time offered to Perceval, but must have remained in the
Castle, with its resoldering always as the test of success in the case of
each questing Knight.   Now, either Chrétien had conceived a different
history of the putative Hallow or he had told the wrong story ; for the
cousin-german of Perceval testifies in his poem that the Rich King

---

[1] *Op. cit.*, pp. 212, 213.   It is said (1) that CRESTIENS DE TROIE began the story of
Perceval ; (2) that it was left unfinished because of Chrétien's death ; and (3) that
Gerbert *a reprise l'œuvre . . . selon la vraie estoire.*

Fisher was wounded in the thigh with a spear. When Gerbert intervened he left Chrétien's intention dubious, and substituted another Sword, which was not a Hallow, though, like that of his predecessor, it was one that had been forged specially—would break in one peril only and must be resoldered where it was made. After the triumph of his welcome, as related already, Perceval came to a Castle in which a smithy was set up under the guard of serpents ; for this was the place of the Craftsman who forged the weapon, and he did not wish it to be mended. The duty of the serpents was to destroy any one who brought the pieces to the smithy. The reasons—if any—are not explained by Gerbert, but it may be said that in certain codices of Chrétien the life of a Smith is somehow dependent on a Sword, and its reforging foreshadows his death approaching. If we can suppose that Gerbert's continuation began at a much earlier point than is now established, some explanation might be possible, though his own evidence seems to be against this view. Perceval conquered the serpents, and the weapon was duly reforged.[1] It does not appear to serve him in any special event subsequently, and as thus nothing follows from the episode we must conclude that its introduction is idle ; that in this respect Gerbert did not know what to do with materials which had come into his hands ; and this is perhaps the conclusion that we should desire in respect of the Sword.

The next episode in Gerbert is a kind of addendum to that of Mount Dolorous in Manessier, and to this again no consequence attaches, except that it is an accident by which the hero is brought to Caerleon and to the Court of King Arthur, when the poet gives us a new and revolutionary explanation concerning the Siege Perilous of Arthurian Romance. The Siege is a decorative Chair of jewelled gold sent from Fairyland—possibly that of Avalon—for occupation by the Best Knight in the World, and by him only with safety. For others who sit therein, the earth opens and swallows them. This Chair is taken by Perceval, as at a great Rite of Exaltation, and the earth does open ; but the Siege remains suspended in middle air ; and the result of this achievement is that the previous ill-starred heroes, who have been engulfed but not destroyed, are restored to light and air.[2] Perceval's next adventure is intended to illustrate his continence when tempted by a demon in the guise of a very fair woman. He emerged unsullied, and reached the abode of his Sister, to her unspeakable joy and comfort.[3] They visited the tomb of their Mother, and then set forth together. Some time after they arrived at the Castle of Maidens, where Perceval in fine left her in hands of safety. Here there was an office of healing,[4] which is of medicine rather than of anodyne ; but though all the ways of wonder lead to and from the Castle of the Holy Grail, the King of that Castle knew too well the fatality by which he was encompassed to

---

[1] Potvin, *Op. cit.*, VI, pp. 167–169. [2] *Ib.*, pp. 171–173. [3] *Ib.*, pp. 175 *et seq.*
[4] *Op. cit.*, VI, 177. Perceval had been wounded seriously while protecting his Sister in a casual encounter and was healed by an ointment in the Castle, his own magical Tablet having passed from Gerbert's memory for the time being.

seek, for he would have sought vainly, his relief thereat. Within the merciful precincts of her new asylum Perceval's Sister was enrolled henceforth as a ministering spirit, and thereat the adventuring Knight learned something more concerning the antecedents of his Quest and also of his own family. The Castle of Maidens received wanderers, but sheltered women only in its ordinary course ; and a reverend Dame— under whose rule the whole Company abode—declared herself a kins-woman of Perceval, being his Mother's Cousin. The name of his Mother was Philosofine, and they two had entered Logres together, carrying the Sacred Hallow ; but this event of the past was evidently a part of the Historical Mystery, and was not to be declared even to the Knight of Quest until he had proved himself. He knew now that even from his very beginning he was a Scion of the Sacred House ; and he might have rested content in his heart that the House would at length receive him. He learned also that it was the sinful state of the land which had caused the Holy Grail to be placed in a Concealed Sanctuary under the ward of the good King Fisher.

Meanwhile the Closing had been taken in the Degree of his duty towards his Sister ; and, in the next place he was called to a subsidiary work in the region of filial duty. With whatever offence he could be charged in respect of his Mother, she was past the reach of his atone-ment ; but his Father in Chivalry, now in the distress of Sorcery—as at the hands of those Sorceresses of Gloucester whom we shall meet with in a late Welsh Romance—demanded his vengeance. This incident is one of several which would make the investigation of Gerbert's materials a quest of high enchantment if only the road were open. Of the duty which was thus imposed and accepted in all the honour of his knighthood, Perceval acquitted himself with credit, his forgotten Brief from the Earthly Paradise coming to his aid, and the providence attached thereto. The episode, however, has a second object, more important to Perceval than itself, which is to aid in recalling a relation-ship between Blanchefleur and his Father in Chivalry—as the same is recorded by Chrétien—and so forward to the root-matter of the poem, which is the Marriage of Perceval, as the condition on which he will learn the Secrets of the Grail and Lance. As regards this Marriage there are two noticeable points, outside the fact that the union itself was the head and crown of exile ordeal.[1] There is (1) the ideal set before the poet, which was to preserve the continence of Perceval till he had accomplished the Quest of the Grail ; and (2) the promise that at some time subsequently—when that was removed which hindered the consummation of the Marriage in chastity—there should arise, as issue from those high nuptials the Mystical Genealogy of the Swan Knight, whereby the Holy Sepulchre would be delivered. It is for this reason that—by a covenant which was made between them—Blanche-fleur remained a maid on the night of her bridal.[2] Of such was the

---

[1] Potvin gives the Marriage at full length, VI, pp. 189–213.
[2] " Pucele i coucha voirement,
Ensement pucele en leva."—*Ib.*, p. 211.

Marriage of Perceval, and thereafter he who was Lord henceforth of all her lands, holding the sworn fealty of many Princes and Barons, went forth again into the world to prosecute the Great Quest. Of the Virgin Bride we hear nothing further, but there can be no doubt that if he had finished with her, as he seems to have planned, Gerbert would have recounted, and did perhaps, the re-union of Blanchefleur and Perceval.

I do not conceive that there is any object in prolonging this summary of a narrative which is protracted in various ways, but has reached its proper term. Some of its later, and, as one would say, redundant episodes occur or recur in the LONGER PROSE PERCEVAL ; but we have no criterion of judgment by which to decide whether one drew from another or both from that inevitable source to which they appeal both, under their respective veils. At the end of his probation Perceval is again at the Grail Castle, ostensibly for the third time ; he makes the Sword perfect ; and the last lines of Gerbert repeat, as they stand in **my** text, those which are last of Wauchier. I have stated my opinion **already**, under the necessary reserves, that Gerbert carried his sequel **further** and produced a conclusion which did not impose upon Perceval —under the genius of Manessier—yet another pilgrimage outwards, but as in the PARZIVAL of Wolfram, reconciled his own institution in the Grail Castle with the healing and concurrent prolongation of the Old King's life. As regards the sources of the CONTE DEL GRAAL in what is termed early historical matter, it is only at a late stage that we reach accounts which are not interpolated obviously, and then they connect with the GRAND SAINT GRAAL and not with the simpler history of Borron.[1] This is true of Manessier and true in part of Gerbert, but on the understanding that the story of Perceval's Mother—in the latter case—does not represent any other extant narrative, more especially in respect of the circumstances under which the Fisher King became the Guardian of the Grail. On the other hand, Wauchier gives a few indications which are of the matter of the Vulgate Cycle.[2]

VI

IN WHICH MONSEIGNEUR GAWAIN IS CONSIDERED BRIEFLY AS A COMPANION OF THE HOLY QUEST

THERE are three that give testimony on earth concerning the Mystery of the Grail—Perceval, Bors and Galahad— and the greatest among these is Galahad, on the authority of the High Quest. This notwithstanding, as there are persons who, through a certain mental deviation, turn aside from the highways of Christendom and look for better paths, out of the beaten track, in the issues of obscure heresy, so it has happened that scholarship,

---

[1] See *ante*, Book II, § 2 ; Book III, § 4.   [2] *Ante*, Book III, § 3.

without setting aside the great heroes of research, has discovered some vague predilection for the adventurous and courtly Monseigneur Gawain. They have been led even to think that he was the first hero of the Grail Quest. In order to strengthen the view, imagination has supposed as usual certain convenient versions, now more lost than regrettable, which present Gawain more fully as a Quest Knight than any document which is extant in Northern French. In such event these versions were like the poem of Chrétien de Troyes, as it was judged by Wolfram—that is to say, they told the wrong story. At the same time there are several accessory considerations which call for mention. Gawain was exactly the kind of character who would be disposed to initiate and undertake all kinds of quests, high and low. That he was a popular Grail hero might mean that some of his chroniclers did not see exactly why his methods and mode of life should create a barrier. It happened, moreover, that in the CONTE DEL GRAAL he is not deserving of harsher judgment than Perceval in the matter of continence.[1] I think further that the old romancists had in their minds a distinction between the continuity of the sin in Lancelot and the sporadic misdemeanours of Gawain, as also between the essential gravity of the particular offence in the two contrasted instances. There is the fullest evidence of this in respect of Guinevere, when considered side by side with other heroines of the Cycles. Moreover, the Romances reflected the unquestioned concensus of opinion at the period regarding the barren woman ; and it seems clear that the unfailing fidelity with which plenary favours were granted by maidens in the matter of a covenant fulfilled, and the frankness which permitted such favours to rank as the term of reward, had its root in the sentiment that, except in Houses of Religion, the womb which bore no fruit was under a greater interdict than that which conceived without consecration by the Sacred Offices of the Church. This must be remembered when the literature suggests, as it does, that the Chivalry of King Arthur's Court translated in an inverted manner the Institutes of Heaven ; that it was not very particular about marrying and giving in marriage ; and that it seemed to have assumed to itself an indulgence, both general and particular, to follow the untinctured office of Nature without much consciousness of a stigma attaching thereto. Finally, it is just to add that the Vulgate Romances manifest a set purpose to depict Gawain in blacker colours exceedingly than any earlier texts warrant.

For the rest, and from the mystical standpoint, it seems pertinent to say that while there is no period at which it was customary on the part of the Church to impose celibacy as an ideal on those who lived in the world, and while from most of the higher standpoints the grace of chastity is less in its simple possession than in its impassioned recovery, we have to remember that the Great Masters do not marry because of

---

[1] Had Perceval acted differently in respect of the Lady of the Chess-Board and had he kept faith with Blanchefleur, Gerbert might not have been moved to produce his so-called interpolation of the CONTE.

the Divine Union. The connection in Chrétien between Gawain and
the Grail Quest arises out of a challenge which he had accepted to clear
himself of a charge of murder,[1] as to which it became, later on, a point
of agreement that if he could find and bring back the Lance which
bleeds he should be excused from returning to withstand an ordeal by
battle. Out of this condition a Montpellier codex of the CONTE presents the visit of Gawain to the Grail Castle very early in the version
of pseudo-Wauchier.[2] He beheld, firstly, a bier and, secondly, all the
Hallows, asked the required Question, and was told by the Royal
Warden that if he could weld the Broken Sword he should know (1) why
the Beautiful Maiden who carried the Sacred Vessel was dissolved in
tears ; (2) why a Bier formed part of the Pageant ; and (3) whose body
was laid thereon. These points are peculiar to pseudo-Wauchier and
his connections. The experiment with the Sword proved, however, a
failure ; Gawain learned nothing ; he fell asleep after hearing the
discourse of the King, who explained what was wanting in him ; and
on awaking next morning he discovered himself in the open country,
with his horse and his arms close by him. It is obvious that he had
found the Lance, but he had not carried it away, and for this reason he
set out to take up the challenge. King Arthur intervened, however,
and the matter was settled in peace.[3]

The codex which embodies this account gives more extended
particulars of another visit which was paid by Gawain to the Castle ;
but it is obvious that they are exclusive mutually, and the alternative Mons version which omits the first visit, and determines in a
different sense the question of the accusation and the ordeal, are for the
Quest of Gawain the logical and preferable texts. Second or first, on
this occasion, nothing was farther from the mind of the character-in-
chief than to go on the Quest of the Grail, nor was he concerned with
the covenant of any challenge. He assumed the responsibility of a
Knight who was slain by a hand invisible when riding under his safe
conduct. The identity of this Knight is never disclosed ; but Gawain
assumed his armour and was carried by his steed, who had mysterious
fore-knowledge of the way, to a destination of which he himself could
dream nothing.[4] He arrived at his term in due course, but what took
place was the reception of a masquerading neophyte, who was unintro-
duced, unwarranted and unqualified. In place of being he that was to
come, they had still to look for another ; but his harness for a moment
deceived the Company about him.

Chrétien knew nothing of a bier and a dead body, in that place

[1] The episode of the challenge begins at l. 6125, *Op. cit.*, II, 205, and the connected
adventures of Gawain proceed as far as l. 7589, when the story returns to Perceval. For
the agreement respecting the Lance see *ib.*, p. 250, ll. 7488–7502.
[2] See *Op. cit.*, III, 369–372 for the Montpellier MS. version of this episode.
[3] It follows that Gawain was one of the heroes who beheld the Vision of the Holy
Grail. In the CONTE, however, it is to be noted that the Sacred Vessel was *glorieus* and
the Sacred Vessel was *sains*, but the election thereto was that of the Best Knight or his
nearest co-heir in normal Chivalry, and not of one who was resplendent in Spiritual
Achievement. Gawain was in this sense scarcely less eligible than Perceval.
[4] *Op. cit.*, Vol. III, pp. 352 *et seq.*, onward from l. 19655.

where the sign of arch-natural life abode in perpetuity. But, according to pseudo-Wauchier and the Mons MS., the bier was in evidence at this visit of him who was unexpected, and a Procession of Canons and Clerks recited thereover the Holy Office for the Dead, with a great ceremony of solemn voices intoning. The King also visited the bier and lamented over it. The Pageant of the Grail was manifested, after the manner which I have described elsewhere, and Gawain saw it openly. At the conventional feast it was the Sacred Vessel which served so far as the food was concerned, but the sacramental communication was in one kind only, since the wine, as we have seen, was brought round by the butlers. Gawain, as in the previous case, asked all the necessary and saving Questions, and was invited to solder the Sword ; but he failed, as before, in this ordeal and learned only concerning its History. A stroke which was dealt therewith destroyed the Realm of Logres and all the surrounding country. In the midst of this narrative Gawain fell asleep at the table, and was left to repose. When he awoke there was neither Hall nor Castle, neither King nor Chivalry about him, but a fairly garnished land lying on the brink of the sea and restored by so much of the belated question as he had asked the King. The common folk blessed him, and the common folk accused him, because he had not finished his work or insured their full felicity.[1]

Of such is the Quest of Gawain as it appears in the CONTE DEL GRAAL, even as the Pillars of a Temple which was never finished. It intervenes between the first and second visit of Perceval to the High House of the Hallows, but on Perceval's own Quest it has no effect whatever, and the narrative of the one ignores that of the other. It is said in some old fable—which is not, I think, of the Grail,—that Arthur and Gawain at last reposed in Fairyland. There are two classes of Knighthood—that which goes in and returns, and thereof is Ogier le Danois ; that which enters but does not come back evermore, and thereof is Launfal. Now, Arthur returns in the fullness of the times that are to come, and, however these dreams may be, it is certain that the Peace of the King is not the peace of Gawain. In conclusion as to the CONTE DEL GRAAL, after every allowance has been made for one statement in Chrétien, from which it follows that the Father of the Fisher King was, as we have seen, sustained by a Sacred Host taken from the Holy Grail, the keynote of the whole Cycle is that it has no sacramental connections such as we find elsewhere in the literature. On this account, if indeed on no other, the CONTE DEL GRAAL has nothing to tell us which signifies in respect of our true affair, except by way of its echoes and reflections from sources which do concern us nearly, and are better and fuller witnesses. It has every title to possess in perpetuity the kind of Perceval which it has helped materially to create—in whom the Parzival of Wolfram has little and the transfigured Knight of the HIGH HISTORY has next to nothing at all.[2]

[1] Ib., p. 364, ll. 20003 et seq., to end of vol. Also IV, pp. 1–6, ll. 20149–20328.
[2] It is to be noted that the adventures of Gawain in Manessier have nothing to do with the Grail.

BOOK IV

THE CYCLE OF ROBERT DE BORRON

THE ARGUMENT

I. THE METRICAL ROMANCE OF JOSEPH OF ARIMATHÆA.—The characteristics of Robert de Borron—The Metrical Romance presented in General Synopsis—Specific Considerations of the Story—The Source of the Text—The Sacred Vessel as it is understood in the Poem—The Divine Communion in the Tower of Joseph—The Secret Words and the Theological Position of the Text—The Institution of the Holy Table—The Mystery and Fate of Moses—The Branches to follow—The Marriage of Alain and the Succession of Keepers. II. THE LESSER HOLY GRAIL.—Its Critical and Literary Position in respect of the Metrical Romance—The Distinctions on Matters of Importance between the two Texts—Concerning the Sacramental Service at the Last Supper—Concerning the Secret Words and their written form—Concerning the Triple Guardianship—Of Words in Eucharistic Consecration—Concerning Joseph of Arimathæa—The Conversion of Britain. III. THE EARLY HISTORY OF MERLIN.—In what sense this Branch follows from the Metrical Romance of Joseph—The Bare Outlines of the Story—The Story as a General Introduction to the Romances of the Round Table—Its Palmary Characteristics as an intermediate Grail Romance—The Hermit Blaise—The Grail in Northumbria—The Secret Records of the Hermitage—The Round Table, its imputed connection with that of the Lord's Supper and with the Table of Joseph—The Void Seat—The Lacuna in the Succession of Texts—Of him who was to come, and whether Galahad or another—Some Implicits of the Legend. IV. THE DIDOT-MODENA PERCEVAL.—The Higher Considerations of the Quest—The Outlines of this Quest—Points of Correspondence with the Early Epochs—Place of this Quest, if any, in the Triad of Robert de Borron—Claims of the Questing Knight—Analogies with preceding Texts of the Trilogy—Discrepancies in the Legend of Moses —Of Merlin's Close in Sanctity and not in Enchantment—Conclusion as to the Lesser Chronicles.

BOOK IV

THE CYCLE OF ROBERT DE BORRON

I

THE METRICAL ROMANCE OF JOSEPH OF
ARIMATHÆA[1]

ROBERT DE BORRON was imbued, and even deeply, with the religious spirit of his period. I think also that in him there was a spiritual tincture which must have been a little rare at that epoch among courtly Minstrels. He had seen, according to his story, some part at least of the Great Book of the Legend, and perhaps it had changed his life. After the manner of his time, he was attached to a patron, and he wrote his poem for the *preux* and noble Chevalier Walter Montbéliard—a Crusader when the Temple was at its glory. The poem opens with an account of the circumstances which led ultimately to the Incarnation of Christ and is based on the notion that prior to this event, and prior indeed to the descent of Christ into Hades, good and bad were alike in Hell and less or more in the power of the evil hierarchy. The root-matter of the story can be expressed in a few words, and may be so offered to simplify the issues which are important to our purpose and must be dealt with therefore more fully.

The Vessel in which Christ performed His Sacrament, according to those words of the text with which we are acquainted already, was taken from the house of Simon by a Jew and delivered into the hands of Pontius Pilate, for no assignable reason except the exigencies of the story. Joseph of Arimathæa, with the assistance of Nicodemus and by permission of Pontius Pilate, took down the body of Jesus after the Crucifixion. The permission was a reward asked by Joseph in return for years of military service, and Pilate gave him in addition the Vessel which the Jew had brought him. In that Vessel Joseph received the Blood, which flowed again from the wounds of Christ when the body was being prepared for burial. He laid the body in a Sepulchre prepared for himself, and he concealed the Vessel in his house. After the Resurrection the Jews sought Nicodemus, who eluded them by flight, and Joseph, whom they seized and imprisoned in a dark tower. The only issue therefrom was at the summit, and this was sealed effectually by

[1] Appendix I, Note 9.

a heavy stone. Christ came to Joseph in the tower, brought him the Sacred Vessel[1] and communicated to him certain Secret Words which were the grace and power thereof. Joseph remained for forty years in his prison and was sustained by the Blessed Vessel, as if in a condition of ecstasy and apart from any normal consciousness concerning the flight of time. In other words, it nourished both body and soul, and this is the high sense in which the Grail appears as a Feeding Vessel in the earliest historical text. Towards the end of the forty years, Vespasian, the son of Titus, being afflicted with leprosy—and a pilgrim who reached Rome having recounted the wonderful miracles of Jesus, of which he had heard in Palestine—a commission was sent to Jerusalem in search of some relic of the Master, if the report of His death were true. The commission in due time returned with St. Veronica, who carried the *Sudarium*, or Sacred Face-cloth, and this effected the desired cure immediately. Titus and Vespasian proceeded with an army to Palestine, to avenge the death of Jesus. It was in this manner that Vespasian found Joseph still alive in the tower : the stone was removed from his sepulchre, and he who had been entombed, like Christ, like Christ also arose. After this rescue was effected, the Emperor's son was converted by Joseph.

The vengeance on the Jews being in fine accomplished, Joseph collected his Relatives as well as certain Companions who had embraced Christianity at his instance, even as those had done ; and by the will of God the party started Westward, carrying the Holy Grail. For a considerable period they took possession of a certain district, not otherwise indicated, and placed it under cultivation. At length a part of the Company fell away from grace, with the result that a scarcity followed in the land : the Vessel was invoked,[2] and it separated the good from the evil within the ranks of the people. By instructions thus obtained, a Table was dight after the manner of that which served for the Lord's Supper, and the Vessel was set thereon. Before it there was placed a single Fish, which the Divine Voice of the Grail had directed Brons, who was the brother-in-law of Joseph, to catch in a neighbouring water. Between Joseph and Brons there was left a vacant place, corresponding to that which had been made void by the defection of Judas Iscariot. A certain part of the Company, being those who had kept in a state of grace, and believed in the Holy Trinity, sat down at the Table, while the rest who gathered about were of those who had lapsed into sin. The good people experienced all spiritual delight and inward refreshment, but the evil were not filled, and they could not even see that which was in full view, the Holy Vessel. When a question, put to them by one who was named Petrus, had elicited this fact, they were denounced as those who were guilty, and they departed in shame. It is to be inferred that soon after

---

[1] Presumably therefore it had remained in the house of Joseph.
[2] That which Joseph invoked before the Holy Grail was the Holy Spirit ; but it was Christ Who answered.

they separated from the Company once and for all. The one exception was a certain Moses, who manifested great sorrow, though he was really an unbeliever at heart.[1] His prayers in fine obtained him permission to take a place at the Table ; but the Void Seat was the one which was alone available, and when he sat down thereon the Siege and its occupant were both swallowed by an abyss which opened beneath him. Meanwhile the Office of the Table had become a daily, as it were, a Divine Service,[2] and so continued till the Company was divided further to continue the journey Westward, even the farthest West, in successive parties, as ordained by Christ Himself, speaking from the Grail. Alain, the Son of Brons, and his eleven Brothers under his guidance were the first to start, he carrying a certain proportion of what must be termed the revealed knowledge of the Holy Grail ; but it did not include apparently the Secret Words. The communication which had been made to Alain was because when the time came for Brons and his wife to seek some kind of settlement in life for their twelve boys, the eleven had elected to marry and were provided therefore with wives, but Alain, the youngest of all, chose the vocation of celibacy. It came about that for this reason he was put over his brethren and was taken by Joseph into his heart after a special manner. This party was followed by that of Petrus, whose connection with the family of Joseph, if any, is not stated ; but he was favoured in another manner which would seem to be more distinctive, since he carried a Brief or Charter sent down from Heaven itself. Unfortunately, the account given of this notable document contradicts and stultifies itself.[3] The chosen destination of Petrus was the Vaux d'Avaron. The last to depart was Brons, apparently with the remanent of the people, and to him Joseph, by Divine Ordination, delivered the Sacred Vessel and communicated the Secret Words. Joseph of Arimathæa remained behind—though the text is corrupt at this point—his mission being accomplished, and is promised *la joie perdurable* of the Paradise which is above.[4]

The theology of the poem is in part of the popular legendary character and may seem a little fantastic even within these limits. For the Early Church and the writers thereto belonging, in places remote from the centre, the world of Christian Doctrine was a world not realised ; and Rome might well have been astonished at certain things which were said and sometimes taught with all innocence of intention on the verges of the horizon Westward. It would be easy to furnish examples

[1] A lacuna follows at this point in the only extant manuscript, but the missing episodes are supplied by the Prose Version.

[2] It was held, as explained already, at the hour of Tierce and was called the Grace of the Grail. We may remember that this was the canonical hour for the Mass-in-Chief of the day.

[3] It is said that the communication licensed Petrus to proceed wheresoever he pleased, but afterwards that it was to remain unread till the coming of a Son who would be born to the supposed celibate Alain, which Son would apparently break the seals and divulge the content.

[4] According to a later statement, Joseph "remained in the land where he was born "—which, however, he and his Company had left long since and gone Westward. Obviously, the later statement is also a late addition.

of elements in Borron which are not less than heretical from the doctrinal standpoint ; but there are indications also of curious learning and traces of strange sympathies. Among the latter may be mentioned a certain tenderness towards Pontius Pilate, the difficulty of whose position as the Procurator of Judæa, when acting almost under the compulsion of a Jewish faction, was from any point of view undeniable. The important point, however, is that the sympathy reflects at a far distance the Apocryphal Legends[1] which represent Pilate as one who was converted ultimately, who became a Bishop of the Church and sealed his testimony with martyrdom. More noticeable than this, perhaps, for the ordinary reader is the writer's seeming ignorance concerning the Jewish Doctrine of rest in the bosom of Abraham for those at least of the faithful departed who died in the peace of Israel.

In the kind of research with which we are concerned here, we must be careful not to mistake the unintended blunder for an express doctrinal view. As a rule, it is easy to distinguish simple errors, but occasionally a specific point may puzzle the most careful reader. While Borron seems wholly unconscious of opposition to the claims of Rome, there is, of course, very full indication of a Secret which inheres in the Grail and some ground for thinking that the rumour of this Secret had gone forth abroad in the world prior to his poem. It is, however, a verbal formula, not apparently a doctrine. " Those who can learn and retain these words," says Christ to Joseph, " shall be virtuous among people and pleasant unto God ; they shall not be forejudged in court, nor conquered in battle, so only that their cause is just."[2] Speaking also of the common hell into which all souls went prior to the coming of Christ, Robert de Borron says : " It was necessary that the ransom of our first fathers should be provided by the Three Divine Persons Who are one only and the same substance". Now, the identity of the Three Persons in Christ is unquestionably a heresy ; but, as it happens, this is a recurring Doctrine of Swedenborg, for whom Christ was the manifested Trinity. It is curious to recall the analogy, though the notion could at no time have formed part of any Secret Teaching, supposing that this were otherwise to be found or expected in Borron. So also we must not interpret as a trace of any Secret Doctrine the implicit of his comparison between the conceptions of Eve and the Most Holy Virgin. He says in effect that Eve conceived in suffering ; that the posterity of our first parents were, like them, doomed to die ; and that the possession of their souls was claimed by the demon as his right. To purchase them from hell our Saviour was conceived in the womb of the Virgin Mary, and in this manner the sin of generation according to the common course of Nature was annulled by a virginal conception. But in the analogy there is no ulterior motive, no *arrière pensée*.

The apostolic priority of Rome has been held to underlie the following

---

[1] See Book IX, § 2.
[2] LE ROMAN DU SAINT GRAAL, ed. by F. Michel, pp. 39, 40.

statement, which is put into the mouth of our Saviour : " I leave this example to Peter and to the Ministers of the Church." Comparatively early criticism looked upon it as equivalent to an acknowledgment of St. Peter as the Official Chief of the Catholic Holy Assembly, and it was remarked that no such admission is found in the GRAND SAINT GRAAL, which, it should be said, is however untrue. If we pass now to the consideration of the Sacred Vessel and to the question what Borron designed to signify thereby, we may note in the first place that, by the hypothesis of the poem, it is not visible to evil-livers, though it is evident that they encircled the table at which they could not sit on the occasion when it was first manifested to the elect. The correspondence of this will be found much later on in the PARZIVAL of Wolfram, wherein the Talisman which answers to the Grail was invisible to a pagan, though he was a man of noble life and a kinsman of the Secret House. Borron speaks by implication (1) of a Vessel,[1] not otherwise named, in which Jesus washed the feet of His disciples ; (2) of that passing fair Vessel, already described, in which Christ made His Sacrament, though the Ritual Institution of the Eucharist is not mentioned more specifically ; (3) of yet another Vessel in which Pilate washed his hands to signify that he was not responsible for the judgment which he had pronounced unwillingly. As regards the second, I have explained in the summary that a Jew carried it from the house of Simon, when Jesus had been led forth therefrom, and brought it to Pilate. At a later stage Pilate took the Vessel, and remembering thereof that it was beautiful, he gave it to Joseph, saying : " Much hast thou loved this man." Joseph answered : " Thou hast said truly." But the gift was less an instance of generosity than of the procurator's desire to retain nothing which had belonged to Jesus, whereby it was possible that he might be accused. Either the present state of the text or the poet's method of expression leaves things so much in confusion that a further question has arisen whether the *piscina* used for the washing of the feet was identical with that Vessel which became ultimately the Grail. It has been suggested, and we have seen already, that for the last word in the line

" Ou Criz feisoit son sacrement,"

what was written and intended originally was the word *lavement* ;[2] but this is extremely unlikely in view of the general content and is certainly not countenanced by the LESSER HOLY GRAIL. It has been suggested further (1) that St. John does not mention the Institution of the Eucharist[3] and is the only Evangelist who does describe the washing of the Apostles' feet ; (2) that Robert de Borron knew only the

---

[1] It is *une grande piscine* according to the prose version of his poem, while the latter mentions the water used for the purpose but says nothing of its container.

[2] It is made by Paulin Paris in his very inaccurate version of the Metrical Romance. See LES ROMANS DE LA TABLE RONDE, Vol. I, p. 127.

[3] It is mentioned, however, in the poem, whence it follows that Borron was acquainted with at least one other Gospel than that of St. John.

Fourth Gospel, possibly through that of Nicodemus in the Christian Apocrypha. But these questions are settled by the text itself in the discourse of Christ to Joseph at the beginning of his imprisonment in the Tower. It is there said (1) that at the Last Supper on the Thursday Christ blessed the Bread and the Wine, and told His disciples that they partook in those Elements of His Flesh and Blood ;[1] (2) that the Table of that Supper should be represented in many countries ; (3) that the Sacrament should never be Consecrated without commemoration of Joseph, who had taken down the Divine Body from the Cross and laid it in the Sepulchre ; (4) that this tomb should be signified by the Altar ; (5) that the winding-sheet in which the Body was wrapped should be called the Corporal ; (6) that the Holy Vessel in which Joseph received the Blood should be called the Chalice ; (7) that the stone with which the Sepulchre was sealed should be signified by the Paten. Nothing can be more express, both as to the Mass and the Eucharist. Unfortunately, nothing can be clearer also in the mind of the poet than the content of the Palladium of his Legend—being the blood of Three Persons in one God. And this, I think, is all that need be said in this place concerning the Cup of the Holy Grail according to Robert de Borron.

That Christ had in nowise forgotten one who had at need befriended Him was shewn by Him bringing it into the prison, holding it in His own hands, while the tower was illuminated by its great light ; for it was full of the Holy Spirit.

The Divine Discourse which occurs in this tower between the visionary Christ and Joseph is remarkable from several points of view, and especially by the categorical assurance that the Risen Saviour brought none of His disciples to the conference, because none was acquainted with the great love which subsisted between Himself and His auditor. It seems, however, to have been a prototype of that love which is the immanence of Christ in the believing soul, and the Palladium in Joseph's care was the symbol of the Redeemer's death, as it is the Eucharist in the external Church. The specific and material explanation is that Joseph took down the body of Jesus from the Cross, and for this reason he was to be a partaker in all glory. Of the colloquy there were, in any case, no witnesses, and the Gospel narratives could offer no contradiction. I suppose that I should add an implicit which seems almost evidently to have been in the poet's mind—that Joseph had made the Resurrection more, humanly speaking, possible by preserving the body as nearly intact as the circumstances of the Crucifixion would permit. The difficulty which seems to have been present to the sub-surface mind of Borron was perhaps not unrealised by one Gospel narrative which is careful to indicate that the bones of Christ were not broken on the Cross.[2]

The especial direction to Joseph was that he should guard well the Sacred Vessel, committing it only to those persons who were designed

---

[1] Michel, *Op. cit.*, pp. 38, 39.   [2] St. John : XIX, 31–33, 36.

thereto, and by these it should be taken as given in the Name of the Father, and of the Son, and of the Holy Spirit. The possessors were to be three and no more, because of the Trinity ; they were : (1) Joseph ; (2) Brons ; and (3) the grandson of Brons, who was to be born in the fullness of time. It must be said that this enumeration appears to omit one person who, according to the text itself, was intended for some High Office. When Joseph prayed before the Cup for guidance over the future of his Company—recalling an ordinance which had told him that at what time soever he desired Secret Knowledge, he should come into the presence of the Reliquary wherein was the Glorious Blood—he was answered by the Voice of the Grail that the celibate son of Brons was to be shewn the Sacred Vessel, so that he could see the content thereof. Now this son was Alain, and it might be supposed that the venerable charge would pass to him from his father, more especially as, in spite of his choice, he was to beget the Keeper in fine, and was not dedicated therefore to permanent celibacy, but held rather in Maidenhood for a Marriage which was predestined already. The instruction to Petrus announced that he was to await the arrival of Alain's Son, who would reveal to him the virtues of the Holy Vessel— being something omitted in his undeclared Brief or Charter, or some- thing hidden therein till the last Legate of the Mystery arrived in Arthurian days—and would make known to him what had become of Moses.

As to this ill-starred personage, who had suffered so strangely for parading a spurious election, with intent to deceive those who were chosen in truth and faith, it is decreed that he shall be heard of no more in song or story till the Knight comes who will fill the Void Seat. In this dubious manner it seems to be indicated that the wrath of the Grail would not be visited to everlasting.

After the departure of the several bands of pilgrims, the poem comes to its conclusion for want of written materials. The author had carried it so far on the evidence of the Sacred Book to which I have cited already the chief reference. He leaves it in the expectation that he will recount later on as follows :—[1]

(1) What became of Alain, whither he went, whom he married, and what heir was born to him.

(2) Whither Petrus proceeded.

(3) The fate of Moses, so long lost.

(4) The destination of Brons, who, outside all inferences of the logical understanding, had received the title of the Rich Fisher, on account of that single occasion when he angled in a certain water and caught one fish.

---

[1] Criticism supposes that these propositions form part of an Epilogue which begins at or near line 3461 and was composed later. It is allowed, however, to be of the same authorship. The contradiction mentioned in a previous note bears other testimony on one point of the Epilogue.

Meanwhile, Robert de Borron had apparently the records of the Fifth Branch, and to that he passed on, so producing a Metrical Romance concerning the Prophet Merlin. Let us therefore on our part conclude also as follows : (1) the formulary which incorporated the Great Secret of the Grail was, without evasion apparently, recorded in the prototypical chronicle by which the poet was guided. (2) The Secret was itself denominated the Grail, as if by a general title, the name not being applied exclusively to the Sacred Vessel.[1] (3) The last directions to Joseph regarding Brons, the Second Keeper, are these : " Tell him how God did communicate unto thee the Holy Words, which are sweet and precious and gracious and piteous, which are properly called and named the Secret of the Grail."[2] (4) There is no real evidence in the poem that they belonged to the Eucharist and were those of Eucharistic Consecration in any form whatever.

The METRICAL ROMANCE OF JOSEPH is the nearest and earliest reflection of all that which could have been imputed as historical in any lost book. It is unalloyed by folk-lore admixtures, for no two things can be less alike than any pre-Grail Feeding-Dish and the Hallow of Robert de Borron's Christian Legend. The distance between the old Myths and this devotional poem is too great for us to say that the latter is the archetypal state of the former after its assumption by Christianity : there is in truth no kinship. It is that from which the Lesser Chronicles and the Vulgate Cycle draw at their respective distances, though they gathered certain elements from otherwhere. Here at least there are no adventitious Hallows : it is the Grail as the one thing only. And the Holy Grail is a symbol of the Angel of Great Counsel made visible.

---

[1] Michel, *Op. cit.*, p. 40, ll. 935, 936.
[2] *Op. cit.*, p. 140, ll. 332–336 :

> " Les seintes paroles dist t'a,
> Ki sunt douces et precieuses
> Et gracieuses et piteuses,
> Ki sunt proprement apelées
> Secrez dou Graal et nummés."

Nutt and others have suggested that the Secret Words are or may be Christ's explanation to Joseph of " the Mysteries of the Grail in its relation to the Sacrament " (STUDIES p. 73), meaning the artificial and not too consistent analogies instituted between Altar and Sepulchre, Winding-Sheet and Corporal, Chalice and Joseph's Reliquary of the Precious Blood, Stone before the Tomb and Paten. Michel : ROMAN DU SAINT-GRAAL, *Op. cit.*, pp. 38, 39. That they are obviously not the poem shews clearly, giving the place of record as a certain Great Book, which Borron had seen with his own eyes. The prose version is still more express, as will be seen in the next section : the Secret Words are uttered at the Great Sacrament performed over the Grail. Obviously therefore they are not an unprofitable description of figurative analogies.

II

THE LESSER HOLY GRAIL

THE first and only editor of this text[1] put it forward as the original Prose Romance from which the poem was produced subsequently by some unknown hand, not so much writing ostensibly under the name of Robert de Borron as reflecting in rhymes and measures the actual words of the original.[2] This view did not obtain at its period any special acceptance and has been long abandoned. The codex as it stands is an accurate rendering of the poem, *plus* certain variations and expansions, of which some are important to our purpose and must be recited briefly. But any literary or other distinction between the metrical story and its disposition in a prose vesture leaves the narrative untouched, both versions working from the same beginning to the same term, so that any general description of LE PETIT SAINT GRAAL would be superfluous in this place.

The circumstances under which certain Secret Words were communicated originally, their transit Westward and a scheme designed for their perpetuation constitute the Mystery-in-chief of the Metrical Romance, and we have reserved for later consideration the important question whether these Words were a formula of Eucharistic Consecration.[3] It is to be observed that they were not used by Joseph when he had occasion to appeal for guidance to the Divine Voice which spoke from within or about the Sacred Vessel, or when he separated the grain from the tares in his band of pilgrims. But the artificial and unconvincing analogy which the text indicates between the Sacrament of the Altar and the Vessel, with its antecedents and environments, suggests that they may have belonged to a Mass ; and it happens that their Eucharistic character is made much more explicit in the LESSER HOLY GRAIL, where it is said, speaking of the Discourse in the Tower : " Thereupon did Christ Jesus teach him those words which cannot be spoken or written, should any one wish to do so, except he have read the Great Book wherein they are recorded, and this is the Secret which is uttered at the Great Sacrament performed over the Grail, that is to say, over the Chalice ; and I—Robert de Borron—do, for God's love, pray all those who shall hear this present book in the reading thereof that they ask no further herein concerning the said matter ; for he who should try to say more might well lie concerning it, since more he could in nowise tell, and such falsehood would profit him nothing."[4]

[1] Eugène Hucher : LE SAINT-GRAAL, OU LE JOSEPHE D'ARIMATHIE, 1875, Vol. I, p. 12 *et seq.*
[2] Hucher regards Borron as a pious Trouvère rather than an Adventurous Knight and as a friend of ascetics rather than a man of the world. *Ibid.*, I, p. 164.
[3] Hucher speaks in his preface of *les secrètes paroles du Sacrement du Graal. Op. cit.*, I, 10. But this is the point at issue, and it can be determined only when the literature has been surveyed in full.   [4] *Op. cit.*, I, pp. 175 and 227.

That the Secret Words were committed therefore to writing is witnessed by both versions, and seeing that these Words are found in neither, it follows that the " Great Book " of the prose version is not the record of Borron's Metrical Romance, though a late addendum to the latter suggests that he and no other was the first to write of the Grail.[1]

The additional light which is gained concerning the Holy Vessel is (1) that it was the blessed and very object wherein Christ sacrificed[2] at the Last Supper ; and this is more express than the words *feisoit son sacrement*, which I have quoted more than once from the poem ; (2) on the other hand, the prose version makes it plainer than the poem that the Vessel brought by the Jew was given to Pilate after the death of Christ, or coincidently therewith, for which reason it could not have been used by the Procurator to wash his hands[3] before he pronounced Sentence, as stated by Paulin Paris ; (3) the Vessel is described by Christ as *la sénefiance de ma mort*, which might apply to a Reliquary containing the Precious Blood, but more obviously to the Sacrifice of the Mass.

Among points left dubious in the poem we have seen that there is the question whether Joseph of Arimathæa remained where he was, not proceeding further Westward than the point of separation determined for the whole Company. Now that which is left doubtful in the poem is carried into triple confusion by the prose version. One of its codices —following the addendum to Borron's poem—says that Joseph went into that country wherein he was born ; another says that he departed and came to his term in the land whither he was sent by Jesus Christ ; yet it seems to follow from this second text that the whole Company was already in *la bloie Bretagne* and that Joseph had converted it newly to the belief in Jesus Christ.[4]

It will serve no purpose to enlarge upon minor debatable points which occur in the prose version, as, for example, on the doubt which it creates whether (1) the Third Keeper of the Grail will be the Son of Brons, by which we should understand Alain ; (2) whether he shall be the Son of his Son, as in the Metrical Romance ; and (3) whether the triple Guardianship, corresponding to the Holy Trinity, should be enumerated after Joseph has surrendered the symbol of his mission, which is the reading of one prose codex. It is sufficient to state in conclusion that as regards the Second Table, and the reason why it was established, the texts in verse and prose are both in agreement that whatever the needs of the Company there was (1) no miracle in the multiplication of food ; (2) only a spiritual refection ; (3) the Office of which was to fill the participants with Grace ; (4) one proof being that the Fish of Brons becomes wholly symbolical and figures continually at the Service.

---

[1] Here is further, final and conclnsive evidence that the so-called Epilogue is the work of one who blundered so seriously over his author's text that it might be questioned whether he had read it.

[2] Hucher, *Op. cit.*, I, p. 216.   [3] *Op. cit.*, p. 128.   [4] *Op. cit.*, I, 262.

III

THE EARLY HISTORY OF MERLIN[1]

THE Mystery of the Holy Grail was a Mystery of Grace Abiding in a Hidden Sanctuary till the time came for it to be manifested at the period of the Quests; and among the texts in which it is exhibited, as if working from afar and vaguely, there is that which I have termed for convenience the EARLY HISTORY OF MERLIN, being the transcript in prose of another Metrical Romance by which Robert de Borron proceeded, for want of intermediate materials, from the History of Joseph to the period which just antedated the birth and life of King Arthur. The Tradition of the one Romance is brought over by the other, and as such it is at once extremely interesting and important for our purpose. With the story itself we are concerned only in the least possible degree. It narrates, in the first place, a conference of demons, summoned—immediately or soon after the Descent of Christ into Hell—to consider the best means of minimising the opportunity of human redemption which had been inaugurated by the sudden translation of all the just of old from the supposed power of Infernus into the joy of Paradise. The conclusion attained was that if only some emissary of theirs could be born on earth, having for his father one of the ₄vil *personæ* and for his mother a woman in the flesh, they would recover some part at least of the patrimony which they claimed in souls. There was one in the council, belonging to that Averse Hierarchy which is termed the Powers of the Air, who had the gift under certain conditions to make earthly women conceive; and he went forth upon this mission. What he did, however, was to surprise a pure maiden, apart from all knowledge of hers, at an unwary moment. After this manner was Merlin born into the world, in the accomplishment of which plot we are translated, with no suggestion or manifest sense of the intervening centuries, from the days that followed the destruction of Jerusalem to the reign of Vortigern in Britain. The device of perdition went, as usual, astray, without let or hindrance; for the mother was saved spiritually by her innocence and, on the discovery of her predicament, by recourse immediately to the Offices of Holy Religion. She was accused indeed before the judges of the country; but the child himself saved her; for, being a babe, he yet spoke—now with the cunning which might be ascribed to his father in Sheol, and now with the subtlety and foresight which suggested the intervention of another and higher power, as if this had taken him for its own purpose into its safe custody.

Throughout the story Merlin, in virtue of his dual origin, is in part like true steel and in part as clay. Robert de Borron borrowed

[1] Appendix I, Note 10.

from antecedent materials which we can trace in their larger proportion ; but the high spirit of his religious disposition worked upon that which he assumed, and wrought a great change therein. His Merlin has come and manifests as if in the power of a Mission which had been imprinted with a Divine Seal ; and though he is at best an admixture, and though the character of some of his actions is stained enough, he who has created him in literature more even than he has derived, does not weary of saying that God, Who spared Merlin's mother in the body of her, was able to save him in the soul, while she contributed thereto, because of her perfect reconciliation with Holy Church. She had sinned indeed not at all, but had once, under great stress, forgotten to pray, and the visitation which came upon her was the hand of a providence rather than a hand which chastised. According to another tale, to which we shall refer later, she became at length a nun, and so passed in holiness. To pass thus also was doubtless Borron's intention as to the son's destiny, and at the end of these Lesser Chronicles we shall see how it was fulfilled. Meanwhile, the expressed mission of Merlin was after an unwonted manner to teach the love of Jesus Christ and the life everlasting.[1] The note of this intention occurs early in the story, when it is said that God took the fiend-born child to His own use, though the Mystery is the manner of that use ; his double nature was such and was so allowed to be, that he might yield to God His part and to the fiend also his own. There are other stories which tell how Merlin dwelt amidst illusion, and how at the end he passed therein ; but these are not of Robert de Borron.

The exigencies of motive rather than of the story itself take Merlin to Britain[2] at a period which, according to his years, would be early out of reason for his work ; but he who was never a child was more already than a man. There is no need to recite under what circumstances, initial and successive, he became the high councillor and worker of many miracles for four kings, each after the other : Vortigern, Pendragon, Uther Pendragon and Arthur. What remains to be said of his history will best fall under the considerations which now follow.

It is perhaps the Merlin Cycle which offers the most curious among what I have termed the Lesser Implicits of Grail literature. I must put them at a certain length because of their apparent importance, and will say in the first place that on Robert de Borron's part, as on that of certain other and unknown writers, there were two tangible purposes in full view : (1) To connect Merlin with all that Grail Mystery which was antecedent to the ascribed epoch of the Prophet ; (2) to identify his function with the termination of Grail marvels under the pretext of Times of Enchantment or Times Adventurous. We are drawn through far tracts of speculation in seeking to understand what sub-surface disposition of mind could have actuated these purposes ; but at the

---

[1] The text may be consulted *passim*. Merlin is eloquent in recalling to his hearers *la joie del autre siècle, la joie perdurable*, lest they forget.

[2] Merlin was born in Carmarthen, according to Geoffrey of Monmouth and Giraldus Cambrensis ; but this EARLY HISTORY places the birth in Brittany.

moment we are concerned only in ascertaining how they are carried out in the story.

There was a Hermit named Blaise, to whom the mother of Merlin had recourse in her unexpected difficulties, who had been also her spiritual adviser previously. The text says that this Hermit was an exceeding good clerk and subtle, for which reason Merlin prayed that he would become the recorder-in-chief, not only of all his deeds but of things heard and seen which he might well think that no creature could describe. A consent was obtained only after the holy man had conjured the querent in the Name of the Divine Trinity that he should deceive him in nowise ; whereupon Merlin answered that the Records would rather keep him from sin than dispose thereto. It is in this way that Blaise is one of its characters even from the beginning of the Romance ; but his chronicle itself opened long prior to the birth of Merlin ; for at the instance of him who was to prove himself a Prophet in Britain, Blaise wrote first of the great love between Christ and Joseph of Arimathæa ; of the lineage of Joseph ; the names of those who were to be the Guardians of the Grail ; of Alain and his Companions, and whither they journeyed ; of the departure of Petrus Westward ; of the transmission of the Holy Vessel from Joseph to Brons ; and of the death of Joseph. The history of these things was to be joined with that of Merlin, and the two recitals were to form a single book, complete in respect of everything, save only the Secret Words revealed to Joseph by Christ. Of these it is certified that Merlin could say nothing ; and the reason of this is to be inferred from the Quest-matter of the Lesser Chronicles, namely, that he had not received them.[1]

In accordance with the general trend of the earlier history and of the personages concerned therein, Merlin announced his intention to go West—that is, apparently out of Brittany into the land of Vortigern, or Greater Britain, and Blaise was also to follow, betaking himself to Northumbria, where it is said that the Guardians of the Grail were then dwelling, though they are not specified by name.[2] The first recompense of Blaise in this life was to be united with these Wardens, but thereafter it was to be *joie perdurable*. The Grail is the Talisman of the whole story, and hereof is the repose of the Grail—that they who have achieved the search shall have rest in the term thereof. And the book made by Blaise was to be called while the world endured the BOOK OF THE SEYNT GRAAL. In this manner did Merlin, though he was not at that time in any sense a Custodian of the Hallows, make a certain claim upon them in the dispensation of their graces and rewards. It was not, in the symbolical sense, of an idle nature, not the artifice of an impostor : rather it was of set purpose and as if the external sign

---

[1] It will be seen in this manner that the EARLY PROSE MERLIN derives directly and only from the METRICAL ROMANCE of Borron. In fidelity hereto, and to Borron's affirmed want of sources, it says nothing as to the fate of Moses, the distinction of Peter or the Marriage of Alain.—*Lestoire de Merlin* in Sommer's VULGATE VERSION OF ARTHURIAN ROMANCES, II, 18–20.

[2] The place is full of vast forests, parts of which have never been explored.

of some Secret Warrant, in virtue of which the Borron branch of the Grail History and Quest is connected indissolubly with Merlin. He laid the scheme, and the Hallows conformed thereto, the end being the termination of those dubious times, the dereliction of which we have heard of so often and can as yet understand so little.

Of such is the Grail in the EARLY HISTORY OF MERLIN. But this is also the first Romance which, in the chronological succession of texts, apart or not from priority in time of literary production, introduces the Third Table and the Mystery of the Siege Perilous. It may be held to constitute another side of its particular claim concerning the British Prophet. Those who have followed so far the History of the Second Table may have recalled perhaps already that a vacant seat was left of old at the Passover for the unexpected guest, and it is left still by the Jews. There is also that custom, beautiful and piteous, of leaving a vacant seat for the Angel of Peace. I do not know what memories of this kind—if any—were present to the mind of Borron when he borrowed from those who had preceded him the idea of the Round Table and attributed its foundation to Uther Pendragon, not to King Arthur, Merlin, however, being in either case the instigator of its Institution.[1] With his reflex of the spirit of sanctity, as conceived by the British Prophet, the Knightly Table was something more than a substitute ; and assuredly, in some later aspects, it reflected on earth that which belongs to Heaven.

In the course of his proposal, Merlin told Uther Pendragon the story of Joseph of Arimathæa, and how in the desert places, the sowing of which had become void through the sin of some who went forth, the Second Table had been instituted to separate the good from the evil. The Third was to be established by Uther in the name of the Trinity, and it was to be set up at Cardoil in Wales, for a certain Feast of Pentecost—that is to say, of the Holy Spirit. As there was a place vacated by Judas and a place that was void at the Table of Joseph, so there was to be one now, which should not be filled in the days of Uther Pendragon, but in those of the King who would succeed him. The Knight who would then fill it was not as yet born, which is colourable enough as a pretence in respect of the Perceval who was to follow as Questing Knight according to the Lesser Chronicles. But the codices have been edited in variant interests and the English rendering, represented by an unique text and drawing from what source I know not, adds words as follows which could apply only to Galahad : " Ne he that shall hym engendere shall not know that he shall hym engendere."[2] On the other hand, the HUTH MERLIN[3] says that he will be engendered by him who ought so to engender him, but as yet he has not taken a wife, nor does he know that he ought to engender him—a passage which, after much circumlocution, comes to

---

[1] Appendix I, Note 11.
[2] See MERLIN, OR THE EARLY HISTORY OF KING ARTHUR, edited for the Early English Text Society by W. E. Mead, 1899, p. 61.
[3] Gaston Paris, *Op. cit.*, I, p. 98.

little. The same codex suggests otherwise that before the predestined hero takes the void seat he must accomplish the adventures of the Grail,[1] which is contrary to all the texts, historical and otherwise. The VULGATE MERLIN says in effect that he who fills the one will fulfil the other. But the English version : " And he that shall a-complysshe that sete must also complysshe the voyde place at the table that Joseph made."[2] This seems to create on the surface an almost insoluble difficulty and can be left at that ; but the meaning is not impossibly that in the Secret and Holy Place where the Grail abides, the Service of the Second Table is held still, as it was in the days of Joseph ; that he who enters into the House shall take the seat reserved for him, and that the Table shall be in fine complete.[3]

Of such was the second mission of the Prophet Merlin ; but the third was the conception of Arthur and the conduct of all those events which should lead to his high coronation as King of Britain. I need not reproduce in this place the familiar story of Ygerne,[4] the faithful wife of the Duke of Tintagel, and of the sorcery by which she received Uther Pendragon in the likeness of her husband and so brought forth the Great Ruler who was to come. These circumstances and that of the Imbedded Sword which led to his ultimate recognition, though he had been reared as the reputed son of a simple Knight, are or ought to be familiar.[5] It was to achieve his prophetic purpose that Merlin assisted Uther over those things which led up to the conception of Arthur, since the latter was to consummate the great intent of the Round Table which was begun by his Father. The conception was one of a triad— of Merlin, of Arthur, of Galahad—which all took place under false pretences, according to Arthurian Romance. Merlin was conscious that he had sinned in respect of this business, and it may be speculated that he sought to make amends by assisting the subsequent marriage between Uther and Ygerne and by his arrangements in respect of the charge of Arthur in childhood.[6]

It should be noted in fine (1) that no Keeper of the Grail is mentioned in the EARLY HISTORY OF MERLIN, though the locality of its abode is indicated ; (2) that there is only a covert reference to Moses ; (3) that certain sources are obvious for certain texts, but there are important respects in which all the early Romances seem echoes from far away of a book that had never been seen by their writers, though it had been heard of by a general report ; and (4) that this statement is intended to override all their references, actual or imaginary, to mysterious sources of information which are not—if they were ever—extant.

[1] Op. cit., p. 68.   [2] Mead, Op. cit., p. 61.
[3] There is no doubt that this suggestion is in accord with the logic of the subject, though it corresponds to nothing in the Quests. We hear of many Tables at the Grail Castle, for the visitor is fed invariably—except in the case of Monseigneur Gawain in the Romance of Galahad—preternaturally or otherwise ; but no Table has a Siege Perilous, except in the Palace of the King, be he Uther Pendragon or Arthur.
[4] See any unbowdlerised version of Malory's MORTE D'ARTHUR, Book I, cap. 2.
[5] Ibid., cap. 3.
[6] It is evident, however, that in and through all he was shaping plans for a great event to come, and this was the manifestation of the Grail.

IV

THE DIDOT-MODENA PERCEVAL[1]

FROM the MERLIN of Robert de Borron there follows directly the DIDOT-MODENA PERCEVAL as the Merlin Quest *par excellence*, but it gleams dimly through a vague species of cloud ; and as there is much which preceded the Romance of the Prophet, and much that remains among the implicits of the literature, so there are things undeclared but self-suggesting as sequels to follow the Quest, things within and without the rewards held in reserve for those who practise holiness.

There is no doubt that up to a certain point the DIDOT-MODENA PERCEVAL connects logically with the two poems which, by the particular hypothesis, were designed to lead up thereto. Its ascription to Robert de Borron, by the secondary and reflective way of a prose version, has been rejected by certain students in the past ; while a recent view regards it not alone as a late Quest but as an attempted restoration of Perceval to the position of Grail Winner after he had been supplanted by Galahad.[2] In any case the anonymous author set himself to complete the work of Borron, which enabled him to provide his hero with indefectible titles and to place his own construction on the trilogy thus created. He worked so well that it is difficult to read the opening portion without feeling that here is a genuine third part of the whole undertaking ; while the fact, so frequently exemplified, that Perceval remains throughout a *virgo intactus*, is in perfect harmony with the mind of the Metrical Romance.[3] The EARLY HISTORY or first part of the VULGATE MERLIN follows directly from the poem of Joseph of Arimathæa, and so far as we can ascertain it closed for Robert de Borron at that stage, when it could, without any violation, be merged in a Perceval Legend, by which the Tradition is continued without a break of any kind. One other favourable point, and assuredly these points are several, is that—unlike the GRAND SAINT GRAAL, which mades an effort in this direction but fails manifestly—it does not seek to fill every gap left by Borron's missing branches : as to Brons, it says only that he is old and full of infirmity ; as to Alain, he is dying. Of their intermediate past it tells nothing ; and I say this, remembering that one of the unprinted

---

[1] Appendix I, Note 12.

[2] See H. Oskar Sommer : MESSIRE ROBERT DE BORRON UND DER VERFASSER DES DIDOT-PERCEVAL, Halle, 1908, pp. 39 *et seq.*, and cf. Bruce, *Op. cit.*, I, p. 113.

[3] If the work is posterior to the Vulgate and Huth later Merlin texts, part of the intention was assuredly to connect the Prophet more intimately with the Grail Mystery and to provide another and very different ending to Merlin's life-story. A similar plan was conceived also respecting Perceval's early history as related in Chrétien. From these points of view the contribution of the DIDOT-MODENA PERCEVAL to the Grail Subject is not without consequence.

Merlin codices speaks of a text which contains the Marriage of Alain.[1]

To conclude as to this question, the Early History of the Prophet specifies at the term thereof that Arthur, after his Coronation, held the kingdom of Logres long in peace, while it leaves Merlin as his Councillor. The PERCEVAL opens with an account of the Prophet's instruction to the King concerning the Round Table and the Grail Mysteries which went before its institution : it is only at the term of the Quest that Merlin passes into voluntary and, as one would think, ascetic retirement, free from personal enchantment and having delivered Britain from spell. The later Merlin texts, on the contrary, intern the Prophet, and then, and not after, lead up to the Galahad Quest. It is difficult therefore to say that the DIDOT-MODENA PERCEVAL does not reflect, from at hand or afar, a possible lost Romance which completed the trilogy of Borron, and was metrical like those that preceded it.

Perceval was the son of Alain le Gros, the grandson of Brons, and the third of that earthly trinity which was destined to possess the Grail. While Arthur was holding high festival at London and was listening to the counsel of Merlin, the Voice of the Holy Spirit[2] spoke to Perceval's Father—he being near his end—and informed him that Brons, the Rich Fisherman and the Warden of the Grail, was in the Isles of Ireland—" in one of the fairest places of the world," according to the Modena text—and that the Holy Vessel was with him. He was old, as I have said ; but he could not obtain refuge in death till he was found by the Son of Alain, had communicated to this Son the Grace of that Vessel, and had taught him those Secret words which he learned himself from Joseph.[3] To express it more nearly in Language of Romance, the Quest, which is the intention of the story, must be fulfilled in all perfection. Thereafter the infirmity of Brons would be healed, and he would receive the Medicine of Eternity, or, as the text says, would enter into the great joy of that Father in Heaven Whom he had served always in time. The youth, Perceval, was directed therefore by the Voice to the Court of King Arthur, and it was

[1] This Marriage is foreordained from the beginning in the Metrical Romance of JOSEPH and so also is the fact that its issue, described as " the Son of Alain "—whether Perceval or another—was to be the third Keeper of the Sacred Vessel and would be qualified as such to make Petrus acquainted with its virtues, as well as to read the Brief or Charter which came into his hands from Heaven. It happens, however, that the DIDOT-MODENA PERCEVAL ignores Petrus and the elected term of his pilgrimage in the Vales of Avalon.

[2] There is no Voice of the Spirit speaking to Alain in the Modena codex. The renown reaches him wheresoever he is—no place being mentioned. He talks about it to his Son, who is apparently a lad, and says that when the boy has grown up he shall be sent to the Royal Court with rich appointments. But Alain dies in his day. Perceval remains with his Mother for yet a little while, then arms himself bravely, mounts his horse and rides away secretly, leaving her to bewail his loss and die. He reaches King Arthur's Court, salutes him proudly and offers himself as one of his household. He is made welcome, is knighted and proves himself so well—though he knew nothing when leaving his Mother's side—that he is called to the Fellowship of the Round Table, which in this text consists of twelve peers only.

[3] It may be noted that the Holy Spirit says nothing to Alain about the Sacrament of the Grail.

promised him that in this place he should hear such tidings that he would be brought in due season to the House of the Rich Fisher. When Alain had heard on his own part, he bowed his head and entered himself, as one who arrives beforehand, into the Company of Christ.

Perceval, in his outward seeming, has little title to participate in the Mysteries, except the title of his geniture. He is brave, savage and imperious ; he is also chivalrous, but he is without the Spiritual Chivalry which we find in the Great Quest. He was left with his widowed Mother, who, as we learn subsequently, sought to dissuade him from the journey ; but obeying the Divine Voice, which had come also to him, he set out for the Court of King Arthur : there he abode for a season ; and there he received the High Order of Chivalry. At the Court he saw Elaine, the sister of Monseigneur Gawain and a niece also of the King. The text says that she loved Perceval with all love that was possible, because in addition to his bravery he was also beautiful. It came about later on that she sent him red armour to wear on her behalf at a tournament : in this manner he was accounted her Knight, and she shared in the glory of his achievements. But hereafter nothing follows concerning her. Perceval was proclaimed the Best Knight of the World after overcoming Lancelot and others of the High Company, it being then the Feast of Pentecost. There was feasting in the hall after the tournament, and Perceval, now enrolled in the Fellow-ship, desired to occupy the Seat left vacant at the Round Table for the predestined third Custodian of the Holy Grail. King Arthur endea-voured to dissuade him, remembering the fate of Moses, but the prayers of Gawain and Lancelot prevailed with the monarch. A tremendous confusion ensued notwithstanding, over which rose the Voice of an Invisible Speaker, bearing once more the same witness which the Voice of the Spirit had borne recently to Alain,[1] but revealing further that the healing of the Rich Fisher depended on a visit to his Castle which must be paid by the Best Knight of the World, who must ask further concerning the Secret Service of the Grail.[2] By the instructions which would follow, a period should be put to the Enchant-ments of Britain. The Voice spoke also of the dolorous death of Moses, who, according to the text otherwise, was to remain in the abyss until the Day of Judgment. The Quest was undertaken by Perceval, and indeed the whole Fellowship of the Round Table ventured forth therein ; but it is stated that of how they fared the Book, which is the prototype, says nothing. Our texts shew, however, on their own part that one at least of the Knights was slain. King Arthur deplored the Quest, as he does in the Romance of Galahad.

The course of Perceval's adventures covers many of those incidents

---

[1] It testified also that Perceval should suffer for his audacity and that the abyss would have swallowed him—as it engulfed Moses previously—were it not for the high and holy titles of Alain his Father and of Brons, the time-immemorial Keeper of the Great Palladium.

[2] The formula of the Question is, according to the Modena MS. : *de quoi li* GRAAUS *a servi et de quoi il sert.* Compare the Didot text : *Et convendra que cil chevalier demande de ce vessel que hom en siert.*

with which we are acquainted already in the CONTE DEL GRAAL. There is, for example, the now familiar story of a maiden lamenting over the body of her Knight, who has been slain by Orguelleus de le Lande, with all that follows thereon. There is the visit to that strange Castle wherein Perceval plays chess with an invisible opponent, and is mated. From this follows some part of the episodes which concern the quest of the Stag's Head in company with a hound belonging to a maiden of the Castle. For our purpose it is more pertinent to record that Perceval arrived after three years of rather casual questing at the Manor where he had lived with his parents and where his Sister abode now, *en le gaste forest*. From her he learned the story of their father, his own early history, and the prophecy concerning the Grail. He heard further that his Mother had died in grief for his departure, and though, under the direction received according to the Didot text, he cannot be said to have deserted her, it is accounted to him somehow as a sin, after the confused manner of materials drawn from many sources. He visited his Uncle, a Hermit, who is a Brother of Alain, and is consequently one of the twelve Brethren who were children of Brons. It is obvious therefore that again the note of time is wanting, as for any purpose of the story this perpetuation of ordinary life through the centuries has no meaning. The survival of Alain himself is in like case, the trinitarian scheme of the Keepership requiring only the excessive longevity of Brons. Perceval confessed to his Uncle and heard from him that at the Table instituted by Joseph—he also assisting—the Voice of the Spirit commanded those who heard it to journey far into the countries of the West, and ordained in particular that the Rich Fisher should go forth into those parts where the sun sets. Furthermore, the Hermit told him how—as son of Alain le Gros—he, Perceval, was *ab origine* Heir of the Grail, by decree of the Holy Spirit, speaking at the Table of Joseph in days of old. To this end he must heal the present Warden, Brons, by visiting his Court, when the Blessed Vessel containing the Precious Blood would be placed in his hands. The Uncle continued to speak of that peculiar and holy service to which the youth had been called ;[1] but he did not, as in other Quests, advise him to beware of idle talking or of the curiosity which leads to questioning.

After these things Perceval continued his Quest, and among other adventures he met with a Knight who, owing to this encounter, had missed by seven days the Crown of the World's Knighthood. He saw, moreover, the wonder of two children disporting themselves in a tree : they spoke to him of the Terrestrial Paradise and of the Holy Spirit ; they directed him also on his Quest, so that he fared better according to this story than he did in the corresponding episode of the CONTE DEL GRAAL. On the threshold of his journey's end, three men in a boat on a certain water—one of whom is Brons—offer him good hostel, after which manner Perceval reached in fine the Castle of his Grandfather,

---

[1] There is also a counsel of chastity delivered to Perceval in the Didot version, namely, *ne de gesir avec fame, quoi c'est un peche luxurieus.*

the Rich Fisher, where he was received after the mode of Chivalry, and the Warden of the Grail was borne into his presence in the arms of sergeants. They sat down to table and the Procession of the Hallows entered ; but Perceval asked nothing concerning them. He is said to remember one counsel of caution which he had received from his uncle[1] in the matter of questioning, from which it is to be inferred either that the text follows some prototype which it does not reproduce faithfully, or that the author has omitted something which he intended to record earlier.

Moreover, Perceval was outwearied by the vigils of two previous nights, and his host, when he noticed this, directed the table to be removed and a bed to be prepared for the Knight, who retired thinking deeply of Lance and Grail, and promising himself that he would inquire of the pages to-morrow. The Voice of the Invisible Speaker which had directed him and the others with such utter plainness at the Court of King Arthur had lapsed apparently from his mind, and from that fatal inattention he passed into the forgetfulness of sleep. On the morrow he went down into the courtyard, to find his horse and arms awaiting him, but there was no one else to be seen. He sallied forth in fine, but only to be cursed by a Maiden in a forest adjoining the Castle, and to be told that, if only he had asked the Question, the Prophecy of our Saviour to Joseph would have been accomplished. It is to be noted that of this Prophecy we find no particulars in any antecedent texts. She affirmed further that the Fisher King would have been restored to youth as well as to health ; and that there would have ceased those Enchantments of Britain the nature and cause of which still fail to appear.

Perceval sought in vain to rediscover the Castle, for over the whole land he could find its trace no longer. As in the CONTE of Chrétien, he returned to the Maiden of the Chess-Board, with the dog to her belonging and the stag's head. She desired him to remain in her company, but he left, with a promise to return, saying that otherwise he would be false to the vow which he had made. In this manner he preserved his desired continence,[2] but he fell into other evils during a pilgrimage of seven years which followed thereafter. Through distress at being unable to find the Fisher King, he lost all memory of God until he met with that Pilgrim Company on Good Friday, when he was asked, again as in Chrétien, why he rode armed for purposes of destruction on such a sacred day. His better nature then returned to him, and before long he was knocking once more at the door of his Uncle the Hermit, to whom he confessed all. It was his intention to revisit his Sister ; but he was told that she was dead these two years past.

[1] From his Mother, according to the Modena MS., which fails, however, to cite the advice in question at the time that she parted from Perceval. It seems obvious that such a caution on the part of the Hermit would have stultified his own scheme, which was to impose on Perceval the mission of healing Brons.

[2] On the occasion of his first visit, the Modena text represents him as expecting and intending to obtain his reward when he had fulfilled the behests of the Maiden.

After certain further episodes—including a tourney at the White Castle—he met with Merlin, who reproached him bitterly for neglecting the Quest, much as he was chided by a certain huntsman in one of the *additamenta* to the poem of Wauchier.   Perceval heard also that the health of the Rich Fisher was still such that he remained at the point of death, though he could not pass away.[1]   But his prayers were going up for his grandson, and by the will of God he was yet to become the Guardian of the Precious Blood.   The authority throughout is the Record of Blaise, to whom Merlin returned after this conversation and recounted that which had passed, as he does so continually in the course of his own Romance.

Perceval reached at last the Castle of the Rich Fisher for the second time : again he beheld the Grail, and on this occasion asked concerning its service, at which the King was made whole ; and in a moment, in the twinkling of an eye, all was changed about him.   The relationship between them was declared ; and Perceval being instructed in the History of the Hallows was led into the presence of the Holy Vessel, where the Voice of High Counsel told Brons to communicate the Secret Words.[2]   In the fulfilment of this command the ancient Warden might have been still speaking when the soul passed from his body ; and Perceval saw how the Angels bore it to the Kingdom of Heaven, unto the Father whom he had served so long.[3]   Perceval remained in the Castle, practising wisdom, and there was an end to the Enchantments of Britain, in common with those of the whole world.   It was as if an Interdict had been imposed and a Legate had removed the Interdict.

While things were so ordered in the Secret Sanctuary, there were events in the outer world which led up to the passing of Arthur, who was carried into Avalon to be healed of his grievous wounds by his sister, Morgan le Fay.   Merlin was still in evidence, passing to and fro between the King's Court and the Sanctuary of the Holy Vessel, where then, as subsequently, Perceval seems to have divided his Office of Warden with the Scribe of the Records thereof.[4]   After the transit of Arthur, Merlin appeared for the last time, recounting the woes which had befallen, whereat the place of Hallows became a House of Mourning and a Chapel for the Office of the Dead.   The Prophet took leave of the Wardens, because it was God's will no longer that he should go to and fro in the world, and he would betake himself therefore, as if for a last refuge, to a hermitage without the forest which encompassed the Castle. It follows that the term of Merlin is revolutionised in this Romance :

[1] On the hypothesis at its value that there could be only three Wardens of the Holy Grail and that the last must be invested during Arthurian days, it is obvious that the life of Brons must be protracted through centuries.

[2] That is to say, *les paroles segroies de notre seygnor que je ne vous puis dire, ne ne doie ; et li mostra tote la créance notre seygnor et coment il (l') avoit véu mort et vif, etc.*— Hucher, *Op. cit.*, I, pp. 483, 484.

[3] In the Modena MS. the passing of Brons occurs on the third day after his healing and delivery of the Vessel.

[4] The same text says that Merlin was required to redeem his pledge that Blaise should abide with the Sacred Vessel, whereupon he conducted the Scribe to the Grail Castle.

he does not pass in enchantment, inhibition and the folly of morganatic ties, as he does in more familiar texts, but seeking the peace of God and choosing the life of contemplation. Thereafter he was seen no longer, and there was no further story concerning the Holy Grail.[1]

The DIDOT-MODENA PERCEVAL and the PARZIVAL of Wolfram are the chief texts which leave the last Warden alive and dwelling in the Sanctuary.[2] It should be noted also that the Quest in this instance does not involve the destruction of Logres or a fatality to the Round Table, though this fatality occurs. The point is important, because it is another note of correspondences between the DIDOT-MODENA PERCEVAL and the EARLY MERLIN. The secret conspiracy, planned, as one might say, in the Sanctuary, against the Great Chivalry was undreamed of by Robert de Borron and is peculiar to the Vulgate Chronicles. The unanimity of the Lesser Chronicles resides further-more in the fact that they are all texts of the Secret Sanctuary, and that they emanate by the hypothesis therefrom. They suggest no public office : there is no travelling of the Grail. Britain suffers during the Quest period from an Enchantment, but it is not described, and it is to be doubted whether Britain knew of it—at least, in such terms. It is the most occult of all processes and the most withdrawn of all localised Mysteries. Brons and Alain have done nothing in the land ; they are aliens of sanctity, with the burden of the years of the *Juif errant* upon them ; and they abide in seclusion.

The DIDOT-MODENA PERCEVAL is scarcely at peace with itself over some of its elements, nor is it at peace unbroken with those antecedent texts from which it follows that the Third Keeper will (1) meet with Petrus, who carries the Sacred Brief, and with him compare their knowledge in common of the Grail Mystery ; (2) find Moses, and this under circumstances which suggest some palliation at least of that which he has suffered through the ages.[3] I do not think that these points make void its place in the trilogy, apart from date and author-ship, because there are several respects in which all the Grail Books, like other Romances of Chivalry, are conventions of the cohorts of sleep, and there is sometimes a distracting spirit moving through the various dreams.

---

[1] Nor yet of Perceval, the Warden thereof. It does not follow that the Records were discontinued, but there was no emissary abroad in the world to proclaim their tidings : they were Records henceforward of Hidden Life alone.

[2] We shall see that, according to Albrecht, the Perceval of Wolfram continued as Warden for seven years, even in the far East, and that another Keeper followed him.

[3] For additional omissions and certain contradictions, see Bruce, *Op. cit.*, II, pp. 106 *et seq.*

BOOK V

THE VULGATE CYCLE OF THE HOLY GRAIL

THE ARGUMENT

I. THE GREAT BOOK OF THE HOLY GRAIL AND, IN THE FIRST PLACE, CON-
CERNING THE PROLOGUE.—The Claims and Defects of the Text regarded
generally—The Secret of this Cycle—Its imputed Authorship—Its hypothetical
Divisions—The Hermit of the Legend—What he Saw and Read at a Mass of
the Presanctified—Disappearance of a Secret Book—The Quest of its Recovery
—The Time of the Transcript thereof.   II. A NEW CONSIDERATION CONCERN-
ING THE BRANCHES OF THE CHRONICLE AND CONCERNING ITS MAJOR
BRANCHES.—Divergence of the extant Manuscripts—The Incorporation of
Robert de Borron Elements—The point at which their Tradition is broken,
and this completely—The Arrival at Sarras—Events which lead up to the
Conversion of this City—The Spiritual Palace—The Ordination of Joseph II
—His Later Life—Of Evalach, the King of Sarras, who was afterwards
Mordrains—Of Queen Sarracinte—Of Seraphe, who was also Nasciens—
Of Celidoine, the Son of Nasciens—The Ship of Solomon—The Building of
Corbenic.   III. THE MINOR BRANCHES OF THE CHRONICLE.—The Later
History of Joseph of Arimathæa—The Life of Petrus in Britain—Of Brons
and Alain—Variations in the History of Moses—Of Simeon and his Brethren
—Concerning the first Galahad—The Genealogies—Conclusion as to the
GRAND SAINT GRAAL.   IV. THE VULGATE MERLIN.—Its Antecedent
History—Merlin as the Chief Promulgator of the Grail Mystery—The House
of the Holy Vessel—Of the Second Nasciens and his History—King Pelles
of Lystenoys—The Maimed King—The Daughter of the House—A Son of
King Pelles—Tidings of the Grail in Britain.   V. THE GREAT PROSE LANCE-
LOT.—The Antecedents of the Story—An Undeclared Mystery of the Grail
—Of Perceval in the Great Quest—Particular Grail Traditions—Missing
Elements of Quest—The Genealogy of Lancelot—His Life in Faërie—Of
Moses and Simeon—Of Monseigneur Gawain at Castle Corbenic—Of Lancelot
and the Lady of the Bath—Elaine, the Maiden of the Grail—The Concep-
tion of Galahad.   VI. A PREFACE OR INTRODUCTORY PORTION APPER-
TAINING TO ALL THE QUESTS.—Claims of the Questing Knights—And
further concerning Gawain—A Pentagram of Chivalry—The Mystery of
Divine Providence manifested in flesh.   VII. THE QUEST OF THE HIGH
PRINCE.—Of the Generation of Galahad—Of some things which followed
thereafter—The Circumstances of his first Manifestation—Its Mystical
Environment—Of the Eucharist in the Quest—Of Arch-Natural Feasting—
The Quest in brief outline—The Liberation of Simeon—The Release of King
Mordrains—The Voyage in the Ship of Solomon—The Term of Quest at
Corbenic—The Mystery Unveiled—The Ascent of Galahad—The Doom of
Earthly Knighthood.   VIII. THE WELSH QUEST OF GALAHAD.—The
Position of this Version—Its Variations in summary—Wanderings of the
Grail—The Dolorous Stroke—Episodes of the Last Scene—Additamenta to
the Vulgate Chronicles.

THE VULGATE CYCLE OF THE HOLY GRAIL

I

THE GREAT BOOK OF THE HOLY GRAIL AND, IN THE FIRST PLACE, CONCERNING THE PROLOGUE

THE GRAND SAINT GRAAL is the most conscious, most cumbersome, most artificial Romance in the literature. It is that also which is beyond all prodigal of wonders, and its wonders are the least convincing. In so far as concerns the History of the Sacred Vessel, it must be said that it materialises the Symbol and it distracts also the Legend. Robert de Borron finished his Metrical Romance by confessing that for want of materials he must, for the time being, hold over those branches of his Chronicle which were intended to deal with the further Adventures of Brons, Alain, Petrus and other characters of the story. In the meantime he proceeded to the Life of Merlin, bridging the gulf of centuries by a promise to retrace the path when he had obtained the necessary data, though it is possible enough that the intervening distances of time may have spelt little to his mind. All that could be construed as wanting is supplied by the GRAND SAINT GRAAL, leaving nothing undone, but working through I know not what mazes of manifold enchantment. I have said that the artifice of the design—which obtains also for its expression—stands forth in full manifestation, even upon its surface. A hand more sparing might have worked greater marvels and left some sense of realism, at least in the order of Faërie. And yet the prolix History has a certain magian touch, all paths of disillusion notwithstanding.

From whatever point of view it is approached, the text will prove otherwise to be sown with difficulties—curious things in truth of the worlds within and without ; but even as difficulties these have also their occasional secret charm. There are vast sections of unnecessary matter which suggest an imperfect art of mere story-telling, while there are materials also which do not belong, more especially at their period, to the horizon confessed by that art. Moreover, nothing in reality is finished, for, as one of the sub-titles indicates, the Romance is presented as a First Branch of the Records of the Round Table, or rather it is a Prolegomenon to these. A Cycle of the literature of Chivalry is supposed to follow thereafter, which might obviously mean (1) that the author had a mind to go further or, alternatively, (2) that his intention was to establish the collated antecedents leading up to other documents which in one or another form were already in being. The second is the actual position, and in this sense there follows from the prolix introduction a great cloud of chivalrous narrative, offering herein a first point of distinction from the Trilogy ascribed to Robert de Borron. The latter lies, comparatively speaking, within a narrow compass, though it has a claim on completeness according to its own measures. There are other differences, however, which are not less marked in their character and are very much more important. The account which I propose of the memorial will differ from ordinary critical and textual apprehension by way of direct summary, since it is actuated by exclusive objects connected with the design of this study.

As the Borron Cycle of the Holy Grail is concerned with the reservation of a Secret comprised by an alleged Sacramental Formula, so there is also a Secret in the GRAND SAINT GRAAL, but it is of a different kind ; and herein is a second distinction that we are called to make between the two Cycles. That particular form of Eucharistic Mystery which is veiled *ex hypothesi* by Robert de Borron and his line of anonymous successors is made void by the later Romance. As if it had planned to shew that there were no Secret Words of Consecration, an actual Mass-Formula is given in full ; and although it is that of a Liturgy which is other than the Latin Rite and betrays Oriental influences, the variations are local and accidental, wearing no aspect of importance, except for Liturgical History.[1] At the same time, when the Hermit of the GRAND SAINT GRAAL is first received into that state of vision from which the transcript of the text follows, what he is promised by Christ is a revelation of the Greatest Secret of the whole wide world. That revelation is, however, a Book and one which is spoken of invariably as very small—so small indeed that it can lie in the hollow of the Hermit's hand. This notwithstanding, it is the greatest marvel that man can ever receive.[2] It was written by Christ Himself, Who committed to writing only : (1) the Book in question ; (2) the Lord's Prayer ; (3) the words written in the sand, according to the New Testament. To pronounce aloud the sentences contained in the Book would convulse the elemental world, and it must be read therefore with the heart.[3]

Not exactly on this consideration but not for less cogent reasons, the first thing which is apparent concerning it is that although the Hermit is covenanted to transcribe the volume and to occupy in this task the period which intervenes between the fifteenth day after Easter and the day of the Ascension ; although further he states expressly that what he wrote down is that which follows his Prologue ; the Secret Book committed to his charge seems obviously not that which he transmits as a memorial for those who come after him. I suppose that in registering this with a certain touch of fantastic gravity,

[1] Appendix I, Note 13.
[2] It is said also that the Adventures of the Grail exceed the knowledge of mortals.— Sommer's Vulgate Text, I, p. 119.   [3] *Ib.*

my motive will not be misconstrued : we are dealing with a parable or pretence, and the point is that it is not especially consistent within its own lines.[1] After making every allowance for the possible variations of late editing, both intentional and otherwise, it remains that the text of the story voids the claim of the Prologue, and this to such an extent that a substitute only is offered—so to speak—for that which was brought from Heaven for the assumed illumination of Logres.[2]

The Book of the Transcript is, by the hypothesis of the Prologue, divided into four Branches, of which the First concerns the lineage of the Hermit himself ; and on the assumption that the HUTH MERLIN is correct in identifying the latter with that second Nasciens who, in the days of the Enchanter and those of Uther Pendragon, was at first of the Order of Chivalry and afterwards a Holy Recluse, it will follow that the entire Romance corresponds to this designation rather than an individual part. The Second Branch is that of the Holy Grail, which is a title of the collection itself, LI LIVRES DU SAINT GRAAL or LESTOIRE DU SAINT GRAAL, and it cannot be allocated to a section. The Third Branch is called the Beginning of Terrors, while the Fourth is the Beginning of Marvels, which in like manner will not assist towards any logical classification, as we are concerned with something that answers in all its modes and pages to the title of a Wonder-Book.[3]

The most express, most ordered, most reasoned part of the entire History is assuredly what is termed the Prologue : it is there that the Hermit accounts for the manner in which he came for a period into the possession of the alleged original text. It reads in certain passages like a story of Initiation. The parti pris is quick to self-deception, and one sees too easily that for which one is looking ; but here are words which are exceedingly like a Sign of Recognition in some Secret Society : " The first Knight," says the Hermit, who has found refuge in a House of Chivalry, " recognised me, as he believed, by a Sign which I bore about me : he had seen me in a place which he named". But the Hermit evaded disclosures, for he was bent on concealing his mission, even as through the whole of his narrative he veils also his personality, though perhaps for the express object that it should transpire in the subsequent texts.

The circumstances under which he came to begin his story took place in Britain, 717 years after the Passion of Christ. It is to be inferred that prior to his mission he knew nothing concerning the Mystery of the Holy Grail, though he did know of his lineage, which may be intended according to the flesh or according to the mystical spirit, if its reference is to the Grades of his Initiation. On Maunday Thursday,

[1] One does not produce memorials for those who come after and then advise a presumed reader that they are likely to convulse the cosmos by their mere recitation ; but we see that this is an affirmation of the text.

[2] I suggest that what is written in the GRAND SAINT GRAAL can be a substitute only, to save the preposterous situation created by the Hermit's claim, namely, that the text put into his hands was the work of Christ Himself. My proposal is not to be understood over seriously.

[3] See Sommer's VULGATE VERSION OF THE ARTHURIAN ROMANCES, I, pp. 5, 6.

after the office of *Tenebræ*, the Grand Master awoke him from sleep and gave him a Book to ease his doubts on the subject of the Trinity.[1] His immediate experience thereafter was the possession of a further gift, which was that of an infinity of tongues. He began reading the Book but laid it by on Good Friday, to celebrate a Mass of the Presanctified. Between the breaking of the Host over the Chalice and his reception of the Elements, he was transported to the Third Heaven, and there was enabled to understand the Trinitarian Dogma by a dilucid contemplation of the Blessed and Glorious Trinity, with its distinction of Persons combined in the Mystery of their Unity.[2] In other words, this was an ecstasy of the Eucharist consequent upon his initiation into the Sacramental Power and Grace enshrined in the Secret Book. After Mass he placed the Book in the Eucharistic Dovecote, or Tabernacle, with the intention not to reopen it till Easter Sunday, when he found that it had been abstracted strangely ; and he undertook a wonderful pilgrimage in search of it.

That he might be directed rightly on his journey, the Hermit was led by an animal which combined the characteristics of the Lamb, the Dog, the Wolf and the Lion :[3] it recalls in fact that Questing Beast which appears in other Romances and, according to its figurative sense, is explained by the PERLESVAUS. Ultimately he recovered the Book, having found it reposing on the Altar in a certain fair Chapel. This restoration was followed by a vision of our Saviour, Who ordained its transcription. On Ascension Day the original was reassumed into Heaven. It will be seen that no pains are spared to exalt the work which follows this introduction : *ex hypothesi*, it is of mysterious and divine origin ; a parchment copy is produced for earthly purposes by the highest of all ordinations ; and as regards its source and nature it must take precedence of everything, even the Canonical Gospels. That which follows, however, is the extravagant story with which we are about to deal.

The Doctrine of the Trinity was the great crux and mystery which seems to have exercised the minds of those who had entered the Path of Sanctity at the period immediately preceding the literature of the Holy Grail. There was a triumph of Faith in accepting it, and he for whom it presented no difficulties had attained a very high Grade of Illumination. The Hermit of the Prologue to the GRAND SAINT GRAAL is moved profoundly by the question, and to recover a supposed memorial concerning it is that which actuates his pilgrimage in search of the vanished Book.[4] We should remember that in the year 1150 the Church had established the Festival of the Most Holy Trinity ; and it was a quarter of a century later that the Grail Legends began to manifest on the horizon of romantic literature.

---

[1] Sommer, *Op. cit.*, I, p. 5.
[2] The Mass is suspended by command of an Angel and so also is resumed.
[3] *Op. cit.*, pp. 9, 12.
[4] It happens to be nothing of the kind, either in fact or pretence, beyond the claim of the Prologue.

II

A NEW CONSIDERATION CONCERNING THE BRANCHES OF THE CHRONICLE

NOT the least difficulty attaching to the GRAND SAINT GRAAL, regarded as a work of "truth in the art" of its particular Mystery, is the divergence exhibited by the extant manuscripts. These differences meet us, perhaps chiefly, at the inception of the story, though they are with us even at the end. In respect of the latter there are texts that incorporate a distinct Romance which is impertinent to the design of the story. In respect of the former, it should be understood that it is of the essence of the whole design to make a beginning from the same point of departure at which Robert de Borron started his Metrical Romance ; and all recensions present therefore some kind of prose version reflecting his narrative. One of them—and it is the most available of the printed texts—has only moderately grave variations from the LESSER HOLY GRAIL up to that epoch of the story when the company of Joseph of Arimathæa set out on their journey Westward ; but another presents a brief summary which scarcely stands for the original. It is not part of my province to express opinions belonging to the domain of textual criticism ; but I think that the design of the GRAND SAINT GRAAL is represented better and more typically by a manuscript like that which was made use of by Dr. Furnivall for the *Early English Text Society*, and this is the summarised form, than it is by a manuscript like that which Hucher selected for the first printed edition, and this is the extended version.[1]

The incorporation of Borron elements serves one purpose which is material from my own point of view, as it sets in relief the distinction *ab origine symboli* between the actuating motives of the two Cycles of literature. It will be remembered that in the Metrical Romance and its later reflections the narrative is broken rudely at that moment when the horizon has begun to expand by an inspired resolution of the Company to part into several groups and proceed Westward separately. Three divisions were involved hereby, and Robert de Borron promised to unfold their stories in due order when he obtained reports concerning them. We have seen also that the author of the GRAND SAINT GRAAL undertook to supply these missing Branches ; but as the results differ, and in no light manner, from the manifest intent of Borron, it may be deduced that they are not the real history, as this might

---

[1] See F. J. Furnivall's uncompleted edition of the GRAND SAINT GRAAL turned into English verse by Henry Lovelich, *circa* 1460, pp. 1–100, in French, replacing what is missing from the Lovelich MS. Furnivall used a British Museum text in the King's Library, specified as B.R. XIV E 3. For the extended version mentioned above, see Hucher, *Op. cit.*, Vols. II, III. For present purposes I am following the edition of Sommer, VULGATE ARTHURIAN ROMANCES, Vol. I.

have been set forth by the pious minstrel. On his part there was assuredly no design to bring Joseph of Arimathæa either to the *Vaux d'Avaron* or another part of Britain. The doubtful meaning of some of his lines must be taken in connection with the general scheme, namely, to establish the Mystery of Sanctity in great seclusion under the government of a single Keeper, with a life protracted through the centuries, until the time of its possible manifestation came. The prose version, or LESSER HOLY GRAIL, is a moderately faithful transcript of his nearly complete poem, though it is doubtful regarding Joseph's final destination. The EARLY HISTORY OF MERLIN is faithful also to what remains of Borron's second Metrical Romance. Of the DIDOT-MODENA PERCEVAL we cannot speak so certainly; but in several points about which we have materials for judgment—and more especially regarding Moses—it does not correspond accurately. We have accepted indeed and enforced the almost unanimous conclusion of later scholarship, according to which the DIDOT-MODENA PERCEVAL is a speculative completion of the Trilogy, characterised by remarkable insight and the work of an unknown hand.

It must be understood therefore that the GRAND SAINT GRAAL, or the elaborate Romance which follows the parable of the Prologue, begins with a short account of the chief incidents in the Life of our Saviour and the condition of Palestine at that period. It repeats the familiar story of the LESSER HOLY GRAIL, but sometimes, as we have seen, only by way of summary, and always with many variations. The fact that Joseph is married and has a Son in his infancy at the time of the Passion of Christ may be taken as the first important point of difference. He is named after his Father, and to distinguish between them the orthography adopted by the Romance to designate the Son is Josephe or Josephes, for which in the the present account I shall substitute Joseph II.[1] The next point of difference, with which we are acquainted also, concerns the identification of the Holy Grail with the Dish of the Paschal Supper—*en quoi li fiex dieu avoit mangie*—instead of with the Eucharistic Vessel of Sacrifice;[2] but it should be said that there is another text, and this follows the description in the LESSER HOLY GRAIL. The circumstances under which the Great Palladium was discovered, after the apprehension of Christ, also vary, and in place of its abstraction by a Jew, who carries the Hallow to Pilate, it is found by Joseph himself in the House where the Pasch was eaten, and is removed by him to be kept for a memorial of the Master. As in the other Romances, it is used to collect the Blood, which, however, is done no longer on Càlvary, but in the Holy Sepulchre itself. The general lines established by Robert de Borron are followed as regards the imprisonment of Joseph, the circumstances under which he was released by Vespasian after a term of forty-two years, and the

---

[1] Sommer, *Op. cit.*, I, p. 19, containing the first reference to Joseph II. The voice of an unseen speaker tells the Father that his Son will never take a wife.
[2] *Ib.*, p. 13.

vengeance wreaked upon the Jews. All lapse of years notwithstanding, Joseph is reunited to his Wife and Son, is baptised, with a great number of his relatives, and he is directed by Christ to go with those who will follow him into distant countries, carrying neither gold nor silver, nor any material possession except the Holy Grail. It is after this point that the prototype of Robert de Borron is abandoned once and for all. The first destination—reached by way of Bethany and a certain Wood of Ambush—is the City of Sarras, situated in a country of the same name on the confines of Egypt.[1] From this land it is stated that the Saracens originated : the people are described as worshippers of the Sun, Moon and Planets. It is also this place which is termed in later Romances the Spiritual City, though it is not on account of the faith found in its citizens—who appear to have been a perverse race at the beginning and end—but because, according to the story, it contained a *Palais Esperiteus*, which name was given it by the Prophet Daniel, who inscribed it on the door thereof. The story is of course apocryphal, but the design is to shew that even the Seers of Israel were aware of the coming of the Grail, since it was in this Palace that the Eucharist was first consecrated. It was the witness on the dry land, as a certain Ship of Solomon was the witness on the open sea.

At Sarras Joseph found Evalach, its aged King, in great trouble through an invasion of his country by the Egyptians under Ptolemy.[2] Joseph commended his conversion as a certain guarantee of victory ; but the King, though not disinclined, was not baptised actually until his enemies were dispersed with great slaughter. The power operating in his favour rested chiefly in a Cross painted on his shield by Joseph. The story of the war and its wonders occupies a substantial part of the narrative, and before Joseph continued his journey Westward the whole population of the country appears to have embraced Christianity. Several Churches were built in the City or its vicinity ; Bishops and Priests were Ordained ; and Masses were celebrated therein.

England is, however, the Promised Land which the special providence of the story has allocated to the spiritual and physical lineage of Joseph of Arimathæa ; and after the departure from Sarras the sole concern of all the involved Adventures is, separately or collectively, to bring the various characters to this country and to reunite them therein, the evangelisation of the existing inhabitants being the palmary term of all. Speaking of the rank and file, apart from several of the most important personages, the good Christians are transported hither miraculously on a garment belonging to the second Joseph, but those who are imperfect come by ship. A few of the chief heroes arrive independently, under circumstances which will be described in the considerations allotted to each. Joseph of Arimathæa reaches the general bourne ; and though the superior importance of his Son causes him to be almost effaced, we hear of him from time to time during long years

[1] *Ib.*, p. 21.   [2] Sommer, *Op. cit.*, I, p. 21 *et seq.*

of continued existence. At length he left this world to be united with Christ, unto Whom all his love was dedicated. He was buried at the Abbey of the Cross in Scotland, for which one codex substitutes Glastonbury.

There is a general sense in which the GRAND SAINT GRAAL—like the Metrical Romance of Borron—is a Book of the Divine Voice which speaks from the Sacred Vessel, though this is not used to pronounce oracles or to separate the good from the evil as it is in the earlier text. The difficulties raised by the story regarding that Mystery of Faith which it exists to shew forth are so grave and so numerous that I must be satisfied with the registration of the fact and its illustration by one instance. The whole notion of the Eucharist is changed by the supposition that, on occasion, it is administered by Angels ; for on no hypothesis is Christ their Saviour or are they His Priests.

Seeing that there is no clear division of episodes in the story, so that one section can be separated definitely from another, I shall attempt only a general grouping. The Master-Branch of the whole prodigal Romance is that which embraces the mission of Joseph II : this is of the essence, and all else is, in comparison, of an accidental order. About his central figure the wonder of the Grail converges and the confused cloud of marvellous incidents : from the first even to the last, he is thus steeped in a Light of Mystery that " never was on land or sea." Prior to the arrival at Sarras a command was received from the Son of God to build an Ark,[1] similar to that of the Old Covenant, for the reception of the Holy Vessel. Public devotions were to take place before it ; but only Joseph and his Son had a right to open the Shrine, to look into the Reliquary and to take it in their hands. Two chosen men were deputed to carry the Ark on their shoulders when the Company was on the march. The design was evidently to invest the new symbol with the same authority as that Palladium which once belonged to Israel. To provide sustenance for the band during their travellings, each disciple—after the Daily Service of Prayer—found in his lodging the food which he desired in abundance ; but it is not said that this sustenance was provided by the Holy Grail.

While the conversion of the King and the issue of the war were pending still at Sarras, things of far other importance were taking place in respect of the Sacramental Mystery under the charge of Joseph and his Son. The Pilgrims had been lodged on their advent in that building which was named the Spiritual Palace. The inhabitants of Sarras did not know why it had received this designation ; but the arrival of the Christian Cohort was to reveal the Prophetic Mystery— firstly, by the presence of the Ark and the Grail therein and, secondly, by the sacred marvels which accompanied the Ordination of Joseph II, with Christ manifested visibly as the Celebrant-in-Chief.[2] In that Palace, on the day following their arrival, the Holy Spirit advised Joseph the Father that his Son had been chosen to guard the Grail, as

---

[1] Sommer, *Op. cit.*, I, pp. 20, 21. [2] Sommer, *Op. cit.*, I, pp. 31–41.

the Aaron of the new Rite ; that he was to be Ordained by the Highest Consecration and must transmit the Priesthood to those whom he deemed worthy. Joseph II received also the power of handing on the Sacred Vessel to whomsoever he would. It is as if Christ said to his successor : " My peace I leave with you ; My peace I give unto you ".

When the Company were worshipping before the Ark in the Spiritual Palace, the Holy Spirit descended in still fire, as at another Pentecost, and entered into the mouth of each one of them, like the Eucharist of some final dispensation which has not been declared on earth. It communicated, however, a Gift of Silence instead of the Gift of Tongues. A Voice spoke also and though apparently it was that of the Spirit, it was also the Voice of Christ. The discourse was memorable enough ; but I can speak only of its end, when the younger Joseph was directed to approach and receive the most great honours which could be conferred on earthly creature. He opened the door of the Ark and beheld a Man clothed in a terrible vestment of scarlet flame. There were also five Angels apparelled after the same manner, each having six wings of fire, recalling the four of Ezekiel. In their right hands they held various symbols of the Passion—about which we have heard already—and each in his left carried an ensanguined sword. The human figure was that of Christ, with the five wounds upon Him. It is said by the text that the Ark had been magnified strangely, so that it could hold the Divine Personalities of the vision : but I conclude rather that when the door was opened, those who were empowered to behold looked as into a seering-glass, which contains at need the earths of the universe and the earths of the starry heavens, with all that dwell thereon. The state of the Second Joseph is shewn by the words addressed to his Father, praying that he should touch him in nowise, lest the speaker be drawn from the joy of his entrancement. That which he beheld next was the Crucifixion itself, presented in Ritual form, with the Angels for actors therein. It seemed even as in one of the Greater Mysteries which I have seen with my own eyes, when the Adept Master is set on a Cross of Dedication and the Officers of the High Ceremonial are those who combine to immolate him. But the design in the case under notice was rather to certify concerning the Vessel of the Grail, for the side of Christ was pierced and the *sang réal* poured therein. The scene closed and a new scene was opened, this time more especially before the eyes of Joseph the Father. That which he beheld was an Altar, within the Ark, draped in white over red, bearing the Sacred Dish, the Nails of Transfixion and the ensanguined head of the Lance. These objects were arranged on the Epistle and Gospel sides, but in the centre—or Place of Consecration—and covered with a white corporal, there was a Rich Golden Vessel with covercle, also of gold, and it is recorded that all precautions were taken that the contents should remain hidden. A Procession of Angels entered with lights, aspergillus, thurible, incense-boat and then—but not in all texts—one carrying a Head, as I suppose, on a salver, and another with a Drawn Sword. This Pageant went about the House, for a Rite of High Consecration, the Grail being also carried, and Christ entered, even as the Priest of the Rite, clad in Sacramental Robes for the Celebration of Mass. The Circumambulation being finished, for the cleansing of the whole place—which, in spite of its name, had been the abode of evil and the spirit thereof—Christ told Joseph II that he was to receive the Eucharist and, as if constituted a Secret Pope, that he was made and Ordained, Sovereign Bishop, reigning over the World of Christendom.[1] He was clothed with rich Episcopal Vestments and set in an Episcopal Chair, which the text says was still preserved at Sarras, where it proved to be another Siege Perilous, for whosoever sat therein was maimed or destroyed utterly. Joseph was anointed by Christ, and with the oil which was used for this purpose the Kings of England were hallowed in later years up to the time of Uther Pendragon ; but it was missing at his coronation. The Ring of Investiture, given to the new Prelate, thus enthroned strangely, could be counterfeited by no human skill, nor could words express the virtues contained in its jewel.

When the Ceremony was at length over and the Divine Discourse had explained one by one the spiritual significance of each part of his clothing, Joseph II was instructed by Christ to Consecrate the Elements, and it came about thus that the people of the new exodus communicated for the first time : but the Host which was elevated by Joseph was the body of a child and that which was received by the faithful, in the mouth of each one among them, was living and undivided flesh. The administration to the cohort of worshippers was performed, however, by Angels, one of whom took the Paten together with the Chalice and placed both of them in the Holy Vessel of the Grail.[2] Whether the Precious Blood adhered to the Eucharistic Vessel and the content of the Reliquary thus suffered diminution we do not know, nor the purpose otherwise of the Ceremony, which, fortunately for the spiritual side of *la haute convenance*, is not repeated either in the Romance itself or anywhere in the literature.

Thus was the Second Joseph Consecrated in the Super-Apostolical Degree, and thus did he see—at least in the sense of the story—all Christ's Mysteries openly. The issues which are raised by the narrative are much more complicated than will be gathered from the preceding summary. Scholarship has paid little heed to the importance of the Sacramental Question and all connected therewith ; but it has not overlooked entirely the Pontifical Supremacy which is ascribed to the reputed founder of Christianity in Britain. While the ecclesiastical consequence to these islands is perhaps the only thing which can be

---

[1] According to the remarkable words put into the mouth of Christ, the Second Joseph became the *nouvel evesque de ma crestienté nouvele*—as if an older Christianity were about to be supplanted. The real meaning is that Christianity was new in the world.

[2] Sommer, *Op. cit.*, I, pp. 40, 41. This is the kind of Transubstantiation : it is perhaps more likely to have been denounced than approved by the Council which met at Lateran in 1215 for the formulation of the Dogma, supposing that it had been brought forward. It should not be inferred that communicants received in both kinds.

said to stand forth clearly, it must be added that if the intention was to make void one claim of the Papacy, there was never a design so clouded and veiled so sedulously.   The Brief for any Secret Pontificate is proclaimed much less openly than the general brief for the Official Church, with all its ways and laws, as we are acquainted with its body —politic and spiritual—at the period.   Still it is said expressly, in words ascribed to the Master : (1) that Joseph has been chosen as the first pastor of a new flock;   (2) that his eminence is comparable explicitly in the New Law with that of Moses, the Leader of Israel, in the Law which now had been superseded ;   (3) that wherever he went, converting people and places, he was there to consecrate Bishops and ordain Priests, who would have power to bind and loose, even as the Apostles ;[1] and that, in fine (4), to the Younger Joseph was committed the government of souls but to the elder that of bodies—the spiritual and temporal powers.   It does not appear especially that the latter ever exercised his prerogative ; but it may be recalled that whereas the first issue of the temporal power was after the spiritual kind, the second was after the political—on the one hand, Joseph II, who never married, whose Office was devised by election ; on the other, Galahad le Fort, a later Son of the original Joseph, who became an earthly King, who was anointed with the mystic oils by his Brother and who reigned gloriously.[2] We may speculate, though it will be all in vain, as to what was in the mind of the author when he substituted an elder Son for the Father and, as if further to confuse the issues, gave both of them the same name.   Whatever the explanation may be, from that moment when the younger man assumed the reins of government in the spiritual degree, the older ceased to retain even the shadow of power. As regards Galahad le Fort, his birth took place in Britain, and it was foretold to his Brother in a vision that he would be the ancestor of a holy lineage of many men of religion, who should maintain the Name of our Saviour in all honour and all power throughout these islands.[3]

His great election and his association in the highest notwithstanding, the Second Joseph was not intended to escape without the purgation of suffering.   When he and his Company were at Orcauz, in the district of Sarras, he was punished for attempting to bind a devil who was hovering over the dead bodies of certain Saracens : for this indiscretion, a Great Vindicating Angel, with a marvellous countenance, drove a spear into his thighs and left the weapon therein. Subsequently, he was healed by another Angel, who drew out the head of the spear.   That which Joseph II should have effected was apparently the conversion of the heathen and having failed in this he was not to

[1] At the beginning of his Pontificate he is said to have Consecrated thirty-three Bishops—a considerable number under all the circumstances ; but unfortunately we hear nothing further concerning them.

[2] *Op. cit.*, p. 282. An example of the Church creating and investing Kings.

[3] Here is a note of intention, the fulfilment of which is wanted.   The said Galahad becomes King of Hocelise-Gales or Wales, and founds an Abbey.   Among his descendants were Urien, Iwain and above all the true Galahad—the Son of Lancelot and last Grail King. Of the " many men of religion " we hear no more in the Vulgate Cycle.

intervene between the destroyer and the victims. I mention these matters, firstly, because the office of wounding in the thighs recurs so continually in the romances, and, secondly, to note that for some obscure reason the injury in question never befalls the Questing Knights. The Lance used on this occasion is also important because of its after-history, for it was destined to prove the beginning of those great marvels which would occur in the land of Britain. At that time it is said that the Lance will drop blood and will strike—also in both thighs—another personage of the Mystery, a Knight full of charity and chastity, who will suffer for as many years as Joseph had carried the weapon in his own wound for days.[1] These, on the computation of the victim, proved to be twenty-two. The reference is here to King Pellehan, whose wounding is narrated, as we shall find, in the HUTH MERLIN, and who is healed in the QUEST OF GALAHAD : the wounding in question is the Dolorous Stroke inflicted by the poor Knight Balyn ; and it follows that the GRAND SAINT GRAAL gives an origin of the Lance-Hallow which either differs from that of all other texts or it has omitted to mention that the Angel of the Judgment used the Spear of the Passion.

When the Company of Pilgrims at length reached the sea-shore, from which they must cross over to Britain, those who bore the Ark of the Grail on their shoulders walked over the intervening waters as if upon dry land : of the others, those who were in a state of grace crossed on the shirt of the Second Joseph, as if on a raft ; but the evil livers were left to fare as they might till ships could be found to carry them. I am not concerned with the events which followed the arrival of all and sundry in the promised land of their inheritance ; but as regards Joseph II, his evangelical journeys through England, Scotland, Wales, Ireland and, as it is said, other strange countries, continue through the rest of the narrative, till at last he visits King Evalach in an abbey which had been founded by the latter and informs him of his own immediate death on the following day.[2] This occurred accordingly at the Hour of Prime next morning, and he was buried in the Abbey. So was Joseph II gathered into the Kingdom of the Father ;[3] and I pass now to the history of one who was designed as a witness through the centuries to that Mystery which was from the beginning of Christian Times and who could enter into his rest only in the arms of Galahad—the High Prince who was to come in the days of Quest.

King Evalach received the name of Mordrains in Baptism, and he remained in his Kingdom after Joseph and his Company continued their journey Westward. The design of the story, as we have seen, is, however, to bring all its characters into *la bloie Bretagne ;* and with this object it puts the most complicated machinery to work for some of the

---

[1] Sommer, *Op. cit.*, I, pp. 77–81.
[2] *Ib.*, p. 284.
[3] The dying Pontiff invested Alain, the Son of Brons, with the Holy Grail, p. 286.

chief heroes. I must speak only concerning the term and its attainment, omitting in the present case the visions and bodily transporta-
tions which befell Mordrains for his further instruction and purgation.
He left Sarras ultimately and for ever, taking his wife with him and
three hundred barons, and proceeding to the rescue of Joseph, who—
as a revelation told him—was imprisoned by the King of North Wales.
His own realm was committed to the charge of the good Knight
Aganore, who was to be King in his place, and so to remain if he did
not return himself. He carried with him the White Shield by the help
of which he overcame the powers of Egypt, so that this passed also
into the West and was kept in perpetuity as one of the Lesser Hallows.
The journey took place by ship in the ordinary way ; Joseph and his
people were rescued in due course ; and of all their enemies not one
was left alive. For this providence public thanksgivings took place
in the presence of the Grail, the Ark of that New Covenant being set
open for the purpose. Evalach, who had experienced already the
delicious effects which followed an Exposition of the Sacred Vessel,
desired to see with his own eyes the interior of the Sanctuary from
which the Grace appeared to emanate. Though incapacitated by
wounds received in the recent combats, he went to the door of the Ark
and he saw the Holy Dish and the Chalice used for Eucharistic purposes.
He saw also Bishop Joseph clothed in those beautiful vestments in
which he had been consecrated by Christ. The Romance says that no
mind could conceive and much less any tongue express all that was
discovered to him. So far, he had been kneeling with head and
shoulders bent forward, but he arose now and pressed nearer. In vain
a voice issued from a burning cloud and warned him to desist : he
advanced his head further, when paralysis and blindness overtook him.
Of all his members he preserved only the use of his tongue, and the
first words which he pronounced were those of adoration, even for the
misfortune which had befallen him and which he recognised also that he
deserved for surprising Divine Secrets. At the price of his health, and
of age-long suffering thereafter, he would not have renounced the
knowledge which he had attained in the Ark.[1] One of the spectators
asked what he had seen, and he answered : " The end of the world, the
Marvel of all marvels, the Wisdom which is above wisdom, the King
of every king." The last wish recorded on the part of Evalach, who
henceforth was to be termed Mehaigné—that is to say, the Maimed
King—was that he should be carried to a certain Hermitage far from
other habitation, as the world and he had no further need for one
another. The second Joseph approved, because the day of Evalach's
death would not be witnessed even by his children's children. He was
taken on a litter to the Hermitage and placed before an Altar—
presumably in a Chapel thereof—where he would be in the presence of
the Body of the Lord whenever Mass was celebrated. Upon the site
of the Hermitage a fair Abbey was built subsequently, and there

[1] Sommer, *Op. cit.*, I, pp. 241–243.

Mehaigné remained till the coming of the younger Galahad—or, as the chronology of the story states, for 200 years. On the day which preceded the death of Joseph II that First Bishop of Christendom anointed the King's White Shield with his own blood, thus making a second Cross upon it. It was reserved for the High Prince Galahad, and should anyone attempt to use it in the meantime he would repent it quickly. Mehaigné regained his sight so that he could behold this Shield and the Ceremony of the Unspotted Sacrifice.

With the story of Evalach there is connected that of his wife, Queen Sarracinte. While her husband was in warfare with the hosts descended from Egypt, she sent for Joseph to ask news concerning him, praying the Apostle to intercede with God that He would turn him to her own belief. Her mother had been converted through the offices of a certain Hermit, and this, assisted by a vision, caused her to be Christened herself. Thereafter she was permitted to see a white box which was kept by the elder lady among treasures of jewels ; and this on being opened proved to contain the Christ under the Element of Bread. The mother took the Host in her presence, for she was departing this life. She charged her daughter to keep the box secretly, in the hope that she also might have Christ in her company. When the mother was dead, Queen Sarracinte went to the hermit and obtained from him another Consecrated Host, as a Sacred Treasure, keeping it in the same Tabernacle and performing her devotions in its presence.[1] Outside this amazing Reservation, the point of importance is that although Joseph II was, by the hypothesis of the story, the first Priest to Consecrate the Elements of the Eucharist, this was being done already—apparently long before—by a Hermit in Sarras, who must have derived from the ordinary Apostles. There is a suggestion of strange implicits in the names of the next character which is placed on my list for inclusion in these major branches. He was Seraphe, in his days, as a paynim, carrying an axe keen as a serpent of fire and evoking at his need the vision of a White Knight mounted on a White Horse and dealing arch-natural destruction. In Baptism, with the others who elected to be redeemed out of Sarras, he assumed the name of Nasciens, as if in a new generation he had been received into the *militia crucifera evangelica*, with a mission to enter the West and preach the Gospel with his sword. Seraphe was the Son-in-law of Evalach the King—a large man, strong-boned and broad-shouldered. Great and many were the miracles which brought him by slow stages to the Isles of Britain ; but I will speak only of his sojourn on the Turning Island, from which he was rescued by that Mystical Ship of Solomon which fills so important an office in the QUEST OF GALAHAD.

Nasciens watched the Vessel coming to him fast over the sea : it was " richer " than any other in the world, but no one was visible therein.[2] He prepared to go on board, when he saw golden letters in the Chaldaic tongue giving warning that those who entered must be

---

[1] Sommer, *Op. cit.*, I, pp. 70, 71.   [2] Sommer, *Op. cit.*, I, pp. 120–137.

full of faith and clean in every respect. He was deterred at first
but after fervent prayer he entered, believing that the strange Ship
had been sent by God. He found therein a Mysterious Couch, having
at its head a Crown of Gold and at the foot a marvellous Sword, which
was drawn ten inches out of the scabbard. Connected with the Bed
there were three Spindles of strange colourings, though not as the
result of artificial tincture : one was red, another white and the
third green. The story of the Ship is recounted at great length, but
to summarise it shortly, the Royal Prophet of Israel had learned
by a Message from Heaven that the last Knight of his lineage would
exceed all other Chivalry as the Sun outshines the Moon. By the
sage counsel of his wife, Solomon built this Ship so that it should
endure for 4000 years, with the double object of making known to
Galahad not only the royalty of his descent but the fact that the Wise
King was aware of his predestined birth in a due time to come. The
building was accomplished in six months, and then the Queen told him
to provide King David's Sword as an arm of might for his descendant.
It was adorned with a new handle, pommel and sheath—all of great
virtues—and a writing about it said that no man should draw it with
impunity, save one who passed all others in prowess and perfection of
virtue. Solomon would have provided rich hangings also, but was
deterred by his wife, who testified that they must be foul and of her
own making, till another woman should, in the coming time, substitute
draperies that were glorious. The High Office was reserved therefore
for the most fair, faithful and unearthly Sister of Perceval. In this
connection, I may say that one of the side-problems of the whole
narrative is that in spite of the wonderful counsel which Solomon
receives from his wife, and in spite of the sacred, exalted meaning
attached to the Ship which was built by her directions, she is described
as a woman who had deceived him and had embittered him regarding
her sex.

The wooden bed seen by Nasciens was placed also in the Ship, and
the Sword was laid thereon as well as the Crown, which was also that of
David. By the same unaccountable directions the three Spindles were
of wood derived from the Tree of Knowledge in the manner here following. Adam and Eve ate the forbidden fruit ; the apple which she
gathered brought with it a branch ; the fruit was separated by Adam
and the branch remained with Eve, who preserved it in their exile as a
memorial of her misfortune. It was planted by her and became a great
tree, which—both within and without—was white as snow. One day,
when they were seated beneath it lamenting their unfortunate condition,
Eve called it the Tree of Death ; but a voice bade them comfort one
another, for life was much nearer than death—whereupon they termed
it by substitution the Tree of Life. They planted cuttings thereof,
which grew and flourished : these were white like the parent tree, but
after the conception of Abel they turned green, bearing flowers and
fruit. It was under the first tree that Abel was murdered—when it

changed from green to red and no longer bore flowers or fruit : in later times it was called the Tree of Counsel and of Comfort.

When the Ship was garnished fully Solomon placed a letter beneath the Crown, giving warning to his descendant against the wiles of women and asking to be held in his remembrance : he recounted also the building. The Ship was launched ; the King saw in a vision how a great Company of Angels descended and entered therein, as it sailed far out of sight.

Nasciens learned further that the Ship typified the Holy Church of Christ ; and as the latter has only faith and truth therein, so in its symbol no faithless men could have part : confession and repentance were necessary qualifications to enter Church or Ship.[1] The inscriptions in the Vessel were Holy Scripture : in a word, as the text suggested, it was a Symbol rather than a Ship. The sea over which it sailed signified the world ; the bed was the Holy Altar, on which the Divine Son is consecrated and offered daily : in another sense, it was also the Cross of Christ. The white spindle meant Christ's virginity, the red one His humility and love, while the green one signified His patience.

So far as regards the Ship of Solomon ; and in respect of Nasciens himself, before closing his story, I must speak of two visitations which befell him. Soon after his conversion he was filled with the same desire to know the Mysteries of the Grail for which Mordrains paid afterwards so heavily and yet was recompensed so well. He raised up the Paten which covered the Sacred Vessel and by his own account he beheld the foundations of knowledge and religion, the beginning of all bounty and all gentility.[2] We may remember here the old poet who said that Christ was " The first true gentleman that ever breathed " ; and doubtless the Sacramental Mystery is also a Mystery of Courtesy. Nasciens was blinded for his presumption and remained in this affliction till the healing of Joseph II from the wounding of the Angel. His second visitation occurred on board the Ship of Solomon, wherein he had been united with his Son and subsequently with King Mordrains. To the latter he shewed the Sword of David ; but when the King took it in his hands the weapon broke in two pieces and rejoined as suddenly. At this moment they were warned to leave the Ship, and in the act of obeying Nasciens was wounded grievously between the shoulders by the Sword.[3] He regarded this as a chastisement in loving-kindness for his sins ; but the episode is made more intelligible by another codex, which shews that he was tempted to draw the Sword from its sheath and use it as his defence against a giant when no other weapon was available.[4] It broke in the mere brandishing and so remained till it was rejoined, unaccountably enough, by the handling of Mordrains. The wounding follows also in this case. Towards the close of the story a certain King Barlans finds the Sword

[1] Sommer, *Op. cit.*, I, p. 139.
[2] *Ib.*, pp. 79, 80. It was therefore no Dish but a Chalice. It is said otherwise that Nasciens saw the wonder of all wonders—that is, God the Almighty.
[3] Furnivall's text of Lovelich, p. 470.   [4] Sommer, *Op. cit.*, I, pp. 161–163.

of David in the Ship of Solomon and uses it to slay Lambor, who was one of the twelve sons of Brons and at that time Keeper of the Grail. There followed great sorrow and suffering in the lands of both rulers ; both were ruined by the stroke, and Barlans, on restoring the weapon to the Ship and sheathing it therein, fell down dead. It will be seen that a kind of Enchantment thus befalls these parts of Britain, though the GRAND SAINT GRAAL is rather the Cycle of Adventures than that of Enchantments. The Sword was to remain sheathed until drawn by a Maiden—that is to say, by the Sister of Perceval.

There is another tale of a Sword which belongs properly to a different branch of the Romance ; but it may be mentioned in this place. Joseph of Arimathæa is wounded, as usual, in the thigh by a false steward, leaving half of the sword in the wound. With the upper half Joseph heals a Saracen Knight, whom he has converted newly, and then uses it to withdraw the point from his own flesh : it comes out unstained by blood, and Joseph foretells that the two parts shall not be joined together till he arrives who shall end the Adventures of the Grail. This is the Hallow which is resoldered by Galahad at Corbenic when the Holy Quest has ended.

So far as Nasciens is concerned the remainder of the story deals more especially with his deeds of valour in connection with the conversion of Britain, which he reached at length by ship and was instrumental in bringing over those who had been left on the further shore by reason of their lapse from grace. His death took place prior to that of the Second Joseph, and he was buried in the abbey of white monks where Mordrains awaited his end.

Celidoine, a son of Nasciens, is in one sense a lesser character, but in the symbolism of the story he seems to stand for something that is important. He is said to have been born under the happiest of starry influences and was himself a reader of the stars,[1] from which he drew presages and on one occasion insured a Christian victory in consequence. The meaning of his name itself is explained to be the Gift of Heaven. One day Mordrains had a vision concerning him, and therein he was represented by a lake, into which Christ came and washed His hands and feet. This signified that God visited Celidoine daily because of his good thoughts and actions. Nine streams issued from the lake, typifying the boy's descendants. Into eight of them Christ passed also and made a similar lustration. Now the ninth was troubled at the beginning— foul even and turbulent—but in the middle it was translucent as a jewel and at the mouth more sweet and pleasant than thought can picture. Before entering this stream Christ laid aside all His vestments and was immersed wholly—that is to say, in the good works of Galahad. The troubled source signified the stain on that Knight by reason of his conception, and the removal of the vestments meant that Christ would discover to the *haut prince* all his Mysteries, permitting him in fine to penetrate the entire Secrets of the Grail.

[1] Sommer, *Op. cit.*, I, pp. 291, 293.

The external life of Celidoine, who reached Britain by himself in a boat, does not concern us except in broadest outline. As his father wrought with the Sword of earthly Knighthood in the cause of Christ, so did the son fight with the Sword of the Spirit—that is to say, with the tongue of eloquence, and paynim clerks and sages could not withstand him. Among many others he converted the Persian King Label and was married to his daughter. As he was a prodigy from the beginning and was knighted in his eighth year, he is comparable to a more sainted Merlin.

One section of the Romance which calls to be included among the major branches, and may be considered by some as most important of all, has been reserved here till the last ; and this is the permanent House of the Holy Grail. During the Keepership of Joseph II the Vessel and the Ark which contained it shared in the travels of the Apostolate ; but it found a place of rest during the reign of his Successor, who was Alain, as we shall learn later. With a hundred Companions he had proceeded to *Terre Foraine*, where the King was a Knight of worth but a paynim and also a leper.[1] He inquired whence his visitors came and was told, from Jerusalem. He asked further whether his disease could be cured and was informed that this was more than possible if he forsook the Evil Law and became a Christian. Hereunto the King consented and after his Baptism he was healed by the sight of the Grail, this being the only occasion on which the Sacred Vessel was shewn to a stranger. It is important also to note that though Alain was Keeper of the Hallows he was not an Ordained Priest and employed one for the purpose of baptising. It follows therefore that the Episcopal Functions of Joseph II did not devolve on his Successor, while it is certain also that there was no sacerdotal character attributed to still later Wardens and, among others, to King Pelles, who was Keeper in the days of Galahad. The new convert was Christened Alphasan, and he proposed to build a Castle for the reception of the Grail, to marry his daughter to Joshua, a brother of Alain, and to make him the heir of his kingdom if the Grail remained therein. Hereto Alain consented : the Castle was built ; and at its completion they found an instruction emblazoned in red letters on one of the gates, saying that it should be called Corbenic, the meaning of which, as we know, is the Treasury of the Holy Vessel.[2] This is on the authority of the text and it is not an unreasonable persuasion to believe that the author knew what he intended to convey by a word which he seems to have compounded ; but as it has not given universal satisfaction we have variants, of which some are as follows : Carbonek=Caer Banawc —the Castle of the Corners, or the Square Castle, but this has nothing to commend it ; Corbenic=*De Corpore Benedicto*, which is high phantasy, but is convincing in that sense ; Cor-arbenig=the Sovereign Chair, which is perfect past all desiring if the House of the Grail was the seat of a Secret Doctrine.

---

[1] Sommer, *Op. cit.*, I, p. 286 *et seq.*   [2] Furnivall, *Op. cit.*, pp. 331, 332.

The Holy Vessel was placed in a fair chamber, as if on an Altar of Repose ; and on the next Sunday Joshua was married to the King's Daughter. His coronation also took place, and in the feast which followed the Company was replenished by the grace of the Grail with all manner of delicacies. That same night the King made the fatal mistake of sleeping in the palace which he had built, and he awakened to witness a Mass of the Grail, celebrated in his room apparently. It was, I suppose, at the term of the Service that the Vessel is said to have been removed suddenly, and there appeared one wearing the likeness of humanity but composed as if it were of flame. He upbraided the King for reposing in a House so holy as that where the Vessel was worshipped ; and as a warning to all who should come after he smote him through both thighs with a Sword. The Sword was withdrawn, the figure vanished, and Alphasan died ten days afterwards. It was in this way, and at first by the voice of the victim, that Corbenic came to be called the Palace of Adventure :[1] many knights attempted to sleep therein subsequently ; but they were always found dead in the morning, one strong hero of Arthur's Chivalry excepted, and he suffered for it otherwise.[2]

III

THE MINOR BRANCHES OF THE CHRONICLE

THE things which remain over for consideration at the term of this inquest are chiefly derivatives from the Metrical Romance of Robert de Borron, including those further Adventures and Histories which he promised to provide if he could. It was not sufficient for the unknown author that England was the Spiritual Patrimony guaranteed to the Eldest Son of the new Church of Christ and the first Bishop of Christendom : that he might exalt it further, he transferred thereto several episodes which had been allocated in the work of his precursor to regions on the hither side of Syria, or wherever he brought the Company of Joseph to its first prolonged halt. The most important of these postponements is the doom which befell Moses : it is told also differently and is connected with a collateral story concerning one who was fated to suffer a similar punishment, of which the Lesser Chronicles know nothing. This personage is Simeon, who is said to be the father of Moses and is first referred to when the Company are crossing the Channel on their way to Britain. Simeon and his son sink then into the water because they have broken their vows of continence, and they have to be saved by the others.[3] Long after the arrival of the whole Fellowship at the term of their voyaging we hear first of

---

[1] Sommer, *Op. cit.*, I, p. 289.   [2] The reference is to Monseigneur Gawain.
[3] LESTOIRE DEL SAINT GRAAL in Sommer's VULGATE ARTHURIAN ROMANCES, I, 211.

the Grail Table, at which Joseph II and Brons sit together, with a wide space between them ; but the explanation of the Empty Seat differs from that of Borron, signifying the place occupied by Christ at the Last Supper.[1] It can be so occupied only by one of greater sanctity than are those at the Second Table. It follows that for the purposes of this Romance the merit of Galahad was greater than that of the First Bishop of Christendom, who held the Warrant of his own Ordination from Christ Himself. When the fact was made public, Simeon and Moses speculated as to its truth and reason. Being sinners, they regarded it as false, and Moses undertook to occupy the seat if permission could be obtained from Joseph II. The latter was told by those who were parties to the conspiracy that a man counted among the sinners was worthy to take his seat at the Grail. Joseph was astonished, knowing under what circumstances he had crossed over to Britain ; but his informants persisted, and though he could not believe in the goodness of Moses, he gave him leave to try. This was without reference to the Voice of the Grail, which was consulted on the occasion according to Robert de Borron, and it illustrates my previous statement that in the later Romance the Sacred Vessel rarely pronounces oracles or acts as a touchstone. Joseph, however, warned Moses himself, when the time came for the trial, not to make the attempt, unless he knew that he was worthy, as he would repent thereof, seeing that it was the Place of the Son of God. Moses was struck with terror but persisted, and, before he had sat long, seven burning hands came from Heaven, set him on fire like a dry bush, and carried him off through the air. Shame fell upon his sinful companions, who inquired whether he was lost or saved : they were told that they should see him again, and that then they would know his fate.[2]

At a later period, when the Company were approaching the forest of Darnantes, they were directed that they must enter therein, and were told that they should find Moses. In a valley they came presently upon a great house and, passing through open gates, they entered a spacious hall, wherein burned a great fire. Out of the fire came a voice, which begged Joseph to pray for the speaker, that his sufferings might be alleviated by the mercy of God. This was the voice of Moses. Joseph II, who was present, demanded whether he was saved or lost, and the answer was that still he had hope of grace. He had been transported by devils, who meant certainly to plunge him in hell ; but a hermit compelled them to release him, as in spite of his sin he had not deserved endless torment. The fire was destined to encompass him till he was delivered by that Good Knight who would end the Adventures of the Grail. Alain, who was present also, asked more specifically who he was, and was told that it was his cousin Moses. Simeon also spoke to him, when he was advised, and Canaan—another of the evil

---

[1] It is obvious indeed that when the time of the Quest arrives Galahad, in taking the Siege Perilous, is given the place of Christ.

[2] Sommer, *Op. cit.*, I, pp. 247–249.

fellowship -that they should seek to be better than they were, and to be cleansed from sin by the Bishop. Joseph II and Alain prayed for Moses, that his suffering might be lessened. A beneficent rain came down into the fire, softening its fervour by extinguishing half thereof, so that the poor sufferer was eased greatly.[1] Simeon inquired how long such flames might endure, and was told by Moses that it would not be so long as he deserved, because he would be released by Galahad, who not alone would end the Adventures of the Grail but all those of Britain

In spite of the counsel which came to them from a source that illustrated so bitterly the neglect of warnings, Simeon and a certain Canaan not only remained without grace but made haste to complete that which remained for them to do in the order of heinous offence. Joseph of Arimathæa and some part of the Christian cohort had entered Scotland, where we have seen long ago that they were sustained by the Holy Grail. In this benefit of refection Simeon and Canaan were precluded by their condition from sharing, with the result that they had nothing to eat for two days and nights.[2] Simeon claimed that he had done more for God than either Joseph or Petrus, and that he was suffering for their sins.: on the other hand, Canaan declared that he was punished for the deficiencies of his own immediate kindred. Simeon covenanted to take vengeance on Petrus and Canaan on his brethren. The issue was that, grievously and almost incurably, the Petrus of Borron's story was wounded in the neck with a poisoned knife, and the twelve brothers of Canaan were despatched with a sword. The visitation of these crimes is varied strangely in respect of severity, and it illustrates, I think, some vague and undeclared sanctity in the mission of Petrus. If so, it is a reflection from Robert de Borron, though in the later story there is no Brief from Heaven, or other Warrant, as the evident Seal of Mission. In any case, he who only wounded Petrus was transported, like Moses, by spirits of fire, while he who was a twelve-fold fratricide, by the comparative mercy of earthly judgment, was buried indeed alive, but with time to repent before death overtook him almost in the ordinary course.[3] Long and long afterwards, when Galahad le Fort, who had become King of Wales, was riding through that country, he saw a great fire burning in a dry ditch. A voice came therefrom and it proved to be that of Simeon, who was expiating in this manner his outrage on Petrus. At the same time— and again like Moses—he was not beyond redemption, and he entreated his auditor to found a place of religion, wherein monks could pray for his soul. Galahad le Fort promised to erect an abbey and to be buried himself therein. Simeon said further that his torment would cease when a Pure and Worthy Knight should come and extinguish the flames. This again would be he by whom the Adventures of the Holy Grail should be brought at last to their term.[4]

[1] *Op. cit.*, pp. 260–262.   [2] *Ib.*, p. 263.
[3] *Op. cit.*, pp. 262–267.   [4] *Ib.*, p. 283.

It is towards the close of the story that Petrus is mentioned first in the GRAND SAINT GRAAL, and is described merely as *Pieres uns parens Josephe*. He is licensed on one occasion to carry the Holy Grail.[1] After the assault of Simeon, the wound of Petrus was examined and a healing by herbs was attempted ; but this did more harm than good. He was left at length in the charge of a single Priest, while the Company proceeded on their way ; but, seeing that he expected to die, he asked to be carried to the seashore and to be placed in a ship which was found lying thereby with its sails set. The Priest was not allowed to go further, and the vessel put out presently with its solitary occupant. He was taken to the Isle of Orkney, where ruled the Pagan King Orcaut, whose Daughter witnessed his arrival. She went on board the ship and so contrived that Petrus was healed in the end by a Christian prisoner who was in the hands of her father. As the issue of the whole adventure, the heathen King was converted ; Petrus married the Daughter ; he lived a long and worthy life as the successor of Orcaut ; and he had a valiant Knight for his heir. He died in fullness of years and was buried at Orkney, in a Church dedicated to St. Philip.

It will be seen that if the author of the GRAND SAINT GRAAL designed in this account to supply the missing branch of Robert de Borron concerning Petrus, he again—and quite manifestly—told the wrong story, for setting aside all question of the written Warrant, the true destination of Petrus was not Orkney but Avalon, and there is no correspondence otherwise with the intimations of the Metrical Romance.

In nearly all those incidents which, from other points of view, are similar to some of Robert de Borron, the part assigned by the poem to Joseph of Arimathæa is transferred to the Son in this prose Romance which is its wresting rather than its extension. A notable instance is the demand for advice by Brons concerning his twelve boys. It is late in the story and long after the arrival of the Pilgrims in Britain that the question arises which appears pregnant with consequence in the Metrical Romance. Brons has been himself so insignificant throughout that his name appears scarcely, though he is entitled to sit with Joseph II, each on one side of the Vacant Seat at the Second Table. As in the earlier text, eleven of the sons expressed a desire to marry while the twelfth—being Alain le Gros—elected to lead a life of virginity.[2] Joseph II manifested great joy at the choice thus made and foreshadowed the reward which was to follow. It is indicated further by the fact that the Son, and not Brons, was directed to fish in the lake and obtain that slender catch which gave him thenceforward the title of the Rich Fisher. In this case, however, it was used by a miracle to feed those whose desert did not allow them to share in the graces and favours of the Holy Table.[3] When Joseph II was dying there stood Alain by his bedside, and, being asked why he was weeping, he answered that it was because he was to be left like a sheep that has lost its shepherd. He was told, however, that he himself should be the

---

[1] Sommer, I, p. 250.　　[2] *Op. cit.*, p. 249.　　[3] *Op. cit.*, pp. 251, 252.

shepherd after Joseph, having the Lordship of the Sacred Vessel, with power to deliver subsequently to another inheritor full of grace and goodness, on condition only that the Hallow remained in the land.[1]

We come in this manner to speak of the successions and genealogies, and in the first place concerning the Keepers of the Grail. Alain, by a curious disposition, died on the same day as Alphasan, the builder of Corbenic, and both were buried in a Church of that city dedicated to our Lady. The text at this point is a little vague in expression and has been interpreted wrongly; but the succeeding Warden was evidently Joshua—that brother of Alain who was most loved by him. He was followed in due course by his son Eminadap, who married the daughter of a King of Great Britain and had Carceloys as issue. The latter begot Manuiel, and from him sprang Lambor, whose death and that which followed I have mentioned previously. This was the first Maimed King of the Grail, and on him followed immediately one who was the Maimed King *par excellence* of suffering and miracle of final healing— that is to say, Pellehan. But the GRAND SAINT GRAAL says that his wounding was in the battle of Rome, and it knows nothing therefore of the Dolorous Stroke inflicted by Balyn. Seeing, however, that both texts testify that Galahad will heal, and he only, I think it must be inferred that the two accounts refer to the same person, who must be distinguished from King Pelles, though there is an inclination in some criticism to conclude otherwise, and I have shared it tentatively. The genealogy is quite clear that King Pelles was son of Pellehan, and there is not any real difficulty about the son succeeding in the life of the father, as this occurs in the case of Joseph II and is the rule rather than the exception in the counter-succession of the Perceval Quests. It follows from the GRAND SAINT GRAAL that four of the Kings whom I have enumerated were called Rich Fishers in succession and that all of them reigned in *Terre Forayne*, which the VULGATE MERLIN terms— or for which it substitutes—Lystenoys.

The other genealogies are useful only in so far as they shew the descent of the persons-in-chief who appear in the Vulgate Chronicles. The most important is that of Nasciens, which leads up through many names—but they are names only—to King Ban of Benoic, the father of Lancelot, and hence to Lancelot himself, as well as Galahad. The *Haut Prince* was descended therefore on the male side from the royal line of Sarras, over which he reigned himself after the Quest was finished; on the female side he was descended from Joseph of Arimathæa, through Galahad le Fort, as the ROMANCE OF LANCELOT shews. Sir Gawain also is represented as coming from this root, which was that of King David; but his descent was through Petrus, the genealogy of whom is clouded rather deeply in the text; [2] as it is indeed in the Romance of Borron.

At the conclusion of the GRAND SAINT GRAAL the story professes to turn to the life of Merlin. Two of its codices contain a long interspersed

<hr>

[1] *Ib.*, p. 286.   [2] *Op. cit.*, p. 281.

digression concerning the two countries belonging to Mordrains and Nasciens after they had departed therefrom. Their power and influence were much increased under Grimaud, the son of Mordrains. When Sarras was destroyed, with the exception of the Spiritual Palace, it was rebuilt more splendidly than ever. These things do not concern us, for in dealing with the great prolix Romance I think that my summary has been confined, in accordance with my design, to those matters which belong to the Mystery of the Grail as it is manifested in the Vulgate Cycle, and, where it has been possible, to the Eucharistic side of that Mystery as the most holy motive of all my long research. On this subject there is one thing further to say. The doctrine of Transubstantiation, as it is presented in the GRAND SAINT GRAAL, and its continual transition into the notion of physical sustenance, are things which scandalise rather than discounsel the soul ; but as we saw in the poem of Borron that Eucharist and Reliquary were alike understood spiritually, so here it will be found in the last sifting that the spiritual side emerges also and becomes at times prominent. When Joseph II, in obedience to the Heavenly Voice, departed from Sarras and its King, that he might preach the new faith to the Gentiles, it came about in the course of the journey that provisions were wanting. In this extremity he knelt before the Ark, wherein was the Holy Vessel, and implored the help of God. Following the directions which he received, cloths were laid on the greensward, and the people took their places. The elder Joseph, pursuing his care of the physical bodies, ordained that his Son should take the Grail in his hands and follow him round the cloths while he circumambulated three times, when—this being accomplished—all who were pure of heart would be filled with the rare sweetness of the world. This Office took place at the Hour of Prime ; the Father and Son sat down, with a vacant place between them —as if something were lacking which at a fitting time subsequently would make perfect all holy ministry ; the Vessel was covered with Paten and Corporal ;[1] and the result was that those who were privileged to take part were filled with Divine Grace, " so that they could neither conceive nor desire anything beyond it." That was a refection in which material nourishment shared not at all, and though the episode does not occur in all the codices, there is something that corresponds to its equivalent. An instance in point is found in Mordrains, the King, who, after he has attained all earthly knowledge, and has received as the price of attainment the orbicular wound of Plato, is nourished through the centuries by the Eucharist, as Anfortas in the German Cycle and the *alter ego* of both in the CONTE DEL GRAAL. There are otherwise indications, and they obtain throughout the Vulgate Chronicles, that the proximity of the Holy Grail transformed the earthly festival into an experience *in extasis* and that the good things here below became as *bona Domini in terra viventium.*

---

[1] The Holy Grail was therefore a Chalice, or at least was used as such.

IV

THE VULGATE MERLIN

A CONSPICUOUS break notwithstanding between the EARLY HISTORY OF MERLIN, which ends by saying that King Arthur held his land and kingdom long in peace, and the VULGATE MERLIN, which begins by reciting how the nobles who had acknowledged him unwillingly went against him into prolonged rebellion, does not hinder the Vulgate codification from prefixing the EARLY HISTORY to its later text. But the main derivations, as it stands, are from the GRAND SAINT GRAAL and the appurtenances thereof, including the prose LANCELOT. We are concerned only with the text in respect of its Grail references, and of the content otherwise it will be sufficient therefore to say that there is embodied an exhaustive account of King Arthur's Wars with the Saxons, a certain group of adventures of the less indubitably romantic kind,[1] and thereafter the various circumstances which lead up to the internment of Merlin, through the wiles and enchantments of Vivien. In this manner it is the close of the Prophet's chronicle, though it is still only the early history of Arthur.

Here, as elsewhere, the re-editing of Romances in the Grail interest is to be distinguished from innumerable alterations made otherwise by various transcribers but to which no ulterior motive need be attributed. Perhaps the most signal instance of all the major editing is the production of two sequels executed independently, to the MERLIN of Robert de Borron, both of which were made less or more exclusively in the interests which I have mentioned, while both also are ascribed falsely to the same hand. We might elucidate better the VULGATE and HUTH MERLIN could one of them be accepted as carrying further forward the Borron Tradition and thus leading up to a Perceval Quest, whether that of the Didot-Modena manuscripts or another—as, for example, the PERLESVAUS, itself presupposing an early history of the Welsh hero. But the derivatives of both texts offer insuperable difficulties in respect of this course. At the same time the process of codification is nowhere complete in the literature. We must assume, for example, on the basis of textual criticism, that the prose LANCELOT had in some form enriched already the Cycle when the VULGATE MERLIN came into existence ; but in several particulars the Merlin allusions in the LANCELOT do not correspond with anything in those later Merlin stories with which we are concerned here. These, on the other hand,

---

[1] As for example (1) the circumstances under which Arthur begot Mordred on the body of his half-sister, wife of King Lot of Orkney ; (2) those of his own marriage to Guinevere, daughter of Leodegan, King of Cameliard ; complicated (3) by the fact that the latter had a natural daughter of the same name whom a plot attempts to substitute for the Bride chosen by the King. It may be added that in the HUTH MERLIN Mordred is the lawful son of Lot and a daughter of the Duke of Tintagel. See the French text, p. 120, but it is contradicted by *ib.*, p. 147.

when they reflect elements that are particular to the LANCELOT, may be reproducing in mere summary or they may offer new materials by way of variation over details.

The VULGATE MERLIN says that God has given to the Prophet that skill and discretion which he possesses so to assist him that he shall accomplish in fine the Adventures of the Holy Grail, which Adventures are predestined to take place in the time of King Arthur, while Blaise, the Hermit and Scribe, shall live to behold the end. This is true in respect of the DIDOT-MODENA PERCEVAL but not of the other Quests, in which this personage is forgotten, or is lost at least among many recording clerks. But as it follows from the reference, by intimation, that Merlin will not himself survive, the Vulgate text cannot be said to lead up to that document. In the interminable account of the Wars with Rion, a Saxon King, there is some stress laid on the achievements of Nasciens, who is the second of that name and not only had been famous in the reign of Uther Pendragon but still surpassed all others in Chivalry. His admission into the Fellowship of the Round Table took place in Arthurian days. He was, moreover, (1) a cousin of Perceval le Gallois, (2) of near kinship to Joseph of Arimathæa, (3) a cousin of Celidoine, and (4) a relation of Pelles, King of Lystenois. Here the derivation is of course from the GRAND SAINT GRAAL ; but the genealogy is a little distracted. Subsequently Nasciens is said to have had Galahad in his keeping, which statement is reflected into the Welsh Quest.[1] Later still, he had the story in his charge, and by ordinance of the Great Master he announced that which he found therein—otherwise, in the Record of Blaise.

There is more than one reference to Elaine, the Daughter of King Pelles of Castle Corbenic, the niece of King Fisher and of Alain, who was wounded through both thighs by an avenging spear. She was the fairest lady in the land and had the Blessed Vessel in her keeping till the time of Galahad's conception.[2] After what manner she was dispossessed of her High Office the text covenants to declare at a later time ; but seeing that it fails herein, it shall be reserved on my own part for the Branch which belongs to Galahad. We hear also concerning a son of King Pelles who—as in the ROMANCE OF LANCELOT—is named Eleazar. At the age of fifteen years he told his father that he should never be made a Knight till the best Knight of the World should give him his arms and the accolade after three years of service. In return for the dignity of Chivalry he believes that he shall take the Knight to the country of King Pelles and the House of the Grail. At this time the King's Daughter, though Bearer of the Sacred Vessel, is only seven years old.[3] Seeing that Galahad during his brief career

---

[1] The reference may be to what must be called the hidden life of Galahad before he came to Court : in any case Nasciens does not figure in the Great Quest.

[2] It is said also that she was the wisest woman of *la Bloie Bretaigne*, surpassing even Guinevere, the wife of Arthur.—See LESTOIRE DE MERLIN in Sommer's VULGATE VERSION OF THE ARTHURIAN ROMANCES, II, p. 159.

[3] *Ib.*, p. 346.

of Knighthood does not confer the High Order on any Squire in his service, save only Melyas de Lyle, Son of the King of Denmark, and much less on one who would be his uncle according to the flesh, whom also he was destined to meet in the Grail Castle at the term of all, we have here a variant of the Legend which differs in certain respects from any extant chronicle of the Perfect Knight. It is otherwise obvious that the *Haut Prince* is not the Best Knight in question ; nor is it in fact Perceval, on whom the title is conferred in his own stories. It comes about indeed that in the end Eleazar serves Gawain and receives the accolade from him, though he was never Best Knight of the World, nor did Eleazar ever conduct him to the Grail Castle.[1]

I do not know what construction is to be placed upon the position of King Pelles : to all intents and purposes he is the Warden-in-Chief of the Grail in the QUEST OF GALAHAD ; but neither there nor in the VULGATE MERLIN is he called the Rich Fisher, which is the character-istic title of the Warden. The Romance with which we are here and now concerned tells us, this notwithstanding, that he is spoken of as the Rich King, which seems by way of alternative : he is also a full noble Ruler and a true one. But there is under his charge King Pelle-nore of the Welsh Lands, that is to say, Pellehan, who is sick and will never be healed till there is manifested one who shall bring to an end the Adventures of the Holy Grail. This comes to pass at the close of the times of Galahad. But there is another brother, who is Alain of the *Terre Forayne* : he is in sickness also, and will never be cured till the best knight of all Britain shall ask him why he is stricken by that malady and what it is that will help him. It follows that there is here an analogue of Perceval's Question ; but it is never asked in the sequel, nor do we hear further of Alain.

In the VULGATE MERLIN the place of the Grail is Corbenic ; it is situated in the realm of Lystenois, which might signify Lyonesse ; and just as we know that the Castle is one of perilous and even fatal adven-ture, so the kingdom to which it belongs is in nowise a region of peace ; and I have said already that its Ruler is a King in Warfare. The Romance contains few other references to the Sacred Vessel and the History or the Quest thereof. The tidings of the Grail in Britain are still tidings only ; the Quest is still not a search after the place of the Hallows, but of Knights who are proper to undertake it.[2] On matters of so-called early history we hear that Joseph of Arimathæa received the Blood from the side of Christ into the Sacred Vessel when the body was still hanging on the Cross—representing a Tradition that differs from the Lesser Chronicles, though it is reflected from one of the visions in the GRAND SAINT GRAAL. We hear further that the Grail came from Heaven above into the city of Sarras, which may be a description by inadvertence, or it may represent a reflection from some

---

[1] *Op. cit.*, p. 389.

[2] It is evident that the rumour grows from more to more ; and seeing that Vessel and Lance can be found only by the best and bravest Knight, all those who are of fair report are drawn to the Court of King Arthur.—*Cp. cit.*, p. 335.

source which corresponds to the antecedents of Wolfram—if any, outside Chrétien.   The Spear which opened the side of Christ was brought to Logres, presumably—for it is not stated—by him who was the first to Consecrate and offer the Eucharistic Sacrifice : that is to say, by the Second Joseph.

So far in fine as the VULGATE MERLIN can be said to end at all[1]— seeing that it stops or breaks off without redeeming its pledges—the close is taken soon after the enchantment of Merlin by arts of his own instruction given to the Lady of the Lake.[2]   The Record of Blaise ceases for want of materials ; but in the meantime the clerks of the Court of King Arthur have taken up the story in a sense, though their task is confined to registrations of prowess exhibited by those who are admitted newly to the Round Table, and are therefore at once Pro-tagonists of earthly Chivalry spiritualised and possible seekers for the Grail.

V

THE GREAT PROSE LANCELOT

BY many ways do all the antecedent texts of the Vulgate Chronicles lead up, in the hands of their editors, to the Romance of Lancelot.   Therefrom, or therein, all reflect, according to their respective measures, and itself is the great text which goes before the Romance of Galahad, as a Royal Prince may herald the King of All.   The pseudo-base of the story in respect of early Grail History is the GRAND SAINT GRAAL ; but some of its refer-ences have no authority in that document.   In comparison with its vast extent, the allusions to the Sacred Vessel are rare and brief.   I will take all the necessary points in their order,[3] beginning with two pregnant statements, the first of which is conclusive as to the historical source ; for it is said that the Holy Grail was that Dish in which Christ ate the Paschal Lamb with His disciples.   But the story is late chrono-logically in the sequence ; it reflected much ; its ambition was to include all Arthurian Chivalry in its province ; and none knew better than the successive authors, who are thought to have welded it into one whole, that the true Service of the Sacred Vessel took place at no festival of earthly meats, but at an Arch-Natural Mass.   It is haunted therefore with the same idea as we shall find in the LONGER PROSE PERCEVAL—that what besides it was, the Grail was also a Chalice, and it is so described accordingly in one of the later branches.   In evidence

---

[1] The last recorded event is the birth of Lancelot. *Ib.*, p. 465.
[2] That is to say, Vivien.   But it may be noted that Morgan le Fay, who is one of Arthur's sisters, learns many of Merlin's crafts. *Ib.*, p. 254.
[3] There are many others and many casual references which trench on familiar ground.   It is said, for example, that the Adventures of the Siege Perilous and the Holy Grail will put an end to those of Logres.   Sommer's Vulgate LANCELOT, II, p. 26.

of this it may be noted that it is apparently the Dove's Censer in the Story of Lancelot which brings the good meat and drink. The second statement occurs in a printed codex, and scholarship, which misses so little within its own province, has contrived to overlook this : the book says, however, that the Natural Grail is to be distinguished from that which is Supernatural ; and this I take to mean that on the one side there is the Festival of the Feeding Dish and on the other the Feast Mystical of Transubstantiation, at the revelation of the whole mystery in the QUEST OF GALAHAD, foreshadowed, as a thing done out of due season, at the Ordination of Joseph II in the old time of Sarras. Beyond both, there is the last experience of the *Haut Prince* in the so-called Spiritual City.

It will not be found, otherwise than as I have here specified, that the Grail elements differ so much from the earlier versions as the actuating sentiments regarding the heroes of the Quest and the qualifications thereto belonging. A certain new spirit has entered—perhaps even a higher quality of the Secret Life of the Church—and it has moderated, among other things, the final aim regarding the Stewards of the Grail and the persons with and for whom it is represented as sojourning on earth. Speaking of the Romance as a whole, it may be said that it is a Wonder-Book rather than a Book of Initiation, though at certain points it embodies very high Mysteries. According to its own description, it is a branch of the Great Book of the Holy Grail ; but the implied reason is that Lancelot was the Father of Galahad. Make as it may for confusion, it is just to add here that, in this connection, one of the unprinted manuscripts speaks of Perceval as the leader and term of all stories told about other Knights : it was he who achieved the Great Quest ; but his story also is a branch of the High Story concerning the Grail, which is the head and crown of all stories. This would seem to indicate that Galahad was not the final hero of the Quest, so far as this codex is concerned, but it may mean also and more probably that he had his own great place at the last consummation, or that he was an intermediate seeker, as were Lancelot also and Gawain.

We shall find in the HUTH MERLIN, firstly that it has allusions to various occurrences in the QUEST OF GALAHAD which are missing in the extant Romance, and, secondly, that much of its material is derived from the GREAT PROSE LANCELOT. So also in this text there are refer-ences to a succeeding branch of the Quest which we have now no means of checking ; but they are not identical throughout with those in the HUTH MERLIN. It is said (1) that the story will recur in this part to the Knight Meliadus, but we hear nothing concerning him ; (2) that it will speak of Helain the White, who became Emperor of Constan-tinople, but this it does not do ; (3) that many marvels concerning the Tower of Merlin will be recounted therein, but we hear nothing ; (4) that Orpheus, a certain enchanter, is doomed to remain in the Castle of the Holy Grail, with two snakes about his neck, until the Quest has been achieved ; but he is forgotten entirely therein. These items may

be contrasted with those which have been specified in respect of the
VULGATE MERLIN : if there are others, as a more exhaustive analysis
would find, and this assuredly, I believe that my purpose has been
served within the measure of reason ; and I will turn therefore to some,
further Grail references found in the LANCELOT, and of which we hear
otherwise.

There are several intimations concerning the close of the Adventurous
Times in Great Britain,[1] and the occupation of the Siege Perilous at
the Round Table : the commencement of these times was on the
occasion of the war declared by Uther Pendragon against King Urien.
There is also a certain Knight, named Elias, who carried two swords,
after the manner of Balyn : one of them was enclosed in a priceless
scabbard, and is said to be that in the old days which pierced the loins
of Joseph of Arimathæa and was broken therein, as narrated in the
GRAND SAINT GRAAL. It was destined not to be resoldered except by
the Lord of Chivalry, who was to put an end to the Adventurous Times,
with all the Wonders and Mysteries of the Holy Vessel.[2]

A few other points will be taken best with the personal history of
Lancelot, though it is not within my province to provide a formal
analysis of the Romance itself. Lancelot was the son of King Ban of
Benoic, and his mother Helen was of the race of Joseph of Arimathæa,
through whom she was of the line of King David. It is said therefore
that, through his Mother, Lancelot had the same blood in his veins as
the King of Heaven Himself had deigned to take.[3]

His baptismal name was Galahad, and, according to the HUTH
MERLIN, Lancelot was that which he received in Confirmation, though
I find no record concerning this Sacrament in his own Romance. He
was carried away in his infancy by one of the Ladies of the Lake :[4] she
is really that Vivien who deceived Merlin, and who, under a cloud
of poetic modernism, is familiar to the readers of Tennyson. The part
which she plays through all the Tale of Chivalry is out of true kinship
with what we have been disposed to conceive as she is pictured in
the departed laureate's glass of vision. By the knowledge which she
derived from Merlin she entered that unincorporated Hierarchy of
Fairyland of which we hear in the Books of Chivalry : she became a
fay-lady, which signifies not an extra-human being of some minor or
elemental order, but a woman proficient in Magic. It should be noted
here that whereas, in the ordinary acceptation, a fairy may correspond
either to male or female, the term is never used in the Arthurian
Books except with reference to a woman. For example, the Fountain
of Fairies, which is mentioned once in the LANCELOT, received that name
because beautiful unknown ladies had been seen thereat.[5] The Lake

[1] Sommer, *Op. cit.*, III, p. 88 ; IV, p. 27.
[2] *Ib.*, IV, p. 324 *et seq.*
[3] *Op. cit.*, III, 12–17.
[4] *Ib.*, 22. The lake was no lake but an illusion of enchantment which concealed
and shielded also the Lady of the Lake's abode.
[5] Compare the Prologue to the CONTE DEL GRAAL, Potvin, *Op. cit.*, Vol. II, at the
beginning.

into which the child was carried was therefore a Lake of Magic, concealing from public view the Palace or Manor in which his guardian dwelt, and the great park-land about it.   The account of the region within this water of enchantment recalls one of the romantic episodes in LE ROMAN DE JAUFRE ; and, speaking generally, there are distinct analogies between this comparatively unknown Provençal poem and other Tales of the Round Table.[1]

Lancelot remained in the charge of the Lady of the Lake until he was eighteen.   About this period she told him the story of his ancestor Joseph, and also of Joseph's son, the first Galahad, who became a King of that country which afterwards was called Wales.[2]   She referred to King Pelles of Lystenoys and his brother, a second and later Alain le Gros, who had never ceased to maintain themselves in high honour and glory before the world and in the sight of God.   As regards his own future course, she forewarned him that he was called to carry to their term many wonderful adventures, while those which he did not achieve would remain over for a Knight who was yet unborn, that is to say, for the last and true Galahad.   But of the Grail she did not tell him, though at a later time he heard of the tomb of Lucan, connected with a House of Religion, wherein was buried the godson of Joseph of Arimathæa, who was once charged with the guardianship of the Sacred Vessel.   The HUTH MERLIN says, however, that it was a granddaughter of the First Keeper, which seems to accord better with the General Tradition.

Before parting with Lancelot, the Lady of the Lake gave him a wand or ring[3]—for the codices differ—which had the power of dissolving enchantments, presumably other than her own ; and it served him in good stead at many junctures.   Thus equipped, she led him forth into the world, accompanied by an amazing retinue,[4] and repaired to the Court of King Arthur, where he was Knighted,[5] and where, in due time, he was entered as a Companion of the Round Table, a reception which was characterised by considerable ceremonial grandeur.   So passed he into the World of Chivalry ; but through the glory of his after-life, and through the scandal of his unhappy, over-measured, too faithful love, we have no call to follow him.   Before we come—in another section— to the great event of his history, outside these particular vocations, there are only three further points to be noted.   On one occasion he has a vision of his ancestors, namely, Nasciens, Celidoine, the second Nasciens, Alain le Gros and Jonas, who begot the first Lancelot, who was himself father to King Ban of Benoic.   But it will be observed that this is on the male side, and is therefore without prejudice to his derivation on the mother's side from the *radix Jesse*.   On another occasion Lancelot visited the tomb of the first Galahad, King of Wales.[6]

---

[1] See Marie Lafon's prose translation entitled : LES AVENTURES DU CHEVALIER JAUFRE ET DE LA BELLE BRUNISSENDE, pp. 122–135.   1856.
[2] Sommer, *Op. cit.*, III, pp. 117, 118.
[3] *Op. cit.*, III, p. 123.
[4] Appendix I, Note 14.
[5] Sommer, *Op. cit.*, III, p. 127.
[6] *Op. cit.*, IV, p. 175.

He saw also the burning sepulchre of Simeon, and spoke with that victim of the centuries, who told him that the Knight who should deliver him would be of his own kindred, and as nearly as possible the very flesh of Lancelot.[1] It is said in explanation that Simeon was the father of Moses and the nephew of Joseph, all which is in opposition to Robert de Borron, though it reproduces literally the GRAND SAINT GRAAL. Moses was tormented in a similar tomb ; but owing to the prayers of Joseph both had experienced a certain mitigation, and their delivery in thirty years was insured at last.[2] Lancelot removed the body of the first Galahad, which was transported to Wales and reinterred with great honour. The third point concerns the visit of Gawain and Hector to a certain graveyard which they are counselled not to enter unless one of them is the recreant knight whose evil living has caused him to forfeit the honour of achieving the Adventures of the Grail.[3] The reference is to Lancelot, and in the graveyard is a marble tomb which contains not only Simeon but his accomplice Canaan and the twelve brothers whom they immolated. While this appears to stultify the previous account of Simeon's place of purgation it is conclusive as to the disqualification of Lancelot for the Great Quest. Had he never loved the Queen, he would not have begotten Galahad, for whom no office would have remained, seeing that he himself was the Exotic Flower of Chivalry, Palm of Faith and Cedar of Purity. But, as things were, the great light of Lancelot was clouded deeply, nor ever shone freely until that term of all when he was received into a Priestly Sanctuary of the Official Church and was clothed at last in incense. It is certain that, speaking generally of the Vulgate Chronicles, there was no true light of Gawain, though some of the Romances issued from the ministry of Nature have pictured him in glowing colours. Subject to one great and cryptic exception, the day of Chrétien and Wauchier had given way to the day of the prose LANCELOT, and Gawain had been stripped of nearly all his graces, a process first begun in the ROMANCE OF TRISTRAM. Perhaps it may be said that albeit he saw something according to the CONTE DEL GRAAL, therein is an episode of personation, on which I have dwelt shortly, though it was not consciously to the hero himself. In Heinrich's poem he enters only into a world of ghosts. In the prose LANCELOT he is characterised by a constitutional incapacity, to which the Galahad Quest adds impenitence in evil-doing. The picture of Sir Bors—on the other hand —is one of great beauty ; but it does not carry with it any particular significance, except that of a witness on his way back into the world. Among the Grail heroes we are reduced therefore, as we have seen and shall see otherwise further, to Perceval and Galahad. Of these two there is little doubt that Perceval was the first in time, or that in a certain sense Galahad was an afterthought. I use the expression so that I may introduce the more acceptable view that this Elect Knight represents a later but exceedingly express intention, as if it were the

---

[1] Sommer, Op. cit., IV, p. 176.   [2] Ib., p. 177.   [3] Ib., pp. 339–341.

design of the Legend to say that a day would come when that Arthurian Sacrament of which I have spoken previously, would be communicated at last not only to the world without, but that the Official Church would receive also, on its knees, acknowledging that there are Great Consecrations. If, without seeming too fantastic, I may refer to an old symbol which has no special connection with the present order of ideas, Galahad is like the horn of the quintessence in the microcosmic and alchemical star, while the four other horns are the four aspects of the Symbolical Legend of Perceval, being (1) the DIDOT-MODENA PERCEVAL; (2) the CONTE DEL GRAAL ; (3) the LONGER PROSE PERCEVAL ; and (4) the PARZIVAL of Wolfram. It does no real outrage to the order of time if I say that these aspects represent, figuratively speaking, the growth of the Tradition. The DIDOT-MODENA PERCEVAL may be doubtless later than Chrétien, and from him may have borrowed something ; but the two texts are near enough in time to make the question of priority, at least to an extent, unimportant. Let me endeavour to compare for a moment the intention of this strange pentagram in literature. Collectively or individually its documents are best taken in connection with one another, and in conjunction also with those which lead up to them. It is only the LONGER PROSE PERCEVAL which stands to some extent alone in the Northern French Cycle, though it has certain connections with the GRAND SAINT GRAAL. In the German Cycle the PARZIVAL is by no means without antecedents, for apart from the alleged hand of Kyot de Provence we can trace at least the analogies with Chrétien, though Wolfram scouted his version. Finally, we have the Galahad Legend, as if the closing were taken in a superlative Grade of Romance.

As in the CONTE DEL GRAAL, so in the Romance of Lancelot, there is one visit paid by Gawain to the Grail Castle, and it begins abruptly with an adventure at a pavilion by a certain fountain.[1] Gawain, who is actor-in-chief, reached a Castle subsequently in some annex or quarter of which he found a maiden in the durance of a scalding bath, wherefrom no one could save her except the highest typical example of Earthly Knighthood.[2] Gawain was not Lancelot—for whom the adventure was reserved—and he failed therefore, for which he was promised shame to ensue quickly. He was received with pomp in the Castle, and came into the presence of the King, by whom he was welcomed after the true manner of Chivalry. In a word, he was at Corbenic, the Grail Castle, and the herald of the secret ministry entered in the shape of a Dove, bearing a censer in its beak. This vision was momentary only, and was not repeated ; but it served as a sign for the Company to take their seats at the tables, and this was followed by the entrance of a Maiden —their daughter, fairest among women—who carried the Chalice of the Grail, in her passage through the hall replenishing the dishes and filling the place with sweet odours. After what manner this multiplication of loaves and fishes takes place does not appear—a feature which

---

[1] Op. cit., IV, p. 341.   [2] Ib., p. 342.

characterises nearly all the coincident Legends of this particular type. It is worth a passing note that the LANCELOT is the only text in which the Grail Bearer is unaccompanied entirely. So much was Gawain bespelled by the Maiden's beauty that he had no eyes for anything else. She departed at length ; and he, coming to himself, found that, for some fault which he could not identify, he only was left without refection of any kind—even as the evil doers in the Company of Joseph. The meal proceeded in complete silence, and was disconsolate enough for the hero, who began to feel already the working of that shame which was promised him. At the end of the supper the whole Company departed, still without any word, and a dwarf—who tried to chastise him, because of his presence in that part of the building—bade him at length go in search of some other chamber, where no one would see him. He remained, however, in the hall, and there had a certain partial vision of a Grail Service. The presence of the Sacred Vessel healed him not only of a grievous wound which he had received from a spear a little earlier in the narrative, but also of various hurts in a long combat with an unknown Knight in the hall. I omit any special account of this meeting, except that there again Gawain was attacked because he refused to depart. I omit also a clumsy parable concerning a dragon who gave birth to a vast progeny and afterwards strove with a leopard, only to be destroyed in the end by her own children, who perished likewise in the struggle. In a state of exhaustion Gawain at length fell asleep, and found on waking in the morning that he was being drawn through the public streets of the city in a vile cart. After being pelted with filth, he was released ultimately, and arrived at the hold of one whom men termed the Secret Hermit. From him he ascertained that he had been at the Grail Castle, which appears to be new tidings. Of the Sacred Vessel and its Mysteries he learned nothing, though it was foretold that he should know soon ; but this promise does not seem to be fulfilled.[1]

Of such is the message of the literature as it moves slowly and heavily towards the greater heights of its root-conception. It should be added that whereas in the prose LANCELOT Gawain is covered thus with disdain, the Romance of Galahad paints him in darker colours. I do not know why there was such a revulsion of feeling in respect of one who in certain texts appears as the Knight of Earthly Courtesy, and who assuredly in the CONTE DEL GRAAL is scarcely less entitled to consideration than Perceval himself.

After another manner is it dealt to another Knight, who visited the Castle also, but he was the Diadem of Chivalry which at that time had been exalted in the world of Logres.[2] By this I mean that he was Lancelot, and he arrived not only as an expected guest, but as one whose advent had been decreed and led up to from the first times of the Mystery. It was then that the great parable of the adventurous Times

---

[1] Sommer, *Op. cit.*, IV, pp. 343-348. Note also concerning the Praise of Gawain, p. 358.   [2] *Ib.*, III, p. 105 *et seq.*

passed into that other parable concerning Times of Enchantment, because it was understood before everything, and was accepted also, that the faith of King Ban's Son was with the heart of the Queen for ever, and so utterly that, in the sub-surface mind of Romance, it had even moved somewhere as if towards a lower sacramental order ; or— without being condoned therein—it was thought to have carried within it an element of redemption.   Dedicated and vowed as he was, no other willing union was possible ; and hence the offices of Enchantment were needed to bring about the conception of Galahad by the Daughter of the House of the Grail, with Lancelot as the morganatic Father, thus insuring the genealogical legitimacy of the last Recipient of the Mysteries.

Of this conception I propose to speak in another section, because the LANCELOT dissolves into the QUEST, of which the first condition is the birth of Galahad.

VI

A PREFACE OR INTRODUCTORY PORTION APPERTAINING TO ALL THE QUESTS

THERE is a certain sense in which we can say that the Knight of old was consecrated like the Priest of old, and the PON-TIFICALE ROMANUM perpetuates to this day the official mode of his hallowing. There is an arming in its high observance and there is an authentic accolade.   Declared or undeclared, the intention was that even warfare should be dedicated to the high ends of the Church, as if the implied covenant of battle were that a man should be so prepared through all his days that no sudden or violent death should find him unfitted for his transit.   The causes of strife are many, and some of them are doubtful enough ; but clothed thus in the armour of salvation the natural-born hero experienced a kind of rebirth and came forth, so far as he himself was concerned, a Soldier of the Cross. One section at least in the romantic literature of Chivalry was devoted to this ideal, and better than any formal Catechism of Doctrine and Conduct did it uphold the Greater Purpose of the Church and illustrate the hypotheses of its practice.   That section was the Quest of the Holy Grail in its proper understanding, and on the authority of this fact I can say that the branch itself became a search after high sanctity expressed in the form of Romance : as such it does not differ from the Quest-in-chief of holiness.

These statements—which are introduced like an interlude or a section apart and as if extra-judicial—would sound strangely in the ears of those who have preceded me, and it must be understood that, of course, I am speaking of things as they are found at their highest in the great texts ; but the evidence is there : it is there also in terms that it is impossible to elude and impossible also to discount. In respect of the CONTE DEL GRAAL, we must surrender to Nature the things which are Nature's; but the LONGER PROSE PERCEVAL says that of God moveth its High History;[1] and I say likewise—but in a more exalted degree still—concerning the QUEST OF GALAHAD. Were it otherwise, the literature of the Grail would be like the records of any other princes of this world, and my predilections would have nothing therein.

It was only by slow stages that the course of the literature rose up to that height at which it found rather than created the ideal of Galahad. We may take as our most obvious illustration of the developing process one crucial point which characterises the earlier Perceval Quests, and this is the loves of the hero. The earlier branches of the CONTE DEL GRAAL shew little conscience on the subject of restraint, the deportment of the hero being simply a question of opportunity. I know that we are dealing with a period when the natural passions were condoned rather easily, though the Church had intervened to consecrate the Rite of Marriage after an especial manner. Hence it was no great stigma for a hero of Chivalry to be born out of wedlock, or to beget sons of desire who would shine in his light and their own subsequently. The ideal of virginity remained, all this notwithstanding, so that the makers of Romance knew well enough where the instituted Counsels of Perfection lay. It is comparatively late in the Cycles that ascetic purity became an indefectible title to success in the Quest of the Holy Grail, about which time Gawain and Lancelot were relegated to their proper places—ridicule and confusion, in the one case, and final, though not irreverent, disqualification in the other.

The DIDOT-MODENA PERCEVAL offers a frigid quality of abstinence, apart from either sympathy or enlightenment, and without one touch of grace to make it kindred with the ardours and solitudes of the Divine Life. The poem of Gerbert preserves the hero's virginity even on his marriage night; but the precaution—considering the texts which he had elected to follow—has the aspect of a leap in the dark. Wolfram insures the chastity of Parzival by introducing the marriage of his Questing Knight at an early stage. The LONGER PROSE PERCEVAL is like Heaven, knowing neither marriage nor giving in marriage, or at least nuptials are so utterly made in Heaven that they are not reflected on earth. Blanchefleur has disappeared entirely; and it is never supposed that the Quest would be achieved in perfection by one who was not a virgin. If we turn now to the story of Galahad, we shall find that the Quest of the Holy Grail has become an unearthly experiment. There is illumination, there is sanctity, there is ecstasy; and the greatest of these is ecstasy, because it is the term of the others. All the high researches end in a rapture, and thereby is that change of location which does not mean passage through space. I believe that the author

---

[1] *Et de Dieu si vient* (*si muet*, according to the Berne MS.) *li hauz contes del Graal.* Potvin, *Op. cit.*, I, p. 2.

of the Great Quest knew what he was doing when—leaving nothing outside—he so transmuted all, and assuredly in the order of Romance he spoke as no man had spoken before him.

Now, seeing that all subjects bring us back to the one subject ; that in spite, for example, of any scandalous histories, every Official Congregation calls us, from afar or near, to the Secret Church ; so, at whatever point we may begin, I affirm that every Quest takes us ultimately to that of Galahad. It would seem therefore that this is the crown of all. If Galahad had come in the good time instead of in the evil, the Grail would have been set up for adoration before the whole face of Logres. But the Quest says that the world was not worthy, though the PARZIVAL seems to say : " Behold, I am with you always."

Of Perceval and his great expeiiment there are several phases : of Galahad there is one only, led up to by many Romances, but represented in fine by a single transcendent text. This is the quintessence and transmutation of everything, allocating all seekers—Perceval, Bors, Lancelot, Gawain—to their proper spheres, over whom shines Galahad as an Exhalted Horn in the Great Pentagram of Chivalry. Of the Perceval Quest there are two major versions ; one of them, as I have noted already, is like an alternative conclusion to the Cycle of the Vulgate Chronicles ; and one—which is the German PARZIVAL—all antecedents notwithstanding, is something set apart by itself in a peculiar House of Mystery. It is the story of the natural man taken gradually to the ethical heights. There is also a third quest, that of the DIDOT-MODENA PERCEVAL, which, amidst many insufficiences, is important for several reasons after its own manner—that is to say, because of its hypothetical genealogy. The fourth is the CONTE DEL GRAAL, and this—apart from Gerbert—is of no importance symbolically, though it is a great and powerful talisman of archaic poetry. The truth is that for all the high things there are many substitutes, after the manner of colourable pretences, and many transcripts, as out of the Language of the Angels into that of man, after the same way that the great external Churches have expressed the Mysteries of Doctrine in words of one syllable for children who are learning to read. But the absolute and direct message of the things most high, coming in the name of these, is commonly alone. In fine, it sometimes happens that as from any corner of the veil the prepared eyes can look through and perceive something of the immeasurable region which lies beyond the normal faculties of sense, so there are Mysteries of Books which are in no way sufficient in themselves, but they contain elements and portents of all those great things about which it is given the heart to conceive. Among these are the Grail Books in the forms which present the Legend at its highest.

VII

THE QUEST OF THE HIGH PRINCE

LET us now set before our minds the image of the Grail Castle, having a local habitation and a name on the mountain-side of Corbenic, somewhere in South-West Wales.[1] The dweller-in-chief of this Sanctuary is the Keeper of the Hallows, holding by lineal descent from the first times of the Mystery. This is the noble King Pelles, behind whom is that undeclared type of consecrated royalty, which was the maimed King Pellehan, whose hurt is to be healed by Galahad. The Maiden who carries the Sacred Vessel in the Pageant of the Ceremonial Rite is the Reigning King's Daughter, the *virgo intacta* Elaine. To the Castle on a certain occasion there comes the Knight Lancelot, who—as we know already—is the son of King Ban of Benoic, while his mother Helen is issued from the race of Joseph of Arimathæa, and through him is of the line of King David. It is understood by the Keeper Pelles that to bring to its final term the Mystery of the Holy Grail, his Daughter must bear a child to Lancelot, and the destined event is accomplished under circumstances of enchantment which might seem to have eliminated from the Maiden all sense of earthly passion. It cannot be said that this was the state of Lancelot, who believed that his partner in the mystery of union was the consort of Arthur the King, and to this extent the sacramental imagery offers the signs of failure. In the case of Elaine also the symbolism is stultified at a second meeting with Lancelot under almost similar circumstances. I need not specify them here, except in so far as to say that there was a plenary incursion of common motive into that which belonged otherwise to the foreordained side of things, so far as she was concerned. I can imagine nothing in the whole course of literature to compare with the original renunciation of this Maiden, on whom the pure light of the Grail had fallen for seasons and years, and who was called upon by the exigencies of the Quest to make that sacrifice which is indicated by the great Romance.[2]

The motherhood of King Pelles' Daughter, because of her consanguinity with the Mysteries, of which she is an Assistant-Guardian under the Hereditary Keeper, occurs as the result of an intercourse which has some aspects of a Magical Marriage, and, considering all its

---

[1] As the Vulgate Cycle stands in its artificial sequence, it creates an impression that the building fluctuated in the mind of Romance. We have the authority, at its value, of the GRAND SAINT GRAAL that it was *fort et bien séant* externally and a fair house within, but there is no suggestion of vast extent. Elsewhere we hear of a township within the walls ; but when Lancelot pays his first visit thereto he beheld a *petit chastiel*. Sommer, *Op. cit.*, V, p. 105.

[2] At a High Festival of the Grail, when she no longer could bear the Sacred Vessel, Elaine upbraided her father who had caused her to lose that which could never be recovered. King Pelles answered that it was done for a high purpose. Sommer, *Op. cit.*, V, p. 142.

circumstances, it is difficult or impossible to speculate about all that lies behind it. We may say almost that the Lesser Mysteries took flesh for a period under an ordained enchantment and were ill at ease in their envelope. Having regard to Galahad's election, the response which he made thereto, and the achievement which in fine crowned it, the manner of his birth is no longer even a stain : it is a triviality, the sufficing cause of which removes the suggestion of profanation in respect of the Holy Place which by that unusual conception drew to the term of its ministry.[1] I can understand that the mind unversed in the harmony of the whole scheme may think that the generation of Galahad should have been left in a cloud of uncertainty and himself without declared father or mother, like the mystic King of Salem. We have to remember, however, that what we now term bastardy does not rank in the Romances as a stain of necessity upon origin : it seems almost a conventional mode of begetting heroes-in-chief, and that which obtains for Galahad obtains for the ideal Hero and King who was son according to the flesh of Uther Pendragon. As no Romances ascribe a higher importance to chastity, and even to virginity, than some of the Grail Legends, so—antecedently at least—their writers had every reason to attach its proper degree of value to the pre-eminence and sanctity of the nuptial bond ; but there was that in the antecedents and genealogy of Lancelot which made him—*ex hypothesi*—the only possible Father for a yet more exotic Flower of Chivalry, who was the predestined Grail Winner ; but at the same time nothing could insure that possibility except in the absence of his marriage.

So therefore Galahad was begotten in the fullness of time, and was seen by Sir Bors when the latter paid his first visit to Corbenic.[2] He is described as a very beautiful child of some two years old, who, according to King Pelles, would accomplish the Adventures of the Holy Grail, as testified by prophecies of saintly men. The days went on, and Bors saw Galahad again, to his great joy, when Elaine attended a great Court summoned by King Arthur at Camelot to keep the Festival of Whitsuntide.[3] The result of this visit was that Lancelot was driven forth by Guinevere and became mad through grief. In this state he reached Corbenic after a long time and was healed by the Holy Grail,[4] when he took up his abode in an island accompanied by Elaine and her suite but not apparently by Galahad, who remained at the Castle. Later on the lad expressed a wish to be near his Father and it was arranged that he should be placed in a Convent at no great distance from Camelot, where the sister of King Pelles was Abbess.[5] Meanwhile Arthur's Queen had repented or changed her mind and had summoned back Lancelot to Court. He prepared to depart, and being again at Corbenic, apparently saw his Son for the first time. Galahad subsequently was taken to the proposed Convent and there remained till

---

[1] The arrangements were made at Corbenic, but the act of intercourse took place at a Castle in the vicinity. *Op. cit.*, V, p. 109.

[2] Sommer, *Op. cit.*, V, pp. 296, 297.

[3] *Ib.*, pp. 376–380.   [4] *Ib.*, p. 400.   [5] *Ib.*, pp. 407, 408.

he was eighteen according to the Vulgate text, for which other manu-
scripts substitute fifteen or " fifteen and over ". He was seen frequently
by his Father, as also by Bors and Lionel, on the witness of the Lancelot
Romance, which, it must be said, does all in its power unconsciously to
commonise the story of the HAUT PRINCE. It is very different with the
Great Quest, which sees that a veil of concealment covers his early days.
When we meet him first therein he is among the Pageants and Holy
Places of Official Religion.[1] Subsequently he is taken to Court by one
who seems a Steward of the Mysteries,[2] and when the Quest begins he
passes at once into a world of parable and symbol, having been
consecrated firstly as a Knight by his own Father, who does not seem
to know him, who acts under the direction of the Stewards, while
Galahad dissembles any knowledge that he might be assumed to
possess. It is all as if he had come out of Hidden Places of the King.
He bears the outward signs of the Mysteries and passes through
Adventures as one passes through Vision : his very battles are like
passages in the Spiritual Combat. The Grail of which he is in quest is
more especially the Secret of High Sanctity and he moves through a
realm of Masses, more sacred and more efficacious than were ever heard
in Logres. He himself is the Mystery of Spiritual Chivalry exemplified
in human form : his history is one of Initiation, and his term is to see
God. As compared with the rest of the literature, we enter in his
Legend upon new ground, and are on the eminence of Mont Salvatch
rather than among the normal offices of Knighthood. It is more
especially this Legend which is regarded by some scholarship as the
last outcome of an ascetic element introduced into the Grail Cycle ;
but it is not understood that throughout the period of the Middle Ages
the mystical life manifested only under an ascetic aspect, or with an
environment of that kind. The Galahad Romance is not ascetic after
the ordinary way, or as the term is accepted commonly : it has an
interior quality which places it above that degree, and this quality is
an open sense of the mystic life. Those who have talked of asceticism
meant in reality to speak of supernatural life, of which the Galahad
Romance is a kind of archetypal picture. The atmosphere of the
Great Quest gives up Galahad as the natural air gives up the vision
from beyond. It is the story of the arch-natural man who comes to
those who will receive him. He issues from the place of its Mystery,
as Lancelot came from Fairyland, or at least a World of Enchantment.
The atmosphere is that of Great Mysteries, the odour that of a
Sanctuary withdrawn behind the Hallows of the outward Holy Places.
Galahad's entire life is bound up so completely with the Quest to
which he is dedicated that apart therefrom he can scarcely be said to
live. The desire of a certain House not made with hands has so eaten
him up that he has never entered the precincts of the halls of passion.
He is indeed faithful and true ; but earthly attraction is foreign to him,

---

[1] Sommer, *Op. cit.*, VI, p. 4.
[2] *Uns preudons a une robe blanche viex et anchiens. Ib.*, p. 7.

even in its exaltation. Even his meetings with his Father are shadowy
and not of this world—a characteristic which seems the more prominent
when he is the better fulfilling what would be understood by his filial
duty. It is not that he is explicitly outside the sphere of sense and its
temptations, but that his actuating motives are of a transmuted kind.
In proportion, his Quest is of the unrealised order : it is the working of
a Mystery within the place of a Mystery ; and it is in comparison therewith that we may understand the deep foreboding which fell upon the
heart of Arthur when the flower of his wonderful Court went forth to
seek the Grail. In this respect the old Legend illustrates the fact that
many are called but few are chosen ; and even in the latter class it is
only the rarest flower of the Mystic Chivalry which can be thought of as
chosen among thousands. Of the Perceval Quest—I have said—there are
many versions, but of Galahad there is one story only. So are the peers of
the Round Table a great company, but Galahad is one. So also, of the
High Kings and Princes, there are some who come again, and of such is
the Royal Arthur ; but there are some who return no more, and of these
is Galahad. He has not been understood even by great poets, for there
could be scarcely a worse interpretation of his position than a poem,
like that of Tennyson, in which he celebrates his strength on the
ground that his heart is pure. Let me add, in conclusion of this part,
that at the time of his coming the Grail went about in the land, looking
for those it belonged to, and that in this respect Galahad had the true
secret of *le moyen de parvenir*. It has its secret place of abiding, its
Altar of Repose at Corbenic, the Grail Castle ; but it appears at the
King's Court—and this is exclusive to the story. The voice of the
Quest passed through all Britain, in part by common report—because
all or nearly all the Arthurian Knighthood bound itself to assume the
task—but in part also by the miracle of unknown voices and of holy
foreknowledge. The Grail itself is not the Official Sacrament, or it is
that and something which exceeds it. If it were otherwise there would
be no sense in the declaration made by a Hermit that certain Knights
may seek but shall never find it. On the Eucharistic side, it is the
Vision of Christ Himself, and the Mystery of Divine Providence is manifested strangely therein. It works through Faith, represented as the
Way of Attainment and the Gate of Things Unseen. In the poem of
Borron and other early versions, the Sacred Vessel is invisible—and that
utterly—to persons of evil life ; but, though still under its due veils,
it is shewn in the Quest more openly, and on one occasion even to all
who are present—good Knights and indifferent. The vision imposes
silence, and this seems to have been always its office ; but it is that
kind of silence which comes about by the mode of ecstasy ; and in the
case of Lancelot it is described rather fully, as if there were a particular
intention discernible in his advancement through those Grades of his
partial Initiation, when he sees without participating. One form of this
ecstasy seems to be connected with the working of the Holy Spirit. But
there is no assurance to be inferred from favour to further favour, since,

on another occasion, the Grail is invisible to Lancelot when it is seen at the same time and in the same place by a Company of White Knights.

Of such is the Vessel of the Legend and as regards the search after it, the Elect Knight is told that God entered into this world to free men from the Wearisome Adventures which were on them and from the evil belief. A close parallel is instituted between the Knight and Christ, since Galahad came to terminate the adventurous and evil destinies in the island of Britain. For this reason he is likened to the Son of the High Father, who brought souls out of thrall ; and even a demon confesses to him as the way of truth.

I conceive that there is little occasion to recite the story of the Quest, which is available after so many manners of English vesture to young and old alike. At the Vigil of Pentecost, Lancelot was carried by a gentlewoman to a Holy House,[1] where he was required to knight the Son of his own body, but, as we have seen, without learning his name or recognising him after any manner. Galahad, who " was semely and demure as a dove, with all manner of good features," was acquainted, undoubtedly, with his geniture ; but he made no claim on his Father. After this mode, at the beginning of his progress, was he consecrated by the secular order and received into the Life of Chivalry. He came forth from the sacred precincts, being a nameless convent of white nuns, wherein it is said that he had been nourished, and was brought to the Court of King Arthur by " a good old man and an ancient clothed all in white," who saluted the company at table with words of peace.[2] Against this arrival the palace had been prepared strangely by the emblazonment of letters of gold on the Siege Perilous—testifying that the time had come when it should be occupied at long last—and by the appearance of a great stone in the river outside, with a Sword embedded therein, which none present could withdraw. The ancient man uplifted the draperies of the Chair, and there was found a new emblazonment : " This is the Siege of Galahalt the High Prince." The youth is seated accordingly, as a royalty who was not of this world, and it was seen that he was clothed in red arms, though without sword or shield. But he had begun to move amidst enchantments : the sword implanted in the stone was to him predestined, and by him it was withdrawn, after which he revealed by the word of his own mouth that it was that weapon wherewith the good Knight Balyn had slain Balan, his brother. At the festival which followed this episode the Grail, under its proper veils, as I have said, appeared in the hall, illuminating all things by the grace of the Holy Ghost and imposing that sacred silence—already mentioned—which obtains in the presence of the Great Mysteries. As the light enlightened them spiritually, and to each uplifted the countenance of each in beauty, so the Sacred Vision fed them abundantly in their bodies ; but because of those draperies which shrouded the Vessel,

---

[1] She came in the name of King Pelles, Keeper of the Holy Grail. Sommer, *Op cit.*, VI, Les Aventures ou la Queste del Saint Graal, p. 1.

[2] Also he announced Galahad as the " desired Knight," of King David's high lineage, who was to achieve the Adventures of Logres and of realms beyond. *Op. cit.*, p. 7.

the Great Chivalry vowed to go in quest thereof, that they might see it more openly. After this manner began the fateful inquisition which, by a messenger from Nasciens the Second—who was the early Keeper of Galahad according to the VULGATE MERLIN—was forbidden to natural women, like that of Masonry, though the ministers of the Grail were Maidens.

The first adventures of Galahad were those which befell him at an Abbey of white monks, when he who was as yet without a shield received that which Joseph II gave in the far past to Evalach, that' he might prevail against the King of Egypt—that also which Joseph crossed with his blood on his death-bed. It was a sign that the Evil Adventures would be ended by Galahad. Previously, it had been a shield perilous to all who used it, because it was predestined to one ; but I do not find that it has a special office in the later part of the Legend.

Of the Grail and the other Hallows, of their Ministry and Mystery, and of all things connected therewith, we have heard in their proper sections otherwise. After what manner Lancelot, Perceval and Bors passed through Worlds of Parable—as through places of purification— I do not speak here, and even in respect of the High Prince, I am concerned only in so far as his story completes the things which were left over from other branches of the Vulgate Chronicles : the healing of Mordrains, the King-Penitent of all the centuries ; the release of Simeon ;[1] and the manumission of the unfaithful Moses. But of this last I find nothing in the Quest. As regards Simeon, the Abbey which was visited by Lancelot was reached by Galahad towards the close of his time of Quest, and there he beheld a burning wood in a croft under the Minster. But the " flaming failed, and the fire staunched " as he drew thereto, and so paused for a space. The voice of Simeon from within greeted him in a good hour, when Galahad was to draw a soul out of earthly pain into joy of Paradise. It said also that he who spoke was of his kindred, and that for three hundred and fifty-four years he had been purged thus of the sin which he had done against Joseph of Arimathæa—or rather not against him but the High Office of the Grail. Galahad took the body in his arms, bore it into the Minster, had service said over it, and interred it before the High Altar. Of such was the rest of Simeon.

It was at another Abbey that he came upon the age-long vigil of King Mordrains.[2] Galahad had hands of healing, and seeing that he was born in the Sanctuary, it may be said that in this Romance the healing comes from within. These were the words of the King : " Galahad the servant of Jesus Christ whose coming I have awaited so long, now embrace me and let me rest on thy breast, so that I may rest between thine arms, for thou art a clean virgin above all Knights as the flower of the lily, in whom virginity is signified, and thou art the rose the which is the flower of all good virtues, and in colour of fire. For the fire of the Holy Ghost is taken so in thee that my flesh which was of dead oldness,

<hr/>

[1] *Op. cit.*, p. 186.   [2] *Op. cit.*, pp. 184, 185.

is become young again." When Galahad heard his words, he covered his whole body in a close embrace, in which position the King prays Christ to visit him, wherein and whereafter the soul departed from his body. So was the curious impertinent, who had been called but not chosen at that time, after his long penance, at length forgiven the offence, and was taken into the great peace, fortified with all Rites of the Most Secret and Holy Church of the Hidden Grail.

The Ship of Solomon had, prior to these episodes, conveyed the Questing Knights—Galahad, Perceval and Bors—from point to point in their progress ;[1] it had taken Lancelot a certain distance in his Son's company, till they commended each other to God for the rest of their mortal life ; it had borne the Sister of Perceval, who of her own hair and of silk, combined with precious stones, had braided the true and proper girdle for the Sword of David, to replace the mean girdle attached to it by the wife of Solomon. But she had yielded her life before Mordrains had passed in God, and her body had been placed by her proper desire in another ship, with a covenant on her part that it should meet the Questers at Sarras, when the Ship of Solomon brought them to that bourne of their voyaging. It remained only that those three should now gather at Corbenic for the healing of the maimed King Pellinor or Pellehan, about whose place and identity we have seen that the text offers some elements of minor confusion. This is he whom we must suppose to have received the Dolorous Stroke at the hands of Balyn.

As the Path of Quest drew towards its central point, the three, who had traversed various converging roads, met, as it is said, at travers, knowing that the Adventures of Logres were at last achieved. They entered the Castle, and King Pelles greeted them with great joy.[2] In this as in some other Romances grave importance is attached to resoldering the Broken Sword, and that which was brought by Eleazer, the King's son, was that with which Joseph II was once stricken through the thighs. It was set perfectly by Galahad when the others had essayed in vain, and was then given to Bors, as a good Knight and a worthy man. What followed thereon was the sustenance of the elect Grail Knights after a spiritual manner, to the exclusion of the general assembly, who were dismissed from the presence. Those who remained were three and three, namely, Galahad, Perceval and Bors, for the first triad ; for the second, King Pelles, his son Eleazar, and a Maiden who was the King's niece, as also the Grail Bearer in succession to Elaine after the conception of Galahad. To these were joined certain pilgrims who were Knights also, namely, three of Gaul, three of Ireland, and three of Denmark. Finally, there was brought in the Maimed King, and thereon a voice said that two of those who were present did not belong to the Quest, at which words King Pelles—although he was the

---

[1] It is said in one place that Galahad and Perceval were together for five years, during which they achieved The Adventures of Logres ; but these are not recounted.
[2] Sommer, *Op. cit.*, VI, pp. 187 *et seq.*

Keeper—rose up with his son and departed. They were therefore thirteen in all ; and according to the text of Malory, one of these was a woman, who was present with them when Joseph II, the first Bishop of Christendom, came down with Angels from Heaven, and celebrated an Arch-Natural Mass in the Holy Place. After the Kiss of Peace given to Galahad, and communicated by him to his fellows, the Celebrants dissolved ; but out of the Grail itself there came the Saviour of all, with the signs of His passion upon Him, and communicated to them all in the Eucharist. He also vanished, and Galahad, who had received his instructions, went up to the maimed King and anointed him with the Blood flowing from the Hallowed Spear. Thereupon, he, being healed, rose up and gave thanks to God. It is said that, in the sequel of time, he united himself to a company of white monks.[1]

" Sir," said Galahad to the Great Master at the close of the Mysteries, " why shall not these other fellows go with us ? "—that is to say, unto Sarras, the reference being to the Nine Mysterious Knights. The answer hereto was significant : " For this cause : for right as I departed my apostles, one here and another there, so I will that ye depart, and two of you shall die in my service, but one of you shall come again and tell tidings." So, therefore, the Company of Adepts dissevered ; but we have seen how Galahad, Perceval and Bors were carried by the Ship of Solomon to Sarras, " in the parts of Babylon," called an island in the Quest. There met them, in accordance with her covenant, that other barque, which bore the body of Perceval's most holy Sister. We have seen also how the soul of Galahad departed, and it rests only to say that Perceval died in a hermitage ; but Sir Bors returned to Logres, bearing the messages of his brethren, especially of Galahad to his Father : " And when he had said these words Galahad went to Perceval and kissed him and commended him to God, and so he went to Sir Bors, and kissed him, and commended him to God, and said : " Fair Lord, salute me to my Lord Sir Lancelot, my Father. And as soon as you see him, bid him remember of this unstable world."

The bodies of Perceval and Galahad were buried in the spiritualities of Sarras, which may have been in some sense a City of Initiation, though until their coming it was ruled by evil rather than good. It was not the abiding place, but that of the final trial for the Stewards of the Mystery, and at first they were imprisoned therein ; though Galahad was afterwards made King. The Spear was taken into Heaven, together with the Holy Vessel, but Bors returned—as it has been intimated—carrying the resoldered Broken Sword, as if grace had been removed, but not that which now may have symbolised the coming destruction of the Round Table. Of the Sword of David we hear nothing further, nor do we know what became of the Ship of Solomon. As the symbol of Faith, it may have continued voyaging ; but on other considerations it had done its work : there was perhaps no reason why it should remain when Galahad had gone.

[1] *Op. cit.*, p. 191.

Perhaps the saddest mystery of all is the end of King Pelles himself, and how it fared with him after the departure of the Grail. It will be seen that the Quest versions offer many alternatives, but there is one text only which says that the Hereditary Keeper was dispossessed utterly and left in an empty Sanctuary.

VIII

THE WELSH QUEST OF GALAHAD

IT is considered that this translation, the only manuscript of which is referable to the early part of the fifteenth century,[1] was (1) made from another codex than that which was used by Malory for the MORTE D'ARTHUR or by Furnivall for the Roxburghe Club ; (2) that it is the transcript of an earlier copy ; (3) that the Welsh rendering was the work of Siencyn ab John, who is said to have flourished three centuries before Caxton. As this date is mythical, we may be content to note (1) that the French original—like other QUESTE texts—embodied material from the GRAND SAINT GRAAL ; (2) that outside all evidences of mistranslation, the WELSH QUEST differs in several particulars from codices which are known to scholarship, while (3) it seems fairly probable that the variations are not those of invention. On the one hand, there is a slight but not inappreciable attenuation of the-mystical atmosphere with which we are lovingly familiar in the old Caxton text, though the general features remain : for example, the strange enhanced knowledge of one another which is attributed in the Malory version to the Knights who beheld the Holy Vessel, under the veils thereof, at the King's Table, is wanting in the Welsh version.[2] Alternatively, there are other respects in which there is an added disposition to dwell on the spiritual side of things found in the French source, and this is manifested plainly in a few crucial cases. The Table of the Lord's Supper is described as that which fed the body and the soul with Heavenly Food, while the Grail itself is said to provide a Spiritual nourishment, .which is sent by the Holy Ghost to him who seeks in Grace to sit at the Table thereof.[3] The intimate connection between the Sacred Vessel and the Office of the Divine Spirit—which is so evident in the Metrical Romance of Borron—is apparent also, and one who is on the Quest is told that by falling into sin he'will fail to see that Spirit, even as Lancelot failed.[4] Outside those rare wanderings of the Holy

[1] Y SAINT GREAL, edited by the Rev. Robert Williams, being Vol. I of the Hengwrt MSS., 1876.

[2] MORTE DARTHUR, Book XIII, cap. 5. Cf., however, LA QUESTE, Sommer, Op. cit., VI, p. 13. It is Malory who enhances the atmosphere.

[3] Hengwrt MSS., I, p. 495. The wording is vague and elusive : (1) " The Holy Spirit will send," (2) " to him that seeks by Grace," (3) " to sit at the Table of the Holy Grail ". It suggests almost an inward experience, as if the Grail comes to a seeker who follows its Quest within. Cf. LA QUESTE, same edition, p. 113, omitted in Malory's abbreviated version.

[4] Hengwrt MSS., p. 470. The words are : " Thou wilt fail to see the Holy Ghost," referring to the Blessed Vessel. It follows that he who sees the Grail sees also the Holy Spirit. Cf. the QUESTE, Op. cit., p. 58, which speaks only of failure in the Quest.

Grail which are recorded in the French text, there are vague, aloof references to its manifestation at sundry places in Logres—or there more especially, if not there to the exclusion of other regions. Finally as to this part, I recognise an added atmosphere of suggested Mystery as regards the House of the Hallows.[1] This was the permanent Shrine of the Holy Vessel ; but whether the latter was visible always to those who dwelt within, or only at certain times and seasons, is not clear from any extant text : it remains indeed doubtful on the evidence of all the French Cycle.   Hence it is open to question whether it was the daily nourishment of the House, or whether its varied ministry was contingent on the arrival of a stranger who was prepared so far sufficiently that he was admitted within the gates.   It was the latter probably, because Lancelot abode in the House for four days ; but it was not until the fifth day, and then in the midst of a supper, that the Grail appeared and filled all with the meats most loved by them.

The Welsh Quest, like its prototype of Northern France, draws— as already noted—from the GRAND SAINT GRAAL, but not always from one of those codices with which we have been made acquainted so far by the pains of scholarship.   For example, the account of the Second Table is given with specific variations, though there is nothing to justify their enumeration in this place, except that the Son of Joseph is said to have occupied the Seat which corresponded to that of Christ, and no one ventured to take it after him.   It was not so occupied in the parent historical text ; and we know, of course, that the Siege Perilous in other presentations of the Legend is that of Judas Iscariot.

What appears to be regarded as the Dolorous Stroke in the WELSH QUEST misreads the same source as follows : (1) King Lambor was father of the Lame King, and was at war with King Urlain, formerly a Saracen.   (2) Lambor was forced to flight, followed by his pursuer, and in doing so reached the seashore, where he found the Ship of Solomon. (3) He took up the Sword therein and smote Urlain, so that he and his horse were cut in two pieces.   This occurred in England, and was the first blow that was ever given with the weapon.   (4) The King who was slain is said to have been so holy that great vengeance was taken by God for that blow.   (5) In neither kingdom—meaning those of the two combatants—was there found any fruit for a long time, everything being dried up, so that the territories are called to this day the Decayed Kingdom.   It is to be observed that this is in direct contradiction to the particulars in the GRAND SAINT GRAAL concerning the death of Lambor, who was Keeper at that time of the Sacred Vessel.[2] The story of Balyn and Balan was of course unknown to the Welsh translator.

As regards the Lame or Maimed King, he was an Uncle of Perceval,

---

[1] It must not be supposed that the Welsh version presents new things, in the order of episodes or otherwise.   It has a certain manner of treatment which leads me to dwell briefly upon a few points which have been passed over or barely cited in my account of the Vulgate QUESTE.

[2] It is in equal contradiction as regards the French QUESTE itself. Cf. Sommer, *Op. cit.*, VI, pp. 146, 147. Cf. Malory, Book XVII, cap. 3.   Urlain was a newly converted " Saracen " and the " holy " King was Lambor.

and so good was his manner of living that his like could not be found in the world. One day he was hunting, and came to the seashore, where he also found the Ship of Solomon. In spite of the warning written therein, he entered without fear, and drew the Sword partly from the scabbard. He was struck by a spear in the thighs, and was maimed from that time forward. In the French QUEST OF GALAHAD this episode is attributed to Pellinor.[1]

As an illustration of general intention prevailing through the Welsh Quest, and reflected from the French text, a hermit reminds Gawain that the dignity of Knighthood was conferred upon him—among other things—for the defence of the Church,[2] and as this specific statement is part only of the general atmosphere through which the Romance moves, it will be for most an eloquent commentary on the alleged underlying hostility to official ecclesiasticism which is some-times traced in the literature, though it is conceivable that others may be asking which Church is intended. In any case, the condition of Wales at the time of the Quest, as it is depicted in the Welsh text, is not an encouraging report regarding the last stronghold of the Celtic Church ; but it is possible that the worst particulars are things which the translator has interpolated.

Whether in their agreement or variation, the details of the story do not call to be scheduled here ; but there are a few points which may be noted with all brevity. Galahad is introduced at the Court of King Arthur, not alone as the desired Knight descended from David and Joseph of Arimathæa but as one on whom rest all the Adventures and Wonders of Great Britain and all countries.[3] He is called the Son of the Daughter of King Pelles ; but the later story speaks invariably of the Grail Castle as that of King Peleur, whom I should identify—*sub nomine* Pellehan—as the maimed and abdicated Keeper who was healed by Galahad in the French version, of which, however, there is no mention in the Welsh Quest. The manifested Festival of the Grail in the hall of Arthur is heralded by an unknown messenger—a " gentle and fair young Maiden " on a white palfrey, who gives warning concern-ing its advent, and this is found also in Malory's version. So great are the delicacies at the table, by the provision of the Sacred Vessel, so much are they dwelt on in the Welsh version, that the resolution of the Knights in respect of the coming Quest has the aspect of material appetite : they resolve not to rest till they can eat at another table where they will be fed as rarely. According to Gawain, there is no such place on earth, except the Court of King Peleur. When the Quest is thus undertaken Galahad says nothing. All this is an accident of aspect ; for elsewhere it is stated (1) that no one shall see the Holy Grail except through the gate which is called Confession, and this is obviously the gate of the Eucharist ; (2) that the final return of Bors

---

[1] To Pelles, in the version of Malory ; but when the Quest ends at Corbenic Pelles is whole and sound. However, there is another maimed King, who is not named in the story, but is obviously Pellehan.

[2] Sommer, *Op. cit.*, VI, p. 39.　　　[3] *Ib.*, pp. 7, 8.

was designed to exhibit the spirituality of that good which at the last end of things was lost by so many on account of their sins.

The time comes when Galahad swears upon the Relics with the others to maintain the Quest, and, apart from this position—which has not been understood by scholarship—there are episodes and intimations which seem intended to shew that the natural child of the Sanctuary was not permitted to know all—though he had that which was implied in his heirship—until, in common with the others, he undertook the great enterprise. The Knights proceeded on their journey weeping and in great sorrow—that is to say, with failing hearts, foreboding the discounselling of so many and all the disaster coming after : *Euntes ibant et flebant.*

There is one reference to Eleazar, the son of King Pelles, and one to a Knight named Argus, who, by an unthinkable confusion, is said to be the son of Elaine, as if this Daughter of the House had married or begotten subsequently. The Hermit, Nasciens II, whose identity is so important for the GRAND SAINT GRAAL, is misdescribed as the son-in-law of Evalach, no extant text disclosing that he in fact is the witness of its PROLOGUE, except the HUTH MERLIN. He is found on one occasion by Gawain in a very poor cell or hermitage, with a small chapel attached.

When the Questing Knights arrive at the Grail Castle, it is not said that they see either Pelles or Peleur, nor are these or Eleazar present at the manifestation of the Holy Grail. The Maiden who remains in the text of Malory is bidden also to depart, following in this respect the chief French manuscripts. He who comes down from Heaven as the first Bishop of Christendom is distinguished rightly from Joseph of Arimathæa, and is therefore the Second Joseph. When he celebrates the Secret Mass of the Grail, he takes out a wafer from the Vessel, which shews that it was used as a Ciborium. In the Divine Discourse thereafter, it is said by Christ that many a good man has come to the Castle through the Grace of the Holy Ghost. As regards the nine mysterious Knights who are not to accompany the three on their journey to Sarras, the parting of those with these takes place amidst great brotherhood, and each of them says who he is ; but the nine are not named in the text. Galahad asks them to salute Arthur if they go to his Court, and they reply that they shall do so gladly ; but they do not say that they will go. Probably they went back by another way into their own countries.

Now, these are the chief points which I proposed to set forth ; and there is one thing more only—that the Spear was not taken to Sarras, nor was it removed to Heaven with the Sacred Vessel. In conclusion as to the QUEST OF GALAHAD, the presence of that Maiden who was niece of King Pelles at the great vision of the Grail seems without authority in extant French texts : it is therefore peculiar to Malory and the version which he followed.

BOOK VI

OTHER AND LATER TEXTS OF THE GRAIL LEGEND

THE ARGUMENT

in a House of the Templars—His Marriage and Enthronement—Exposition
of the Hallows—Alleged common source for the SONE and PARZIVAL—Futility
of this Hypothesis.   VI. VESTIGES OF THE GRAIL IN ITALY.—The Pageant
of Romantic Chivalry—The *matière de Bretagne* in Italy—The Grail Story
took no Root therein—The Grand Palamède—Meliadus and Girone il
Cortese—Le Grand Perceforest—The Prophecies of Merlin—The Italian
Tristram—The Tavola Ritonda—Its Tristram form of the Galahad Quest
—The Grail in Decadence.   VII. SPANISH AND PORTUGUESE QUESTS.—
Migration of French Arthurian Literature—No Original Texts in Spain or
Portugal—The pseudo-Robert de Borron Cycle—A Version of the Quest of
Galahad in Spanish Translation—Another in Portuguese—Of Galahad as
an Earthly Knight—Degradation of the True Quest and its Motive Spirit—
Recurrence to the Provençal Kyot—Hypothesis of Schulz.   VIII. THE DUTCH
LANCELOT.—Date of this Compilation—Outline of its Contents—The Quest
of Perceval—His Failure and Penitence—His Restitution—His Inclusion
with Galahad in the Quest.

OTHER AND LATER TEXTS OF THE GRAIL LEGEND

I

THE LONGER PROSE PERCEVAL

AMIDST much that is dubious and belonging to the seeming of enchantment, one thing is certain—that the Perceval Quests leave behind them the Grail Castle and that nothing is taken absolutely away, for even the CONTE DEL GRAAL presents the Removal of the Hallows as a point of speculation rather than a thing of certitude.[1] So much is true also of the only prose Perceval Romance in the Northern French Cycle which leans towards greatness. I have given it a name which is descriptive rather than its exact title, for, like the CONTE, it is PERCEVAL LE GALLOIS, the PERLESVAUS of modern scholarship, while for him who in recent years recreated rather than rendered it, the proper designation is THE HIGH HISTORY OF THE HOLY GRAAL. By its own hypothesis it is based upon and was drawn into Romance out of a Latin book said to have been written by Josephus, otherwise Joseph II of the GRAND SAINT GRAAL— that first Priest who sacrificed the Body of the Lord.[2] So therefore, as the Lesser Chronicles derived from a Secret Book referable to the first Joseph, does this reflection of the Legends draw from the Records of his Son. But the one is not rendered into the other, for the other derives from the one many points of reference which it does not set forth actually.

The LONGER PROSE PERCEVAL is an echo of many texts, including the CONTE DEL GRAAL, and of things unknown which might suggest Kyot de Provence, or the group which may be covered by his name. It would seem also that the author, though there was much that he remembered, had either forgotten not a few episodes of the antecedent Legends, or alternatively that he scouted some things and was bent on inventing more. We have seen that, according to Wauchier, the failure of Perceval to ask a vital Question involved the destruction of Kingdoms ; but the LONGER PROSE PERCEVAL is the one story in the whole Cycle which, firstly, accounts for the King's languishment, by this failure,

---

[1] A pregnant intimation among the last words of Manessier is that the Grail henceforward was not seen so openly.

[2] Potvin, *Op. cit.*, I, p. 113 ; HIGH HISTORY, Branch IX, Title 8.

as the sole actuating cause, and, secondly, represents King Fisherman as dying in the middle way of the narrative, unconsoled and unhealed, before the word of power is spoken. It is never spoken in the PERLES-VAUS : the Question is never asked. Further, it is the only story which describes the Secret Sanctuary as the Castle of Souls, or which specifies an Evil Brother of King Fisherman under the title of the King of Castle Mortal, though this character has analogies with the Klingsor of Wolfram.

There is little need to dilate on the story itself, which is available to every one in the best of all possible versions ;[1] but it should be understood that its entire action is subsequent to the first visit paid by Perceval to the Grail Castle and the consequent suppression of the Word. In the course of the story such suppressions are several. For example, when the dismembered Pageant of the Grail is going about the land, a certain Damosel of the Car wanders from place to place, carrying her arm slung at her neck in a golden stole, and lying on a rich pillow. As to this, Monseigneur Gawain, who meets and converses with her, fails to inquire the reason, and is told that no greater care will be his at the Court of the Rich King Fisherman.[2] That reason, however, is explained to him subsequently, namely, that she was the bearer of the Sacred Vessel on the occasion of Perceval's visit, and nothing else will she carry till she returns to the Holy House.[3] It will be seen that the Romance has strange vicarious penances besides its strange Quests. It does not appear why the Damosel of the Car is constrained to wander on account of Perceval's silence. But we are moving through-out the narrative in a high region of similitude, and although it is con-cerned so chiefly with the perpetuation of a Mystery which is so Divine, it creates no secret from the beginning as to the nature and origin of that Mystery, nor does it fail to make plain the fact of a figurative significance which underlies many of its episodes and adventures. Sometimes its dealings in allegory are drawn from materials belonging to another side of the Grail Legend, as in one reference to King Pelles, who for the great love of his Saviour had renounced his kingdom and entered into a hermitage. It is said that his son Joseus slew his own mother at a certain Castle, which from that time forward continued burning, burning ; and it is testified that from this hold and from one other there will be enkindled the strong flame which in fine shall consume the world.

Again, there are many intimations concerning the Earthly Paradise, which lay behind the Castle of the Grail, shewing that this House was like a place of Initiation—the gate of something that was beyond it. According to Josephus, the soul of any person who passed through the

---

[1] It may be said almost of Sebastian Evans that he made up a new language as another vesture for the HIGH HISTORY.

[2] Potvin, *Op. cit.*, I, pp. 34, 35 ; HIGH HISTORY, Branch II, Title 4.

[3] There is no record of her return, though she is clothed again in all comeliness as the story draws to its finish. See *Ib.*, I, p. 346, and HIGH HISTORY, Branch XXXV, Title 26, where Perceval on revisiting the Grail Castle finds his Mother and Sister, they having been brought thither by the Damosel of the Car.

Castle went to Paradise, from which those who are disposed[1] may infer what Grades of Advancement were conferred within its penetralia. The true Spiritual Place was therefore not at Sarras—which in this story has gone utterly out of being—but at the Grail Castle, though before the Earthly Paradise becomes the Home of Souls it must be assumed into a Higher Garden of Eden. There is another facet of this jewel of meaning which says elsewhere that the Red Cross symbolises the Redeeming Blood, meaning that it is the tincture of the Divine Virtue by which the Tree of Universal Disaster becomes the Tree of Life. There are other allusions, designed—as one would imagine— to exhibit the proximity of this world to the next, and it happens sometimes that one side of the world beyond thus realised is not of a desirable kind. Perceval visits a certain Castle of Copper, which is a stronghold of evil faith and an abode of perverse spirits. Beside it there rages a water called the River of Hell, which plunges and ploughs into the sea with a fell hissing, so that it is a place of danger to those who sail by the stars.[2]

The story has many adventurers, and he who attains to the Keeper-ship is not he who can be said to enter the Mysteries at a saving time. As King Arthur is accused at the beginning of falling into a supine state, ceasing from deeds of Chivalry and scattering the flock of his Knighthood, so a certain poetical justice is done to him by the assign-ment of an important place of vision in the finding of the Grail. It is to be noted otherwise that the PERLESVAUS is not a Quest of the Grail but a record of Quest failure. Prior to the death of King Fisher-man, the latter received a visit from Gawain, who, in accordance with the prophecy uttered by the Damosel of the Car, failed in his turn to ask the vital Question, though scarcely—as the Romance confesses— through his own fault ; for at the sight of the Grail and the Lance he fell into an ecstasy, and, for the first and only time recorded of him in all the literature, the thought of God overflowed his whole con-sciousness.[3] Lancelot also visited the Castle prior to the King's death ; but there was no manifestation of the Sacred Vessel on this occasion, because of that which had been and was between him and Arthur's Royal Consort, the reason apparently being less on account of the past than of his long impenitence in the heart.[4] By the evidence of several texts Gawain had led an evil life, almost *ab initio ;* but here he is pictured differently and, moreover, for the purposes of the Quest he had been prepared and cleansed by Confession. It is just to add that the Exalted Legend of Galahad is not so severe upon Lancelot, permitting him to see all save the inmost heart of the Mystery. For such a measure of success as rewarded his presence at the PER-LESVAUS Grail Castle, Gawain was indebted to the prowess by which, as a preliminary condition, he was enabled to wrest from an unlawful

[1] *Ib.,* I, p. 249 ; HIGH HISTORY, Branch XXII, Titles 1, 2.
[2] Potvin, *Op. cit.,* I, pp. 202–204 ; HIGH HISTORY, Branch XVIII, Titles 9–13.
[3] *Ib.,* I, pp. 87–89 ; Branch VI, Titles 18–20.
[4] *Ib.,* I, pp. 128–132 ; Branch X, Titles 9–12.

custodian the Sword of St. John the Baptist. Speaking generally, he was the favoured recipient of many Episodical Mysteries in this Romance to each one of which a suitable interpretation is allocated. In one case his adventures proved to be an excursion into the mystical domain of the Fall of Adam and that of the scheme of Redemption. In another he beheld Three Maidens grouped about a fountain ; but they dissolved ultimately into a single Maiden, as though they were another symbol of the Holy Trinity and the superincession of the Three Divine Persons. If, this notwithstanding, he was allotted no better success than Perceval on his first visit, he learned much, and more indeed than he was qualified to understand fully.[1]

The PERLESVAUS History is dolorous enough in its consequences even to worthy heroes and others illustrious who undertake it without indubitable election. The Realm of Arthur was left sufficiently dis-counselled when he set forth on that great errand ; the King suffered even the death of his Queen, in defiance of the whole Tradition of the Cycle. He is a pathetic and haunting figure moving through the Pageant of that one Romance which has enrolled him—however informally—among the Knights of Quest ; and though he saw the Grail in its processional travels when it was uplifted like a Monstrance over the World of Logres, he did not reach the Castle till after the second entry of Perceval, as another King in warfare, had been ratified by the return of the Hallows. Then he was welcomed by Perceval and was led into the Presence of the Grail, or at least into the Chapel where it abode and was accustomed to appear at the serving of the Mass. It is at this point that the Mystery of the subject deepens and that Arthur is said to have beheld the five changes, corresponding to the five wounds which Christ received upon the Cross. But the vision had a more withdrawn meaning, which is kept in utter reserve, because it is the Secret of the Sacrament. It was through his experiences in the Hidden House that Arthur, on his return to Cardoil, was enabled to furnish, as we are told, the true pattern for Eucharistic Chalices, previously unknown in his Kingdom, and, in like manner, of Bells for Church Offices.[2]

It is scarcely possible to say that the numerous allusions to the Sacred Vessel tend to the increase of our knowledge on the descriptive side of the object ; but on that which may be called historical there is ample evidence that the story draws from some form of the GRAND SAINT GRAAL, while its specific additions and extensions do not distract its harmony in respect of this source. It is clear from several statements that there is to be no rest in the land until the Grail has been achieved ; but the tremor of Adventure and Enchantment which stirs Logres in its

---

[1] It is to be noted that the PERLESVAUS is an antithesis to the Vulgate Cycle in respect of Monseigneur Gawain. His character is exonerated in this laudable Romance. It is said, for example, (1) that he never left a hostel without hearing Mass, " if so he might " ; (2) that he ever had pity of discounselled Dame or Damsel ; and (3) that he never did churlishness to other Knights.

[2] Potvin, Op. cit., I, pp. 248–251 ; HIGH HISTORY, Branch XXII, Titles 1, 3. Gawain accompanies the King but does not apparently see the Mass.

dream is not characterised clearly by either of those diagnoses which are found in the Vulgate or Lesser Chronicles. Prior to the first arrival of Perceval, and during his Keepership subsequently, those Maidens and Holy Hermits who, in one or another way, have been concerned with the Grail Service have a devotional refuge therein which carries with it a species of youth renewal. Yet the Vessel itself still lies under a certain cloud of mystery, and during the period of research there is no man, however well he may be acquainted himself therewith, who can instruct another in the Quest or in the attainment of the Castle of Desire. The will of God alone can lead the seeker.

Though encompassed by sacramental protections, the Grail and its Companion Hallows were not without danger from the assaults of workers of evil. We learn rather early in the story that King Fisherman is challenged by the King of Castle Mortal in respect of Grail and Lance.[1] The fact of this claim and the partial success which follows it constitutes a departure from the Tradition of the whole French Cycle, in so far as it is now extant ; but we shall meet with its remote correspondences in the German Cycle, and shall find that, as they do not derive from one another, they seem like branches with a common root which lies beneath the surface of the literature. The King of Castle Mortal is described as he who sold God for money ; but although there is a full account of the evil ruler taking possession[2] of the Grail Castle, we know nothing of his antecedent life, except that he was a brother of him who was sealed with sanctity and was hence the Rightful Custodian of the Sacred Objects. It follows from this that the King of Castle Mortal was reared, so to speak, in the Sanctuary and must have either betrayed the Sanctuary or have been cast out therefrom. His usurpation takes place after the death of King Fisherman, which seems to have created the opportunity ; but when the enemy of the Laws of Light entered into the Hidden House of God, the Chapel of the Holy Grail was emptied of its Hallows, which were taken into deeper retreat.[3] The Sanctuary was not destined, however, to remain under the powers of darkness ; and as in other Romances Perceval returns in fine to ask the postponed Question ; as by so doing he restores health to the King and joy to the Hidden House ; so here he visits the usurper with arms of the body, arms of the soul in purity, invincible arms of grace ; and by his conquest of the Castle he comes into possession of the Kingdom, while the self-destruction of the false King follows on that victory. Then are the Hallows restored, though the witness does not say whether by hands of men, hands of Angels, or borne by the Wind of the Spirit. The sepulchre of King Fisherman was before the Altar, and it was covered with a jewelled Tabernacle, which seems to have been moved by a miracle.[4]

[1] Potvin, *Op. cit.*, I, p. 137 ; HIGH HISTORY, Branch XI, Title 2.
[2] *Ib.*, I, p. 185 ; *ib.*, Branch XV, Title 32.
[3] It is to be noted that there was no Keeper after the death of King Fisherman and during the siege of the House, nor indeed until Perceval cast the usurper out and so read himself in.
[4] Potvin, *Op. cit.*, I, 209–217 ; HIGH HISTORY, Branch XVIII, Titles 24–36.

Perceval abode in the Castle, except in so far as his toilsome life called him temporarily away, and there also were his Mother—who did not die at the beginning of his adventures, as in several of the other texts—and his Virgin Sister, till they were called at length from earth. The call came also to Perceval, but not in the guise of death. He was instructed, as we have seen in another branch of our inquest, (1) that the Grail would appear no more in the Chapel or Castle ; (2) that Perceval should know well—after a brief space—the refuge into which it had been taken ; (3) that he was to divide the other Hallows between certain Hermits who possessed the " building word " for Churches of all things holy and Houses dedicated to sanctity. But Perceval was still in the flesh, and it follows therefrom that the Grail in this story does not in reality depart, but is removed and remains—as it would seem—in some undeclared Sanctuary—somewhere in the " lands " or the " islands." Perceval was not instructed, and made no disposition in respect of his Kingdom or the Castle ; for there began the ringing of certain joyful bells, as if for a bridal. Into the harbour there entered a ship having white sails emblazoned with the Red Cross, and therein was a fair Priestly Company, robed for the celebration of Mass. The anchor was cast, and the Company went to pray in the Chapel of the Holy Grail, bearing with them glorious vessels of gold and silver, as if on the removal of those things which were without price in the order of the Spirit there were left, for a sign of goodwill, the external offerings of precious metals of this world. Perceval took leave of his household and entered the ship, followed by those whose high presence made his departure a pageant.[1] He went unto the Grail, and the Most Holy Grail received him.

There can be no question that in spite of several discrepancies this version of the Grail Legend is the most significant of all its renderings into the fair Language of Romance, that being excepted only which is the exalted Quest of all. I record in conclusion as follows : (1) That there is no genealogy given of the Grail Keeper ; (2) that among the discrepancies, or as something that is out of reason, there must be included the allocation of the King's illness to the paralysed inquisition of Perceval ;[2] (3) that so far as Enchantments of Britain are mentioned in this text, the LONGER PROSE PERCEVAL draws a certain reflection from the Lesser Chronicles ; (4) that the final abrogation of the Question through the King's death in misease, and the winning of the Grail by the seeming chance of war are things which place this branch of the Grail literature apart from all other branches.

I should mention further that the Shield borne by Perceval is said to have been the Shield of that Joseph who " took down the Saviour of the world from hanging on the Rood ", and that Joseph set in the boss thereof a Relic of the Precious Blood, with a piece of the Seamless

---

[1] Potvin, *Op. cit.*, I, pp. 346–348 ; HIGH HISTORY, Branch XXXV, Titles 26, 27.

[2] The story demands this criticism, because in the absence of the King's illness there is presented no alternative use for a Question imposed on seekers who visited the Castle of Hallows.

Garment. It seems obvious that there is a reflection from the GRAND SAINT GRAAL concerning the Shield of Evalach ; but we know otherwise that this was reserved for Galahad. In fine, as regards the Question, with all that followed in respect of the King's languishment, it should be noted—as a suggestion of deeper Mystery behind one unaccountable Mystery—that, on the evidence of King Fisher himself, he would have been whole of his limbs and his body, had he known that the visitor at the Grail Castle was Perceval, and his own nephew.[1]

II

THE HUTH MERLIN

THE story of Balin and Balan, "two brethren born in Northumberland, good Knights "—so described at the termination of the Second Book of Malory's MORTE DARTHUR[2] —is a sufficient title to immortality on the part of the HUTH MERLIN, so called because it was once included among the treasures which enriched the Huth Library, long since dispersed. The text is otherwise alternate to the Vulgate version, replacing its unending, sanguinary battles with so-called Saxon Saracens by a sheaf of wild adventures, high enchantments and pageants marshalled gorgeously. After what manner this distinction appealed to those who came after is evident from the use which was made of the text by Malory. Among all and above all the sublime and terrible tale just cited constitutes its great outstanding contribution to Arthurian literature. An extrinsic interest attaches also to the question of its alleged authorship, though this has prompted here and there the wrath of scholarship. The Huth like the VULGATE MERLIN lays claim upon Robert de Borron, and in a much more express and recurring manner than the earlier medley. The claim is not only put forward with a clear personal note which is rare, if not unique, in Arthurian Romances, but we are introduced also to a supposed collaborator and kinsman, Hélie de Borron, to whom, in virtue of a putative concordat, the false Robert has reserved for himself unconditionally all that part of his subject-general which belongs to the High Scripture, to the Mystery of the Holy Grail.[3]

The period of the work as it stands, according to the first and only editors, Gaston Paris and J. Ulrich, is between 1225 and 1230,[4] for which more recent critical speculation has substituted a more uncertain

---

[1] Potvin, Op. cit., I, p. 131 ; HIGH HISTORY, Branch X, Title 11. In this manner the explanation of his languishment, given on the same page, is completely stultified.

[2] See the 1819 edition of THE BIRTH, LIFE AND ACTS OF KING ARTHUR, having the Introduction of Robert Southey, I, p. 69.

[3] See MERLIN, ROMAN EN PROSE DU XIIIᵉ SIÈCLE . . . D'APRÈS LE MANUSCRIT APPARTENANT À M. Alfred Huth, par Gaston Paris et Jacob Ulrich, 1886, II, pp. 57, 58, 172, 173, 198. On the other hand, that which leads up to and is connected with what is called the BRAIT DE MERLIN, the voice of his last testimonies, uttered from the tomb of his enchantment, is made over to Hélie de Borron.

[4] Op. cit., I, p. LXIX.

date " between the early thirties of the thirteenth century and 1250 ",
with a disposition to favour " the second half of this period ".[1]
It is divisible into five sections : (1) a prose version of Borron's
JOSEPH OF ARIMATHÆA ; (2) the redaction, also in prose, of Borron's
Metrical Romance of Merlin ; (3) that later History of Merlin which
is exclusive to this manuscript ; (4) a Quest of the Holy Grail, of
which two fragments only remain in the French language ;[2] and (5) *ex
hypothesi* only, an addendum or epilogue containing a summarised form
of the MORT D'ARTUS. As regards the fourth branch, we know that it
was a Quest of Galahad, and we are enabled to check a few of its
variations from the authentic Vulgate text, firstly by allusions in the
HUTH MERLIN itself and secondly by those cited already from the
VULGATE MERLIN. There are also the French fragments already mentioned, while those who desire to go further will find materials for their
purpose in Portuguese and Spanish translations, as will be seen in due
course. It may be accepted that the first part, as we have agreed to
call it, offers no deviation of consequence from other texts of the
LESSER HOLY GRAIL, and that it reflects therefore almost literally
the Metrical Romance of Borron. It has not, however, been printed.
In the second part also there are no important differences ; but when
Blaise is engaged by the Prophet to write the History of Joseph and
therewith to incorporate his own proposed Records, it appears that
the Custodians of the Grail had their independent memorials, to which
access was possible apparently, and these also were to be embodied
by the scribe.[3] In other words, he kept the Minutes of the Mystery,
and the claim is hence that there was a great Grail Book in the form
of a general prototype. As regards the third part, with which we are
concerned in the present section, our attention need be directed only
to intimate things of the Sacred Vessel and the appurtenances thereof.
Merlin moves through the story as an Ambassador rather than a
Messenger of those who are the Guardians of the Grail ; but the
advertisements concerning it are still as of a Parnassus which is remote.
About the time of a certain Tourney held in Logres, a great rumour
passed over the land regarding the Blessed Reliquary and its location
in Britain. Where it abode was unknown, for if Merlin spoke in season,
he told little ; but the grace of its discovery and the limit of the
Adventurous Times were reserved for the Best Knight of the World.
The Companions of the Round Table set themselves—as they do also
in the VULGATE[4]—to follow the Quest of such Knight through many
lands, and—as again they do therein—to report concerning any Good
Knight unknown heretofore among them. If one were found, he was
straightway led to the Court, his Chivalry was proved—as if a stranger

---

[1] J. D. Bruce, EVOLUTION OF ARTHURIAN ROMANCE, I, 479 *n.*
[2] *Ib.*, p. 469.
[3] The HUTH MERLIN, I, pp. 32, 33.
[4] See LESTOIRE DE MERLIN in Sommers' VULGATE VERSION OF THE ARTHURIAN
ROMANCES, II, pp. 334, 335. Cp. the Early English Text Society's MERLIN, OR THE
EARLY HISTORY OF KING ARTHUR, II, pp. 502, 503.

knocked for admission at a Lodge of the Craft Degrees—and on with-standing the tests, he was received into the Great Company. Each Knight who returned from the Quest recited his adventures ; and these were reduced into writing by four clerks retained in the service of the Queen. In this manner they were transmitted to later times.[1] It was an age of Secret Chronicles, of their sealing and the breaking of seals. On the pre-viewed approach of his doom, and before finally parting from Blaise, Merlin indited that prophecy concerning the Times of the Quest, to which I have referred previously. It opened as follows : " This is the beginning of the adventures in the land of Britain, whereby the mighty Lion shall be overthrown : these adventures shall be taken to their term by a King's Son, who shall be chaste, and the Best Knight of the World." After this manner did he who instigated the Quest seem to encompass thereby rather than foresee the destruction of the Round Table, its King also and its Chivalry. It is said further—and still on the ground that he had not much longer to remain in the world —that Merlin engaged King Arthur to record all the occurrences which took place at the Royal Court, and that fifty clerks were set aside for this office.[2] Finally, as regards such memorials, another book was written by the own hand of the Prophet, giving before the event an account of the death of Arthur and of Gawain. It was in the keeping of Morgan le Fay ; but with its contents she was not acquainted, because of the doom which would befall her or any other woman who, according to Merlin, should know of such deaths beforehand.[3]

The Hidden Life of the Holy House is a prolonged Mystery of the Ages through all the literature ; and if one corner of the veil is lifted for a few moments by the VULGATE MERLIN in its unconcerted allusions to King Pelles, the Huth Manuscript does not compete with even this vague quality of candour, nor is there any certain ray of light cast upon the Grail itself. It is only the two great texts of Tran-substantiation in the days of Quest which can claim to have drawn aside the Curtains of the Temple and to have manifested the Secret Things, though they continue to say that these should be kept covertly, and thus even in the unveiling they suggest that there is a deeper hiding. In the GRAND SAINT GRAAL Corbenic is not more accessible because it is portrayed so openly, and it is not perhaps more withdrawn because it is in nowise named by the HUTH MERLIN. This text has allusive and hinting methods which are particular to itself, and there is one among them which seems to suggest a wilderness of strange meaning behind its simple words. When Bademagus, like other of the Knights to whom no attainment was destined, was concerned for a period in the Quest, he found a branch of an Holy Herb, which was a sign of the SAN GREAL, and no knight came upon such token unless his life was good.

The Tradition of the Third Table is carried over from the EARLY HISTORY OF MERLIN, in which Robert de Borron narrates its Institution by Uther. The HUTH text, following the prose LANCELOT, represents

---

[1] HUTH MERLIN, II, pp. 97, 98.   [2] Ib., p. 100.   [3] Ib., pp. 227, 228.

it as having passed into the charge of King Carmelide, the father of Guinevere. According to the VULGATE MERLIN, the Knights of the Round Table, being weary of the evil estate into which all the country had fallen, retired to the realm of Leodegan. It does not add what appears to follow from the text of the HUTH MERLIN, namely, that the material Table itself was in the Palace at Carmelide. The story of the Siege Perilous is given much after the usual manner, but with a few omissions and variations. Stress is laid upon the fact that each Knight on rising from the table finds his name inscribed miraculously upon the seat to him belonging—an incident which, according to the mind of the Romance, exhibits the high pleasure taken by God in the Institution of the Round Table.[1] Among the signs and tokens which go before, or are conterminous with the Quest, there is the appearance of that strange, nondescript animal, which is a combination of many creatures, and is called the Questing Beast, because within her there is a noise of hounds baying. In the HUTH MERLIN she appears, as if it were out of due season, during the reign of Uther, who is told by his great counsellor that she concerns one of the Adventures of the Grail.[2] It will be explained to him by Perceval le Gallois, the Son of a Knight who at that time is following the beast in question. As Perceval, however, is unborn and as Uther dies in his day, the prophecy does not come to pass ; but it serves to introduce Pellinore, who is represented now as a King and again as a Knight, and he it is who follows the Questing Beast. After his death, we know from Malory that she was long sought by Palamedes, in both cases, to no purpose apparently, for nothing comes therefrom. It is in the LONGER PROSE PERCEVAL—as we have seen—that an allegorical interpretation of the interminable pursuit is given to Perceval himself.

I have said that Pellinore had not begotten a son in the days of Uther Pendragon ; and though on his first introduction in the days of Arthur, his jousting seems to have constituted a kind of guerilla warfare against the Chivalry of the Court, he is married ultimately to one of the King's sisters, and when the Round Table is sent by Leodegan of Carmelide as his daughter's dowry,[3] he is chosen by Merlin to fill one of two empty seats which had been left thereat by the prophet's ordinance. Moreover, when other seats fall vacant, owing to death, he assists the King to fill them, and he serves him also in warfare. Pellinore was slain in fine by Gawain, whose father had fallen at his hands. It should be added that the genealogy of Perceval, according to this Romance, makes void that of the Lesser Chronicles, as it does also the corresponding account in the LONGER PROSE PERCEVAL.

These things connect with the Holy Grail, though it is in a subsidiary sense only ; but the root and centre of the story is the great device by which the HUTH MERLIN brings war upon the House of the Hallows, devastation on the surrounding country, and a living death upon one

---

[1] HUTH MERLIN, Op. cit., II, p. 68.
[2] Ib., I, p. 160. See also ib., pp. 161, 177, 258.   [3] Ib., II, p. 62.

of the Hereditary Wardens by means of the Dolorous Stroke.[1] Of this fatality I have given some account already in a previous section, and I must speak of it here without covering precisely the same ground. The Romance shews that the Secret Powers of Avalon were hostile in respect of King Arthur even from the beginning. From those realms of dream and faërie the Lady Lilith or Lylle—otherwise a Lady of Avalon—brought a mysterious Sword to the Royal Court, then being held at London.[2] The weapon was her great encumbrance ; but she was condemned to carry it till some Knight should succeed in unsheathing it. Arthur and all his Companions made the attempt in vain ; but the poor Knight Balyn, who had just been released from prison, fulfilled the task easily. He refused to restore the Sword to the damosel; and though he was told that it would cause his own destruction, he agreed to take the risk. Thereupon a Lady of the Lake entered and demanded either the head of the Knight who had won the Sword or that of the maiden who brought it. Balyn, however, cut off her own head, saying that he had been in quest of her these three years past, she having slain his mother by her arts of enchantment.[3] In this manner he saved the other damosel, though Merlin shewed that she was of evil ways and life, never appearing for good, but for great harm only. Here and thus begins the story of Balyn and Balan, as a tale of dole from the first, and such it remains to the end. But the Dolorous Stroke itself came about through a Knight who had the power to ride invisible, and thus had others at his mercy. Balyn was in chase of this Knight, to put an end to his evil deeds, and after the episode of the Sword he overtook him in the Castle of his Brother, who is the King Pellehan.[4] There he destroyed him in open court at a festival, and he was pursued by the King from room to room of the building to avenge what appeared to be an act of wanton murder. They met in a richly dight bed-chamber, where there was a table of gold on four pillars of silver, and on the table a marvellous Spear, strangely wrought. Therewith Balyn smote his pursuer, who fell down in a swoon.[5] The Castle roof and walls broke and caved in. Merlin appeared and prophesied that King Pellehan would remain sorely wounded for many years—that is to say, until Galahad healed him in the Quest of the Holy Grail. Merlin added that there was preserved in the Castle a part of the Precious Blood of our Lord Jesus Christ which Joseph of Arimathæa had brought into this land, while the Spear was that of Longinus, and the King himself was nearly of Joseph's kindred. Balyn rode subse-quently through fair lands and cities, of which many inhabitants were slain on all sides, while those who remained cried out piteously against him. Such was the visitation of the Grail—a strange and unheard-of enchantment. The story continues, multiplying dole and doom, with

---

[1] It is foretold that this stroke will initiate the marvels of the Holy Grail in Great Britain, obviously because the wounding of the Grail King brings about those Quests by which alone he can be healed. *Op. cit.*, I, p. 264.

[2] *Ib.*, p. 213.   [3] *Ib.*, p. 219.   [4] *Ib.*, II, pp. 23-31.

[5] Britain henceforth is called *La Terre Gastée*, or *Terre Foraine*.

greater doom foretold, till the two Brethren, Bayln and Balan, destroy one another unwittingly—truly Adventurous Times, from which all might pray to be delivered.

The opening incidents of this story are found in the CHEVALIER AS DEUX ÉPÉES,[1] and, so far as these are concerned, it may have drawn from some unknown source which is common to both. On the other hand, the passing of Merlin through the arts of Vivien or Nivienne, that other Lady of the Lake who was the Foster-Mother of Lancelot, owes something to the Great Romance which is concerned with Lancelot's story.[2]

When the HUTH MERLIN ceases to speak of the Prophet's interment, it promises to be concerned henceforth only with the Grail ; but in the imperfect state that we possess the text it ceases to speak at all. As a final word on my own part, the fact may be cited that the Knight Pelleas is said to be one of great worship and one also of those four who achieved the Holy Grail. It follows herefrom that the missing Quest of the HUTH MERLIN had grave variations from that with which we are acquainted, because it is not to be assumed that Pelleas was one of the Nine Knights, mostly unknown, who presented themselves, demanding and receiving admission, in the Temple of the Grail Castle at the term of the Holy Quest.

My readers must be dissuaded from supposing (1) that it is possible to pursue the question of these variations except in a study which would appeal only to scholarship, or (2) that for general purposes it would in any sense repay the task. The few words that I propose to offer on the subject will be reserved of necessity to a section on Spanish and Portuguese texts. We shall find that the Galahad of the false Robert de Borron is a caricature of the hero-in-chief of all the Holy Quests and that he shews in the same distorted light under which he appears in what is called the cyclic Romance of Tristram, to the consideration of which I proceed in the next but one section.

III

THE PROPHECIES OF MERLIN

THOSE who know—as should all literate persons—the ever famous Geoffrey of Monmouth and his HISTORIES OF THE KINGS OF BRITAIN[3]—HISTORIA REGUM BRITANNIÆ—will remember that Book VII of that enchanted Chronicle is concerned with the PROPHECIES OF MERLIN and that it incorporated a Latin tract which preceded the HISTORIA under the title of LIBELLUS

[1] A Metrical Romance of the early thirteenth century, edited by Wendelin Foerster, Halle, 1877.
[2] She was the daughter of a King of Northumberland.
[3] Readers who may shrink from the Latin original may be recommended the limpid translation of Dr. Sebastian Evans, which is available to all and sundry in EVERYMAN'S LIBRARY.

MERLINI. The magical birth of the Prophet is recited in Book VI ; and in Book VIII, which contains some further Prophecies, we learn how Merlin's arts encompassed that meeting between Uther and Ygerne or Igrayne, Duchess of Tintagel, which led to the conception of Arthur. Thereafter we hear no more of Merlin in Geoffrey's story. But a mighty brood of Prophecies was generated in later years, and on the testimony of various Romances we owe their preservation to a long succession of *notatores* or Scribes. We may be content on our own part to remember Blaise of the Borron Grail Cycle, who is first and only in that group of texts.[1] Southey said long ago, with a touch of *naïveté*, that " the Prophecies of Merlin are usually sought for to accompany the Romance "—meaning the Vulgate version—and he cites a Rouen edition in his Preface to the MORTE DARTHUR of 1817. There is, however, the *editio princeps* of Paris, *anno* 1498, which was followed " with unimportant omissions or transpositions of chapters "[2] by the following later issues : (1) Paris, 1505, third volume of the ROMANCE OF MERLIN ; (2) Paris, 1507, where the Prophecies are in the second volume ; (3) Paris, n.d., but *circa* 1510, Prophecies in the third volume : (4) Rouen, *circa* 1520, also undated ; (5) *Ib.*, n.d., but *circa* 1526 ; (6) Paris, 1526 ; and (7) *Ib.*, 1528, in the third volume.[3] Miss Paton has given us an edition of extraordinary value and interest, " leaving nothing undone "—as Southey says of Sir Walter Scott. It is based on a manuscript in the BIBLIOTHÈQUE MUNICIPALE DE RENNES and is the most notable contribution to our textual knowledge of Arthurian literature which has appeared since Dr. Sommer produced his VULGATE VERSION OF THE ARTHURIAN ROMANCES.

With the Prophecies, however, in any shape or form we are concerned only in so far as they may touch upon Grail matters ; and from this point of view they can be examined and dismissed within a brief space. We hear (1) of the strange adventures which will take place in Great Britain in the time of King Arthur, *pour la venue du Saint Greal* (Miss Paton, I, 91) ; (2) of the Lady of the Lake commending chastity to Bors, then in his youth and a *biax enfes* (*bel enfant*), because he " will be chosen by our Lord Jesus Christ for one of those who shall behold the great wonders of the Holy Grail " (227) ; (3) that the Sister of Perceval will die a virgin in the service of the good Knights, that is, Galahad, etc. (237) ; (4) of the Coronation of Galahad in the City of Sarras (249) ; (5) of a certain Pentecost and the beginning of the " Festival of the Holy Grail " (323) ; (6) of a Tourney proclaimed by Arthur at the request of the Rich King Fisher, because he knew that on this occasion the Grail would be seen at the Royal Court—a glimpse for one moment behind the scenes of Corbenic and its Mystery (422) ; (7) of a Maiden sent by King Arthur to Pelles the Grail King, inquiring whether a particular valiant Knight " can be he who will fulfil the Adventures of the Grail ", and of Pelles' reply " that he probably is not

---

[1] See Miss Paton's study on the Scribes in LES PROPHECIES DE MERLIN, II, pp. 301–327.
[2] *Op. cit.*, I, p. 40.   [3] *Ib.*, I, pp. 39, 40—summarised in the text above.

himself the Grail Hero, but that he may beget him "—indicating the purpose beforehand on the part of the Grail King (434) ; (8) of the valorous Knight Segurant and his disenchantment by the power of the Grail—an episode otherwise unknown (442). Galahad, the Perfect Knight, appears on times and occasions but in connection with events that are more than familiar in the LANCELOT and the QUESTE. We hear, for example, (1) of the Sword fixed in the *perron*, a weapon which none could draw forth save he (1, 206) ; (2) of his beauty above that of all other Knights (226) ; (3) of a precious stone in the crown which Galahad is destined to wear when he is made King at Sarras (248) ; (4) of the wonders of Logres which are to be achieved by him (II, 132) ; but nothing is added even in the way of decoration, nor is there any suggestion which increases the significance of things and episodes. The Prophecies are also not without interest for the character and Quest of Perceval, mainly in connection with Galahad but also—by inference —for his own individual achievement, as recorded in the Didot-Modena texts. It is almost needless to say, having regard to the MERLIN in which the Prophecies are, so to speak, embedded, that the CONTE DEL GRAAL might never have come into being, so utterly is it set aside in depicting the Son of King Pellinor.[1] Perceval is *virgo intactus* through-out and always : he comes forth as such at his birth and so remains to the end, in order " to achieve the High Quest of the Holy Grail " *et s'en ira avecques le bon chevalier es parties de Jerusalem* (I, 237). Although tacitly rather than otherwise, Perceval is characterised by the same virtue in the Didot-Modena Quest, and Miss Paton cites an instance when the author of the PROPHECIES had this text in his mind, that is to say, when a certain *Sage Clerc* committed to Perceval a " valued book of Merlin ", being the Record of those Prophecies which had been written down by the Hermit in question. This took place at the Court of King Arthur (I, 231), and subsequently the prayers of Perceval are instrumental in saving the *Sage Clerc* from destruction in some pro-longed magical experiments which need not be specified here, as they do not belong to my subject, approximately or remotely (231–236). Readers of Southey's Preface, already cited, may remember his refer-ence, by which it appears that the *Sage Clerc* " was a very remarkable personage, who travelled through the air, over land and sea, upon a huge stone, having a devil in its centre like the kernel of a nut. This devil was the unlucky fiend who had Merlin for his son ; and it is to his credit that he speaks well of a son so unlike himself and all his father's family " (MORTE DARTHUR of 1817, pp. xiii, xiv). Occasional adven-tures and deeds of arms on the part of Perceval are to be found in other MSS. of the Merlin Prophecies, outside that of Rennes, and they are summarised by Miss Paton (I, 380–382, 387, 388, 390) ; but it would be idle to speak of them here.

The Prophecies contain no record of a Grail Quest achieved ; Perceval

---

[1] Perceval is the son of Pellinor according to the Vulgate Cycle, but the son of Alain according to that of Robert de Borron.

is with us continually, but seldom to our real purpose, except in
didactic description ; Bors appears from time to time : we are
present, for example, at his Knighting by a Son of the Rich Fisher who
is dwelling in a Hermitage but has not yet assumed a Hermit's garb
(I, 410–412, from Miss Paton's SUMMARIES OF EPISODES IN THE MSS.
OF GROUP I).   This has been brought about by the Lady of the Lake,
who counts Lancelot, Lionel and Bors as her *trois enfants* (I, 485).   It is
the only episode that calls for mention here.   As in the LANCELOT and
QUESTE, Palamèdes follows the Questing Beast (I, 377, 435, and II, 260,
261) and might be following him still so far as the Prophecies are
concerned, as he reaches no term therein.   Joseph of Arimathæa is
the " noble chevalier " who took " our Lord Jesus Christ from the true
Cross " (I, 198), and the Lord sent him to England with the Dish—
escuelle—containing His Precious Blood (307).   Joseph II is Bishop
of Sarras, consecrated by Christ Himself (198), and he accompanies his
Father for the conversion of England, the overthrow of idols and the
building of Christian Churches (307).

Miss Paton reminds us (II, 325) that, according to the Didot-Modena
texts, Merlin had Perceval under his special protection ; that he was
throughout his " fairy guardian " ; that he knew of him " long
before his birth " ; that he " created the Round Table and destined the
Perilous Seat for him " ; that he " guards him on his way to the Grail
Castle " and leads him to achieve the Quest.   But the Prophecies come
out of the Vulgate Cycle and in all their Arthurian references return
continually thereto.   The Quest for them is therefore the Quest of
Galahad, and they are for myself at least an eloquent testimony to
the influence and importance of that crown of the Grail literature.
This is their office, and it is for this reason that I have included the
PROPHECIES OF MERLIN among the later texts of the general Grail
Cycle.   Miss Paton has proved that the Rennes MS. is of Italian origin
and probably the work of a Venetian.   In the present connection her
text is the more interesting and significant on that account.   By
whomsoever written, it is certain that the author had a wide acquaintance with the Vulgate Chronicles, not to speak of the PALAMÈDES, or
its main sections, MELIADUS DE LEONNOIS and GUIRON LE COURTOIS.

IV

THE GRAIL IN THE TRISTRAM LEGEND

THE PERLESVAUS and the QUEST OF GALAHAD are sealed with
sanctity, whatever may be thought and felt and said of the
ascetic element which rules therein.   It was the way of the
world to God in those old days, but other ways have opened.
Having ceased to be a beaten track, we may see the path no longer ;
but about the quality of sanctity in these Romance Records there is no

doubt or question. So also Transubstantiation Doctrine illustrated by miraculous Masses may fill our souls with loathing, much as if we were called to witness and share in a cannibal feast ; but behind such prohibitive *signacula* some of us, at least a few, may discern the authentic *signata*, and that after all the gross symbolism is seeking in its laidly manner to shadow forth the Mystery of Divine Communication to the soul of man. We have to look at this subject later on under other aspects and in another light. Meanwhile our study of texts having brought us to the high eminence of the Grail subject, we have to survey its decadence, and the development of the Tristram Legend must be offered for consideration in the first place, because it is the descent at its beginning, and there is still some vestige of the old atmosphere, the savour of incense in the Sanctuary.

My readers may be dissuaded from supposing that we are concerned with the Legend itself, with the workings of a sorcery philtre and the amours of Tristram and Iseult. It was in great vogue in those days, and in the hands of successive editors it became a cyclic Romance which incorporated material from all quarters of the Arthurian theme, including most especially the Cycle-general of the Holy Grail. It is of no consequence to our purpose that for those who know the texts the result is heterogeneous, that the elements do not mix. Our object is only to see what happens to the Grail itself, how it fares with the Galahad and Perceval of the authentic memorials, and what new spirit abides in the Hidden Church when those who bear witness concerning it are no longer the Priests of the Mystery but ministers of a carnal synagogue. The Cup of the Eucharist has no part in love-philtres and the Host hallowed in Heaven, or by those who come down therefrom, has no part in the love-scenes betwen Tristram and Iseult. The maxim appertaining thereto is : What God has set asunder let no man join together. He shall do it at the peril of the subject, and " a story told for one of the truest and holiest that is in this world " shall be recited henceforth in brothels and in an Alsatian den of thieves.

The Cyclic Romance[1] begins with the marriage of the Sons of Brons, in accordance with the counsel given by Joseph of Arimathæa, as if the story throughout were an integral part of the matter of the Holy Grail. That Helain le Gros, who is Alain of the Metrical Romance[2]

---

[1] It should be understood that the story of Tristram was told originally in verse, by Thomas, an Anglo-Norman poet, by Béroul his successor and by Chrétien de Troyes. There are fragments remaining of the first two, but the ISEUT LA BLONDE of the third is utterly lost. The prose Romance which followed some time in the thirteenth century is represented by numerous manuscripts and by several printed editions which appeared between 1489 and 1586. The evolution of the Tristram story has been studied by Dr. E. Löseth in his excellent and exhaustive analysis of twenty-six manuscripts and several of the published texts, under the title of LE ROMAN DE TRISTAN, &c., 1890. The work embodies also an examination (1) of the ROMAN DE PALAMÈDE, to which we are indebted for the Romance of MELIADUS DE LÉONNOIS, the father of Tristram, and GUIRON LE COURTOIS ; (2) of the compilation by Rusticien de Pise, extracted from the unprinted and now imperfect PALAMÈDE. It is to be understood further that the prose TRISTRAM in all its forms is later than the Vulgate Arthurian Cycle and draws therefrom.

[2] I refer of course to the metrical JOSEPH of Robert de Borron, which is the root of all Grail Histories in the French Cycles and is presupposed by all their Quests.

and has declined to wed, is promised by Joseph the guardianship of the Vessel after his own death. It does not appear that this promise is fulfilled[1] and as a fact we hear no further concerning him. The subsidiary object is to shew that Tristram descends lineally from one of the twelve Sons, being he who is named Sadoc in the cyclic story. The early days of Tristram are recited and a version of the familiar Château Orgueilleux episode may be taken as the beginning of his adventurous life. Here as otherwhere it is the hold of Arthur's enemies, but is represented as having been demolished by Uther Pendragon and rebuilt subsequently. Its evil customs, being the treatment of prisoners belonging to the Round Table, are to be suppressed by Tristram, though only for the time being : it is foretold that the task will be resumed by Galahad and afterwards by Blioberis.[2] The Questing Beast, with whom most of us have made our acquaintance under the auspices of Malory, moves through the whole story and Palamèdes is represented as following it for fourteen years. We have seen that according to the HUTH MERLIN it connects intimately with the Grail and its Quest. On the other hand, the TRISTRAM unveils its pseudo-real story, which may be compared with the PERLESVAUS explanation. The monstrous creature is the progeny of King Ypomenes' daughter, who is enamoured of her own brother and, being repulsed by him, accepts the offers of a beautiful stranger who is in reality the devil in disguise and claims power to help her. The disgraceful episode may be left at this point adding only that all concerned therein come to an evil end.[3]

When Perceval appears on the scene he is the Squire of Agloval, who is represented as his brother. He is brought to the Court of King Arthur to receive the Order of Knighthood. This takes place accordingly and jousting follows, in which Perceval is elevated by the success that he attains and at the subsequent feasting he makes plain his ambition to occupy the Siege Perilous. At the end of a heated debate he is allowed to do so, with the result that the earth opens , the seat is suspended above the deep abyss, and he is saved vicariously in view of his genealogy and the valour of his father King Pellinor. This amazing episode is at issue with a later event, when the Silent Maiden of the other Perceval stories hails him in Arthur's Hall as Servant of Jesus Christ and as a Virgin Knight. She bids him take the Siege Perilous as one who is destined thereto and then leads him thither. When the silk which covers it is raised it is found that his name is inscribed upon it. She tells him also of another and greater occupant to come, when he—Perceval—will sit on the right-hand seat beside it

---

[1] We have seen elsewhere that the promise in question is not an invention of the TRISTRAM story. It seems obvious also from the JOSEPH poem that the logical heir of the Grail was Alain and not Brons.

[2] See *Op. cit.*, p. 56, where the forecast is furnished with details, but the task is undertaken by none of the Knights named, while nothing further is heard of the Castle itself.

[3] *Op. cit.*, p. 420.

and Bors upon the left.[1] Of such is the exaltation of Perceval ; and we hear little further concerning him—except that he is defeated on one occasion by Blioberis and is healed by the Holy Grail—till the hour of the Great Quest begins, which is that of Galahad and preserves the authentic lines, amidst commonising variants.

King Arthur knows beforehand that at the decreed Pentecost to come the great event will begin, for the consummation of the great marvels which obtain in the Kingdom of Logres and are mentioned everywhere in the texts but never described anywhere. As regards the early life of the palmary Quest Hero, it is the Fisher King himself who administers the potion to Lancelot on the night of Galahad's conception. King Pelles subsequently takes the child to an Abbey where he remains with an aunt till he is twelve years old. He is knighted by Lancelot in due course, is brought to the Court of King Arthur and occupies the Siege Perilous. Prior to this episode an election to the Round Table was made void if the name of the chosen Knight did not appear on the seat to him assigned. Galahad has many adventures, in the course of the Quest, which are unknown to the original text. They are chiefly concerned with combats in which he exhibits nothing but earthly prowess. His war-cry throughout is : CORBENIC, CORBENIC, which notwithstanding he is overthrown on one occasion ; on another the issue is doubtful ; on a third he defeats Lancelot no less than three times. He suffers imprisonment once, but is delivered speedily. To make an end of this tabulation, he does battle with two hundred knights, using one spear only and emerges victor. We hear soon after that— chronology having passed into abeyance—Charlemagne has a statue erected to the glory of Galahad. As regards the Quest itself, amidst a multitude of other adventures which do not belong to our purpose, Galahad, who just recently has prayed to behold the Secret Things of the Grail, pays a visit to King Pelles, when the latter is celebrating the anniversary of his coronation ; but nothing follows thereon, except that he meets Perceval's Sister and a Cousin of hers, who recovers her reason through the mere fact of his presence. After times and happenings he is again at Corbenic, where he heals Pelles, who is apparently the Maimed King in this version, solders the Broken Sword and asks his Grandfather to tell him the meaning of the Grail and the Bleeding Lance. The latter consents, and it will be seen that in this manner the object of the Galahad Quest is confused with that of the Perceval Cycles. King Pelles reminds him significantly that he knows it well already, which is obviously true, seeing that he was born in the Castle. The story which follows varies from the authentic version. It is a woman, for example, who receives the Precious Blood in the Paschal Dish when Christ is hanging on the Cross. The Saviour is represented also as appearing before his disciples, on the day of the first Pentecost,

[1] The base of this episode, as we have seen, is the DIDOT-MODENA PERCEVAL, which knows nothing, however, of the Silent Maiden in this connection and much less of the greater occupant to come of the Siege Perilous. See Hucher, *Op. cit.*, Vol. I, pp. 426–428.

bearing the Grail and Lance. Afterwards he delivers them to Joseph, who brings them ultimately into Britain. Finally, Galahad meets his mother at Corbenic on the great day of consummation but repulses her caresses, as if she also represented that " deadly flesh " from which he desired to be released.

Tristram takes the pledge of the Quest in his own manner, swearing to maintain it like the others for a year and a day ; but the account is disconnected, the pledge in his case seeming long subsequent to the Manifestation of the Grail at King Arthur's Court. He is delayed, moreover, by the accident of an imprisonment and thereafter falls ill. In any case he reaches Corbenic on two occasions, but to no purpose—*pour sa luxure*, as the text says. He cannot set foot in the Chapel of the Holy Grail on the first visit and on the second, when he is accompanied by Iseult, he is reproached for his disloyalty to King Mark. Under these circumstances it is not surprising that later on he bewailed the ill-starred Quest, about which it has been foretold already that it will cause his death. He dies with Iseult at the end of his story, but not on account of the Grail.

We may pray to be delivered assuredly from the Quest of Galahad according to the TRISTRAM codex ; but other Grail versions await analysis, and one of them in contrast herewith is like darkness compared with moonlight.

V

SONE DE NAUSAY

IT has been settled by the most recent voice of scholarship—or " until the times do alter "—that the vast metrical recitation which passes under this name belongs to the second half of the thirteenth century. It seems the fashion in France and England to neglect or exclude Grail texts which are or may be *post* 1250 from the canon of Grail literature. Hence it follows that the SONE DE NAUSAY—VEL NANSAI[1]— has suffered the same fate as DER JUNGERE TITUREL of Albrecht and has met with little attention, except from Miss Jessie L. Weston,[2] who adopted, developed and adapted an unconvincing thesis of Goldschmidt. He discovered supposed veridic traces of Kyot de Provence in the belated poem from the Netherlands. The SONE DE NAUSAY has been printed once only,[3] and then in the

---

[1] Nansay is Miss Weston's variant, given without explanation in her LEGEND OF PERCEVAL, Vol. II, 1909, and in ROMANIA, Vol. XLIII, 1914. In reality, however, she is following Prof. K. Nyrop and his study of the poem in ROMANIA, Vol. XXXV, 1906. I observe that Dr. Bruce ignores the revised orthography in his EVOLUTION OF ARTHURIAN ROMANCE, Vol. I, pp. 350–353. Cf. the poem itself, p. 2, ll. 41, 42, where the older spelling is in harmony with the terminal rhymes :

Terre ot en la marche d'Aussai,

Siens fu li castiaus de Nausay.
[2] See in particular the LEGEND OF PERCEVAL, Vol. II, which seems more dogmatic on the subject than the later contribution to ROMANIA, cited above.
[3] SONE VON NAUSAY, edited by Moritz Goldschmidt. Tubingen, 1899.

forbidding form which is characteristic of German antiquarian output.[1] It is by no means so dull as it looks on the crowded leaves of a Tubingen octavo series, and is indeed of no little importance for reasons which have escaped official scholarship.

The poem derives indubitably from the GRAND SAINT GRAAL in its account of the Sacred Vessel. It embodies a Conversion Legend, and he who converted Norway—the scene of action—is Joseph of Arimathæa. But it would be difficult to exaggerate the distinction between Joseph in the Metrical Romance of Robert de Borron and his reflection in SONE DE NAUSAY, where he figures as a fond old widower who becomes enamoured of a pagan princess, and is pictured otherwise performing deeds of valour as a Knight-at-arms. It follows herefrom and is manifest in additional respects that as the developed Tristram Romance represents the decadence of the Quest and its heroes, so does this poem correspond to a vulgarisation of the Grail Mythos. It is to be observed in the first place that the Sacred Vessel is divorced from its old familiar setting. There is a maimed Warden or King in the person of Joseph himself ; [2] but his healing is not postponed till some elect visitor arrives and asks an arbitrary Question which performs its work automatically. He is cured in fact by a Knight who has skill in medicine. In the second place the Grail and its future stewardship are not the term and crown offered to those who go on the Quest thereof. It is not a treasure in the hands of Hereditary Keepers belonging to a single family. It is set apart from the PARZIVAL absolutely by the fact that there are no TEMPLEISEN ; otherwise, there is no Chivalry to guard the Talisman. It is in the charge of Monks with an Abbot at their head and is kept in an ivory box.

Norway is far outside the geographical field of Grail Romance, though the Hermit of the Prologue to the GRAND SAINT GRAAL is led thither by a strange beast when in search of the Book from Heaven which contains the Grail story and has been written by Christ Himself. The fact which has no consequence and means nothing in the Vulgate ESTOIRE may have suggested his unconvincing Conversion Legend to the author of SONE DE NAUSAY. For the rest, the Round Table and its Chivalry appear nowhere, nor is Arthur mentioned in the poem. The Hallows are four in number, being (1) the Sacred Vessel itself ; (2) the Lance of Longinus ; (3) one of the candelabra carried by Angels at the Nativity of Christ ; and (4) a Processional Cross containing a True Cross Relic. As in Chrétien, the Grail in its manifestation gives forth a great light : *Tous le pays en raluma*. But it must be said of one

---

[1] It appeared as Vol. CCXVI of the BIBLIOTHEK DES LITTERARISCHEN VEREINS IN STUTTGART.

[2] He conquers Norway by the force of arms, converts the people by the sword, destroys the reigning monarch, becomes King in his place, baptises and marries his daughter, who remains a pagan at heart and hates her father's murderer. Divine punishment overtakes him for these follies ; he is stricken with complete and painful incapacity, can neither feed nor help himself, and so becomes a *Roi Mehaigné*, in imitation of the other Romances. He takes refuge also in fishing and so becomes a Fisher King (l. 4823). His healing is accounted for, however, in a single colourless line, as if God proposes but man disposes.

and all these objects that the sense of mystery is removed.[1] They are exposed before the people for worship and the Grail itself is like any other Reliquary.

Nausay—otherwise, Nansai—is identified by Gaston Paris with Nambshein in Alsace. Sone=Suennsen in Old German, according to the same authority. The hero's ancestor was Count Anseis of Brabant, who married the daughter of the Count of Flanders, and their eldest son was Lord of Nausay, as if a hereditary fief or title. At the age of twelve years and five months the lad is not only a miracle of learning, who has been instructed by four masters, but is also so well-grown that, being at the Court of the Emperor, he falls wildly in love. However, he fares so badly therein that he sets forth on his travels or adventures, passing through England, Scotland and Ireland. From Ireland he proceeded to Norway—then in a state of siege—and performed great feats of arms, defeating and driving out the combined forces of the Kings of Ireland and Scotland, described as invading Saracens. Prior to the combat the King of Norway, whose name is Alain, takes him to the Holy Island of the Grail, which is four-square, with towers at each angle and the Castle in the centre. He sees the Hallows and is girt with a Sword of Joseph,[2] the latter being Alain's ancestor and Patron Saint of Norway. With the aid of this glaive Sone overcomes the King of Scotland and slays the Irish King. He goes forth again on his wanderings, revisiting Ireland, where the people rise up against him to avenge their Ruler's death. He finds sanctuary in a House of the Templars;[3] but he comes into the presence of the Queen, who falls in love with him and ultimately bears him a son. This notwithstanding, the *wanderlust* returns and presently he is again in Norway. Alain has died and his daughter Odee is Queen in his place. The memory of Sone's valiant deeds is with her and with the Court about her. He weds Odee and himself ascends the throne. The Marriage and Consecration take place at the Grail Island, and after these Ceremonies there is a Solemn Exposition of all the Hallows. They are carried in Procession before an adoring crowd, the new King himself uplifting the Grail.

Three sons are born to the marriage and meanwhile Margon, the Master of the Irish Templars, brings to him the illegitimate boy who is the fruit of his amour with the Queen. She has attempted to destroy the child in her rage at Sone's desertion. The four are brought up together. When years have elapsed the Monarch is summoned by the

---

[1] Cf. Bruce : " The last veil of secrecy about the Grail has disappeared : the Grail Service is conducted in the sight of the whole people," etc. *Op. cit.*, I, 352.

[2] It is not any Sword which is included among Hallows of other texts but that with which Joseph defended his realm as King of Norway.

[3] It is on this basis and one other episode mentioned below and arising herefrom that Miss Weston discerns a Templar element in SONE DE NAUSAY and compares it with that in the PARZIVAL. (See ROMANIA, *loc. cit.*, p. 412.) Obviously it is nothing of the kind in either case. The alleged element in the PARZIVAL is confined (1) to the name *Templeisen* and (2) to the fact that the Grail Chivalry is clothed like the Knights Templar, a simple matter of imitation from which nothing follows. On the other hand, the SONE shews only that there was a Templar Preceptory in Ireland and that the Master or Preceptor saved the life of a child.

Pope to drive out Saracens from Italy, after which he is crowned as Emperor. His four sons, the eldest being the offspring of his Irish adventure, become respectively Kings of Sicily, Norway and Jerusalem, while the fourth is elevated to the Throne of Peter. They appear to survive him, and he himself is succeeded at his death by the son of his elder brother.

The dream of a common source for the SONE and PARZIVAL, made evident by the poems themselves, is perhaps the most slender plea which has been yet put forward to substantiate the claim on Kyot de Provence advanced by Wolfram. It lies within the limits of two points, (1) the presence in both cases of the Swan Knight Mythos[1] and (2) the alleged analogy between the vengeance of Heaven which overtook Anfortas owing to his amour with the Lady Orguelleuse and that which befel Joseph for his own second marriage. It has been well pointed out that the Swan Mythos was of general knowledge both in Germany and the Netherlands at the respective periods of the two poems ; and for the rest that there is no real connection between the liaison of Anfortas and the espousals of Joseph, which were within the law and the order. Other supposed analogies are too flimsy to excuse enumeration. They are set out at full length by Miss Weston in her contribution to ROMANIA, already cited. She was preceded by Prof. Singer in Germany[2] behind whom is Goldschmidt, who glances at the subject briefly in an introduction to the poem which he edited.

VI

VESTIGES OF THE GRAIL IN ITALY

SOME of us remember to this day, after how many lustrums, and with a certain still joy, the first rumours which reached us of old folios, done in the sixteenth century and prolonged without let or hindrance through hundreds of black-letter leaves. Some of us saw excerpts, translated out of the old French, perhaps even a summary account, or were haunted by a mere title put into free English—as it might be, " The Most Elegant, Mellifluous and Delightful History of Perceforest, King of Great Britain." Later on we were told, it may be, of that most excellent curator of a Paris Library who fled from the burning building with a single mammoth volume, crying in his triumph : *J'ai sauvé le Grand Perceforest.* We

---

[1] As regards the Mythos in the poem itself, it is never mentioned ; but a son of Sone is said to have married a cruel Lady of Bohemia, named Matabrune, in connection with whom a prose summary of the work recites the Swan Story in three considerable paragraphs—not in eight or nine lines, as Bruce suggests. Whether the anonymous précis is by the same hand as the anonymous poem is another question ; but it happens to be denied by Bruce, though he gives no reason. *Op. cit.*, I, p. 353. For the reference to Matabrune in the poem, see ll. 20807–20810, p. 538.

[2] See ZEITSCHRIFT FUR DEUTSCHES ALTERUM, Vol. XLIV, 1900, pp. 330 *et seq.*

read also in his glorious English the introduction of Robert Southey
to a certain edition of Malory's MORTE DARTHUR, and became rich in
many names of books—LANCELOT DU LAC, MELIADUS DE LÉONNOIS,
GUIRON LE COURTOIS and LA QUESTE DU SAINCT GREALL. Were we
not haunted long and even inspired perhaps when Southey told us
that the last and best of these was the favourite book of Muno
Alvarez Pereira, who " endeavouring as far as possible to imitate the
character which he admired "—Galahad, namely—" became himself,
the fair ideal of a perfect knight ". It was long after, maybe, that
we came to see these books, to find that the Holy Grail figures in the
Romance of Perceforest[1] and to learn—let us say—at long last that
PERCEFOREST, MELIADUS and GUIRON, though never drawn into
English, have existed for centuries in old Italian versions. So did
we serve our apprenticeship before making acquaintance more directly
with Tales and Legends of Arthur in the Italian Peninsula, gathering
from there and here, till the day came all recently when Professor
Edmund G. Gardner has opened a door leading into almost plenary
knowledge on this subject.[2] The *matière de Bretagne*, as it happens,
was imported into Italy too late for it to have or acquire direct bearing
on our theme, which is that indeed of Arthurian literature, but solely
and only in so far as it connects with the Holy Grail. It happens also
unfortunately that, according to Professor Gardner, the Grail story
took no root in Italian soil : " Its mysticism was of a kind alien to the
Italian genius ".[3] But this is not to say that we shall learn nothing
to our purpose by glancing briefly at how it stood with the Mythos
in that country. There is one poet and one only in the thirteenth
century who could or did claim that he knew well the Lance and the
Grail.[4] The Italian MELIADUS and GIRONE IL CORTESE were printed
in the sixteenth century but offer nothing to our subject, though we
know from the French original that Guiron belonged to the lineage of
Joseph of Arimathæa on his mother's side. These Romances are part
of a GRAND PALAMÈDE, the report of which has sounded far back in our
ears and is scarcely less talismanic than the GRAND PERCEFOREST ;

---

[1] We are told how it comes into Britain in the care of Alain, its Keeper, and performs
a miracle of healing, on which a conversion follows. Corbenic is already in existence as a
Royal Palace or Castle ; but the King of *La Terre Foraine*—otherwise, the new
convert—builds a Chapel for the Grail within the precincts and is present at a Mass
therein. He sees the Holy Grail, which is covered with red samite. Unaccountably
enough, so far as the King is concerned, Mordrains is also brought in—he who is the
Maimed King—lying on a rich bed, and he receives the Sacred Host at the hands of the
Grail Bishop Gamiel, who is unknown in the Grail Cycles. As in these, Mordrains is
waiting through the centuries the coming of him who is to fulfil the Adventures of the
Holy Vessel and to behold its Mysteries unveiled. It will be observed that the King of
La Terre Foraine is identical with him who became Alphesem in Baptism ; but it
does not appear that he is slain subsequently for sleeping in his own Castle. PERCE-
FOREST has been referred to *circa* 1350 and later. It was printed twice at Paris, in 1528
and 1531. An abridged Italian version appeared at Venice in 1556–1558. The Romance
is concerned with an age of Chivalry preceding that of the Round Table.
[2] See THE ARTHURIAN LEGEND IN ITALIAN LITERATURE, 1930.
[3] *Ib.*, p. 20.
[4] *Op. cit.*, pp. 31, 32. The poet in question was Ruggieri Apuliese. It is affirmed
further that he knew about the Round Table, Tristram and Iseult the Fair. He belonged
to the second-half of the thirteenth century.

it has never been printed in full and does not exist at this day " as an organic whole ". It was used by Rusticiano da Pisa when compiling " the earliest Arthurian Romance written by an Italian ".[1] But of this there are fragments only. The Palamède was a source also for the French PROPHECIES OF MERLIN, a work—as we have seen—which is now shewn to have been written at Venice or at least by a Venetian, between 1274 and 1279.[2] It was laid under contribution by the TRISTANO RICCARDIANO towards the end of the thirteenth century, and this has been edited at Bologna in recent days.[3] It is based on the French TRISTRAM, is unfortunately incomplete and contains no Grail allusions ; but readers of Malory[4] will remember the Weeping Castle on an Island of Giants where Christianity was preached by Joseph of Arimathæa : it appears to derive in the TRISTANO from the French source used by Malory. An unprinted TRISTANO and LANCILOTTO PANCIATICHIANO of the early fourteenth century give part of the Galahad Quest and part of the MORT ARTUS. As regards the first of these, when the Holy Grail enters the Banqueting Hall of the King's Palace it is not borne by unseen hands but is set between the horns of a white stag which is led in with chains of gold by four men in white raiment. We may compare the memorable Procession of the Grail in the LIVRE D'ARTUS, where the Sacred Vessel is carried on the back of a white stag, having a red cross on its forehead and lighted tapers on its horns.[5]

The TAVOLA RITONDA belongs to the middle of the fourteenth century[6] and is described as " the most important Arthurian Romance written in Italian,"[7] a cyclic compilation which derives from Rusticianus da Pisa, the PALAMÈDE, the TRISTANO RICCARDIANO and other sources, and includes a Tristram form of the Galahad Quest, depending from the French text but shewing variations therefrom. This also is the Grail story in decadence.

VII

SPANISH AND PORTUGUESE QUESTS

WE have seen that the migration of French Arthurian literature from its native soil into Italy is mainly of reflective interest. Possibly in the nature of things and certainly in the point of fact, it casts no light upon texts belonging to the source itself. Above all it does not help us to understand the originating mind of the Grail and its Mystery in France.

---

[1] It is, however, a compilation in French and is in fact the French MELIADUS, to which reference has been made previously.

[2] See the Introduction to Miss Paton's PROPHECIES DE MERLIN, 2 vols., 1926, 1927.

[3] See IL TRISTANO RICCARDIANO, edited by E. G. Parodi, 1896.

[4] See also MORTE D'ARTHUR, Book VIII, caps. 24, 25.

[5] See Sommer's VULGATE VERSION OF THE ARTHURIAN ROMANCES, Vol. VII, pp. 244–246.

[6] Gardner, *Op. cit.*, c. IX *passim*. The Italian text was edited by F. L. Polidori in 2 vols., 1864, 1865.　　　　　　　[7] Gardner, *Op. cit.*, p. 152.

Moreover, Italian imagination bodied forth nothing on its own part which can be called of living consequence to our subject. Even the TAVOLA VECCHIA of the TAVOLA ROTONDA compilation, which has been termed " a peculiar feature of the treatment of the Arthurian Legend in Italy ",[1] has its roots in the prose version of Robert de Borron's MERLIN. Dante has Arthurian motives ;[2] the DITTAMONDO of Fazio has allusions which can be traced to their sources in the " matter of Brittany " ;[3] Boccacio has Arthurian connections ;[4] the spirit of the Arthurian and spirit of the Carolingian Cycles were fused together under the auspices of Boiardo and Ariosto.[5] But these things belong to the great story of Italian literature and are not of our purpose otherwise.

The position is similar as regards the Spanish and Portuguese Cycles of Arthurian Romance : there is no original literature ; there are translations and imitations only. Both are of great importance for the pseudo-Robert de Borron sequence of Grail texts, and especially for its lost Galahad Quest, which is known in its French original by two fragments only, as we have seen. The GRAND SAINT GRAAL, with slight abbreviations, certain extensions and omissions, is represented by a manuscript LIVRO DE JOSEP ABARAMATIA, which ends with the conversion of Evalach. A MERLIN Y DEMANDA DEL SANTO GRIAL is on record as appearing at Seville in the year 1500 ;[6] but no known copy is extant. It is therefore a matter of speculation whether it was reprinted in LA DEMANDA DEL SANCTO GRIAL : CON LOS MARVILLOSOS FECHOS DE LANCAROTE Y DE GALOS SU HIJO, Toledo, 1515. It was divided into two parts, (1) EL BALADRO, which has been identified with a publication of Burgos in 1498,[7] and this is described as " an incomplete version of the lost CONTE DEL BRAIT," ascribed by the HUTH MERLIN to Hélie de Borron. (2) A version of the Quest of Galahad.[8] LA DEMANDA DEL SANCTO GRIAL appeared at Seville in 1535, a reprint apparently : in any case both texts are held to contain the Spanish version of the pseudo-Robert QUEST and MORT ARTHUR.[9]

Among Portuguese texts, the National Library of Vienna has a fifteenth-century manuscript entitled HISTORIA DOS CAVALLEIROS DA MESSA REDONDA ET DA DEMANDA DO SANTO GRAAL. It was partly printed by Carl von Reinhardstoettner in 1887 : a complete edition has been long promised and expected. It is held to be the pseudo-Borron QUEST indisputably.[10] There is also a sixteenth-century Lisbon

[1] Gardner, *Op. cit.*, p. 155.   [2] *Ib.*, p. 130 *et seq.*
[3] *Ib.*, pp. 222–228.   [4] *Ib.*, p. 228 *et seq.*
[5] *Ib.*, *cap.* XIII *passim.*
[6] See THE ARTHURIAN LEGEND IN THE LITERATURES OF THE SPANISH PENINSULA, by William J. Entwistle, 1925, p. 153.
[7] *Ib.*, p. 160.   [8] *Ib.*, pp. 146 *et seq.*
[9] The Spanish DEMANDA DEL SANTO GRIAL was edited in 1912 by A. Bonilla y San Martin. There was also a previous edition under the same care, published at Madrid in the first of two volumes entitled : LIBROS DE CABALLEROS. The DEMANDA is itself in two parts, being (1) IL BALADRO DEL SABIO MERLIN and (2) the DEMANDA proper, specified as describing the feats of Lancelot and his Son, Galahad.
[10] Bruce, *Op. cit.*, I, p. 470.

manuscript, referred in the text to 1313 and containing a Portuguese version of LIVRO DE JOSEP ABARAMATIA.[1] Finally there is a HISTORIA DE LANCELOTE in an unique Seville manuscript, but unprinted and undescribed, so far as my knowledge goes. We are therefore much in the same position concerning it as we are respecting a Spanish printed book called HISTORIA DE PERCEVAL DE GAULA, CABALLERO DE LA TABLA ROTONDO ET CULA ACABO LA DEMANDA Y AVENTURES DE SANTO GRIAL, of which no copy exists. It is said to have appeared at Seville in 1526, on the authority of Bonilla.[2] It was once thought to be based on the 1530 French prose version of the CONTE DEL GRAAL, but the settlement of the year of its publication in Spanish puts an end to this speculation.

It is to be understood that I am citing only texts belonging to the matter of the Holy Grail and am omitting therefore all reference to other Arthurian translations. The Tristram story was popular in Spain and Portugal and is represented by several manuscripts and more than one printed work.

I have shewn that the Galahad Quest, in so far as it enters into the cyclic version of the Romance of Tristram, is the Quest in decadence. That of the pseudo-Robert de Borron Cycle is in worse case, but I prefer to summarise its position on authority other than my own. According to Bruce, (1) the Grail theme practically disappears from view ; (2) Galahad differs from other Knights in being hardest hitter of all ; (3) Corbenic and its Spiritual Palace in the Vulgate text have lost their titles to the name ; (4) it is visited by Galahad as he might arrive at any other hospitable abode ; (5) the conception of the Grail and its Castle is cheapened further by establishing a Sorcerer in the latter ; (6) the episodes which make up the bulk of the work are like the most threadbare and extravagant among those encountered in the LANCELOT ; (7) the profoundly religious spirit of the Vulgate Quest has vanished from the imitation.[3] The views of Mr. Entwistle are equally strong and searching. As regards the Castilian DEMANDA he describes the so-called Robert de Borron as " wholly insensible to the logic of the Legend " and repeatedly turning away from it " to lose himself in a catalogue of fantastic happenings and insensate battles ".[4] The Quest is " a scatter-brained narrative which adds to the true Grail the Knight-errantries of Galahad, passages in detraction of Gawain and copious extracts from the Tristram and Palamèdes."[5] In the Portuguese DEMANDA, " nobody cares for the Holy Vessel ; nobody has any purpose save cuffs and blows. Galahad is as absurdly pugilistic as any other Knight."[6]

It remains to be noted otherwise that the witness of the Holy Grail which reached the Spanish Peninsula was of Galahad and not another. The German TEMPLEISEN, the Stone, the Hierarchy of Fallen Angels

---

[1] Bruce, *Op. cit.*, I, p. 460 ; II, p. 289.
[2] *Ib.*, II, p. 291 ; Entwistle, *Op. cit.*, p. 183.
[3] *Op. cit.*, I, pp. 470–472.
[4] Entwistle, *Op. cit.*, p. 148.
[5] *Ib.*, p. 149. See also pp. 151–153.
[6] Entwistle, *Op. cit.*, p. 165.

have no part therein. There would be a certain intellectual consolation in knowing that the Quest of Galahad passed into the life of Spanish and Portuguese Romantic Chivalry, were it not for the kind of version which drifted therein.

Before parting with the Spanish Peninsula, it shall be excused if I recur for a moment to the Provençal Kyot, for whom I have been looking all my life, since I knew anything of Wolfram, and whom I have placed among literary myths with an aching heart. We know that in 1820, on the evidence of Fr. Jayme de Villanueva, there were large collections of unedited Provençal poets in the archives of Spanish Churches. This is readily explained (1) by the intimate union between the Court of Provence and that of Barcelona; (2) by the union of the Crown of Provence and the Crown of Aragon in the person of Alphonso the Second; and it is Aragon that once at least was especially rich in such manuscripts; (3) by the popularity of Provençal poetry in Catalonia during the twelfth and thirteenth centuries. A poem breathing the Provençal atmosphere and inspired by the Provençal spirit, whether written or not in the *langue d'oc* would have drifted surely into Spain from Provence and left some trace behind it : it is for this trace that I have followed a vain quest through so many years.

There was also at one period a great movement of literature from Southern to Northern France and through Northern France to England at the time of Henry II. He married Eleanor of Guienne, who is said to have brought Provençal poets in her train. Could we suppose therefore that Kyot de Provence and his poem antedated other Grail literature, as held by some in the past, when he was regarded still as an historical personality, it would be possible to account for the subsequent appearance of the Cycles in Northern French. He has faded, however, from the fore and the background, and were it otherwise the explanation has the disadvantage of fatal facility, for Kyot, *per se*, as we have heard concerning him, seems incapable of accounting for Grail Romance outside the one text which he is claimed to have influenced in Germany. It was on an illusory assumption of this kind that the Perceval Legend was classed as Celtic by Schulz but the Grail, on the other hand, as Provencal. The Grail of Kyot is not the Grail of Northern France. The marriage of Schulz's two classes is said to have been contracted about 1150 ; but it is difficult to believe that any Sacramental Mystery had developed at that or any approximate period in Southern Romance : in any case, only a shadow of the Eucharist is found in Wolfram. The value of such a possibility is shewn by the traditional hostility to the Church of Rome on the part of most Troubadours, while the comment at large hereon is the Albigensian Crusade. After all, the analogy of Troubadour poetry with Grail literature seems exceedingly slight : if we set aside the CONTE DEL GRAAL, the love element therein is only an accident of the Cycle ; and it is totally absent from two of the highest texts. The mystical side of human love in poetry and its Provençal reflections are like a light of Moslem ecstasy.

VIII

THE DUTCH LANCELOT

WE shall find at a slightly later stage that Italian, Spanish and Portuguese texts of Arthurian Romance cast light upon those of Northern France as translations or imitations of variants now no longer extant, and that they are of importance for the same reason in respect of the Grail Cycles. As I am speaking of a great literature to those more especially who are unversed otherwise therein, it is not only desirable but needful to say something of all the branches, derivative as well as direct. The DUTCH LANCELOT demands a brief consideration from this standpoint and might indeed repay further treatment than it is possible to give here.[1] It is a compilation which is known only by a single text, and this is incomplete unfortunately, the first part out of four original divisions being now wanting. The authorship is unknown and the date of composition is speculative, though it lies somewhere between 1250 and 1350, with a preference on the part of Bruce for the second half of the thirteenth century. So far as we can judge of what is wanting, it may be said to have taken a most considerable field of Grail Romance for its province. The missing first volume must have contained, almost indubitably, the earlier life of Lancelot, while it may have included some part at least of the Quest and initial failure of Perceval at the Grail Castle. The second Book embodies adventures of Agravain, the brother of Gawain, a Knight of pride and violence ; and this is the last division of the French Prose LANCELOT, presented in metrical paraphrase.[2] It is in this section that Lancelot pays his first visit to Castle Corbenic and that the conception of Galahad is encompassed. The poem reverts thereafter to dealings with Perceval and has vestiges of a Tradition which is not extant in the Romances of Northern France. There are variations, for example, in the development of the tasks proposed by the Messenger of the Holy Grail to the Knights of King Arthur's Court.[3] Correspondences are traced (1) with diversities

---

[1] ROMAN VAN LANCELOT, edited by W. J. A. Jenckbloet, 2 vols., 1846, 1849. Described by Bruce as a " collection of Arthurian Romances." There are 87,296 lines extant.

[2] It contains in addition to its excerpt from the French LANCELOT (1) part of Chrétien's CONTE, being mainly that section which is devoted to the adventures of Gawain ; (2) the Romance of MORIEN, which has been edited separately and translated into English by Miss Weston : it is not of importance for Grail purposes ; (3) an account of Lancelot's combat with a Knight named Yder on account of a damsel's mantle : it connects with an old story of a mantle which serves as a test of chastity ; (4) an account of Lancelot and Bohort rescuing a maiden who has been bound to a tree by a gang of evil knights ; (5) a version of a French Romance entitled RICHARS LI BAUS, otherwise LE CHEVALIER À LA MANCHE ; (6) a story of Gawain and Kay ; and (7) a story derived from a supposititious French original, speculatively entitled LANCELOT ET LE CERF AU PIED BLANC. The second Book of the Dutch poem is the longest of all, comprising some 47,262 lines.

[3] The reference is to the visit of the Laidly Damsel, who comes to denounce Perceval for not having asked the all-important Question at the Grail Castle.

in the Montpellier MS. of the CONTE DEL GRAAL; (2) with the Vatican German Perceval; and (3) with Wolfram's PARZIVAL, but at a long distance. The Quest of Galahad occupies the third Book, and the fourth brings all to its term in the MORTE D'ARTHUR. The Dutch Metrical Romance is an exceedingly composite work; but a logical purpose seems to prevail throughout, combining the Perceval and Galahad Cycles of Northern France and shaping them towards a harmonious end. Among many other points there may be noted the fluidic analogy which it offers with the poem of Heinrich in its judgment on Perceval. Therein—as we shall see—the Lord of the Hallows and those by whom he was encompassed had great hopes of the latter; but because he had entered the Castle and did not ask the Question he was discarded once and for all. As regards the episodic or biographical Romance of Morien, to which I have referred in a note, he is the son of Agloval and the nephew of Perceval, and is a Black Knight, recalling Feirfeis, who is Perceval's half-brother in the Romance of Wolfram. The correspondence once suggested to scholarship a lost French poem as the source of both. Unlike Feirfeis, however, Morien is a Christian when he arrives in the realms of the West in search of his father, to whom he is in fine united and whom he causes to marry his mother according to Christian Law. It is in the course of his story that we learn as follows concerning the Holy and Sacramental Mystery :—

(1) King Arthur—who here, as otherwhere, manifests his unfailing love and anxiety for Perceval—is represented as lamenting his loss because he has gone in search of the Grail and the Sacred Lance, and because there is no news regarding him. Now, the text states—and this is on the part of the King, as if by prophecy or foreknowledge— that he will never find them, that is to say, upon earth. (2) The same conviction may have entered into the zealous heart of the Widow Lady's Son; but Sir Gareth, also a brother of Gawain, is he who announces the reason, which is not on account of his failure but because Perceval sinned in leaving his mother to die of grief at his absence. On this score he might search till the Kingdom which is above descends on the Kingdom which is below, but his pains would be his only meed. We see here that a responsibility which should be transient only and is such always in the French Cycles is pictured as permanent and insuperable : fortunately it proves in appearance only. (3) Perceval, on his part, has become convinced of his sin and has embraced the life of a hermit as the proper path of atonement. (4) But Arthur and Gareth notwithstanding, the intention of the tale is to restore Perceval forgiven to the Higher Life of Chivalry, and we have accordingly (5) a vision of Sir Agloval, who speaks of a Golden Staircase seen therein, which, by interpretation, is more than the sunbeam whereon the Grail enters in the Great Quest; for it symbolises the Sacred Vessel as another Ladder of Jacob leading to the Throne and the Kingdom, and this is also for Perceval as the days of the life of him. It followed that he should yet have his place in the Quest, and it was affirmed that

in such high service he should pass to his reward on high. That which is foretold here is of course fulfilled to the letter in the part which follows thereafter—that is to say, in the QUEST OF GALAHAD.

The DUTCH LANCELOT is in some respects that which I indicated at the beginning, an attempt to harmonise all the cycles by dealing (1) with the Quest of Perceval and its initial failure ; (2) with that of Gawain, corresponding to the Montpellier intercalation of the CONTE DEL GRAAL ; and (3) finally with the union of Galahad, Perceval and Bors, according to the plenary inspiration of the Great Quest. The DUTCH LANCELOT offers the position of a text which had every opportunity to profit in universals and not in particulars only by the poem of Wolfram ; but, though it is under the obedience of the prototype created by the CONTE DEL GRAAL for the early history of Perceval, it redeems him only at the close, by a kind of *tour de force*, in its adaptation of the story of stories.

BOOK VII

THE GERMAN CYCLE OF THE HOLY GRAIL

THE ARGUMENT

I. THE PARZIVAL OF WOLFRAM VON ESCHENBACH.—Its valuation by Recognised Criticism—Alleged Theological and Ecclesiastical Position— Evidence of the Surface Sense—Specific Analogies with French Romances of the Perceval Cycle—The Triad in the Keepership of the Grail—Geniture of Parzival—Of Gamuret and Herzeleide—Of Parzival's Cousin Sigune— At the Court of King Arthur—The Red Knight—The Brother of the Grail King—Queen Kondwiramur—The Marriage of Parzival—The Fisher King —The Castle of Mont Salvatch—The Pageant and Bewrayed Question— Of things which followed thereafter—Of Kundrie, the Grail Messenger— Parzival hardens his Heart—The Pilgrim Band—The Hermit's Story of the Grail—Parzival's Election—The King's Healing—Specific Distinctions from Romances of the French Cycle—The Morganatic Union of Gamuret—The History of Kundrie—The Magician Klingsor—Of Feirfeis, the Brother of Parzival—His Union with the Maiden of the Grail—Of Prester John—The Story of Lohengrin—The Grail in Wolfram's Poem—Its Quasi-Sacramental Connections—Its Feeding Qualities—Its Antecedent History—The Bleeding Lance—The King's Wounding—Of the Duchess Orguelleuse—The Castle and its Chivalry—The Source of Wolfram—The Story of Kyot de Provence —The Judgment on Chrétien de Troyes—The LAPIS EXILIS—Of a Second Sense in the Parzival. II. THE QUEST OF KYOT DE PROVENCE.—The Testimony of Wolfram—The Story betrays itself—Alleged Evidence of the SONE DE NAUSAY for the existence of Kyot's Poem—Failure of this Testimony—Alleged Identity of Kyot de Provence and a Bishop of Durham —What follows therefrom—The Source of Chrétien—Chrétien as the Source of Wolfram—The Religious Position of Wolfram. III. THE CROWN OF ALL ADVENTURES.—The Quest-in-Chief of Monseigneur Gawain—Heinrich and Chrétien—Heinrich and the alleged Kyot—Keynote of the Story—The House of Glass—The Companions of the Quest—The House of Death—Its Dream of Splendour—The Banquet in the Castle—The Grail Vision—The King's Sustenance—Wine of Forgetfulness—The Question Asked—The Hidden Secret—The King's Release—The Vanishment of the Grail—Conclusion as to this Quest. IV. THE TITUREL OF ALBRECHT.—Literary History of the Poem—The Incorporations from Wolfram—Its Reversion to the Cycle of Northern France—The Grail as a Chalice —Pretensions of the Poem as a complete History of the Sacred Vessel and its Wardens—Religious and Ecclesiastical Aspects—Removal of the Grail to the Land of Prester John— Subsequent Removal of the Ancient Sanctuary—Parzival as the Heir of the Priest-King—The King's Legend—King Arthur's Search for the Grail. V. THE GRAIL IN DESECRATION.—How the Talisman became a Place— The Other World of Heroes—A Heathen Earthly Paradise—The Grail and Juno—The Grail and the Paradise of Venus—The Venusberg—The Grail Diabolised.

257

THE GERMAN CYCLE OF THE HOLY GRAIL

I

THE PARZIVAL OF WOLFRAM VON ESCHENBACH

THOSE who in recent times have discussed the poem of Wolfram with titles to consideration on account of their equipment have been impressed not alone by the signal distinctions between this German poem and the Perceval Legends as we know them in Northern France, but by a superiority of spiritual purpose and a higher ethical value which are held to characterise the knightly epic. For the moment, at least, it can be said on my own part that we are in the presence of a poet whose work is full of gorgeous pictures, all rude diction notwithstanding, and all contemporary reproaches made upon that score. To me—but as one who on such subjects speaks with a sense of remoteness—the traces of Oriental influence seem clear in the poem, partly in its decorative character and partly in its allusions to places—after every allowance has been made for geographical confusions. Such traces are admitted, and they are referred to the source of Wolfram, about which I must say something in this section to introduce the separate inquiry which will follow hereafter. But we are asked in our turn to recognise that the PARZIVAL is the most heterodox branch of the whole Grail Cycle, though it has been said to be the work of an ecclesiastic. The major proposition is put forward in authoritative statements on the part of scholars who have scarcely produced their evidence, and in sporadic discursive remarks on the part of some other writers who could have been better equipped. In this manner we have (1) the negative inference drawn from a simple fact—as, for example, that the PARZIVAL does not exhibit such hostility towards Mohammedan people and things as characterised Crusading Times—but as much might be said about other texts of the Grail ; (2) the positive opinion that the Chivalry of the Grail Temple resembles an association formed without the pale of the Church rather than within—which on the authority of the poem itself seems untrue, and this simply. Those who expound these views look for an explanation to the influences exercised theoretically by Knights Templar and the Sects of Southern France—which possibilities will be considered in their proper place in respect of all the literature. As a preliminary, by way of corrective, I desire to record here that if the PARZIVAL is heterodox, its elements of this order have been imbedded below the surface, and then deeply ; but whether it implies in this manner any secret religious claims which are not of normal Sect or Heresy is another question. On the surface it would be easy to make a tabulation of many points which manifest an absolute correspondence with Church Doctrine and Ordinance ; but it will be sufficient for the moment to say that Mass is celebrated and heard as it is in the other Romances ; that Baptism is the first gate to be opened by or for those who would see the Grail ; that Confession is not less necessary ; while so far as there is allusion in particular to dogmatic teaching, that it is of the accepted kind, as of the conditions and day of salvation : Mary is the Queen of Heaven, and the Lord Jesus dies as Man on the Cross ; the Divinity of Three Persons is included in one God. Sometimes there is an allusion which looks dubious, but it is mere confusion, as when a Hermit speaks of a soul being drawn out of hell, where the reference is of course to the purgatorial state.

The story of the Quest in Wolfram may be considered in the interests of clearness under two heads, the first of which is designed to develop the specific analogies with other Romances of the Perceval Cycle, and especially the CONTE of Chrétien, while in the second there are exhibited the specific points of distinction. As regards the analogies, it is to be understood that I reserve the right to omit any or every episode which does not concern my ultimate purpose. It is to be understood further that all analogies are under their own reserve in respect of variation. Let it be recalled, in the first place, that the historical side of the Perceval Legend in the CONTE DEL GRAAL of Chrétien is in a certain state of confusion. . That poet left so much to be desired on the score of clearness about the early life of his hero that another poet prepared some antecedent information ; but he spoke according to tradition and forgot that the matter with which he intervened was not in complete accordance with Chrétien's own account, so far as he had gone. All continuations of the CONTE were either too late for Wolfram or were for some other reason unknown by him : but it has been held that Wauchier and Manessier produced their romantic narratives following several prototypes, not of necessity connected with their character-in-chief, *ab origine symboli*. Gerbert was either under the obedience of a prototype peculiar to himself in the Northern French Cycles or he invented much and greatly, unless anyone can suffer at this day the suggestion that he derived from the dubious Kyot de Provence, of whom we shall hear shortly at length. In any case he knew something of the Lorraine Epic Cycle and its Legend of the Swan Knight. With the DIDOT-MODENA PERCEVAL Wolfram has only those points of concurrence which belong to any common primordial source, and with the PERLESVAUS or LONGER PROSE PERCEVAL his features of likeness are in so far as both texts stand together by themselves. Under these qualifications, the salient lines of correspondence by way of likeness with the French Cycle may be collected as follows.

The genealogy in the PARZIVAL is simple : it is the triad, which is permanent on earth as the Holy and Undivided Trinity is eternal in Heaven. But in most texts the Trinity of the Grail Keepership is by way of succession and therefore the analogy is thin. Wolfram, on the other hand, ends with a perfect symbol in the union of those who have reigned with him who shall reign henceforward, whereas all other Quests of Perceval leave him alone in his kingdom at the end absolute of the great adventure. The German Kings of the Grail are Titurel, Frimutel and Anfortas. The first is the founder of the dynasty—in respect of the Grail Keepership—and he remains alive, like Brons in Robert de Borron, the maimed King Pellehan in the QUEST OF GALAHAD, and that nameless hidden sovereign who anteceded King Fisherman in the CONTE DEL GRAAL.[1] The second has died in war, which was not in the cause of the Grail, and it is partly for this reason that Perceval must intervene to renew the triad. The nearest analogy to this is in the DIDOT-MODENA PERCEVAL, which after the achievement of the Grail pictures the Questing Knight abiding in the place of the Hallows with Blaise and Merlin as two substituted Keepers, though at the close it detaches the prophet and puts him into mystic retreat, as if at the term of the ages—when Avalon gives up its exiles —he might again manifest and testify. There is also another analogy, but this is of the implied kind, for in the PARZIVAL and the DIDOT-MODENA PERCEVAL he who has achieved the Quest remains, and the Sacred Vessel—in apparent perpetuity—that is to say, in the House of the Hidden Hallows. Both Elect Knights—shadows of a single personality—arrived, that they might stay in fine.

The father of Parzival was a King's Son—as he is occasionally in the other Romances—and it is said in more than one place that he came of faërie lineage. In the natural order he was, however, a Prince of Anjou. It was on the Mother's side that the youth was by generation a Scion of the House, and entitled therefore, supposing that he was prepared otherwise, to return therein. She was Herzeleide, Sister of the Grail King and Queen in her own right of Wales and Norgales. The father—who had been married previously in the East—was named Gamuret ; but in the course of Knightly Adventure he was slain shortly after the birth of his only Son in respect of the second union. That he may be saved from the violent end which in those days was involved by the Life of Chivalry, there follows—with many variations—the concealment of Parzival by his Mother in the wild places and woodlands. It does not appear what she did to insure the rule of her kingdoms, including the heritage of her Son, but the result was that the three countries fell into other hands. She who had been born an inbred Daughter of the Holy House might have acted better and more wisely to have reared her Son—in the spirit and intention at least—as a

---

[1] Potvin : CONTE DEL GRAAL, II, pp. 260, 261.

child of the Sacred Talisman instead of a wild boy of the woods, denied
all knowledge of God in his early years. Far otherwise than she did the
twice-born Hermit Nasciens, who had Galahad in his keeping ; far
otherwise did they of the White Abbey, among whom Galahad was
found by Lancelot. But the fatality was working with greater power
because she strove the more ; Parzival met all the same with Knights
of King Arthur's Court, and rode forth as usual—not with her consent
indeed, but with the dangerous folly of her cautions—in search of the
Order of Chivalry. Almost immediately after her parting with
Parzival, she died in the grief of his loss. He, as in other stories,
reached the pavilion of the Sleeping Lady, and he took not her ring
only but also a buckle. In this instance she seems to have been
unwilling throughout, and the youth behaved brutally.[1]

Before reaching the Court of King Arthur he met with his Cousin
Sigune, and it should be noted here that there is no Sister in this
version of the Quest. Of her he learned his proper name and so much
of his genealogy as was requisite to assure him that he was the legitimate
King of North Wales, in the defence of which right there perished her
own lover, whose body remained in her charge after the mad manner
of the Romances.

As geographical names signify little or nothing, the Court of King
Arthur was held at Nantes, and on the youth's arrival thither we meet
with the old episode of the Maiden who could not laugh until she
beheld the Best Knight in the World.[2] She was struck and insulted
by Kay for paying this honour to one of Parzival's outlandish appearance, and a considerable part of the story is concerned incidentally—
like the CONTE—with the youth's resolution to avenge her and a certain
Silent Knight who, after the manner of the dwarfs, found speech to hail
his advent and was also chastised. The Red Knight is on the scene, as in
the CONTE, and Parzival—whom Arthur has knighted—obtains his
armour. The story is the old story, that the Knight had taken a cup
from the Round Table and spilt wine upon the robe of the Queen.
But the secondary detail was a matter of accident and one regretted
deeply, for in this story only the Red Knight is a hero after his own
true manner : he is also the youth's kinsman, and his death—which
occurs as previously—is a stain on Parzival rather than to the glory of
his prowess.

So proceeds the story, and so far as it follows the long weariness
of the worn way, even its decorations can lend it only a secondary
interest. I think also, and it must be said, that even in his exaltation
the hero kindles little sympathy, whereas Galahad enthrals for ever.
The next incident in our scheme is Parzival's Instruction in Chivalry,
which took place at the Castle of Gornemanz, who was a Brother of
the Grail King, though this relation was not declared to his pupil.
Like Gonemans de Gohort[3] in the CONTE, he is responsible for the

---

[1] Cf. Potvin, *Op. cit.*, II pp. 62–67.
[2] *Ib.*, pp. 76 *et seq.*, to the death of the Red Knight.   [3] *Op. cit.*, p. 104.

fatality of the unasked question, and in both cases there is the same want of logic on the surface, whether or not it covers a secret intention. The result otherwise of the instruction was that Parzival ceased from his folly.

The experience completed, he asked his teacher at their parting to give him his Daughter when he had done something to deserve her ; but it appears to have been more in conformity with her father's implied wish than through a keen desire of his own, and we hear nothing further of either. His next task brought him to Belrepaire— in siege by sea and land and wasted by famine. There he succoured the Queen Kondwiramour, who corresponds to Blanchefleur,[1] and there also he married her. We are now in that region which we know to have been travelled by Gerbert,[2] and as for him the espousals left the lovers in virginity, so, according to Wolfram, the marriage was not consummated till the third night. But—whereas a high motive actuated the two parties in the French Romance—in the German poem there was no mutual concordat but a kind of spurious chivalry on the hero's side which he overcame in the end. Few, however, were the days reserved to love : the voice of duty called the Son to see how it fared with his Mother, and Parzival set forth. But the Mother was dead ; the purpose fades away ; he meets with the Fisher King, whose Castle is close at hand, like all things that are greatest. As regards his qualifications for the visit, it would seem that, even in the Holy Place, he thought chiefly of knightly combats and wondered how he should find them in such surroundings. The Fisher King was Anfortas, the Maimed King, and the Procession was that which I have described previously, at needed length. The Castle was full of splendour and Chivalry, but it was full also of sadness : the story is one of suffering and sorrow. The relation between Host and Guest was that of Uncle and Nephew ; but as usual it did not transpire on this occasion. Parzival failed also to ask the vital Question ; but it should be noted that, although grievous sin is attributed to him on this account, he has not been warned so distinctly—either here or in the CONTE DEL GRAAL—that there would be a Question to ask as he is in the DIDOT-MODENA PERCEVAL. He went forth unserved from the Castle ; but there is no suggestion of any external enchantment, nor did he find that the whole country had been laid under a mysterious interdict which had rendered it utterly waste, or that the inhabitants were abandoned to various forms of distress. On account further of the normal offices of Nature, it is to be understood that he left the Castle as a Knight who has finished his visit—that is to say, he rode away : it was not the Castle which left him by a sudden process of vanishing.[3] In the world outside he was reproached by his kinswoman Sigune, who still had the body of her lover.[4]

The familiar pursuant adventures must be mentioned briefly. The

---

[1] Cf. Potvin : CONTE DEL GRAAL, II, pp. 98 et seq.

[2] Ib., VI, pp. 189–213. Cf. Miss Mary Williams' complete text of Gerbert, Vol. I, pp. 191–215, ll. 6225–7020.

[3] See Potvin, Op. cit., II, pp. 142–154.   [4] Ib., pp. 154–163.

Lady of the Pavilion was exonerated fairly by Parsifal[1] and sent with her vanquished spouse to the woman who could not laugh at the Court of King Arthur, where she proved to be the Knight's Sister, so that Kay was put to shame. Arthur rose up and set forth on the quest of Parzival, who was found in the love-trance of Chrétien's poem and brought to the royal tent. There he was made a Knight of the Round Table, and thither came the laidly Kundrie—that baleful messenger of the Grail, who was also God's minister—to curse and denounce him for his ill-fated course at the Castle.[2] She told him much which belongs to another branch of our subject, but also of his Mother's death, by which news he was overwhelmed, and by the shame of the messenger's wrath tempestuous. He departed from that Court as a man who had lost his faith, yet he went—*pro forma* at least—on the Quest of the Grail. After long wanderings he met again with his Cousin Sigune, whose lover had found a sepulchre, near which she lived as an Anchoress and received food from the Grail, brought her by the Sorceress Kundrie. At a later period, Parzival, being still in his sins, and cherishing no thought of God, encountered the pageant of pilgrims on Good Friday; but his better nature did not return to him so quickly as in the other stories.[3] In due course he reached the hold of a Hermit, who—here as there—was his Uncle, to whom he confessed everything and from whom he learned—subject to certain variations—the story of the Grail in full.[4]

When he is heard of next in the poem, the chance of war had brought Parzival in collision with Gawain, and they failed to recognise each other until the latter suffered defeat. The victor was restored in this manner to the Court of King Arthur, passing henceforth to and fro between that world and the more external world of adventure. To the Court on a certain occasion, with no preface or warning, again there came Kundrie, Sorceress and Messenger, carrying the news of Parzival's election to the Holy Kingdom of the Grail.[5] Thereat he rose to his feet and recited the secret story of the Great Palladium, as he had learned it from the lips of the Hermit. He told how none could attain it unless he was called thereto; and in virtue of that calling, in his own case, he took leave of the Chivalry for ever. He reached the Consecrated Castle, beheld the Hallows therein, and asked the necessary question, to the King's healing and the joy of those who were delivered from the thrall of his long suffering.

I have left out of this summary all but one reference to Gawain, who occupies a third part of the whole story, and whose marriage is celebrated therein. He undertook the Quest of the Grail, and though much followed thereupon in the matter of High Adventure he did not attain the term. To say this is to indicate in one word an important point of difference between this text and the post-Merlin stories of the Vulgate Cycle. There are other variations, but I will mention this only, that

---

[1] Potvin, *Op. cit.*, pp. 163–185.   [2] *Ib.*, pp. 200–203.
[3] *Ib.*, pp. 254–257.   [4] *Ib.*, pp. 258–264.
[5] Cf. the CONTE DEL GRAAL, Potvin, VI, pp. 149, 150.

I may have done with any extraneous matter ; it concerns the character of Gawain, which is one of knightly heroism and all manner of courtesy and good conduct.   Wolfram knew nothing apparently of that later fashion of calumny which was set by the ROMANCE OF LANCELOT.

The reader is now in a position to understand how far this summary corresponds with the general outline of Chrétien and with the brief Quest in the DIDOT-MODENA PERCEVAL.   At a later stage of our research, he will trace also certain salient analogies with the WELSH PEREDUR, and, in a lesser degree, with the English SYR PERCYVELLE.   In fine, he will see that so far as the schedule reaches, it has no correspondence in adventure with the LONGER PROSE PERCEVAL, which is the second part only of a Knightly Quest or a supplement thereunto, though the two Romances converge—as suggested previously—in the path of their greatest divergence from other texts.   We have now to establish the points of distinction in the PARZIVAL—which are a much more serious question—and I shall do so under three subdivisions, the first of which will deal with romantic episodes, the second with the Grail itself, including its concomitants in symbolism, and the third with the source of Wolfram, thus leading up to the considerations of my next section.

A morganatic union was contracted by the Father of Parzival, prior to his Marriage with Herzeleide, as one consequence of a journey East-ward in search of adventure.   He was the means of salvation to a heathen Queen Belakané, whom he wedded and whose throne he shared for a period.   It may be advanced that this union was not one which the Church would recognise ; but Gamuret is not exculpated, because it is quite clear that he had every opportunity to convert her and to lay the Christian Religion like a yoke on the neck of her kingdom.   He would be responsible therefore for not making the attempt, an episode which does not correspond to a high sense of Christian duty at the period ; while his subsequent Marriage—which is not challenged by the poet—would be thought little less than disgraceful if the hypothesis of scholarship had not allocated the poem of Wolfram to so high an ethical level.   The fruit of the first union was the pagan Prince Feirfeis, who, being born in the East under such circumstances, is harlequined— that is to say, is represented as half black and half white, to indicate his dual origin.   The death of Gamuret was the result of a second visit to the East.   He heard that Baruc the King of Bagdad was beset by the Princes of Babylon, and having served him in his youth he was impelled to go forth to his rescue.   In one of the ensuing battles he took off his helmet and laid down for a few moments on account of the heat.   A Pagan Knight poured thereon the blood of a he-goat, and that which was previously like diamond in its hardness became soft as sponge. The result was that the King of Alexandria cut with his spear through the helmet and penetrated the brain.

I have mentioned here the first point of distinction between the more narrative part of the poem and the other Quests of Perceval :   the second concerns Kundrie, who acts as the Messenger of the Grail.   She is

described as faithful and true, possessing all knowledge—according
to the institutes of the period—and speaking all tongues. But she was
repellent in appearance beyond the physical issues of Nature, as a
combination indeed of gruesome symbolic animals. She was a Sorceress
also, as we have seen, though this is perhaps a technical description
of the period, expressing only the sense of her extraordinary knowledge. She is not, however, to be identified with the evil side of the
powers of Avalon, concerning which we hear so much in the LANCELOT
and later Merlin texts, nor is she exactly a Fay Woman—that is to say,
the Daughter of a School of Magic—as conceived by the French
Romances, since she does not practise Magic or weave enchantments.
Her impeachment of Parzival at the Court of King Arthur turned
mainly on his failure at the Grail, and was interspersed with prophecy
which future events made void.[1] I must say that her discourse reads
only as the raving of one distracted, and that by which she was
distracted was the sorrow in the House of the Grail. As Parzival might
have disarmed her by the simplest of all explanations—being that
which he gave subsequently to the Round Table itself[2]—and as thus he
had at least his personal justification reposing in his own heart—it is
curious that he should take her reproaches so much more deeply into
his inward nature than his counterpart in the CONTE, and that he held
himself shamed almost irretrievably, though the Court did not so hold
him. The effect was greater than this, for it hardened his heart against
God and converted one who had never been ardent in faith, who had
never so far experienced a touch of Divine Grace, into an utterer of open
blasphemy. Other stories say that he had forgotten God, but in
Wolfram he remembers and rebels.

The PARZIVAL does not give us an intelligible history of Kundrie ;
it does not explain why the Messenger of the Grail was or had become
unlovely ; or why it connects, however remotely, that Sacred Object
with one whom it terms a Sorceress.[3] We see only that she comes and
goes as she pleases, or is commissioned thereby, in and about the Holy
House : she carries the palliatives administered to the wounded King
to a place where they become available for Gawain, and she brings—
as we have seen—the Food of the Grail to Parzival's Cousin, Sigune,
after her lover is buried and she has become a recluse in a hermitage
beside his sepulchre.

[1] He was (1) sealed, signed and delivered to the hands of hell ; (2) the future horror
of heroes ; (3) one who would be the scourge of happiness ; and (4) so diseased in honour
that no physician will have the power to heal him. Cf. the " laidly Damsel " of the
CONTE DEL GRAAL, from which all this is imitated and exaggerated. Potvin, *Op. cit.*,
II, pp. 200–203.

[2] He cited, that is to say, the warning against loquacity and impertinent questions
received from his instructor Gornemanz at the beginning of his career. There is no
parallel justification offered in the CONTE.

[3] It is said only at a later stage that she and her Brother, who is not less hideous
than herself, were gifts to the Grail King on the part of a Queen Secundilla, the Pagan
wife of Feirfeis, whose rivers flow with jewels and whose mountains are of gold.—
PARZIVAL, Book X. Having regard to her Consecrated Office, it is obvious that this
explains nothing and is indeed a hindrance rather than a help. Cf., however, the
Prester John Mythos, which will be examined at a later stage.

The intervention of a problematical Magician named Klingsor in the story leaves us also in doubt as to what he represents in the scheme. He came of the race of Vergil—whom Mediæval Tradition presents as a potent enchanter—and was originally a duke of noble life till he was ensnared by unholy passion, for which he was visited heavily, being deprived of the instruments of passion. Those who know anything of Occult Traditions will be aware that this affliction would have been an almost insuperable barrier to his success in Magic ; but Wolfram, who knew only by hearsay, and then at a very far distance, says that he became a Magician by his maiming, meaning that he visited the Secret City of Persida, the Birthplace of Magic—on its averse side apparently —and received initiation in full, so that he could work all miracles. He erected a Keep of Wonders, which is a sort of contradiction, in terms of diabolism, to the Castle of the Holy Grail, as his own life is an analogy by travesty of that of the King of the Grail, who had sinned also in his senses, at least by the desire of his heart.[1] CHATEAU MERVEIL, however, seems to lack intention, for the Magic which built it was not proof against the personal bravery of Gawain, who put an end to the enchantments and became Lord of the fortress. It should be added that Klingsor himself does not appear in the poem, so that he is like a King in hiding.

There is little cause to delay over the history of Feirfeis, the brother of Parzival, who came with a great host Westward in search of Chivalry and his Father, only to learn that the latter was dead when he and Parzival had nearly slain each other. Feirfeis married before leaving his native land ; but as Wolfram von Eschenbach begins his knightly epic with one cruel adultery, so he ends it with another, eclipsing his previous record by uniting Feirfeis, within the sacred walls—after his Baptism— to the pure and wonderful Maiden who through all her virgin days had carried the Holy Grail. Now, I pray that God may preserve us from these high ethical values which we have known under rougher names. To make bad worse, when the wedded pair proceed on their journey Eastward, the news of his first wife's death is brought to Feirfeis, which soothes and gladdens the quondam Grail Lady, though it seems a poor satisfaction. I have read some weird criticisms which are designed to depreciate it, but—while God continues willing—I set my own heart on the QUEST OF GALAHAD. In fine, as regards this Marriage the issue was a Son, who received the name of John the Priest—that is to say, Prester John, the great, legendary, sacerdotal, Christian King of the farthest East, the rumour concerning whom went forth over Europe at the end of the twelfth century.

After the union of all the characters of the story—who are within the sphere of election—at the Castle of the Grail, which, as in Chrétien

---

[1] See *ante*, Book VI, sect. 1. As stated there, in my study of the PERLESVAUS, there is a curious correspondence between Klingsor, the Magician of Wolfram, and that King of Castle Mortal who sold God for money. It does not appear, however, that he was evil *ab origine* by Nature, like the Brother of the Rich Fisher in the particular French Romance.

so here also, is never the HOLY GRAIL, the poet passes to the history of Lohengrin—the Son of Parzival and Kondwiramour. He became the Knight of the Swan, whose Legend was transferred by Wolfram from what is termed the Lorraine Epic Cycle. We shall hear further concerning him and the transmission of the Sacred Talisman to Prester John in the YOUNGER TITUREL, of Albrecht. Kardeiss, the second of Parzival's twin Sons, was crowned in his infancy as King of those countries which were the more earthly heritage of his Father.[1]

A few matters of lesser importance may be grouped here together : (1) There is an account of the Mother of King Arthur which is the reverse of the other Legends : it is related that she fled with a clerk who was versed deeply in Magic—one would have thought a reference to Merlin, who otherwise at least is unknown to Wolfram. The reference, as a fact, is to Klingsor. Arthur is said to have pursued them for three years.[2] (2) There is no Siege Perilous and no reference to Lancelot. (3) Parzival is elected to his Kingdom by the fiat of the Grail itself. (4) The mystic Question in Wolfram seems to be the most natural and ineffective of the literature, its words being : What aileth thee here, mine uncle ? (5) It is essential that this Question should not be prompted ; but Parzival's Uncle on the Mother's side gives him the information in full and so makes void the condition ; yet Parzival asks in the end, and all is well with the King.

I pass now to the matter of the Grail itself, to the Hallows—imputed or otherwise—connected therewith, and the subsidiary subjects, in so far as they have not been treated in the considerations of the Second Book. It will clear the important issues in respect of implicits if I say that in the German Cycle there are no Secret Words, there is no strange Sacerdotal Succession, while the religious side of the Mystery is distinct, and so utterly, from that of the French Romances. The Grail is not a Chalice—and much less a Chalice containing the Blood of Christ : it is a Stone, but this is not described specifically when it is first beheld by Parzival. It is carried on a green cushion and is laid on a jacinth table over against the Warden. It is called the Crown of all Earthly Riches, but that is in respect of its feeding properties, of which I shall speak presently. It is not termed a Stone, which is the current account regarding it, till the Knight hears its history from the lips of his Uncle Trevrezent. The names which are then applied to it are Pure and Precious, *Lapis exilis*[3] (literally, *Lapis exilix*, but this is a scribe's mistake and is nonsense), and it is

---

[1] We do not learn how they came back into his possession.

[2] It came to nothing at the time ; but in Book XIII Arthur and his host reach the Keep of Wonders after its conquest by Gawain, and there the King meets his Mother, with no particular astonishment on either side. She has been long held in durance by Klingsor. It is to be noted that the root-matter of the Keep of Wonders, Château Merveil, is of French origin.

[3] It may be noted that this title is given to the Stone of Alchemy in a citation under the name of Arnoldus. It is the only instance that I can remember in the literature of the subject. See Mangetus : BIBLIOTHECA CHEMICA CURIOSA, 1702, II, p. 88.

also that Stone which causes the phœnix to renew her youth. No
man can die for eight days after he has seen it, and—although this
virtue is forgotten in the case of Titurel, who is described as an ancient
of days—those who can look on it daily remain in the appearance of
youth for ever. It is subject, apparently to a periodical diminution
of virtue, and it is re-charged like a Talisman every Good Friday by the
descent of a Dove from Heaven carrying a Sacred Host : she deposits it
thereon, and so returns whence she came. It follows that the Mystery
of the PARZIVAL suggests an Eucharistic Mystery, although at a far
distance, seeing that it never communicates Supersubstantial Bread.
What it does distribute actually we have learned elsewhere ; for at the
supper-table in the Castle it acts as an inexhaustible larder and superb
hotch-pot, furnishing hot or cold, wild and tame, with the wine-cups of
an eternal tavern. As a peace-offering to the rational understanding,
there is a vague suggestion that the Stewards of the Castle provide
the salt, pepper and sauces. Wolfram von Eschenbach describes this
abundance as (1) earthly delight in the plenary realisation thereof,
and (2) joy which he is justified in comparing with the glories of
heaven's gold bar. Long researches dispose the heart towards patience
—perhaps because of their weariness : let me be satisfied therefore
with repeating the bare fact that this story is supposed, by those who
know, to be the High Spiritual Quest of all, on which authority I am
casting about me for the arch-natural side of an alderman's dinner.
The writing on the Grail Stone might well be : *esurientes implevit bonis*.

   The sacred character of this wonderful object—which solves for those
who are called the whole difficulty of getting a material living—is
explained by the antecedent part of its history. It was brought to this
earth by a company of fallen angels, who gave it into the charge of
certain baptised men, the first of whom was Titurel. In the Northern
French Cycle the origin of the Sacred Vessel is explained in a manner
which, within its own limits, is quite intelligible : it may be almost said
to begin in Nature, though it ends in a Great Mystery. To the Cup
used by Christ at the Last Supper no unusual qualities attach ; Robert
de Borron says that it was *mout gent ;* but it is only in the sense of an
utensil at the period. This is probably the earliest description which
we have, and it is left by most of the later texts in similar comparative
simplicity. The arch-natural character resided solely in the content.
To sum up, the Paschal Dish of the Galahad Quest began on earth and
was taken to Heaven ; but the history of the German Hallow is the
converse of this : its origin is celestial, but in the end it is left on earth.
Let it be remarked in conclusion that there is no reason assigned for
the bringing of the Grail to earth, nor do we hear of its purpose or
nature prior to this event.

   The Lesser Hallows of the story have scarcely a title to the name,
as they have no connection with the Passion of Christ or any other
Sacred History. The Grail King was wounded in ordinary warfare
by a poisoned spear, and this was exhibited in the Castle, but not as a

memorial or a symbol of vengeance to come, for the heathen who smote him died at his hands in the joust. We know already that the Lance has a prodigal faculty of bleeding ; but it is to no purpose. The Sword seems to be merely an ordinary weapon of excellent quality and temper ; it was used by the King before he fell into sickness ; it is given to Parzival—as a mark of hospitality apparently ; it will break in one peril and can be made whole by the virtues of a certain spring, which comes to pass later.[1] No Dish is specified as part of the Official Procession ; and the two silver knives, though they have a certain history, for they were made by the smith Trebuchet, serve only a surgical purpose in connection with the King's sufferings.

As regards these, we know that the sin of Anfortas, for which he has been punished full long and in which he awaits the help of the Mystic Question, was a sin of earthly passion. The Grail is an Oracle in Wolfram, as it is in Robert de Borron, but according to the latter it spoke, while here it writes only. In this manner it calls maidens and men from any place in the world to enter its service ; but the maidens it calls openly and the men in secret. It appoints also the Successor of the Reigning King and the Wife whom he must take unto himself. With his exception, a life of celibacy is imposed on all the Chivalry of the Castle. With the women it seems to have been different ; but those who married went out into the world. The sin of Anfortas, which led to his grievous wound, was—as I have just said—a sin of earthly passion, but not apparently of that kind which had been consummated literally in the term of service. There were expectations, however, in that direction, and hence the doom that followed. The Grail, moreover, had not announced that this Keeper should take a Wife, and he had gone before its judgment by choosing a Lady for his service, in whose honour he went beyond the precincts of his Kingdom in search of knightly deeds. She was the Duchess Orgeluse, who became subsequently the Wife of Gawain. In accepting the service of Anfortas, as later that of her future Husband, she was pursuing only a mission of vengeance on one who had destroyed the Prince to whom her love had been dedicated from the first days of desire. The King of the Grail was abroad on these ventures when he met in a joust with a heathen, who had come from the region about the Earthly Paradise and cherished the ambition of winning the Grail. We have seen that the unqualified aspirant after the secret knowledge died in the tourney, but Anfortas went home carrying the poisoned spear-head in his flesh, and thereafter he abode as a King in suffering and even in punishment. It follows that the cause of battle was honourable according to all Rules of Chivalry, but the motive which brought about the catastrophe was, I suppose, the root of offence, and for that he was bruised grievously. All the resources of healing were sought in the world of Nature and

---

[1] Cf. the corresponding episode in Gerbert—Potvin, *Op. cit.*, VI, pp. 168, 169, where the Sword broken by Perceval on the threshold of the Earthly Paradise is made whole by the smith who wrought it, but of course by the fire of his forge, instead of running water.

that of Magical Art : the Grail itself in vain ; in vain the Waters of Paradise ; the blood of the Pelican, the heart of the Unicorn ; that Bough which the Sibyl gave to Æneas as a Palladium against Hades and its dangers ; and the Magic Herb which springs from the blood of a Dragon—but these too in vain. Finally, the appeal was referred to the Sacred Talisman by Offices of Prayer, and a writing which appeared thereon announced the condition of healing—to wit, the visit of a Knight who should demand knowledge concerning the Woe of the Castle. It is the only version in which this Mystic Question is shewn to originate from the Grail itself. It is also the only version in which sin enters the Sanctuary ; and it is therefore important to shew that it is a sin of sense in the least degree : it is rather a transgression of obedience. There are stated periods in the story for the increase of the King's suffering, being the close of the wandering of Saturn, causing frost and snow in summer on the heights where the Kingdom is situated. The cold is agony to the Keeper, and it is then that the Poisoned Spear is used to pierce him again : it re-opens the wound ; but it keeps him alive, for it draws out the frost in crystals—which crystals are removed by the Silver Knives of Trebuchet.[1]

The Castle of Wolfram is supposed to have been situated on a Northern slope of the mountains of Gothic Spain, while on the Southern side, or in Moorish Spain, was the Castle built by Klingsor—that is to say, the Keep of Wonders, containing the LIT MERVEIL of the other Romances. The name allocated to the first was that of the eminence itself—Mont Salvaage, Salvasch, or Salvatch. There is no account of the building or of the incorporation of the Chivalry ; but (1) the Grail Knights are chosen, as we have seen, by the Grail itself as opportunity offers or circumstances seem to require ; (2) they may be elected in childhood ; (3) they constitute an aggressive Military Order, going sometimes on long missions ; (4) they cannot be regarded as a perfect nor yet as an invincible Chivalry, for one of them is overthrown by Parzival in combat, when on his Quest of the Castle ; and here, as in other respects, (5) they recall and are practically identified by Wolfram with the Knights Templar, having also the same Order name. Scholars who have investigated this part of the subject trace a connection between the House of Anjou and the Templar Brotherhood : it should be added that the lineage of Anjou is the subject of continual reference in Wolfram's poem, and Parzival is of that legitimacy.

At the beginning of his Chronicles Wolfram testifies to a single prototype from which alone he drew ; he cites its authority several times in the course of his poem : in one place he gives a very full account of it ; and he testifies concerning it at the end. He knew otherwise of Chrétien's version, but he suggests that it was the wrong story, with which the fountain-head might be reasonably indignant. The authentic text was the work of Kyot de Provence, and from that region it was

---

[1] When Parzival is called to become the King of the Grail and has reached its Castle the periodical crisis has attained its extreme height.—Book XVI.

brought into the German fatherland. It was not invented by Kyot, but was found by him under circumstances the account of which is in one respect a little out of harmony with itself. It lay rejected or forgotten in the city of Toledo, and being in the Arabic tongue, the first task of Kyot was to learn that language. This he accomplished by the sacramental grace of baptism and the holy illumination of faith. Without these aids to interpretation the tale would have remained in concealment, for, according to its own testimony, no pagan talents could have expressed the Great Mystery which reposes in the Grail. This is so far clear ; but the difficulty is that it was written in the first place by one who ranks as a heathen for Wolfram—that is to say, one who on the father's side was a worshipper of idols, though on the mother's, apparently, of the royal line of Solomon. This was in the days which preceded Christ, and the alleged Jew was the first in this world who ever spoke of the Grail. That which enabled him to do so was his gift of reading the stars, wherein he saw wondrous secrets ; for the story of the Grail was written in a celestial galaxy. On this basis the scribe wrote more especially concerning the descent of Angels to earth, carrying the Sacred Object, and concerning certain baptised men who were placed in charge thereof. This being the record attributed to a Son of Israel before the first dispensation had suffered supersession, no one will be surprised to learn that his name was Flegetanis, but here ends the account concerning him. Kyot may have been dissatisfied, reasonably or not, with the transcript from the starry heavens ; but he confesses only to anxiety about the identity of those who had been appointed the Wardens ; and after consulting old Latin works, he went in quest of their records through France, Britain and Ireland, but did not attain what he wanted until he arrived in Anjou, where he found the story of the Keepers faithfully and truly registered—that is to say, concerning Titurel, Frimutel and Anfortas. It seems clear therefore that the Jew of Toledo told the Early History of the Grail but gave no version of the Quest. I deduce from these data two conclusions, one of which is speculative and personal to myself at the moment : (1) The appeal of Kyot, like other Grail romancers, is to an antecedent authority and, like some of them, to a primordial text ; (2) the story of Flegetanis has suffered what is termed contamination by the introduction of extraneous matter, being all that which was not included in the record of the starry heavens, for which reason I set down as a tolerable presumption that neither Kyot nor Wolfram told the true story, however ample the evidence on which the version of Chrétien was condemned. I suppose that I shall be accused of fooling or alternatively of preternatural gravity ; but I mention these matters because of what will be said hereafter concerning a Lost Book of the Grail. Two points remain to be mentioned here : (1) Kyot seems to have cautioned those who reproduced his story to hide the chief matters until the end thereof, and this is cited by Wolfram, though it can be said scarcely that he carried out the injunction ; (2) if Wolfram followed Kyot, and him only, it seems certain that Kyot himself recounted several adventures to which his translator alludes merely in passing : however, they do not concern us.

II

THE QUEST OF KYOT DE PROVENCE

IT was not in the least essential that the minstrels and prose writers who spoke and wrote of the Grail, as indeed of other matters, at the epoch with which we are dealing, should have their own names perpetuated in or with their stories. The note of such personal ambition is curiously wanting, as contrasted with our own ultra-self-conscious period. On the other hand, there was an unqualified need that the Sagas which they made and told should be accepted as very truth, to insure which they made innumerable claims on the past, appealing to its real or imagined archives. Chrétien de Troyes had a " best story " behind him ; Robert de Borron cited a great book ; later Merlin Romances had the Prophet's own memorials ; while that which they told of the Grail came from the House of the Grail, to which a scriptorium was evidently attached. So also in the Palace of the King there was a driving of many pens to bring and keep up to date the Chronicles of the Round Table. The authorship of the PERLESVAUS is a concealed mystery for ever, because it must come forward forsooth under the auspices of him " who first consecrated the Body of the Lord ".[1] Walter Map, writing to Giraldus Cambrensis, has a touch of regret in recording that want of time prevented him, the preacher, from putting many pens to paper, yet a whole Cycle of Romance passes under his name ; while a pseudo-Robert de Borron and his kinsman, a supposititious Elias, are connected with another sequence.[2] It was desirable also on occasion that an alleged source and authority should be put back into the past at some considerable distance. I have given Wolfram's account of his Provençal Master Kyot apart from comment, except for foot-note references to corresponding episodes in the Perceval Myth of Chrétien. So far as the latter poet had carried his putative version of the *mellor conte qui soit contés en court roial*, he accounts for everything in the PARZIVAL ; but Wolfram was going much further and must have a source behind his manifest pattern and original : otherwise he would be " making up " on his own part, instead of reproducing a real story drawn from

---

[1] *Cist hauz estoires nos tesmoigne et recorde que Joseph qui nos en fet remembrance fu li premiers prestres qui sacrefieat le cors Notre Seignor, et por itant doit l'an croire les paroles qui de lui viennent.*—PERCEVAL LE GALLOIS : LE ROMAN EN PROSE. Potvin, I, p. 113. Cf. Sebastian Evans : THE HIGH HISTORY, Branch IX, Title 8.—" This high history witnesseth us and recordeth that Joseph, who maketh remembrance thereof, was the first priest that sacrificed the body of Our Lord, and forsomuch ought one to believe the words that come of him."

[2] See *ante*, Book VI, § 2, *s.v.* THE HUTH MERLIN. There was a disposition at one time to accept Hélie de Borron, possibly because of his alleged Kinsman's intriguing testimony to their companionship in arms and letters ; but it became evident on later research that the " Kinsman " was a false Robert.

authentic regions. The great imaginative poet bent upon telling "things unattempted yet in prose or rhyme" created therefore Kyot de Provence, giving reins to his unbridled fancy for the greater exaltation of his theme. It was wholly insufficient that the said "illustrious Master" had himself invented : he appears as a channel only, having seen with his own eyes the Adventures of Parzival "written in a pagan tongue". Behind Kyot there was pictured Flegitanis, descended from the wise Solomon and one who was renowned[1] for his knowledge, especially concerning the stars, he being an astronomer above all things. It came about therefore that behind Flegitanis were all the starry heavens and that by his ability to read therein he became qualified to affirm the existence of a "prodigy" called the Grail. It has been said in the past by hostile criticism that Wolfram invented these things to conceal the fact that his sole source was Chrétien.[2] The explanation is futile. Wolfram was in search of a warrant for another and greater story than ever had entered into the thought of the Northern French poet, and hence Kyot, with all his celestial signs revolving in heaven above him. The Provençal poet is a glorious invention, but I would burn many candles to the Virgin at any Church of Toledo, would only the lost planet of his poem at length "swim into our ken".[3] However, that poem is the PARZIVAL and Kyot is the Lord of Eschenbach. He could have done much better in one respect, unless indeed he intended to betray his own invention : he need not have made Flegitanis a pagan who worshipped a calf ; he need not have put him far back into pre-Christian days ; or he might have remembered in doing so that when a "legion of angels" brought the Grail to earth, they could not in the nature of things have gone about to discover "baptised" Guardians for the Talisman.[4] It would be ridiculous to say that the story betrays itself, even at every point : it is a great betrayal throughout of the fact that Wolfram devised it out of his own head : that fact is written all over it, from A to Z.[5] That a few in the past have hoped to find the poem somewhere in Southern

[1] Obviously in the sense of a "reader," and in the sense of the *astronomia* of Paracelsus, who theosophised thereupon.

[2] It has not been suggested that Wolfram knew the GRAND SAINT GRAAL ; but Flegitanis is curiously reminiscent of that text and of its many references to a Duchess Flegetins, who was (1) the Sister of Evalac, who became Mordrains in Holy Baptism ; (2) the Wife of Nasciens ; and (3) the Mother of Celidoine.—Sommer, *Op. cit.*, I, pp. 51, 52, and elsewhere in several places. See *ibid.*, Supplementary Volume, being Index of Names and Places, *s.v.* Flegentine, Flegetine.

[3] Toledo is specified because—as readers will remember—it was there that Kyot found the Arabic manuscript, written by the "great astronomer" and was able to understand as well as read it, by the virtues of Christian Baptism and a knowledge of Necromancy. Presumably Kyot evoked Flegitanis, as the Witch of Endor called up Samuel.

[4] That he could have forgotten may seem incredible, were it not for the fatality or providence which insures, with almost unfailing precision, that forged documents and false ascriptions should always betray themselves, at some "unwatched portal of the wall."

[5] We have only to consider for a few moments in summary form. It supposes (1) that Kyot, being a Provençal, wrote in French ; (2) that there was a pre-Christian Arabic manuscript concerning the Grail ; (3) that it was written by a Pagan of Jewish descent —apparently on the mother's side ; (4) that, being an astronomer, he discovered by signs in heaven the existence of a prodigy called the Grail ; (5) that it was brought to

France or in a Spanish Monastery is a testimony to the capacity for dreaming on the part of scholarship : so also is the learning which has identified Kyot laboriously with Guiot de Provins[1] and even with a Priest of the Church in Britain who died Bishop of Durham.[2]

It has been maintained also with zeal and enthusiasm that the SONE DE NAUSAY gives evidence of sources that were used previously by Wolfram, who did not therefore derive solely from Chrétien. The alleged evidence is of two kinds. There is firstly the fact that the Grail King—Joseph of Arimathæa—in SONE DE NAUSAY—was smitten by God because of his foolish marriage, while Anfortas, the third Grail King of the PARZIVAL, is maimed in the course of adventures undertaken to win and to keep the favours of Orgeluse, described as a Lady of Logres. It is said secondly that there are allusions to the fable of the Swan Knight in both poems. If these points survived the test of examination they would prove nothing, except that the anonymous author of the later text had borrowed from Wolfram, the latter belonging to the first decades and the former to the second half of the thirteenth century. The correspondences however are phantasmal. The visitation of Joseph is represented as Divine in its origin, while Anfortas is wounded in warfare. Joseph is healed by a Knight who has skill in medicine, but Anfortas was to wait through long years the advent of one who will ask him an arbitrary question. Joseph in fine is married to a pagan who has passed through the Rite of Baptism but remains a heathen at heart, while Anfortas has an illicit amour with a noble Christian Lady. As to the Myth of the Swan Knight, it does not exist in the SONE DE NAUSAY ; but the author of a later prose summary attached to the poem recites the story briefly in connection with the text's account of a marriage between Sone's son and a Lady of Bohemia.[3]

The PARZIVAL of Wolfram emerges therefore with a debt to Chrétien which is not altogether unlike that of Shakespeare to the folk-story of Lear. It is a great creative and decorative poem, with an elaborate plot which is developed logically throughout. It is a work of imagination carried triumphantly to its term. For myself it seems too often overloaded and cloyed, decoration for the sake of decoration, spangles

---

earth by a legion of Angels, who then returned to the skies ; (6) that they seem—for it is not stated definitely—to have placed it in the hands of certain baptised scions of a pure race, this amazing fact being noted apparently in the pre-Christian Arabic text ; (7) that Kyot discovered this text lying neglected at Toledo ; (8) that what with the illumination of faith, the grace of baptismal water and the most abhorred of occult arts, he contrived to read it ; (9) that he went in search of the Grail Wardens through the Chronicles of various countries, including Britain, France and Ireland ; (10) that at long last he learned in those of Anjou concerning Titural, Frimutel, Anfortas and his Sister Herzeleide, who became the Mother of Parzival—a likely research indeed, a likely finding, altogether a likely tale.

[1] The hypothesis is that Kyot should be read as Guiot and that Wolfram mistook Provins for Provence. Guiot de Provins is famous for a satirical poem known as the BIBLE GUIOT, an attack on contemporary manners and vices.

[2] The Prelate in question is Philip of Poitiers, while the author of this proposition is Paul Hagen in WOLFRAM UND KIOT. See ZEITSCHRIFT FÜR DEUTSCHE PHILOLOGIE for 1906. Those who care to check the alleged evidence will find it in Bruce, *Op. cit.*, I, pp. 318, 319.

[3] SONE DE NAUSAY, *Ed. cit.*, p. 554.

or gold everywhere, for all is not gold that glitters on its garish vesture. Pageant is for the sake of pageant, apart from further purpose. The fact is illustrated conclusively by the Grail Procession in the Banqueting Hall of the Grail Castle, largely a procession of supers carrying this and that, including the legs of a table, while there are others who bear nothing but merely swell the numbers. The Grail of Wolfram is perhaps the supreme unreason of the whole ornate device. It is (1) a family oracle which has no office whatever outside the family and (2) a family larder which provides food in season, ready-cooked and dressed, apart from cost or toil, except possibly that of a few hypothetical scullions in the kitchen of the King : these may wash the plates, the dishes and polish the jewelled goblets. What part has God therein, that God should send down the Grail ? What office has a Sacred Host, consecrated at some Mass in Heaven and thence conveyed, that the family may eat for ever ? What kind of life is led in the Grail Castle ? There is no Priesthood of the Grail and there are no Divine Offices. The life is not one of religion and the Chivalry called to the Service has only to guard the marches against all cowans and intruders. There is a suggestion, I think, in one place of services performed beyond ; but it leads nowhere.

It has been suggested—as we have seen—that there is a sub-surface hostility to Rome and all its ways, especially those of doctrine ; but it is difficult to agree so far as the open sense of the poem is concerned. There are no Priests in the Castle, but their ministry is available at the precincts. Baptism is an essential Rite, and in a notable case Feirfeis, the Brother of Parzival, cannot see the Grail till that ceremony has been performed upon him. Confession is also practised and Masses are heard occasionally, as for example by Parzival and Konduiramour towards the end of all. There is heresy here and there, but it suggests a layman's blundering rather than design. Trinitarian teaching would seem indispensable, as in the PERLESVAUS, and, as in that story, the three Divine Persons are held to be incarnate in Christ ; though in both cases I tend to infer that the respective authors would have been astonished to learn that this is not good Roman Theology. Stress has been laid on the fact that Saracens are not regarded with horror and are not evidently excluded from the Round Table ; but after all the respective positions of Moor and Christian are made clear enough in the case of Feirfeis.

It must be added that much of what has been said on the ethical value and pregnant significance of Wolfram's poem will have to be taken back. The repudiated marriages of Gamuret and Feirfeis are eloquent and in fact final on the first count. The test of value in respect of Christian faith is found in the conversion of the Pagan Prince. It was any profession and any belief and any manner of gods in order to possess the Grail Maiden, for whom also he would have been willing to put away any number of wives and favourites. The test of value also as regards the Grail object is provided by the kind

of transaction which bartered the Elect Virgin for the advantage
of such a conversion enacted to the accompaniment of broken marriage
vows. With reference to the second count, the TEMPLEISEN are not a
Great Chivalry comparable to the historical Templars at their best and
highest. They are family retainers belonging to a supposed branch
of the House of Anjou which possesses a Magical Palace. The women of
the Castle could go forth and be married as and when it was possible
and if and how they pleased. The men, on the other hand, were
pledged to celibacy, except the Grail King, but why so pledged there
is no reason given and there is none in the nature of things.

It is to be noted also that after all the sufferings through his years
of maiming Anfortas has been King of the Grail ; but he is deposed as
soon as he is healed on the reiterated ground of unworthiness, and
Parzival reigns in his stead by the ordinance of the Grail itself. After
this manner is a youthful indiscretion punished as if to everlasting.
It would be unwise at this point to examine the titles of Parzival,
whether they are valid or flimsy : it must be held sufficient to remember
that Anfortas returns to a life of active Chivalry, by the hypothesis
of the story, and for the rest that the royal dignity is merely titular
to all intents and purposes. There is no obvious office, there is no
special prerogative ; Anfortas remains in the Castle. What does it
signify which of them is called the King ? Titurel also remains, with
the weight of the years upon him and illustrated in particular by an
unyielding form of gout. " Nothing to do and all one's life to do it in "
seems the last inscription which might have been written on the Magian
Stone : it has been primarily responsible for the supreme follies (1) of
the Question that must be asked for the sake of the healing of Anfortas
and (2) its antithesis, the Question which must not be asked if Lohengrin's wife is not to be deprived of her husband and left with no power
to sue for the restitution of conjugal rights. The PARZIVAL is told
grandly, but if ever a wrong story was proffered concerning the Grail,
the case is that of Wolfram's epic.

III

THE CROWN OF ALL ADVENTURES

THE implicit, I must suppose, of every succeeding Quest was
that some earlier singer of *le meilleur conte qui soit conté en
cour royale* had told the wrong story, in one or another
manner, and that a yet far higher flight of pure Romance
must justify the material which came into the hands of each later
poet—whether in the mode of records or that of the mind's imagining. The most interesting contrasted instance is the LONGER PROSE
PERCEVAL, put forward as an alternative to the QUEST OF GALAHAD, as
if by one who cleaved to the old Tradition concerning the Hero of

Achievement and yet had every intention of profiting by the high light of sanctity which overshone the symbol of Galahad. The least comprehensible contrasted instance is the competition instituted—*circa* 1220—in the name of Gawain by Heinrich von dem Türlin in his poem of Diu Crône.[1] The ambition seems impossible after the Parzival of Wolfram, but that poem was not appreciated—on account of its setting chiefly—by the general Profession of Minstrelsy. The instance further was, in its way, a certain exoneration of Chrétien, who was followed in several respects and often appealed to by Heinrich. That Diu Crône justifies any claim to existence I do not think ; but this notwithstanding it is a very curious Romance, so much under veils of enchantment that the whole action seems transferred into a Land of Faërie, while the gifts and dotations which are offered to the elect hero might have made any Quest of the Grail almost a work of superfluity on his part.[2] In place of the Castle of Maidens there is pictured a Wandering Island of the Sea wherein dwell Virgins only ; and the Queen of this wonderful people, exercising a royal privilege, offers the possession of herself in marriage and the rule of her Kingdom to Gawain as her Chosen Knight ; yet if this be incompatible with his purpose, she will tolerate their parting at need and will bestow upon him, as her token of goodwill, an elixir of unfading youth. The hero exercises his admitted power of choice in favour of the second alternative, and with good reason probably, since the island was doubtless one of those dreaming places where a thousand years are even as a single day, and after a moon of sorcery he might have issued bearing on his shoulders an age past all renewing, even by the Holy Grail.

The keynote of the story is in one sense the Disqualification of Perceval, who—because he had failed once—had forfeited his vocation for ever. The opportunity is transferred to Gawain, and Heinrich is indebted to Chrétien for the substance of those inventions by which he is covenanted to enter on the Quest of the Holy Grail. We, on the other hand, may be indebted to his own imagination for the aids that the Powers of Faërie combine to provide by means of telesmas and other wonder-working objects which safeguard the way of the Quest. Seeing that the failure of Perceval to ask the all-important Question is held insufficient as a warning in the case of Gawain, when he seeks to follow in his footsteps, he is reinforced by a particular caution at the Castle of Wonders. What he receives is indeed a dual counsel : he is not only to ask and to learn, but, in order that he may behold the Grail, he is urged to abstain at the table from all refreshment in wine. The Maiden—described as a goddess—who proffers this advice proves to be she who carries the Sacred Vessel in the Pageant at the Castle thereof. The analogy by opposition hereto is Wauchier's story of the trick played upon Perceval by the Daughter of the Fisher King when she carries off

[1] The poem is in Middle High German, and nothing seems known of the author. Bruce suggests that he was " probably of Steiermark " but offers no reason.
[2] We hear of draughts in cups which are proffered to test chastity, of those who may go invisible by means of girdles and of sleep produced by images.

the stag's head and basset to punish Perceval for not asking the Question.

We have had scant opportunity to appreciate Gawain's share in the great adventurous experiment within the horizon of Wolfram's poem : we have seen also in the CONTE DEL GRAAL how and why, as a part of his own vindication, he set forth to seek the Bleeding Lance ; but the Quest proved a failure. Except the promiscuous proposal and fleeting undertaking in the Galahad Quest, Gawain does not figure as a Knight in search of the Grail in the French Romances till we come to the period of the LONGER PROSE PERCEVAL. Even in Wauchier the fullest account of his visit to the Castle of Hallows is apart from all note of intention, as he is simply a gallant of the period in attendance on Guinevere, who herself is awaiting the return of King Arthur after the reduction of Castle Orguellous. On the other hand, Heinrich's DIU CRÔNE pictures him expressly, and as if in real earnest, seeking to achieve the Grail, enduring also many adventures because of it.[1] After the poem of Wolfram, his success does not seem to improve upon his failure in the other stories ; it is by way of superfluity, and it may be said para-doxically that Heinrich takes him for another, as he was hailed also for a moment in pseudo-Wauchier's poem.

In the course of his progress Gawain arrived at a bountiful and smiling land, as if it were the precincts of an Earthly Paradise, and on the further borders thereof he beheld a Vast Fiery Sword keeping the entrance to a Fortress with walls translucent as glass. I do not know, because it is difficult always to adjudicate in his case, why he should have regarded that wonder in the light of an evil omen ; but this is how it impressed him, and he missed perhaps one among the highest Adventures when he retired so incontinently—whether it was a way of entrance into the Lower Eden guarded by Kerubim, or into the fascina-tion of a False Paradise. Great as are the accomplished enterprises of Grail literature, I think that greater still are some of those which therein are hinted only, remaining unachieved or unrecorded. It seems clear that this Fortress, at no indefinite distance from the Grail Castle, is like unto that which Perceval would have entered in Gerbert's poem, and his incontinent eagerness contrasts favourably with the terror and the flight of Gawain.

The Knight continued to traverse a land flowing with milk and honey, and he rode for yet twelve days, when he came upon Lancelot and Calogrenant—another Companion of the Round Table—both in a manner on the Quest.[2] So these three shadows of those who should finish the experiment in utter reality came at last to their bourne. It

---

[1] Nutt suggests that Heinrich presents the most archaic form of the Unspelling Quest —STUDIES, p. 182. As a fact, Gawain undertakes to seek the Grail as the outcome of a Chessboard episode, in which he plays with a Maid and has to defend himself with the Board subsequently.

[2] The story of Queen Guinevere's abduction by Meleagant, Son of King Bademagus, and her rescue by Lancelot is reproduced in DIU CRÔNE from Chrétien's CONTE DE LA CHARRETTE. It may be noted also that Caleogrenant appears in Chrétien's YVAIN.

may have been a region of Sorcery which encompassed that abode, which we know to have been a House of the Dead ; but it was assuredly like the intermediate region of occult speculation between the life of this world and the life everlasting. There are few things in literature which savour so strangely of that visionary astral region, full of great simulations and full of false joy, which does not attempt to conceal its bitter heart of sorrow. The Knightly Company depicted on a meadow without the burg, performing evolutions in pastime, was like the " midnight host of spectres pale " which " beleaguered the walls of Prague." But the places of death are not in this case, places of silence ; the burg itself had a noisy throng within it ; and so had the Castle or Palace—that Ghost's House and House of the Dead Alive. The Companions were brought under safe guidance into the Hall in chief, which was like the Kabbalistic Sphere of Venus—a pomp of external splendour, heavy with the crushed-out fragrance of heaped roses—as some mansion in an Eastern Fairyland. In the Hall of Roses there was seated the Host who was to receive them—another patient sufferer of the ages, diverted in his pitiful weariness by youths playing chess at his feet and jesting in the course of the game. That game is a feature which in one or another form is inevitable in all the stories till the highest of the high Quests intervenes and makes void so many of the old episodes. We know that it is played elsewhere by pieces having self-moving powers ; but here it is played by the dead, amidst shadowy sport and raillery : betwixt the one and the other there is perhaps suggested some vaguely mystical side of the old war in mimicry.

The Questing Knights had not been received to no purpose : there was a work which they were required to perform, supposing that they were prepared properly ; for the unspelling quest is followed even to the grave. Lord or Prince of the Castle, it is not said till the close whether the host is old or young ; he is not termed the Rich Fisher, and his genealogy is unknown. So also are most antecedents of the Hallows. The guests were treated royally and were entertained at a banquet ; but at that time the Master of the House neither ate nor drank. On his part, remembering the warning which he received, Gawain ate only, and this in spite of solicitations on his entertainer's side, the doom of whom seems to have been working more strongly, seeing that it drew to its term, and he was compelled to entreat that which would operate against his salvation. Lancelot and the other Companion quenched their thirst with wine, which overcame them immediately, as if it were nepenthe devised for that express purpose ; and they fell into heavy sleep. The Lord of the Castle fulfilled his office zealously, and again tempted Gawain ; but, finding no better success, he desisted, and thereafter began the high pageant, the foremost in which were maidens ; and she who was fairest among all—the Crowned Priestess who carried the Most Holy Vessel[1]—was recognised as her

---

[1] It is borne on a cloth of samite and reposes on a jewel for its base, as a Reliquary may rest on an Altar—a suggestion of Dr. Bruce.

who had counselled Gawain previously—counselled him above all, like other wandering Messengers in the Romances of Perceval—not to forget the Question did ever he come to the place. If he could not be compelled therefore, he could at least be prompted, and the convention recalls that indicible word which *ex hypothesi* cannot be spoken or written and yet is communicated to the Initiate of many Mysteries, when he finds that he has been acquainted always therewith.

Before the Company—which was numerous within as without—had taken their places at the table, a page of the chambers brought in the Hallow of the Sword and laid it at the feet of the Master. The inference is that this was the fatal weapon which, in the midst of the strife of kinsmen, had somehow brought woe on the Castle—as we shall learn shortly ; but the particulars are not given, and of itself the weapon would be nothing to our purpose, except that it is the antithesis of other Swords in the Legends. Not only was it perfect then but would so remain for ever : it was adjudged to the successful Quester and would break in no peril—an office of relaxed observance which shortened and simplified the Quest.

Now, the Company in the Castle had feasted gallantly, like the guests who sat with the Master ; though dead, they yet spoke—and that, it would seem, volubly—interchanging questions and answers, as if in mockery of the Real Question ; but the strong wine of the banquet had no effect on them, and the Lord of the plenty meanwhile, as I have said, had fasted. But the appearance of the Grail procession was the signal that he was to receive a certain shadow of nourishment—as if, after some Necromantic Supper, an astral Eucharist were communicated to one who had not partaken previously. We know already that the Vessel contained the semblance of a Host, as from the Lance there exuded Blood into a Salver—neither more nor less, in this case, than those three mystical drops which tincture all the Legends and connect them, as if undesignedly, with other and older Mysteries. In the story of Wolfram the first nourishment drawn from the Grail at the banquet in the Castle Hall is described as Bread, and Heinrich—as if profiting by a caution in respect of the Feeding Dish—converts the Sacred Object into a simple Ciborium. The Master of the Castle received therefore in Bread ; but of the Bread he took only a third part, as if it were the efficient oblation at a Sacrifice of the Mass. He drank also the Blood from the Salver, no one but himself sharing in these Elements of a substituted Eucharist. He was fed sacramentally and super-substantially in some sense ; for this his only nourishment was administered once in a year. Therefore Gawain arrived at a happy season, to see and to speak ; and on contemplating these things, he overflowed in himself with the wonder and the mystery of it all, so that, acting on the spur of the moment, importunately he asked that which was vital to those who were suffering from death in life—namely, the Mystic Question, the most conventional of all formulæ : What does it mean ?

There was no effect to begin with—no sudden change, I mean, from life to death or from death to life ; but if before there was the chaffer and light talk at a feasting, now it was the hubbub of a joy beyond suppression, as if the closing at last were taken in a Great Grade of Long Sorrow.

Gawain has asked indeed ; but as regards the Secrets of the Grail he is not told anything : it has come forth out of Mystery and it passes away therein. It is said to be God's Mystery—one of the Secrets of the King, and Heinrich has written about it : *abscondere bonum est*. Of the woe, the wasting and the endurance, when brother warred upon brother, he learned something,and we have heard enough ; of Perceval's failure and the deepened misery therefrom he was told also, and lastly the indispensable condition of release resident in the Question. But the King himself was guiltless, and so also were the Maidens ; he, however, was dead, with all the men of his household ; but they were alive in the flesh and they would go forth in the morning. When that dawned presently, the released speaker vanished, the Grail also with him, and its Mystery, never to be seen more.

The following points may be noticed in conclusion of this study : (1) There is no question anywhere of feeding properties in the Sacred Reliquary, except as regards the King—and him it feeds sacramentally ; (2) the Spear does not distil blood until it is laid on a table, with the head apparently over the Salver ; (3) the recession of the Grail seems to have been adjudged because it has performed its work of feeding the dead Master, keeping him in the semblance of life ; and once this office was perfected it went like a ghost. After what manner the variations which are introduced thus into the shifting pageant of the Legend can be said to elucidate its object will not be determined easily, if indeed at all. The doom that involves the dwellers in the Castle changes the symbolism but certainly does not exalt it. The Romance, for the rest, is the work of one who has resolved to give the palm to Gawain at the express expense of Perceval, to the Knight of This World in place of the Knight Celestial. It is the experiment of an inventor who possibly may have adapted some old materials to another purpose, at once indeterminate and undesirable.

The date ascribed to the poem is about 1220, and its ingarnering as a whole is regarded as a little chaotic. It reaches some 30,000 lines ; and though we hear generally concerning King Arthur's Court and the Round Table, Gawain is the hero-in-chief. After his completion of the Grail Quest, various pageants of Chivalry bring him back to his Uncle and the Fellowship, the story in this manner reaching its natural close.

IV

THE TITUREL OF ALBRECHT

THE Secret Doctrine of Kyot de Provence and the High Tradition of the Starry Heavens not only failed to convince the minstrel world in Germany concerning the titles of PARZIVAL—of which one example is Heinrich—but it failed to hold even those who had no alternative and more elect hero to offer—of which the example, within certain limits, is Albrecht.[1] It came about that towards the end of that century which had seen the light of Wolfram there arose the succeeding light of him who was to follow ; and, having regard to the welcome which he received, the German world was looking evidently for another. He came to announce, like the French Romances before him, that the Grail had been taken away. Albrecht was an Austrian or Bavarian poet who wrote between 1250 and 1275, but of whom absolutely nothing is known. He undertook to carry the whole experiment to its term, which he did in a vast production of 45,000 lines, written in the obscure style of his predecessor-in-chief, whence—and for other reasons—the distinct individualities were confused for a considerable period. He incorporated various materials, first among which is the unfinished work of a completely anonymous and, if possible, more unknown poet than himself. Secondly, he appropriated and extended certain so-called TITUREL fragments which were the work of Wolfram himself. About the first author it can be said only that he is affirmed to have projected a complete Chronicle of the Grail and its Keepers, drawing for this purpose on the assumed source used by Wolfram. It is a matter of speculation at what point he broke off and for what reason ; but his mantle fell upon Albrecht. The materials left by Wolfram are two in number, and the opening lines of the first fragment explain why they have been termed a TITUREL poem. They are really, by Wolfram's evidence, parts of the early history of Sigune and Schionatulander— respectively, the cousin of Parzival and her lover, who was his cousin also and whose embalmed body she carries with her so long in the PARZIVAL poem. It appears from the fragments that the lover met his death in satisfying a whim of his mistress, who desired to possess a Brackenseil.[2] Albrecht incorporated and extended these fragments,[3]

[1] There was once a disposition, now abandoned, to identify him with Albrecht von Scharfenberg, also in the thirteenth century, whose MERLIN survives in a very late redaction. Its sources are the MERLIN of Robert and the GRAND SAINT GRAAL.

[2] " Simrock has alluded already to the fact that Wolfram's TITUREL, were it finished, would form a curious contrast to the PARZIVAL, the hero of which pursues the highest adventure, whereas Schionatulander sacrifices his life for the possession of a Brackenseil." Franz Pfeiffer in GERMANIA, IV, pp. 298 *et seq*. Brackenseil, *i.e.*, a lead for a sporting-dog.

[3] Writing in the Review GERMANIA for 1862, San Marte points out that Albrecht transfers from Wolfram (1) " all that relates to Sigune's youthful love " ; (2) thence proceeding to depict her life after the death of her lover ; and (3) changing " the passionate, sensuously loving woman into a religious devotee." There is, however, the PARZIVAL's testimony that she became an Anchoress and was fed by the Grail—surely an advanced instance of devotion to spiritual things. Albrecht is exonerated assuredly.

as I have said, and in many other ways the YOUNGER TITUREL, as it is called, covers much of the ground belonging to the earlier epic, carrying the History of the Grail to its final term. It has been explained that the lateness of the poem has excluded it in the mind of English scholarship from the canon of the Grail : alternatively it has been simply neglected ; but German thoroughness has done it ample justice, and its consideration will help us better to understand the position and claim of the German Cycle. To that Cycle it makes a real contribution, and it differs in this respect from the Metrical Romance of LOHENGRIN, which is ascribed to the year 1300.

This is an important document for the Legend of the Swan Knight, but its allusions to the Holy Grail are of an occasional kind. It should be understood that Lohengrin issues from the House of the Great Talisman and that he returns in fine thereto. Here is the first point, and the second offers a revolution of the whole Arthurian Cycle respecting the close in disaster of all those chivalrous times. The star of the King's destiny does not set in blood and warfare—

" In dark Dundagel by the Northern sea——"

owing to that frightful fatality by which Arthur begot Mordred on the body of his half-sister. Other stars intervened to avert the doom and vengeance for that which was done in ignorance. In place of the dubious mercy of healing at the hands of Morgan le Fay in the mystic island of Avalon, the King—at the head of his whole Chivalry— accompanies the Grail to India, where he and they are its presumable Guardians—as well as the TEMPLEISIN—at some remote, undeclared place of the Eastern world.[1]

One important point with regard to Albrecht's share in the TITUREL undertaking is that he sets aside the antecedent history of the Holy Grail, bequeathed by his earlier German peer in poetry, and reverts for his thesis concerning it to the more orthodox Traditions of Northern France. In a word, the Sacred Object is no longer a Stone, whether that in the Crown of Lucifer or that which consumes the Phœnix and at the same time incubates the egg which the bird has laid. It is the Sacred Vessel of Joseph II, of the GRAND SAINT GRAAL and the Quest of Galahad, so that once again—and but once in the German Cycle— we can kneel in spirit where the Great Reliquary is exposed for veneration on the Second Mystical Table, while seeing that here as there the Paschal Dish is so connected with the Cup that it seems ever to dissolve therein, we may assist also at a SuperEfficacious Mass said in the Sanctuary, looking towards that time

---

[1] It may be noted that the TITUREL differs from a manuscript concerning Parzival and the Round Table which is preserved among the treasures of the Vatican, being the sole copy that is known. It was written a little earlier than the year 1336, and it incorporates Manessier's conclusion of the CONTE DEL GRAAL with materials derived from the PARZIVAL and Albrecht's TITUREL. It was composed by Nicholas Wisse and Philip Colim, a goldsmith of Strasburg. They dedicated it in 1336 to Ulric, Lord of Rappottstein in Alsace.

when we also, at the Words of Consecration, shall behold the five changes.[1]

The TITUREL claims to provide the perfect and rectified History of the Vessel and its Wardens from the beginning to the end thereof. Considering that the first Grail King is the real centre of interest, an excessive space is devoted to Sigune and her Lover. At the inception there are given the generations of the Secret Dynasty from the days of Vespasian, when Berillus of Cappadocia, who had great possessions and was moreover of the Christian Faith, took service with the Roman General at the Siege of Jerusalem and followed in his train subsequently when he was called to the throne of the Empire. Berillus married Argensilla, the daughter of the Emperor, and a considerable part of France was assigned to him thereafter in fief. He had as issue Titurisone, who married Elizabel of Arragon, and of her—after long years and precious offers in pilgrimage at the Holy Sepulchre, because of their childless condition—there was born Titurel, this name being a contraction of the parental designations. It will be seen that the genealogy takes back the so-called Angevin Dynasty to a very early period of the Christian centuries, as well as to the Holy Fields. The remaining succession in the Keepership follows the indications of Wolfram.

At this point it is desirable to establish the ecclesiastical position of DER JÜNGERE TITUREL. For San Marte, who was A. Schulz and who wrote on the subject in 1862, the PARZIVAL of Wolfram was the product of an anti-papal spirit which preceded the Reformation, the poet himself being " penetrated by an evangelical, apostolical spirit ". From this point of view the earlier poet was at the poles asunder from Albrecht, who is " the Ultramontane Priest compared with the Gospel Knight ". It will be observed that I have failed to read Wolfram or interpret him altogether on these lines. So far as the surface of his text is concerned and having regard more especially to his twice implied agreement with the Roman valuation of marital contracts between Christians and Pagans, he casts a dubious light on San Marte's thesis. On the other hand it is now seventy years since San Marte wrote, and it calls to be said that during the intervening period his view of the PARZIVAL has been approved implicitly by later scholarship : equivalent theses expressed in variant terms have been with us to this day. So far as Albrecht has remained a subject of critical judgment, I suppose that agreement continues on San Marte's TITUREL estimate, whether or not a survey of the text would make an opposite opinion difficult. For Albrecht (1) the Catholic Priesthood is " raised above every class " ; (2) the Church as the teacher of true faith is " above the Grail " ; (3) the Grail Temple is in fact a glorified Church, with " the

[1] When the anonymous poet who has been mentioned opens the story he follows Wolfram in his PARZIVAL and TITUREL fragments. The Grail, however, is carried by Angels instead of a human being, and it gives no written instructions. Afterwards messages appear on the surface of the Stone and a Maiden is the Grail-Bearer. It follows that Albrecht was content to remain at issue with the precursor whom he incorporated.

TEMPLEISEN as its custodians "; and (4) a solemn significance is assigned to all its parts. So also as regards Prester John, " who is known in Heaven by his great virtue and by his invincible power on earth ". Fourteen crosses are carried before him when he goes forth to battle, while at table he is waited on by Kings and Princes, those who are seated with him being Archbishops and other Prelates of Holy Church. Here is a question of fact arising from the poem itself ; but San Marte fails to observe that, all this notwithstanding, the Hierarchy in the person of its Eastern Vicar receives the Grail Messengers with the utmost humility and not alone does Prester John offer his crown to Perceval but he is dispossessed thereof by the written ordinance of the Grail. It follows in the logic of things that the Keepers of the Sacred Vessel are above the Church and its Custodians—a point to be marked for review at a later stage.

As regards the recession of the Grail, the TITUREL describes an evil time which fell upon things outside the precincts of the Temple in its mountain fastness between France and Spain ; and it was in pursuance of their own counsels of prudence rather than by an instruction from without that the Keepers of the Holy Vessel convened in fine the cohort of the Templar Chivalry and that Parzival, accompanied by them and carrying the Hallows of the House, went in quest of his Brother Feirfeis, so reaching India.

The PARZIVAL of Wolfram indicates that Prester John was the issue of this Brother, but Albrecht represents him as an independent Ruler in the East, and gives such an account of himself and his wonderful kingdom that the reigning Keeper is minded to place the Grail in his care. When, however, Parzival came into his august presence, bearing the Holy Vessel, the Priest-King offered his realm and crown, as we have seen, to him who was the Grail-King. Parzival, however, desired to enter his Brother's service, for report had assured him that all material and spiritual riches abode with Prester John, even the Seven Gifts and the Twelve Fruits of the Divine Spirit of Counsel. It remains to be said that Parzival's decreed reign lasted for ten years only and was closed then by his death, the reason that it was not perpetuated for a longer period being his guilt in respect of his Mother's unhappy end. He was succeeded by the son of Feirfeis.

At the prayers of the Keeper, the Castle and Sanctuary of the Grail were transported in a single night to India, so that the Great Palladium had again its proper Asylum. It was this, I conclude, that led to the whole Chivalry remaining as they were in the East, whereas, if they had relinquished their trust, they might have returned whence they came.

It is to Ethiopia, Turkey, Armenia, the farther side of Persia and the yet more remote East that other Legends refer the retreat of Prester John, which really was " built in the unapparent ". There is hence no need to co-ordinate rival versions, nor would such a task be possible in the cloud of conflicting accounts. To vary the issues of confusion,

I will mention only that, according to the DUTCH LANCELOT, the Priest-King appears to have been Parzival's Son. It is thought that the reticence of Wolfram on the whole subject is explicable by the fact that there were few materials at his period, while in the fifty subsequent years, the rumours of the Eastern Legend had extended and were available to Albrecht. But it should be remembered that the first rumour is referable to 1156,[1] and before the end of the twelfth century it had the support of Maimonides as well of the wandering Israelite, Benjamin of Tudela. The seat of Peter had done more than confess to an attraction when an Embassy was sent to Prester John bearing a written communication from Alexander III ; and before 1180, or about this time, the Emperor of Constantinople, the Pope of Rome and St. Louis King of France are supposed to have received a celebrated letter in which the mysterious potentate announced his own existence with consummate grandiloquence. It was an impossible document in the worst style of false seeming ; but it created great interest and great wonder.[2] It concerns us only because it may have provided certain materials both for Wolfram and Albrecht. The Palace of Prester John is like the Grail Castle of Mont Salvatch drawn out into a greater " wilderness of building " ; and the PARZIVAL allusions to the Earthly Paradise are recalled by an account of that Spring which is three days' journey from the Garden of Eden. Whosoever can drink of its water will have, through all his later life, the aspect of thirty—precisely that appearance which was maintained by the Templar Chivalry owing to the presence of the Grail. The myth of Prester John has been noticed exhaustively by several writers : it never required exploding, but that work was done in the seventeenth century by Julius Bartolocci in his MAGNA BIBLIOTHECA RABBINICA.[3]

There is only to add concerning Albrecht and his TITUREL (1) that in the earlier part of the fourteenth century it was not alone allocated to Wolfram, as we have seen, but was held to be his master work ; (2) that all assertions notwithstanding, the precarious hypothesis of Albrecht's acquaintance with the poem of Kyot has been abandoned some time since ; (3) that the TITUREL represents King Arthur and his Knights as travellers in search of the Grail after it had been taken away. It was a vain journey, of which Parzival had calculated the probabilities beforehand when he took leave of the Round Table, and at long last the Chivalry returned whence it came. The Adventure, which seems to have extended through many countries, is the root-matter of that other fable which was conceived subsequently, as we have seen, by the author of the metrical LOHENGRIN.

[1] See the CHRONICLE of Otto of Freisinger, *sub voce* 1145.—*Lib.* VII, Cap. 33.
[2] Appendix I, Note 15.
[3] *Ib.*, Note 16.

V

THE GRAIL IN DESECRATION

WOLFRAM VON ESCHENBACH died *circa* 1220, leaving
the magnificent TITUREL fragments as his last witness
on the Grail subject. We have seen that they were
appropriated by the authors of a later TITUREL who
carried the Grail to the East and the Land of Prester John. Albrecht,
who completed this vast experiment, is supposed to have written
between 1250 and 1275. Thereafter the fame of the Talisman assumed
another aspect. My authority-in-chief on its subsequent disastrous
story affirms that between the hostility of the Church—which naturally
had no toleration for a Secret Knightly Order independent of itself and
without ecclesiastical elements—and between the sensual attractions
pictured in the Palace of the Grail, the mythos declined with great
rapidity " from the level of the PARZIVAL to a significance which was
purely carnal ".[1] For a time it was celebrated by German Minnesingers
as the Other-World Home of heroes : when they were overtaken by
death, it was said that they " went into the Grail ".[2] The Talisman
became in this manner a place instead of a Stone. Later on it was
adopted as the name of a heathen Earthly Paradise and (or) as " a
symbol for those forbidden delights which in popular thought gave to
that Paradise its great attraction ". The CHRONICLE OF MAGDEBURG
gives account of a Festival held in that city, some sixty years after
the death of Wolfram, namely, in 1281 under the title of Grail Festival.
A certain learned man is said to have made a Grail, otherwise undescribed but alluding presumably to the staging of the feast itself. He
invited many merchants of various cities to visit Magdeburg, if they
wished to practise " the Knightly Art ".[3] A beautiful woman,
denominated Dame Feie, would be given to him who fought with most
valour and manhood. The Grail was set up on a marsh amidst tents
and pavilions. On the day of celebration, after the guests had heard
Mass, it is said that they went before the Grail, to look thereon. Each
was permitted to touch a visitor's shield—these being hung on a certain
tree—when its owner came forward and fought with him who had thus
given the challenge. An old merchant, however, won Dame Feie and
married her off, giving her enough to leave her wild life. About 1478
Gert van de Schuren says that the Knight Elyas " came out from the

---

[1] Philip Stefan Barto : TANNHÄUSER AND THE MOUNTAIN OF VENUS, New York,
1916, pp. 8, 9. Cf. B. ten Brink : GESCHICHTE DER ENGLISCHEN LITERATUR, II, p. 216.
" Back of the entire belief there seems to be the idea of a Mystical Church independent
of the visible and established Church, a Church in fact which had its own apostles and
servants." Quoted by Barto.
[2] Barto, *Op. cit.*, pp. 8, 113, citing F. von der Hagen, III, pp. 150, 151, 376, with
Minnesinger extracts.
[3] *Ib.*, pp. 9, 10, 114, 115, on the authority of the CHRONIKEN DER DEUTSCHEN STÄDTE,
VII, pp. 168 *et seq.*, *sub anno* 1281.

Earthly Paradise which some call the Grail ".[1] The last Minnesinger, Oswald van Wolkenstein, uses the term as a synonym for sexual pleasure. A fair lady, parting from her lover at daybreak, calls him her " highest Grail, which covers all my sorrows ".[2] John Veldenaer, writing about 1480, says that according to certain Chronicles, the Knight of the Swan came out of the Grail, " as the Earthly Paradise was called ".[3] Johann Frisch quotes a work of the fifteenth century according to which the Grail meant a dance or carousal.[4] Casper Abel terms it a sort of festival or game of a merry and ribald nature.[5]

These are like accidents of the subject in its gross degeneration ; but it came about that popular tradition placed the Grail Paradise in the depths of a hollow mountain. Arthur is King of such a realm in the WARTBURGKRIEG.[6] Many heroes were with him, as well as the goddess Juno and a daughter of the Sibyl. There is no need to say that this Other-World Faërie was under the ban of the Church or that any communication therewith was apostasy of the worst kind. In 1410 Dietrich of Neim speaks of a mountain in Italy, near Puteoli, and says that it was called the Grail by many deluded Germans, according to whom it was the abode of those who were " given over to dancing, to wantonness and the practice of Magic Arts ".[7] In 1583 Johann Fischart identified the supposed Paradise with the Mountain of Venus ; but there is evidence that the mysterious realm began to be called by this name at an earlier period. It is first mentioned by Johann Nider, as one speaking from afar and asking whether there is any truth in the Mount of Venus story where men are said to be leading " a life of ease and lustful pleasure in company with beautiful women ".[8] A mountain of the Sibyl in the Appennines was known also by this title : in both cases it is to be understood that there was no Grail connection. It would seem also that as this denomination grew it displaced the old name, which moreover had not passed into Italy. But even in Germany, when the DEUTSCHE HELDENBUCH testifies that the famous Eckart is still in front of *frau Venus berg* and will be there till the crack of doom we hear nothing of the Grail in this familiar Saga. The task of Eckart is to warn those who would enter of that which awaits them and its dangers : it is presumably for this reason that he is called " the faithful Eckart ".[9] Its attractions are depicted with relish by Hermann von

[1] Barto, *Op. cit.*, p. 10. Cf. Blöte : ZEITSCHRIFT FÜR DEUTSCHES ALTERTUM, XLII, p. 4.   [2] See Wolkenstein, edited by Schatz, No. 11.
[3] W. Hertz : PARZIVAL, 1898, p. 465.
[4] TEUTSCH-LATEINISCHES WÖRTERBUCH, *sub nomine* GRAL.
[5] SAMMLUNG ETLICHER NOCH NICHT GEDRUCKTEN ALTEN CHRONICKEN, p. 56.
[6] See Simrock's edition, stanzas 83–87. They are translated by Barto, pp. 11, 12. It appears that those who dwell in the mountain have flesh and bones, as when they lived on earth. Moreover, Knights are sent forth occasionally therefrom to the aid of Christendom.
[7] We have Professor Gardner's authority that the Grail never took root in Italy, and the " deluded Germans " are responsible probably for the Grail ascription. The eminence in question was known as MONS SANCTÆ BARBARÆ, according to Schilter : THESAURUS ANTIQUITATUM, Vol. III.   [8] Barto, *Op. cit.*, p. 18.
[9] This denomination is familiar in the PHANTASUS of Ludwig Tieck ; but long previously Hans Sachs praised him as " true Eckart."

Sachsenheim, who tells of its many diversions, its harps and horns and pipes, its gold and precious stones, etc.[1] So also does Altswert in DER TUGENDEN SCHATZ.[2] Felix Faber, *circa* 1483, locates the Mountain in Cyprus, where it was sewn with lustful plants. There were caverns for the worship of Adonis and gardens for pleasure and revelry. He tells also of a Mountain in Tuscany where the Court of Venus was held. There is lastly his story of Danhuser, a noble Swabian, who was in the Mountain with Venus but being stirred by repentance, contrived to leave it and make his confession to the Pope. He was refused absolution and returned thereupon to the Mountain.[3]

It may be added that the Mount of Venus in Italy is mentioned by Paracelsus, who accepts the myth as literal.[4] Later still German references thereto are found in the poems of Hans Sachs.[5] The fable was hawked about by travelling scholars and became ultimately a theme of ribaldry. There is no occasion to multiply the stories further or to speak of the Tannhäuser Saga, which lies beyond my province. It is held to be of German origin, the tales of Tuscany and Cyprus notwithstanding.

Barto concludes thus his thesis of origin : " the Venusberg is of German birth and is but a later appellation for the ancient German Paradise, to which the first name attached was that of the Grail ". He fails to shew, however, that the denomination is of real antiquity. All his citations of the term in connection with the Mountain of Venus are of a date posterior to the periods of Wolfram and Albrecht. In conclusion the German Grail may have come from Heaven and may have been carried subsequently to the Land of Prester John, but its last destination was the *descensus Averni* under the designation of Mount of Venus. In the French Cycle it was desecrated sufficiently under the auspices of the Tristram Legend and the pseudo-Borron Quest ; but it was not diabolised.

---

[1] Barto quotes from a poem of Sachsenheim entitled DIU MÖRIN.

[2] He speaks of varied grace and beauty—a wondrous round—and testifies that one might travel far on earth to find such joys elsewhere.

[3] Barto, *Op. cit.*, pp. 22, 122, 123.

[4] The Strassburg collected edition is cited, but I know only that of Geneva, 3 vols. in folio. Paracelsus affirms that Venus is dead, the Mount of Venus notwithstanding, and that her Kingdom has perished with her. On the other hand, the Tannhäuser Legend is genuine and not a mere fiction.

[5] Barto cites NEUDRUCKE DEUTSCHER LITERATURWERKE, IX, pp. 13, 16, 20.

BOOK VIII

WELSH AND ENGLISH TEXTS

THE ARGUMENT

I. THE WELSH PERCEVAL.—How it was held to have existed in an Earlier Form—Qualifications and Reversal of this Judgment—A Reflection from French Sources—Absence of the Grail Talisman—The Peredur of Wales as the Perceval of the Conte del Graal—Correspondences with the other Hallows —The Stone and Spear—The Bowl filled with Wine—The Question of the Story—Early History of Peredur—The Episode of the Tent—The Red Knight and the Golden Goblet—Peredur at the Court of King Arthur—The Dwarfs and Kay—Destruction of the Red Knight—Peredur is taught Chivalry by an Uncle—A Rich Fisher—Another Uncle in his Castle of Talismans—The Broken Sword and the Bleeding Spear—The Head swimming in Blood—Peredur asks nothing—He leaves the Castle next morning—He is Reproached by a Beautiful Maiden—A Besieged Maiden who corresponds to Blanchefleur in the Conte—An Unwelcome Suitor Vanquished—Peredur's Love Trance—Second Visit to the Court of King Arthur—A Third Visit— The Secret of a One-Eyed Lord—The Mound of Mourning—The Stone of Wealth—Peredur Conquers the Addanc—He is Entertained by an Empress for Fourteen Years—Returns to the Court of King Arthur—The Laidly Damosel—The Fatality of the Question—Peredur goes in search of the Lance and its Story—He is Upbraided for Bearing Arms on Good Friday— He Visits a Castle of Wonders—The Chess-Board Episode—Return to the Castle of Talismans—The Question is Forgotten and there is no Exhibition of Talismans—He is Commissioned to Destroy the Sorceresses of Gloucester —The Story left Unfinished. II. THE ENGLISH METRICAL ROMANCE OF SYR PERCYVELLE.—A Later Text than the Mabinogi of Peredur—Similar Claim to Antiquity made on its behalf—Same Result in Last Conclusions of Scholarship—Another Reflection from Chrétien—The Antithesis of Grail Romances—Absence of any Question and any Hallows—Perceval's Early History in this Text—Recurrence of the Red Knight Episode—Perceval at the Court of King Arthur—Death of the Red Knight—Destruction of his Mother—Perceval is Entertained at a Castle—A Messenger from the Maiden Land—Position of the Lady Lufamour—Perceval goes forth to her Rescue— His Battle in her Cause—Arrival of King Arthur and his Companions— Perceval is Knighted by the King—He Weds Lufamour and Becomes Ruler of her Country—He sets off to Find his Mother—Success of this Mission— He Brings her to the Maiden Land and she Abides therein—He goes to the Holy Land and Dies there in Warfare.

BOOK VIII

WELSH AND ENGLISH TEXTS

I

THE WELSH PERCEVAL

THIS is one of the two texts which have been held to offer independent proofs of a pre-Christian and pre-Grail period of the Quest ; but in their present state they are among the latest documents of the literature. It is perhaps more perilous to speak of the MABINOGI concerning Peredur, the son of Evrawc, than of anything extant among authentic Grail texts : its dimensions are small, but it has offered a field of debate for more than fifty years. The RED BOOK OF HERGEST, of which it forms one of the stories, is found in a Welsh manuscript which belongs probably to the beginning of the fourteenth century ; but the contents of the collection were long held to have existed in a much earlier form, now as usual unknown. The voice of criticism concerning the PEREDUR became less assured, however, as time went on, and has at length reversed its judgment. We are concerned in the first place with the story itself, admitting that the wildness of old Welsh manner and atmosphere might suggest to an unfamiliar mind its correspondence in essentials with the claims once made respecting it—or that it is among the oldest of the Quests. On the other hand, there is nothing to support the unimaginative and frigid panegyric which, because the plot turns on a conventional and not very purposeful vendetta, terms the narrative logical and straightforward. On the contrary, it is confused and disconcerting. It is indeed among the idlest of stories and leaves several of its episodes unfinished. There was in fact something to be said from the beginning for an alternative construction placed on the document, that instead of an intermediate between folk-lore and Grail literature, it is demonstrably a chaotic reflection from a single French source. It is, however, to all intents and purposes an undigested medley of several elements ; for while it derives in the main and beyond all contradiction from the CONTE of Chrétien, we must remember that behind that poem there is the almost world-wide Mythos of the Great Fool, that story of the half-wild boy who becomes a great hero. It follows that the earliest and unfinished Grail Quest has this root in folk-lore. It must be remembered also that long after Chrétien, or *circa* 1227, Manessier's conclusion of the CONTE effects the healing of the Grail King by introducing the Vengeance Legend, which is another folk-lore element, though an almost ridiculous stress has been laid upon this fact on the part of scholarship.[1]

The PEREDUR at its value is a version of the Great Fool Mythos and is also a tale of vengeance,[2] though the presence of the latter motive signifies as much and as little for explanatory values as does its absence from the PERLESVAUS, the Galahad QUEST and the DIDOT-MODENA PERCEVAL. It includes therefore some part of those elements which belong to the Grail literature, though much was abandoned when the Quest was carried into transcension.

Whether regarded as a Sacrament or Telesma, it is to be understood that there is nothing in the Welsh Perceval which answers to the Holy Grail, as this is described and manifested in any of the Grail Cycles ; but it has been brought into the category of the literature for three palmary reasons : (1) Because it embodies the idea of a Quest ; (2) because this Quest is connected with asking a Conventional Question concerning certain Talismans ; (3) because these Talismans are in the House of a King or Lord who is maimed and whose healing would have resulted from the Question. Outside these specific correspondences, it is obvious that Peredur of Wales is the Percival le Gallois of the CONTE DEL GRAAL and some other Grail Romances, while, all variations notwithstanding, the History of the one, in a broad sense, is also the History of the other. As regards variations, some important points may be scheduled at once as follows : (1) The motive of the Quest does not enter into the story until nearly its very end ; (2) the Question is never asked ; (3) there is no record that the King is ever healed ; (4) the one accredited Talisman of the whole story does not figure as that weapon which caused the maiming of the story.

It should be noted, however, with due consideration for what has been said to the contrary by criticism, that shadows of the characteristic Grail Hallows are to be found in the story for the further confusion of the issues ; but they serve no purpose therein. (1) THE CUP : there are, in fact, two Cups, both filled with wine and presented with their contents to Perceval, on condition that he fights with their bearers. (2) THE BOWL, also filled with wine, and this passes on similar conditions. Perceval slays the bearers ; and we shall see that he is afterwards entertained by an Empress for fourteen years. This incident has no analogy with anything in the other documents. (3) THE STONE, which is guarded by a serpent and is carried on the tail of the reptile.

---

[1] The vendetta motive belongs to folk-lore because it belongs to human history *ab origine* and will do so *ad sæcula sæculorum*. There is no excuse therefore for affirming that Manessier and Heinrich—who has also the vengeance motive—were indebted for the introduction to folk-lore, when they drew obviously from the wells of human nature. The Vespers of Palermo, for example, are not referable to folk-lore, nor are the records of Scotland Yard.

[2] There has been recognised also of comparatively recent years the fact that it represents an undigested amalgamation of three different stories.

The virtue of this Stone is that whosoever possesses it and holds it in one hand may have in the other as much gold as he desires. The analogy is therefore rather with the purse of Fortunatus than with a Feast of Good Things ; but incidentally it recalls the latter. (4) THE SPEAR : this is of mighty size, with three streams of blood flowing from its point to the ground. It is the only so-called Talisman of the story, the only one which appears in the Castle of Talismans, and its purpose is to occasion the Question which, if answered, will lead to the King's healing. Why it is a spear and why it distils blood the story does not explain.[1] It has either been transferred from some other Legend, as, for example, a genuine Grail Romance, and placed without much reason in its present setting, or there is no better instance of such an alleged transfer in the whole Cycle. The Spear is seen once only, and on that occasion is accompanied by a large Salver in which is a man's head, surrounded with a profusion of blood.

The Question which Peredur should have asked was the meaning and the cause of these wonders. He is cursed the next morning by his foster-sister, but it is not because he forbears at the instance of his maternal uncle. It is only after long years that his silence is denounced by a boy disguised as a laidly woman ; but at the end of the whole business the Question, as we have seen, is not asked. Apparently it is too late, and Perceval had only a single chance, as he had in the poem of Heinrich and, after another sense, in the LONGER PROSE PERCEVAL. The penalty of his original failure is (1) that " the lame king will have to endure battles and conflicts " ; (2) that his knights will perish ; (3) that " wives will be widows, and maidens will be left portionless." It does not appear that any of these disasters come to pass ; but certain Sorceresses of Gloucester, who caused the King's lameness among other misdeeds, are destroyed, which does not heal the King, so that the Vendetta is a vain affair.

The father of Peredur was Evrawc, who owned the earldom of the North and had seven sons, with six of whom he was slain, for they began in the folly of tournaments and so ended.[2] Peredur, the surviving and youngest son, was taken by his mother into the wilderness, where he could see neither horses nor arms, lest he also should become a great warrior before the face of the Lord, and die in battle, with all that violence which signified the perfection of valour in those days of harsh adventure. His companions were the women of his mother, with some boys and spiritless men. In spite of such precautions he was destined, however, to depart from the house of his childhood in the wild and solitary ways, where the life which he led was like that of a savage hermit. He was the cutting of a fruit-tree and was sadly in need of grafting : grafted he was in the end on the Great Tree of Knighthood, yet he behaved throughout with the thoughtlessness of the impassioned

---

[1] There is no elucidation in Chrétien.

[2] I am reproducing the Early History at some length to make evident its substantial identity with the CONTE of Chrétien.

man. It is only in the Grail Romances that he puts forth many blossoms, and sometimes splendidly ; but even then he does not bear the good fruit after its own kind in anything but the latest texts.

One day Peredur saw three knights, and his Mother said that they were Angels.[1] He decided to become an Angel; but the questions which he put to them subsequently having obtained a more reliable account, he resolved further to follow their vocation. Finding that she could not dissuade him, his Mother gave him some notable instructions, as, for example, that he should pay court to a fair woman, whether she would or not, and that if he obtained anything precious he should bestow it, and so earn fame for his largesse. In fine, she told him to repair to the Court of King Arthur. He mounted a sorry hackney and began a long journey. Arriving at a rich tent in a glade, he mistook it for a Church and repeated his *Pater noster*, having little else of religion ; but the tent contained a beautiful lady, who gave him refreshment and allowed him to take a ring from her hand.[2] Now, he who was the lord of the glade became angry because of Peredur, and said that the lady, who was his wife, should not rest two nights in the same house till he had visited vengeance upon him.

As the youth drew towards the Court of King Arthur, a Red Knight entered the Palace, and seeing how the Queen was served with wine by a page from a golden goblet, he dashed the liquor in her face[3] and smote her on the face also. But, despite this challenge, such was the unknightly condition of the Round Table that all present feared to avenge the insult, believing that the aggressor had magical protection ; and so he retired with the vessel. Peredur then rode in, and asked for the honour of Knighthood ; but because of his outlandish appearance, he was treated with indignity by Kay and others of the household. A male and female dwarf, who had dwelt in the palace for a twelvemonth, uttering no word, found their tongues suddenly to praise him as the Flower of Chivalry, for which they were beaten by Kay. When Peredur demanded the accolade, he was told jeeringly to follow the Red Knight, recover the goblet, and possess himself of his horse and armour. He found no difficulty in obeying, and by slaying the Knight he accomplished his first mission of vengeance, which contains a more important implicit than the vindication of Arthur's Queen ; for, unknown to himself, the Red Knight was he who had slain his Father. The removal of the armour he could not accomplish till Sir Owain of the Round Table came to his help, after which he assumed it and mounted the dead man's horse. He restored the goblet to Owain ; but to return and receive Knighthood at the King's hands he refused until he had punished Kay for the insult which he had offered to the dwarfs. In this manner he began his second mission of vengeance, the implicit

---

[1] Cf. CONTE DEL GRAAL, ed. of Potvin, II, p. 41.

[2] The text emblazons the original accounts freely : for example, at this point the Lady is said to be seated on a golden chair, near the door of the tent. Cf. the CONTE, *ib.*, II, pp. 62–67.

[3] Compare the version of Chrétien, in which the King is the victim.

whereof involved his own vindication, because he, too, had been treated injuriously. After various encounters, the result of which is that many were sent to place themselves at King Arthur's mercy,[1] on account of the dwarfs, he met with an ancient man, richly vested, whose attendants were fishing on a lake, and who was therefore the substituted Rich Fisher of the Grail stories.[2]

It does not seem to follow that the servants caught anything; but if they did it was not to our purpose. The ancient man was lame, and he is therefore an alternative of the Maimed King. He retired into a Castle at hand, whither Peredur followed, and being there welcomed he learned that the host was his own Uncle. By him—in the space of a few hours—he was taught Chivalry, was cautioned, for no apparent reason, against asking questions, and was assured that any reproach involved by his silence should not fall on the boy but on himself only. It is as if this uncle said : " Do not explore the Concealed Mysteries : I will account." He accounts so badly, however, that the disgrace is ultimately on Peredur.

The next day the youth reached another Castle where he found a second Uncle, at whose bidding he smote a great staple three times with a sword, and both were shattered. The first and second time he rejoined the pieces of the sword, and the staple was also made good, as if automatically. The third time neither would unite, and we thus have an alternative of the Broken Sword in the Grail Legends ; but nothing follows in the Welsh story, nor is the weapon heard of afterwards. What next occurred at the Castle was a Rite as of a Lodge of Mourning. Two youths entered the hall bearing a mighty Spear, from which poured torrents of blood : and at the sight of this all the Company present fell into grievous lamentation. Two Maidens followed carrying a large Salver, whereon was a man's head ; and this, which was swimming in blood, as we have heard previously, caused another great outcry. Peredur, however, had been counselled well, and he asked nothing concerning these marvels, which fact constitutes the Great Mystery of the Voided Question and the prolonged sorrow of the Lord.[3] Now, either the two Uncles are distinct persons inhabiting two Castles, in which case (1) the story identifies them afterwards, although vaguely ; (2) the relations are working one against the other, unless there is some cryptic understanding between them ; or (3) they are one person strangely confused, while the Castles are one Castle, in which case the lame Uncle himself issues that decree of silence which will delay his healing indefinitely and testifies to his separate existence as the Brother first seen by his guest. Whatever alternative is chosen, the story rests distracting.

On the morning that followed these occurrences Peredur rode away from the Castle, and while still in its vicinity he came upon a beautiful

---

[1] No less than sixteen Knights are said to have been vanquished in a single week : contrast the comparative sobriety of the French story.

[2] Confused, however, with Perceval's instructor in the CONTE. *Ib.*, II, pp. 86 *et seq.*

[3] *Op. cit.*, II, pp. 143–150, ll. 4264–4488.

Maiden, who was watching by the side of her dead husband, who has been slain by the Knight in the woodland glade. She told the youth that she was his foster-sister, that he was responsible for his Mother's death because of his desertion, and that he had therefore become accursed.

We shall see in the sequel that he was under interdict after two manners, but in neither case does it appear to carry a consequence. After this meeting, in which he does everything to assist the distressed lady,[1] and to recognise a relationship for which there is nothing to account in the story, he continued his journey and reached yet another Castle, wherein was a high-born Maiden, also in stress and besieged by an earl whom she would not consent to wed. The unwelcome suitor was vanquished by Peredur, who sent him to the Court of King Arthur, restored all her possessions to the despoiled Lady, and after the space of three weeks again rode away. It should be noted that this Maiden is the Blanchefleur of the CONTE DEL GRAAL, the bride-elect of the hero according to Chrétien de Troyes, his wife in the conclusion of Gerbert, and so also in the PARZIVAL of Wolfram.

At this stage, as might be expected, Peredur encountered for a second time the Lady of the Tent or Pavilion, only to find her in sorry straits through her lord's treatment, owing to the intrusion of the youth in the early part of the story. He overcame the Knight in due course, enforced the usual pilgrimage, and pledged him to deal loyally with the Lady in future, she having been at fault in nothing. In the Adventure which next followed, he found that a whole country had been wasted by nine Sorceresses of Gloucester, and they were now attacking the sole remaining Castle, for no object assigned or assignable. Over one of them Peredur prevailed, and she—though aware from of old of all that they must suffer at his hands—invited him to their palace. During three weeks he led a hidden life among them for the ostensible purpose of learning Chivalry, which he knew already by its practice and otherwise by the instruction of his Uncle : it is thus certain that they could teach him little thereof, and of honour or virtue nothing.[2]

By this time Peredur had sent so many Knights as hostages to Arthur's Court, in part to justify the dwarfs, that the King determined to seek for him. The search began accordingly, and after he had taken leave of his imputed instructors, the youth was found by the Companions of the Round Table at the moment when he was wrapped in the now familiar love-trance, thinking of the lady of his heart. Kay, among others, disturbed Peredur rudely, and was chastised with violence. In this manner was accomplished the second mission of vengeance, or rather its implied part. Gwalchmai, who is Gawain, approached Peredur gently and courteously, and so brought him to the King.[3] All went to Caerleon, and there Peredur, who, by inference

---

[1] He inters the body, overcomes the Knight of the glade and covenants him to marry her whom he has made a widow—thus following but contradicting the CONTE. See *Op. cit.*, pp. 156, 157 and 160–163.

[2] It will be observed that this futile episode is not in debt to the CONTE.

[3] The literal identity with Chrétien's account will be noticed throughout this episode. *Op. cit.*, II, pp. 186–197.

from his trance and a certain period of tarrying, may be supposed to have loved previously the Lady of the Castle, became deeply enamoured of another Maiden ; but seeing that she failed to respond, he vowed himself to silence in all Christendom till she should love him above every man. He left King Arthur's Court and passed through various Adventures, which are devoid of analogy with those of the other Romances. The time came when he yearned to revisit Caerleon and again have the Maiden's society, besides that of the Chivalry. At the Court on account of his silence he suffered further indignity, still on the part of Kay ; but after many signal examples of valour, the Lady of his affections, although she did not recognise him, confessed that if only he could speak, she should love him best of all men, as she did indeed already, his dumbness notwithstanding. So was he delivered from his vow ;[1] and as he had sent many gifts to the male and female dwarfs, after a votive manner, it is to be inferred that his second vengeance was further and fully accomplished by the disgrace which his deeds reflected upon the unworthy Kay.

At a later period, he being again on his travels, Peredur arrived at a Castle, where the Lord was a Black Man who had lost one of his eyes, and it was his custom to destroy every visitor who went to the place unasked. One of the Lord's daughters interceded vainly, when he who at the time of need neglected to question his own uncle demanded now an explanation of the circumstances under which his present host had been deprived partially of sight. For this he was informed that he should not escape with his life. However, in due course, he conquered the Black Master of the House and slew him, after learning his secret. That secret caused him to visit another Castle, the knights in which rode out daily to do battle with an obscure monster, which is termed an Addanc in the story ; their bodies were brought back by the horses, and they themselves were raised up again nightly by the women of the household.[2] Peredur, as will be expected, went forth to destroy the monster and, in return for the pledge of his future love, he was presented by a Strange Woman with a Stone which insured his success. As regards the covenant between them, he was told when he next sought her to seek in the East—that is to say, in India ; but we hear nothing more concerning her. Omitting an intermediate episode on which little depends, he came to the Mound of Mourning, where three hundred nobles guarded a serpent until the time should come for it to die. The explanation is that the tail of the serpent contained that Mysterious Stone to which I have referred already—the Stone of Wealth Inexhaustible—and the intent of the whole Company was to compete for this jewel. Peredur destroyed the serpent, which they did not dare to attempt, and, having compensated the other seekers, he bestowed the prize on a Knight who had been in his service, thus fulfilling

[1] And so ends the second love-episode, left at a loose end like the first : nothing further is heard of either Lady.
[2] See Book IX, § 1, concerning a Scottish Vessel of Balsam and the Cauldron of the Blessed Bran.

one behest of his Mother. He next reached a galaxy of tents, gathered about the pavilion of the Empress Cristinobyl, who was resolved to wed the most valiant man in the world, and him only. This was the unknown Enchantress by whose aid he was enabled to conquer the Addanc. The place was filled with competitors for her hand ; but Peredur overcame them all, and was entertained by the Empress for fourteen years, as the story is said to relate : it is the only appeal to some antecedent source which occurs in the whole text—and it has not been identified. In this way the hero's variable affections find their rest for a period—by inference, in such a Land of Faërie as was visited by Ogier the Dane.

Peredur came back at length to the Court of King Arthur, without having attracted apparently any surprise at his absence ; and, almost immediately after, the Palace was visited by a Laidly Damosel, through whom it transpired what misery followed the failure to ask the Question at the Castle of the Lame King.[1] It is to be noted that so only, almost at the end of the story, does the hero learn anything concerning his omission and the fatality which it involved. He was reproached, as we have seen, bitterly by his foster-sister, but not about this matter ; and the inference is that so far he had only reason for satisfaction in having followed the counsel of his first uncle—until the time came when he forgot the injunction at the Castle of the one-eyed Lord. Being now undeceived, he vowed to rest never until he knew the story of the Lance. He departed accordingly, while, at the suggestion of the same visitant, Gawain went in quest of a Castle on a high mountain, wherein it is said that there was a certain Maid in prison, and the fame of the world was promised to him who released her. This is the only instance, and a shadow at that, in which any Quest is allotted to the hero of all gallantry in this story, though his adventures occupy so large a space in the CONTE DEL GRAAL. We hear nothing, however, as to the term reached by Gawain. Peredur, after long wanderings in search of the Laidly Maiden, whom he seems to have regarded as a guide, was accosted by a Hermit, who upbraided him for bearing arms on so holy a day as Good Friday.[2] Recalled to that shadow-sense of religion which he had forgotten apparently, he responded in a becoming manner and received some directions which brought him ultimately to the Castle of Wonders. The first marvel which he saw therein was the inevitable chess-board, whereon automatic pieces were playing the game by themselves. The side which he favoured was defeated, and in his anger he cast both board and men into a lake. The Laidly Maiden appeared thereupon and reproached him. He was set certain tasks, under the pretext of recovering the playthings.[3] They included that Adventure of stag and hound with which we have made acquaintance previously ; but the term of all was to bring him for a second time to

---

[1] Potvin, *Op. cit.*, II, pp. 200–205.
[2] CONTE, *Op. cit.*, II, pp. 254 *et seq.*
[3] *Ib.*, Wauchier's continuation, IV, pp. 76–83.

the Castle of his maimed Uncle and to the end of his Quest. Thither Gawain had preceded him ; and in this manner, as in several of the Grail Romances, the Knight of earthly courtesy is somehow connected with the Quest—whether he has undertaken it himself, or by accident, as in this instance.

Peredur found no Lance, and we have seen that he asked no Question ; but he was told by a yellow-haired youth, who begged the boon of his friendship—since they two were Cousins—that it was he who in the far past carried the Ensanguined Talisman, that he bore also the Salver, and—at the end of Peredur's long years of Adventure, long years of Faërie Life—that he appeared as the Laidly Maiden. As the Question had passed into the limbus of desuetude and, all his vow notwithstanding, as he asked and learned nothing concerning the Lance, it is possible, as I have suggested, that the opportunity of asking and of receiving knowledge was not granted a second time to the seeker. With these things also withdrew the Foster-Sister of Peredur, his dubious alternative Uncle and the first Lady of his Love. No one thought further about them, though the seeker did learn that the Head on the Dish of Blood was that of another Cousin, who was killed by the Sorceresses of Gloucester. It was they also who lamed his Uncle, and for this he was to wreak vengeance upon them. Here therefore was the third and final Vendetta which Peredur accomplished, with the assistance, curiously enough, of Arthur and all his Household, by the destruction of the nine Priestesses of Evil Magic. Whether this restored his Uncle or relieved the land and the people is not told in the story, nor do we learn anything further concerning the hero, or what, in fine, became of him. Perhaps in the Castle of his Uncle he completed a third period of hidden life.

I have not entered into the Quest of the Holy Grail for the unsatisfying purpose of reproducing the Romances in full Synopsis, all repetition notwithstanding, and those more especially which are outside the issue of my real concern. But because of the claims which were once advanced respecting it, as the last reflection of some primordial type of Quest, and because of that later criticism which rejects such earlier findings, the Welsh Perceval has called for adequate analysis. It is a story without an end, even as its French model, the CONTE DEL GRAAL. It reproduces Chrétien's story, in combination with material drawn from Welsh sources now unknown, producing an inextricable jumble : it contributes nothing therefore to the understanding of the Grail subject. From my own point of view, the fact is perhaps regrettable, as it can never be unprofitable to find the beginning of a Myth or even an earlier state and stage. As things are, we are left with the CONTE DEL GRAAL of Chrétien as the first record in literature regarding Perceval le Gallois. I could do better, as it seems to me, with an early Celtic Saga behind his story.

II

THE ENGLISH METRICAL ROMANCE OF
SYR PERCYVELLE

WE have seen that the non-Grail Quest of Peredur does not contain the fibrous roots of a Legend which is earlier than the Grail period of literature. There is, however, the English poem of SYR PERCYVELLE, which belongs to the late fourteenth century, being therefore long posterior to the MABI-NOGIÓN of the RED BOOK, though there is said to be an Italian story which is even later still.[1] A similar claim to antiquity has been made and maintained on behalf of this text and, as will be found, with the same result in the last conclusions of scholarship. From one point of view there is of course no question that it is in the position assigned thereto : that is to say, the poem is a *circa* 1370 presentation of an older story, being the CONTE of Chrétien, modified there and here, and brought briefly to a suitable conclusion. For the rest, its elements are those of a plain tale, primitive and characteristic as such of the period to which it belongs. It is less disconcerting and aimless than the Welsh PEREDUR, is, moreover, in perfect harmony with itself, has a conclusion proper to its beginning and intervening incidents which so work together that the term indicated at the start is brought consistently to pass.

It is the antithesis of any of the Grail Romances : there is only the shadow of a Quest, and it is found at the end of all ; moreover, there is no Question ; there are no Hallows of any kind, either Lance or Sword or Cup ; and, finally, there is no Enchantment of Britain. It is a savage story—naked and not ashamed : it calls on the kingdom of blood to be manifested about the hero, and he ensures its coming.

The mere skeleton of the poem will exhibit its points of contact with Chrétien and the Welsh Peredur, as also its variations therefrom. The Father of Perceval, who bore rather curiously an identical name, was married for his valiant deeds to a Sister of King Arthur. She gave him only the one son ; for a great tourney was held to celebrate the birth, and thereat the Father was slain by a Knight in Red Armour. As in the Grail Romances, his widow fled into the wilderness, taking the child with her, so that he should know nothing about deeds of arms. He was brought up in the fell and the wild wood, with wild beasts for his companions. However, as the boy grew up the Mother allowed him a small Scotch spear, and with this he became so dexterous that nothing could escape him. He was clothed in skins, and for a long time seems to have been reared as a heathen ; but it came about at length that the

---

[1] I have failed to trace this story, nor does it perhaps signify. Prof. E. G. Gardner says in another connection that the sole allusion in Italian literature to Perceval's failure over " the fateful Question " occurs, so far as he has found, in a poem of Guittone d'Arezzo, who belongs to the thirteenth century.

Lady taught him some prayers to the Son of God,[1] and shortly after he met with three Knights of King Arthur's Court, namely, Gawain, Yvain and Kay. He inquired which of them was the Great God about whom his mother had taught him, and threatened to slay them if they refused to answer.[2] He was told who they were, and then asked whether King Arthur would knight him also. Being referred to the Monarch himself, he seized a wild horse, took leave of his Mother, and rode to Court clothed in skins of beasts, nourishing a firm resolution to destroy the King if he would not grant his request. At parting the Mother had given him a ring to be kept as a token, and had promised that she would await his return. On his road he reached a Pavilion wherein was a Lady asleep. He kissed her and exchanged a certain ring which she wore for the one that had been presented to himself. He arrived at the Court of all Chivalry, and King Arthur recognised the boy's likeness to that older Perceval who had received his own sister as wife. The King, however, and apparently the whole Chivalry had been reduced to recurring distress through fear of a Red Knight, who came regularly to rob the Monarch of the Cup out of which he was drinking. Perceval's arrival was coincident with another visitation of this kind, being the fifth during as many years. The Cup was of red gold, and it was seized while the Royal Feaster was in the act of putting it to his lips. Perceval, who was a witness, offered to bring back the vessel if Arthur would knight him, and the King promised to do so on his return.[3] He went to fetch armour for the child ; but Perceval in the meantime departed. The Red Knight did not wish to do battle with so sorry an opponent ; but in the end there was a momentary combat, Perceval slaying the Champion by throwing his dart, which passed through one of his eyes. For what it is worth, we have here a fortuitous shadow of that Vengeance Legend, examples of which in the Grail Literature have been studied with zeal by scholarship. I have said that Perceval slays the Red Knight ; but, as in the WELSH PEREDUR, he does so without knowing that the victim was responsible for his Father's death : his sole and simple object is to wipe out an affront offered to the King. After the encounter Perceval, with the assistance of Gawain, who had followed and come upon the scene, stripped the body of the armour, and the youth was clothed therein. He did not return to claim the promised reward of Knighthood, and Gawain was the bearer of the Cup to the Palace. Perceval's next office was to destroy a witch who was the mother of the Red Knight, and on account of his armour he was taken then and subsequently for that personage himself. He was entertained later on at the Castle of an old Knight, to which there came presently from the Maiden Land a Messenger who was on his way to

---

[1] The poem says that this took place at the age of fifteen.
[2] He supposed Christ to be a person who could be met, as natural man meets man.
[3] It would seem that the High Order of Chivalry was acquired rather quickly and cheaply in those days and at that Royal Court, for Arthur was proposing to confer it upon Perceval in the midst of a daily meal when he was prevented by the intrusion of the Red Knight.

King Arthur, entreating assistance for his Mistress, the Lady Lufamour. She was being oppressed by a "Sultan" who desired her for his wife, and because of her refusal he had not only slain her father and brother but had wasted her lands, so that she had only one Castle left in which to take refuge. To this retreat Perceval asked his way, with the intention of destroying the "Saracen"; but the Messenger preferred to continue his own road and get help from the King. Perceval, on his part, determined to discover it for himself, and three sons of his host insisted on accompanying him, which they did for a certain distance, after which he contrived to shake them off. Meanwhile the Messenger reached the Court and had a very indifferent answer from Arthur, who, together with his Chivalry, appears in a pitiful light throughout all the early portion of the story. The King, in fact, tells him that there is no Lord in his land who is worthy to be called a Knight. However, on hearing a description of the valiant youth who was seen by the Messenger from the Castle on his road to Court, the King concluded that this was Perceval, whereupon he called for horses, arms and three Companions of his Table[1] to follow in quest of the hero, fearing that he might be slain before they could reach him. By this time Perceval had arrived at the Maiden Land, and found a host of pavilions marshalled about a city. He set to and slew many, his ingenuous warcry being apparently that he had come to destroy a Soldan. He slept in the open field, with his dead strewn about him. The Lady Lufamour came to survey the slaughter from the height of her walls, and descried the knight whom she supposed to have effected it. She sent her Chamberlain to bring him into the city : therein she made him good cheer, and fell in love at first sight. He returned to do battle in her cause, she promising herself and the Kingdom if he destroyed the Soldan. He behaved in a manner which recalls the worst combats in Spanish Romances of Chivalry, wherein one Knight scatters a thousand Paynims. Meanwhile, King Arthur and his Companions arrived, but were mistaken by Perceval for enemies, and he fought with Gawain. However, ultimately they recognised each other and embraced. All proceeded to the Castle, where Arthur recounted to the Lady the early history of Perceval. The next morning he was Knighted by the King, and again went forth against the Soldan, whom he slew finally. He was made King of the country, and wedded Lufamour. Being still in the first year of his marriage, he remembered his Mother, and rode away to find her. This is the Quest of the story, and on the way he had to champion the Lady of the Pavilion, who had fallen into the hands of her husband for the business of the ring.[2] He reconciled

---

[1] They are those whom he met in the forest, namely, Gawain, Yvain and Kay.
[2] He heard the cry of a distressed woman and found her tied to a tree. He who was her Lord, otherwise, the Black Knight, had so done because, twelve months since, as she lay on her bed, one whom she did not see came into her pavilion and took her ring in exchange for his own. It was a ring of many virtues and whosoever wore it could not suffer death or be maimed. Perceval knew then that this was his doing. Subsequently the Black Knight would have died at his hands ; but the Lady begged for his life and it was granted on the condition that she was forgiven freely, as one who had done no wrong.

them *vi et armis*, and learned that the ring which he borrowed had strange magical powers. He proposed to exchange again ; but the husband had given that which was Perceval's to the Lord of the land, a Giant of whom none would dare to ask it. He was, indeed, the Brother of the Soldan, and there is no need to say that Perceval in due course not only defeated but dismembered him. He recovered his ring at the Giant's Castle, and learned from the Seneschal that his master had offered it to a Lady whom he besought in marriage ; that she recognised it as her Son's ring, and, supposing that he had been slain by the Giant, she fled distracted into the forest hard by. Perceval was now close on the track of his Quest-object : he assumed a garment of skins, that she might know him the more easily ; and it was not long before Mother and Son met and were henceforth reunited. They repaired to the Giant's Castle, till the Lady was restored to health and sanity. In fine, he carried her home, where she was welcomed by his Queen and the Great Lords. This was the good end of Perceval's Mother ; and in this way the story describes its perfect circle. The end of Perceval himself was in the Holy Land.

It will be seen that the English SYR PERCYVELLE is not what is called an Exile and Return Story, nor is it in any legitimate sense to be regarded as a Tale of Quest. It is so manifestly another variant delineation, *plus* an original completion, of Chrétien's CONTE that it has been deemed unnecessary to illustrate the fact by recurring annotations. The poem is another and original way of recounting the same Saga. It belongs to the Romance of Adventure rather than to Myth. If the Great Fool Story is behind the CONTE—as it is presumably—it is also behind SYR PERCYVELLE at a much later stage. And having reached this point in respect of our Welsh and English texts it seems opportune to clear the issue by adding that the far-spread Saga of the heroic simpleton is like its two late reflections—of no purpose to the Christian Mystery of the Holy Grail, which is the one and only subject of our present research. A misguided person—an American, I think—once wrote a book about Sixteen Crucified Saviours, and there may have been as many or more ; but the research concerning them is of no purpose to those who are seeking the life of high experience in the Mystical Christ.

BOOK IX

CRITICAL APPARATUS IN RESPECT OF THE GRAIL
CYCLES: CELTIC HYPOTHESIS

THE ARGUMENT

I. THE ANTECEDENTS OF THE LEGEND IN FOLK-LORE.—Summary of the Past Research—Proposed Apparatus of Criticism—Pre-Christian Folk-lore Hypothesis—Forerunners of Grail Talismans—Present Position of Proposed Grail Antecedents—Irish and Welsh Legends—The Tuatha de Danann—The Irish Avalon—The Myth and its Talismans in Wales—The Cauldron of Bran—Folk-lore and Grail Talismans—The Legend of Perceval and the Lay of the Great Fool—The Welsh Mabinogion—The Peredur Story—Survival of Old Mysteries in Christian Britain—Revival of Welsh Literature—Celtic and Latin Rites—Folk-lore Transmutations—Of Celtic Christian Hagiology. II. THE ENVIRONMENT OF THE GRAIL LITERATURE.—That which encompassed externally the Grail Subject—Heritage of Minstrels and of Druids—Power and Portent of the Latin Church—Great Doctrinal Debate on the Eucharist—Of Reservation—Of Communion in One Kind—The Grail as a Symbol of Catholic and Christian Faith—Theory of Transubstantiation—The Grail as a Reliquary—Hallows of Other Relics—Relics of the Precious Blood—Legendary Chalices—The Fable of Fécamp—The Sacred Lance in Legend—The Crown of Thorns—The True Cross—The Sacred Nails—The Shroud of Christ—A Word on Apocryphal Gospels—The *Sudarium* of Veronica—The *Volto Santo*—The Sword of St. John the Baptist—Caput Johannis —Other Environments of the Grail Subject. III. THE HOLY GRAIL IN THE LIGHT OF THE CELTIC CHURCH.—A. A POSSIBLE ORIGINATING CENTRE OF THE WHOLE MYSTERY.—The Celtic Church as an environment of the Grail literature—Its traces of Eastern influence—Of the spirit of the East in the Grail Legend—Its implicits as reflections of the Celtic Church—The source of British Christianity independent of Rome—Reference to the Johannine Rite—Certain considerations which would determine the present inquiry. B. THE FORMULÆ OF THE HYPOTHESIS SCHEDULED.—Of Britain as a microcosm of the world—An analogy from the Apocalypse—Celtic religious sympathies—The hypothesis under review—Celtic origin of the Grail Legend—The Legend as an ecclesiastical growth—The Grail Church—St. David and his miraculous Altar—The Fish Symbol and the Rich Fisherman—The Secret Words as an evasive reference to the Epiclesis Clause—Nature of this Clause in Eucharistic Consecration—Celtic Hereditary Keepers of Relics —General characteristics of the Celtic Relic—Of Mass Chalices—Of Mystic and Holy Cups—Of the Columbarium and the Grail Dove—The disappearance of St. David's Altar—Withdrawal of the Celtic Rite—The Celtic Church and the Druids—Cadwaladr and Galahad—The return of the British King —Claims connected with Glastonbury—The substitution of Joseph of Arimathæa for St. David—Further concerning Fish Symbolism—And concerning Mass Chalices—Of Mystic Bells—A Church consecrated by Christ —Super-Apostolical Succession—The House of Anjou—A Mystery of the Celtic Mass—Summary of the whole matter—The Dream of a Secret

Mass-Book. C. IN WHAT SENSE THE PLEA MUST BE HELD TO FAIL.—Some Preliminary Admissions—The Secret Tradition of the Epoch—Further concerning Super-Apostolical Succession—The Church in Britain—Absence of Passion-Relics in the Welsh Church—The Epiclesis Clause does not explain the Secret Words—Greek Mode of Consecration—Distinctions between Cadwaladr and Galahad—Fantasy of the VIR AQUATICUS—The Altar of St. David a false ground of comparison—Substitutes for the Sacramental Cup—True position of the Glastonbury claims—No substitution of Joseph for St. David—The Second Joseph—Another light on King Arthur's Chalice—And on the Mystery of the Celtic Mass—Further concerning a Secret Book of the Mass—The Pan-Britannic Church and the Grail Literature—The Celtic Church and the Literature. D. THE VICTORY OF THE LATIN RITE.—Of Rome and the other Assemblies—Why Rome prevailed—The conclusion that we must go further.

CRITICAL APPARATUS IN RESPECT OF THE GRAIL CYCLES: CELTIC HYPOTHESIS

I

THE ANTECEDENTS OF THE LEGEND IN FOLK-LORE

WE have now passed in review every text constituting and belonging, directly or indirectly, to the Grail literature, including two late documents which scholarship has connected therewith, though the Grail itself does not appear therein. My next task is to present the apparatus of criticism on the Grail subject, including the various hypotheses by which it has been sought to account for the origin of the Mythos and to explain its meaning. On the surface it is a Christian Mythos, and in the Cycle-General of Northern France its central Palladium and most of the other Talismans which are grouped about it are Relics of the Passion of Christ. It is otherwise with the German Cycle, the chief text of which was supplemented, however, by another poet who, many years subsequently, restored to the Grail of Wolfram that place in Christian Legend from which it was removed in the PARZIVAL. All this notwithstanding, it has been contended that the origin of the Grail and the Quests which arose therefrom are to be found in folk-lore rather than in Christian story, whether or not the latter should be regarded as pious legend, fable or parable. It has been held in particular to have originated in folk-lore of the Celtic race, even if the peculiar *matière Celtique* proves on examination to have its independent analogues somewhat widely distributed. As this hypothesis was adopted and favoured for a considerable number of years, it is that which calls for consideration in the first place. But seeing that at the present time the fashion of it seems passing away, I am tempted at the beginning of this section to assure my readers that it shall be approached on my own part in no spirit of prejudgment, more especially as my position in respect of the Grail and its literature remains unaffected by the hypothesis itself and by any conclusion which may be reached on its validity.

The beginnings of literature are like the beginnings of evolutionary life : they are questions of antecedents which are most commonly past finding out, and we may come perhaps to see that they do not signify vitally, because the Keys of many Mysteries are to be sought in the comprehension of the term of these rather than in their initial stages. Textual and literary scholarship was disposed for some decades to lay great and almost exclusive stress on alleged Celtic forerunners of the Grail Talismans and on certain Welsh and other supposed prototypes of the Perceval Quest in which the Sacred Vessel does not appear at all. As regards such affiliations, whether Welsh, Irish or English, I do not think that sufficient allowance has been made for the following facts : (1) That every archaic fiction and every Legend depends, as suggested previously, from prior Legend and fiction ; (2) that such antecedents are both explicit and implicit, intentional and unconscious, just as in these days we have wilful and undesigned imitation ; (3) that the persistence of Legends is frequently by the way of their transfiguration. We have done nothing to explain the Ascension of the Grail to Heaven and the Assumption of Galahad when we have ascertained that some possible centuries before there were Myths about a Cauldron of Ceridwen and that of the Dagda, any more than we have accounted for Christianity if we have ascertained, and this even indubitably, that some Ecclesiastical Ceremonial is an adaptation of pre-Christian Rites. Here, as in so many other instances, the essence of everything resides in the intention. If I possess the true Apostolical Succession, then, *ex hypothesi* at least, I do not less Consecrate the Eucharist if I use the Latin Rite, which expresses the words of institution in the past tense, or some Oriental Rite, by which they are expressed in the future, and which includes, moreover, the EPICLESIS Clause, being an Invocation of the Holy Spirit.

There is in any case no question that the Grail antecedents in folk-lore have been reduced to very slender proportions by late findings of research. Were it otherwise, I should be the last to minimise their consequence, after their own kind, just as I might not feel called to abandon some particular Official Church because I have been received into the Greater Church which is within. There was a time when I thought that certain old Myths were taken over for the purpose of Christian Grail Symbolism under the influence of a special although inexpressed motive and that subsequently to such appropriation they assumed importance. This is still an intelligible proposition, having regard to the third fact enumerated above ; but opinion has fluctuated of recent times to such an extent that even the antiquity of the Myths themselves seems under an implied challenge, as will be seen later. I am convinced also, with others who have preceded me,[1] that the faculty of invention was militantly alive in the twelfth and thirteenth centuries and that it is folly to account for its creations by the prodigal multiplication of supposititious lost texts which were held to contain the inventions in some variant or identical

---

[1] The most recent and fullest exponent of this view is Dr. J. D. Bruce, though he was preceded by other writers whom he cites in brief.

form. Subject to these qualifications, I proceed to place my readers in possession of the bare elements which were held to have been carried over from pre-Christian times into the Grail Mythos, as follows.

I. We hear of an Irish Legend concerning a Cauldron of the Dagda, from which no Company ever went away unsatisfied.[1] It was one of the four Talismans which a certain godlike race—that of the Tuatha de Danann—brought with them when they first came into Ireland.

The Talismans were a great Treasure according to an old Irish BOOK OF INVASIONS, which, however, in its present form has been referred to an undetermined date in the twelfth century.[2] The Talismans in question were (1) the LIA FAIL, otherwise, CLACH-NA-CINAANHUINN, the Stone of Fate or Destiny, now as alleged the Coronation Stone in Westminster Abbey, brought thither by Edward I.[3] (2) The Sword of Lug the Longhanded, Luga of the Long Arm, the Invincible Sword, and he who wielded it was called the Redeemer of his people.[4] (3) The Magic Spear, and this was the Spear of Lug. (4) The Cauldron of the Dagda, who is termed the good god[5] and the head apparently of the Irish Olympus.[6] The variations of its Mythos confer upon it many magical properties. Hosts of men might be fed therefrom without impairing its content.[7]

The Tuatha de Danann came from very far away, for according to one of their Legends, during the course of their wanderings, they learned Magic in Greece and thereafter migrated to Lochlann on the shores of the Baltic—Denmark and South Sweden—thence to Scotland and to Ireland in fine.[8] An alternative account says, on the authority of Tuam—that in all probability they came from Heaven.[9] Another story and one which might apply in either case speaks of a magic cloud by virtue of which they were wafted to Erin in a state of invisibility.[10] All testimonies agree that they were skilled in Magic, besides being excellent builders, poets and musicians. Their breed of horses could not be surpassed in the world, being moreover shod with silver and having golden bridles : no slave was allowed to ride them.[11] The Tuatha de Danann Knights are described as a splendid cavalcade : seven-score horsemen, all sons of Kings, wearing green mantles fringed with gold,

---

[1] See Nutt, *Op. cit.*, p. 184.

[2] W. Ralph Hall Caine : ANNALS OF THE MAGIC ISLE—that is, the Isle of Man, 1926, pp. 69 *et seq.*   [3] Cf. Nutt, *Op. cit.*, p. 184.

[4] Hall Caine, *Op. cit.*, p. 68. Luga was King of the Tuatha de Danann. See Alexander Macbain : CELTIC MYTHOLOGY AND RITES, p. 168.

[5] Nutt, *Op. cit.*, p. 185.

[6] According to Edward Clodd, he was the god of fire, and his Cauldron was the vault of the sky. Quoted without reference in ELDER FAITHS OF IRELAND, I, p. 347.

[7] Hall Caine, *Op. cit.*, p. 69. As regards the variations mentioned above they are not only those of the Cauldron *per se*, for we must include also those of the folk-lore Cup, the lore of which belongs to the same root. The Vessel and its content are said by Campbell to be common in Celtic Traditions : they are Cups taken from fairies, Cups giving all kinds of drinks, the Cup of Fionn which healed diseases and was analogous of course to the Hidden Cauldron of the Feinne and the Vessel of Balsam.—POPULAR TALES OF THE WEST HIGHLANDS, IV, p. 351.

[8] P. W. Joyce : OLD CELTIC ROMANCES, 1879, p. 401.

[9] Hall Caine, *Op. cit.*, p. 68.   [10] *Ib.*, p. 69.

[11] See Lady Wilde's ANCIENT LEGENDS OF IRELAND, 1888, p. 93.

having golden helmets on their heads, greaves of gold about their limbs and golden spurs on their heels.[1] There is a Legend of Edain, the King of Munster's Queen, which tells of the sorcery in their music.[2] They overcame the Firbolgs and drove them to Innismore, one of the chief Western Islands. The Firbolgs were dark and the Dananns fair, warlike, energetic but acquainted also with the healing art and skilled in Druidism. From these two races the Faërie Mythology is said to have sprung.[3] But after two hundred years the Dananns were overcome by the Milesians, whereupon they transformed themselves into Fairies, having escaped annihilation solely by their magic art and the consequent veil of invisibility. It is said that they retired to lonely places, but their repute as magicians followed them, and they were held to live in splendid palaces, hidden in the interior of pleasant green hills.[4] This catastrophe occurred in the age of the world 3500=1029 B.C. Another version speaks of their life in caves as continuing to this day and as destined to go on without death intervening until the Day of Judgment.[5] On the other hand, the twelfth-century BOOK OF LEINSTER contains the Myth of Oengus, one of the Tuatha de Danann, who has a faërie palace in the Irish Avalon called Tir-na-n-Og, or Tairrngire, the Land of Promise, the Land of Never Ending Youth, in which Oisin once dwelt for three hundred years. It is sometimes identified with the Isle of Man.[6]

II. The Myth travelled to Scotland or some of its analogues arose independently therein. There also, as in Ireland, we find sometimes a Vessel which brings the dead to life and in one case is in the keeping of an old woman. It is then a Vessel of Balsam.[7] It is otherwise a Cauldron which is filled with plants, and a King's son is put therein. He has been clothed with a magic shirt, which becomes now a great encoiling serpent : it is destroyed by virtue of the stew, and this destruction liberates the Prince from the spell.[8]

III. The Myth and its Talismans passed also into Wales, and the Cauldron recurs frequently in the poems which are extant under the name of Taliesin.[9] Among other properties, it gave melody to Bardic lays.[10] The Cauldron of Awen is the Cauldron of that Goddess. But there was also the Cauldron of Ceridwen, which was full of melodious

---

[1] Cf. J. F. Campbell : THE CELTIC DRAGON MYTH, quoting the *Geste* of Fraoch, which mentions lances like candles, having knobs of burnished gold and spear-points of inwrought carbuncle, p. 2.

[2] Lady Wilde, *Op. cit.*, pp. 93–96.　　　[3] *Op. cit.*, p. 337.

[4] Joyce, *Op. cit.*, pp. 401, 402.　　　[5] Lady Wilde, *Op. cit.*, pp. 93–96.

[6] Nutt, *Op. cit.*, pp. 191, 192. Cf. Hall Caine, *Op. cit.*, pp. 108, 109, concerning the Shining Land and the Tree of the Shining Land. Its leaf is breath of life, its bloom is youth and its fruit is fulfilment of desire. The boughs of the Tree seem to be of silver, its blossoms are white and the fruits are golden apples. The Shining Land is the Land of the Living Heart, the Land of Manannan, whose Magical Stone recalls the Cauldron of the Dagda : it was a Stone of Everlasting Store, pp. 202–209. For Manannan mac Lir, see Nutt, pp. 192–194.

[7] Campbell, *Op. cit.*, I, XLI.　　　[8] *Ib.*, XLVI.

[9] Edward Davies : MYTHOLOGY AND RITES OF THE DRUIDS, 1809, p. 16. Davies at his early period accepted the poems as genuine, notwithstanding their acquaintance with Ovid's METAMORPHOSES, Pythagorean doctrines and reflections of Greek, Roman and Jewish history, to which Macbain calls attention. *Op. cit.*, pp. 102, 103.

[10] *Ib.*, p. 21.

song,[1] and is, moreover, a source of mystical lore.[2] It happened that Gwion the Little, having been set to guard the Vessel, found three drops of its water alighting on one of his fingers, when he put it hurriedly into his mouth, as one scalded. It is said that " every event of futurity was opened to his view."[3] The Cauldron itself was divided into two parts, but the whole of its water was poisonous, the drops in question excepted. A multitude of ingredients entered into the decoction, according to the poem called TALIESIN'S CHAIR. Most important of all is the Cauldron of Bendigeid Vran, who is Bran the Blessed, the son of Llyr, whose story is told in one of the Welsh Mabinogion, among other places. Its property was that if a man be slain to-day and cast therein, to-morrow he will be as well as he ever was at the best, except that he will not regain his speech. He remains therefore as if in the condition of Perceval when that hero of the Grail stood agaze in the presence of the Mystery with a spell of silence upon him. It would follow that the Druidic Mysteries, as we find them in Welsh Legends, are like other Initiations : the Candidate is passed through the experience of a Mystical Death and is brought back, as, for example, by the Cauldron of Bran or that of Ceridwen, to a new term of existence ; but although in this sense the dead are raised, they are not in such cases restored with the gift of tongues : there is life but no word of life. In other language, the silence of the great pledges is imposed henceforth upon them. The dead rise up, but they do not begin to speak.[4]

The Cauldron attributed to Bran was used by the Irish in their fight about Branwen, and it was destroyed by Evrissyen, who was the source of all the strife. He cast himself into the Cauldron of Renovation, as it is termed in the Saga, rent it into four pieces and burst his own heart in the act. It is on this memorable occasion that Bendigeid Vran, who is Bran, gave orders to the sole seven who survived the warfare that they should cut off his head, carry it to the White Mount in London and there bury it, with the face towards France. But seeing that this would be a long journey, they had licence to feast for seven years in Harlech. The birds of Rhiannon should sing to them the while, and the Head of Bran would be the same pleasant company as when he was alive in the body. Thereafter for fourscore years they should sojourn at Gwales in Penno, the Head being still uncorrupted, and so continue unless and until they opened the door that looks towards Aber Henvelan and Cornwall. They must then set forth for London and bring the Head with them. It was arranged after this manner : they feasted for seven years at Harlech and for fourscore years at Gwales in Penno, remembering nothing of their sorrows.[5] However, at long last Heilyn son of Gwynn, curious to see what might befall and

[1] *Ib.*, p. 20. [2] *Ib.*, p. 26. [3] *Ib.*, p. 214.
[4] See BRANWEN, THE DAUGHTER OF LLYR, *passim*, from the Red Book of Hergest, edited by Lady Charlotte Guest. There are many editions.
[5] Cf. the Crown of Forgetfulness which Morgan, Queen of Faërie, gave to Ogier le Danois in Avalon, where trees are always green, the flowers do not fade, the sun never sets and cometh not storm or cloud. See POPULAR ROMANCES OF THE MIDDLE AGES, by G. W. Cox and E. H. Jones, 1871.

whether it was a true story, opened the door which looked towards Cornwall, thus proving that they did remember one thing at least of the past. They became conscious now of all their old evils and journeyed in great perturbation to London, where they buried the Head in the White Mount.

Except in so far as the Cup of the Grail Legend concerns, as we have found, a Mystery of Speech and its Suppression, it is difficult to trace its correspondence with this Cauldron and that of the Dagda. If such things can be considered as the raw material out of which the Grail story issued in fine, the fact extends rather than reduces the seeming miracle of transformation, whereby the Holy Vessel of Christian Symbolism was brought forth from a Druidic Cauldron, which is sometimes that of Ceridwen and sometimes of Bendigeid, being at once the Fountain of Bardic Inspiration and the provider of a feast of good things.

The Cups and Cauldrons were many in Celtic lore, not to speak of other regions, almost the wide world over. There is the Caire of the King of Alba, which boiled sufficient meat and no more for each given Company, whatever amount of food was put therein ;[1] but there is obviously no comparison between this story and that of the Feast-providing Grail, into which nothing was put. We may remember further, at its value, the milk-white cow of the Iolo MSS., which gave enough milk to every person who desired it. Those who drank were healed from all disease, became wise if they chanced to be fools and had wickedness eradicated from their natures. It happened, however, that certain natives in the Vale of Towey resolved to kill and eat her ; but she vanished from their hands and was never seen again.[2] It would serve no purpose to recite further examples or multiply those which correspond to the other Talismans.[3] The Grail Sword, as we have seen,

---

[1] Bruce, *Op. cit.*, I, p. 270.

[2] THE IOLO MANUSCRIPTS, 1848. According to Grimm, the Grail cannot be more celebrated than Sampo in the Epic of the Finns. Fashioned by the god Ilmarinen in Pohjola, it was a joy to live in the land that possessed it. The fields were covered with standing corn and hanging fruits. Now, there came a time when the gods planned to retrieve it, and the theft succeeded. But the Princess of Pohjola pursued them in eagle shape and overtook the fugitives on the open sea and strove to regain the Vessel. It fell in the struggle on the water and was broken, the lid remaining in her hands. The result was that wretchedness and famine have reigned ever since in the land. One of the thieving gods found certain fragments on the shore, and these being sown grew into trees, one of them becoming a lofty oak which darkened the sun. Jacob Grimm says : "We gather from all these examples, still far from complete "—he has quoted a cloud of instances—" how under the veil of sensuous images—Spear, Hammer, Hat, Helmet, Cloak, Horn, Goblet, Necklace, Ring, Ship, Wheel, Tree, Rod, Flower, Cloth, Meat and Drink—lay hidden the spiritual virtues of Victory, Happiness, Peace, Healing, Fertility, Riches, and Poetic Art." It is to be questioned whether the lesson arises from the Sampo itself. See TEUTONIC MYTHOLOGY, English Translation, II, p. 873.

[3] The cited and citable examples get further away from Cup and Cauldron notions when a full enumeration is attempted, as the following cases shew : (1) In the KALEVOLA there is a mill which gives a perpetual supply of flour. (2) In the VOYAGE OF MAILDUN and his Companions, the travellers reach an Isle of the Four Precious Walls, where a maiden gives them food from a small Vessel. It looked like cheese, but " whatever taste pleased each person best, that was the taste " he found therein. They had precisely the same experience at the Palace of the Crystal Bridge. (3) There is also the Feast of Gobnann, the Dedanann Smith, instituted by Mannanan Mac Lir. Whoever was present and partook of the food and drink was set free from sickness, decay and old age.

not being a Passion Relic, occupies usually a false position in the sequence, while supposititious analogies in folk-lore connect with these solely as so many further and less or more notable instances of magical weapons. Among these may be mentioned the White Glaive of Light, which MacIain Direach is set to keep in order by command of the Seven Big Women of Dhiurrath, and with which he tries to run away but fails. They are willing to exchange it for the Yellow Filly belonging to the King of Erin. Now this King will part with it only for the King of Farne's daughter ; but the hero of the story manages to get the daughter for himself, she abetting, and also the Glaive of Light, the office of which is to keep off foes, presumably by its mere exhibition.[1]

In addition to these somewhat phantasmal but still subsistent consanguinities, we have seen at full length that there are two versions of the Quest or Mission of Perceval into which the Mystery of the Grail does not enter as a part, and that in their extant forms they are much later than any of the Grail literature in Northern French. One is the story of Peredur, the son of Evrawc, in the Welsh MABINOGION, while the other is the English Metrical Romance of SYR PERCYVELLE, both of which have been analysed at due length in the immediately preceding section. Scholars have compared them with the LAY OF THE GREAT FOOL, being a Myth of wide diffusion, of which these are the latest developments. This Myth is not alone much older than either but is earlier than the Grail form of the Saga in the CONTE DEL GRAAL. It is in fact a primitive Mythos, a characteristic example of which will be found in Campbell's collection and must be left therein for consultation by those who are concerned. There is no Quest, there is no Question, there is no Wonder Vessel : there is not even a Sword or a Lance in many versions. The relation of this Lay and its scattered variants to the Perceval le Gallois, the Didot-Modena texts, not to speak of the PERLESVAUS, is the relation borne by certain other old fables to some of the Shakespeare plays. In other words, the originals are of no consequence in the light of their developments.

It does not follow from these considerations, so far as they have now proceeded, that the Grail texts had no folk-lore antecedents or that these were other than Celtic. My task has been only to place them in their true light and leave them to stand at their value. Another point arises at this stage, and the most recent view on its subject may be taken to represent the past of independent criticism which lies behind it. It is an old story that there is as yet no certain canon of criticism to distinguish the genuine memorials of Welsh archaic literature from a vast mass of false seeming which wears only the vestures and mask of antiquity. It is now many years since M. Villemarqué, the Breton, illustrated what it was possible to do in the production and extension of Armorican remains, and in the Principality there have been more

---

[1] Campbell, *Op. cit.*, I, XLVI ; II, pp. 332 *et seq.* In another version the Glaive of Light belongs to the King of the Oak Windows. I, p. 3. It seems also to give vision before and behind, obviously by casting light in both directions. I, p. 263.

than one Villemarqué—*fabulatores famosi*—whose obtained results, if not calculated to deceive even the elect, have made the specialist wary, sometimes about rejecting but always of accepting anything in the definite and absolute sense. Dr. J. D. Bruce has brought forward the results of his inquiries into all aspects of the subject, and I am proposing to summarise them at this point as practically the latest and certainly the most mature and competent, having regard to his intimate acquaintance not only with the entire field of the Grail subject but with all critical opinion which has unfolded thereupon. It is to be understood, however, that his researches and decisions on the Celtic hypothesis concern me only as belonging to the scholastic apparatus, for reasons which will emerge at the close of the present section.

In respect of the Welsh MABINOGION, it is affirmed that three of these tales are derived undoubtedly, and in the most direct manner possible, from three French Romances, namely, (1) OWEN, or THE LADY OF THE FOUNTAIN, which corresponds to Chrétien's YWAIN, otherwise LE CHEVALIER DU LYON; (2) PEREDUR AB EVRAWC, corresponding to his CONTE DEL GRAAL; and (3) GERAINT AND ENID, which answers to his EREC. Their French origin is unmistakable, in the coherent structure of the stories and the character of the life reflected, its social spirit included, which is that of the twelfth century in France. It is indicated also that in this triad as a whole the localisation is vague and shadowy, whereas in the genuinely Welsh stories the movements of the heroes through the land of Wales can be followed even at this day. Bruce affirms further (1) that in the Chrétien and Welsh trilogies the incidents concur throughout and also in their successive order, with one exception only in the LADY OF THE FOUNTAIN. There is further no need of calling into existence those imaginary and much earlier French sources which were loved by scholarship in the past to account for the MABINOGION cited : Chrétien will suffice.

The debt of the Galahad Quest and the PARZIVAL to the folk-lore Bowl of Plenty is qualified by the considerable doubt which is cast on the antiquity of the Irish TUATHA DE DANANN Tradition, with its Cauldron of the Dagda, Stone of Destiny, Spear and Sword of Lug : it is pointed out that we know of this grouping only through the seventeenth century Irish historian Keating, who, moreover, does not define their nature, saying only that the Stone of Destiny was that which was brought by Edward I from Scone in Scotland and is now in Westminster Abbey. It is suggested that the other Talismans may have been no more marvellous. On this question of date it will be seen that the whole problem of Celtic influence on Grail literature is thrown open to debate. So also Bruce says that " the debt of the French Romances to Irish sources seems to . . . have been greatly exaggerated ".[1]

As regards the PEREDUR story, Campbell said of old that it exists in many languages, including Icelandic,[2] which is certainly true in respect

---

[1] Bruce, *Op. cit.*, I, pp. 46, 47, 71, 94, 270, 273, 274.
[2] Campbell, *Op. cit.*, IV, p. 281.

of the Great Fool Saga. He was an admirable and enchanting scholar for his period, but the connection which he instituted between the PEREDUR and the CONTE DEL GRAAL as between root and branch has passed utterly away. Nutt was his disciple and followed him till he was corrected by Zimmern and abandoned the point of view.[1] It follows that there is no older system shining through the MABINOGION " as clearly as these shine through the French and English Romances," and much less that their " ultimate source is in the East ".[2]

When the Celtic hypothesis was most flourishing as an explanation of Grail origins, and when it was presented by some of the later exponents, like Miss J. L. Weston, with an assurance recalling the triumphant dogmatism of Professor Tyndall's Belfast Address, it left the great texts of the Grail literature unaffected, since the fact remained that Secret Words of Eucharistic Consecration and the Arch-Natural Ordination of Joseph II owed nothing to pre-Christian Celtic lore and dream. Above all and more than all the last Grail Mass at Sarras and the last Communion of Galahad had no root in such sources. It remains, however, to say that notwithstanding the change of view on the part of more recent and fully equipped scholarship, summarised in the name of Bruce, the story of the Great Fool is suggested most assuredly by Chrétien's first Romance of PERCEVAL LE GALLOIS, though I am disposed to think that the prototype was little more than a vague and floating recollection in his mind. So also the Magical Cauldron is not only of Irish, Welsh and Scottish Tradition, for its independent stories are all the wide world over. There is every reason to think that some of them were abroad in Northern France at the Grail period, but that which follows therefrom is less than little. We can still agree with Bruce that no one as yet has brought forward a folk tale, Celtic or otherwise, corresponding in incident and setting to the Grail story ;[3] that the debt of Arthurian Romance to Celtic Sources has been exaggerated greatly ; and that " personal invention was the most important factor " in its creation.[4] It was not the reflection of a great body of Oral Tradition " in any essential degree ". Bruce cites Foerster and Golther as predecessors who took this view. In a word, the authors of the Romances " were primarily poets, not transcribers of folk tales ". In final conclusion on this theme, the last words of Bruce, in which the Celtic folk tale origin of the Grail Legend is set aside as unsatisfactory,[5] may be compared with my own detached and reasonably moderating position. After all the moils and batterings, something remains to be said for reflections brought over from the past and corresponding broadly speaking to the Celtic hypothesis which has held the field so long. It is difficult to believe that the Grail Dish or Stone of Plenty owed nothing to the Cauldron of the Dagda, Cauldron of Ceridwen, Stone of Mananann, so on and so forward, supposing that on the question of date they could have been known to the veiled

[1] Bruce, *Op. cit.*, I, p. 269.
[3] Bruce, *Op. cit.*, I, p. 275.
[2] Campbell, *Op. cit.*, IV, p. 277.
[4] *Ib.*, pp. IV, V, 4.
[5] *Ib.*, p. 275.

author of the Galahad Quest and to Wolfram von Eschenbach, failing which something may have come to them from much further away. Alternatively, those who invented so much may well have invented more, and having regard to their theme it would be almost of necessity in the likeness of those who had preceded, but with due allowance for variations in mode and form and purpose.

Supposing therefore that certain antecedents of folk-lore passed into the literature of the Grail, undergoing—as they did assuredly—some great transmutations, so also did more than one element of old Druidism merge into Christianity. Rite and Myth and Doctrine were tinged by Tradition and Doctrine and Rite ; for things which co-exist may tend to dovetail, at least by their outer edges ; and there are traces, I think, of a time when the Priest who said Mass at the Altar was sometimes a Druid at heart, and in his heart saw no reason for the Druid to be less a Priest. Long after the conversion of the Celt, enigmatical fables and mystical Rites lingered in Gaul and Britain. There were Masters of Lesser Mysteries, old arts and pseudo-sciences, whose knowledge, it has been claimed, was perpetuated under the shadow of the Celtic Church and even within the pale thereof. By the evidence of some who spoke on its part of old, the Bardic Sanctuary opposed no " Precious Concealed Mysteries " ; and the Church not improbably received into its general alembic much that was not of its matter, expecting to convert it therein and turn it out in a new form.[1] In the fourth century there were Professors at Bordeaux who had once at least been Druids, and for the Doctrines of their later reception the heart of their old experience may have been also an alembic. St. Deuno in his last moments is recorded to have exclaimed : " I see the Trinity and Peter and Paul, and the Druids and the Saints "—a choir invisible, the recognition of which would, if known, have imperilled his canonisation, supposing that its process had been planned at Rome.

At a much later period, even in the twelfth century, we have still the less or more vague intimation of perpetuated Mysteries, and there is no doubt that the belief in these was promoted generally by the Bards. The twelfth century saw also the beginning of a great revival of literature in Wales. I have cited certain Iolo Manuscripts which are late and of dubious authenticity ; but accepting their evidence under all necessary reserves, they refer the revival in question to Rhys ap Twdur, who assumed the sovereignty of South Wales, bringing with him " the system of the Round Table, as it is with regard to Minstrels and Bards ". And when the time came for the last struggle between the Celtic and Latin Rites over the independence of the British Church, I can believe well enough that all which remained, under all transformations, of that old mixed wisdom of the West was fighting also

---

[1] It is an old story that Pope Gregory the Great counselled Augustine on the eve of his journey to Britain that what it was possible to take over and adapt should so be suffered and treated, rather than destroyed. Doubtless a similar course was followed instinctively by those who came previously to convert the land and the islands. Doubtless also it has been a key of conquest in the hands of other religions.

for its life. When pseudo-Taliesin prophesied the return of Cadwaladr, who had passed into the unmanifest like Arthur, and like Arthur was destined to come back,[1] I believe also that this allegory of rebirth or resurrection, if it referred on one side to the aspirations of the Celtic Church, did not less embody on another the desirable notion of a second spring for the Mysteries which once dwelt in Wales, which even after many centuries were interned rather than dead.

We can imagine—though perhaps at a far distance—what kinds of medley resulted from such interpenetration of Doctrine and Practice as I have here indicated : the shadowed sacrifice of human victims in Ceremonial Observances on the one side ; the Eternal Sacrifice of the Victim Who is Divine and Human on the other ; the renovation of the Candidate as the term of Symbolical Ritual ; and the Resurrection of Christ as the first-fruits of the redeemed in the signal degree. With these as the analogies of or between opposites, there were meeting-points and enough in the Lesser Mysteries, while encircling as an atmosphere there were, on the one hand, the presages, the signs, the omens, the vaticinations, the inspirations dark and strange of Seers and Bards ; but on the other there were the Great Consecrations, the Holy Objects, the Sacred Traditions, the Inspired Writings and all the Annals of Sanctity. In fine, against the Solemn Pageants of Pagan Ceremonial Performances there was the Great Mystery of the Faith in Christ, the White Sacrifice, and the Clean Oblation of the Eucharist. I confess that if there were otherwise any evidence, it might be imagined that Secret Words, exceeding *ex hypothesi* all Words of Institution in the Ordinary of the Official Mass-Book, and strange claims of a Priesthood which had never been authorised at Rome, might issue from so enigmatic and dubious a Sanctuary.

Speaking still in my detached manner, the earlier Welsh literature, whatever its dates, is a little like the wild world before the Institution of the Sacraments ; the poem of Chrétien is a little like the natural world with its interdict just beginning to be removed : it is also like the blind man restored in part to sight, seeing all things inverted and devoid of their normal proportions. The LONGER PROSE PERCEVAL, or PERLESVAUS, occupies a middle position between the Great Quest and Wolfram : the Enchantments of Britain—as if Logres were this visible Nature—have dissolved : Grace is moving through Nature ; the Great Mystery is being declared and testified to everywhere. In the PARZIVAL the things which are without suffer a certain renewal ; and yet the German Epic is in no sense a near correspondence and equivalent of the Galahad Quest.

From all this matter of fact, matter of aspiration and high matter of dream, we can infer that wherever the cradle may be of the Grail and its root Legend—Gaul, Armorica or Wales, but the last as a possibility

---

[1] Cf. IOLO MSS., p. 525. Cadwaladr the Blessed lies buried in Rome, and when his bones are brought thence to the Isle of Britain, then shall the Cymry regain their crown and sovereignty.

apart in a world of shadow—there was at work, less or more everywhere in the Celtic region, what I have called the alembic of transmutation. I care not what went therein—Cauldron of Ceridwen, Cauldron of the Dagda, Head of Bran and Poisoned Spear which smote him, Lay of the Great Fool, Expulsion and Return Formula, Visitations of the Under-world, and so forward for ever and ever—for that which came out was the Mystery of Faith manifested after a new manner, and the search for that Sanctuary wherein, among all waste places of the cosmos, the evidence of things unseen became palpable to the exalted senses of the Great Quest. Little and less than little does it matter how that began which reaches this high term ; and for us therefore, who " needs must love the highest when we see it ", we can only guess the beginning which brought the term we find. However, its work is done, and it is not a living concern of ours.

In our childhood we passed through the sorcery of fables, from Bidpai to La Fontaine ; but these were not everlasting dwellings. In our youth there may still have been some of us who looked to see great lights in L'Origine de tous les Cultes and in The Ruins of Empires ; but again there was no abiding place. At this day it seems weariness, and is almost idle, to go back to the scrolls of Mythologies, or otherwise than with great caution to folk-lore, when in far different flights we have touched the hem of His garment. I do not propose to include the study of folk-lore in the same category as the imaginings of Dupuis, Volney and Godfrey Higgins ; but unless we can presuppose a certain enlightenment it may prove a morass sometimes rather than a pathway. However this may be, in seeking for a new scheme of inter-pretation, it is necessary rather than desirable that we should make a beginning by doing justice to old schemes, the office of which is at once recognised and reduced by the entrance of an overlord into his proper patrimony. It must be said otherwise that the old appeal of scholar-ship to the derivation of Grail Legends from folk-lore and the anxious collection of fresh data from this source have acted in the past upon several groups of students like the head of Braid's lancet on his hypnotic subjects. They are pretexts which entranced them. There was never an occasion in which folk-lore was more important at the beginning—if only to get out of the way—and mattered in finality so little ; it is a land of enchantment, withal somewhat dreary, and through it the Unspelling Quest passes laboriously to its term.

An old metaphorical maxim of one of the Secret pseudo-Sciences once said : " The stone becomes a plant, the plant an animal and the animal a man " ; but it did not counsel its students to consult the stone that it might better understand man, though the stone remains a proper subject of investigation within its own limit. I leave readers who are after my own heart and within the classes of my proper school to apply this little parable to the question that is here at issue respect-ing the Grail in folk-lore. It remains to be said otherwise that one field of Celtic Research has been neglected so far, and it is that precisely which may—by a bare possibility—throw light on the Christian aspects of the Grail Legend apart from the aspects of old non-Christian Myth. If there are analogies in the root-matter between the Hallows of Cup and Glass and folk-lore Talismans, there are others which are far more intimate between the lesser matters of the literature and Celtic Christian Hagiology. It seems a commonplace to add at the moment that particular Christian Tradition has for its environment the general Traditions of Christianity ; and for explanatory purposes that may be best which lies the nearest : at least it enters reasonably into any full consideration of the whole subject.

Apart from the fixed purpose in the direction which I have specified —that purpose which having exhausted, and this too easily, the available fields of evidence, begins to imagine new ; apart from the thousand and one things which, by the hypothesis, might be referable to folk-lore if the wreckage of that world had not been disintegrated by the mills of the centuries ; the antecedents of the Grail in folk-lore have been a wide field for patient research : it has offered also an opportunity for great speculations which go to prove that the worlds of enchantment are not worlds which have passed like the Edomite Kings ; but as it is certain that there was a King afterwards in Israel, I have concluded at this point to abandon those quests which for myself are without term or effect and hold only to the matter in hand, which is the development of a cosmos in literature out of those strange elements that strove one with another in pre-Christian Celtic literature.

II

THE ENVIRONMENT OF THE GRAIL LITERATURE

IT is impracticable to approach the literature of the Holy Grail for any purpose of special consideration in the absence of a working acquaintance with that which encompassed it externally in History, in Church Doctrine, in Popular Devotion and in Ecclesiastical Legend. As an acquaintance of this kind must not be assumed in my readers, I will take the chief points involved as follows : (1) The doctrinal position of the Church in respect of the Holy Eucharist ; (2) the passage of Transubstantiation into dogma, and other circumstances which led up from the date of its definition to the Institution of the Feast of Corpus Christi in 1264 ; (3) the Cultus of the Precious Blood ; (4) the mind exhibited by the higher life and the mystical literature of sanctity ; (5) the status of Minstrelsy ; (6) the horizon filled by coincident Schools of thought within and without the Church ; (7) the state of the Official Church itself, and more especially (8) the position of the Church in Britain, including its connection with the ambition of an English King ; (9) the Legendary

History of certain Relics ; (10) the voice of Catholic Tradition regarding Joseph of Arimathæa ; (11) the aspects of coincident heresies
which have been connected with Grail literature ; (12) the discovery
of the SACRO CATINO in 1101 ; (13) the Invention of the Sacred Lance
at Antioch ; (14) the Traditional History of certain Imputed Relics of
St. John the Baptist.

The consideration of some of these points must be reserved for the
time being ; but the particulars hereinafter following will enable an
unversed reader to approach the literature with a knowledge of several
elements which entered into its creation and were concerned in its
development.

A great literature may arise in part or otherwise out of folk-lore,
primeval fable and legend ; but albeit in this sense it will have antecedents in that which was at first oral and passed subsequently into
writing, it does not happen that development can proceed without
taking over other elements. That such elements were incorporated in
the case of the literature of the Holy Grail is too obvious to call at this
stage for further recitation in the absence of a particular motive.
Those who in the later twelfth and the early thirteenth century
produced the body-general of the Grail Cycles—being makers of songs
and endless tellers of stories—knew something, as we have seen, at
however far a distance of Celtic wonder-lore. It was the heritage of
the Minstrel from long antecedent generations of Druids and Scalds and
Bards. But there had come to them the hints and reflections at least
of another and higher knowledge—a Tradition, a Legend, the rumour
of a Secret perpetuated, possibly from far away ; above all and more
than all, there had come over them something of the divine oppression,
the secret sense of a Mystery which lies behind the open symbols of
Christian Doctrine. Let us take in the first place the power and the
portent of the great Latin Church, with its abiding presence of the
Sacraments, its unfailing growth of Doctrine, its generation of New
Doctrine, not indeed out of no elements, not indeed by the simple
fiat lux of the Seat of Peter, for the Councils were many besides those
which laid claim on an Œcumenical Title ; but in the Western
countries of Europe—at so great a distance from the centre—the growth
may have been almost unsuspected and often seemingly unprefaced, as
if there had been spontaneous generation. Ever magnified and manifold in its resource, there was the popular devotion, centred about a
particular locality, an especial holy person and this or that individual
holy object. Under what circumstances, and with what actuating
motives, we have to learn if we may ; but it can be understood in the
lesser sense how far the singers and the songs which they drew from the
past underwent a great transformation ; how the Bowl of Plenty—
if this indeed had preceded—became the Chalice of the Eucharist ;
how the Spear of many battles and the Sword of destruction became
the Lance which pierced our Saviour and the weapon used at the
martyrdom of His Precursor. I set it down that these things might

have intervened naturally as a simple work of causation which we can
trace with comparative ease ; but they would not for this reason have
assumed the particular complexion which characterises the Cycle at
large of the literature : we should not have its implicits, its air and
accent of mystery, its peculiar manifestation of Sacred Objects, or its
insistence on their final removal. For the explanation of these things
we shall have to look further afield ; but for the moment I need note
only that the writers of the literature have almost without exception
certified that they followed a book which had either come into their
hands or of which they had received an account from some one who
had seen or possessed a copy. We can trace in the later texts and
can sometimes identify the particular book that they followed respectively ; but we come in fine to the alleged document which preceded
all and which for us is as a centre of research.

Amidst the remanents of mythical elements and the phantasmagoria
of popular devotion, the veneration of Relics included, there stands
forth that which from Christian time immemorial has been termed the
Mystery of Faith, the Grace not less visible because it is veiled so
closely, and this is the Real Presence of Christ—after some manner—
in the material symbols of the Eucharist. Seeing that the literature of
the Holy Grail is, by the hypothesis of its Hallow-in-chief, most
intimately connected with this Doctrine and the manifestation thereto
belonging, it is desirable and essential before all things to understand
the Eucharistic position at the period of the development of the
literature. We have plenary records therein of two schools of thought,
though the evidence of the one is more clamant than that of the other :
they are respectively the School of Transubstantiation and that which
is alternative thereto, namely, the Spiritual Interpretation of the Grace
communicated in the palmary Sacrament of the Altar.

The great doctrinal debate of the closing twelfth and the early
thirteenth century was that which concerned the Mystery of the
Eucharist, and in matters of Doctrine there was no other which could
be called second in respect thereof. It filled all men's ears, and there
can be no question that the Sodality of Minstrelsy was scarcely less
versed than the outer section of the Priesthood in its palmary elements.
Of this debate France was a particular centre, while Languedoc, in
the person of the Albigenses, was a place of holocaust, the denial
of the Eucharist being one of the charges against them. As regards
the debate itself, its *terminus ad quem* was reached when the Doctrine
of Transubstantiation was decreed by the Council of Lateran in 1215,
under Pope Innocent III. The words of the Definition are : " The
Body and Blood of Jesus Christ are truly contained under the Species
of Bread and Wine in the Sacrament of the Altar, the Bread being
transubstantiated into the Body and the Wine into the Blood ".[1]
Long anterior to this promulgation there can be no doubt that the
Doctrine represented the mind of the Church at the seat of its authority

[1] C. G. Coulton : FIVE CENTURIES OF RELIGION, Vol. I, p. 104.

and power. In contradistinction thereto were the views of the protesting sects, and there was the feeling of a minority which held, so
long as it dared and could, to a spiritual interpretation of the Real
Presence and yet, so to speak, was at work within the Sanctuary.[1]
The external devotion to the Eucharist which was manifested more and
more by the extremists on the side of the Church would be checked
scarcely by the exponents of a middle way. At the dawn of the
thirteenth century the Consecrated Elements were beginning to be
elevated for the adoration of the people : the evidence is regarded as
doubtful in respect of any earlier period. It must have become a
custom in 1216, for a constitution of Honorius III speaks of it as of
something which had been done always.[2] In 1229 Gregory IX devised
the ringing of a bell before Consecration as a warning for the faithful to
fall on their knees and worship Christ in the Sacrament.[3] Still earlier in
the thirteenth century, Odo, Bishop of Paris, regulated the forms of
veneration, more especially when the Sacred Elements were carried in
procession.[4] Hubert, Archbishop of Canterbury, had taken similar
precautions at the end of the twelfth century.[5] It seems to follow from
the Constitutions of Odo that some kind of Reservation was practised
at his period, and it is possible that the custom had descended from
earlier times. There is nothing, however, in the Romances to shew that
this usage was familiar : the Perpetual Presence was for them in the
Holy Grail, and apparently in that only. Church and Chapel and
Hermitage resounded daily with the Celebration of the Mass. In one
instance we hear of a Tabernacle on the Altar or some kind of receptacle
in which the Consecrated Elements reposed.[6] The most usual mediæval
practice was to reserve in a dove-shaped Repository which hung before
the Table of the Lord. The GRAND SAINT GRAAL has one noteworthy
example of Reservation, for it represents a Sacred Host delivered to the
custody of a convert, one also who was a woman and not in the vows
of religion. It was kept by her in a box, and the inference of the writer
is that Christ was, for this reason, always with her.[7] The reader who is
dedicated in his heart to the *magnum mysterium* of official faith may

---

[1] Berenger combated the theory of Transubstantiation as far back as 1050.

[2] There is no trace of it in the Gallican Mass, as described by St. Germain de Paris
(Migne : PATROLOGIA LATINA, *tom.* LXII) or in Warren's invaluable attempt to reconstruct the Ritual of the Celtic Church.

[3] The PERLESVAUS tells us on the authority of its mythical Josephus (1) that there
was no bell in Greater or Lesser Britain during the days of the Grail ; (2) that people
were called together by a horn and other devices ; (3) that King Arthur rejoiced when he
heard a bell apparently for the first time ; (4) that he heard one daily on his pilgrimage
to King Fisherman's Castle ; (5) that a bell was in evidence also at the Grail Mass in the
Castle. Potvin, *Op. cit.*, I, pp. 227, 249, 250. HIGH HISTORY, Branch XX, Titles
6, 7 ; XXII, 2, 3.

[4] Having regard not only to the devotion of the period but to the passion for
spectacles, those which were connected with wealthy Churches must have been decorative and impressive sights. Some of the Grail Pageants may embody reminiscence as
well as invention. It will be observed that these Processions in public imply Reservation.

[5] Not-only on account of the crowd of witnesses but the crowd which followed.

[6] They were reserved for the use of the sick as well as the absent in the Celtic Rite.
See F. E. Warren : THE LITURGY AND RITUAL OF THE CELTIC CHURCH, 1881, pp. 138,
139.   [7] LESTOIRE DEL SAINT GRAAL in Sommer, *Op. cit.*, I, p. 70.

be disposed to regard this as something approaching sacrilege, and I confess to the same feeling ; but it was a frequent practice in the early Church, and not, as it might be concluded, a device of Romance.

As regards Transubstantiation, the voice of the literature in the absence of an express statement on either side seems to represent both views. The Vulgate Chronicles of the Grail are as text-books for the illustration of the Doctrine ; but it is absent from the Lesser Chronicles, and outside this negative evidence of simple silence there are other grounds for believing that it was unacceptable to their writers, who seem to represent what I have called already a Spiritual Interpretation of the real Presence, corresponding to what ecclesiologists have termed a body of Low Doctrine within the Church.[1]

There was another question exercising the Church at the same period, though some two centuries were to elapse before it was to be decided by the central authority. It was that of Communion in both kinds, which was finally abolished by the Council of Constance in 1415, the decision then reached being confirmed at Trent in 1562. The ordinance of Communion in one kind was preceded by an intermediate period when ecclesiastical feeling was moving in that direction ; but there was another and an earlier period—that is to say, in the fifth century—when communion under one kind was prohibited expressly on the ground that the division of the Great Mystery could not take place without sacrilege. As a species of middle way, there was the practice of the intincted or steeped Host which seems to have been coming into use at the beginning of the tenth century, although it was forbidden at the Council of Brago in Galicia, except possibly in the case of the sick and of children. The custom of mixing the Elements was defended by Emulphus, Bishop of Rochester, in 1120, and Archbishop Richard referred to the intincted Host in 1175. All these problems of Practice and Doctrine were the religious atmosphere in which the literature of the Grail was developed. There were great names on all sides ; on the side of Low Doctrine there was the influential School of Berengarius ; on that of Transubstantiation there was the name of Peter Lombard, the Master of Sentences, though he did not dare to determine the nature of the conversion—whether, that is to say, it was " formal, substantial, or of some other kind " : on the side of communion under one element there was that of St. Thomas Aquinas, the Angel of the Schools, in connection with which it is to be observed that there is no instance throughout Grail literature of Wine being administered to any Knight of Quest on those rare occasions when he was permitted to receive the Bread.

With an environment of this kind it was inevitable that Poetry and Legend should take over the Mystery of the Eucharist, and should exalt

[1] After what manner it was related to and distinguished from that of Berengarius, which was condemned, cannot be discussed here. It is to be observed only (1) that when the Vision of Christ in the Tower explained the Symbolism of Mass Vessels to Joseph of Arimathæa, he heard nothing concerning Transubstantiation, nor (2) does it appear in the EARLY MERLIN or DIDOT-MODENA PERCEVAL.

it and dwell thereon. In any case, from the moment that the Eucharist entered into the life of romantic literature, that literature entered after a new manner into the heart of the Western peoples. Very soon, it has been said, the Grail came to be regarded as the material symbol of the Catholic and Christian faith, but in the proper understanding it was really the most spiritual symbol : I believe that it was so considered, and the statement does little more than put into English the inspired words of the Ordinary of the Mass. In the middle of the mistaken passion for holy wars in Palestine ; through the monstrous iniquity of Albigensian Crusades ; the ever-changing struggle notwithstanding between Pope and King and Emperor ; within the recurring darkness of interdict, when the Sacraments were hidden like the Grail ; the Legend of the Holy Grail grew and brightened, till the most stressful of Adventurous Times, the most baleful of all Enchantments, shone as it seemed in its shining, and a light which had been never previously on the land or sea of literature glorified the Spirit of Romance. It was truly as if the Great Company of singers and chroniclers had gathered at the High Altar to partake of the Blessed Sacrament and had communicated not only in both kinds but in elements of Extra-Valid Consecration. The thesis of this section is that God's immanence was declared at the time of the literature through all Christendom, by the Mystery of Faith, and that the development of Eucharistic Doctrine into that of Transubstantiation was only an extravagant recognition of the corporate union between Christ and His people. That immanence was declared also by the high Branches of Grail Romance, even as by the quests of the mind in philosophy—after which manner Romance, in fine, became the mirror of Religion, and the literature testified, under certain veils, to a Mystery of Divine Experience which once at least was manifested in Christendom.

As the theory of Transubstantiation did not pass into dogma till a late period in the development of the canon of the Grail, so it can be said that romantic texts like the GRAND SAINT GRAAL, the LONGER PROSE PERCEVAL and the GALAHAD QUEST, but the last especially, which contains the Higher Code of Chivalry, were instrumental in promoting that dogma by the proclamation of a Sacrosaintly Feast of Corpus Christi maintained for ever in the Hidden House of the Grail, till the time came when the Festival of Exaltation and the Assumption into Heaven of the Sacred Emblems was held in fine at Sarras. There was thus a correlation of activity between the two sides of the work, for it was out of the growing dogma that the Grail Legend in the Vulgate Chronicle assumes its particular sacramental complexion.

Passing from the doctrinal matters expressed and implied in the literature to the Sacred Palladia with which it is concerned more especially, we enter into another species of environment. Out of the Doctrine of Transubstantiation and the congeries of devotional feelings connected with it there originated what may be termed a cultus of the Body of God and of His Blood, understood in the Mystery of the

Incarnation, and the instinct which lies behind the veneration of Relics came into a marked degree of operation. Such veneration is instinctive, as I have just said, and representing on the external side, invalidly or not, the substance of things unseen in Religion, it is so rooted in our natural humanity that it would be difficult to regard its manifestation in Christendom as characteristic more especially of Christianity than of some other phases of belief. The devotion which, because of its excesses, is by a hasty and unrooted philosophy termed superstition —which no instinct can ever be—manifested early enough and never wanted its objects. There can scarcely be any call to point out that in the considerations which here follow I am concerned with questions of fact and not with adjudication thereon. The veneration of Relics and cognate objects, to which some kind of sanctity was imputed, became not only an environment of Christianity at a very early period, but it so remained almost to the present day for more than half of Christendom. It may be among the grievous burdens of those ecclesiastical systems in which it prevails and in which it is still promoted, but having said what the sense of intellectual justice seems to require, that it may be exonerated from the false charge of superstition, I have only to add—and this is to lift the Grail literature out of the common judgment which might be passed upon memorials of Relic worship— that the instinct of such devotions, as seen at their best in the Official Churches, has always an arch-natural implicit : it works upon the simple principle that God is not the God of the dead but of the living, and the reverence, by example, for the Precious Blood of Christ depends from the doctrine of His immanence in any memorials which He has left.[1] I need not add that, on the hypothesis of the Church itself, the sense of devotion would be better directed, among external objects, towards the Real Presence in the Symbols of the Eucharist ; but in the Grail literature it was round about the Sacramental Mystery that the Relics of the Passion were collected, operating and shining in that light.

We know in a plenary sense that the Sacred Vessel of the Legends was in the root-idea a Reliquary, and as such that it was the container and preserver of the Precious Blood of Christ, though as time went on we hear less and less of the content in its original form, for at the Miraculous Masses it is the Body of God in the human figure of the Christhood which comes forth from the Dish or Chalice. In any case, the romantic passion which brought the Reliquary into connection with the Sacrament which communicated the Christ Life to the believing soul and the doctrinal passion which led to the definition of Transubstantiation interacted one upon another. John Damascene had said in the eighth century that the Elements of Bread and Wine were assumed and united to the Divinity by the Invocation of the Holy

---

[1] The Grail at the Mass of the Grail in the Great Quest provided the Feast of Food in Christ, and the Reliquary itself, containing the Precious Blood, answered to the ordinary Chalice of Wine which was and still is adored by the laity but of which only the Priest partakes in the Roman Rite.

Ghost, for the Spirit descends and changes.[1] The Venerable Bede has said that the Lord gave us the Sacrament of His Flesh and Blood in the figure of Bread and Wine. And again : " Christ is absent as to His Body, but is present as to His Divinity ". And yet further : " The Body and Blood of Jesus Christ are received in the mouth of believers."[2]

For those who out of all expectation translated the problems of Doctrine, as they best could, into the language of Romance—out of the Latin, as they said in their imaginative fashion—the Palladium of all research was that Vessel of Singular Election which contained in their ingenuous symbolism the Blood of Christ. But seeing that they were in haste to shew how those who were worthy of receiving Arch-Natural Sacraments did participate at the Grail Mass in corporeal and incorporeal elements adequate to sustain both body and soul, so did the Reliquary become the Chalice, from which the Christ came down to communicate His Own Life. They collected also, under ecclesiastical and monastic ægis, certain other Relics about the Relic-in-chief. Now, the point concerning all is that most of the minor Hallows were known already as local objects of sanctity no less than the palmary Hallow, but the sanctity ascribed to the latter and the devotion thereto belonging were beginning to prevail generally. It is difficult to trace the growth of this kind of cultus ; but as to the worship of spiritual devotion there was offered everywhere in Christendom the Mystical Body and Blood of Christ in the Sacrament of the Altar, so at many shrines—as if the more visible symbol carried with it a validity of its own, a more direct and material appeal—there was the reputed *sang real* of Christ preserved in a Reliquary. Some of these local devotions were established and well known before the appearance of any text of the Holy Grail with which we are acquainted—probably before those texts which it has been customary to postulate as antecedent to the extant literature.

We have at the present day the Feast of the Precious Blood, which is a modern invention, and perhaps for some even who are within the fold of the Latin Church, it may be classed among the unhappy memorials of the Pontificate of Pius IX. This notwithstanding, it is what may be termed popular, and has in England its confraternities and other systems to maintain it in the mind of the laity. It has the London Oratory as its more particular centre, and it is described as an union and an apostolate of intercessory prayer. Without such assistance in the Middle Ages we can understand that the cultus had its appeal to the devotional side of the material mind, for which flesh and blood profited a good deal, in spite of asceticism and the complication

---

[1] That is to say—or at least more especially—by virtue of the *Epiclesis* Clause in the Mass Formula of Consecration. It seems obvious that John Damascene was not teaching Transubstantiation.

[2] The citations are interesting in their contrast, for if Christ be " absent as to His Body," the latter is not received " in the mouth of believers." The truth is that no one really knew what happened at the Mass-Consecration till rigid definition intervened, and they contradicted themselves occasionally, as well as others.

of implicits behind the counsels of perfection in the religious life of the age.

The historical antiquity of the local sanctities which centre about certain Relics is shrouded like some Masonic events in the vague grandeur of time immemorial, and a defined date is impossible. Because the Legends of the Grail are connected with the powers and wonders of several Hallowed Objects belonging to the Passion of Christ, it is essential rather than desirable to ascertain whether at the period when the literature arose—and antedating it, if that be possible—there were such Objects already in existence and sufficiently well known to respond as a *terminus a quo* in respect of the development of the Legends. The places which appear as claimants to the possession of Relics of the Precious Blood are, comparatively speaking, numerous ; among others there are Bruges, Mantua, Saintes, the Imperial Monastery at Weingarten, and even Beyrout. According to the story of Mantua, the Relic was preserved by Longinus, the Roman soldier who pierced the side of Christ. Within the historical period, it is said to have been divided, and some part of it was secured by the Monastery of Weingarten, already mentioned. This portion was subdivided and brought from Germany by Richard of Cornwall, the brother of Henry III. Fractional as the portion was, it is affirmed to have been a large Relic, and the fortunate possessor founded a Religious Congregation to guard and venerate it. Later on, however, it was divided again into three parts, of which one was retained by the Congregation, one was deposited in a monastery built for the purpose at Ashted, near Berkhampstead, and the third in a third monastery erected at Hailes in Gloucestershire. All these were foundations by Richard of Cornwall ; and to explain such continual division, it must be remembered that this was a period when the building of Churches and Religious Houses was prohibited without relics to sanctify them. Now, the story of Richard himself may be accepted as tolerably well founded ; but there is much doubt concerning the Relics at Weingarten and at Mantua itself. The alternative statements are (1) that in 1247 the Templars sent to King Henry III a *vas vetustissimum*, having the appearance of crystal and reputed to contain the Precious Blood ;[1] (2) that in the same year, and to the same King, there was remitted by the Patriarch of Jerusalem a Reliquary termed the Sangreal, which had once belonged to Nicodemus and Joseph of Arimathæa.[2] Now it is obvious that at the period of Henry III the canon of the Graal literature was almost closed : and these stories are obviously a reflection of that literature ; it was also the time when (1) the *Sacro Catino* of Genoa may have begun to be regarded as the Grail, and when (2) a similar attribution was given to a

---

[1] The story is told by Matthew Paris in his HISTORIA ANGLIÆ. See the Paris edition of 1644, p. 493.

[2] The testimony of Matthew Paris shews that the two stories are in reality one ; that the authenticity of the Reliquary sent by the Templars, or rather *Magister Templi*, was vouched for by the Patriarch in question as well as by certain Abbots and other " magnates of the Holy Land."

Sacred Vessel which had been long preserved at Constantinople ; but these objects, whether Dishes or Chalices, were not Reliquaries. It will be seen that the claim of Mantua remains over with nothing to account for its origin. Of Beyrout I have heard only, and have no details to offer. But the Relic of Bruges has a clear and methodical history, passing from Legend into a domain which may be that of fact. The Legend is that Joseph of Arimathæa having collected the Blood from the wounds of Christ, as the literature of the Grail tells us, placed it in a phial, which was taken to Antioch by St. James the Less, who was the first Bishop of that city. The possible historical fact is that the Patriarch of Antioch gave an alleged Reliquary about 1130 to a Knight of Bruges who had rendered signal services to the Church in Antioch. It was brought back by him to his native place, and there has remained to this day. One dubious element in the story is the gift of such a Relic under any circumstances whatever, while a point in its favour is that the Vial has the character of oriental work which is referred by experts in ancient brass to the seventh or eighth century.[1]

In comparison with this simple and fairly consistent claim, there is a monstrous invention connected with the Monastery of the Holy Trinity at Fécamp in Normandy. Here there is—or there was at least in the year 1840—a Tabernacle of white marble, decorated with sculptured figures and inscribed : " HIC SANGUIS D.N., I.H.V., X.P.I." It is called therefore the Tabernacle of the Precious Blood.[2]

The story is that Joseph of Arimathæa removed the Blood from the wounds of Christ after the body had been taken down from the Cross, using his knife for the purpose and collecting the sacred fluid in his gauntlet. The gauntlet he placed in a coffer, and this he concealed in his house. The years passed away, and on his death-bed be bequeathed the uncouth Reliquary to his nephew Isaac, telling him that if he preserved it the Lord would bless him in all his ways. Isaac and his wife began to enjoy every manner of wealth and prosperity ; but she was an unconverted Jewess, and seeing her husband perform-ing his devotions before the coffer, she concluded that he had dealings with an evil spirit and denounced him to the High Priest. The story says that he was acquitted : but he removed with the Reliquary to Sidon, where the approaching Siege of Jerusalem was made known to him in a vision. He concealed therefore the Reliquary in a double tube of lead, with the knife and the head of the Lance which had pierced the side of Christ. The tube itself he hid in the trunk of a fig-tree, the bark of which closed over its contents, so that no fissure was visible. A second vision on the same subject caused him to cut down the tree, and he was inspired to commit it to the waves. In the desolation which he felt thereafter an angel told him that his treasure had

[1] The Reliquary is in evidence, is carried annually in Procession and Bruges is not far away for those who are concerned with approving or rejecting the views of experts. Whether some of the latter have pronounced counter-views is another question.

[2] See Le Roux de Lincy : ESSAI SUR L'ABBAYE DE FÉCAMP, 1840.

come to shore in Gaul and was hidden in the sand near the valley of Fécamp.[1]

I do not propose to recount the various devices by which the history of the fig-tree is brought up to the period when the monastery was founded at the end of the tenth century. The important points in addition are (1) that the nature of the Reliquary did not satisfy the custodians, and, like the makers of Grail books, they wanted an Arch-Natural Chalice to help out their central Hallow ; (2) that they secured this from the Priest of a neighbouring Church who had celebrated Mass on a certain occasion, and had seen the Consecrated Elements converted into flesh and blood ; (3) that a second knife was brought, later on, by an angel ; (4) that a general exposition of all the imputed Relics took place on the High Altar in 1171 ; (5) that their praises and wonders were celebrated by a Guild of Jongleurs attached to the monastery, which guild is said to have originated early in the eleventh century, and was perpetuated for over four hundred years ; (6) that the story is told in a Metrical Romance of the thirteenth century, though in place of Joseph the character in chief is said there to be Nicodemus ; (7) that there are other documents in French and in Latin belonging to different and some of them to similarly early periods ; (8) that there is also a Mass of the Precious Blood, which was published together with the poem in 1840, and this is, exoterically speaking, a kind of Mass of the Grail ; but I fear that a careful examination might create some doubt of its antiquity ; and, speaking generally, I do not see (1) that any of the documents have been subjected to critical study ; or (2) that Fécamp is likely to have been more disdainful about the law of great inventions than other places with Hallows to maintain in Christian—or indeed in any other—times.

So far as regards the depositions which it might be possible to take in the Monastery concerning its Tabernacle ; and there is only one thing more which should be mentioned in this connection. It has been proved by careful research among the extant codices of the CONTE DEL GRAAL that in some copies of the continuation by Wauchier the episode of Mont Douloureux is said to have been derived from a book written at Fécamp.[2] It follows that one important text at least in the literature of the Holy Grail draws something from the Monastery of the Holy

---

[1] The author just cited is not only the authority-in-chief on the claims of Fécamp, its archives and its history but he is the first, I believe, to connect its Reliquary with the Grail Legend. Heinrich followed after a lapse of fifteen years, so it was a fairly old proposition when Miss Weston took it up with enthusiasm in comparatively recent days, but fared rather badly at the hands of German criticism. The question is naturally unimportant from my own point of view. Fécamp is one of many places which claim the possession of Reliquaries containing the Precious Blood or were in a position to do so in the past. It is not impossible that the sum total of their content would exceed the blood capacity of any human being ; but it is quite certain that the question signifies little. Europe was a storehouse of Relics when Grail literature was evolving : it lived and moved and had its being among them, was itself largely a record of Relics drawn into Romance, and in a sense it was in debt to all. There is no reason why Fécamp should be excluded ; but it is eminently desirable that its influence should not be exaggerated.

[2] Miss Weston regards the statement not only as made by Wauchier and not as interpolated into certain MSS. but imagines that the alleged book or story was a developed Grail Romance.

Trinity ; but, lest too much consequence should be attributed to this fact, it may be noted in conclusion (1) that the episode in question has no integral connection with the Grail itself ; (2) that the Tradition of Fécamp which I have characterised as monstrous, by which I mean in comparison with other Legends of the Precious Blood, is distinct from that of the Holy Grail in the texts which constitute the literature ; and (3) that this literature ultimately passed out of Legend into the annunciation of a mystical claim. It is the nature of this claim, the Mystery of Sanctity which lies behind it and the quality of perpetuation by which the Mystery was handed on that is the whole term of my quest.

We have seen how at Fécamp there occurred a curious intervention on the part of an Arch-Natural Chalice, being that Vessel into which the Grail passes by a kind of superincession, if it does not begin and end therein. But there are other Legends of Chalices and Dishes in the wide world of Reliquaries ; and in order to clear the issues it may be stated that the Table of the Last Supper is said to be preserved at St. John Lateran, with no history of its migration attached thereto. The Church of Savillac in the diocese of Montauban has also, or once had, a *Tabula Cœnæ Domini* and the Bread used at that Table. As regards the Chalice itself, there is one of silver at Valencia which the Catholic mind of Spain has long regarded as that of the Last Supper ; but I have no records of its history. There is one other which is world-wide in its repute, and this I have mentioned already, as if by an accidental reference. The *Sacro Catino* is preserved in the Church of St. Laurence at Genoa, and it is pictured in the book which Fra Gaetano di San Teresa dedicated to the subject in 1726.[1] It corresponds by its general appearance—which recalls, broadly speaking, the calix of an enormous flower—more closely to the form which might, in the absence of expert knowledge, be attributed to a decorative Paschal Dish than a wine-cup ; but there is no need to say that it is not an archaic glass vessel of Jewry. The history of so well-known an object is rather one of weariness in recital ; but at the crusading sack of Cæsarea in 1101 the Genoese received as their share of the booty, or in part consideration thereof, what they believed to be a great Cup or Dish carved out of a single emerald : it was about forty centimetres in height, and a little more than one metre in circumference ; the form was hexagonal, and it was furnished with two handles, polished and rough respectively. Now, Cæsarea was near enough to the Holy Fields for the purposes of a pious identification in the hearts of crusaders ; and moreover the vessel had been found in the mosque of Antioch, which might have helped to confuse their minds by suggesting that it was a stolen relic of Christian sanctity. But at the time when the city was pillaged there is no evidence that the notion occurred to the

---

[1] IL CATINO DI SMERALDO ORIENTALE, GEMMA CONSAGRATA DA N.S. GESU CRISTO NELL' ULTIMA CENA DEGLI AZIMI, *etc.*, published at Genoa in the year mentioned, an exhaustive work and of voluminous proportions.

Genoese, or that it was on some dubious ground of the kind that at the return of some of them it was deposited in their Church as a gift. It may well have been a thank-offering, and this only ; but I confess to a certain suspicion that, vaguely or otherwise, they had assumed its sacred character, and that its identification, not certainly with the Holy Grail, but with the Dish or Chalice of the Last Supper, may have begun earlier than has been so far supposed—antedating, that is to say, the first record in history. This record is connected with the name of Jacobus de Voragine, author of the Golden Legend, at the end of the thirteenth century.[1] Later on the Grail rumours passed over from France into Italy, with the results already seen. The claim of a Grail connection could not be put forward by the Wardens of the *Sacro Catino ;* but its identity with the Vessel of the Last Supper may have originated in this manner, to the increase of its value. The heaviest fines, and even death itself, were threatened against those who should touch the Vessel with any hard object. A cruel but belated disillusion awaited, however, its Wardens when it was taken to Paris in 1816 and was not only broken on the way back but, having been subjected to testing, was proved to be glass instead of emerald.

Second in importance only to the Talisman of the Holy Grail was the Sacred Lance of the Legend, and as in the majority of texts this is also a Relic of the Passion, our next task is to ascertain its antecedent or concurrent history in the life of popular devotion. We know already of the thesis manufactured at Fécamp ; and the alleged shaft of the Spear used by Longinus is preserved in the Basilica of St. Peter's. According to Roman Martyrology the Deicide was suffering from ophthalmia when he inflicted the wound, and some of the Precious Blood overflowing his face, he was healed immediately—which miracle led, as it is told, to his conversion. Cassiodorus, who belongs to the fifth century, says that the Lance was in his days at Jerusalem ; but this was the head and the imbedded part of the shaft, the rest being missing.[2] He does not account for its preservation from the time of Christ to his own. Gregory of Tours speaks of its removal to Constantinople, which notwithstanding it was discovered once more at Antioch for the encouragement of Crusaders, under circumstances of particular suspicion, even in the history of Relics. This was in 1098. There is also a long story of its being pledged by Baldwin II to Venice and of its redemption by St. Louis, which event brought it to Paris ; but this is too late for our subject.[3] A Holy Lance with an exceedingly confused history—but identical as to its imputed connection with the Passion—

[1] See CHRONICON GENUENSE, *cap.* XVIII, in Muratori's RERUM ITALICARUM SCRIPTORES, IX, pp. 32 *et seq.*, Milan, 1726. It may be mentioned that the marvellous Dish was a genuine emerald on the authority of Jacobus. He was Archbishop of Genoa. The earliest reference to the *Sacro Catino* is that, however, of William of Tyre in his BELLUM SACRUM, Bk. X, *cap.* 16.

[2] It is not of consequence from the Reliquary standpoint and could be replaced at need, because the head only pierced the side of Christ.

[3] St. Louis came to the Throne in 1226 and died in 1270. At the period in question, even the TITUREL of Albrecht was in existence, the last text of the Grail canon.

came also into the possession of Charlemagne.[1] That any history of such a Hallow is worthless does not make it less important when the object is to exhibit the simple fact that it was well known in the world before Grail literature, as we find it, had as yet come into existence. According to St. Andrew of Crete, the head of the Lance was buried with the True Cross, but it does not seem to have been disinterred therewith.[2] It is just to add that some who have investigated the question bear witness that the history of the Hallow is reasonably satisfactory in the sixth century and thence onward.[3]

The next Relic which may be taken to follow on our list is the Crown of Thorns; it figures only in one Romance of the Grail, but has an important position therein.[4] The possession of single or several Sacred Thorns has been claimed by more than one hundred churches, without prejudice to which there are those which have the Crown itself, less or more intact.[5] This also is not included among the discoveries of St. Helena in connection with the True Cross, and there is no early record concerning it ; but it is mentioned as it stands by St. Paulin de Nole at the beginning of the fifth century.[6] One hundred years later, Cassiodorus said that it was at Jerusalem,[7] and Gregory of Tours bears testimony to its existence. In the tenth century part of it was at Constantinople, which was a general centre, if not a forcing-house, of desirable Sacred Objects. The alleged portion had been there for a great period, as it is affirmed that St. Germain, Bishop of Paris, was in that city and received part of it as a present from the Emperor Justinian.[8] Much later the Patriarch of Jerusalem is supposed to have sent another portion to Charlemagne. In 1106 the treasure at Constantinople is mentioned by Alexis Comnenus. Another Crown of Thorns is preserved in *Santa Maria della Spina* of Pisa.

The Sacred Nails of the Passion appear once in the GRAND SAINT GRAAL, and these also have an early history in Relics.[9] Some or all of them were discovered by St. Helena with the True Cross, and,

---

[1] According to the GESTS OF CHARLEMAGNE in the Hengwrt MSS., vol. II, p. 440, the great King, during his Pilgrimage to Jerusalem visited the Church at Mount Olivet " in which it is believed that the Lord and His Twelve Apostles first said the Lord's Prayer " and received from the Patriarch a certain portion of the " Relics of Jerusalem," namely, among many others, " the Shroud of Jesus Christ, and His Knife and His Cup and one of the Nails that were driven into Him on the Cross ; and the Crown of Thorns."

[2] According to the MASS OF GOOD FRIDAY in the Hengwrt MSS., vol. II, p. 620, the Sacred Nails were discovered miraculously long after the Invention of the Cross, but in the same place.

[3] Meaning, of course, that the migrations and duplications of the Lance can be traced from that period.

[4] The PERLESVAUS, that is to say. See the HIGH HISTORY, Branch XIV, Title 2 ; XXI, 3, 14, 15, 22 ; XXII, 1. The Crown of Thorns figures also in the Provençal Romance of FIERABRAS, which is as rich in Passion Relics as the Grail story under notice.

[5] It is put up for competition as a complete Relic at a Tournament in the PERLESVAUS, and is borne away by Perceval, who brings it to the Grail Castle.

[6] The growth of Churches as Christianity itself grew promoted the need of Relics, and the need multiplied examples.

[7] Flavius Magnus Aurelius Cassiodorus, Senator, A.D. 490–585, was the author of various works including INSTITUTIONES DIVINARUM ET HUMANARUM LITTERARUM, an encyclopædia of literature and the arts, designed for the use of monks.

[8] Germanus was born *circa* A.D. 469 and died in 576.

[9] Sommer, *Op. cit.*, I, pp. 32, 33.

according to St. Ambrose, one of them was placed by her in the diadem of Constantine, or alternatively in his helmet, and a second in the bit of his horse.[1] In the sixth century St. Gregory of Tours speaks of four nails, and it seems to follow from St. Chrysostom that the bit of Constantine's charger was coupled with the Lance as an object of veneration in his days. As regards the diadem fashioned by St. Helena, this was welded of iron and became the Iron Crown of Lombardy, being given by Gregory I to Theodolinde in recognition of her zeal for the conversion of the Lombard people. Charlemagne, Sigismund, Charles V and Napoleon I were crowned therewith. Muratori and others say that the Nail which hallowed it was not heard of in this connection till the end of the sixteenth century, and the Crown itself has been challenged. Twenty-nine places in all have laid claim to the possession of one or other of the four nails, and there are some commendable devices of subtlety to remove the sting of this anomaly. It is sufficient for our own clear purpose to realise that the Relics, if not everywhere, were in " right great plenty."

It is also in the GRAND SAINT GRAAL, and there only, that we see for a moment, in the high pageant of all, a vision of an ensanguined Cross, a blood-stained Cincture and a Scourge or Rod, also dyed with blood.[2] Of the *Crux vera* and its invention I need say little, because its relics, imputed or otherwise, are treasured everywhere, and we shall see that their multiplicity, even at the earliest Grail period, made it impossible to introduce the Cross as an exclusive Hallow in the Sacred House of Relics. The Traditional Loin-Cloth is said to have been in the possession of Charlemagne and was given by him to St. Namphasus, who built the Abbey of Marcillac and there deposited the Relic. It is now in a little country Church called St. Julian of Lunegarde.[3] According to St. Gregory of Tours, the Reed and the Sponge, which had once been filled with vinegar, were objects of veneration at his day in Jerusalem.[4] They are supposed to have been taken to Constantinople, which notwithstanding an informant of the Venerable Bede saw the Sponge with his own eyes, deposited in a silver cup at the Holy City. He saw also the shorter Reed which had served as a derisive symbol of the Lord's Royalty.[5]

The Shroud also figures in the History of Relics and occupies a

[1] Alban Butler's LIVES OF THE SAINTS, *s.v.* August 18, may be consulted on the Invention of the True Cross and Nails—obviously, however, from no critical standpoint.
[2] Sommer's edition of the Vulgate Texts, vol. I.
[3] It is not to be supposed that I am concerned personally with the history of Relics as such. My object is to shew how those of the Passion were in great evidence at the Grail period. I have mentioned here and there the recent whereabouts of a few, but am not in a position to affirm whether they are actually in same place at this date. Those who are concerned can satisfy themselves with a little pains.
[4] It is obvious that if Passion Relics were to justify their claims they had to begin at Jerusalem, though it is not less certain that if they were to serve any practical purpose they must be brought Westward. Even the Holy House of Loretto was caused to travel miraculously.
[5] The point is interesting, as shewing that the Holy Fields produced their own Relics on occasion, so that Legends concerning those of the Passion did not originate always far away and assign Palestine as their fountain source.

considerable place in the PERLESVAUS, where it covers the Altar in
a Chapel of a mysterious and perilous Grave-yard. It is said concerning it that " the cloth is of the most holiest, for our Lord God was
covered therewith in the Holy Sepulchre, on the third day when
He came back from death to life."[1] The Sister of Perceval has to
obtain part of it in order to save her Mother and herself from the
King of Castle Mortal, who is laying siege to one of her Castles. It
is necessary that she should enter the perilous place alone and withstand its evil hauntings. Even her brother must leave her on the
threshold to dree the weird in virtue of her own spiritual strength
and her prayers. Thereafter the story of the Shroud is left at a
loose end and we know not what becomes of it.[2]

The Relics of the Cross of Christ were growing freely at the Grail
period, and it must have been more and more obvious to the mind of
Romance that it would be impossible for it to figure bodily in the
Great House of Hallows. As a fact, however, it does not appear at
all : we hear only of a fragment in the boss of a shield mentioned
once in the PERLESVAUS. Now the Cross has not merely its Relics in
" right great plenty " but also its Legends, and in this manner we are
brought to a brief consideration of certain Apocryphal Gospels which
are to be placed on the documentary side of that environment amidst
which the literature of the Holy Grail was developed. Chief among
these is the so-called GOSPEL OF NICODEMUS—otherwise and more
especially the ACTS OF PILATE—of which there are various recensions
in Greek and Latin, as well as Coptic, Syriac and Armenian versions.[3]
It contains the root-matter of Early History Grail stories in verse
and prose. Whether by direct acquaintance with one of the Latin
codices, by some Northern French rendering or—and perhaps most
likely of all—through the channel of popular preaching, Robert de
Borron derived therefrom (1) the bare elements of his Myth concerning the imprisonment of Joseph of Arimathæa and of the visit paid him
by Christ in the dark Tower ; (2) the fact of his miraculous sustenance—not, however, by the ministry of the Holy Grail ; (3) the story
of the Descent of Christ into Hell for the liberation of the Fathers ;[4]

---

[1] Potvin, *Op. cit.*, I, pp. 173–177 ; HIGH HISTORY, Branch XV, Titles 12–20.

[2] The Shroud of Christ was the subject of an elaborate study by Paul Vignon, and
this was translated into English so far back as 1902. The Relic with which it is concerned
is said to have been known historically in the East since 1353 and belonged to the Royal
House of Savoy for a long period, dating from the middle of the fifteenth century. It
was shewn at an Exhibition of Sacred Art in Turin on May 1st, 1898. The volume
contains an exhaustive examination and defence of the Relic as authentic in all respects.
It was photographed at the time mentioned and the negative revealed what is termed a
" positive portrait," *ex hypothesi*. The examination of this photographic evidence lasted
for more than a year and a half and was then made public. It is not the only Shroud in
the Christian world of Relics : there was that also of Besançon, but it was pronounced
fraudulent and the ecclesiastical authorities, we are told, gave orders that it should be
converted into lint.

[3] The German reader may be referred to the texts printed by C. Tischendorf in
EVANGELIA APOCRYPHA, and others to Dr. M. R. James' excellent APOCRYPHAL NEW
TESTAMENT published by the Clarendon Press in 1924 and reprinted in 1926.

[4] It is said that a Latin version of the Descent into Hell has been the parent of others
in every European language. James, p. 95.

(4) the healing of a Roman Emperor by the Face-Cloth of St. Veronica ; (5) the Emperor's conversion ;[1] (6) the vengeance wreaked upon the Jews, including the derisive story that they were sold at 30 for a penny. As regards the Cross, it is said in the second part of the Gospel (1) that the Cross of Christ was placed in the midst of Hell, to remain there for ever as a sign of victory.[2] But the cross of Dysmas, the penitent thief, was carried by him into Paradise.[3]

The Last Relic of the Passion of which we hear in the Books of the Grail is the *Sudarium*, which all men know and venerate in connection with the piteous Legend of Veronica. The memorials of this Tradition are on a moderate computation as old as the eighth century, but the course of time has separated it into four distinct branches. The first and the oldest of these is preserved in a Vatican manuscript, which says that Veronica was the woman whose issue of blood was healed by Christ and that she was also the artist who painted a likeness with which another account is concerned.[4] She was carried to Rome with the picture for the healing of the Emperor Tiberius.[5] The second branch is contained in an Anglo-Saxon manuscript of the eleventh century ; and this says that the Relic is a piece of Christ's garment which received in a miraculous manner the impression of His countenance.[6] The origin of the third Tradition seems to have been in Germany : it is preserved in some metrical and other Latin narrative versions. The likeness of Christ is said to be very large, apparently full length. It was in the possession of Veronica, but without particulars of the way in which it was acquired. According to a variant which is perhaps of the twelfth century, the Emperor who was healed is Vespasian, and Christ Himself impressed His picture on the face-cloth which He used when He washed before supper at the house of Veronica. She had asked St. Luke, whom tradition represents as an artist, for a copy of the Master's likeness. The fourth and last variant is the familiar Calvary Legend, wherein the holy woman offers in His service the cloth which she has on her arm when Christ is carrying the Cross, and she is rewarded by the impress of His countenance thereon. The noticeable point is that the story of Veronica, of the *Sudarium*, and of the healing of a Roman Emperor is the root-matter of the earliest historical account of the Holy Grail ; and this fact has led certain scholars to infer that the entire literature has been developed out of the Veronica Legend, as a

[1] It is to be noted that in the Gospel of Nicodemus the Emperor in question is Tiberius, but is Vespasian according to the Metrical Romance of Robert de Borron.
[2] The reference is obviously to the Hades of the Fathers and not to " the bottomless pit " into which Satan was cast by Christ.
[3] The Hengwrt Welsh MSS. include a fragment from the Gospel of Nicodemus concerning the Tree of Life in Paradise and the sowing of three seeds from an apple of the Tree. They produced three saplings which went through many vicissitudes and were planted ultimately in the Temple of Solomon, where they formed a single tree. This also had strange experiences in the course of the centuries, being cast at one epoch into the River Jordan. It was used in the end for the wood of the Cross of Calvary.
[4] That of the *Volto Santo*, traditionally the work of St. Luke.
[5] See *ante*, Book IV, sect. 1, for the version of Robert de Borron, which is concerned with another Roman Emperor.
[6] It is alternative therefore to the Shroud of Turin.

part of the Conversion Legend of Gaul, according to which the holy woman, in the company of the three Maries and of Lazarus, took ship to Marseilles and preached the Gospel therein. They carried the *Volto Santo* and other Hallows.[1]

I approach now the term of this inquiry, and there remains for consideration the Sword of the Grail Legends, which is accounted for variously in respect of its history and is described also variously ; but it is not under any circumstances a Hallow of the Passion. A Romance which stands late in the general Cycle, so far as chronology is concerned, connects it with the martyrdom of St. John the Baptist. I have found no story in the world of Relics to help us in accounting for this invention, though there are traces of a Sword of St. Michael. In this respect, as indeed in other ways, the Hallow is complicated in the literature. It embodies (1) matter brought over from folk-lore ; (2) deliberate invention, as when one story affirms it to be the Sword of David, but another that of Judas Maccabæus ; and (3) the semi-devotional fable to which I have referred above, which can be taken in connection with the Legends of the Head of St. John, served to Herodias on a charger to satiate her desire for revenge on the precursor of Christ, he seeming to have reproached her concerning her manner of life. It will be plain from the enumeration subjoined that the Relics of St. John are comprehensive as to the person of his body. (1) A Martyrology tells us that some of his blood was collected by a holy woman at the time of his decapitation, was put into a vessel of silver, and was carried into her country of Guienne : there it was placed in a Temple which she erected to his honour. (2) The body was, according to one account, enshrined in a temple at Alexandria, which was dedicated to the Saint. Another says that the Head was interred at first in the sepulchre of Eliseus at Samaria. During the reign of Julian the Apostate it was redeemed from possible profanation and sent to St. Athanasius, who concealed it in a wall of his Church. At the end of the fourth century the entire remains were removed to a new Church, built on the site of a temple of Serapis. Subsequently they were divided and distributed. (3) The *Caput Johannis* was carried to Antioch by St. Luke, or alternatively to Cæsarea. From whichever place, it was removed afterwards to Constantinople and brought finally into France, where it was divided into three parts, one of which is at Amiens, another at Angély in the diocese of Nantes, and the third at Nemours in the diocese of Sens. A distinct account states that the Head was found in Syria in the year 453, and that the removal to Constantinople took place five centuries later. When that city was taken by the French in 1204, a Canon of Amiens, who was present, transported it into France, where it was divided, but

---

[1] The story is that after the first persecution, when St. James was slain by the sword, his followers were thrust into a boat without oars or sails on the coast of Palestine, not far from Mt. Carmel. It contained St. Mary, wife of Cleopas ; St. Salome, often called St. Mary Salome ; St. Mary Magdalene ; St. Martha ; the maid Marcella ; Lazarus and Joseph, with many others. The boat drifted to Provence and up the Rhone to Arles. THE COMING OF THE SAINTS by J. W. Taylor, 1911, p. 126.

into two portions apparently, one being deposited at Amiens and the other sent to the Church of St. Sylvester in Rome. I have seen also a report of two heads, but without particulars of their whereabouts.

So much concerning the *Caput Johannis*, but I should not have had occasion to furnish these instances were it not for the apparition of an Angel carrying a Head upon a salver when the wonders of the Holy Grail were manifested originally at Sarras.[1] But this vision is not found in the story which connects the Hallowed Sword with the Head of St. John the Baptist. The Charger or Salver, with its contents, is supposed to be a complication occasioned by the intervention of folk-lore elements concerning the head of the Blessed Bran. In any case, a Dish or Platter apart from any Head, is almost always the fourth Hallow in the Legends of the Grail ; and in those instances when the Grail itself is a Chalice it may have answered to the Eucharistic Paten, or alternatively to the Paschal Dish of the Last Supper.

It follows from the considerations of this section that whether or not there has been a passage of folk-lore materials through the channel of Grail literature—which passage has less or more involved their conversion—the real importation into Romance has been various elements of Christian Symbolism, Doctrine and Legend : it is these above all that establish the authentic subject-matter of the whole Mystery. It must be understood, this notwithstanding, that the literature is not to be regarded as an extension of the History of Relics into the World of Romance. Certain compilers of encyclopædic dictionaries and handbooks have treated the value of such Legends, and of the claims which lie behind them, in a spirit which has been so far serious that they have pointed out how the multiplicity of claims in respect of a single object must be held to militate against the genuineness of any. One early critic took the pains, centuries ago, to calculate how many Crosses might be formed full-size from the Relics of the one True Cross, and an opponent not less grave took the further trouble of recalculating to prove that he was wrong.[2] So also Luther, accepting a caution from Judas, lamented that so much gold had gone to enshrine the imputed Relics when it might have been given to the poor.[3]

It is desirable now to notice a few points, for the clearance of certain issues. (1) The German Cycle of the Holy Grail has the least possible connection, as we have seen otherwise, with Christian Relics ; speaking of the most important branch, it is so much *sui generis* in its

---

[1] The reference is to the *Grand Saint Graal*, not, however, to the Vulgate version printed by Sommer, *Op. cit.*, Vol. VI. Cf. Nutt's summary, based apparently on Furnivall's text : " Seven Angels issue from the Ark . . ., an eighth carrying the Holy Dish, a ninth a Head so rich and beautiful as never mortal eye saw." STUDIES ON THE LEGEND OF THE HOLY GRAIL, p. 55.

[2] Similar concern has not been shewn about other Relics of the Passion; but, as in the case of the Shroud, the Church intervened occasionally to make away with things which interfered one with another.

[3] Robert de Borron and the *Grand Saint Graal* connect Judas more especially with the general indignation of the Disciples, according to St. Matt. xxvi, 8, over the waste of the precious ointment by the " woman having an alabaster box " and the money represented thereby. It was on this account that Judas " went unto the Chief Priests " and sold the Master.

symbolical elements that it enters scarcely into the same category as the Northern French Romances. (2) No existing Reliquary and no story concerning one did more than provide the great makers of Romance with raw materials and pretexts : the stories fell into the background, and the symbols were exalted by their genius. (3) The imaginary or vanished books to which they appealed were not of Fécamp or any competitive Monasteries, Abbeys or other Holy Houses, but the rumour of something unknown and withdrawn " far in the unapparent ". The growing literature of the Grail drew from the life of devotion in its application to the Mystery of the Eucharist, owing little in reality to the secondary veneration of Relics ; and on its own part it contributed a secret life to stimulate and extend the central Doctrine of the Mystery.

Investing this Mystery in chief of the faith in Christ which is thus the only real concern of the Holy Grail, there are other environments which will appeal to us, though their time is not yet in our methodical scheme of progress. There is (1) the state of the Official Church, so glorious in some respects, so clouded in others, like a Keeper of Sacred Things who has been wounded for his own sins, or like a House of Doctrine against which he who " sold God for money " has warred, and not in vain, for at times he has invaded the precincts and entered even the Sanctuary, though the holy deposit has not been affected thereby, because by its nature and essence it is at once removed from his grasp. There is (2) the Church in Britain and its connections of the Celtic world, having aspirations of its own, as there is no question—having a legitimacy of its own, as none can deny at this day—but with only a local horizon, a native mission, and used, for the rest, as a tool for ambitious kings, much as the all-embracing claim of the Church at large was the tool of the Popes at need. There is (3) the resounding rumour and there is the universal wonder of the high impossible quest of Holy Wars in Palestine, without which we might have never had the Grail literature, the Romances of Chivalry, or Secret Treasures of the disdainful East brought to the intellectual marts and houses of exchange in the restless, roving, ever-curious kingdoms of the West—kingdoms in travail towards their puberty. There is (4)—and of five things to be enumerated, I count this the head and crown—there is the higher life of sanctity and its annals at the Grail period, as the outcome of which the West went to the East, carrying what it believed to be the missing talent of gold, without which, as the standard of all values, all other talents were either debased or spurious. It was the age of a thousand reflections, at centuries sometimes of distance, from Dionysius (so-called), Augustine and the first great lights of Christendom ; it was the age of Hugo de St. Victor, of Bernard, of Bonaventura ; it was the age which Thomas of Aquinas would take up later as plastic matter in his hands, and he shaped the religious mind of the world after the image and likeness of his own mind in the high places of the Schools ; it was the age of many doctors, some of whom might have known in their heart of hearts the real message of the Grail and where its key was to be sought.   (5) There is in fine a fifth branch, but this is the sects of the period, because more than one division of the Christian World was quaking and working towards emancipation from a yoke which was none too sweet and a burden none too light.   As to all this, it seems needful to say at the moment that if the Books of the Holy Grail are among the most catholic of literature, they were not for such reason laid at the feet of Innocent III or those after and before in the Chair of Peter.

III

THE HOLY GRAIL IN THE LIGHT OF THE CELTIC CHURCH

A.—A Possible Originating Centre of the Whole Mystery

AMONG all external organisations there is one Institution—and there is one only—which might be expected to offer some of those signs and warrants that we should look for in a Sodality, Association or Church which could and did connect with the idea of the Holy Grail, as something approximate to its source, if not indeed a centre from which the Mystery originated.

The Early History of the Holy Grail, as distinguished from the several Quests undertaken for the discovery of that Sacred Object, is one of Christianity colonising.   We know that in the French Cycles, by the universal voice of the texts, it was a Mystery which was brought into Britain, and supposing that the Legend as a whole—apart or otherwise from anything involved by its implicits—could be regarded as of Celtic origin, its religious elements, in the absence of special and extrinsic claims, might be accounted for most readily by the fact and characteristics of the Celtic Church.

" That is best which lies the nearest," according to an old maxim, and the Celtic Church is much closer to our hands than anything which has been suggested alternatively,[1] while it was unquestionably that environment in which some of the Legends developed.   Those who have recognised previously, in their imperfect and dubious way, that some of the Grail Legends have a mystical aspect, and that hence they are probably referable to something in Instituted Mysticism, have put forward bare possibilities, and, independently of these, scholarship has itself gone much further afield.   ·It has thought of the Far East as the home of the Holy Grail, and some who are mystics by more than a predisposition on the surface, know certainly—even if it is in a certain

---

[1] It is to be observed (1) that the Grail Castle is in a remote fastness of Northumbria according to the Borron Cycle, where Celtic Church influences lingered long after the victory of the Roman Rite ; and (2) that in the Vulgate Cycle the Grail Castle of Corbenic is in South-West Wales, as if it were a Celtic Sanctuary.

sense only—that there is a country deep in Asia. Now, albeit the limits of our evidence concerning the Celtic Church are circumscribed somewhat narrowly, there seems no doubt that this Church bore traces of Eastern influence—by which I mean something stronger and plainer than resides in the common fact that Christianity itself came to us from the oriental world.[1] If, therefore, the Holy Grail has any marks and spirit of the East, it might be accounted for in this manner by way of the most colourable inference. If, however, we prefer to consider without any longer preface what is the palmary claim of all, and if therefore we appeal to the veiled suggestion of pre-eminence in the Grail Priesthood in respect of an extra-valid form of consecrating Eucharistic Elements and of a Super-Apostolical Succession, it may be advanced that here is simply an exaggerated reflection of that which was claimed actually by the Celtic Church and more especially by that Church in Wales.[2] The claim was that it had a title to existence independently of Rome, Christianity having been established in these islands for a long period prior to the arrival of St. Augustine, which arrival, from this point of view, was an incursion upon territory already conquered and held to a defined extent as well as a sacred endeavour to spread the Gospel of Christ : it brought therefore spiritual war besides the light of truth. I have classed these two points together—that is to say, the alleged oriental origin and the original independence of Rome—not because I regard the second as important in comparison with the first, but because as a fact we know that the Celtic Church had a certain autonomous existence long before any Legend of Joseph of Arimathæa was devised in the local interests of Glastonbury.[3] It was not therefore at the beginning a question of Angevin ambition. Further, we can understand, I think, very well how this claim may have been exaggerated in Legend, so as to cover—as I have said— the special implicits that are traceable in Grail literature and therefore to account for it within, as the general characteristics of the Celtic Church may account for it reasonably without. I propose now to set forth some other specific analogies from which we shall be enabled in fine to draw a general conclusion, namely, whether we can be satisfied with the evidence as it stands or whether we must go further. Let us remember, in the first place, that the earlier point, if it can be taken apart from the later, would mean probably an origin for the Holy Grail independent of Celtic environment, and would not of necessity exclude that of some Eastern heretical sects which passed into Southern France ; otherwise a derivation through Spain ; or, as an alternative

---

[1] C. F. E. Warren : THE LITURGY AND RITUAL OF THE CELTIC CHURCH, 1881, p. 55.
[2] We have also to remember that (a) the Arthurian Romances were called *matière de Bretagne* on the Continent, a denomination which persisted when the French texts passed into Italy, Spain and Portugal ; (b) that in the Northern French Cycles the heroes of Arthur's Chivalry moved continually and rapidly between Logres and Brittany ; and (c) that Brittany was another region in which the Celtic Church survived.
[3] Dr. J. Armitage Robinson concludes that 1191 is the earliest possible date for the legendary connection of Joseph with Glastonbury, *Op. cit.*, p. 50. But there seems little question that *circa* 1250 is in his view nearer to the literal truth.

for both, the transit, for example, of Johannine Tradition Westward. But if we abandon the earlier and have recourse to the later point, then the Legend of the Holy Grail—because it contains elements which are foreign to the mind of Romance, though they find expression in Romance form—must belong to that class of fable which has been invented in an external interest, and its position is not much better than one of forged decretals : it might be indeed a decretal in litera-ture, put forward in many guises and with many variants, and it would be useless to look therein for any secret intention beyond that of the particular pretence which it was designed to support. With the merits and defects of Celtic Christianity in Britain one is acquainted suffi-ciently to deal rather summarily respecting the value of any mystical suggestions which are discernible in the Cycles or in remanents of literature that must be regarded as belonging thereto. The hypothetical implicit with which I am dealing, if found to obtain, would signify therefore the closing of the whole inquiry.

B.—THE FORMULÆ OF THE HYPOTHESIS SCHEDULED

There are traces in the Anglo-Norman Romances of a certain fluidic sense in which Britain and its immediate connections, according to the subsurface mind of their writers, stood typically for the world. They were familiar enough with the names of other regions—with Syria, Egypt, Rome—above all, with the Holy Places in the Jerusalem which is below ; but their world was the Celtic World, comprised, let us say, between Scotia and Ireland on the one side and central France on the other. This region came, I think, to signify symbolically, and so we hear that the failure to ask " one little question " involved the destruc-tion of kingdoms, while the belated interrogation seems to have lifted a veil of Enchantment from the world itself. The cloud upon the Sanctuary was a cloud over that world ; its lifting was a glory restored everywhere. But as the Enchantment, except within very narrow limits, and then *ex hypothesi*, was only of the imputed order, so the combined restoration of Nature in common with Grace was but imputed also : the woe and inhibition were removed as secretly as they were imposed. So again, when the Chivalry of the Round Table—according to the Vulgate Cycle—covenanted to go forth on the Quest of the Holy Grail, the universal and proclaimed object was to terminate those hard Times of Adventure, which had become intolerable : *pour deliveir nôtre pais des grans mervelles et des estrainges auentures qui tant y sont auenues, lonc tans a.*[1] The whole position reminds one of that chapter in the Apocalypse which presents a sheaf of instructions to the Seven Churches of Asia. No one knew better than the Jews not only concerning Rome, Greece and Alexandria, but of the world extended further : this notwithstanding, when the Great Book of the Christian

---

[1] Cf. the *Queste* in Sommer's text, *Op. cit.*, VI, pp. 7, 8, 10. It affirms that the Adventures of the Quest are significances and demonstrations of the Holy Grail.

Secret Mystery was first written, the World of Christendom was confined chiefly within narrow limits in Asia, and this was the World of the Apocalypse. Recurring to the fact out of which this analogy arises, it should be added, as a matter of justice to the hypothesis under consideration, that within this Celtic World the first and most natural sympathy in the religious order would be indubitably with its own aspirations : I set aside therefore for the time being all speculation as to anything rich and strange in Rite and Doctrine which may have been brought from the Eastern world by those—whoever they were— who first planted Christianity on the known confines of the West. The chief points of the hypothesis may be collected into a schedule thus :—

(1) It has been affirmed that the Grail Legend is of Celtic origin and making, because of the Celtic attributions of the Romances and their Celtic *mise-en-scène* and characters ; because of the Celtic names, disguised and otherwise, even in those which belong to the Teutonic Cycle ; and because of imagined derivations into Grail Legend from Welsh folk-lore.

(2) The Romance of the Holy Grail, regarding the Cycle synthetic-ally, is a great Ecclesiastical Legend of Celtic origin ;[1] while there are other Ecclesiastical Legends, referable to the same source, which suggest the Grail atmosphere. The " Grail Church " was in its earlier stages the Celtic Church contrasted with the Saxo-Roman.

(3) The nucleus is to be found in a story concerning St. David and his Miraculous Altar. The Apostle of South Wales, with some other Saints, made a pilgrimage in the Legend to Jerusalem, where the Patriarch of the Holy City invested him as Archbishop and gave him " a consecrated Altar in which the body of our Lord once lay." It was transported to Wales and performed innumerable miracles ; but after the death of St. David it was covered with skins and was never seen by any one. According to a variant of the Legend, this Altar—and possibly some other Hallows—was carried through the air to Britain, and hence was often described as *e cælo veniens*. Though apparently it was the rock-hewn sepulchre mentioned in the New Testament, no man could specify its shape, its colour, or of what material it was fashioned : in addition to its other wonders, it gave oracles—that is to say, a Voice spoke therein, as it did, according to the Romances, in the Grail itself. St. David died about 601 A.D. ; he gave the Mass to Britain ; he was of the lineage of Our Lady ; and his birth having been foretold by the finding of a great fish, he was termed the Waterman—*vir aquaticus*— which recalls the Rich Fisherman of later Legends. It might be said that this title was applicable especially to him, as one who was rich in the conversion of souls to Christ and in the greater gifts of sanctity. His ancestors bore the name of *Avallach*, whence that of the King of

---

[1] My old friend Arthur Machen believes that the Grail Myth is a glorified version of early Celtic Sacramental Legends, married to certain elements of pre-Christian folk-lore. See *The Secret of the Sangraal* in a collection entitled THE SHINING PYRAMID, p. 90.

Sarras seems to be derived certainly ;[1] and he is said to have provided Sacred Vessels for the Celebration of the Eucharist.[2]

(4) The Secret Words of the Robert de Borron Cycle refer to the *Epiclesis* of the Greek Rite.[3] The form of Eucharistic Consecration in the Latin Rite is actually the Words of Institution—that is to say, the New Testament's account of the Last Supper. In the East, however, Consecration is effected by addition of the *Epiclesis* clause—that is, by the Invocation of the Holy Spirit. In its more usual form, it is a petition for the descent of the Comforter, firstly, upon the worshippers, and, secondly, upon the Altar Gifts, that the Elements may be converted into the Divine Body and Blood. The Liturgy of St. John Chrysostom may be consulted on this point : indeed from one passage it would seem to follow that what was communicated was the Holy Ghost, an idea in which all that attaches normally to the Eucharistic Office seems dissolving in a higher light.[4] The evidence, however, is confessedly somewhat indirect, as no Gallican or other connected Liturgy gives the Words of Institution ; but they are found in a North Italian, perhaps a Milanese Liturgy, and elsewhere, outside the Greek Rite. It has been said that between 750 and 820 A.D. certain words in the Celtic Rite vanished from the Consecration of the Eucharist, corresponding presumably to the intervention of the Roman Rite.[5] The Celtic was abolished formally about 850, but is said to have survived even to the period of the Grail literature.[6] The Welsh in this case might have learned from the Crusades that the LITURGY OF THE HOLY SPIRIT was still used in the East.

(5) The notion of Hereditary Grail Keepers, so strongly emphasised in the Romances, is derived from the Hereditary Relic Keepers of the Celtic Church. Mr. J. Romilly Allen has said : " The vicissitudes through which the Relics passed in the course of centuries were often of a most romantic description. The story was generally the same. The book, bell or crozier belonging to the founder of the Church was supposed to have acquired peculiar sanctity and even supernatural properties by association with him ; and after his death it was often enclosed in a costly metal shrine of exquisite workmanship. Each

---

[1] Avallac=Evalach in the GRAND SAINT GRAAL, according to this hypothesis. He was the son of a poor cobbler, who served Tholomer-Ptolemy, King of Egypt and whose valour brought him the crown of Sarras. Sommer, *Op. cit.*, I, pp. 47, 48. He became Mordrains in Baptism. *Ib.*, p. 75.

[2] Cf. the PERLESVAUS : Potvin, *Op. cit.*, I, p. 272, and HIGH HISTORY, Branch XXVI, Title 4.

[3] Appendix I, Note 17.

[4] See L. Duchesne : ORIGINES DU CULTE CHRÉTIEN, and in particular the fifth, revised and enlarged edition of 1920, which approximates the Liturgy of the Gallican Rite to the Syriac of the fourth century and reconstructs the latter on the basis of *Catechesis* 23 of St. Cyril of Jerusalem, the CONSTITUTIONES APOSTOLORUM and the HOMILIES of St. John Chrysostom. The *Epiclesis* follows the Words of Institution, and the transformation—spiritual or otherwise—of the Bread and Wine is operated by the descent of the Holy Spirit thereon, and Christ is among His believers under mystical veils in a veritable communion, as One in many and the All in one. *Op. cit.*, pp. 57–63.

[5] The inference is obviously that the *Epiclesis* Clause was removed.

[6] According to Arthur Machen, a remanent of Culdees in the twelfth century are reported as celebrating " some kind of barbarous Rite " in a corner of a Scottish Church. *Op. cit.*, p. 117.

Relic had its hereditary custodian, who was responsible for its safe keeping and who in return received privileges, such as . . . the title to inherit certain land, of which the Relic constituted the tenure."[1] The preservation of Relics under hereditary guardianship seems to have been common among Celtic families : it was the case with the Banner of St. Columba.[2] So also the Relics of certain Saints belonging to the Scoto-Irish Church were in the care of families of Hereditary Keepers : these were consecrated objects, not human remains, and they were regarded as of great virtue when borne in battle by a person who was free from deadly sin. Sometimes a Venerable Cup was deposited in a special Shrine ; sometimes the Book of the Gospels was enclosed in triple cases—as of wood, copper and silver. The custody of such an object became an office of dignity from generation to generation in a single family. The general characteristics of the Celtic Relic may be enumerated as follows, but it is not intended to say that every Sacred Object possessed all the qualities : (1) It came from Heaven, like the Grail ; (2) it was of mysterious and incomprehensible matter ; (3) it was oracular ; (4) like the Grail, it had the power of speech ; (5) it healed the sick, as the Grail did also occasionally, though this was not its specific office ; (6) like the Grail, it must not be seen by unqualified persons ; (7) it had the power of miraculous self-transportation, and the Holy Cup, in certain Romances, was also a Wandering Vessel ; (8) it acted as a guide ; (9) it was a Palladium ; (10) it executed judgment on the wicked and profane, which is the characteristic in chief of the Grail in the Metrical Romance of Robert.

(6) In the PANEGYRIC OF ST. COLUMBA, a document ascribed to the last years of the eleventh century, it is recorded among his other good works that—like his peer, St. David of Wales—he provided a Mass Chalice for every Church—presumably within his special sphere of influence or perhaps even in the islands generally. Readers of the prose PERCEVAL LE GALLOIS will remember that Chalices were so uncommon in Arthurian days that the King, during a certain Quest, seems to have met with one, and that miraculously, for the first time in his life. One explanation is that wooden bowls may have been used previously for purposes of consecration. I allude to the Mass of the Grail, which Arthur was permitted to see at the Grail Castle—that is to say, after the accession of Perceval to the Office of Keeper.[3] We should remember at this point that it is only at the close of the Cycle in Northern French—that is to say, in the Romance which I have just mentioned, in that of Galahad and in the GRAND SAINT GRAAL—

---

[1] The possessive sense in these matters seems a little like that of the Bardic Secret itself. See J. Williams ab Ithel : BARDDAS, Vol. I, 1862, pp. 65, 66. It was not lawful to utter " the Secret Word of the primitive Bards . . . to any man in the world, except to a Bard who is under the vow of an oath." So it was reserved and so also transmitted, like the Blessed Relics.

[2] In like manner, the Grail Castle is ever a House of Relics, and they multiplied more and more as the literature extended towards its term. The PERLESVAUS embodies a long list and may compare almost with the wealth of the Provençal FIERABRAS.

[3] Potvin, Op. cit., I, p. 250 : HIGH HISTORY, Branch XXII, Title 3.

that the Sacred Vessel, its other uses notwithstanding, is connected expressly with the Administration of the Eucharist, though it is not always the Vessel of Communion.

(7) There are historical memorials of Holy Cups, possessing great virtues and preserved in old Welsh families. Among these is the Holy Cup of Tregaron, which was made *ex hypothesi* from the Wood of the True Cross, and its healing virtues were manifested so recently as the year 1901.[1] The curious thing in the Romances is that the Holy Grail has healing power, but not for the Keeper himself, who in most texts of the Perceval Cycle can be cured only by a Question,[2] and in the Galahad Legend—but here it is a former Keeper—by the magnetic touch of his last lineal descendant.

(8) In England during the Middle Ages,[3] the Eucharist was reserved, as we have seen otherwise, in a *Columbarium*, or Dove-House, being a Vessel shaped like a Dove. This was the Tabernacle of its period, and it recalls (a) some archaic pictures of a Cup over which a Dove broods ; (b) the descent of a Dove on a Grail Stone in Wolfram's poem ; (c) the passage of Symbolical Doves in connection with the Grail Procession as told by several Romancers, but especially in the Quest of Galahad ; and (d) the Office of the Holy Spirit in the Grail Legend.[4] But it is suggested also—and this, I believe, by Huysman—that the Tabernacle was frequently in a form of an Ivory Tower, to symbolise Christ in the womb of the Virgin, who is herself called *Turris eburnea*.

(9) The vanishing of the Grail refers (a) to the actual disappearance of St. David's Altar after the death of its custodian ;[5] (b) to the disappearance of the Celtic Church before the Roman ; and (c) to the subjugation of the British by the Saxons. The Welsh Church was pre-eminently a Monastic Church ; and, in spite of the existence of Bishops, its government was in the hands of Monks. The claim of the ancient British Church generally, including its Legend that the first Church of Glastonbury was consecrated by our Lord Himself,[6] may

[1] It must be confessed that the last point cannot be verified. I find no reference in my papers : it may well have been a newspaper report.

[2] Except, *e.g.*, in the PERLESVAUS, and in this anomalous text the Keeper is stricken because the Question is not asked. Cf., however, DIU CRÔNE, in which all the men of the Household as well as its Head are suffering not from disease or maiming but from a state of death in life. In Manessier the head of his Brother's destroyer heals the Grail King.

[3] In the Celtic Rite the Reserved Sacrament was carried to the sick in a " chrysmal," or in a satchel suspended from the neck. Warren, *Op. cit.*, p. 138.

[4] Not only does the Voice of the Holy Spirit speak from the Grail in the Metrical Romance of Robert de Borron, but it is heard *in articulo mortis* by Alain according to the DIDOT PERCEVAL and by Perceval himself in the Modena text. It must be remembered also that the Dove is the Symbol of the Spirit, and it precedes the manifestation of the Grail at Corbenic in the LANCELOT and at the Royal Court in the QUESTE.

[5] It might refer also and perhaps as easily to the migration of some proscribed Sect Eastward, and the Grail Refuge of the PERLESVAUS might be the impregnable and almost inaccessible Citadel of Montségur, the last stronghold of the Cathari and their Holy Church of the Paraclete.

[6] This is the Church built of wattles, erected by Joseph of Arimathæa and his disciples, " thirty-one years after the Passion of our Lord and fifteen after the Assumption of the Virgin " and " dedicated to His Mother by the Lord Himself." Dr. Armitage Robinson, *Op. cit.*, p. 28. The authority is an introductory chapter prefixed to William of Malmesbury's DE ANTIQUITATE, *circa* 1250.

help us to explain the undertone of dissent from Rome which can be noted here and there in the subsurface of the Grail literature, but especially in the LONGER PROSE PERCEVAL. To appreciate the position fully, we have to remember that the Latin Rite gained ground and influence with the Norman Conquest, though independently of that Rite there were monasteries in remote valleys where the old Liturgy and its supposititious ancient form of Consecration may have been used still, and where also the ancient wisdom of the Druids was preserved, though—in spite of certain testimonies—it could have been scarcely considered consistent for a man to be a mystical Druid and also a Christian. The Druidic Secret was symbolised by the term *Afalon,* which means the Apple Orchard. The last Welsh Archbishop of St. David's died in 1115, and was succeeded by a Norman, that is to say, by a Roman prelate.

(10) Cadwaladr is Galahad. Galahad took away the Holy Grail, because, according to the WELSH QUEST, the world was not worthy.[1] His prototype, in despair of his country, removed certain Relics, and, by the testimony of one Tradition, he died in the Holy Land, as if he also had departed to Sarras, with the intention of proceeding further. Another story says that he projected the reconquest of Britain in a fleet furnished by his kinsman Alain of Brittany, where he was then in exile ; but an Angel warned him to desist. He was to seek the Pope and confess, and he would be canonised after his death—which, according to his Legend, occurred at Rome. This chieftain, who loomed so largely in Welsh imagination, who, like Bran of another mythos, is termed the Blessed, was regarded as of the Royal Line of David : he is thought to have been the custodian of Holy Relics belonging to his family before him, and when he died—in reality, as it seems, of the Yellow Sickness—in 664 his second advent was expected confidently. So many Legends grew up around him that he appears to have drawn into himself all the aspirations of Celtdom. His return is associated with a second manifestation of his Relics and with the final felicity of the Celts. Awaiting that event, the entire British Church, for reasons not fully explicable, began to droop and decay, till a Welsh revival was inaugurated in the year 1077 by the return of Rhys-ap-Teuudwr from Brittany.[2] Bards and Druids were at white heat, for

[1] The Welsh translator varies the QUESTE that he may bring the state of things home to his own countrymen. " For at that time so bad was the country of the Welsh, that if the father was ill in his bed, the son would come to him, and would pull him from bed, and drag him out, and kill him. And so also would the father do with the son ... And when the father was seen killing the son, and the son the father, in that manner, all went armed to tournaments and combats, and so they were killed, and because they were killed in arms, they were said to be gentlemen." HENGWRT MSS., I, p. 476.

[2] Cf. G. M. Harper in THE LEGEND OF THE HOLY GRAIL, 1896. He says (1) that no poetical influence was half as widespread as that which started from Wales at the end of the eleventh century ; (2) that it was occupied by free Celts at the beginning of Norman rule in Britain, but they lost their independence when little more than a century had passed away ; (3) that at the beginning of the twelfth century they remembered their original possession of the land and that their Christianity was older than that of Saxon or Norman ; (4) that their old Mythology revived in noble song ; and (5) that they may have remembered their independence of Rome in earlier times, as the Irish remembered long generations previously. *Op. cit.,* pp. 7–9.

Rhys himself was a descendant traditionally of Cadwaladr the Blessed, who was to restore all things. He even claimed identity with that departed hero.

(11) When the particular set of claims connected with Glastonbury began to be manufactured about 1150, to centralise a wide field of interest at a defined point, Joseph of Arimathæa was substituted for St. David.[1] There was the supposed body of Joseph ; there were the Vials which he brought, containing the imputed Precious Blood ; there also was the body of King Arthur and the so-called *Sapphirus*, the Lost Altar of the Welsh Apostle, the last of these recalling rather plausibly the *Lapsit exillis* or *exilix* of Wolfram. From this point of view it is worthy of close attention (*a*) for its sacramental connection ; (*b*) for its association with the Body of the Lord ; and (*c*) for the mystery attaching to its form, with which we may compare the vagueness which characterises nearly all descriptions of the Grail Vessel.[2]

(12) The hypothetical descent of the Grail *prima materia* from folk-lore no more explains the Christian Legend of the Grail than the words *vir* and *virtus* explain the particular significance attaching to the term *virtuoso*. The Mythological Salmon of Wisdom as a prototype of the Fish in Robert de Borron's poem is a case in point. The true approximate progenitor is the primitive Christian Fish-Symbol which was familiar to Celtic Christianity ; and seeing that the latter was much like the Church at large of several centuries earlier, so it may have preserved things which had passed elsewhere out of memory—the *Ichthus* Symbol among them. This signified Christ, and especially the Eucharistic Species. It symbolised also the *Disciplina Arcani* and was the most general of Christian Emblems : it passed into a defined form of expression for concealment of more interior Mysteries, and to partake of the Fish was an evasion for the Reception of the Sacrament.

(13) His connection with the Quest of the Grail not only enabled King Arthur to furnish Chalices for Churches but Bells, also, which seem to have been unknown previously in Logres. In the Celtic veneration for Relics they bear, however, a conspicuous part, the examples being far too numerous for recitation in this place. I can say only that their cultus, their care, the keeperships instituted in connection with and the wonders ascribed to them are common to ancient Wales, Scotland and Ireland.

(14) Reverting once more to St. David, it is reported traditionally that the first Church which he built was situated at Glastonbury, and in connection with this ascription we shall do well to remember that primitive structure which is said to have been consecrated by Christ Himself. This in more senses than in one sense merely was a source and fountain of all religion in the Kingdom of Britain, as affirmed by

---

[1] It would seem that the statement obtains only in respect of Glastonbury, where William of Malmesbury tells us that he came only as a visitor and built another Church.
[2] I have said that it might be even a Lamp in Chrétien, and the word Grail bore this connotation in Northern France. It is said to be the Paschal Dish in the Galahad Quest ; yet it served as a Pyx in the last Masses at Corbenic and Sarras.

William of Malmesbury. It was therefore among ecclesiastical structures what the Second Joseph was among the Bishops of Christendom. If ever there was an Arch-Natural Mass celebrated and a Noumenal Eucharist administered at a specific place in Logres, assuredly with these warrants it would have been only at Glastonbury, the connection of which with St. David raises one further point. The Celtic Church is said to have held that the Roman Pontiff was the Successor of St. Peter, but the Patriarch of Jerusalem—who ordained the Apostle of Wales—was the Successor of Christ. The subsurface intention which created this Legend seems to have been nearly identical with that which put forward the Super-Apostolical Succession of Joseph II, and it follows that Celtic Imagination at work in the field of Hagiology furnished the makers of Romance—and the author in particular of the GRAND SAINT GRAAL—with an ample groundwork. The substitution of the Man of Arimathæa for the original Patron of Wales was the appropriation of an independent Legend, and it served the ecclesiastical side of Angevin ambition without affording a handle to the troublesome Principality on the Western side of the vast dominions of Anjou.

(15) And now as regards the summary of the whole matter, the argument may be expressed as follows : (a) The Grail Legend is demonstrably of Celtic stuff—in part of Celtic folk-lore which has turned good Christian, but more largely of Ecclesiastical Legend ; (b) it derives from the story of St. David and his Altar ; (c) the original Grail Book was probably a Legend following a special and peculiar Liturgy ; (d) the Legend told of the Conversion of Britain by St. David, the celebration of the Christian Mysteries on the Saint's Miraculous Altar, which was claimed to be the Sepulchre of Christ, of the wonders wrought by this Altar, of the coming of the heathens, the ruin of Britain, the flight of its King—who was St. David's last descendant —bearing with him the Altar Relic to the East. There he died, thence he shall yet return, again bearing the Relic. The Britons shall triumph, the Saxons shall suffer expulsion and the Mystical Words shall be uttered once more over the Thaumaturgic Altar.

It is obvious that, according to this hypothesis, the Book, which was far older than any Grail literature, remained in concealment in Wales and perhaps was unearthed at the Norman Conquest of Glamorganshire, when it was modified, varied, exalted, transformed and allegorised by successive makers of Romance, being adapted specifically as an aid to the House of Anjou, in its struggle with the Pope, by the author of the GRAND SAINT GRAAL—whether Walter Map or another. But Rome proved more than one part too strong and by more than one interest too many for the ambition of Henry II, while as regards Wales, it had long and long already succumbed to the Latin Rite.[1]

[1] That is to say, between 750 and 809, according to Machen (p. 120) ; but according to Warren (p. 4) North Wales conformed in 768 and South Wales in 777.

C.—IN WHAT SENSE THE PLEA MUST BE HELD TO FAIL

Let us suppose it indubitable for a moment, even in a plenary sense, that folk-lore provided its elements as the crude matter of the scheme of the Holy Grail. Let us admit it to be true also that many accidentals of the Celtic Church became accidentals of the literature ; and that they were worked into the Grail Cycle as well as the pre-Christian elements, the process arising in the most natural of possible manners. It would not be exactly that the most early Romancers took the matter which was nearest into their hands, but rather that there was no other : the external aspect of religion was by necessity therefore a reflection of the Celtic Church. But as mere folk-lore does not explain the Christian Grail and the high experiments of sanctity connected therewith, so the contributory memorials on the Celtic Ecclesiastical Side do not explain it either. To justify and expound this statement, be it noted (1) that Christianity existed in Britain during the Roman occupation and that three British Bishops were present at the Council of Arles, about 350 A.D. ; (2) that the extent of its diffusion is doubtful, but it was probably the religion of Romans and Romanised Britons in and about the garrison towns ; (3) that it became diffused more widely in the early fifth century, which was the beginning of an age of Saints ; (4) that it is doubtful whether the Celtic Church[1] at this period was a descendant of the Roman-British Church or a colonisation *de novo* from Gaul, but it may have combined both sources ; (5) that an episcopal mission from Gaul into Britain is certain, and its object is supposed to have been the extinction of Pelagian heresy, or Pagan, as it has been suggested alternatively ; (6) that the derivation *ab origine symboli* was possibly from Ephesus through the Johannine Rite into Southern Gaul, and thence into Britain ; (7) that, also possibly, there were other Oriental influences, and particularly from Egypt, in the fifth century, the evidence being : (1) The derivation of Celtic ornament from Egyptian ornament ; (2) the commemoration in ancient Irish books of " Holy Egyptian Hermits " buried in Ireland ; (3) the correspondences between the Celtic monastic system and that of Egypt ; (4) the practice, attributed to St. Columba, of removing his sandals before entering the Sanctuary, an observance known otherwise only in Egypt.

As regards the hypothesis put forward in the previous sub-section, it is observable that we have not been invited to consider in the Celtic

---

[1] According to Warren " there are no substantial grounds for impugning the orthodoxy of the Celtic Church. On the contrary, there is unimpeachable evidence the other way." The fact that Pope Gregory commissioned Augustine to impose his personal jurisdiction not only over all Bishops ordained by him but over all Priests in Britain —presumably there already—" that they might learn the rule of believing rightly and living well from his life and teaching " (Bede's ECCLESIASTICAL HISTORY, I, 29) is explained by the Pontiff's slender acquaintance with the faith of the British Church. *Op. cit.*, p. 26. It happens that Pelagius was of British birth and that his teachings obtained a certain credence in his native country rather early in the fifth century.

Church any traces of a particular theological or doctrinal Tradition—such as might, for example, be inferred from the supposed Johannine Rite—or of an evasive or concealed claim : it is not suggested that in Wales, Scotia or Ireland there is any trace of an Ecclesiastical Legend concerning a Relic which at any distance might be held to offer correspondence with that of the Holy Grail or even one of its companion Hallows, because the essential condition of the analogy must be indubitably the existence of memorials of the Passion of our Lord. Of these it is certain that there were none, because otherwise it is certain that they would be adduced. We are asked, on the contrary, to assume that a variant liturgical reading, the Legend of an Historical Apostle, after passing under a specific transmutation, and the mythical restitution of a Welsh King are the first matter in combination of the complex cycles of literature which are comprised in the Grail Legend. If this hypothesis can be taken with such high seriousness that we may suppose it put forward—shall I say ?—as an equivalent by analogy for that which has offered St. Dominic and the enchanting fable of a question which should have been put to the Pope as a real explanation of the Perceval-Grail Myth,[1] it will be sufficient, I think, to deal with it on general lines rather than by an exhaustive process of criticism in detail. Let us put aside, in the first place, all that part which is purely in the region of supposition, and take the actual facts as things for valuation in the schedule. Question of *Epiclesis* or question—as we shall see presently—of a particular tense, it is obvious that the oriental terms of Consecration, when those prevailed in the West, were the secret of no particular Sanctuary as distinguished from all other Holy Places in Britanny, Britain and Wales.[2] They were catholic to these countries and also to a great part of that which we understand by Scotia, Ireland and Gaul. They connect in themselves with no Keepership and with no Hallows. We know that the Roman Rite colonised all these countries, and that in the course of time it prevailed. But the period between the public use of the Words now in question and their final abrogation was one of centuries, and although during a portion thereof—*ex hypothesi*—they may have been perpetuated in concealment, there is no doubt that they had fallen into complete desuetude long before the third quarter of the twelfth century. It is impossible to suppose that there was at that time any one concerned in their perpetuation sufficiently to put them forward as a Great Mystery of Sanctity inherent in the heart of Christianity, while it is impossible, mystically speaking, that they should carry this significance. The Secret Words do not emerge in the Metrical Romance of Joseph as in any sense the material of Romance : they appear with all the marks of

---

[1] See Dr. Sebastian Evans : IN QUEST OF THE HOLY GRAIL, 1898.
[2] They were secret to all Sanctuaries in the sense that the words are said in a low voice. All Low Masses of the Roman Rite may be called secret, being said in an undertone, not to speak of a language which is largely unknown to the laity. The same affirmation can be made of the Greek Rite. As regards the *Secreta* of the Ordinary, the undertone is reverential.

a particular claim advanced for a special reason and maintained through more than one generation by the successive production, firstly, of a prose version of the Early Metrical MERLIN and, secondly, by the similar derivation or independent invention of the DIDOT-MODENA PERCEVAL, which carried on the same Tradition, though it seems left unfinished, perhaps from the standpoint of narrative and assuredly of the term of its intention. In the second place two concurrent claims appear, and the second—which is stronger than the first—abandons the claim in respect of Secret Words. It does this so explicitly that it makes public the Words of Consecration, by which we are enabled to see at once how little they could ever have signified, if indeed it were possible to suppose that these are the Lost Words of Grail literature.[1] Moreover, by a particular fatality, they do not happen to contain the *Epiclesis* Clause. In its place, as we know so well already, we have the claim of the GRAND SAINT GRAAL on a Super-Apostolical Succession— as I have said, a much stronger claim and one for which there is little precedent in the dubious history of the Celtic Church. It is out of this pretension that the Galahad Quest arises, though at a period when the notion itself seems to have passed out of sight. We are agreed that, so far as there is a true story at all, it is the Quest of Galahad, with the LONGER PROSE PERCEVAL as its competitor on the same level, and the question of Secret Words never entered into the heart of either. It is useless to put forward the assumed fact of their existence in the Celtic Rite of Institution as something which is explanatory of the literature.[2] In this connection it is of importance to remember (1) that the only prose PERCEVAL which is of any consequence mystically is that which depends from the GRAND SAINT GRAAL rather than from Robert de Borron, and is of course the PERLESVAUS ;[3] while (2) the only Metrical Romance of Perceval which ethically may be also important is that of Wolfram. The first has abandoned the Words and the second all earthly Eucharistic connection. The first puts the Roman Dogma of Transubstantiation in its most materialised possible form. It will be seen therefore that the Celtic hypothesis fails along what must be regarded as the most vital line. I submit that the pretention to a Super-Apostolical Warrant is either part of a fraudulent scheme for pre-eminence as an argument for autonomy in the case of the British Church, with the advisers of a King for its spokesmen, or it belongs to another order of concealed sentiment and event, the details and motives of which are wanting on the manifest side of things. In the first instance it is not of our concern and is explanatory only of

[1] *Laiens fist iosephe le premier sacrement qui onques fust fais a cel pueple mais il lot moult tost acompli. Car il ni dist fors que le parole seulement que ihesus dist a ses disciples, quant il sist a la chaine, tenes et mangies cest li urais cors qui pour vous & por maintes gens sera liures a tourment ; & autre tel dist il del uin ; tenes & si beues tout car cest li sans de ma nouele loy li miens meismes qui por uos fu espandus en remission de uos pecies.* Sommer, *Op. cit.*, I, p. 40.

[2] It might as well be suggested that the whole Northern French Grail Cycle came into existence to promote the practice of Communion in one kind, for so the Knights communicate in the Great Quest and inferentially or otherwise through all the texts.

[3] By its recurring appeal to Joseph II as he who first sacrificed the Body of the Lord.

one branch of a large literature ; in the latter we must go much further, and if we can supply the missing events or motives[1] from certain hidden sources, we shall be in possession of at least a provisional explanation of things most important in the literature and—*donec de medio fiet*—it must be allowed to hold.

The distinctive note of the Latin Eucharistic Rite is that, like the Gospels of St. Matthew and St. Mark, it gives the first Words of Institution thus : *Accipite et manducate ex hoc omnes. Hoc est enim corpus meum*—" Take and eat ye all of this. For this is My body ". Hereto certain Oriental Rites added other words, which should read in Latin : *Quod pro multis confrangetur*—" Which shall be broken for many ". The GRAND SAINT GRAAL in the Hucher text gives : *Venes, si mangies et chou est li miens cors qui pour vous et pour maintes autres gens sera livres a martire et a torment*—the substantial equivalent of *pro multis confrangetur*. Compare the Gospel of St. Luke in the Latin Vulgate, which uses the present tense : *quod pro vobis datur.*

So far as regards the really trivial question of tense. The mode of Consecration by *Epiclesis*, or the Invocation of the Holy Spirit, will be unknown to some of my readers, and I extract one example therefore from the LITURGY OF ST. JOHN CHRYSOSTOM.

THE PRIEST (saith).—Blessed art Thou, Christ our God, who didst fill the fishermen with all manner of wisdom, sending down upon them the Holy Ghost, and by them hast brought the whole world into Thy net, O Lover of men : Glory be to Thee.

R. Both now and ever, &c.

THE PRIEST (saith).—When the Highest came down and confounded the tongues, He divided the nations ; when He distributed the tongues of fire, He called all to unity ; and with one voice we praise the Holy Ghost.

The Deacon, pointing to the Holy Bread, saith in a low voice :

DEACON.—Sir, bless the Holy Bread.

The Priest standeth up, and thrice maketh the sign of the Cross on the Holy Gifts, saying :

PRIEST.—And make this bread the Precious Body of Thy Christ.

DEACON.—Amen. Sir, bless the Holy Cup.

PRIEST.—And that which is in this Cup the Precious Blood of Thy Christ.

DEACON.—Amen. (*And pointing with his stole to both the Holy Things*) Sir, Bless.

PRIEST.—Changing them by Thy Holy Ghost.

DEACON.—Amen, Amen, Amen.

PRIEST.—(*After a pause*) So that they may be for purification of soul, forgiveness of sins, communion of the Holy Ghost, &c.

---

[1] The events, if they signify validly, will be those of inward experience.

I believe that in the Mosarabic Rite, which is thought to be in near consanguinity with the Celtic, the *Epiclesis* formula is used on occasions only. It is missing altogether from the so-called LITURGY OF ST. DIONYSIUS, which only survives in the Latin. I should add that the existence of the clause in the Celtic Rite—whatever the strength of the inferences—is a matter of speculation, for the simple reason that no such Liturgy is extant.[1]

The other analogies and possibilities are a little attractive on the surface, and are of the kind which are caught at rather readily ; but they seize upon a single point where they can be made to apply, and the other issues in a long sequence are ignored. The name Cadwaladr naturally suggests that of Galahad, and on the appeal to certain laws of permutation, it seems for a moment justified, but it is not justified in the Legends. The last King of the Britons had indeed the Hallows of his family by the right of inheritance ; but there was no antecedent Keeper whom he was required to heal, and there was no Quest to undertake in order that he might secure his own. But this healing and this Quest inhere in the Grail Legend, and are manifestly at the root of the design, so that there is no connection possible between the two cases. Moreover, Cadwaladr is destined by his Legend to return, while it is of the essence of that of Galahad that he comes back no more. The same remarks will apply to all traceable instances of HereditaryKeepership in Celtic families, whatever the object reserved. It is even more certain that any comparison of St. David the Waterman with the Rich Fisherman who is wounded is highest fantasy : neither physically nor symbolically did the Saint suffer any hurt, but, again, one of the foremost Grail intentions resides in the King's wounding. The symbolical term Fisherman signifies the Guardian of the Holy Mysteries ; it can have nothing to do with DEVERUR=Waterman. We do not know why a great fish is said to have heralded the birth of the Welsh Apostle. To help out the argument, we may affirm that he was a Guardian of the Christian Mysteries in the land to which he was commissioned ; but we do not in this manner account, either in the historical or symbolical sense, for the fishing of Brons or Alain in the lake, or for the title of Rich Fisherman applied to the Wardens of the Grail. It is true that they also were Guardians of Mysteries, but this is an instance of concurrence and not of derivation. The LESSER HOLY GRAIL may create a comparison between the Sacred Vessel and the Sepulchre in which Christ was laid ; but it does not for this reason institute any analogy between that Vessel and St. David's Altar, nor is the appeal to Wolfram useful except in the opposite sense, for the Grail Stone of the PARZIVAL, whether or not it was once in the crown of Lucifer, can tolerate still less the institution of its likeness to " a sepulchre that was hewn in stone, wherein never man before was laid."

[1] It is to be noted that the GRAND SAINT GRAAL gives the Formula for the Consecration of Wine. But *ex hypothesi* the Chalice was the Grail itself, the Reliquary of the Precious Blood, which no human being, including the first Priest who sacrificed the Body of the Lord, would dare to Consecrate. Another Vessel was therefore used.

The Altar of St. David is an interesting fable of its type, as preposterous as that of Fécamp, and between the Tomb of Christ, *ex hypothesi* transported to Wales, and the Sacramental *Ciborium* likened to the Holy Sepulchre there is no analogy in any world of correspondences.

It remains therefore that in this literature we have seen how evil fell upon the House of Doctrine ; how it overtook also the Keeper of Secret Knowledge ; after what manner he was healed at length ; how the Hidden Treasures passed under the care of his saviour ; and how at the term of all they were removed, because of a fell and faithless time. That might be a very pleasant scheme of interpretation which could say that the House of Doctrine was the Celtic Church and that the wounded Keeper signified the Church in desolation ; but it remains that we must go further in our search for a Key to these Mysteries.[1]

[1] I went further on a day long since, when dream moved up towards vision, but did not reach that state : it broke therefore and dissolved. But a few of my fellow-watchers in the precincts may find some glints of suggestion among the shards, so they are drawn here together, carrying no title. It is true that I went further, and not without remembering that dreams lead sometimes unto great awakenings, in others and even us, when it may happen that we exceed their measures. It seemed to me then at a venture that, as the sum total of many mystical aspects, the desire of the eyes in the Seeking and Finding of the Holy Grail may be re-expressed as follows : Temple or Castle or Palace—Mont Salvatch or Corbenic—wherever located and whether described as " a wilderness of building," crowded burg or simple hermit's hold, there is one characteristic concerning the Sanctuary which is essentially the same, amidst all variations of the accidents : the Keeper of the Great Hallows has fallen upon evil days ; the means of restoration and of healing must come from without. They are those of his predestined successor whose office is to remove the Palladium, so that henceforth it is never seen so openly. Taking the Quest of Galahad as that which has the highest significance spiritually, I think that we may speak of it thus : In the last analysis it is the Inward Man who is really the Wounded Keeper. The Mysteries are his ; on him the woe has fallen : it is he who expects healing and redemption. His body is the Grail Castle, which is also the Castle of Souls, and behind it is the Earthly Paradise as a vague and latent memory. He who enters into the consideration of this Sacred and Immemorial House by contemplation, under fitting guidance, shall know why it is that the Grail is served by a pure Maiden and why that Maiden is ultimately dispossessed. Elaine is the Soul, and the Soul is in exile because all the high unions have been declared voided : the Crown has been separated from the Kingdom and experience from the higher knowledge. So long as she remained a Pure Virgin, she was more than a Thyrsus-Bearer in the Mysteries ; but the morganatic marriage of mortal life is part of her doom. This is still a high destiny, for the Soul out of earthly experience brings forth spiritual desire, which is the Quest of the return journey ; and this is Galahad. It is therefore within the law and the order that she has to conceive and bring him forth. Galahad represents the highest spiritual aspirations and desires passing into full consciousness, and so into attainment. But he is not reared by his Mother, because Eros, which is the higher knowledge, has dedicated the true desire to the proper ends thereof. It will be seen also what must be understood by Lancelot in secret communication with Elaine, though he has taken her throughout for another. The reason is that it is impossible to marry even in hell without marrying that seed which is of Heaven. As she is the Psychic Woman, so is he the Natural Man, or rather the natural intelligence which is not without its consecrations, not without its term in the highest. Elaine believes that her desire is only for Lancelot ; but this is because she takes him for Eros ; and it is by such a misconception that the lesser Heaven stoops to the earth : herein also there is a sacred dispensation, because so is the earth assumed. I have said that Lancelot is the Natural Man ; but he is such merely at the highest : he is born in great sorrow, and she who has conceived him saves her Soul alive amidst the offices of External Religion. He is carried into the lesser Land of Faërie, as into a garden of childhood. When he draws towards manhood, he comes forth from the first places of enchantment and is clothed upon by the active duties of life, as by the Vestures of Chivalry. He enters also into the unsanctified life of sense, into an union against the consecrated life and order. But his redeeming quality is that he is faithful and true, because of which, and because of his genealogy, he is chosen to beget Galahad, of whom he is otherwise unworthy, even as we all, in our daily life, fall short of the higher aspirations of the Soul. As regards the Keeper, it is certain that he must die and be

If the Legend of the Holy Grail were the last light of the Celtic Church before it expired in proscription, one would confess that it was glorious in its death. But the most that we can say actually is rather that it left elements which in fine served a better purpose. The PERLESVAUS, the poem of Wolfram, and the sacred and beautiful Quest of Galahad, these are three records which bear witness on earth of the secret things which are declared only in the Heavens. There are Three Tabernacles wherein Transfiguration takes place.

In the extrinsic Celtic remains the only substitute which offers for the great Legend of the Holy and Sacramental Cup is an obscure and nameless Vessel which is subject in its latest history to the irreverence of a pedlar, and this it was deemed worth while to avenge. From such inefficiencies and trifles it is certain that we must have recourse, even if for a moment only, to the Glastonbury Legend, which did invent high fables to glorify the British Church. This recourse must fail us however in its turn, because Glastonbury is (1) of very small moment throughout the Grail literature, except in the PERLESVAUS ; (2) is never the place of the Sacred Vessel, for even its most mythical allocations—as, for example, Corbenic—cannot be identified therewith ; and (3) it knows nothing of the Second Joseph. The GRAND SAINT GRAAL does in one of its codices speak of Glastonbury as the burial-place of the elder Joseph, though it only says " *Glas* in England," for which other texts substitute Scotland. I doubt very much whether the Glastonbury Legend was intended for more than the praise of a particular Monastery : it represents Joseph of Arimathæa as the chief among Twelve Apostles sent by St. Philip to Britain, and they carried a Vial or Vials containing the Precious Blood. The Grail notion might have gratified Henry II, who concerned himself with things Arthurian, but beyond this we have only Romance of History. It is certain in any case that St. David was not transformed into Joseph of Arimathæa, so far as Glastonbury is concerned. He and his *apostoli coadjutores*, his Staff and his Relics, belong to another story, brought over from the Continent when St. David had passed into desuetude. Even so, of the Joseph claim, as we have it in the Grail Romances, there is little enough trace in historical writers of the time. The Abbey of Moienmoutier[1] in the Vosges laid claim to the original possession of Joseph's body ; but it disappeared or was stolen, as some said, by the

replaced by another Keeper before the true man can be raised, with the holy things to him belonging, which Hallows are withdrawn indeed, but it is with and in respect of him only ; for the Keepers are a great multitude, though it is certain that the Grail is one. The path of Quest is the path of upward progress, and it is only at the great height that Galahad knows himself as really the Wounded Keeper and that thus, in the last resource, the physician heals himself. Now this is the mystery from everlasting, which is called in the high doctrine *Schema misericordiæ*. It is said : *Latet, æternumque latebit*, until it is revealed in us ; and as to this : *Te rogamus, audi nos.*

[1] See THE MYSTIC VISION by Miss Fisher, p. 49. The theft is referred to Glastonbury by Paulin Paris. Miss Fisher is a little vague respecting the Relics : possibly the reference is to the two Vials. It does not seem that other Relics than these were claimed by Glastonbury, except that it was the burial-place of Joseph. Miss Fisher says that it appropriated Joseph " bones and all " (p. 50). Its claim rests, however, on his supposititious evangelisation of Britain, beginning A.D. 63.

Monks of Glastonbury. If it be affirmed that the Second Joseph, who is a creation of the GRAND SAINT GRAAL, signifies some move in the curious ecclesiastical game which was played by Henry II, the evidence is in the opposite direction, so far as it can be said to exist : it is obvious that any game must have worked better with the original Apostolical Joseph than with his imaginary Son.[1]

It is time to close these reflections, and there are only two points which remain, as I have not covenanted to deal with the *minima* as a whole. If King Arthur was enabled to make Chalices for ordinary Sacramental Uses in Official Churches from the prototype which he saw in his vision, being an Arch-Natural Chalice, this occurred after the same manner that the Pilgrim Masons who discovered the body of the Master Builder were enabled to bring away certain things in substitution for the Secrets that were lost at his death ; and there are thus other analogies than the natural and reasonable gifts of the Welsh Apostle ; but there is no need to dwell upon them in this place.

The quotation which I have given from the LESSER HOLY GRAAL raises an interesting point, and, without being versed in the ecclesiastical side of things, we can all of us believe that a Church so strange as that which once ministered in Wales had also some curious things belonging to the Liturgical World ; but the extract in question must be read in connection with the original Metrical Romance, where the symbolism is expressed differently.

> " Aussi sera representée
> Cele taule en meinte contrée.
> Ce que tu de la crouiz m'ostas
> Et ou sepulchre me couchas,
> C'est l'auteus seur quoi me metrunt
> Cil qui me sacrifierunt.
> Li dras où fui envolepez,
> Sera corporaus apelez.
> Cist veissiaus où men sanc méis
> Quant de men cors le requeillis,
> Calices apelez sera.
> La platine ki sus girra
> Iert la pierre senefiée
> Qui fu deseur moi seelée,
> Quant ou sepuchre m'éus mis."

The Blood is mentioned therefore and the analogy is complete ; it is also gracious and piteous, as the poem might say itself ; and, in fine— apart from forced analogies of a material kind—it is a true, catholic and efficacious comparison, which exhibits for those who can read in the heart one other side of secret Eucharistic symbolism —even the deep mystery of that mystical death which is suffered by the Lord of Glory in the assumption of the Veils of Bread and Wine, that He may arise into a new life in the soul of the reborn communicant.

---

[1] We have seen that Glastonbury would have nothing to do with Joseph II and substituted its own Vials for the Holy Grail.

I do not propose to speak of any original Grail Book, because this s for another consideration ; but supposing for a moment that a Secret Liturgy or Missal were at the root of the Legend my conviction would be that it was not especially Celtic and still less Welsh especially. Behind the hypothesis of the *Epiclesis* Clause there lies for me a deeper speculation, because there are traces of a rare and wonderful Office of the Holy Spirit here and there in Grail literature ; it may be—not impossibly—that this is one of the keys as to its source and Doctrine, could only we find the lock for which it was wrought in Romance. Would it open some gate, I wonder, leading back to that Johannine Rite,[1] the rumours of which have reached us from strange and doubtful quarters ?

It has been noted already that if we accept the hypothesis of a Pan-Britannic Church, its evidence lies substantially within the measures of the GRAND SAINT GRAAL. Of Chrétien's intention we can discern little, nor does it indeed signify : it seems fairly clear that he had no religious, much less ecclesiastical implicits. Wauchier and his anonymous precursor are in the same position ; Manessier is concerned only with a Vengeance Quest ; Gerbert offers a few significant allusions, but his end is a thing frustrated. There is nothing so remote from all ecclesiastical programme in the official order as the Lesser Chronicles, notwithstanding their Secret Words. Finally, the PARZIVAL of Wolfram renders to God all that can be offered by ethics—like another Cain, though not of necessity rejected, offering the fruits of earth—and to the spiritual Cæsar appears to deny nothing. If the PARZIVAL has an ulterior motive it is not of the Celtic Church, nor yet of the House of Anjou, about which methinks that it protests too much, either for the alleged Provençal Kyot or the Lord of Eschenbach. There remain therefore only the VULGATE CHRONICLES and outside the primary text in place, which happens to be last in time, may those come forth and testify who can find a Pan-Britannic Church in any MERLIN codex, the LANCELOT or the QUEST.

The debate must end here : there is another point of view from which one cares but little on what materials the makers of Grail

---

[1] There is something to be said on this subject at a later stage ; but the pitfalls of occult reverie are about it on every side. It has been suggested, for example, that there is a chain of " evidence " passing through Spain and the Knights Templar to St. John the Divine, so onward to the Essenes, after whom there is the further East. This is the fable of a few who look to India as asylum-in-chief of all veridic Mysteries ; but it has been found more convenient to state the fact of the evidence than to produce it. At an earlier stage Abbé Grégoire affirmed that our Saviour placed His Disciples under the authority of St. John, who never quitted the East and from whom certain secret teachings were handed on to his successors, the Johannine Christians, leading after many centuries to the Institution of the Templars. Again, the evidence is wanting on all the counts. The broad speculation has found, however, some favour with a few critics of the Grail literature ; and Simrock in particular put forward, as will be seen in another section, the idea of the Sacred Vessel as belonging to the root-matter of alleged Templar Secrets. He suggested also a connection between that Chivalry and the Essenes, postulated as repositories of a concealed science confided by Jesus to His Disciples and, in fine, by them communicated to Templar Priests. Those who are acquainted with the claims of German Masonic Knights Templar in the late eighteenth century are likely to be looking for the problematical personality of Johann August Starck in the shadows behind Simrock.

Romances may be held to have worked, since it is clear that they imported therein a new spirit. If anyone persists in affirming that Cadwaladr, who went to Rome or Jerusalem, is to be identified with Galahad, who went to Heaven, he can have it that way at his pleasure, understanding that on my part the judgment is reserved. I know that the one has suffered a high change before he has passed into the other. I know also, in any case, that of God moveth the PERLESVAUS and the GALAHAD of the King of All. I know that every literature has its antecedents in some other literature, and that every religion owes something to a religion that preceded it. Sometimes the consanguinity is close and sometimes it is very far away. Only those who affirm that the one accounts for the other, and this simply and only, seem to be a little unwise. Christianity arose within Jewry and doctrinally out of Jewry, but this fact only brings their generic difference into greater relief. So also the Grail literature rose up in the Celtic Church ; its analogies may be found therein ; they may be many also in folk-lore ; but there are also as many ways in which the one, as we know it, does not account for the other, as we have it actually.

The Celtic Church has assisted us, however, to see one thing more plainly, though we know it on other considerations, namely, that in fine there is but a single Quest, which is that of Galahad. We must make every allowance for the honest findings of those past scholars, for whom the Holy Grail, as it was and it is, has never spoken, for whom it is only a Feeding-Dish under a light cloud of imagery, and by whom it is thought perhaps in their hearts that the paraded intervention of Christianity among wild old pagan myths is on the whole rather regrettable. They turned naturally to those quarters whence issue the voices of purely natural life, and therefore they chose Gawain and Perceval in his cruder forms, because these spoke to them in their own language. Unmanifested now but still discerned darkly, if a lost proto-Perceval should be found at length, even that which went before the PEREDUR and the English Metrical Romance ; and if, as there is no doubt, it should be devoid of all elements belonging to Grail or Quester, our case would be proved the better, being (1) the natural succession of the Galahad Quest after the GRAND SAINT GRAAL ; (2) the succession of Perceval in the sequence of Robert de Borron, but rather as the scion of a less exalted legitimacy ; (3) the introduction of the late prose PERLESVAUS or PERCEVAL LE GALLOIS as a final act of transmutation in the Anglo-Norman Cycle, which so far assists our case that it manifests the unfitness, realised at that period, of Perceval as he was known by the earlier texts ; (4) the derivation of the Wolfram PARZIVAL in part from Celtic elements, in part from some which are, or may have been, Teutonic, but also with speculative derivations through Provence from Spain.

D.—THE VICTORY OF THE LATIN RITE

The hypothesis of the Celtic Church has been put forward in the last section as it has never been expressed previously : I have diminished nothing and any contrary inferences have been proposed so far temperately ; but the issues are not entirely those of the Grail Legend, and in view of all that comes after a few words in conclusion of this part may be stated in plainer terms. It should be on record, by example, for those who have ears, that the Welsh Church with its phantom and figure-head Bishops, its Hereditary Priesthood, its fighting and sanguinary Prelates, and its profession of sanctity as others profess trades, seems a very good case for those who insist that the original Christianity of Britain was independent of St. Augustine, which it was, and very much indeed ; but on the whole, as a counsel of despair or otherwise, there may be some of us who will prefer Rome.[1]

There may be insufficiencies and imperfect warrants in the great Orthodox Assemblies ; there may be and there are indeed a thousand scandalous and appalling histories encompassing the Roman Orthodoxy ; but the Celtic Church—innocuous in these respects—recalls nothing that we can regret. Gildas and St. Bernard at their values are eloquent witnesses concerning it. The Latin Rite prevailed because it was bound to prevail, because the greater absorbs the lesser. For the rest, we know that the True Church has never been built on earth, except in the hearts of the Elect ; that after Rome and Greece and Canterbury, we are looking like the Joachists for the Reign of the Holy Spirit. On the other hand, and now only in respect of the Legends, let us say lastly, using a tongue of symbolism, that the Ascension of Galahad is without prejudice to the second coming of Cadwaladr. It does not signify for our purpose whether Arthur ever lived, and if so whether he was merely a petty British Prince. The Grail is still the Grail, and the Mystery of the Round Table is still the sweet and secret spirit of Universal Knighthood.

It has been proposed that the Grail Symbols are to be found in the Greek Mass : the Cup, the Lance, the Platter or Sacred Dish, the Lights and so forth. In reality it is a fantastic reverie which reduces the Hallows and replaces the mighty Spear—a blood-dripping Talisman—by a small instrument used for dividing bread and called, also fantastically, the Lance of Longinus, which is obviously the sole ground on which the comparison has been made. We must remember in these connections that the Pageants or Processions in the Grail Castle have no relation to a Mass of any kind whatsoever. If they are comparable with any Church Observance, it is with the Catholic Ceremony of Corpus Christi and the modern Procession of the Blessed Sacrament, which forms on special occasions a part of the Rite of

[1] Apart from its official history, apart from the poisoning Borgia and his Host efficacious unto death ; apart from the Legate of Innocent III and his holocaust of men, women and children of Provence, leaving God to find out His own.

Benediction. We may remember also the Procession of the Precious Blood at Bruges, which is at least some centuries old.

It is obvious that there is a Mass of the Grail in certain texts, though not in any branch of the CONTE DEL GRAAL, not in the DIDOT-MODENA PERCEVAL, and not of course in Wolfram. It is found in the Galahad QUESTE and in the PERLESVAUS. In these it is a Wonder-Mass, and no other Hallows ever occur therein, an accessory Chalice excepted, or that which corresponds thereto. Miss Fisher, among others, has been misled by plausible but quite empty analogies between the Church Mass and the Grail. Such correspondences are obvious enough, but they account for nothing which distinguishes the Grail Service from an Ordinary of the Latin Mass or from any of the Orthodox Liturgies. The Ordinary was heard daily in every Minster and was said in Hermit's Chapels. It is met with continually in Grail texts ; but it was not the Grail Mass which Arthur heard and saw in the PERLESVAUS and which Galahad heard with his peers at Corbenic or at the end of all in Sarras.

It is to be noted further that an attempt at identification of the Secret Words communicated by Christ to Joseph with any part of the VERE DIGNUM or the official SECRETA is like explaining the Rosicrucian *absque nube pro nobis* as a simple confession of faith : it covers no part of the ground. The MYSTERIUM INEFFABILE does not lie within the compass of a Roman penny Catechism.

BOOK X

FURTHER CRITICAL APPARATUS:
THE SCHOOLS, THE CHURCHES, AND THE SECTS

THE ARGUMENT

I. Chronological Sketch of the Critical Literature.—Early Studies of Arthurian Romance in England—Arthurian Antiquities in Wales—Views of Thomas Warton derived from the German Grail—Gorres on the Lohengrin Legend—Speculations of Dunlop—Fauriel on Provençal Literature and the Grail therein—On Kyot de Provence—On Earthly and Heavenly Knighthood—On the Grail and Apocryphal Christian Legends—Various editions of the Parzival—Modernised versions of Schulz and Simrock—Their variant points of view—The historicity of Kyot—Legend of the Baptist's Head—Alleged identity of Kyot de Provence and Guiot de Provins—Opinions of Rosenkranz and Rochat—The Younger Titurel—Templar Speculations—Criticism of San Marte—Clash of opinion on Celtic origins—Furnivall and Campbell—Vogue of Baring-Gould in England—Paulin Paris and his rendering of the Prose Lancelot—Opinions of Potvin—Bergmann on the San Greal—Rejections of Zarncke—The praise of Birch-Hirschfeld—His views on the Borron Cycle and Celtic Fables—On the Question in Perceval Romances—Counter views of M. tin—Conclusions of Herz—The Studies of Alfred Nutt—Miss Weston's Contributions to the Criticism of Grail Literature—Bruce on the Pageant at the Grail Castle in the Conte of Chrétien. II. The Claim in Respect of Templar Influence.—An Illustration of the Romance of History—The Templars and the Latin Church—After what manner the Temple has been brought within the Chain of a Secret Tradition—The Grail and Templarism—A note on one Hypothesis—Templar Symbolism in Grail Literature—The Temple and the Parzival—Estimate of the alleged connection—The Templars and Catholicism—The Grail and the Church—A Matter of Personal Confession—Summary of Templar Hypotheses in respect of the Grail Literature—Grail Knights and an Order of San Salvador—The Baphometic Mystery—Von Hammer's Grail Reveries—Abbé Grégoire on a Secret Doctrine of St. John the Divine—The Speculations of San Marte—Judgment thereupon—Simrock on alleged Templar and Grail Traditions—Purpose of Grail Romances according to Eugène Aroux—Papal Interdiction of Grail Romances according to Moland—Religious Opinions ascribed to the Templars by Naef—Miss Weston's affirmations on the Templar Debate—Papal Charges against the Knights Templar—Questions of Heresy—Inferences and Conclusions based hereon—True position of the Order—Saint Bernard's Ideal regarding it—The Hypothesis Abandoned. III. The Sects of Southern France.—Albigensian Sects and the Grave Misconceptions Concerning them—Old Protestant Apologists—Occult and other Speculations—Attempted connection of the Sects with the Grail Subject—Its critical examination—Albigenses as Manichæans—Waldenses as Donatists—Paulicians and Cathar—The Albigensian Crusade—Simon de Montfort—His war of extermination—His death—The Crusade and the Holy Inquisition—The Last Stronghold of the Catharists—Judgment on this business—The Story of Enforced Confessions—The Sects and their Sacramental Teaching—A French Understanding of Chivalrous Romance—The Theses of Aroux—The Grail as signifying a Secret Association—Canon of Criticism in respect of Chivalrous Literature—Supposed Intervention of Secret Orders in the development of the Grail Subject—An Authentic Record of Albigensian Belief—The Cathar Ritual of Lyons—Incarnation of the Mystical Christ in perfect believers—Eckbert on the Cathar Sacrament—Testimonies collected by Schmidt—Views in contradiction—Joinville's Story of Montfort and of Albigensian Bread and Wine —The Albigensian Book of John the Evangelist.

FURTHER CRITICAL APPARATUS:
THE SCHOOLS, THE CHURCHES, AND THE SECTS

I

CHRONOLOGICAL SKETCH OF THE CRITICAL LITERATURE

IT will pass, I suppose, unquestioned that a notable impetus was given to the study of Arthurian Romance in England by the publication in 1817 of the first reissue of Caxton's MORTE DARTHUR by Sir Thomas Malory, printed originally in 1485 and made available thus early in the nineteenth century, with an admirable introduction and notes by Robert Southey.[1] It will be understood that at this day the introduction is rather of memorial than of critical value : it spoke of the sources of Malory, as they could be ascertained at that date, and offered to those who were concerned a first acquaintance with the wealth of Arthurian literature in Northern French, as represented by the printed editions of the fifteenth and sixteenth centuries. Scott had preceded the English Poet-Laureate with his edition of Thomas of Ercildoune, including an investigation of the so-called Luce de Gast Cyclic Romance of Tristram, "with his usual ability and erudition, leaving nothing undone", as Southey testifies. Edward Davies was also in evidence, unfolding his Arkite Mythos and other reveries of the period in dissertations on Celtic Druids and Celtic Mythology, embodying amazing translations of Welsh triads, Taliesin Poems and so forth, drawn from Cambrian Archives and accepted of course at the value of their own claim on an almost prehistoric past.[2] They served, however, to make known something of Arthurian antiquities in the Principality of Wales, as did also Sharon Turner from the attempted historical standpoint. As the days drew on Thomas Warton appealed to Continental sources in his HISTORY OF ENGLISH POETRY, which is not without value even at this day and delightful in any case as a storehouse of reference. He was acquainted with a mangled version of the GRAND SAINT GRAAL under the name of Robert de Borron and with the SAINT GRAAL as a Reliquary containing the Precious Blood. He regards it, however, as a Breton or British

---

[1] Appendix II, Part I.   [2] THE MYTHOLOGY AND RITES OF THE DRUIDS, 1809.

account and passes to German Romance for a different version of its history. In this way we are furnished with a moderately accurate and graphic account of the PARZIVAL scheme, having special reference to the Kyot de Provence fable, by which Warton was greatly attracted, more particularly with the discovery of the Grail depicted mysteriously in the skies. He regards the claim made on an Arabian source as supported by the internal evidence exhibited in the poem of Wolfram. " The scene for the most part is not only laid in the East but a large proportion of the names are of decidedly oriental origin." Like so many who succeeded him, Warton was impressed also by the almost fraternal communication between Christian and Saracen, the absence of religious animosities, and by the fact that Christian Knights were enrolled frequently under the Banners of Eastern Caliphs.

According to Wolfram the Grail came down from Heaven, but Warton points out that according to his assumed Armorican, British and even Provençal Legends, it was brought Westward from the Eastern World, in connection with which he is reminded of that other Traditional Cup which occupies, as he says, a conspicuous place in Jewish Law. He traces its descent from the Patriarch Joseph to Solomon the King as to " the great object of Hebrew veneration and glory ". From this point there begins to open before him a wide field of mythos. The Jew who discovered and contrived to read the Toledo Arabic manuscript is said to have descended from Solomon on the maternal side, a fitting genealogy, in Warton's view, for him who was destined to write the first story of the Grail in any language of the West. Historical difficulties notwithstanding, the Blessed Vessel is connected at once with that other miraculous Talisman which Persian fable bestows on Jemshid, a " pattern of perfect Kings during whose reign the Golden Age was realised in Iran ". Favoured by Ormuzd and his legitimate representative on earth, Jemshid discovered a Goblet of the Sun when digging the foundations of Persepolis, " and it brought him unbounded knowledge of both terrestrial and celestial affairs ". The Goblet passed on from the founder of the Persian Monarchy to " the hero of all later oriental fiction ", namely, Alexander the Great, for whom it was " the auspicious emblem of his victorious career ". It became for Eastern poets a symbol of the world and of " the fecundating powers of Nature ", as also a source of divination and even of the Philosopher's Stone. Warton remembers further that a Goblet of the Sun is found in Grecian Fables and that a Golden Chalice, also of the Solar God, is connected with the name of the Theban Hercules. The analogy between these things and the Holy Grail is instituted by affirming that " the Sacred Vessel of modern fiction is no less distinguished for its attributes ", at which point it may be wise to leave the question.

Warton's account of the PARZIVAL is derived probably from J. Gorres, to whom he refers and who produced in 1813 the POEMA PARCIFALI ET LOHENGRINI from a text compiled by Glokle of two

Vatican manuscripts.[1] Gorres prefixed an elaborate introduction which is not without interest at the present day as regards the Lohengrin Myth, many variants of which are collected. On the other hand, the PARZIVAL study is not a little confusing and chaotic, for example, identifying the Castle of Mont Salvatch with India and the regions of Paradise adjacent thereunto. The fact notwithstanding that the Grail is for Wolfram a jewelled Stone, it is described as a Cup by Gorres. It fell from Heaven, apparently into the terrestrial Eden, and was sent forth therefrom. So also Colonies of Priests emerged from the same region for the foundation of Sacred Cities over the whole world. For the rest, it is difficult to distinguish when the author is talking of PARZIVAL and when of Albrecht's TITUREL. It was the period of General Vallancey, when all etymologies were possible and all reveries based thereon passed as evidential: he is cited as "incontrovertible" by the German author, who proceeds on his own part to identify Lokrin with Lohengrin. He speaks also of St. Gervasius, an alleged kinsman of Jesus, who lived for 380 years, "which is not so surprising", in the opinion of Gorres, because Charlemagne's Master of the Horse, attained the age of 300, "though not of the family of Jesus" Other speculations suggest the perpetuation of an Ecclesiastical Tradition from old Druidic and Priestly Dynasties— for whom the Grail was a symbol apparently from time immemorial— together with a Secret Teaching of the Knights Templar, the latter belonging, however, to a later stage of the present critical apparatus.

Warton was followed by J. C. Dunlop, whose HISTORY OF FICTION went through several editions and was something of a standard work for a not inconsiderable period. It reappeared on a late occasion under the editorship of H. Wilson, by whom the text was revised and extended.[2] Dunlop regarded the earlier branches of GUIRON LE COURTOIS as "perhaps the finest of all the old fabulous histories of Britain", thus recalling the judgment of Robert Southey, who, speaking also of the earlier sections, recognises therein a certain unity of purpose which distinguishes it from many of the other Romances. Generally also its style is said to be distinctly marked, especially in dialogue, while the "tone of morals is infinitely superior" to all other productions of the kind. There is special reference to the Tristram Legend by Dunlop, together with analyses of the PALAMÈDES and of ISAIE LE TRISTE. These points are worth enumeration only to shew that at his comparatively early date Dunlop had a considerable speaking acquaintance with the literature of Chivalry in Northern French. On his errors and misapprehensions it would be idle to dwell, as they were inevitable at that date and signify nothing at the present day. Nor does the little that he says of the Grail Cycle demand particular reference, for it cannot be held that he contributed anything of consequence to the existing knowledge.

The testimony of Wolfram von Eschenbach to his source in Kyot de

---

[1] Appendix II, Part II.   [2] A fourth edition appeared in 1845.

Provence was not as yet challenged in the first decades of the nineteenth century, and there can be little question that students in
England and France—few and far between—who had some first-hand
knowledge of the PARZIVAL must have been impressed deeply with the
salient distinctions from the Perceval Cycle represented by Chrétien
de Troyes and more especially by the CONTE DEL GRAAL in its prose
version of 1530, the poem being of course unprinted. An example in
point is offered by Fauriel in his HISTOIRE DE LA POESIE PROVENÇALE,
which assuredly marked an epoch and is even now without a serious
competitor in its own tongue.[1] His familiarity with the extant
remanents of Provençal literature shewed him that Kyot was non-
existent outside the witness of his confessed German imitator ; but he
did not regard the fact as justifying a denial of the poet's historic
actuality. The reasons, however, do not prove convincing, being
(1) that the names of many past Troubadours have not come down to
us and (2) that Wolfram among all Minnesingers is of high authority
on the subject of Provençal literature, as it was one of his favoured
studies. It is held to follow that the fact of a great epical Romance in
the *langue d'oc*, with Kyot as author, cannot be called in question. But
it is obvious that the survival of a few anonymous lyrics offers nothing
to the point at issue and that the credibility of Wolfram's claim is itself
the subject of consideration. Moreover, epic poetry was not cultivated
in Provence, notwithstanding the isolated cases of SYR JAUFRE and
FIERABRAS. There is one other argument adduced by Fauriel, and it
happens to have held the field almost to the present day among those
who believe in the alleged source of Wolfram, namely, that the
PARZIVAL, from beginning to end, is sown with evidences of its Romance
origin—for example, in the multitude of its neo-Latin names of places
and persons and things. The value of this supposed testimony has been
discounted now, while that which prevails brings us back to l'Abbé de la
Rue, who in days preceding Fauriel registered his conviction that the
authenticity of Kyot was comparable to that of the Arabic Grail MS.
discovered by him at Toledo.[2] There is no space here or need to
reproduce the grounds of judgment.

For the rest, Fauriel was disposed to conclude that the Grail side
of Arthurian Legend was of monastic origin and that it delineated
above all an ideal contrast, fostered by the Church itself, between
earthly and heavenly Knighthood. So far as Germany is concerned the
basis of comparison was between the Templar Institution, then presumably at its best, and the mundane Knightly Orders. But the Grail
fable, " invented by the Romance writers of the Continent, passed, like
other chivalrous stories, into Great Britain, where it was altered,
modified and localised by Anglo-Norman authors ", who produced the
huge prose fictions of MERLIN THE ENCHANTER, LANCELOT OF THE
LAKE, PERCEVAL LE GALLOIS and above all the GRAIL MYTHOS. The

[1] Appendix II, Part II.
[2] ESSAIS HISTORIQUES SUR LES BARDES, LES JONGLEURS ET LES TROUVÈRES, etc.
3 vols., 1834.

last is characterised by " a much greater religious development, more mystical exaltation and more of sacerdotal influence . . . The two rival Chivalries are constantly opposed to one another therein ; they are at strife pre-eminently in the Quest of the Grail itself ". The same opposition is found in LANCELOT OF THE LAKE, where they are designated openly as respectively terrene and celestial, " It was because he was tainted with love, because he had set all his desires and all his thoughts on Queen Guinevere, because in a word he was a terrene Knight, that Lancelot spent himself vainly in his search for the Grail. The finding of that Holy Vessel and the explanation of its great Mysteries were reserved for those who were pure from all sin—otherwise, for the Chivalry of Heaven ".

Fauriel goes on to affirm that this distinction between the two Chivalries is continually summed up in the same terms. For example, on the threshold of the Great Quest and at Pentecost in the Court of King Arthur, the earthly and heavenly Knights began their contest— a reference to the Tournament prior to the manifestation of the Grail.[1] " The earthly Knights, who had earthly eyes and hearts, wore black robes, that is to say, they were clothed in sin and desecration. The others, who were the Celestial Knights, were vested in white robes, otherwise, in virginity and chastity. The fundamental idea . . . was to celebrate a Chivalry opposed to that of the age, a religious, austere and Christian Chivalry, in accordance with the desire and intent of the Church." So far as it is possible to say, the Romances were not the work of Ecclesiastics but rather of romantic poets, the fact notwithstanding that some manuscripts of the Great Grail Quest indicate that it was composed " by the order of Holy Church ". However this may be, Fauriel is " very much inclined to imagine that the authors of the earlier Grail Romances found their basis and motive either in a lost Legend or in some popular Tradition, like that connected with the arrival, for example, of Lazarus and Magdalene at Marseilles ".

The impressions with which I have dealt up to this point do not represent any serious study of a large literature, largely unprinted. Warton, a poet himself, was concerned through all its centuries with English poetry, and Dunlop with fiction all the wide world over. In his three notable volumes Fauriel dealt exhaustively with Provençal verse ; but it connects with the Grail only through the mythical personality of Kyot de Provence. Apart from this, there is no Holy Grail in the literary remanents of Southern France ; there is no Spear of Longinus ; there is no Quest of Perceval ; and no one hears of Miraculous Masses or of a legendary Bishop—unknown to Church History—who Consecrated the Body of the Lord for the first time after the destruction of Jerusalem, the Apostles appointed by Christ having died in their day and generation without fulfilling the Divine. Command to " do this in remembrance of Me ". These are implications of the claim which obviously are not to be found in any text of the

[1] See Malory's MORTE DARTHUR, Book XIII, cap. 6.

literature and much less in the GRAND SAINT GRAAL itself, to which
we owe the invention of the Second Joseph Myth. We shall see in a
later section that they suggest concealed purpose : the implications
in any case have been missed throughout by criticism.

As regards the impressions of early Grail students they have been
presented at a certain length, as the first explorations on the subject.
It is these which came into the hands of later scholarship, better
equipped as it was because texts were beginning to be published :
the Metrical Romance of Borron in 1841, the CONTE DEL GRAAL
between 1866 and 1871, the Didot Perceval in 1874, together with the
GRAND SAINT GRAAL. Various editions of the PARZIVAL had appeared
also in Germany. Those of Schulz and Simrock are important as rival
versions in modern form which made the root-matter of the German
Grail more readily accessible to those who cared in the Fatherland.[1]
Now, the scholars in question were not only competitive translators
but held mutually exclusive views. San Marte believed from the
beginning in Wolfram's Kyot de Provence, though he identified him
subsequently with Guiot de Provins, the poet of the BIBLE Guiot.[2]
Simrock, on the other hand, sets out at considerable length and
expresses strongly his grounds for rejecting Kyot as a Wolfram
invention, while in respect of Guiot and his BIBLE they could have
furnished only the name of another and not too famous French poet,
under whose cloak Wolfram might do more than distract attention
from his manifest debt to Chrétien. It is throughout a laboured
argument ; but some of the main considerations are exceedingly strong
and justify Simrock's conclusion that the German poet created Kyot
" in order to authenticate his own reshaping of the Saga ", notwithstanding the authority and fame of Chrétien. For the rest, Simrock
connected the Grail in its earliest form with the Legend of St. John
the Baptist's Head, not on account of the Head on a Platter in the
Welsh PEREDUR, nor yet because of that Baphometic Head which
the Templars were accused of worshipping, but because (1) the Blood
in the Grail Vessel is a vital element of the Myth and (2) a symbol of
creative power, as well as of the reproductive virtue resident in the
Blood of the slain God. On this and on other grounds, Wolfram's
PARZIVAL is held to represent the Grail Mythos in its purest and oldest
form.[3] Unfortunately, however, the Grail in Wolfram is a Stone and
not a Vessel ; it does not contain blood ; there is no Head on a Platter
in the Grail Castle ; and there is no allusion to the Baptist, with or
without his Head, in the whole poem. It is to be noted finally that
there is no Reliquary containing blood, precious or otherwise, while
there is nothing which corresponds, literally or figuratively, with a
dead or dying God.

For many years after Schulz and Simrock the work went on and in
Germany was admirable after its own kind ; but it is obvious that there

---

[1] Appendix II, Part I.
[2] WOLFRAM VON ESCHENBACH AND GUIOT VON PROVINS, GERMANIA, Vol. III, pp. 445,
et seq.   [3] Karl Simrock : PARCIVAL UND TITUREL, 1876.

can be no call here to present variations of opinion and the clash of debate, when we are concerned in reality only with final results on origins and intimations on meanings and intentions behind the litera- ture at large. Lachmann and Gervinus had already set aside the identification of Guiot de Provins with Kyot de Provence, while the discovery of Guiot's Lyrical Poems had disposed Wackernagel in the other direction.[1] In 1855 there must be ranged on the side of denial the not unimportant name of A. Rochat. There was that also of Dr. Karl Rosenkranz, who had a great influence on scholars and students, as made evident by San Marte's criticism of certain changed views expressed by his and their " old teacher and friend of our youthful days ". In 1833 he held that the PARZIVAL was completed so early as *circa* 1205, and he was possibly the first to question the identification of that unknown Albrecht who finished the YOUNGER TITUREL, with Albrecht von Scharfenberg. Later on Rosenkranz came to regard the PARZIVAL from a different standpoint and in place of dwelling on its high ethical and even spiritual values we are told (1) that many of its allusions point to heretical doctrine on the origin of evil ; (2) that there is a Gnostic element in its history of Lucifer ; (3) that the Grail itself—as a Stone from the Crown of Lucifer—represents the pre- cosmic genesis of evil, though it is overcome by the love of God incarnate as man. We must deal with this as we can, having regard to the fact that the Stone in the Crown of Lucifer does not happen to be found in the PARZIVAL but at a much later date in the WARTBURG- KRIEGE.[2] There are further grounds of suspicion based on the facts (1) That the Grail placed its *Templeisen* in complete independence, not only because it " clothed and fed its worshippers, bestowed life upon them through their contemplation of it and gave them com- mands in the shape of luminous inscriptions on its rim "; but on the spiritual side (2) that these Templars were themselves Priests (which, however, appears nowhere in the poem) and that they were not in subordination to ecclesiastical superiors, even the Pope ; (3) that the Grail insured their future bliss ; and finally (4) that it chose those whom it willed, according to its own way, and they were enrolled in its secret service.[3] Proceeding further, Rosenkranz institutes a signifi- cant contrast between this so-called spiritual side of the PARZIVAL, culminating in the attainment of its hero, and the worldly or natural side, culminating in Gawain's Adventure at Chateau Merveille, and finds therein something more living and human than is presented by that other aspect, which is " weighed down by the fetishism of an

[1] K. Wackernagel : ALFRANZÖSISCHE LIEDER UND LEICHE, 1846.

[2] See Simrock's PARZIVAL UND TITUREL, *sub voce* Kyot, and also on the Myth of the Grail. According to this poem, which may be referable to the thirteenth century but is obviously later than Wolfram, " sixty thousand Angels, who wished to supplant God in Heaven, had a crown made for Lucifer. When the Archangel (Michael) plucked this from Lucifer's head, a Stone fell from it, and this Stone is the Grail." In such case, it was more likely to be a symbol of false Doctrine and Luciferian knowledge than of Divine Life.

[3] San Marte on Wolfram's PARZIVAL and its critics, in GERMANIA, Vol. VII, pp. 55 *et seq.*

impersonal Relic ". The judgment on Parzival himself assuredly strikes a revolutionary note for that still very early period of Grail criticism. (1) It is not only incomprehensible that the hero asked nothing about the wonders of the Grail Castle, but it suggests dullness of mind. (2) He went about subsequently for years, wherever his horse led him, and had lost all faith in the Providence of God. (3) When he is brought by the Hermit Trevrezent into a better frame of mind and undertakes the Quest of the Grail, he " does nothing really good, beautiful or great to deserve the good fortune which suddenly becomes his and brings his story to a complete spiritual standstill ". (4) In other words, he attains the Kinghood of the Grail, as the *terminus ad quem* of all things desirable, but it is to be observed that this is conferred upon him " without any ecclesiastical mediation ".[1] San Marte was grieved beyond words by these accusations and discoursed at length upon them without affecting their force. This is how matters stood *circa* 1855–1862 ; and, on my own part, I have tried to reduce the laudation of Parzivalian spiritualities within reasonable bounds. It would seem, however, that Rosenkranz produced little impression at his own date except among his individual pupils.

There is perhaps little need at the present day and in view of my particular design to present the various theses which were offered through the years on the Celtic origin of the Grail. When J. F. Halliwell edited the Thorton Romances, so early as 1844,[2] he recognised that SYR PERCYVELLE had its roots in the CONTE DEL GRAAL and that so also had the Mabinogi of PEREDUR. When Furnivall issued the GRAND SAINT GRAAL in 1861, under the auspices of the Roxburghe Club,[3] he denied the Celtic origin. Meanwhile J. F. Campbell was at work on his delightful selection of POPULAR TALES OF THE WEST HIGHLANDS, a treasure at this day for all its fortunate possessors.[4] He offered no dogmatic statements, but in the Lay of the Great Fool, in the destroyer of the Gloucester Sorceresses, in the CHERCHEUR DU BASSIN and in the Perceval who achieved the Grail, Campbell was inclined to recognise a single Celtic hero, with his Myth variously unfolded. Baring-Gould followed in 1867 with his CURIOUS MYTHS OF THE MIDDLE AGES,[5] a deservedly popular work which went through several editions, and so far as regards its essay on the Holy Grail, the Celtic thesis therein, reflected from Villemarqué, was the accepted explanation of origins among the few who were concerned therein.

French scholarship was also at work in the publication of texts and occasionally of modernised versions, having critical studies attached thereto. Paulin Paris produced five volumes of the second class in his ROMANS DE LA TABLE RONDE, unfortunately with some fortuitous interpolations of the Metrical JOSEPH. This notwithstanding, his rendering of the great prose LANCELOT might be pleasant reading enough in English, even at this day and, with a little editing

---

[1] See Rosenkranz : DIE POESIE UND IHRE GESCHICHTELE, 1855.
[2] Appendix II, Part I. [3] *Ibid.* [4] *Ib.*, Part II. [5] *Ib.*

and illustrating, might appeal to young and old as a Tale of Faërie and Chivalry, written out at full length.[1] For Paulin Paris the Grail Legend was of Celtic origin but the *matière de Bretagne*, in the form of " lays ", now no longer extant, was the channel through which it passed to the knowledge of French TROUVÈRES and later prose romancists. For this authority also the Grail reflected and registered the aspirations and ambitions of the British Church. As regards texts and their editors, Potvin considered the PERLESVAUS, published in the first volume of his CONTE DEL GRAAL, not only as the oldest Romance of the Grail Cycles but as going back in its foundation to the eleventh century. On this subject Evans, its English translator, followed the French editor with blind confidence and was entrapped accordingly in his essay attached to the HIGH HISTORY. Potvin furthermore was in agreement with Paulin Paris that the Grail Legend at large embodied or reflected a long struggle between Britain in alleged heresy and the hypothetically orthodox Rome. No one, including myself, seems to have seen at this day the French original of Bergmann's SAN GREAL, which appeared in English at Edinburgh in 1870, with no indication that it was translated matter. Whether he had read or even heard of the PERLESVAUS is an open question. The thesis is contradictory enough, maintaining, for example, (1) that the invention of the Grail Fable belongs of right to the Provençal Kyot, but the particulars concerning him in Wolfram, our only source of knowledge, are largely fictitious or erroneous ; (2) that the myth is not of Celtic origin, yet the Welsh PEREDUR is authentic in the sense that it is an ancient folk-story. The alleged Kyot had conceived the idea of a Sacerdotal Chivalry and Royalty, created to guard the temporal and spiritual welfare of humanity : as this scheme is reflected by Wolfram, the Grail TEMPLEISEN " resemble an association formed without the pale of the Church, rather than a Catholic Community."[2] Bergmann's thesis lies within the measures of a pamphlet, and with its accounts of Kyot, of Mont Salvatch=Mont Salvagge in wild or inaccesible Catalonian ranges, of the Migration of the Grail to India, of Albrecht's TITUREL and the Romance of Prester John, it should have attracted more attention than apparently it did in its place of publication, the Athens of Scotia, or elsewhere. It appealed, however, to the Rev. Walter W. Skeat, when he edited the JOSEPH OF ARMATHIE and other old English Grail and Joseph tracts for the Early English Text Society, in 1871.

In 1876 Zarncke moved the debate a stage further by rejecting alike the Celtic and Provençal origin of the Grail Mythos, substituting an exclusive source in Apocryphal New Testament texts—the GESTA PILATI, VINDICTA SALVATORIS, NARRATIO JOSEPHI, and so forth.[3] With these I have dealt previously ; and the fact that the earliest

---

[1] The LANCELOT transcript occupies three out of five volumes which constitute the work in question.
[2] Appendix II, Part II.   [3] ZUR GESCHICHRTE DER GRALSAGE, 1876.

historicity Grail poem has its root in these, and is itself the historical root of all the Northern French Cycles, has long since passed the region of debate. From this point of view, our problem is no longer as to the source of the Christian Legend but as to that which lies behind its evolution in the World of Romance.

Our next important name is that of A. Birch-Hirschfeld, who was praised so highly by Nutt for his " most searching and exhaustive analysis of the whole Cycle ". It can be left at this, because at the present day the Cycle lies before us within the measures of this volume. It must not be left, however, without a note of regret on my own part that the Didot-Modena text—which presupposes the Metrical Romance of JOSEPH and the EARLY MERLIN—can never again figure in the world of criticism as the earliest Perceval Quest. Even at this late day I have read over the Birch-Hirschfeld arguments[1] in favour of this view, hoping for a way in which they could be made once more into hall-marked current coin of speculative debate. To make an end on this side of the subject, our author held that the Welsh tale of the Lance and Basin—the PEREDUR, in other words—is derived from Chrétien, while there is no authentic analogy between the Cauldron of the Dagda, or similar Celtic Fables, and the Reliquary of the Holy Grail. The latter was sacramental for Borron. There is one thing more : the almost unsearchable problem of the Question which had to be asked to insure the successful termination of the Unspelling Quest, meets with a solution in Birch-Hirschfeld. As Joseph of Arimathæa was com-pelled to make two demands on Pilate for the Body of the Master, so had the Grail-Seeker to come twice in search of its symbol, that out-ward sign of the Christ Life within. Well, it is a solution of sorts, and it may happen that one which is bad is better than none at all. But it is obvious unfortunately (1) that in the PERLESVAUS and DIU CRÔNE Perceval had no second chance ; (2) that he was not on the Quest in Chrétien, on the occasion of his first visit to the Grail Castle, and could not be said therefore to apply ; while (3) the proposition that the Mysterious Question had such an inconsequent source behind it seems fantasia at fever heat.[2]

There rose up E. Martin in 1878[3] to shew cause why the conclusions reached by Birch-Hirschfeld should be set aside for the most part. He was certain that Wolfram had other sources than Chrétien and that hence in so far as the PARZIVAL differs from the CONTE its extraneous episodes and material are important for the Myth in its original guise. This notwithstanding, the oldest extant form of the Grail Mythos is that of Chrétien, but in affirming this Martin includes the several sequels of the CONTE, and so doing he reads himself definitely outside the lists of debate. It is to be understood, however, that the Metrical Romance of JOSEPH is the earliest example of the Christian Grail

---

[1] Appendix II, Part II.

[2] Birch-Hirschfeld suggested otherwise that the Perceval Question was an invention without meaning. Cf. Nutt's STUDIES, p. 171, a severe criticism of this view.

[3] Appendix II, Part II.

Mythos, and that it was composed *circa* 1200 A.D. Yet a Christian origin for the subject itself cannot be accepted, because a flat or open Dish was used at the Last Supper, while the Blood of Christ on the Cross was received in a Bowl; but this is obviously one of the points at issue in the story of Borron. It is said further that the idea of a Cup is one of the latest variants of the Legend; but Borron's story is all the same the tale of a Pyx or Chalice; and if this chaotic argument is to be taken seriously, then the earliest text of the Grail Christianised is later than the QUESTE, according to which the Grail Reliquary was the Dish in which the Lord and His Apostles " ate the lamb on Sher-Thursday."[1] For the rest, according to Martin, the Grail has a Celtic root which is still traceable after the story has turned good Christian.

In 1882 W. Herz published a study on the PARZIVAL and the Grail, in which he agreed with Birch-Hirschfeld that Robert de Borron stands first among the writers of Grail Cycles; but he held further (1) that the Legend took form on British soil and was actuated by the Antipapal bent of the Church in Britain; (2) that Perceval the Seeker belongs to the Great Fool far-diffused Fable; (3) that the PEREDUR version and the Breton PERONNIK derived from Chrétien; while (4) the English SYR PERCYVELLE presents the earliest extant form.[2] These things stand at their present depreciated values; for no one mentions the PERONNIK, because the trail of Villemarqué's inventions is over all his Breton Sagas. We have also estimated sometime since the debt of PEREDUR to the CONTE; we have found—either to our satisfaction or regret—that the question-in-chief regarding SYR PERCYVELLE is as to its high place among English Metrical Romances of the fourteenth century, and not the great antiquity of its root-matter, the evidence of which has failed us; and we are motived in fine by a shrewd suspicion that the faculty of inventing stories has its records the wide world over, from time immemorial, and that their recurring likeness to one another may be due as often as not to simple matters of fact in mere experience. The seemingly foolish fellow who turns out hero or genius has not been found once only in the long course of the ages, so that his tale had to travel in order to be met with everywhere. As a fact he has been found in all times and places, and is so well known that he is liable to have been invented sporadically where he does not happen to have been met.[3]

From 1882 to 1888 is a little like the short pace forward taken with the foot in something called Freemasonry; and it brings us to Alfred Nutt, who first learned " to love Celtic Tradition " through J. F. Campbell and his ever-memorable Highland Stories. We are prepared therefore to find that Nutt's STUDIES OF THE GRAIL LEGENDS—as their sub-title explains—were undertaken with special reference to the hypothesis of its Celtic origin. Nutt was not only a man of learning

---

[1] MORTE DARTHUR, Book XVII, cap. 20.

[2] It is to be observed that we are now in the year 1882, when Hertz published his SAGE VOM PARZIVAL UND DEM GRAL at Breslau, and when the chief texts of the literature were available in printed form.

[3] I have noted elsewhere a similar transparent but neglected point of fact in the case of Vengeance Legends.

in these matters but of notable general accomplishment, and some of his monographs remain of real value. The Grail STUDIES in particular have drawn together a wealth of material, the interest and consequence of which are not reduced materially by any fate of the assumptions which led to their collection.[1] I have intimated, however, that the speculative part is qualified rather than destroyed. It does not follow that Keating, who first published an account of the Tuatha de Danaan and other old Irish themes,[2] made it up out of his own head, any more than Moses de Leon invented the ZOHAR in the thirteenth century, though it was he who edited and he who issued to those who could buy copies. Criticisms vary and fashions of investigation change. Successive hypotheses rise like stars and rule in the speculative heaven of mind ; they set ultimately and yield their place to others ; they leave also their light behind them in the records of the past. I write as one who loves the Celtic " setting ", of which Alfred Nutt talked. There are many things also which I cherish in the garnerings of Sir John Rhys. They do not " charm " alone " the Romantic Spirit of the Middle Ages " about which Nutt wrote ; and I agree utterly with him, in the closing words of his STUDIES, when he testified[3] (1) that " quickened by Christian symbolism they came to express and typify the noblest and most mystic longings of man " ; (2) that the Grail Legend, fashioned by " the poets and thinkers " of that now far-away past " has still a lesson " and still a " meaning " for us ; and (3) that it is part of our " yearning for the truth and beauty of the infinite and undying."

That is better and sweeter and holier than anything which ever came into the written word of Jessie Weston, though she told me once in a letter how, after all, she believed in her heart that it is " the Mass which matters." She was mainly reflective in speculation, though she made her little discoveries there and here. Her LEGEND OF LANCELOT and especially her LEGEND OF PERCEVAL are of lasting value, but mainly in respect of material, for no one knew better the Grail and Arthurian texts.[4] As time went on, she offered much incense on Altars erected to Vegetation Gods, with the GOLDEN BOUGH as her oracle. We are in debt to her always for publishing the MODENA PERCEVAL, and I am thankful on my own part that she wrote FROM RITUAL TO ROMANCE, with which I shall be called to deal in a later section.

It was her last published volume, and we find ourselves brought thereby, as if with a sudden leap, to the year 1920. The publications of some intervening years by her and others have been either the subject of notice elsewhere in my text or are represented sufficiently in the Bibliography which appears at the end. There is a word, however, to add here on the exhaustive work of the late Dr. J. D. Bruce, to which

[1] Appendix II, Part II.

[2] That is to say, he gave very full account of it in a HISTORY OF IRELAND, published originally in the seventeenth century, but a more available edition by Joyce appeared at Dublin in 1880. See Book I in particular. Bruce—*Op. cit.*, I, 274—puts a note of interrogation against the account of Keating on the ground that his sources are unknown respecting the Talismans.   [3] *Op. cit.*, p. 259.   [4] Appendix II, Part II.

reference has been made frequently throughout the present volume. No one has collected more fully or analysed more carefully the Arthurian and Grail texts ; no one has paid more serious attention to the views and variations of views on the part of recent official scholarship ; and no one has set aside more completely the speculations which have appeared, so to speak, in the outer courts and classes. They may be good, bad or indifferent ; but in a comprehensive work one would have thought that the fact of their existence should have been made known at least. There would have been no call, however, to dwell upon this point, except for the noteworthy fact that on one occasion Dr. Bruce has presented his intimations on the meaning which lies behind the subject matter of the Holy Grail ; and no one in the broad thoroughfares, byways or purlieus of—let us say—even occult reveries in Germany, France or England has failed more disastrously. He is discussing a theory of the Eucharistic origin of Chrétien's Grail Procession, in which I disbelieve utterly so far as the CONTE is concerned, or at least his share therein. He proceeds to argue (1) that if the Lance carried in this Procession is that of Longinus ; if the Grail is the Chalice ; if the Silver Platter is the Paten ; it becomes " plain " —God help us—that the Fisher-King is the Crucified Christ, because He has been riven through both thighs in a battle ; while his Father or " double," the " Mysterious King who is likewise lame " and has not left his room for fifteen years, " being sustained exclusively by the holy wafer," is the Holy Ghost.[1] A proposition like this does more than baffle commentary : it outrages contemplation, not alone by the ghastly *non sequitur* of identifying the Fisher with the Christ— Crucified or not—because forsooth he appears in a supposed Procession of the Blessed Sacrament, but because of the blasphemous follies involved : (1) the Divine Spirit becomes also the Eternal Father ; (2) God the Son must be healed by a twelfth-century version of the Great Fool Mythos personified ; (3) he is utterly dependent on being asked an arbitrary Question ; (4) the Fool Transformed is destined to take the place of the Second Person in the Holy Trinity ; while (5) the incapacitated Holy Spirit is nourished by the Body of His alleged Son. The force of mania cannot further go.

II

THE CLAIM IN RESPECT OF TEMPLAR INFLUENCE

I SUPPOSE that there is no one at this day, even on the outermost fringes of the wide world of books, who will need to be made acquainted with the fact that the old and glorious Chivalry of the Temple was instituted as a protection for the Christian Pilgrims who visited the Holy Places of Jerusalem in the first quarter

[1] EVOLUTION OF ARTHURIAN ROMANCE, I, pp. 257, 261, 262.

of the twelfth century. It was a military and religious organisation *ab origine symboli*, differing as such from the Hospital of St. John, which at its incorporation was a healing fraternity, and only assumed arms following the example of the *Militia Crucifera Evangelica* which had arisen suddenly at its side. Templar history is a great storehouse of enchanting hypothesis and also of unreclaimed speculation expanded from writer to writer. I know no greater sea on which ships of imagination and fantasy have launched more boldly : if they have reached no final harbour, they have paused to take in further stores at innumerable " summer isles " of an imaginary Eden " lying in dark purple spheres of sea ; " and if in some undemonstrable way they have slipped their cables and eluded sporadic hostile vessels, this has been because the equipment of the latter has not been better than their own, while as regards credentials the letter of marque carried by the unwelcome visitor would often not bear much closer inspection than their own unchartered licence. Now, an Order which was established in the East for a specific Christian purpose, which embodied ideas of devotion that were ecclesiastical as well as religious, which accepted monastic vows— even those counsels of perfection that qualified for the Quest of the Grail —yet, in spite of these, which became wealthy in the corporate sense beyond the dreams of avarice, insolent and haughty beyond the prerogatives of feudal royalty, and had darker charges looming against it, does assuredly offer a picture to research the possibilities of which are likely to be exploited in all directions. The story of the Brotherhood and the things implied therein have been approached therefore from many points of view, enforced by many considerations and by much which passes for evidence in the absence of a valid title. I speak—as it will be understood—here of the things recognised or divined beneath its external surface, for on that side there is nothing more direct and more simple. We know that the Latin Church has a heavy account to balance in respect of the Order, and by the characteristics of the charges preferred it is responsible also for having brought the Templars —whether warrantably or otherwise, but at least all unwittingly— within the dubious circle of a Secret Tradition in Christian Times, for an unwary proportion of those who recognise the fact of such Tradition. It remains, however, that from this standpoint their story has never been told by anyone who spoke with knowledge on the involved subject. Here is no place to attempt it ; but the Mystery of the Temple in a very minor degree interpenetrated the Mystery of the Grail, and something must be said concerning it in this connection. There is at the present time in England (1) an extending disposition to appreciate remotely and dimly an imbedded evidence that Romance-Literature did somehow shadow forth an initiatory process, as hinted previously, and as it remains over for later consideration at length ; (2) that in some manner not yet understood the Knights Templar and the Grail Legend grew up together, and that they answer with strange voices if set to question one another across the void which intervenes between an Externalised

Chivalry in fact and an Ideal Chivalry in books. In a word, the literature has been held sometimes to represent, within clouds and under curious veils, something of the imputed Templar subsurface-design ; or alternatively certain Grail texts do reflect at least indubitably after their own manner and on their own authority the Knight-hood of the Morning and of Palestine raised from the world of reflections into the world of the archetype.[1] The PERLESVAUS, for example, is not alone a work with an interior motive ; it is not only the story of a Suppressed Word and of the sorrow and suffering which were wrought by that suppression ; it is not only a prototypical correlative of the Masonic Eighteenth Degree in a form not less clear because it can be traced only by a specialist ; but—at least in adventitious ways—it has ever-recurring characters of Templar Symbolism. Now that which wears herein—and so through the French Cycle—little more than an aspect of accident, passes in the PARZIVAL of Wolfram into the appearance of a preconceived plan. Herein is the story of a Confraternity, partly military but in part also religious, connecting by the Legend of its lineage with a kind of Secret History in Christendom written under the guise of Knight-Errantry : it is the Romance of an Order of the Holy Grail whose members are chosen out of thousands, dedicated, set apart, and sometimes terrible in power, almost " like Cedron in flood." I do not wonder that before the face of this picture the criticism of the Grail literature has been haunted here and there with the dream of Templar intervention, and the only question which concerns us is the extent to which such an hypothesis can be justified. Even in the least illuminated circle the possibility has been regarded from time to time with increasing respect by students uncommitted thereto ; and apart from any claims on its own basis it would be difficult for this reason to pass it over entirely. The imputed fact, or the likelihood, that the literature was a vehicle, officially or otherwise, of some Occult or Mystical Tradition, without depending for any one on the merits of this hypothesis, would in certain minds be enhanced substantially thereby. But it is desirable to note, in the first place, that it is now an old speculation ; secondly, that recent years have not brought to light, that I am aware, any new facts on the subject ; and, lastly, that in so far as the contention is put freshly there is a disposition to dwell on the TEMPLEISEN depicted in the PARZIVAL as not only a militant body but also a governing theocracy, and one which above all things was not ecclesiastical. It is just this which impresses me as at least a little exaggerated in tone : I do not find that Anfortas and his Chivalry can be called a governing power[2] any more than the Company overruled by King Pelles of Lystenoys, about whose warfare we hear in the VULGATE

---

[1] Cf. Baron Tschoudy—less or more *passim*—in L'ÉTOILE FLAMBOYANTE, of which there were several editions at Paris, the Hague and so forth, early in the nineteenth century.

[2] The Grail itself governed, calling, choosing and commanding all by the power of the written word. The Chivalry had no voice in appointing the King who was to come, nor did it elect members. Those who were fed by the Talisman were under the yoke thereof, from which there was no appeal.

MERLIN. If Mont Salvatch was anything of the kind, it was obviously a Secret Kingdom ; but as much might be said of Corbenic and the Realm to which it belonged. Seeing also that the Keepers of the Grail and the Cohort of their Ministers had at no time a sacerdotal aspect— some express claims notwithstanding as to their geniture—the ecclesiastical note therein is wanting through all the Cycles. The distinction in chief between the TEMPLEISEN and the other Knights of the Grail is that in Wolfram the former are Theocratically organised, while the latter are either an inchoate gathering or they are like the retinue which would be attached to a Feudal Castle. In one case, which is that of the DIDOT-MODENA PERCEVAL, the House Mystic might be a simple Tower and, from all that we learn about it, little more than a Hermit's Hold.

It is obviously one thing to say that Wolfram modelled his Chivalry on the prototype of the Knights Templar—which is an interesting fact without consequence—and another that the modelling was inspired by familiarity with Templar secret intention ; and it is on this point, which is the motive behind the hypothesis, that reasonable evidence is wanted. The next step is to recognise *tendances suspectes* in the poem of Wolfram and to regard the Templar design—whatever it was otherwise—as anti-Catholic in its spirit. With the first ascription I have dealt when discussing the German Cycle in general ; of the second we can divine little, and then but darkly ; while in respect of the third I recur to that canon of criticism which has served me well already : in so far as the Templar Order is held to be not only anti-Papal but also anti-Catholic, it is antecedently and proportionately unlikely that any evidence will connect it with Grail literature, at that epoch of the world and amidst its strife of sects.

Whatever the origin of that literature, in one and all its forms, it is not merely on the surface a Catholic Legend but in forms of presentation it seems so to have issued from the heart and centre of Catholicity that it is almost in the likeness of an exotic, as if from some Sanctuary behind the external and visible Sanctuary of the Universal Church. If this is the heart of Romance going out in its yearning towards God, there was never a heart in Christendom " which warmer beat and stronger." It is like the voice—at its truest—of that Ideal City, the First City, the Spiritual City, of which Wagner wrote, and it is seldom heard on earth ; it seems to speak from the pictured home of the Soul, the place of pre-existence, with all the mystery and wonder of enchanted Hud and of Irêm in the Land of the Morning. And in the melody of that voice, within the verbal message thereof, we know that the country deep in Asia is not to be found in any Highlands beyond the Himalayas, or in the fabled Sarras. Again, it is the Country of the Soul and of the Soul's Legend : it is the Kabbalistic Place of the Palaces at the centre of the dimensions, sustaining all things.[1] We know also that we shall

---

[1] *Vide* the SEPHER HA ZOHAR in many places and Knorr von Rosenroth in KABBALA DENUDATA, I, *s.v. Palatia.*

look vainly for Corbenic on the wild coast of Wales, and for the local habitation of the Grail Castle of Mont Salvatch at any of the grand passes of the Pyrennees into Spain ; for this also is like the Rosicrucian Mountain of Abiegnus and the mystic Fir-Cone, a Mystery enfolded within and without by many meanings.[1]

But if such is the position in respect of the Holy Grail, and if it follows therefrom that in some hands it has rested under a serious cloud of mis-apprehension, there is something to be said on the same subject, though not in the same sense, in respect of the Knights Templar. The eye which has turned from the Grail literature to the records of the Great Chivalry has been drawn in that direction chiefly because of the charge of heresy which was preferred of old against it. I am not designing to suggest that the side of criticism which is prominent in the open day is interested—or much less concerned seriously—in heresy as such, though I confess—if it be fitting to say so—that next to the truth which is of God and the deeps therein, whereof simple minds dream nothing, I am conscious of few things more fascinating than the ever-varied story of old condemned doctrines and of those who loved, followed and honoured them. It draws the mind for ever with vague and preposterous hopes ; and seeing further that I am on the side of any orthodox faith only in so far as the Old Mule which carries the Mysteries can be shewn to be on God's side—as the PERLESVAUS testifies—I do not doubt that many are the *choses suspectes* which might be gleaned from this book, while many there may still be who could wish to include its writer in the annals carried forward of Smithfield or Tyburn and those who went thither in the days of Mary or Elizabeth.

Here is cleansing confession ; but scholarship, as I have intimated, is detached, subject to its inoculation by the notion of pagan faiths perpetuated through Christian centuries—the stilettos of which virus have pierced me also in both arms. But I believe, apart from such images, that I carry a lamp to enlighten these obscure ways, and much as I may love their crookedness, they do not deceive me. It is on this account that the alleged heresy of the Temple, so far as it concerns the Grail, can be dealt with shortly here, for which purpose I will go back so far as my knowledge of the criticism extends along these lines.

A summary of the views held and of the speculative hypotheses advanced may be grouped chronologically after the following manner. (1) So far back as 1809, Dr. F. H. v. d. Hagen was concerned in the editorship of a MUSEUM FÜR ALTDEUTSCHE LITERATUR and affirmed in the first volume[2] that a connection between the TEMPLEISEN and Knights Templar is not to be doubted, being indicated abundantly by the names. He believed, however, that the two Chivalries were related but not identical and that Wolfram's Grail Knights repre-

[1] GEHEIME FIGUREN DER ROSENKREUZER AUS DEM 16 TEN UND 17 TEN JAHRHUNDERT, etc. Called otherwise an ABC BOOKLET FOR YOUNG SCHOLARS IN THE SCHOOL OF THE HOLY SPIRIT. Altona, 1785.

[2] Other editors were B. T. Doun and J. G. Büsching. The place of publication was Berlin.

sented in reality an Order of San Salvador de Montreal, founded *circa*
1120, by Alphonso III, the warrior King of Arragon and Castile. Moreover, King Alphonso built or fortified a town called Montreal to
resist the Moors in Valencia and there established the Chivalry. Here
—so far as Grail connections are concerned—is obviously pure speculation, not only destitute of evidence but of anything to justify its
promulgation. In a presumably later dissertation Von Hagen appears
to have changed his ground and to have affirmed that all the old
Romances treating of the Holy Grail were written to glorify the Order
of Knights Templar.[1] (2) In the year 1811 the orientalist J. von
Hammer-Pugstall published his well-known and long-remembered
MYSTERIUM BAPHOMETIS REVELATUM, in the course of which he
identified certain Baptismal Fonts or Vases—which he included among
antique memorials of the Templars—as examples of the true San Graal
Vessel ; and since he inter-related Templar Secret Doctrine and Gnostic
Theosophies, he remembered that, according to Epiphanius, the
Marcosians made use of three large Vases in their Celebration of the
Eucharist. They were filled with white wine, which was supposed to
undergo a transformation of colour and other magical changes. He
held also that the poem of TITUREL—presumably that of Albrecht—is
nothing but an allegory devoted to the Society and Doctrines of the
Knights Templar and that the Grail Temple, its Altars and its sculp-
tures, are significant of Templar Churches. He notes further that the
origin of the Holy Grail is referred always to the East, and that the
praises of the Vessel are celebrated throughout the TITUREL in terms of
mystical exaltation, with special reference to its abstruse Secrets.
The Chalice itself is a symbol of the Gnostic Sophia, while its twelve
Seniors or Archons, the instituted Guardians of the Grail, were
Initiates of Gnostic Mysteries. On these and other considerations, he
concludes that this most celebrated Cup of the Middle Ages was not
only a Templar symbol but an outward evidence of an inward Wisdom-
Knowledge preserved and perpetuated in the Order.[2] The Baphometic Mystery itself lies outside our subject, being the question of an
idol which the Templars were supposed to worship ; but it may be
said that on this part of his thesis the views of Von Hammer did not
survive criticism even at his own period. As to the Grail reveries, it is
to be questioned whether any one was at pains concerning them : they
are likely to have passed unnoticed. At the present day, even an
unversed reader will see that they are mere impressions expressed
dogmatically, and as the author had no evidence to produce in support
of his contentions so none has emerged since. The Templars may have
had a Secret Doctrine, but nothing has transpired respecting it and
nothing above all to connect it with Gnostic Theosophies. (3) In the
year 1828, the Abbé Grégoire expressed—as we have seen—a conviction

---

[1] This is cited by Fauriel and is therefore at second hand, without particular reference.
[2] Von Hammer's thesis seems to have appeared originally in DER FUNDGRUBEN DES
ORIENTS, VI, part 4.

that Christ transmitted to St. John the Evangelist a Secret Doctrine which descended ultimately to the Templars.[1] (4) In the year 1834 Gabriele Rossetti affirmed that the Templars belonged to Secret Societies and that they professed doctrines inimical to Rome ; but though much has been hazarded concerning their opinions, nothing has been ascertained conclusively. He held further that they were of Egyptian derivation and that from them the Albigenses emanated, which of all speculations brought forward on the subject in hand is assuredly the most unfounded.[2] (5) Between 1836 and 1841 San Marte—otherwise, Albert Schulz—produced the first modern German version of the PARZIVAL and laid stress on Templar correspondences with the German Grail Mythos in the Introduction prefixed thereto. The denomination TEMPLEISEN not only recalls the Templars but customs followed by these recall the poem of Wolfram. For example, at the Baptism of Feirfeis the Grail Liturgy uses the opening words of the Gospel according to St. John, and it is claimed that these words were an apparently essential part of the Eucharistic Ceremony among the Knights Templar. Moreover, the supposititious Baphometic Idol which the Knights were accused of worshipping and to which they looked not only for wealth but for all the fruits of the earth is in obvious correspondence with the food-providing powers of the Grail Talisman. In a later and revised edition of the work under notice[3] San Marte dwells on the alleged Secret Teaching of the Templars and on the rigidity with which their alliance was shut off from all without its pale, corresponding in these points with the Grail Chivalry isolated at Mont Salvatch from all intrusion, with guarded passes and ruled by Hereditary Kings.[4] He says further that in Spain and the South of France—connected obviously in his mind with the Provençal source of Wolfram—" there were not wanting Spiritual Societies which differed in essential points from the dogmas of Catholic Teaching " ; that soon after 900 A.D. " journeys were undertaken from France and other European countries to the Arabs in Spain " for the study of Islamic sciences ; that schools arose in this manner for the practice of Astrology and Natural Magic, at which Mohammedans, Jews and Christians were, so to speak, bound together and united in one purpose ; that the Grail Saga may have arisen in these centres ; that its Cult and its Kingdom constitute a poetic representation of the Kingdom of God in " the spirit of a knightly layman set free from rigid traditional and ecclesiastical forms ".[5] Finally, in his monograph on Welsh Tradition and its influence, San Marte affirms (a) that the Grail Legend

[1] Abbé Grégoire : HISTOIRE DES SECTES RELIGIEUSES. He seems to have regarded a certain LEVITIKON as so far authentic that it was "an exposition of the Religious Doctrine of the initiated." The initiates, however, were those modern French Templars —circa 1805 and subsequently—who derived from Fabré-Palaprat's notorious Charter of Larmenius.
[2] DISQUISITIONS ON THE ANTIPAPAL SPIRIT WHICH PRODUCED THE REFORMATION, 2 vols., 1834. The translation was by Miss Caroline Ward and appeared concurrently with the Italian original.
[3] Both editions were published at Magdeburg, the second in 1887.
[4] Introduction to the second edition.   [5] Ibid.

did not assume a defined form till after the Institution of the Templars ; (*b*) that as the MILES TEMPLI fought for the honour of the Cross and the protection of Pilgrims, so also fought the TEMPLEISEN for the glory of the Grail and the Sanctuary wherein it was preserved ; (*c*) that the Templars chose their own Grand Master and might appoint one of the most remote members, while the coming King of the Grail was liable to be summoned from " the most distant corner of the earth " by its appointed Messenger, the so-called Sorceress Kundrie ; (*d*) that the Grand Master of the Temple was subordinate to the Pope alone, and the Grail King lived " in angelic purity " in the sight of God upon earth ;[1] (*e*) that only children of pure birth could be chosen as Servants of the Grail and that Knights only, or the Sons of Knights, lawfully begotten of noble ladies, were eligible as Templar Candidates ; (*f*) that everything was in common with the Templars, while the Grail provided TEMPLEISEN with all human necessities. There are other and yet more frivolous analogies which it would serve no purpose to enumerate. It should be obvious to all that if consanguinities can be established on lines like these they might be found everywhere. The GRAND PALAMÈDE and the GRAND PERCEFOREST may be Templar Romances, for no better reason than because they post-date the foundation of the Templar Chivalry ; whosoever has fought for the glory of anything while that Chivalry lasted may have been in the bonds thereof ; whosoever lived in purity under the eye of Heaven was to all intents and purposes a Knight Templar ; and so was every heir to any and every throne who happened to be *in absentia* when his predecessor passed out of this life. There is no need to add that a food-providing Talisman bears no relation to community of goods ; and in this manner we are left only with the law of legitimacy as a ground of union between the German Grail of Wolfram and Albrecht and its postulated source.[2] Now it happens, as regards the Northern French Cycle, that Galahad, the *Haut Prince*, certified as such by the Inscription on the Siege Perilous, was a natural son of Lancelot. I have said elsewhere and maintain that Galahad and the Great QUESTE are the head and crown of the Grail Legend, whatever we elect to think of Parzival and the poet who gave a new and wonderful life to the creation of Chrétien : now, the putative stigma connected with Galahad's birth counts for nothing in the light of his story at large, his dedication and his final

---

[1] One is left to speculate on the supposed ground of analogy between angelical purity and subordination to the Pope alone. Readers who wish to verify the author's text may be referred to AN ESSAY ON THE INFLUENCE OF WELSH TRADITION UPON THE LITERATURE OF GERMANY, FRANCE AND SCANDINAVIA, translated from the German of Albert Schulz. Llandovery, 1841, p. 121.

[2] Compare San Marte's implied counter-views at a later point of the Introduction already cited : the " blessed contemplation " of the Grail on Montsalvatch preserved " the servant of the Holy Vessel from every deadly sin " and herein presumably resides the kind of perfection attained by Parzival in the pleasant married life of his Kingship. It did nothing of the sort unfortunately in the case of his precursor, Anfortas. It may be noted, as a matter of curiosity, that at this stage of his thesis the Grail has become for San Marte an exceedingly conglomerate symbol, being (1) a Stone fallen from the crown of Lucifer, (2) the same Stone converted into a Cup, and (3) as such the Holy Vessel which received the Blood from the side of Christ when it was pierced by Longinus.

attainment. (6) In the year 1852 Dr. Karl Simrock expressed an opinion that the Doctrine and Tradition of the Templars were based on the Tradition of the Grail ; that Christ had been instructed by the Essenes ; that He confided a Secret Knowledge to some of His Disciples ; and that this was imparted subsequently to Priests of the Templar Chivalry.[1] As regards the first point, the Grail owed nothing to the Temple, while in respect of the second it is not suggested that the alleged Secret Knowledge bore any relation to that which *ex hypothesi* may be imbedded in the Grail literature. Simrock, however, cannot be said to have been concerned seriously with the Templar thesis and was inclined rather to look for light on the Grail in the direction of Traditions connected with St. John the Baptist. (7) In the year 1854 it was sustained by Eugène Aroux that all the archaic Romances of the Holy Grail were written to glorify the Order of the Temple and to present its Doctrine in the form of Romance.[2] (8) In the year 1858 the same writer went further in a fantastic work and affirmed that the Templars were parties to a concealed programme for the creation at Jerusalem of a religious and military rival to the power and ortho-doxy at Rome.[3] It would be impossible to present his thesis in any reasonable space, and it has nothing to do with the Grail. As regards glorification of the Temple in the Grail Romances, the affirmation is justified by crediting the Chivalry with Albigensian and other views for which there is no evidence. (9) In 1865 Louis Moland, in his ORIGINES LITTÉRAIRES considered that the Grail Legend and the Templar Order were expressions in literature and life of the same ideal, being the union of Knighthood with Sanctity, and he stated further (*a*) that there was a strange Templar reflection in a literature which was unquestionably and closely related with the principles of that Chivalry ; (*b*) that the Roman Curia interdicted the Grail Romances coincidently with the suppression of the Knightly Order.[4] It will be seen that the root of this thesis is identical with that of Schulz. (10) So far as I am aware, the debate appears to have slept till 1890, when F. Naef published at Nismes a volume of moderate dimensions on the religious opinions which he ascribed to the Templars, in connection with which he had strong personal views on the Grail Legend and that which lay behind it. Taken generally, he traced a decided religious tendency and what he termed a symbolical mysticism in the Romances of the Round Table. As regards the Grail itself, it has next to nothing in common with Catholic Legends, while the Cultus of the mysterious Chalice far surpassed in grandeur and exaltation the relative worship paid by the Church even to the most Sacred Relics. Now, from his

---

[1] The PARZIVAL of Wolfram von Eschenbach, translated into modern German.
[2] See his DANTE : HÉRÉTIQUE, REVOLUTIONNAIRE ET SOCIALISTE.
[3] MYSTÈRES DE LA CHEVALERIE ET DE L'AMOUR PLATONIQUE AU MOYEN AGE.
[4] More than fifty years later, Miss Weston asks whether the Grail Romances were forbidden or whether they were merely discouraged ; and she answers herself by saying that " probably we shall never know." FROM RITUAL TO ROMANCE, p. 177. It is needless to say that we look to Moland in vain for evidence, nor does he enable us to see after what manner Templar principles were reflected into Grail Romances.

point of view, " it is just this exaltation of mystery and of holiness which unveils so clearly the symbol and the allegory " of the entire conception. He goes on to say that the mystical symbolism was a protest raised from time to time " by superior souls, to escape from the scholastic absurdities and the despotism of the Roman Church." Having enlarged further on these and connected subjects, it is proposed that they suggest the idea of Initiation into some Instituted Mystery, and the Order of Knights Templar, being that alone which was ready to his hand at the period, is made to serve his purpose. He rejected the scandals repeated by writers like von Hammer and affirmed that their Secret Doctrine was a Christian Gnosis—whatever the term may mean—" concealed in the mysterious assemblies of the Order ".[1] It was supposed to come from the East, meaning obviously that it was met with in Palestine or thereabouts. Naef adds cautiously that we have no ground of speculation as to its nature. The sole basis on which this reverie rests is the fact at its value that the Templars appear to have possessed a variant version of the Fourth Gospel, a verse of which has survived and is quoted by the author under notice. It occurs at the end of the Gospel and Jesus is supposed to be speaking. The words are : " In truth, I say unto you, I am not of this world. But John will be unto you a Father until he comes with Me into Paradise." They may suggest to some minds the possibility of a Johannine Tradition within the Temple. (11) The dream of the Grail and the Temple—after 1890—passed on, as it may be said, from mouth to mouth and contributions thereto and thereon will be found more especially in occult works and periodicals, the writers, in all cases practically, depending on those who had preceded. They are records of added impressions and sometimes of added inventions which there is no space or cause to cite. Thirty years later Miss Weston published the last word, so to speak, which as yet has been delivered on the subject.[2] She is in the course of affirming that Grail Romances repose on the ruins of an august Ritual and not on a poet's imagination ; but about this, its import and its value we shall hope to ascertain later. The force of religious evolution had driven the august Rite from its high estate into caves and mountain fastnesses, or island isolations, " where those who craved for a more sensible (not necessarily sensuous) contact with the unseen Spiritual Forces of Life than the orthodox development of Christianity afforded, might, and did, find satisfaction ". The accent of assurance may be noted, as if something evidential and exceeding contradiction had come at last into Miss Weston's hands. She goes on, however, to ask a simple question : " Were the Templars such ? Had they, when in the East, come into touch with a survival of the Naassene, or some kindred sect ? " The answer is simple also, after its own manner : " It seems exceedingly probable ". An expatiation follows, and we learn that in such case

---

[1] OPINIONS RELIGIEUSES DES TEMPLIERS.
[2] FROM RITUAL TO ROMANCE, pp. 176, 177.

many problems would be cleared up, as if once and for all. We should understand (1) the puzzling connection of the Order with the Knights of the Grail ; (2) the doom which fell upon them ; (3) why they were held to be heretics ; and (4) in what their heresy consisted. It was something which struck at the root and vitals of Christianity, if the intimations cherished by Miss Weston are based on fact. She affirms also that we can understand in such case why the Church knows nothing of the Grail, and why that Sacred Vessel encompassed by an atmosphere of reverence and " equated with the central Sacrament of the Christian Faith, yet appears in no Legendary, is figured in no picture, comes on the scene in no Passion Play " This notwithstanding, " the Church of the eleventh and twelfth centuries knew well what the Grail was ", and it is possible for us to know on our own part, if we accept her thesis on its genesis : we shall know also why, with all the splendour and wonder of the Grail Cycles, it " vanished utterly and completely from the world of literature ". The explanation is that it belonged to a cult of Vegetation Gods perpetuated into the Christian centuries, passing *ex hypothesi* with the Templars, but still, as we shall see, not wholly beyond recovery for those who know where to look. I have mentioned that this speculation will recur for our inspection later : at the moment we have only to notice that, even from Miss Weston's point of view, the question of Templar connections with strange or Secret Doctrines in the East is only a matter of probability by her own admission. It may prove to be even less.

The summary above has omitted of necessity many allocations and many hazards of hypothesis which might have been collected from other sources. Our next step is to ascertain from the authentic charges made against the Templars during the course of the processes instituted by the Ecclesiastical Courts of France and elsewhere what were the heresies of Doctrine and Practice imputed to the Chivalry in the accusations of the dominant Orthodoxy. Setting aside those which constitute alleged infringement of the Decalogue and sins " crying to Heaven for vengeance ",[1] the major counts were two : that Candidates for Reception into the Order were called upon to deny Christ and offer a ceremonial outrage to the Cross as the Symbol of His Passion. The minor points were many, but after disentangling the alleged Cultus of the Baphometic Head and some other things which may be ruled outside our concern,[2] they are reducible also to two, being (1) the secular

---

[1] It has to be remembered (1) that the Templars were men of action, not men of contemplation ; (2) that they were bound by monastic vows but were leading their life in the world and on fields of battle ; (3) that as Soldiers of the Cross and otherwise, incorporated for perpetual warfare, they were men of great physical power, having all the advantages, all the dangers and temptations implied by that vocation ; (4) that inevitable results in any or all directions must have stared Rome in the face ; and (5) that Roman astuteness would never have proceeded against the Templars on mere charges of incontinence : authentic or fraudulent, they had another and larger dossier.

[2] The ruling obtains definitely in respect of the Head, because the worship of idols lies outside the Grail subject. Those, if any, who wish to pursue the subject will do well to accept one word of warning, avoiding therefore occasional occult dissertations and their source in Von Hammer-Purgstall. They will be threading idle mazes. Let them have recourse to Michelet's Procès des Templiers, 2 vols., 1841–43, containing the Latin

absolution from sin which was said to be given by the Grand Master in
Open Chapter and possibly also by the Preceptors of local Com-
manderies and Encampments ; (2) a practice in respect of the
Eucharist which did not involve exactly a denial of Doctrine but
exhibited hostility thereto. The first is important because in a
qualified form it was the only charge which was held proven against the
Templars as a result of examinations in England ; [1] but it is on the
second that the whole thesis with which we are concerned appears to
break down. The accusation was that in Consecrating the Blessed
Sacrament, the necessary and efficacious Words were omitted.[2] The
evidence adduced on this question included that of an English Priest
who had officiated once for the Templars and who was forbidden to
recite the Clauses of Institution.

I do not propose to report upon the validity of the charges in whole
or in detail : with a single exception, they lie outside our subject, and
those who are concerned must be referred—if they can summons such
patience for their aid—to the Latin Process of the Trial, which was
published many years since in France, and to which I have had recourse
in notes. The Templars have been accused by learned people of Gnosticism, Manichæanism, Albigensianism, not however, on the authority
of those memorials, which speak with another voice. There is no
evidence in either case : it is wanting also for the other speculations
which are included in my summary above ; and, in fine, there is none
also for the suggested Grail connections, though I confess that my
far-off researches were begun in an expectation of the kind. The
Templars, if guilty, as affirmed of old on the worst of all possible
authority, were in the position of some heresies in Southern France :
they reduced, denied, derided, or stood in fear of the Eucharist, and
therefore the abyss intervenes between them and a literature which
exists to exalt it. As regards the German PARZIVAL, it possesses the
putative *tendances suspectes* to which I have referred in more than
one connection. It may be said that the Host which came from Heaven
was a designed antithesis to the Host consecrated on earth ; but I
believe that this is fantasy,[3] because to hear an ordinary Mass was as
much a duty of Knighthood according to Wolfram, as we find it in
the QUEST OF GALAHAD, the LONGER PROSE PERCEVAL and any of the
other Romances.[4] I believe in my heart that the instituted analogy

---

records of the Trials, printed from one of two copies made at the time, the second being
delivered to Pope Clement. It will tell them precisely what the Prosecution understood
by the Head and what they extracted thereupon from their victims, under or after
torture, and otherwise.					[1] C. G. Addison : THE KNIGHTS TEMPLAR.

[2] As if the Templars believed and were afraid—a notable and significant point, on
assuming for a moment that the charge had a ground in fact.

[3] From another point of view, it might be very much more than fantasy, were there
ground for believing that behind the earthly wonders of the *Lapis exilis*, the Stone
which fed and the Stone which clothed, the Oracle which called the Elect and reigned
and ruled in all, Wolfram was intimating another Arch-Natural Eucharist, which came
down from Heaven and communicated Bread of Life and Wine of the Kingdom. But
for this I find no evidence.

[4] We have seen that Albrecht's TITUREL is precisely the kind of creation which would
have been called disdainfully an ultramontane poem in the later nineteenth century.

between the TEMPLEISEN of Mont Salvatch and the great Order of
Chivalry was natural and irresistible in the mind of the poet who
conceived it ; I believe that it is the only connection and, as I have said,
that nothing follows therefrom. I believe that the sole Eucharistic
privilege enjoyed by the Templars was a decree which permitted them
to celebrate one Mass annually in places under interdict ; that there
were next to no instances in which they renounced their faith, much as
they may have dishonoured it by their lives ; and that their foundation
under the patronage of *la doce mère de Dieu*[1] represented their ecclesiastical ideal. I believe in fine that their first principles were expressed
on their behalf in the Epistle of St. Bernard *ad Milites Templi*. It
was written at the instance of Hugo, the first Commander, and this
fact is all that need be derived from the Prologue. The text itself
exhorts the new Institution to strive with intrepid souls against the
enemies of the Cross of Christ, because those to whom death is a reward
and life is Christ need fear nothing. Let them stand for Christ therefore, rather desiring to be dissolved, that they may be with Him. Let
them live in good fellowship, having neither wives nor children. A
later section concerns that external Temple from which their particular
title was taken, and it compares the glories of the House built by
Solomon for the Glory of God with the inward grace of that Inward
Temple to which the Order was attached in the spirit. In other words,
this was for St. Bernard a House not made with hands, since the
Chivalry was itself a Temple, and, like that of Masonry, the edifice was
erected in the heart. The Brethren are in fact described as a Holy City ;
they are connected with the idea of the Church itself ; and the enumerated details of the Holy Place are used for spiritual exhortation
addressed to the Knighthood. The promise to Zion that its wilderness
shall become an abode of all delights, its solitude a Garden of the Lord,
echoing with joy and gladness, with thanksgiving and the voice of
praise, is said to be the heritage of the Order, and to watch over their
Heavenly Treasure should be their chief care—so acting that in all
things He should be magnified Who guides their arms to the battle and
their hands to the warfare.

Whether it profits to add more I question, but this may be said at
least—that I am sacrificing all my predilections and making my task
much harder by throwing over the Templar hypothesis, not alone in
its connection with the Grail on the historical side, but as one of the
Channels through which the Secret Tradition may have passed in
Christian Times.

I have searched many highways and byways with an anxious eye
for evidence, and I have been haunted with the dreams of those who
went before me in the way ; but I have returned so far with empty
hands. I can say therefore only : *magis amica veritas*.[2]

---

[1] Appendix I, Note 18.   [2] Appendix I, Note 19.

III

THE SECTS OF SOUTHERN FRANCE

PERHAPS no Christian sects have been the subject of more unbridled speculation and plenary misapprehension than those numerous groups which pass under the general denomination of Albigeois and Catharist in Southern France during the twelfth and thirteenth centuries. The affirmation obtains in several directions but more especially in that of writers who represent the borderland of occult thought. Against the monstrous iniquity of Albigensian persecution in the past there is the incompetence, not unmixed with dishonesty, of old Protestant apologists—as, for example, the grossly uncritical expatiations of the Rev. G. S. Faber[1] at the beginning of the nineteenth century. We have to deal, however, at the moment with a particular enthusiasm which attempted—between 1854 and 1858—to connect the sects and their exponents with the literature of the Holy Grail and we have to ascertain, if possible, what, if anything, may lie behind it. The initial impulse in this direction is to be found in special pleadings, criticisms and modes of interpretation with which France made us familiar some eighty years since, while their leading was followed much later by certain English exponents who scarcely knew their subject. For the purpose of the present analysis it is immaterial whether the Albigenses and their consanguinities were " pure Christians ", as pure Christianity was understood at the period, according to arbitrary canons, or whether they were Manichæans—to cite one out of many suppositions. The sole and all-important question is as to that light under which they presented Eucharistic Doctrine, and from this standpoint it seems clear, on the surface at least, that they could have had no connection with the development of any Grail Cycle, unless indeed its component texts were so devised that they maintained outwardly that which was denied within. If Albigensians and Catharists were Manichæans at heart and in practice, they had a tinkered Eucharist, from which nothing followed in relation to authentic Sacramental Mystery. If, on the other hand, they were Protestants of their period, they would deny as such most of the Sacraments, while in respect of Doctrine at least they would almost certainly have tampered with the Eucharist.

Postponing for a moment those French speculations which have nothing to tell us regarding Albigensian or Catharist teachings and deal only, as we shall see shortly, with a particular construction of a great body of romantic literature, it may be said—and is needful to note in order to clear the issue—that the merely Protestant standpoint in all matters of this kind, being naturally one of militant

[1] Remembered in perpetuity for the materials apart from the thesis of his ORIGIN OF PAGAN IDOLATRY.

opposition to the Latin Church, ignored or denied the Church theory
that the Sects of Southern France, including the Paulicians, who have
been proposed as their predecessors, were Manichæans, while the
connected Sect of Waldenses, or disciples of Peter Valdo, were originally
Donatists.[1] With these questions in themselves we have no concern,
till we come to the later part of the present thesis, nor yet with an old
contention that there was a line of succession in perpetuity from
Apostolic Times through the Waldensians. There is no reason to
suppose that the hypothesis is valid, and it matters little to our
purpose if it was. There may be placed in the same category a not
less romantic supposition, namely, that the Vaudois had been located
in the Cottian Alps since the time of the Apostles and that their
system had never varied from the tenets and practices of primitive
Christianity. It is not of necessity a seal or mark of favour if these
facts are undoubted ; but actually they are questionable enough,
like that apologetical *pièce de résistance* which accounts for the small-
ness of the Vaudois Community by inferring from the Apocalypse
that the Church, during a certain disastrous period, would be reduced
within very narrow limits and that for this reason—among contentions
not less logical—the Vaudois, Waldenses and Albigenses constituted
during those internecine days the one and truly Catholic Church.[2]
Another field of reverie connects the so-called Waldensian Church with
the Church Primitive through the Albigensians themselves ; and if the
last Sect had really the Paulicians for their ancestors they date back to
a considerable antiquity ; while, as regards distribution, it is said that
the earlier " heresy " had its Houses of Assembly established all the
way from Thrace to Gascony. They came from the East originally, or
this is their Legend, but their early traces have disappeared, supposing
that the story is true outside the imagination of apologists. However
this may be, the Paulicians, so far as history is concerned, arose in
Armenia, where they were founded by one Constantine about the
middle of the seventh century. They were mixed up with the Milesians,
who made common cause with Constantine, but they were proscribed
by the Emperors of Byzantium and the so-called heretic was himself put
to death. The same Paulicians have been identified with the Cathari,
and these are said to have been in union with the Waldenses, whose
first stronghold was among the Alpine valleys of Piedmont. On the
other hand, the Paterins, whose chain of dissemination is affirmed to

---

[1] The ENCYCLOPÆDIA OF RELIGION AND ETHICS recognises the presence both of
Paulician and Manichæan elements.

[2] My readers must be dissuaded from assuming that I am concerned in reality with
the claims or principles of any Official Church or with the construction or destruction of
any thesis which attempts to define Catholicity. I do not think, with old-fashioned
Protestantism, that Rome represents the unity of slumbering intellects, nor with Angli-
canism *in excelsis* that the " Holy Catholic Church " is a denomination applied and
applicable to a general collocation of internecine sects. *Ecclesia Catholica in corde
ædificata est et tabernaculum ejus in spiritu sancto nostro.* Meanwhile, I am concerned
with presenting an exploded thesis on the Grail Legend in the course of a three-fold
exposition of the critical apparatus thereon. We are to ascertain in conclusion that which
arises, if anything, from later lights on the historical side of the subject.

have extended from Bulgaria through Lombardy to the Atlantic, have been represented as a variety of the Albigensian sect, if not identical therewith. These views constitute a cloud upon the problematic Sanctuary, in respect of its origin. Other accounts say that they appeared in Italy during the first years of the eleventh century, with which may be compared the counter-suggestion that their most probable founder was Peter of Lyons more than a hundred years later. Persecution may well have joined distinct elements of sect till they became merged in one another ; it caused them also to move, like the Grail, Westward, and thus they entered Southern France, where those who had pre-existed under more than one name received the title of Albigenses—as it is thought, from their headquarters at Albi. Here also they fell under proscription, and because at that period men believed—and never more strongly—that they were doing God's work by annihilating those who worshipped Him under another code of doctrine, there was not only a crusade of extermination declared against them but we encounter St. Dominic fighting the heresy with other weapons than the Sword of the Spirit—in the belief that this also might be either as the Word of God in activity or its working substitute. This was under Innocent III, who occupied the Chair of Peter between 1198 and 1216 and who—prior to defining Transubstantiation—proclaimed the great Crusade against the Albigenses and their con-sanguinities in 1208, its leader-in-chief being Simon, Count of Montfort, while Folquet, a Troubadour Bishop of Marseilles, was one of its most violent partisans. There is no opportunity and fortunately no need to trace in these pages the merciless career of Montfort, the plunderings and massacres which characterised the war of extermination carried on under his auspices. At Lavarn the widowed Lady of the City, described as the bounteous Giralda, and her daughter were flung into a well and stones rolled down upon their bodies. At the beginning of 1213 Innocent declared the Crusade at an end,[1] but this prohibition was rescinded in the following year, the Pope himself passing to his reward in 1216. He was succeeded by Honorius III, who pursued the policy of destruction with increased vigour. Montfort was killed in the third Siege of Toulouse on June 25th, 1218. The persecution and the war dragged on, and it is said that after 1229 Albigensian history is mainly associated with that of the Holy Inquisition. It was not until 1244 that the last stronghold of the Catharists, the supposed impregnable Montségur,[2] fell into the hands of the enemy, and its Suzeraine, the Princess Esclairmonde de Foix, sealed her faith in her blood—or rather in fire—with many others of the Perfect Brethren. So do Official Churches illustrate their construction of the emblematic paradox concerning that Prince of Peace Who came with a Sword. If ever the Scarlet Woman of Apocalyptic Parable was seated on the Hills of Rome it was in the thirteenth century of the pseudo-Christian

---

[1] According to an alternative account, the further preaching of the Crusade was prohibited by the Council of Lateran in 1215.   [2] Appendix I, Note 20.

era ; and if ever she was " drunk with the blood of the Saints," the place of vintage at that period was in Southern France. It was then and there also, if ever, that the mystery of all iniquity came from the deeps in its power. The literature, the language and great masses of the population were destroyed in the years of ravage ; the remanent of Catharists, Albigenses and the rest fled to Piedmont, Austria, Bohemia and even England, though the last statement has been challenged. But the Sects die hard, like the persecuting Churches : it has been even said that a few of the Perfect Believers survived in Bosnia *circa* 1875.[1]

There is very full evidence that the unremitting persecution brought many individuals into occasional outward conformity and to denials in public of that which they held in secret. On the basis of their enforced confessions, they repudiated Manichæan derivations and principles, claiming to follow primitive Christian teaching as they construed it from the New Testament or certain parts thereof, since it does not appear that they accepted all the Epistles : there are, moreover, persistent rumours about a Catharist version of the Fourth Gospel. A Dominican Missionary and Inquisitor who recounted in a poem which survives his debates with an Albigensian Theologian, accuses the Sect (1) of denying Baptism and regarding Satan as the creator of this world ; (2) of rejecting Confession and teaching that those who had Sons and Daughters were outside the pale of salvation ; (3) of claiming inspiration from the Holy Spirit and making a traffic therein amongst their disciples ; (4) of denying the Resurrection and affirming that the souls of the redeemed would assume a new body, having a certain resemblance to the old and yet differing therefrom ; and in fine (5) of maintaining that the souls of men are those of lost angels—the difficulty about this, in the mind of the Dominican, being apparently that we have no recollection of our past. The importance of this text is that although it embodies accusations included in the proscription of the sect it may also have reflected current fluidic opinions in orthodox circles at the period. Other charges affirm (1) that the Baptism which was recognised by the Albigenses was that of Fire or of the Spirit, recalling the Mysterious Office of the Paraclete which is often a subject of reference in the Grail literature ; (2) that the wandering preachers of the sect distributed nourishment of the body as well as the Bread of Angels—here recalling the two-fold ministry of the Grail ; (3) that they rejected the Books of Moses ; (4) that they regarded this sublunary world as the only hell ; (5) that their subsurface working was that of a New and Secret Priesthood which was to dispossess and succeed the Papal Hierarchy, as if here also there was a special succession from the apostles having kinship with the Super-Apostolic Succession of the Grail Priesthood.

Such fantastic analogies notwithstanding, it is clear on the old findings, for and against, that the sects of Southern France—as

[1] See ENCYCLOPÆDIA OF RELIGION AND ETHICS, I, s.v. Albigenses.

presented by either hypothesis—offer nothing to our purpose. From eclectic Gnosticism, which took over from Christianity that which coincided with its purpose, to Vaudois and Lollards, there is not one which sought to develop, exalt or exaggerate the sacramental teaching of the ancient Church. We know that, on the authority of Origen, the Marcionites taught the communication to the soul of man of a Divine and Sanctifying Spirit added by the Redeemer, Who imparted it in the Eucharist ; and if this meant the Descent of the Paraclete, the perpetuation of such a Doctrine might help us to understand why the Voice of the Grail was that of the Holy Ghost and yet in some mysterious way was that also of Christ.[1] But of such perpetuation there is no trace whatever. As regards the Albigenses, there is no question historically that they denied Transubstantiation, though they accepted some qualified Sacramental Teaching concerning the Lord's Supper, which they commemorated in woods and forests on a cloth spread upon the ground, or in their own houses. On these considerations it would be worse than idle to suppose that they had any hand in the Grail Legend, and this would remain substantially true even if we elected to suppose (1) that the Mythical Kyot was actually a poet of his period ; (2) that he belonged to one of the Sects ; and—going still further—if we suggested (3) that his poem conveyed, after a hidden or an open manner, some part of Albigensian Teaching.

Passing now for the time being from these external questions of fact and doctrine, a word must be said to dispose of that other claim to which I have adverted at the beginning. It took all Chivalrous Romance for its subject, and it claimed to have demonstrated that a large European literature had been written by Albigenses for the edification of Albigenses and to put forth in a veiled manner Albigensian Doctrine. There are certain precursors who do not prepare the way, for they open up issues which end either in a *cul de sac* or take the seeker through by-paths which can be followed interminably without leading to a true goal. The author of this demonstration was Eugène Aroux, who published in 1858 the MYSTERIES OF CHIVALRY AND OF PLATONIC LOVE IN THE MIDDLE AGES. Its inspiration in chief was derived from Gabriele Rossetti and particularly from the ANTI-PAPAL SPIRIT WHICH PRECEDED THE REFORMATION. Both works have exercised an influence on certain later schools of occult thought in England ; but Rossetti does not speak of the Grail, and hence there is no call that here I should speak of him. The monument of M. Aroux was preceded by other of his works designed to shew that Dante was (*a*) heretical, revolutionary and socialistic ; (*b*) connected with an

---

[1] LE ROMAN DU SAINT-GRAAL (of Robert de Borron), edited by Francisque Michel, 1841, p. 103, ll. 2459, 2460. Joseph prays for the counsel of Christ on the need of his people in the presence of the Holy Vessel ; but that which answers is said to be the Voice of the Holy Spirit :

Lors ha à Joseph la vouiz dist,
Ki venue est dou Saint-Esprit.

Joseph, however, receives the direction given as *le commandement notre Seigneur*, p. 107, ll. 2555, 2556.

alleged fusion between the Albigenses, Templars and Ghibellines for the creation of Emblematic Freemasonry ; (c) himself so far implicated in Freemasonry that the DIVINE COMEDY is really Masonic in its purpose. In further support of these views Aroux had translated the whole *Commedia* into literal French verse and had commented on it " according to the spirit." Finally, he had instituted comparisons between Dante and the writers of the Grail Cycle. It came about thus that the products of this Cycle were included by his general ingarnering, but he shews little familiarity with his subject, and he wrote at a period when the literature was still practically unprinted. He puts forward the talismanic proposition that the Holy Grail was a mysterious association[1] and that the mission of its Initiates was " to recover the vessel of truth with luminous characters wherein was received the Precious Blood of the Saviour." According to his peculiar canon of criticism this signified the design of " leading back the Christian Church to Apostolic Times and the faithful observation of the Gospel precepts."[2] M. Aroux wrote as a defender of the Roman Church, and, after all that has been said and done upon the whole subject, it has not occurred to any one—perhaps least of all to him—that the true mission of the Church may have been to get away from apostolic times and to put aside, like St. Paul, in its maturity the things which belong to the child. For the rest, M. Aroux confused in a grotesque manner the Grail Knights with those of the Round Table, and appeared to suppose that Wolfram's PARZIVAL and the TITUREL of Albrecht are representative of the entire literature.[3]

As regards Chivalry, his thesis can be stated shortly : The actual, historical, feudal Chivalry was an institution more or less savage, and the Chivalry set forth in the Romances had no existence on earth. This is equivalent to saying that the heroes and heroines of Mrs. Radcliffe, the modes and manners which she depicts, the spirit which characterises her episodes, perhaps even the scenes which she describes so graphically at hearsay, are never found in real life, though sentimentalism is always sentimentalism, mountains are always mountains, and as regards the Pyrenees in particular they are situated indubitably between France and Spain. The thing goes without saying in each case, for the Romance, one would say, is—well, precisely a Romance, But on the basis of this transparent fact, M. Aroux builds his theory that the Books of Chivalry were the *corpus doctrinale* and literary body-politic of the Protestantism of its period, reduced to this resource because of the intolerant powers that were. And this is just what appears to be so highly ridiculous, not because a

---

[1] Itself described as " an ascetic Freemasonry," meaning presumably that it was an Instituted Mystery. LA COMÉDIE DE DANTE, II, p. 1279.

[2] MYSTÈRES DE LA CHEVALERIE, p. 73.

[3] Aroux depended on Fauriel for his knowledge of the German Grail, and it is to be questioned whether he knew any of the French Grail texts at first hand. Were there anything in his speculations, he should have found a mine of opportunity in the 1530 printed prose version of the CONTE DEL GRAAL ; but seemingly he had not heard of its existence.

literature cannot have concealed motives, or that of the Grail among them, but because it might be shewn in a no less pseudo-conclusive manner that the CONFESSIONAL OF THE BLACK PENITENTS was the final rescript of the followers of Manes. And this seems to be intolerable.

Speaking generally as to the canon of criticism, it is in all respects like that of the late Mrs. Henry Pott in the Bacon and Shakespeare controversy : he, as she, proves far too much for his own credit. If the canons of Mrs. Pott demonstrate that Bacon was the concealed author of the disputed Plays, then the same canons shew—and the claim is before us—that he must have written the works of Marlowe, Massinger, Ford, and the bulk of Elizabethan literature. In the same way, the evidences adduced by M. Aroux are either insufficient to prove his point or alternatively a similar scheme has given us, according to their inward sense, the NIGHTS of Straparola, the NIEBELUNGEN SAGAS, the ROMANCE OF THE ROSE and the entire literature of the Troubadours, to say nothing of the Welsh MABINOGION, REYNARD THE FOX and things innumerable of the German Minnesingers.[1] This is indeed the expressed thesis of M. Aroux, and the only reason that he omitted the Latin literature of Alchemy—which might have proved more to his purpose—is because he had not come across it. There is no need to outline the nature of his evidence ; but, to speak generally concerning it, the same canon might be applied with the same success to Mrs. Radcliffe's ROMANCE OF THE FOREST and to the MYSTERIES OF UDOLPHO. The principle, in other words, would repeat itself everywhere with fatal facility.

I should not have dealt with these fantastic matters except for the interest which they have raised in schools of thought which are not always so far from my own ; because in the last resource they constitute an attempt, after their own manner, to shew the hand of supposed Secret Orders in the development of the Grail literature ; and because there is another point of view from which, after these debates, the Grail subject can be approached in connection with Southern France, whether or not we shall reach ultimately the same term. I conclude for the moment as follows : (1) that the Chivalry of the Romances—Grail, Arthurian and others—was an ideal conception, corresponding as such to the atmosphere, characteristics and subject-matter of other Cycles of Romance ; and (2) that the Historical Chivalry of the period corresponded to the impression which we obtain of the period by reading old Chronicles, like those of Froissart. For the rest, M. Aroux's canon of interpretation is exceedingly simple : (1) any Heroine of the Romances signifies the Albigensian Church ; (2) any Hero signifies one of its Apostles or Teachers ; (3) the enemies of both are the dominant opposing Church ; (4) the Holy Vase of the Grail is its Divine and Hidden Doctrine.

[1] Cf. LES MYSTÈRES DE LA CHEVALERIE, in which these texts are studied : for the *Nights* see pp. 146–154 ; for the Sagas, pp. 110–115 ; for *Le Roman de la Rose*, pp. 138–141 ; for *Reynard the Fox*, pp. 130–137 ; for the Minnesingers, pp. 188, 189.

Against these speculations and these significances, fantastically inread, there is fortunately one fragmentary record of Albigensian Belief which has survived the Montfort Crusade, and defaced though it is it offers some light on the subject which was unknown seemingly to Eugène Aroux, not to speak of the Protestant Apologists. Perhaps in his case it was overlooked rather than unknown, as Schmidt, writing a few years earlier, was acquainted therewith and cited it in his still important work on the Sects of Southern France.[1] I refer to the Cathar Ritual of Lyons, which is now well known among us, having been translated and published in 1898 by Mr. F. C. Conybeare as Appendix VI to THE KEY OF TRUTH, being a Manual of the Paulician Church of Armenia. The Lyons Codex[2] contains (1) the New Testament in the Langue d'Oc ;[3] (2) Latin Prayers which are manifestly Trinitarian, as shewn by the recurring Benediction : *Pater et Filius et Spiritus Sanctus parcat vobis omnia peccata vestra ;*[4] (3) the *Paternoster* with *Panem nostrum super substancialem,* instead of *panem quotidianum :* (4) the Service=*Servitium,* or Prayer ; (5) the Reception of a Believer ; (6) the *Consolamentum ;* (7) certain Prayers for the Sick ; and (8) St. John, I, 1–17 in Latin : *In principio erat verbum,* etc. There is no Eucharistic Celebration. As regards the Believer's Reception, this signifies his Reception of the Lord's Prayer, whereby presumably he became a Member of the Church and was thus qualified for the Office of Spiritual Baptism, termed *Consolamentum.* He could apply for it at once, but in most cases this crowning Ceremonial was postponed to a much later period and was taken often *in examine mortis,* when it served as a Viaticum for the departing soul. Mr. Conybeare institutes a close correspondence between the Albigenses=Catharists and the Paulicians, otherwise the Adoptionist Church, being " a phase of the Christian Church so old and outworn that the very memory of it was well nigh lost " It was held by the latter (1) that Jesus was man only till He received the Baptism of John—whence it follows, however, that John must have been more than man, in that he was able to communicate that super-efficacious Rite which could transform " mere " man into a Son of God. Yet it does not appear that Adoptionists were Christians of St. John, Mandæans and so forth. (2) That we in turn can become the Adopted Sons of God : *et ille Christus et nos Christi.* (3) That " the Paulicians adored their elect ones as living representatives of Christ ". (4) That the Transubstantiation of their Eucharist was not of the Elements but of the bodies of those who partook of them. (5) That it was Celebrated at night, like the Last Supper, in an ordinary house and sitting at a common table. (6) That

---

[1] HISTOIRE ET DOCTRINE DE LA SECTE DES CATHARES OU ALBIGEOIS, by C. Schmidt, 2 vols., Paris, 1849.

[2] The MS. is in the BIBLIOTHÈQUE MUNICIPALE DE LYON. It was published in facsimile by M. L. Clédat, *anno* 1887.

[3] *Il présente des traits dialectaux propres à la région qui comprend le Tarn, l'Aude, la Haute-Garonne et l'Ariège, région qui est celle où les Albigeois étaient le plus répandus.* Louis Palauqui : LA VÉRITÉ SUR L'ALBIGÉISME, n.d., p. 12.

[4] Cf. *Adhoremus Patrem et Filium et Spiritum Sanctum* (repeated three times).

it was not merely figurative, the Eucharistic Meal having a mystical value. (7) That it made use of a single loaf.

We have seen, however, that the Cathar Communion is wanting in the Lyons Manuscript, while the Trinitarian Formula in the Latin Prayers is identical with that of Rome, whereas the Adoptionist Formula appears to have been *In nomine Dei Patris et Filii Spiritus Sancti*, implying—if it can be called translatable—a very curious procession of the Divine Persons.[1] Our other sources of information are in the records and testimonies of the persecuting Church, and they stand at their dubious value, whatever it is. One example is Isaac Catholicos and his summary of Paulician tenets, according to which " Christ did not hand down to us " an instruction to celebrate the offering of Bread in Churches, the homes of the faithful being consecrated sufficiently by the presence of the Elect therein. There is otherwise the evidence of Eckbert on the Cathar Sacrament, identified with that of the Paulicians. The Perfecti were Shrines of the Christ Spirit, the Vessels of Christ, before whom the ordinary believers prostrated themselves. The flesh of the Perfecti was that of Christ, Whose body they were ; and it was therefore one and the same thing to affirm the conversion of Eucharistic Elements into their body and blood or into that of the Saviour. From another point of view the Elements were lifeless in themselves, the change being in the body of the Elect, and their conversion was communicated to the Bread and Wine in the Office of Blessing, comparable seemingly to the tingeing power of the Stone in Alchemy. The points are put more strongly when Eckbert speaks of the heretics whom he found in the neighbourhood of Trèves and Cologne about 1160. It is certified (1) that the Masses celebrated in Churches were disdained by them ; (2) that the true Priests were to be found among them only ; (3) that they alone could " make the Body of Christ at their tables ". The witness, however, was deceitful, from Eckbert's standpoint, as they were not referring to " the true Body of Christ ", born of the Blessed Virgin, but to their own flesh nourished at their own tables and regarded as the Body of the Lord.

Schmidt brings together some important testimonies on the hostile side in his study of Albigensian Doctrines and Customs, dwelling on the simplicity of the cult and its religious usages, the absence of ornaments, statues, pictures and especially of the Cross, which was regarded with horror as the instrument-in-chief of the Passion. His account of the Eucharistic Service is given at some length, citing Gretser, Reinerius, the Council of Narbonne (1243), Canon 29, and other sources. It may be rendered as follows.[2] " Before taking seat at the table the

---

[1] *Les Cathares substituaient au dogme catholique de l'unité de la substance divine et de la trinité des personnes égales entre elles, la doctrine d'un Dieu-Père existant de toute éternité, aux emanations infinies, d'un Fils et d'un Esprit Saint (Paraclet), dieux par origine, mais anges par destinée, inférieurs au Père quoique consubstantiels à lui.* L. Palauqui, *Op. cit.*, p. 16, citing Schmidt and J. Guiraud : CARTULAIRE DE N.-D. DE PROUILLE.

[2] Schmidt, *Op. cit.*, I, p. 129.

Lord's Prayer was said and the Blessing pronounced. Thereafter a Minister or the eldest among the Perfecti, took bread, blessed and distributed it in morsels to all present, saying : May the Grace of our Lord be with you for ever. Each communicant partook thereupon of his portion in silent recollection." This, according to Schmidt, represented the prim tive agape or Love-Feast, symbolical of Brotherhood. In his opinion many believers regarded the Bread as really blessed and termed it Bread of God or Bread of the Holy Prayer. In the days of persecution the Perfecti went about in the houses of the faithful and blessed the Household Bread, so that it could be eaten in private at convenient times, in which manner they were never without the nourishment of souls. Notwithstanding, however, the importance thus attached obviously to the Communion Service and its Office in Bread,[1] Schmidt affirms that the Sect rejected all mystical signification relative to the Body of Jesus Christ, in the sense ascribed thereto by the orthodox Eucharistic System. Above all they recognised no supernatural transformation resulting from the Blessing of Bread, which never represented the material Body of Christ, since this was phantasmatic only, according to Catharist dualism.

In so far as Conybeare is right in his contention that the Paulician or Adoptionist Church was fundamentally one and the same with that of the Albigenses, it will be seen that Schmidt's evidences are at issue therewith, as the following excerpt from the KEY OF TRUTH will establish more clearly. " That our Mediator and Intercessor Jesus Christ, the Lamb of God, took the Bread in His hands and blessed it, this the Holy Evangelists declare. That is to say, He earnestly besought the Almighty Father that He would change the Bread into His (Christ's) true precious Body. This is why the texts say He blessed, that is, He prayed the Lord (Father) that He would change the Bread truly into His (Christ's) Body. And so it was changed assuredly by the Spirit of the Heavenly Father. And when He (Jesus) saw that the Bread was changed into His Body, then He thanked the Almighty Father for having made it into His Body and Blood."[2] If this means anything, the Bread and Wine were transubstantiated at the Last Supper by the Prayer of Jesus, the power of God the Father and of His Holy Spirit into the living Flesh and Blood of the Nazarene Christ. We may compare a further passage from the same text as follows. " Now, our Lord Jesus Christ willed to distribute his Holy Flesh and Blood unto disciples and believers. He began with the following figure. He opened their minds, saying : My Flesh is the true food and my Blood is the true drink. Again he said : I am the Bread of Life which came down from Heaven. He that eateth this Bread shall live for ever. When our Lord had ended these figures, many of the Disciples turned back. Then he said to the remaining Disciples : Do ye go and get ready for us the Table of Holiness, where I shall presently perform the Mystery of Salvation, for My own Believers and Beloved

[1] Ib., p. 132.   [2] Conybeare, Op. cit., p. 123.

Ones. And when it was eventide Jesus went and sat down, and the twelve with Him. He took one loaf and said : Take ye, eat. This is My BODY which for you and many is distributed unto the expiation and remission of sins. (So also saith He in regard to the Cup) ".[1] It will be seen that in this manner the KEY OF TRUTH bears witness in one place to a literal conversion and suggests in another that the words of Christ on the subject were speech in figures. It is not surprising therefore that Conybeare lamented the loss or destruction of the Paulician and Catharist Sacramentaries. In the case of the Paulicians, however, it seems clear on the whole that the Celebrant or Minister not only stood, by his Office, in the place of Christ but was actually trans-figured into Him mystically, from which it would follow that in Blessing or Consecrating the Eucharistic Elements, using the words of the Master, they became, for those who believed, that which they were to the recipients at the Last Supper, whether by way of representation in the Tertullian sense or by the Transubstantiation of Roman Doctrine.

These evidences and counter-evidences may be compared with the Sieur de Joinville's story of certain Albigensians who came to Simon de Montfort and invited him to see with his own eyes the miracle of Bread and Wine, which had become visible Flesh and Blood in the hands of their Priest at the Consecration. Simon answered : See it on your own part, if you do not believe ; but as for me I have firm faith in the Holy Sacrament of the Altar as the Church teaches, and hence I shall look for that blessing in Heaven which awaits those who have not seen and yet have believed. It is said that St. Louis was fond of telling this story, obviously not on account of the alleged sectarian miracle but as an illustration of perfect faith. The Joinville Memoirs belong to the close of the thirteenth century and Montfort died under the walls of Toulouse in 1216, when Louis IX was a child. He succeeded his father in 1226. It would look as if there were strange claims about concerning the Eucharist as practised by some or other of the Sects in Southern France, where the Albigensian Crusade was raging. Many things passed at that period by general and ignorant ascription under the Albigensian name, but they correspond badly enough with all that we know of the Catharists, while the rest are not to be distinguished one from another at this day.

The Albigensian collection at Lyons includes a Provençal New Testament in use by that Sect, and it has been said—not unexpectedly —to be characterised by peculiar features ; but I cannot trace that it has been edited. There remains, however, one other text, the authen-ticity of which does not seem to have been challenged, and it is decisive from the doctrinal standpoint. This is the BOOK OF JOHN THE EVANGELIST, LIBER SANCTI JOANNIS, extant only in Latin and printed originally by I. Benoist in his HISTOIRE DES ALBIGEOIS, Paris, 1691, Vol. I, pp. 283–296. It was transcribed by or for him from the Archives of the Inquisition at Carcassonne, and an inscription on the MS. affirms

---

[1] Conybeare, *Op. cit.*, p. 123.

that " this is the Secret Book of the Heretics of Concorèze, brought
from Bulgaria by their Bishop Nazarius : full of errors." Whether the
heretics in question were pure Albigensians and Catharists must remain
an open question. It was included by J. C. Thilo in his CODEX
APOCRYPHUS N.T., and a variant text was published by Döllinger
in BEITRÄGE ZUR MITTELALTERLICHEN SEKTENGESCHICHTE, from a
fourteenth-century MS. at Vienna, described as imperfect towards
the end. The Archives of the Inquisition at Carcassonne demand and
would repay exploration. My full knowledge of the LIBER is a debt
owing to Mr. M. R. James' APOCRYPHAL GOSPELS, impression of 1926,
which made me acquainted also with the work of Benoist. He describes
the BOOK OF JOHN as a Bogomile production, and in respect of Bishop
Nazarius there is cited his examination by Rainer in CONTRA
WALDENSES, Vol. VI. It follows that there is a connection established
with this Sect, whether or not Nazarius was himself a Waldensian
Prelate. It is obvious that there is no need or opportunity to investigate
or report here upon these obscure questions. The Johannine text
comprises an interlocutory discourse between the Beloved Disciple
and " our Lord Jesus Christ," recorded by the former and revealing
that which be learned as he lay upon the Master's breast.[1] It includes
a hectic account of Satan, his estate before the Fall, the activities
connected with his rebellion and that which followed thereon. At a
certain stage Satan cried to the Father for mercy, on the ground that
he would pay all. It was granted for " even unto seven days," and
during this period Satan made the world, separating the earth from the
waters, kindling the light of the moon and the light of stars, commanding
the earth to produce living things, and finally creating man, apparently
in his own likeness, but whose body of clay was animated by an Angel
belonging to the Third Heaven. An Angel of the Second Heaven
entered into the body of the woman. Satan also made Paradise. The
Fall of man followed, by the evil spirit tempting Adam and Eve to
fulfil the act of sex, begetting in this manner sons of the Serpent and
sons of the devil, " even unto the end of this world." That is to say,
the sex act continues, bringing fallen Angels into the bodies of women
—presumably by the fact of conception—where they " receive flesh
from the lust of the flesh." It is added : " so is the kingdom of Satan
accomplished."

The Mosaic Revelation was the work of the evil spirit and it seems
to have been preceded by a Secret Teaching in sixty-seven Books,
written by Enoch, when Satan had raised him " upon the firmament "
and " shewed him his godhead." They taught " the custom of sacrifice
and unrighteous Mysteries." When the Father sent Christ into the
world His Angel Mary had preceded Him. He " entered in by the ear
and came forth by the ear." To hinder this Divine Mission Satan
raised up his own Angel, " even Elias the Prophet, baptizing with
water." It is added that the " Disciples of John marry and are given

----

[1] Appendix I, Note 21.

in marriage," but not those of Jesus, who are as the Angels of Heaven. The Disciples of Jesus are baptized also with water, and it is their title to see the Kingdom of Heaven. The Albigensian Baptism of the Paraclete is apparently a later revelation and is not mentioned in the BOOK OF JOHN, which proceeds to describe the Last Days and the coming of Christ to Judgment.

There is only one conclusion to be drawn from the evidence thus collected briefly, and it is this, namely, that the attempt to connect the Catharists, Perfecti and other Sects of Southern France, as we know them by the evidence surviving, with the literature of the Holy Grail is a marriage of things which can never be brought together. We may be all of us Catharists at heart in the depths of our sympathy, when we remember the Albigensian Crusade ; but we can have no part in their views, though they may awaken a curious interest, like the latest decoded Babylonian Myth. There is one thing more. On the hypothesis that the Grail Mythos is itself a veil, we must be content to admit that it is like the Veil of Isis which no man can raise rather than tolerate the suggestion that these nightmare faiths are behind it.

It is not manifestly impossible that a cryptic literature like Alchemy, which has proclaimed from the beginning that its use of specific terms is not to be taken literally, may be concerned with a very different object from its supposed transmutation of metals. It is not impossible that some persons who adopted its terminology may have used it on their own part in a sense which differed from others, so that there may have been two schools of practitioners. It is intolerable, however, to propose that the literature of the Holy Grail, though it treats on the surface of Secret Eucharistic Words, of an Arch-Natural Mass and of the most Sacred Relics in all the world of Relics, was committed in reality, but deeply beneath that surface, to denial and rejection of the Mass and disdain of Relics. But this is a highly economical picture of the utter contradiction in terms between outward Grail texts and their inward meaning if Grail literature was put forward, so to speak, in secret by Albigensian and Catharist Sects ; if it was part of a subversive movement in respect of Roman Doctrine and Practice ; if it was heretical on the Person of Christ, heretical on Sacramental Efficacy, on Trinitarian Theology and on the status of the Blessed Virgin. This being the logical position of the case, it is permissible to proceed and indicate that such a thesis has never been advanced by any writer who was adequately equipped in the matter of critical knowledge concerning Grail texts. It is an old story of the past which called to be set aside then on this ground only, and it recurs occasionally, both in France and England, with no better offset. But it serves now, as it served then, to create and magnify an aspect of suspicion about the subject at large, which is sufficiently difficult in view of its own claims, and it has seemed to demand consideration from this standpoint.[1]

---

[1] Appendix I, Note 22.

BOOK XI

FURTHER CRITICAL APPARATUS : THE RITUAL HYPOTHESIS

THE ARGUMENT

I. The Grail and Eleusis.—Inferences from preceding Conclusions—Romance as a Vehicle of deep Experience—Mystical Aspects of the Grail Legend—Transit of the Hallowed Object—The Grail Stone—The Grail and the Instituted Mysteries—Speculations of Simrock—Symbolism of the Vegetation God—The Blood of the Dying God—The Precious Blood of the Christian Mystery—Reveries of Ernst Martin—Nitze on the Fisher King in the Grail Romances—The Grail as an Agrarian Cult—Alleged Derivation from Eleusis—Eleusinian Mysteries—Promise of the Rites to its Candidates —Legend of Demeter and Kore—Seedtime, Harvest and the Story of the Soul—The Soul in the Mysteries—Life in the World to come—Lesser and Greater Mysteries—Safeguarding of Initiated Souls—Their way of Escape—Eleusinian Testimonies on Eternal Beatitude—Nitze on the Fisher King and the Questing Knight—Contrast of Grail Initiations and those of Eleusis —Failure of supposed Correlation between Grail Initiations and those of Eleusis. II. The Grail and the Mysteries of Adonis.—The Story of the Soul in Schools of Western Mysticism—Its Rebirth, Regenerated Life, Mystical Death, Resurrection and Ascension—Search for Analogies of this Scheme in Old Instituted Mysteries—Mr. A. P. Cooke's Speculations on the Neophyte of Egyptian Rites—Initiations and Advancements in the Mysteries offered no Individual Experience—The Search a Failure—Miss Weston's Views—The Grail as a confused Record of Vegetation Rites—Her Search Among Adonis Rites—Adonis, Attis and Tammuz—Observations on the Adonis Legend—Sex-Complex of the Cultus—Alleged Spiritual Teaching of the Nature Cults—Liberation of the Soul—The Philosophumena of Hippolytus and its Naassene Document—Its alleged Justification of Vegetation Rites and their Import—The Time Gulf between Fertility Rites and the Grail Epoch—Suggested Perpetuation of the old Rites—Alleged Survival at the Present Day—The Grail and the Worship of Mithra—Criticism of this Claim—Miss Weston's Position Thereon—Mithraic Rites and their Spiritual Significance—The Mithra Cult and that of Kybele and Attis—The Feast of Spiritual Life—Death and Resurrection of the Candidate in the Phrygian Mystery—Alleged August Nature of the Mithraic Rite—The *Taurobolium* and its Baptism of Blood. III. The Grail as a Mystery of Initiation.—Initiations Suggested by the Grail Quests—Another Point of View Intimated by the Story of Galahad—A Study of the Other Texts—Their Attempted Reconstruction in Ritual Form—The Law of Succession in the Quest of the Holy Grail—The Question and its unsolved Mystery—Percival and the Priesthood—A Place of Masses in the Perlesvaus—Galahad and the Sacred Host—The Host in the Parzival—The Grail as a Mystery of Christian Religion—Its Receptions are as if into a Secret Church—Difficulties of this View—Recurrence to the Removal of the Grail—The Grail as a Testimony of Loss and Dereliction. IV. Israel and its Holy Assembly.—Thought in the Middle Ages—The School of Christian Mysticism—Records of Other Schools—The Voice of the Grail—After what manner it was followed by a Voice of Israel—The Schools of Kabbalism—The Loss of the Word in Israel —Spain and Jewish Theosophy—Scheme of Theosophical Kabbalism—A Great Book of Debates—Ancient Kabbalism as a School of Adeptship— Absence of Ceremonial Forms. V. OF SPIRITUAL ALCHEMY.—Secret Churches and Secret Tribunals—The Law of Silence and the Law of the Sign—An Illustration Drawn from Craft Masonry—A Strange Leaven at Work in Grail Texts—Their Suggestion of a Great Experiment—The Arch-Natural Mass—The PERLESVAUS and the Galahad Quest—The Hope of Theosophical Israel—The Witness of Another School—Physical and Spiritual Alchemists—Heinrich and Khunrath and Jacob Böhme—Their Mystical Understanding of the Hermetic Subject—Way of Attainment in Alchemy—Rise of other Witnesses—an Unincorporated Sodality—Mystical Alchemy a Doctrine of Attainment only—Its Terminology Identical with that of the Physical Alchemists—The Philosophical Stone and the Tingeing Christ—Points of Terminology Common to both Schools—Tentative Experiment in the Explanation of the Mystical Theme—The Art and its Vessel— The Mercury, Sulphur and Salt—The Mystical Stone—The Matter of the Work—Alchemy and the Eucharist—The Grail and the Mystery of Faith. VI. ANALOGIES OF QUEST IN MASONRY.—The Craft Degrees—Judgment on the High Grades—An Old Thesis of Ragon—Manifestation of Doctrine in Terms of Building Symbolism—The Craft Legend and the Alleged House of Doctrine—The Question in the Master Grade—The Substituted Master Grade—The Quest in Masonry—The Word of Life and the Word of Death— The Temple in the Heart—Moses and the Tables of the Law—Sidelights Drawn from High Grades—Grades of the Holy Sepulchre—Of Substituted Restorations—The Substituted Sanctuary—Masonry as an Index-Finger pointing to other Rites—Summary of Secret Things Perpetuated through the Centuries. VII. THE SECRET CHURCH OF ECKARTSHAUSEN.—Intimations of a later Period—A Holy Assembly Behind the Christian Church— After what Manner it Calls to be Understood—The Root Fact behind it —Actuality and Permanence of an Ancient Experiment—The Holy Assembly and the Higher Mystery of the Eucharist—Eckartshausen on the Second Birth—The Process of Regeneration—The Advanced School and the Visible Church—The Inmost Sanctuary—The Communion of Saints—The First Estate of Man and Restoration thereunto—The Stages of Regenerated Life—Separation of the Inner Sanctuary and the Earthly Temple—Their designed Reunion—The Incarnation and Reunion with God —The Royal and Sacerdotal Science—Regeneration and the Mystery of the Eucharist—Testimony of the Chevalier Lopuhin—Errors of Expression in both Witnesses—Summary Observations on the Office of the Secret Church. VIII. SUMMARY.—General Conclusion on all the Schools of Symbolism— Mysteries of Divine Attainment—Evidences of Secret Doctrine in the Grail Literature—The Realm behind Doctrine—Our Consciousness of Loss Everywhere—Of implied Restoration—The Quest Perpetuated—Expectation and Attainment.

BOOK XI

FURTHER CRITICAL APPARATUS: THE RITUAL HYPOTHESIS

I

THE GRAIL AND ELEUSIS

THE Books of the Holy Grail are either of purely literary, antiquarian and knightly interest, or they are more and other. If literary, antiquarian and chivalrous only, they can and should be left to the antiquaries, the critics and the folk-lore societies, without attempting to discover subversive meanings therein. But if they exceed these measures it is not improbable antecedently, having regard to their subject, that the excess belongs to religion on its deeper side, not excluding the mystical element, and to those generally who recognise—being themselves mystics—that the Legends of the Soul are met with in many places, often unexpectedly enough, and that wherever found they have issues outside all that is understood, commonly and critically, by Comparative Religion and the origin of Religious Belief. The mystical element—to repeat the conventional description—outside the considerations put forward, is for such persons of all importance, while it is otherwise and invariably the only thing that is really vital in Legends.

The impression which is left upon the mind by the conclusions already established is assuredly that the " divine event " is not that, especially or only, " towards which the whole creation moves ", but is a term, both here and now, to which souls can approximate and wherein they can rest by the centre. Across the threshold of the Galahad Quest we pass, as if out of worlds of enchantment, worlds of faërie, worlds of the mighty Morgan le Fay into realms of parable and then —all parable transcending—into a region of dual meaning, more deeply unrealised. So also, after having reflected on the external side of the Romances and the preliminary analogies of things that are inward, we pass, as we approach the end of our research, into a world of which nothing but the veils and their emblazonments have been declared so far. No other Romances of Chivalry exhibit the characteristics which we discern in the Books of the Holy Grail at their best and highest ; but if we do not know categorically why and how Romance came to be a vehicle for the expression under symbols of man's deepest experience, we have reasons—and more than enough—to determine that it was not automatic, not arbitrary, and yet that it was not fortuitous : it came about in the nature of things by the successive exaltation of a Legend which had capacity for exaltation into transcendence. The story of Galahad is not like the institution of the Ritual belonging to the Third Craft Grade in Masonry, which seems without antecedents that are traceable in the primitive elements of the early Building Guilds.[1] By successive steps the Legend of the Grail was built up till it reached that stage when the Hierarchies could begin to come down and the soul of Galahad could ascend. It is important to establish this fact, because in that which remains to be said I must guard against any supposition that a conventional Secret Society or Sect took over the Romances, edited them and interpenetrated the texts with mystical elements. That is the kind of hypothesis which occult interests might have manufactured sincerely enough in the old days—had they known their way through the literature—and it would have had a certain warrant, because there is evidence that this is exactly the kind of work which in a few given cases was performed by Concealed Orders.[2] The Grail as a literature came into other hands, which worked after their own manner and worked well, though not, it must be admitted, in harmony with the art of story-telling. They were not, as we shall see, those of an Incorporated Order in the modern notion of the words.

So far I have defined, but in one sense only, the position of the literature. It remains to be said that what has been termed from the beginning the major implicits, as they project vaguely and evasively upon the surface, are integral elements of the mystical aspect. But they must be taken here in connection with one feature of the Quest which is in no sense implied, because it will concern us in an important manner at or towards the close of all. I refer to the Recession of the Grail. There is no need to remind anyone after so many enumerations that the final testimony of all the French Quests is—in one or another way—that the Grail was withdrawn. It is not always by a removal in space ; it is not always by assumption into Heaven. In the German Cycle the Temple was inaccessible from the beginning and the Palladium never travelled, till—once and for all—it was carried, as in a great Procession, to the furthest East. Wolfram left it in primeval concealment ; but this did not satisfy one of the later poets, who married more closely—as we have seen—the Grail Legend to that of Prester John. Now it might be more easy to attain translation, like St. Paul, than to find that Sanctuary in India where, by the assumption,

---

[1] See my NEW ENCYCLOPÆDIA OF FREEMASONRY, Vol. I, pp. 334, 335, 366–368 and elsewhere.

[2] It is proposed, for example, that the Mysteries of Mithra drew something at a late period from those of Attis and later still from Christianity itself. The Rites of Attis seem also to have borrowed from the Mithraic Cult. In modern days Emblematic Freemasonry was developed from old Craft Constitutions with the help of a Hiramic Myth, itself indebted to Jewish Theosophy—at however far a distance—for its idea of a Lost Word.

it must be assumed to remain. Wolfram was within the measures of his own symbolism when he left the Grail at Mont Salvatch, not removing to the East that which in his case did not come therefrom. Albrecht, who tells of the transit, took first the precaution to change the Hallowed Object. It may well be that ultimate removal was inherent to the whole conception from the beginning, concurrently with the Secret Words, and, at a later period, with the peculiar claim concerning Sacerdotal Succession.[1] The testimony itself was twofold, because in addition to the withdrawal of the living Sign, certain texts tell us of the House that is emptied of its Hallows : these are in particular the PERLESVAUS and the Quest of Galahad. There is also Manessier's conclusion of the CONTE DEL GRAAL ; but no very important inference can be drawn therefrom.[2] One of our immediate concerns will be to find the analogies of this prevailing conception elsewhere in the world of symbols. It is at this point curiously that one element of Grail history which has been ascribed somehow to Kyot comes to our assistance, providing—sub nomine Wolfram, or otherwise—an intermediary between the literature of Mystical Romance and—as we shall learn—the obvious text-books of the Secret Schools. It opens, I think, strange vistas of intellectual wonder and enchantment. We have heard already that the Stone which is identified with the Grail in Wolfram was at one time a Stone in the crown of Lucifer ; and seeing that, according to other Legends, the thrones left vacant by the fallen angels are reserved for human souls,[3] it becomes intelligible why the Grail was brought, in the hypothesis, to earth and what may have been signified by the mystical jewel. The Stone in the crown of Lucifer symbolises the great estate from which the archangel fell. It was held by the Fathers of the Church that, when still in the delights of Paradise, Lucifer was adorned by all manner of precious stones, understanding mystically of him what in the text of the prophet Ezekiel is said literally of the Prince of Tyre : *In deliciis paradisi Dei fuisti ; omnis lapis preciosus operimentum tuum : sardius, topazius, et jaspis, chrysolithus, et onyx, et beryllus, sapphirus, et carbunculus, et smaragdus*[4]—nine kinds of stones, according to Gregory the Great, because of the nine Choirs of Angels. And Bartolocci, the Cistercian,[5] following all authorities, understands these jewels to signify the knowledge and

---

[1] The Secret Words were the Mystery of a Mass in the Transcendence, while the thesis of Super-Apostolical Succession—though it ignored the Secret Words—created *ex hypothesi* a Priesthood for the Celebration of a Mass which could be said by no other Ministry in the world of Christendom. These now familiar intimations suggest a Secret Church, as it might be, speaking at a venture, of those who—out of all public view, knowledge or suspicion—put in practice the Mysteries of Inward Experience shadowed forth in the Mystical Theology, *sub nomine* Dionysius. But again it would be no organised Church, equipped with Liturgy and Sacraments, under a Hierarchic Rule. I am devoting some later sections to historical developments of this subject when the canon of Grail literature had closed. They will serve as object-lessons, from which we can look back upon the past to the possibilities of the Grail period.

[2] See Book XII, Sect. 2.

[3] See W. W. Comfort : THE QUEST OF THE HOLY GRAIL, translated from the critical text of Albert Pauphilet, 1923, p. 174. Cf. Pauphilet, *Op. cit.*, p. 215.

[4] PROPHETIA EZECHIELIS, *cap.* XXVIII, 13.

[5] MAGNA BIBLIOTHECA RABBINICA, I, pp. 309–316, and especially p. 312, col. 1.

other ornaments of grace with which Lucifer was adorned in his original state as the *perfecta similitudo Dei*—in other words, the light and splendour of the Hidden Knowledge. It would follow on this interpretation (1) that the Grail Stone in no sense belongs to folk-lore ; (2) that it offers in respect of its origin no connection with the idea of physical maintenance, except in the sense that the things which sustain the soul maintain also the body, because the *panis quotidianus* depends from the *panis supersubstantialis ;* (3) that the Wisdom of the Grail is an Eucharistic Wisdom, because the descent of an Arch-Natural Host takes place annually—even in the Wolfram version—to renew the virtues thereof ; (4) that the correspondence of this is, in other Cycles of the Legend, the Host which is consecrated extra-validly by the Secret Words, and so also the correspondence of the Stone which comes from Heaven is the Cup which goes thereto ; but in fine (5) that the jewel in the crown of Lucifer is called also the Morning Star, and thus it is not less than certain that the Grail returns whence it came.[1]

The various problematical aspects of the Grail Legend, and the several schools of thought which have offered light thereon, having been examined up to this stage, a question arises whether they have points of correspondence with any scheme of the Instituted Mysteries, whether any element which is present in the Romances can be regarded as an approximate or far-off reflection of something which at that time or previously was known and done in any of the Secret Schools. The possibility has presented itself frequently to the mind of scholarship, which, having performed admirable work in its study of the Grail texts, has been and is still in search of some final explanation concerning them. The shadow of the old Order of the Temple has haunted them in dreams fitfully, and they have lingered almost longingly over vague imagined analogies with the Orgies of Adonis and Tammuz. As behind the Christian Symbolism of the extant literature there spreads the whole world of pagan folk-lore—with its Cauldrons, Cups and Talis-manic Stones—so, at least antecedently, there might be implied also some old scheme of Initiation. The examination of this thesis, if not in itself acceptable, may enable us to offer an alternative, under proper judgments of reserve, as something which may be held tentatively until later circumstances of research either lead it into demonstration or furnish a more adequate substitute.

We have seen that in the year 1842 Karl Simrock published a version of Wolfram's PARZIVAL in modern German.[2] In the critical observa-tions attached thereto the Great Reliquary was connected with the Germanized Myth of Herodias and St. John the Baptist, with Myths of Freyja and Odin, the death of Wotan at or about the summer Solstice, the death of Balder, and so backward to the Greek story of

---

[1] I am speaking obviously in the sense of parable, the sense in which Gregory the Great understood Ezekiel and Bartolocci talked about Lucifer. It is not the sense of the so-called level-headed man, for whom the Sacred Host is a wafer of unleavened bread and the Morning Star is a moving light in a mundane sky.

[2] It went through successive editions, the last appearing at Stuttgart in 1876.

Venus and Adonis, the Phrygian Attis and the Egyptian Osiris. The Grail, like these, shadowed forth " the creative power dwelling in the blood of the dying god ". We are brought thus early in the criticism of the Grail subject to the thesis of the Vegetation God as its root and essence. It was pointed out that the blood of Adonis produced the Anemone in the year following his death ; that of Attis brought to birth the Violet ; while the healing Johanniskrant sprang from the blood of St. John the Baptist.[1] It seems obvious that these slender fables belonged to poetic fancy rather than motived Myth ; and so far as I am aware Simrock's suggestion passed unnoticed. As regards the decapitation of the Precursor, it has no connection with the Grail ; a head in a Dish is carried in no Procession except in the Mabinogi of Peredur, which we have found to derive from Chrétien, with the Grail omitted.[2] As regards furthermore the creative power dwelling in the blood of the Dying God, if the Reliquary of the Romances is derived from this Mythos, so also by implication is the whole Christian story of Redemption, following the hypothesis of the reverie, a point which Simrock presumably was not proposing to affirm. It happens, moreover, that the Precious Blood of the Christian Mystery is not creative but redemptive, unless in the sense that it brought forth Children of the Second Birth ; and this, I suggest, is a Christo-Mystical aspect of the subject which was beyond the purview of the German scholar. Finally, neither the Grail nor its content manifests creative power in any one of its aspects. When it figures as a Food-providing Talisman, it may be said to maintain but does not originate life. It answers so little to any scheme of a Vegetation-God-Culture that if and when the failure to ask " one little Question " causes blight in the land, the Reliquary or Talisman can do nothing to mend matters : for the termination of those woes and enchantments, there is one who must return whence he came and fulfil that which was neglected previously ; and through years of adventure, years of Quest and years of God-forgetting, the task remains with him.

I conclude that Simrock's thesis is of the same value as that of Ernst Martin, another PARZIVAL editor, who maintained much later[3] (1) that the maimed King of the Grail was the wounded Arthur, taken for his healing to Avalon and expected to return therefrom ; (2) that Arthur represented the Vegetation God. It happens, however, that in Classical Mythos the God who dies is also the God who rises, and vegetation therefore reappears ; but Arthur has not returned in any Arthurian Saga, whence it follows that seedtime might indeed continue, but no harvest could be reaped. As to the identification of Arthur with the Grail King, again the mania of hypothesis could not further go. It means

[1] We may compare the mysterious undescribed herb which is found in the neighbourhood of the Grail. See Book VI, sect. 2.
[2] We have seen that " a glorious Head " is carried by an Angel in the codex of the GRAND SAINT GRAAL which was used by Dr. Furnivall.
[3] See ZUR GRALSAGE, which appeared at Strasbourg in 1880, pp. 31 et seq. Also the Introduction to Martin's edition of Wolfram, Strasbourg, 1900–1903, pp. lviii et seq.

(1) that the Grail King of the CONTE DEL GRAAL dies when Perceval is with Arthur at the Royal Court, so that there is a dead and living Arthur, of whom the latter attends the Coronation of Perceval, the new King ; (2) that in the Didot-Modena text, Brons, who is Arthur in the dream, dies and is assumed by Angels, which notwithstanding, and at the same time, he is sitting with his Knights at the Round Table : afterwards he is carried over a great water to Avalon ; (3) that he dies also in the PERLESVAUS but subsequently visits the new Grail King, Perceval, at the Grail Castle ; (4) that in the Galahad QUESTE he joins a Company of White Monks, and so ends his days presumably ; that in DIU CRÔNE he is one of the Dead-Alive in the Grail Castle and vanishes when the spell is broken : yet Gawain returns to Court ; (6) that in the PARZIVAL, as in the CONTE, Perceval is with Arthur when he is called to the Grail Kinghood ; but Anfortas, who is Arthur, is also at the Grail Castle, is there healed by Perceval and remains with him. It may seem preposterous to offer this exposure of an exposition which exposes itself ; but I am concerned with elucidating the career of the Vegetation-God-hypothesis in Grail literature, and it is no part of my design to conceal the fact when it fails signally.

Through the days of Birch-Hirschfeld and others of the competent German school the subject slept, or was only stirred in its sleep by a casual reference in some French, German or other class-review, till Prof. W. J. Nitze arose under the auspices of the Modern Language Association of America and produced his elaborate and suggestive study of the FISHER KING IN THE GRAIL ROMANCES, which is the first methodical thesis on the so-called Ritual Theory and is referable to the year 1909.[1] The speculation supposes that the Grail in its origin belongs to an Agrarian Cult and as such connects with Eleusis at a far distance, the intermediaries being Rites practised in later times, on or about the Mediterranean littoral, and finally a Celtic Cultus which apparently had seedtime and harvest for its subject and which drew from that region. As there is no trace of the Rite in any place or time of the Celtic world, it would be idle to examine, from this point of view, the very numerous fashions of Mystery in Herculaneum, Pompeii and other cities of the sea-board in Southern Europe. At the root it seems idle also to discuss the hypothesis itself ; but it must be remembered (1) that my task includes the whole critical apparatus of the Grail subject, and (2) that the Ritual Theory once earned a certain auditorium in England, chiefly through Miss Weston's insistence, and is not to be ignored in consequence. As regards Prof. Nitze, there is perhaps no other theme in which it would be tolerated for a moment to suggest a vital connecting link when there is no evidence for its existence. Looking back upon some of my own researches, what might I not have achieved with the talismanic problems (1) of Spiritual

---

[1] See PUBLICATIONS OF THE MODERN LANGUAGE ASSOCIATION OF AMERICA, Vol. XXIV, pp. 365–418, a desirable collection of materials. A sympathetic and imaginative heart drew me to Nitze when he dared to think, so late as 1903, that the Grail might have had a Latin Original, little as I could share the dream.

Alchemy, if I could have postulated a decisive but vanished text, ante-dating Heinrich Khunrath and Jacob Böhme ;[1] (2) of the Rosy Cross, had I dared to imagine a codex of its Traditional History midwise in the fifteenth century, or perhaps much earlier ;[2] (3) of the Hiramic Myth in Emblematic Freemasonry, if I ventured to postulate an undiscovered Old Constitution—so called—behind it ?[3] There are many yesterdays of reflection and research when things of this kind were possible, but I should be read out of court to-day.

Let us glance, however, for a moment at those Mysteries of Eleusis which lie behind the thesis of Prof. Nitze, remembering that we are not concerned with the Processions and Spectacles but with a bare question of outline. They communicated not only an assured pledge that, for those who received them, a life of bliss followed the experience of death but that it was reserved to them alone. For the Profane there was indeed another life, but it was one of desolation and misery. The guarantee, it is to be remarked, was unconditional,[4] not consequent, for example, on an earthly life shaped thereafter in conformity with the prospect unfolded. The fact of Initiation sufficed. It is useful to dwell upon this and compare the conditions of the Quest in that story " told for one of the truest and holiest that is in this world ", the Galahad story of the Holy Grail. At the same time the experience of Initiates was something more than a sight of the Pageants, of the terror and darkness of Hades, or the splendours and felicities of Elysium. On the authority, at its high value, of comparatively recent research, there were certain secrets revealed to safeguard the progress of the soul on its way through the world beyond ; and these secrets were couched in verbal formulæ.[5] It belongs to the old magical doctrine of words and names which compelled the Gods themselves.[6]

The Legend of Demeter and Kore, otherwise Persephone, is the Legend of Eleusis—its Traditional History, in the modern parlance of Initiations—and Demeter was a Goddess of Agriculture who taught Attica the Mysteries of Seed and Harvest, by which it emerged from savage into civilised life. When the Initiate of Eleusis attained its highest Grade and became an Epopt there was shewn to him by the Hierophant an Ear of Wheat, as the last message of the Rite. It follows that seedtime and harvest symbolised somehow the story of the soul. The dead body descends into the underworld of the grave, but the soul comes forth alive. In so far as late Platonism, testifying concerning the Mysteries with golden mouths, may be held to connote

---

[1] See THE SECRET TRADITION IN ALCHEMY, 1926.
[2] See THE BROTHERHOOD OF THE ROSY CROSS, 1924.
[3] See EMBLEMATIC FREEMASONRY, 1925.
[4] *Pas plus chez les Grecs que chez les Égyptiens, il n'y a l'idée de mérite ou de démérite ; il n'y a pas des bons et des méchants, mais des initiés et des non-initiés.* Foucart : RECHERCHES SUR L'ORIGINE ET LA NATURE DES MYSTÈRES D'ELEUSIS, 1895, p. 22. There is also his MYSTÈRES D'ELEUSIS, published in 1914, and I refer occasionally to LES GRANDS MYSTÈRES D'ELEUSIS which appeared in 1900, and was reprinted like the RECHERCHES from the MÉMOIRES DE L'ACADÉMIE DES INSCRIPTIONS ET BELLES LETTRES.
[5] Paul Foucart : LES MYSTÈRES D'ELEUSIS, 1912.
[6] François Lenormant : LA MAGIE CHEZ LES CHALDÉENS, 1874.

experiences drawn from the Rites of Eleusis, I have shewn elsewhere[1] that, like Plato before them, they beheld the Rites through his
and their own glass of vision, and ascended with him through contemplation to " the Intelligible Beauty ", even " Communion with the
Gods ". There is no need here to retrace this ground and much less to
explore it further. It is mentioned firstly to check the purely automatic
beatitude which Initiation conferred on the Recipient in the world to
come. There was more in the Mysteries for some than was found by
others : they communicated to each as he was able and willing to
receive. It is certain, in the second place, that if Demeter and Kore
were Goddesses originally of a Vegetation Cultus, they must have
suffered a great transformation at Eleusis, for it follows from all the
records that the Rites delineated the *post mortem* story of the human
soul, though without abandoning utterly the first matter or body-
general of the symbolism : otherwise, an Ear of Corn would not have
been uplifted at the close of all, as *Summa totius Mysterii*. It may seem
an inadequate type to invest with high meanings and encompass by
high pageants ; but we must remember (1) that life is life, and life of all
things sacred ; (2) that life is one and is actually that Isis whose veil
has not been raised by any science of man ; and (3) that the Ear of
Corn is the matter of that daily bread which maintains our life on earth.
It is the greatest of all symbols ; but if there is another to compare
therewith, it is Wine beyond all question ; and we know after what
manner a Greater Mystery than Eleusis has found and symbolised the
Latens Deitas within the *Magnalia Signa* of Bread and Wine.

What, however, was the story of the human soul, as delineated in the
Mysteries ? What its life of the world to come ? Has research
discovered anything to justify the striking comparison of Plutarch, who
says (1) that death is like a Rite of Advancement, and (2) that the
after life is even as another Initiation and a celebration of August
Rites ? There were in reality three stages or Degrees of Initiation and
Advancement, of which the First and the Third were like a Prologue and
Epilogue to the elaborate pageant of the Second. The First was the
Lesser Mysteries and conferred the title of *Mustai* on all who were
admitted. It took place at the Eleusinion of Athens for those Candidates who were assembled at Athens, and in the Court of the Temple
for others at Eleusis itself.[2] We know nothing whatever about the
Ceremonies of the first day, except that they began with a Proclamation concerning those who were excluded from Initiation by the Law
of the Mysteries.[3] On the second day the purification of Candidates
took place in the sea, as also that of their living sacrifices, the pigs which
they must offer to Demeter, an observance that would have appeared
to have followed, possibly forthwith or alternatively on the third

---

[1] NEW ENCYCLOPÆDIA OF FREEMASONRY, Vol. I, s.v. Eleusinian Mysteries.
[2] *Ibid.*, I, p. 107.
[3] Persons who were excluded, in addition to so-called Barbarians—being those
outside what may be regarded as the Greek Empire—were above all murderers and
persons who were ritually unclean.

day.[1] So far as we are aware, this completed the Ceremonial Offices of the Lesser Mysteries, and the *Mustai* passed out of view for a period.

The Greater Mysteries took place at Eleusis alone, the statues of Demeter and Kore being carried thereto in procession, with other sacred objects, a solemn ceremonial which started on the fifth day of the Mysteries and ended in torchlight on the sixth, the latter beginning at sunset. In the Hall of Initiation the *Mustai* beheld in dramatic form (1) the Rape of Kore by Pluto, being the known mythological story, with additions and variants peculiar to the Mysteries and reserved to the Initiates alone ; (2) the pilgrimage of the soul in the underworld, with instructions on the methods by which it could be brought to a happy issue. The *Mustai* were caused " to traverse successively the two regions of the kingdom of Demeter and Pluto, the first with its obstacles, its dangers and the monsters which confronted the deceased ; the second, which represented the Elysian fields, with their serene light ".[2] We are assured also that " in the course of the journey the Hierophant instructed the *Mustai* on the route which must be followed in this last and terrible experience, on the Secret Names of the divinities which they would have to prononuce, the all-powerful formulæ which, recited with appropriate modulations, would put enemies to flight and open an entrance to the blessed dwellings ". The result of this instruction inspired them " with no vague hope but the certain assurance of beatified life in the world below ".[3]

The Lesser and Greater Mysteries are grouped together by criticism, as if they were one Degree, the second being that of the *Epoptai*, for which Candidates became eligible originally at the expiration of twelve months, but later—and in the Christian era—after the lapse of five years.[4] Those who were to be made *Epoptai* witnessed therein the marriage union of Zeus and Demeter, ending, as we have seen, with the Ritual Elevation of the Symbolic Ear of Corn.[5] It is the one and only remanent of a seedtime and harvest cultus that research has discovered at Eleusis. The point which concerns ourselves is that the Mysteries had as their single object the safeguarding of initiated souls on the other side of life. This is their claim and by this are they to be judged alone. They revealed a way of escape for those who chose to take it on the conditions offered and at the price demanded.[6] The alternative was to be plunged in slime and " lead therein a wretched existence which deserved not the name of life ".[7] It happens, however,

---

[1] It is more likely to have followed at once, or the sacrificial victims would have needed another purification.

[2] Foucart, LES GRANDS MYSTÈRES, p. 137.

[3] RECHERCHES, p. 53.

[4] According to Foucart, there were two classes of Initiates only—the Mustai and the Epopts. The Lesser Mysteries were a preparation only, the Greater Mysteries imparted the revelation which constituted Initiation, properly so-called.

[5] *Pour figurer l'union du Dieu et de la Déesse, les deux acteurs sacrés descendaient dans une retraite obscure.* Foucart : RECHERCHES, p. 48.

[6] M. Foucart has shewn that the Fees for Reception and the connected expenses were fairly high.

[7] *Ib.*, p. 21.

that the testimonies concerning eternal beatitude in the Elysian Fields compare unfavourably with even the Spiritistic Revelations of Andrew Jackson Davis on the subject of Posthumous Life in the Summer Land. On the authority of Plutarch, the *Mustai* beheld "pure places and prairies resounding with voices and dances." Sacred words were pronounced, and divine apparitions inspired a religious respect. The perfected Initiate was free to go and come : he celebrated Mysteries, wearing a crown on his head, and lived with holy men. Finally, he had the felicity of beholding the uninitiated plunged in mire and darkness. This also is on Plutarch's authority ; but Aristophanes before him had mentioned the bosks of myrtle where, in the midst of a beautiful light, the Initiates danced and sang to the sound of flutes. If there was anything otherwise done and said at Eleusis to justify the later Greek Philosophers and Theosophists, we are without a record concerning it : the inscriptions fail us, like the Greek and Latin authors, those of the Christian faith included.

In the light of this brief and more than inadequate summary, we can return now to Prof. Nitze and his thesis on the Fisher King ; but in the first place to his notion of the Grail Knight, meaning the Knight on Quest, who is the Initiate of the Mysteries coming down from Eleusis. The latter, however, had no single Postulant, as the Candidates came in great numbers.[1] The alleged Grail Knight is therefore not a personality but a type, and this may seem perhaps the worst interpretation which has been offered unto this day of Galahad, Perceval or Bors. It is unavoidable, however, for the same Ritual procedure applies to all comers and does not distinguish between them. As regards the hypothetical Grail Initiate, it is proposed (1) that he was responsible for the success of the Grail Service, which is ridiculous in view of Greek Mysteries ; (2) that in the case of his failure the crops also failed and the springs ran dry. But Athens and Agra knew nothing of these disasters, since the days of the Rape of Kore and Demeter's wanderings, when as yet there were no Mysteries and consequently no Candidates ; (3) That on his long-delayed success he becomes an Epopt, because he beholds the vision and succeeds the Fisher King. But Perceval beheld it in his failure, even as he did in his triumph, and in the Galahad Quest the attaining Knights not only saw the Grail but carried it away, thus putting an end to the Mysteries, once and for all. Finally, the supposed correlation between supposed Grail Initiations and those of Eleusis reaches its crowning anticlimax when we are reminded that the Grail Knight succeeds the Grail King. *Mustai* or *Epoptai*, it did not happen that any one of the multitude who owed and paid their pig to Demeter, or beheld the Ear of Corn, became the next Hierophant. But all were entitled to succeed, according to this hypothesis.

Having been assured categorically that the Grail Knight's failure to

---

[1] We have to remember that Greek Initiation was a business proposition, a source of revenue and a State institution redounding to the credit of the State.

ask the Grail question causes the crops to fail,[1] we are to learn in the next place that the land lies waste because of the Fisher King's infirmity, which not withstanding he is said to be the representative of the other world and the Guide thereto.   He is nothing of the kind in any of the Grail Romances and, if he were, the Greek Hierophant is he who guides, counsels and safeguards the way through Hades rather than one who leads thereto.   Moreover, he is not maimed, he is not without strength in his bones, has no correspondence with " Nature's declining strength " and finds no consolation in fishing.   He is not under the Spell of a Question ; he is not one of whom anyone would dare to ask ; he expounds but does not answer.   Supposing that the Grail Romances at once conceal and offer intimations concerning a Rite of Initiation, that which will least of all suffer comparison therewith is the ceremonial congeries of Eleusis.

It must be pointed out in conclusion that Prof. Nitze misrepresents unconsciously the Records of the Grail when he says that it is primarily a Food-Providing Vessel.   It figures as such only in (1) The prose LANCELOT, (2) The Galahad Quest, (3) The still later GRAND SAINT GRAAL, all of the Vulgate Cycle—and of course in the German PARZIVAL. It has no such office in Chrétien or in the JOSEPH of Robert de Borron. But these are the primary texts.   It has none also in the DIDOT-MODENA PERCEVAL or in the PERLESVAUS.

II

THE GRAIL AND THE MYSTERIES OF ADONIS

THE life of the soul in God and the story of its deep experience have been portrayed in later Schools of Western Mysticism under the symbolism of a Second Birth, a Life of Regeneration, a Mystical Death, a Resurrection and an *Ascensio Mentis vel Animæ in Deo*.   It is implied here and there in Catholic Mysticism—in Eckhart, Tauler and Bona, among others— but was adopted and developed more especially in later types— among the followers of Jacob Böhme and by Louis Claude de Saint-Martin.   It is the life of Christ in the soul and the life of the soul in Christ.   There is no question that these symbolical representations correspond literally with the states and stages of the soul's experience on the path of return to God, answering after its own manner to the

---

[1] The reader may refer at this point to Book II, sect. 9, but the collation therein could have been carried much further, had space availed. It is to be understood that the Land of Logres is described in some texts as wasted, that water ceased to flow in certain cases and that crops once or twice are said to fail. But the sorcery, distress and interdiction are more often on a larger scale. In Pseudo-Wauchier, Perceval's failure to ask the required Question works the destruction of kingdoms ; in Manessier the work of the Broken Sword not only destroyed Logres but all the surrounding country ; in the PERLESVAUS there was war everywhere. But all the desolation and all the waste seems to be purely nominal, a stated fact which is nowhere exemplified.

Eastern recovered knowledge of the Unity. I have been looking all my life for the analogies of this figurative representation in the records of the past ; and as a student of the Instituted Mysteries there is perhaps no need to say that the Doctrine of Rebirth therein, and the pictured symbolism concerning the Death and Resurrection of the God, suggested intimations of analogous experience in pre-Christian days. In this manner I was brought into contact with those past explanatory hypotheses of the Mysteries which supposed that the Candidate for Initiation took the part of the God in his ordeals ; that in him the God died and in him also arose. When Mrs. Atwood wrote her SUGGESTIVE INQUIRY into what was termed by her the Hermetic Mystery, she supposed that adept Hierophants put the Candidate into deep trance and that the soul was led therein through states of inward experience into something that answered for her to intellection of the Supreme Oneness.[1] She did not express it thus clearly, for she was lost amidst a cloud of words and images derived from late Platonism ; but it was and is easy to see that her thesis was false at the root, since it is not by travelling in the Spirit Vision or by a vicarious illumination that any true end is attained. It is a work in one's own life. So also it was easy to see that another and greater scholarship, which explains the Mysteries as presenting in picture fashion the annual story of seedtime and harvest, was reducing them to a hollow show, writing out at full length the judgment of Thomas de Quincey when he affirmed that th Mysteries were the great imposture of the classical world. But if seedtime and harvest are the story of the soul in incarnation, life, growth, and the great harvesting of death, leading to other life, symbolised by the ear of corn exhibited in pregnant silence, as if by the Gods in their Olympus, then the Mysteries are not a cheat but at least the shewing of a vision. And if the Birth, Death and Resurrection of the God are the story of the soul awaking from life and illusion of the senses to an apprehension of the Great Reality ; if the Death of the God is significant of the soul dying to all that itself can perish ; and if the Resurrection is to life in God, then the Mysteries in their own day and after their own manner portray the story of the soul which dies to earthly things, that it may rise into the knowledge and attainment of those things that are eternal. Plotinus, Iamblichus, Porphyry, Proclus—these and the rest of them—testifying to the import of the Mysteries as understood in their days by them, encourage us to look at them from a point of view like this ; but they have left us no evidence that the experience of Candidates was more than that of minor activities and witness in great pageants, in shows that shewed. They took part in Processions, they bore the Thyrsus, they went through Lustrations ; but there was nothing individual. For the rest, they beheld and heard and carried away that which they could and would.

[1] A SUGGESTIVE INQUIRY INTO THE HERMETIC MYSTERY AND ALCHEMY, . . . BEING AN ATTEMPT TOWARDS THE RECOVERY OF THE ANCIENT EXPERIMENT OF NATURE, 1850.

As regards the second Birth, Initiation was its actuating cause by the hypothesis of the Mysteries, and it presupposed a Figurative Death, the Birth itself being also obviously emblematic. Mr. H. P. Cooke reminds us in a recent study[1] that, according to Julius Firmicus Maternus, " the intending *Mystes* of Attis was admitted as *moriturus* " —one who is about to die. But seeing that the Mysteries worked in symbolism, obviously also they could communicate nothing automatically. How should Alkibiades, for example, profit by a Figurative Death ? As much and as little as some and many of those who pass through the Death and Raising of the Third Degree in Craft Masonry. The Initiations of Eleusis took place in crowds, and there is nothing to indicate that even its Greater Mysteries were communicated individually. Mr. Cooke presents a Talismanic speculation on the Neophyte of alleged Egyptian Rites acting " the part of the Deity " ; but there is no evidence before us, except that he quotes John Yarker, who wrote long years ago a chaotic volume entitled ARCANE SCHOOLS,[2] and it was published towards the end of his life by Tait of Belfast.[3] Yarker was one of my occasional correspondents in those days, and so also was the excellent William Oxley, who paid one visit to Egypt, if I remember rightly, and returned with revelations which impressed Yarker and no one else presumably in the wide world of Research.[4] It is difficult to believe one's eyes on finding both or either figuring as speaking with authority on Egyptian antiquities or on any of the Mystery Schools, except Freemasonry in Yarker's case. Even on that subject, which he had followed in every direction, his contributions are stultified by fantastic hypotheses and by the omission of important references which could alone enable some of his most debatable statements to be checked.

I have looked vainly for indisputable records of such Initiations and such Advancements ; but there is only the affirmation of Proclus, according to which the Body of the Candidate was buried in " the most secret of all Initiations ", the head only excepted. Mr. Cooke, who is otherwise of interest, fails therefore—but inevitably—over the most vital point of his thesis, and the subject must be left at this point. There is nothing to help us in the vast collection of Sir James Frazer on the Dying God or in the researches of Sir Wallis Budge on OSIRIS AND THE EGYPTIAN RESURRECTION. According to Graillot, the Candidates for simple Initiation in the Attis Rites were many, but the Rite of Enthronement at a later and higher stage presupposes a single *Mystes*. Unfortunately they are scarcely of my concern in the present collection.

[1] OSIRIS : A STUDY IN MYTHS, MYSTERIES AND RELIGION, by Harold P. Cooke, M.A., 1931.
[2] The work appeared in 1909 and, according to its sub-title, included a General History of Freemasonry.
[3] Yarker on the Holy Grail, pp. 191 *et seq.*, proves an amazing study, a burlesque of blunders, based on casual reading at second and third hand. Chrétien, for example, gave us the Titurel Legend, and his poem is entitled : SIR COULES DEL GRAIL.
[4] EGYPT : WONDERS OF THE LAND OF THE PHARAOHS, *circa* 1886. My impression is that it appeared originally in the columns of the MEDIUM AND DAYBREAK, to which Oxley was a frequent contributor.

It remains therefore that the Birth, Death and Resurrection of the God
in Ritual cannot be affirmed to portray those states and stages of the
soul's experience to which I referred at the beginning. A little mixed
and confusing, their best offering was a lesson of hope to come hereafter
in Elysian Fields.[1] So also the mythological Pageants of other
Mysteries conveyed analogous messages ; but at their best and highest
—as it seems to me—the Epopt's Vision of the Gods has little at
this day to tell those who are in search of the union. Above all, in
those rare cases where the Epopt became the God M. Graillot makes
evident—more or less unawares—how far from the term of veridic
experience was the Candidate's spectacular enthronement.

Here in a sense are preliminary considerations to the critical thesis
which follows in the present section ; and they are offered (1) because
my readers must not be in doubt on my own position respecting those
Ancient Mysteries which have been connected occasionally with the
Grail ; (2) because of that which will be found in my twelfth book to
emerge from the QUEST OF GALAHAD, when its close is reached at
Sarras. I pass now to the more immediate matter in hand.

It has been pointed out that Prof. Nitze is in debt to Frazer, whose
vast collection of instances and examples on matters of primitive
belief and custom, with and without its hypotheses, is a time-saving
source of reference ready to the hands of all. In matters of research
upon points of fact along such lines, it would be folly to go further till
the riches of THE GOLDEN BOUGH have been put under contribution.
Obviously also Prof. Nitze is in debt otherwise to this common source
of knowledge because he reflects therefrom the theory of Nature and
Vegetation Cults, the most accredited exponent of which is Sir James
Frazer. Miss Weston, to whose views and imaginings I proceed in the
next place, described herself as " an impenitent believer " in Frazer's
main theory,[2] and she was such indeed unconditionally, though she
read into the Vegetation Cultus, the Seedtime and Harvest Rites, higher
or deeper intention than had been ever acknowledged by him. It would
enlist all my own interest had she held one ounce of real evidence in her
hands or had even portrayed in adequate outline its supposed measure
and term. But the living nature of its " glorious great intent " does
not emerge in her pages, leading to the irresistible influence that it was
something supposed only but of which she was unable to speak,
except at a distance and vaguely. It is to be understood, however,
that when " fresh from the study " of Frazer's GOLDEN BOUGH, she
was " struck by the resemblance between certain features of the Grail
story and characteristic details of the Nature Cults described."[3]

---

[1] We can imagine a possible inference which could have been drawn from their
experience by some prepared Postulants : that the Death and Resurrection of the God
was in truth their own story, not alone because man dies physically and rises in the
soul to other life, but may die also mystically to that which is evil within him and arise
into Divine Life. There is nothing, however, to shew that this lesson was taught in the
Mysteries, unless we elect to affirm that their Pageants were designed to teach it.
Evidence unfortunately is wanting here as well, so it can be only a devout opinion.

[2] FROM RITUAL TO ROMANCE, p. 10.   [3] *Ib.*, p. 3.

She asked herself finally whether in this " mysterious " Legend " we might not have the confused record of a Ritual once popular and later surviving under conditions of strict secrecy ". Miss Weston pursued her inquiries, making such progress and attaining such conviction that she became qualified at last in her own opinion to affirm that the " origin of the Grail will be in dispute no longer by any fair-minded critics ".[1] It does not appear unfortunately that at or about the date of her chief contribution on the subject she enlisted assent or approval from other scholars, and in 1923 her thesis was set aside more or less definitely by Dr. J. D. Bruce.

However this may be, in the course of explorations after a Grail source in Ritual, Miss Weston reached another conviction, namely, that it was " a fatal mistake to seek in the direction of Eleusis " : the explanation is that she had taken to heart a counsel of Cumont, namely, to remember that in so far as the Mysteries influenced Christianity, we must look to those of Hellenised Asia rather than Greece proper, because the first Christian Communities rose up amidst Oriental, Semite, Phrygian, and Egyptian populations.[2] She turned therefore to " the Phœnician Greek divinity " known as Adonis and to the Rites connected with his death, exile and return or resurrection, though instead of giving an intelligible account of these—so far as available materials permit—she draws, chiefly from Frazer and his sources, miscellaneous examples of supposed Nature Ritual to illustrate " the widespread character of Mediæval and Modern Survivals " of the particular Mystery Cult. It leaves us at a loose end as regards the Cult itself, but it serves to introduce a surprising, if subsidiary thesis on its survival to this day, as we shall find a little later on.

Eleusis is dismissed in a paragraph, and it may be noted in this connection that Miss Weston knew nothing apparently of Foucart's researches, though their latest edition appeared so far back as 1914, while as regards the Mother of the Gods, and as regards Adonis, Attis and Tammuz, she has consulted Baudissin, Langdon, Farnell and others, in addition to Frazer, but has passed over the mine of research in Graillot's CULTE DE CYBÈLE, which belongs to 1912.[3] From this source alone, not to speak of the others, it is possible to estimate the extraordinary complexity which arose from the interpenetration of Cults passing under the names of Adonis, Tammuz and Attis, as well as to realise how slight and inadequate is their treatment under Miss Weston's auspices and how special is the pleading which insists on seeing their reflection everywhere in the Legend of the Holy Grail. I am not speaking as one who has an axe to grind, for I am concerned with the Grail as it appears in Grail Texts, a Christian Talisman which entails a Christian Quest ; and if something of pre-Christian Myth is reflected therein, it is *nihil ad rem meam*, as I have made plain already.

[1] *Op. cit.*, p. 5.
[2] See LES RELIGIONS ORIENTALES DANS LE PAGANISME ROMAIN, p. x.
[3] Henri Graillot : LE CULTE DE CYBÈLE, MÈRE DES DIEUX, À ROME ET DANS L'EMPIRE ROMAIN.

But it has proved—and we have seen also—that the Welsh PEREDUR
is not an antecedent of Perceval in any of his guises, from the Chrétien
section of the CONTE DEL GRAAL to his beatification in the late
PERLESVAUS. It proves also that, while magical Cups and Cauldrons
are far and wide in Myth, not excepting that of Sumerian times,[1] it is
impossible to hold any opinions on the Cauldron of the Dagda, as it is
first heard of in unquestioned record no earlier than the seventeenth
century.[2] It remains now to be seen whether Miss Weston's appeal
to Rites connected with the names of Tammuz, Attis and Adonis can
be held to fare better. We are concerned of course with the case as
presented by herself and not with its possible approach from some other
point of view.

Miss Weston's main thesis opens on a personal note, from which it
appears that she found refuge in Nature Cults as a possible explanation
of Grail origins, (1) because " the theory of Christian origin breaks
down when faced with the awkward fact that there is no Christian
Legend concerning Joseph of Arimathæa and the Grail " ;[3] and
(2) because she had failed to find any folk-lore prototype of the
Grail story, containing " the Waste Land, the Fisher King, the Hidden
Castle with its solemn Feast and Mysterious Feeding Vessel, the
Bleeding Lance ", and the rest.[4] She was in a dual dilemma therefore,
and her research of half a century had turned to ashes in her hand,
though it happens that she had beeen one of the chief English contributors to that side of the subject which insisted on folk-lore explanations. It happens, however, on the side of Christian origin, that the
Grail is of no vital interest if its source is only in Christian Apocryphal
Legends. I have said much earlier that its place in this event is among
the annals of Relics, as a notable development therefrom in the World
of Romance. It is important because of its claim on a Christian Secret
and a non-Roman perpetuation, because of its implicit postulate
concerning a doctrine and practice of which the Church at large knew
nothing, and because of its open affirmation of a direct descent from
Christ instead of from an appointed apostolate. It is more than true
in one sense that " the Church knew nothing of it " : from that point
of view, it could not afford to know. But there is another from which, I
think, that it suspected if it did not know, but kept a politic silence,
leaving such things to pass as figments of Romance. What it would
have done with a Sect presenting such claims there is no need to
speculate, remembering Southern France in the twelfth and thirteenth
centuries.

In any case, Miss Weston took the Nature Cults and drew from
there and here, but always from sound authorities, on Tammuz and
Attis and Esmun and Adonis, but the last especially, regarded as best
known and his Ritual as " the classic form of the Cult " Of the Rite

---

[1] Appendix I, Note 23.
[2] That is to say in THE GENERAL HISTORY OF IRELAND, by Geoffrey Keating, D.D.,
translated from the original Irish by Dermod O'Connor, 1726.
[3] FROM RITUAL TO ROMANCE, p. 2.   [4] *Ib.*, p. 3.

itself I have intimated that she has little to tell, in part because little indeed has come down. She presents some familiar features, including (1) the traditional history of " a fair youth, beloved of Aphrodite, who, wounded in the thigh by a wild boar "—read, in the generative organs —" died of his wounds ". At the prayers of the goddess, he was permitted by Zeus to return for certain months of the year, like Persephone, and (2) thus divided his time between Aphrodite— presumably in Olympus—and Persephone in Hades, by whom he was beloved also.

It would seem therefore that in the underworld, as above, his virility was restored to him, (1) because a maimed youth, however beautiful, would have scarcely appealed to Greek Goddesses, and (2) because Adonis, *ex hypothesi*, " represents in anthropomorphic form the principle of Animate Nature," and an unsexed symbol would not have served the purpose, would not have stood for the " virile activity on which vegetable and human life depends." Miss Weston stresses therefore the sex-complex of the Cultus, with special reference to Baudissin,[1] Bellay,[2] Dulaure[3] and Miss J. E. Harrison.[4] She cites also the evidence of Lucien—if indeed it be he who wrote DE DEA SYRIÆ. He affirms (1) that the women votaries of the Cultus, whose business it was to lament the death of Adonis, had either to be shorn of their locks, an outrage which redounded somehow to the honour of the God, or must sell themselves—for one day only—to strangers, either in the market-place or even in the Temple itself, the profits of this traffic defraying the costs of the sacrifices offered to Aphrodite ; (2) that the Priests of Adonis inflicted mutilation on themselves and thus suffered with their God, a very curious practice in connection with a supposed Fertility Rite. We may remember also that, according to Ovid, the rejoicings on the Resurrection of Adonis degenerated into orgies at Rome.

Miss Weston makes no secret and manifests no reluctance on these points of fact : she cites some of them expressly, though she may not have remembered that, according to Gerald Massey, " Nature is not ashamed of her symbols ". It is ashamed, however, of excesses and maniacal outrage. It may have seemed to her indeed that the excesses were intelligible in view of the Mysteries concerned and were almost emblematic like these. They do not prevent her from maintaining that the Nature Cults—which include the worship of Adonis—were (1) " the medium of imparting high spiritual teaching ", and (2) that " the Vegetation Deities, Adonis-Attis, and more especially the Phrygian God "—who is Attis—" were the chosen guides to the knowledge of, and union with, the Supreme Spiritual Source of Life, of which they were the communicating mediums ". A considerable part of her evidence for these things is found in the Mystery Feast, of

[1] ADONIS UND ESMUN.
[2] Annales du Musée Guimet, s.v. ADONIS.
[3] DES DIVINITÉS GÉNÉRATRICES.
[4] THEMIS, A STUDY IN GREEK SOCIAL ORIGINS.

which the initiated alone were privileged to partake in " the Orgiastic
Ritual of the Priests of Kybele ", worshipped as the Great Mother. The
authority is Cumont, who affirms (1) that they communicated the
aliment of Spiritual life—presumably *ex hypothesi ;* (2) that it was
calculated to sustain the Initiate in his ordeals ; and (3) that for these
and other reasons " the Phrygian fable became a traditional mould
into which subtle exegetes boldly poured " their philosophical speculations, not only on creative and fecundating forces as principles of
material form, but on " the liberation of the Divine Souls plunged in
the corruption of this material world ".[1]

The suggestion is characteristic of the period, and we have seen
how Greek Philosophers were affected by the Rites which they had
presumably received, all which notwithstanding the Attis Initiate may
" have eaten from the tympanum " and may " have drunk from the
cymbals ", but he profited solely and only according to his own
measures. To say otherwise is to rave.

Miss Weston draws also from a Naassene document given in the
PHILOSOPHUMENA of Hippolytus and translated by G. R. S. Mead
in the first volume of his THRICE GREATEST HERMES. But it serves
her only because it identifies Attis, the Son of Rhea, with " Thrice-
longed-for " Adonis, with Osiris, Adama of the Samothracians, and
Pan—otherwise, as she puts it, " all the Mystery-Gods with the
Vegetation Deity, Adonis-Attis ".[2]   In fine the document adds :
" the True Gate is Jesus the Blessed ".   Whether He also belongs to a
Nature Cult is not discussed ; but Miss Weston proceeds to ask
triumphantly whether the Naassene text does not " provide a complete
and overwhelming justification " of those scholars who have " insisted
upon the importance " of Vegetation Rites.   Especially and *per se,*
one would have thought not, because it is so obvious that such Rites
must belong to one another and live in one another's likeness, that it all
goes without saying.   Let us suppose, however, that an affirmative
answer is the right and reasonable and only thing ; that the importance is magnified further when the text compares Aphrodite in love
with Adonis to Aphrodite desiring Soul, and the Mother of the Gods
who emasculates Attis to " the Blessed Nature above of the super-
Cosmic and Æonian spaces which called back the masculine power of
Soul to herself ".

On this understanding at its value we can proceed to the next point.
Pan is dead, with the rest of the Gods in his likeness, and the Rites
to them belonging, though Frazer and other scholars have collected
Fertility practices through all time even to this day, and all the wide
world over.   Who shall bridge the gulf between that death and the
Grail epoch ?   Dr. Bruce calls it a thousand years.[3]   The question is
virtually asked by Miss Weston, and she devotes certain chapters to an
attempted answer.   The result is a consultation of her authorities,

[1] LES RELIGIONS ORIENTALES DANS LE PAGANISME ROMAIN, p. 84.
[2] FROM RITUAL TO ROMANCE, p. 148.   [3] *Op. cit.,* I, p. 284.

already cited, and a selection of mediæval and modern folk customs—mostly modern and mostly crudest mummery, not apart from a mocking spirit—which represents somehow the Death and Resurrection, so called, of the Vegetation Spirit. They are there at their value, curious enough and likeable on that account as a miscellaneous garnering ; but they bear precisely the same relation to the historical Rite of old as the Coronation of a May Queen to that of a Royal Potentate, or a Village Council to a State Parliament.

Above all they are ridiculous when utilised to enforce a suggestion that the old Rites continued, that one of their aspects is to be found in the Grail Mythos, and that they are with us in concealment and not less alive than of old even at this day. It may seem incredible on the part of an accomplished scholar who used to be taken seriously ; but here is the unadorned fact. The beginning of the reverie is in the second volume of her LEGEND OF SIR PERCEVAL, published in 1909; it is reiterated in a little conspectus of the whole subject entitled THE QUEST OF THE HOLY GRAIL, and it appears at full length in her final experiment, FROM RITUAL TO ROMANCE, which is more especially under examination in this section. In presenting so extraordinary a subject I shall be well advised to express it practically in her own words. At the opening of the study in question, Miss Weston informs her readers that having worked out a possible solution of Grail problems on a Ritual basis, she became aware of certain links which were " missing in the chain of evidence " and that the search after these involved her in some nine or ten years of additional research. Between these statements she introduces the following unexpected disclosures : (1) that " no inconsiderable part " of the information at her disposal " depended upon personal testimony ", derived from those " who knew of the continued existence of such a Ritual ", and " had actually been initiated into its Mysteries ", (2) a Ritual namely, of which the Grail Mythos is a confused record.[1] The revelation rests at this till the close of her volume, when she adopts a more oracular tone and affirms (1) " without entering into indiscreet details," that " students of the Mysteries are well aware of the continued survival of this Ritual ", being apparently a Worship of Mithra, " under circumstances which correspond exactly with the indications of two of our Grail Romances "[2] —neither Romances nor indications being specified, presumably for discreet reasons ; (2) at the " risk of startling her readers ", Miss Weston retells the story of the Young Squire in the PERLESVAUS who dreams that he is smitten because of a stolen candlestick of gold and awakens to find a knife in his side, while the precious spoil is hidden in his hose. She affirms that it portrays the test applied to a Candidate for Initiation on " the Astral Plains ", with its fatal reaction on the physical.[3]

It is obvious that from 1909—or even earlier—to 1920 Miss Weston was in the course of being " spoon-fed " by a group of occult students,

---

[1] FROM RITUAL TO ROMANCE, p. 4.　　　[2] Op. cit., pp. 162–164.
[3] Ib., pp. 169–172.

connected with one of those very numerous so-called Orders which were mushroom growths of the period but were paraded invariably among believers who fell into their toils as institutions of remote antiquity. A considerable part of my life has been spent in exploring and exploding the pretentions of their predecessors, in and behind the nineteenth century ; but they were abroad at the opening of the twentieth, and they are abroad and clamorous to-day, especially in America. They work very often by dupes who are sincere on their own part and act as emissaries. Some of them are operating by type-script —of which copies are in my possession—and in this case the emissaries act as local centres from which the scripts are circulated. Sometimes they work in Ritual ; and I suppose there is a baker's dozen extant under the style and title of The Rosy Cross ; for it happens that spurious Masonic Orders and Degrees are neither in fashion at the moment nor to be put forward easily, in view of the vigilance of Grand Lodges, Chapters and Conclaves. An Eastern Source is favoured in certain quarters, for it makes inquiry difficult ; but the best and most baffling refuge is the Astral Plane, because it defies research when a Postulant for Initiation or a Member in the early stages is assured that the Rites and the knowledge derive from that quarter. The Grail has not been forgotten in the manufacture of such Mysteries ; and I have a feeling that somewhere in my archives there is a Mithraic Rite, reflecting in the far distance and with the Bull in the background, so far as sacrificial offerings are concerned. Had I time and inclination for an extended memorial on Modern Occult and Pseudo-Mystical Schools, there might be some rough unveilings. Those who, like Miss Weston, have taken such dreams and inventions seriously may demand our sympathy, but their opinions have ceased to signify. An illustration in her case is the mental state which permitted her to presume and expect credence for her concealed sources of supposititious knowledge, a certain alleged BOOK OF THOTH possibly included.[1]

We are in sympathy also when she who had dwelt so long in the paths of Celtic Scholarship, had reflected so much from its German ingatherings and methods is brought not merely to say (1) that a path which leads only " into a Celtic Twilight can only be a by-path "[2] but that " visits to the Other Worlds are not always derivations from Faërie Lore, because that World " is not a myth but a reality,[3] and because in all ages there have been souls willing to brave the great adventure of its exploration, on the chance of bringing back with them some assurance of the future life. We are in sympathy, but I at least know a little of her inspiring source in the dogmatic part of her statements and that regions of occult practice and their dubious lights amidst Cimmerian darkness are still less an adequate goal for a life's research than any Celtic by-path.

It is time now to make clear in a few words her position on that part of her subject with which alone we are concerned in reality. It can

---

[1] Appendix I, Note 24.   [2] *Op. cit.*, pp. 3, 176.   [3] *Ib.*, pp. 175, 176.

be presented in a plenary sense by her dogmatic statement that " the Grail Romances repose eventually not upon a poet's inspiration but upon the ruins of an august and ancient Ritual ; a Ritual which once claimed to be the accredited guardian of the Deepest Secrets of Life."[1] It is not that of " Adonis, Attis and their congeners ", because these after all—many pages of panegyric notwithstanding—prove to be half-gods. It is therefore either the originally Persian Cult of Mithra, the chief authorities for which are two well-known works of M. F. Cumont, and on these Miss Weston depends in part, or it is something undemonstrable and perhaps a figment of debate in the esoteric circles to which she alludes and into which she may have been admitted personally before the close of her life. Those kinds of doors open rather easily to such as are predisposed and likely to prove *personæ gratæ* by virtue of a believing heart. Her reticence notwithstanding—as if it were needful to confuse a simple issue—I conclude or assume that she refers to " the popular religion of the Roman Legionaries " which celebrated that union of Mithra and the Goddess Anahita, which Miss Weston assures us was regarded as equivalent to the marriage of Attis-Kybele, the Phrygian Deities. There was a time, as we learn from Cumont, when Mithraism lacked the spiritual significance which was subsequently attached thereto—by the philosophers presumably, to whom I have referred previously, and presumably also at that time when it was competing with Christianity for predominance. It is difficult to connect Roman Legionaries with cults " imparting the highest religious teaching " and following " chosen guides to . . . union with the Supreme Spiritual Source of Life."[2] It is impossible to connect them with a God who imposed strict chastity on his Initiates. In any case the " august and ancient Ritual " had perished as such between seven and eight centuries before the Grail literature arose, and this is after making allowance for the Worship of Mithra, which is said to have been still practised during the fifth century in certain remote cantons of the Alps and Vosges.[3] It is to be submitted in all reason that at that period it was no longer an august Rite.

It survives, however, for Miss Weston, firstly in the Grail Mythos and secondly in those alleged esoteric circles which have been considered at some length and put definitely out of court. They belonged and belong now to the class of testimony respecting which no one in their senses can believe any witness, however amiable and personally sincere, except with all archives before us. The head and centre of the august Rite, as laid bare by scholarship, appears to represent a concordat between the Mithra Cult and the sister Phrygian Mystery of Kybele and Attis, and is that which Cumont describes as celebrating a Festival which was " an aliment of Spiritual Life."[4] As such it was common seemingly to both ; but Miss Weston's deposition is a little confused and confusing, so that it is difficult to know when she is dealing

---

[1] *Op. cit.*, pp. 176, 191.   [2] FROM RITUAL TO ROMANCE, p. 149.
[3] *Ib.*, pp. 161, 162.   [4] LES RELIGIONS ORIENTALES, etc., p. 137.

with the one and when with the other. The Feast is said to have become " the centre of the whole religious action."[1] This is on the authority of Dieterich, and Miss Weston terms it "a close parallel with the Grail Romances." It is nothing of the sort because, on her own shewing, in the " Attis Feast " the Initiates " ate and drank " from the Sacred Vessels ; but no one partakes of the Sacred Grail content when this is the Precious Blood. Otherwise, people are fed by Magic, destroying the whole analogy. Moreover, it is folly to look behind the gulf of centuries when a " close parallel " is ready to our hands in the Christian Eucharistic Rites, which recall demonstrably those of the Grail, the latter with a non-Roman Form of Consecration, a non-Roman and a wonder-side. As to the spiritual sustenance and the alleged supernatural communications to the soul, Miss Weston had only to study orthodox Eucharistic *Theosophia* of the Grail period to find all the desired parallels without assuming the secret perpetuation of a dead Pagan Rite.

So also there is an arbitrary parallel instituted between a suppositious Death and Resurrection of the Candidate in the Phrygian Rites and postulated ceremonial in the Grail Mythos. But again there is no analogy, for there is no Death or Resurrection in any Grail literature ; and Miss Weston has to content herself with a phantom substitute in " the healing of the Fisher King ".[2] She dwells much also on the wasting and restoration of the land, on the suspension and freeing of waters in Grail texts, and on their reflections from folk-lore ; but in so far as they are found occasionally they are not of real service on questions of origin, the MATIÈRE DE BRETAGNE being obviously ready to the hands and in the hearts of Grail Romancers, even as I at this day, though I may be writing on the Mystery of Union must give evidence inevitably of a hundred extrinsic issues, because the matter of the twentieth century is not only ready to my hands but has its conscious and subconscious images like a crowded population of my mind.

Miss Weston is keen on affirming the august nature of the Mithraic Rite, but passes over an important feature of the Sister Mystery which may have belonged ultimately to both. Cumont can be consulted here, but his two works on the subject have become rare in these days. There is, however, the CULTE DE CYBÈLE, by Henri Graillot, an exhaustive and admirble study, which may be consulted on the subject of the *Taurobolium* and its revolting Baptism of Blood. The Candidate for its Mystery descended into a pit, so that the Sacrificial Bull

---

[1] FROM RITUAL TO ROMANCE, p. 139.

[2] It is perfectly clear that an infirm King who, whether healed for the moment or not, dies subsequently and is in no case restored to life, has no relation to any Fertility Myth and is still less " a deeply symbolic figure, . . . the essential centre of the whole cult, a being semi-divine, semi-human, standing between his people and land, and the unseen forces which control their destiny " (*Op. cit.*, pp. 128, 129). Miss Weston sets out by stating that her theory will be established on a firm basis if the Fisher King is proved to be an integral part of her Imagined Ritual, while, on the other hand, if he does not fit into the framework, her theory will be seriously incomplete, if not what she terms *manqué*. She has satisfied herself on the affirmative side of her thesis, but it will convince no one else.

was above him. It was immolated by himself in this position, and the blood poured over him ; over body, over face ; and in the mouth itself he received *la rouge pluie*. The genitals of the slaughtered beast were carried into the Temple, where they were consecrated to the Great Mother and were interned in a Holy Place, under a commemorative Altar. The *Taurobolist* who had performed this ceremony became regenerated *ex hypothesi* in his health and vital force. Citing Tobæus and Prudentius, Graillot affirms (1) that the pit was a sepulchre in which the discarded remains of what is termed the old man were left ; (2) that an Office of the Dead was chanted about the Candidate ; (3) that when he emerged from the figurative tomb, a bloody apparition, he was hailed as pure of pure and holy of holies ; (4) that the assistants at this foul business fell down and worshipped before him. There seems evidence even that certain Candidates mutilated themselves in honour of the goddess.[1] To quote once again my old and by now almost proverbial sentence, it is from such orgies, in the view of Miss Weston, that there has come down to us " a story told for one of the truest and holiest that is in this world "—the Quest. of the Hóly Grail.[2] It is small wonder that in one of her craziest dicta Miss Weston lays down that the Quest of Galahad does not, properly speaking, belong to the Grail at all but to the Lancelot Legend :[3] it certainly does not, if the Grail at the long last of all its variant interpretations, emerges as a veiled example of such a Rite.

III

THE GRAIL AS A MYSTERY OF INITIATION

ELEUSIS and the Rites connected with the Name and Myth of Adonis have proved of no effect for our purpose, each in its turn ; but the fact remains that no one acquainted with their peculiar characters and seals, their *mise-en-scène* and atmosphere, can fail to be reminded of Initiations, old and new, when they contemplate the Quest of the Grail. Like the Hermit of the GRAND SAINT GRAAL, it must be recognised among those who know by something borne thereon.[4] They will observe also that it can be distinguished into certain Degrees, as if Lesser and Greater Mysteries, the one ending in failure and the other in a crown of success. So did the Perceval of Gerbert give the wrong Battery on the Gate of the Earthly Paradise, and so did it cost him another seven years of wandering and probation. But the end of the Mysteries is ever to approve their Candidates, if in any wise this be possible, and the end is also to receive them, lest Initiation itself should perish. Thus, in the case

[1] Graillot, *Op. cit.*, pp. 155–157, 158.
[2] It is Caxton's Colophon, Book XVII of Malory's MORTE DARTHUR, at the end of the story concerning the Sangreal.   [3] FROM RITUAL TO ROMANCE, p. 195.
[4] Sommer, VULGATE ARTHURIAN ROMANCES, I, p. 10.

under notice, Perceval is given a test of merit to accompany and aid his return, as we have seen long since. In other texts he fails to ask the Question of the Rite and is covered with seeming ceremonial reproaches ; yet the way back is open and late or soon he receives his call. It is implied early in the CONTE DEL GRAAL and the Didot-Modena Quest when the denunciations of the laidly Grail-Messenger spur the hero to undertake the Quest. In the German PARZIVAL the Grail itself calls him who is foreordained to the Kinghood. A new face of things is presented in the PERLESVAUS, which stultifies the office of the Question and gives the Grail Crown to Perceval by right of conquest, enforced by that of heirship. Finally, in the Quest of Galahad, which revolutionises the whole story, all and sundry are invited to attempt the Quest by the Grail manifesting for that purpose in the Royal Court of Arthur.

The Chivalry of the Round Table goes forth thereon, but only to disastrous failure ; and Monseigneur Gawain confesses in the MORT ARTUS that he who, alone of all, suffered contumely at Corbenic was responsible in his own person for the slaughter—in tourneys and what not—of eighteen Questing Knights. On the other hand, those nine Anonymi who entered, as we have seen, at the beginning of the Sacro-Saintly Festival, when the Mystery was in fine unveiled, took their places unchallenged, as if they were Epopts already, familiar with the Service of the Grail and divinely anxious to share again therein. As if such, they were received by Galahad ; as such they knelt with him and saw the Blessed Vision. But it happens that at this time we are called upon to regard the whole Quest-subject from another stand-point, which is neither that of Eleusis nor Mithra, of Mount Heredom or the Rosy Cross. We pass suddenly from these and their pageants, as if into a Church unknown, which appoints Messengers to carry its glad tidings through the world without. The story of the Secret Words dissolves, the Super-Apostolical Succession passes out of view ; but the same high warrant, the same Man-Christ clothed now in all the symbols of His Passion tells Galahad that even as He appointed Apostles to carry His Gospel through the four quarters, so now He has chosen those nine Anonymi, whose sole Priesthood is that of the Order of Knighthood, to carry the tidings of the Quest achieved—as one might say, over all the world. It is essential to remember this when looking, as I proceed to do, at the Grail as a possible Rite of Initiation.

Palace or Keep or Temple, " wilderness of building " or grey North-umbrian Hold, the House of the Holy Grail is the place of its Hidden Mystery and all that takes place therein belongs—let us say and think —to the Form of Reception for those who are called to partake. In all those Tales of Quest which signify from this point of view, as from others that are more important, the Candidate is a scion of the House, a Royal Heir-at-law, apparent or presumptive. On the surface this is according to the flesh ; but from the Mystery point of view there is that latent within him by which he is or may become duly qualified to receive

Initiation, and for its sacred charge to devolve ultimately upon him. Here, I conceive, is the broad hypothesis of the subject ; and it may not be held impermissible for one who, like myself, is directly and indirectly acquainted with many forms of Initiation, old and new, to affirm that it would be possible on my own part to reconstruct at their value all the Quests in decorative pageants, even the CONTE DEL GRAAL and the Gawain part of the PERLESVAUS, which is its only Quest element. I have been at this kind of work for many years of initiated life, have filled all the offices in all the chief departments and am an old hand with all the stage machinery.[1] It has been worth while to mention this (1) because the great dissimilarity between Rites of which the fact is known publicly and of those which are hidden from the world, between those which exist on a small scale and those which are established on a large, have brought me a diversified experience ; (2) because by virtue of such experience I am qualified to know whether this or that material, if put into my hands, would prove workable ; and (3) because in this manner I have acquired an instinct[2] by which I am enabled to decide whether the Grail literature does represent at a near or far distance something which " once in time and somewhere in the world ", existed as a Ceremonial Mystery.

The first point that is obvious in respect of the Grail literature is that it would be like telling the wrong story if we selected a particular Quest version and decided, on the basis of one or another consideration, that it approached most nearly the original Ritual form. We should inevitably make our choice of this or that text because it seems to us that it is the most capable of successful dramatic rendering. It happens, however, on the hypothesis with which we are dealing, that Grail Ritual preceded the Grail Romances, while having regard to the variety of Quests and to the fact that they exclude one another, we are without any canon of criticism to guide a choice, the modern notion of dramatic values being most probably the worst of all. If we care so to regard it, we have already before us the Book of the Words of Wagner's PARSIFAL, as a German Quest version and a counsel of caution as to what may befall anyone who attempts to reconstruct a particular Quest in the guise of a Mystery Ritual. Wagner, as it goes without saying, had no such scheme in view : as a " great tone-poet ", his task was to translate the spirit of the Grail and its Quest in the tongue of music ; and he gave that to the ages before him which itself could never be put into words, as his own attempt at verbal rendering makes more than clear.

It seems to follow that, from all the Quests and from the histories which lie behind them, our task is to extract a marrow or essence if we are bent, not indeed upon reconstructing a hypothetical Grail Ritual antecedent to all but upon presenting to our own minds, and to those

---

[1] I am not referring to Freemasonry *per se* or especially, in all its Orders or Degrees, though it is to be understood of course that they are included.

[2] Even to one who is acquainted chiefly or only with the ill-explored wealth of Masonic Ritual, or with the Archives of the Rosy Cross, such instinct comes.

who may share our zeal, a presumptive picture of that which took place at the Temple of Grail Initiation when a Candidate came to the Gate. It may be said that the word Grail would not be heard therein, which is likely enough and signifies little enough ;[1] for there was a Vessel of singular election, which may as well be called by that term as by any other. There were also companion Hallows, a Shrine of all, a Guardian of the Shrine, and so forth. In the absence of these it is obvious that there would be nothing to reconstruct : there would be only a wide field for the play of free imagination. The next point which is clear and prevails throughout is that we are concerned with a sacred trust and a law of succession thereto : and this means that the purpose of Grail Initiation differs from all others in the Mysteries of past and present. We have seen that Candidates came in crowds to Eleusis and obtained that which Eleusis had warrants to give ; but no one remained at Eleusis, the hierophants and Priests and Officers of its Rites being drawn from two families. Adonis, Attis and Mithraic Rites received their tens of thousands, multiplied many times over in the course of their long histories ; but no one dispossessed another and became the Ruler of the Rite. We do not dispossess the Grand Master on taking the Master Grade of Emblematic Freemasonry ; and so of the rest. The Supreme High Buffalo, if there happens to be such an exalted personage, abides supreme and high, though recruits innumerable may reinforce the Antediluvian Order, much as Mr. Dick Swiveller would have remained " Perpetual Grand ", whatever new companions might have flocked to the festal board of his own most worthy Rite. A further feature of the problematical subject is that in one or another sense the Grail is always removed or goes into deeper hiding in the Grail Romances, as we have seen over and over again in the course of our research. It is the antithesis therefore of any other Ritual Mystery, supposing that it is such indeed. The Mysteries, on the other hand, always remain, though only Eleusis had specific head-quarters with a notable place in history.[2] The Secret remained always, but was available always for communication under its solemn seals. The Grail has no story after, according to its own records ; there is an utter end of all things, unless and until our own gifts of vision intervene to stultify its rubrics and to make its closings void. I do not pause to think how much further we might prolong these changes and counter-changes of the subject put into our hands ; but there is at least one more point which I must not fail to cite, because it is the pivot of all the events round which the Perceval Cycles move. This is the Question, and its utterly unsolved Mystery.[3] We have seen that it stands alone, or I at least have fared as a pilgrim through worlds of great adventure, through age-long times of adventure, through a

---

[1] It became a purely conventional designation as time went on, for obviously the *Grasal* or Dish had no application to a Mass Chalice and still less, if possible, to the Stone of Wolfram.

[2] While the Rites of the *Mater Deorum* and the Mithraic Rite not only travelled but colonised, Eleusis remained where it was : those who desired its Mysteries came thereto ; it went in search of no one.　　　　[3] Appendix I, Note 25.

thousand ways of faerie and ways of the lore of folk : but neither
in highways nor by-ways have I met elsewhere with the Question
which must be asked : it is found nowhere in the world before it occurred
to Chrétien de Troyes that it should be imposed on his rather painted
and jewelled example of the Great Fool Fable, and it is nowhere in
the world after, except in the Grail poems and romances which
followed his lead. As one speaking out of due time, I have registered
already that he who comes to the Mysteries comes with open ears and
eager eyes, but not with an open mouth : he listens and does not ask.
What kind of Rite went back upon this procedure and held up its main
workings till the Candidate for Admission took that course which no
Candidate was ever allowed to take ? What Kind of Rite sent him forth
in disgrace and exile because he had failed to do what never was done
before ?[1] I know only of one direction in which we can turn for a
solution of this problem, and it is that in which the Instituted Mysteries,
past and present, have never turned themselves. They have never
drawn into Ritual the Great Mystery which lies behind the unconditional allegation of a Master more illustrious than any Hierophant of
old, of Him who said in His plenary mediatorial capacity : Ask and
ye shall receive. But that is another kind of questioning, beyond the
measures of the PERLESVAUS, beyond the highest intimations of the
Galahad Quest. I have said that it has not been drawn so far into any
Ritual, and it has not been drawn into Romance. It is the consecrated
essence of all the verbal talismans ; and the simplicity of its utter
guarantee has the ring of the Word made flesh. It has the music of
all the plain song of all the Masses and high *Epiclesis* clauses ; and
behind it is the music, as it seems to me, of yet another Mass, which
we would give our souls to hear ; but it has not been drawn as yet into
the Liturgy of any known Church. Faintly and far away, it may have
been heard by Lopuhin, somewhere in Russia, and over against, I
think, some great Pasch Candle burning ; less faintly and not so far,
Eckartshausen heard it surely, when a rift shewed light through the
clouds of his Holy Sanctuary. And I in my humility, the last and
least of witnesses, testifying faithfully amidst the world of emblems,
have heard a voice, as one of another ordination ; and it chants over
and over *Mysterium Fidei*, till a Sanctus Bell rings, and the World of
Faith is justified in the World of Reality.

But if this is like a Preface from the leaf of another Missal, though
beginning in the old manner with *Vere dignum et justum est*, it leads
us on to the next clause of this our critical research. The Perceval of the
CONTE DEL GRAAL having in fine fulfilled the Quest, becomes the King
of the Grail and overwatches it in peace for the space of seven years.
He then serves God in a Hermitage, followed by the Sacred Vessel and
the other Hallows. He passes in succession through the Offices of Holy
Church and becomes a Priest : he says Mass apparently for five years
and then is called to his reward in Heaven, the Hallows ascending also

---

[1] It may be asked also : In what other Rite of all the world of Rites does a Candidate
come to heal and save otherwise the desperate situation of a Holy House ?

—or so it is proposed at a venture.[1] The Perceval of the PERLESVAUS, having achieved in his turn, and having guarded the Reliquary in like manner, is carried in a ship by a goodly company, robed as if to sing Mass : they sail away to a place where the Grail has gone before, and this also is a place of Masses.[2] The Lancelot of the Great Prose LANCELOT and the sacro-saintly QUESTE, having drawn so near to the Mystery, as a man of sin may dare, makes at long last an end to a life of sin ; and having been ordained also, it is testified concerning him that " a twelvemonth he sang Mass."[3] Galahad ascends to Heaven, as if with the Sacred Host, hallowed in an Arch-Natural Mass, dissolved between his lips. It may be said that the Host is everywhere. In the PARZIVAL of Wolfram a Host hallowed in Heaven renews from year to year the virtues of the Holy Grail. The maimed King of the CONTE DEL GRAAL is sustained in like manner through the years. There is even a curious Office of Bread in the phantom Quest of DIU CRÔNE ; and I wonder that Miss Weston did not observe more closely the receptacle in which it is carried : it seems dangerously like the Holy Box of Eleusis.[4] What are we to say of these ever-recurring facts on the hypothesis that there was a Grail Ritual, a time immemorial Rite, and its Liturgy, before the Holy Grail was drawn into Romance ? We cannot ritualise the Grail Mythos by an arbitrary process of eliminating its vital elements for the purpose of producing a supposititious non-Christian form. It leaves nothing but a couple of references to dried-up springs and perhaps three to harvest failures. Miss Weston has wearied Heaven with dreams on these subjects—not to speak of her readers ; but there is no material here. And " the Fisher King in the Grail Romances " is not material *per se*, more especially if we remove his healing by Question on the ground that it does not belong to folk-lore or to Vegetation Cults. Throughout the Grail literature, the Grail is a Reliquary containing the Precious Blood of Jesus Christ, except in Chrétien de Troyes, who had not reached the point of explanation concerning it, and except in Wolfram, who derived from the French poet and did not know what the latter was talking about. He had therefore a fine field for invention, in course of which he brought Kyot de Provence to birth, the Jew Flegitanis, as a contribution to Semitic nomenclature, and drew the starry heavens into his creative scheme. Wolfram is one of those witnesses who shine more radiantly in proportion as they lie the more ; but the breach between him and me will never be filled, because he has failed to deceive me. It is to be remembered lastly that the Grail without the Secret Words stultifies the Lesser Chronicles, while the PERLESVAUS and the QUESTE are rooted in the claim that Joseph II was the first Bishop of Christendom and the first Priest who consecrated the Body of the Lord.

But taking all these contributory materials and grouping them

---

[1] Potvin, *Op. cit.*, VI, pp. 152–155.
[2] *Ib.*, I, p. 347 ; HIGH HISTORY, Branch xxxv, Title 27.
[3] LE MORTE DARTHUR of Malory, Bk. XXI, *cap.* 10.
[4] That is to say, the κίστη, which is supposed to have contained Bread, Cakes, etc.

together, let us bear in mind that, by the hypothesis of the subject, we are not dealing with this or that Son of the Quest in Romance.[1] Gawain and Perceval and Bors and Galahad pass from the scene of activity, like Arthur and all his Court. The Candidate for admission within the circle of Mystery has those qualifications which brought them to the term of Quest in the old Knightly Romancēs and have put aside those hindrances which caused some to fail. Let us ask ourselves in the next place : What is the kind of Temple approached *ex hypothesi* in the period prior to Romance by the Grail Aspirant, and what reception awaited him ? It was the place of a Christian Mystery ; the place of a maimed King ; the place of a King in his passing ; the place of a Secret Hierarchy ; the place of Masses said nowhere else on earth ; the place of Secret Consecrations ; the place of Strange Hallows ; the place of reception and the communication of miraculous Eucharists administered by Christ Himself ; the place where unknown Candidates or Epopts, coming from far countries, might enter unchallenged and behold the Mystery unveiled. What again was this kind of Temple ? Eleusis and Samothrace ; Thebes and Memnon ; Dionysiacs and Adonis Rites ; Attis and *Mater Deorum ;* Mysteries of Mithra : it was not of these things and places. It was a Mystery of Christian Religion prolonged into the unknown and the place of a Secret Church. I am not certifying at the moment—or perhaps subsequently—that here is discovered the Mystery behind the Holy Grail ; but it becomes intelligible in this way and no other, if the great diversified literature is more than successive creations of High Romance.

There are many difficulties of detail, and high above all emerges the problem of succession which is not of detail but belongs to the heart of the Mystery. Were it a question of one and no other, per-petuated from age to age, there might be easy travelling, so to speak ; but he who is to come is not in the likeness of him who has reigned previously. It does not happen that folk-lore scholars have taken this subject in hand, and it seems to have escaped also the exponents of Ritual theories. It is the rock on which their explanations would be ships that founder, did they find plain sailing otherwise. I have contemplated long and have surveyed the subject long from different points of view— to no purpose so far. It is not as if a Church in sickness were dis-possessed by another Church or a new sect, for the Candidate, be he Perceval or Galahad, comes not to hurt but heal.[2] It is not as if a dispensation which had lived its day were to be succeeded by another, even if fulfilled therein—e.g., for it belongs to the Grail period and was a great debate beginning therein—the *dispensatio sub nomine Christi* in a *Dispensatio Spiritus Sancti*.[3]

[1] See *ante*, XI, sect. 1, on the inevitable impersonality of the Ritual Candidate.

[2] It may be advanced that the Candidate takes possession and that in several cases the previous Keeper dies. But that of which he takes possession is the old Sacred Object : no change occurs therein. He brings no other Grail to supersede the old.

[3] The influence of the EVERLASTING GOSPEL spread far and wide at a post-Grail period, the work under that title appearing in 1254. It is no concern of our subject, as it looked towards a new age when no Sacraments would be needed. See A. S. Tuberville ; MEDIÆVAL HERESY AND THE INQUISITION, 1920, p. 38.

Second in enumeration here but not less vital among the major problems is the Recession of the Grail, when it happens to be removed actually at the close of a given Quest ; when it is said to be heard of no more ; when it is carried to the country of Prester John, as into a no-man's land ; when certain *Templeisen*, to all intents and purposes, appear to have shut their gates and raised their drawbridge. Substantially speaking, these are variants of the same theme. It is as if some higher authority than a given regnant Church had made a bid for recognition, exhibiting all its warrants, but the scheme had failed and its embassy had been recalled suddenly. It is as if a sect in warfare against such an orthodox regimen had been extinguished in fire and blood, some last and least remanent of its mission putting forth in veiled language an account of what the world had lost. It is none of these things, for the simple reason that there is no trace of any among the manifold activities of the outside world in the twelfth and thirteenth centuries. We have looked in the most likely directions, among the sects of Southern France, and they have failed us utterly. It might prove the same if we had all the Sacramentaries of all the sects in Europe at the Grail epoch. But in their absence we cannot tell for certain.

The question must be left at this point, for the time being. The Initiations have failed us, and the Heresies have also failed. There is only one thing certain in the whole dubious research, that the Holy Grail was removed because the world was not worthy and that the loss is irreparable to the world. If it was a Stone beyond price on which Divine instructions were written in times of need, the unerring *doctor dubitantium* had withdrawn his teaching. But if it was a Chalice of Salvation, the age was left with Rome's dismembered Eucharist, with such a Papacy as would reign later at Avignon, and with the wasted cities of Southern France. But yes, and if it be worth while to say so, there remained the guiding Spirit of the Holy Inquisition. It was loss on every side, and a Matthew Arnold of the period might have said more truly then than later, amidst the desperate complexion of things : Behold, the end is everywhere.

Now, so far as Grail literature is concerned, it was without hope of restoration anywhere. And worm-eaten Hosts wrote their silent commentary on the Doctrine of Transubstantiation,[1] once and for all defined in 1215. " With great pardons to sell for those who paid well, and with small ones for those who paid less," the traffic in Indulgences throve, and the sale of Masses for the Dead. There did not fail, more-over, the hope of worse to come ; since the birth of Alexander VI was still in the womb of time ; and not until a little later than the last Grail poet died did they begin to spoliate and burn the Knights Templar. Who was it that cried long since : *Roma, Roma ! Non è più com era prima ?* But yet it is the same for ever, with due regard to

---

[1] G. G. Coulton : FIVE CENTURIES OF RELIGION, I, p. 111 ; also Appendix II, pp. 481–484.

variations and reductions of opportunity. Some of us have loved it from the beginning and will love it even to the end, because of that which it has thought itself to be, and thinks even yet. But we cannot forgive it, some of us, because it is like Wolfram, that old intimate of my own : it could not deceive us to the end. Yet in fine, and this is to be noted : we may yet desire to die fortified by its last Rites, because, after all the searchings, it may happen that we have not found the Grail, though after all removals and all ascensions, it is said that Gwalchmai saw it.[1]

The Grail literature is in any case a testimony of loss and dereliction ; but it is said of the REX INCLYTUS ARTHUR : *Rex quondam, Rexque futurus*. And there are reasons why in the three following sections it is desirable to look briefly at two later literatures, one of loss only, the other only of attainment, and at a modern Mystery, which is of both loss and recovery. They will shew us that the same things tend to persist in the world of cryptic literature, and that the story of loss is not continued for ever. In this manner we may see the sorrowful message of the Holy Grail to those whom it has left in another and less discouraging light.

It is desirable to recall in conclusion that he who enters a Church may be baptised on the threshold of its Temple, and confirmed at a later stage ; he may receive Eucharistic communication ; he may be even ordained and professed ; but, unlike the Secret Orders, he is not pledged, usually under heavy penalties, to keep its procedure secret. In some papers put into my hands by Mr. Frank Ashton-Gwatkin, who has made a study of the Conversion Legends in Southern France and of the Sects in that region, there are allusions to a Secret of the Church of the Holy Spirit, namely, the Catharist Church ; but the Church itself was not secret, and the Albigenses generally were among the clamant sects of their epoch, with a propagandist spirit at white heat.

IV

ISRAEL AND ITS HOLY ASSEMBLY

THOUGHT in the Middle Ages moved, like external science, through a world of mystery, and the Christ-Light moved through the mist-light filling the bounds of sense with the shapes and symbols of vision. It follows that strange things seemed possible at a period when all was dubious in respect of knowledge ; and apart from the power of Religion, which tinged life itself with the lesser elements of ecstasy, there was the kind of enchantment

---

[1] The words are : " And after his "—that is Galahad's—" death they saw a hand coming from Heaven . . . and the hand took the very precious Vessel which was called the Greal, and departed with it. And from then until to-day, there was no one that could see it on the earth, except Gwalchmai once." Welsh QUEST OF GALAHAD, *Op. cit.*, p. 545.

which dwells always about the precincts of unknown vistas. Apart also from the shapes of imagination, there were the picture-evoking enthusiasms of minds seeking emancipation from regnant law and authority, more especially in matters of faith. Whether or not the Books of the Holy Grail belonged to the last category, they are like echoes from far away, after their own manner, because even as the Secrets of the Greater Mysteries have not passed into writing, while the Holy Assemblies do not issue proceedings, so the inward life of devotion and the experiments towards its term, whether manifested in works of Mystical Theology or in Books of Romance, reach only a partial expression. The value of the Grail Legends at their highest is resident in the suggestions and the lights which they can afford us for the maintenance of that concordat which constitutes the Divine Alliance. Having found that we are dealing with a body of writing which puts forth strange claims and implies concealed meanings, having found also that it exhibits an intention to bring these meanings forward, and being desirous of knowing the peculiar motives at work, we are disposed naturally to look towards other concealed literatures and to ascertain what light—if any—they cast upon the general problem. The great school of Christian mystical thought within the Official Church was concerned with a Mystery of Sanctity, the bourne of which was identical with that object which I am seeking to put forward as the end of the Grail Quest. It was, however, in a very early stage of its public development during the Grail period : the great lights were to come, though those who carried their lamps stood almost on the threshold. So also there were other schools of literature beginning to open their leaves of record, and they offer us certain lights on their own part, because there is a sense in which they had the freedom of the same Sanctuary. It is reasonable therefore to suppose that so far as there are difficulties in one path we may receive help from another and thus attain a better understanding of the whole. It is desirable to consider these extrinsic schools, it being understood that so far as they deal in the one subject it is presented invariably in a different way.

The Voice of the Grail in all its Tales of Quest proclaimed that the Sacred Palladium was lost to the world of Logres or the world at large, with the sole exception of the German Parzival. The story is never told in the same manner. The Grail remains with Perceval in the Didot-Modena text and Perceval abides in seclusion. It ascends to Heaven with him—according to an almost casual proposition—in Manessier's conclusion of the Conte ; but this is a reflection from the Quest of Galahad. It disappears with the Ghosts of Heinrich and passes over a radiant sea with the Son of the Widow Lady in the ever memorable Perlesvaus. But if it abode at Montsalvatch, with its self-chosen *Templeisen*, and was so intended to do in the mind of Wolfram—from time immemorial unto immemorial time—there came a day, very late in the life of the Mythos, when Albrecht concluded that the Lord of Eschenbach had told the wrong story in respect of the term thereof : so he carried the Holy Grail and all its Chivalry to the Land of Prester John. Heaven of the Galahad Quest ; Heaven of the CONTE DEL GRAAL ; undiscoverable fastness of Northumbria ; Summer Isle of the PERLESVAUS ; Bourne beyond the lonely road and its House of Ghosts ; Abyssinia, India or far Cathay—the places and names exist only, as I have suggested, to certify the catholic fact that the Grail has gone. The times of Hard Adventure, the times of Great Enchantment, strange and fell, may have terminated when Galahad and Perceval found the Priceless Talisman and healed the King according to their several modes ; but that which neither ended was the want of worth in the world : the Sacred Presence was removed and its Grace was lost, with no promise of return.

It remains, however, that those who achieved the Grail—found and so achieved—received their guerdon : it could not be taken from them who were with it and of it, its epopts and its saints—initiated, passed and raised thereby and therein. If these things are to be understood as shewing forth under veils a process of receiving Postulants among the people of a Mystery, we have seen that it did not work like receptions celebrated at Eleusis and othcrwhere in the classical and sub-classical world : the reception rather was into the adyta of a Secret Church or Holy Assembly. Now, it happens significantly that when the canon of the Grail was closed and had passed practically out of memory as centuries slipped away, the Voices of other literatures and of one other Mystery rose up in succession ; and it seems desirable to examine them shortly and so ascertain whether—amidst all their differences—they tell something of thc same story.

The Voice of the Grail is a Voice of Christian THEOSOPHIA in the form of Romance theologised ; and when it ceased from speaking another sounded in the world and told its tale of loss ; but this was a Voice of Israel, declaring its Holy Kabbalah, an alleged Tradition of the past, claiming to have been revealed for the first time at the beginning of those terrors and proscriptions which followed the Fall of Jerusalem, being that epoch of waste and desolation when, according to Robert de Borron and ACTA PILATI, the Jews were sold in the market-place by Vespasian at thirty for one penny. In reality its immortal memorial is a MIDRASH of old but uncertain date which grew with the years and generations, becoming a matter of public knowledge to Jewry at large and to a few who had ears in Christendom late in the thirteenth century.

The Schools of Kabbalism can be scarcely said to have done more than emerge partly into public existence when the canon of the Grail literature had already closed : in these Schools there were masters of mystical thought, though more especially perhaps on the intellectual side. Now, in its own way the Theosophical Scheme of Jewry in exile is a story of loss like the Grail, though it is one which ends in expectation—or, as I should say, in mental certitude. The loss in external history and in national life was counterpoised by a figurative loss in the

Sanctuary, much as if the Arch-Natural Eucharist, the Grail which is of all things holy, had been taken away. It was that which was written of old, not only in one galaxy of stars but by the cosmic power of which the worlds themselves were made. The substitution which, according to the Grail Legends, was left with the Christian Church in place of more living sanctities is paralleled by that other Legend which tells how the stress and inhibition of Israel is because the Divine Word has been withdrawn from the Holy Place, and instead of the true TETRAGRAM, the voice of the Rabbi pronounces now only the Name ADONAI. But even as the Eucharist is still a grace of thanksgiving—EUCHARISMA—and the House from which the Grail has departed is still a Holy House, so all sanctity attaches in like manner to the substituted Sacred Name and to the cortex of those letters which represent the Tetragram : יהוה. There was a time when this Name was pronounced in its true form by the High Priest once annually in the Sanctuary : it restored the people of God and maintained the Inmost Shrine, keeping open the channels of Grace, even as the Heavenly Dove, descending on Good Friday, renewed the virtue of the Grail. Afterwards, as I have indicated, there came another time when disaster fell upon Israel, with the result that the essential elements of the Name —the authentic vowel-points—in which its true vocalisation was involved, became lost even to the Sanctuary.

It should not be necessary to say that I am by no means putting forward the hypothesis of a channel of communication, by which something was derived into Romance Literature from implicits which about the same time or subsequently were unfolded in Zoharic Books—and much less *vice versa*. We know that behind the Grail Castle, according to the PERLESVAUS, there was the Earthly Paradise, and that the House of the Holy Vessel was also a Castle of Souls. We know that, according to the ZOHAR, the Garden of Eden is placed in a position which corresponds with that of the Grail itself. We know that both were removed, the Grail into the heavenly regions and the Garden of Eden into that which is no longer manifest. The latter place was connected nearly in Kabbalism with the Great Sanctuary—truly a Castle of Souls —wherein all those who are to come await their incarnation in turn ; for according to Jewish Theosophy the creation of souls is not successive, or dependent on earthly generation, but eternal in the heavens. I know on my own part that there is nothing in literature so like the departure of Galahad as that of R. Simeon ben Yo'hai ;[1] and in spite of uttermost divergencies in the root-matter, the Mystery of the Holy Grail has its sub-surface analogy with the Mystery of the LESSER HOLY

---

[1] A point comes in the story when the voice of R. Simeon ceases. "But afterward a voice cried : ' Length of days and Years of Life ' ; and yet another : ' He seeketh Life from Thee ' . . . Rabbi Abba saw that the holy light, the holy of holy ones, had been wrapped away from the world : he lay upon his right side and a smile shone upon his face . . . It is added that during his obsequies the bier of the deceased saint was raised in the air, and fire shone about it, while a voice cried : ' Enter into the nuptial joys of Rabbi Simeon.' " THE HOLY KABBALAH, by A. E. Waite, p. 147. See also Baron von Rosenroth : KABBALA DENUDATA, *tomus* II, s.v. IDRA SUTRA.

ASSEMBLY. I know that the GREATER and LESSER SANHEDRIM[1] sound like oracular voices speaking in an unknown tongue concerning the Holy House, and we feel that behind the outward offices of religion there was a little Company of the Elect which was like an unincorporated Inner Church of Israel. I know that, according to the involved scheme of the SEPHIROTH—those mystical numerations which are set upon the Tree of Life in Kabbalism—the Waters of Life are in Knowledge,[2] which is also the place of the Cup, and this is reserved always for those who are athirst. But these things, with others and many others, do not constitute the lightest shadow of transmission. No French poet could be expected to know thereof ; no exponent of Christian Legend, even when interpreted mystically, ever looked to Israel for light and leading in those internecine days—however much the name of Provence may suggest a certain difference in mind from the prevalent orthodoxy of the age. That there may be no mistake on this subject among those whom I address more especially, I note further that the peculiar presentation of Grail Symbolism which is connected with the name of the reputed Provençal Kyot—who alone of all might confess to some curious derivations from a course of study at Toledo—is precisely that presentation in which the Sanctuary is not voided and the Grail is not taken away.

It is a matter of common knowledge that, at the period in question, Spain was one place in the world where the Jews were not merely free from raging persecution but where various positions of importance were open to their competition. We know, moreover, that a great light of Moslem learning shone forth in some Spanish Academies. We know finally or may learn that this other and exotic light of which I am speaking had kindled therein among the Chosen People themselves. Palestine and the East generally thereabouts may have contributed its portion, and did indeed do so ; but the heart and marrow of Kabbalistic Theosophy was in Spain. The Jew of Toledo, the Jew of Cordova and of other places in the Peninsula look great figures in the literature, as they do also in certain Academies of Southern France, though there the Jews did not find the same peace in their abodes. For them the asylum was Spain, and that indeed must have been little less than a Terrestrial Paradise realised.[3] And as between the South of France and Spain the channels of communication stood wide open ; as Provence is the supposititious place at its value of the first Grail poem ; as the Ideal Castle, the Holy Place, Mont Salvatch, had its abode unapproachable in the Pyrenees, so the imaginative mind may incline to think that behind the strange Legend of the Jew of Toledo there may be something undemonstrable of a lost Grail connection ; though so far as evidence goes it must be admitted that this is like the stuff of which dreams are made. The analogy between all the Schools in succession is that of the testimony which they bear in

---

[1] Waite, *Op. cit.*, pp. 139–145 and 146, 147. See also Plates I and II.
[2] *Ib.*, pp. 191–195.   [3] *Op. cit.*, pp. 75, 76.

common, while if after other manners they reflected one into another the witness might be weaker in proportion. There is no concert, there is no debt in literature, there is no result in time, as by a course of development from cycle to cycle of books. The scheme of Theosophical Kabbalism is distinct absolutely from that of Grail literature, as of anything else that at any period was drawn into Romance : it is the evidence of two Schools which did not know one another ; and although at the root their evidence is of the same kind the relation between them is that, so to speak, of the pairs of opposites. As I must look to be challenged in the gate over the theses of this book, I assume at this point so much harness as will suffice to dissuade the gentlemen of the counter-guard from supposing that I am open to attack as one who would maintain that generic literature A is the concealed father of generic literature B. Speaking now more seriously as a counsel to some of the Confraternities with which I am affiliated in thought and the pursuit of a term in common : when it is said that " God so loved the world," the counterpart in Kabbalism is that MALKUTH, meaning the Kingdom, is in no sense apart from KETHER, meaning the Crown, and that the progression from ALEPH to TAU is complete, without break or intermission ; yet St. Paul, whom I have quoted, is not for such reason a precursor of the ZOHAR. So also when the Arabian Academies of Spain[1] became the resort of Christian Scholars—" men of curious inquiry ", as one has said concerning them—it does not suggest that from such Schools they brought back Sufic Mysticism and translated it into Romance. It does not mean that there also they met with the *corpus materiale* of the Kabbalah, a final receptacle of the *débris* and drift of all the old Theogonies, Theosophies and occult knowledge of many places and periods, or that learning there how She who is called the Daughter of the Voice was withdrawn from the Sanctuary of Israel, they told in another tongue how, after the departure of the Grail, the dwelling of King Fisherman " began to fall ", though the Chapel thereto belonging never " wasted nor decayed ". The voices say one thing only ; but they do not speak in concert. We know only and realise that Israel is waiting by the waters of Babylon, and it has come to pass that, though we draw from other places, we are also beside her, remembering perhaps more dimly and yet with deeper yearning the glory that was once in Zion.

Of such was the mind of Kabbalism, its appanage, its baggage and its Quest.

Those who revere it at this day continue to invoke ADONAI instead of YAHWE, and till knowledge is restored to the Sanctuary on the Day of Messiah the King, they deplore the loss of Israel, as those who read these pages and I who write them deplore the loss of the Grail. Perhaps also Theosophical Jewry—like a Holy Assembly, but few and far apart —explores as it can, according to its own individual gifts of insight, the deeps of meaning behind the loss of the Word, as we too—a not

[1] See James Finn : HISTORY OF THE JEWS IN SPAIN AND PORTUGAL, 1841.

less scattered Company—are in travail continual over the meaning of the Grail and that which was taken away when it left the world. Perhaps in fine neither they nor we are any too sure on the values of this and that in our findings. Voice of the Holy Grail, Voice of the HOLY ZOHAR, is there anything that voices better " the devotion to something afar from the sphere of our sorrow "?

There is one more word to add : those who read the ZOHAR, which at this long last is assuming some fashion of an English vesture,[1] will find that from beginning to end it is a great book of debates in which the Masters of Tradition unfold their Secret Tradition one to another when and wherever they meet. They are high initiates of Holy Doctrine, holding their various grades of knowledge ; but these have not been communicated in any scholastic curriculum : they are products of individual illumination, and for this reason the wisdom develops among them and grows from more to more, abiding always under the canons of a hidden law. It comes about also that they may meet with a stranger in their travels and may cherish doubts concerning him : in the end, however, it may happen that they fall on their knees before him, and he is hailed as more than a Master. Ancient Kabbalism was most assuredly a School of Adeptship, a Mystery as such ; but no one was received therein according to ceremonial forms : they grew up into their High Grades and—as suggested already—were as if a Secret Church in Israel. Those who entered therein were joined thereto by virtue of their own titles, earned and attained within. After such manner did Galahad achieve the Quest ; and if the Holy Grail could be regarded in its literature as a strange case—after some undetermined manner—of Ritual drawn into Romance, so also Perceval was received, while Lancelot and Gawain were rejected for carrying false titles.

V

OF SPIRITUAL ALCHEMY

IT is to be noted that Mediæval and later scholarship had scarcely troubled itself with the great Books of Jewish Theosophy till it was found or conceived that they could be made to enforce the Official Doctrines of Christianity. Many errors of enthusiasm followed ; but the Books of the Mystery of Israel became in this manner the public heritage of philosophy ; and we are now able to shew after what manner it enters into the general storehouse of mystical knowledge. The literature of Alchemy, in like manner, so long as it was in the hands of certain amateurs of infant science and its counterfeits,

---

[1] THE ZOHAR, translated by Harry Sperling and Maurice Simon; Vol. I, 1931; Vol. II, 1932. There are others to follow, probably five in all.

remained particular to themselves, and outside a questionable research in physics it had no office or horizon until it was affirmed or inferred that some curious texts of the subject had been written in a language of subterfuge ; that in place of a metallurgical interest it was concerned in its way with the keeping of Spiritual Mysteries. There were again errors of enthusiasm, but a corner of the veil was lifted. Now, it is indubitably the message of the Grail that there is more in the Eucharist than is indicated by any Sufficing Grace imparted to the ordinary communicant, and if it is possible to shew that behind this undeclared excess there lies that which has been at all times sought by the Wise, that *est in sacramento quicquid quærunt sapientes*, then the Grail literature will enter after a new manner into our heritage from the past, and another corner of the veil will be lifted on the path of experience. It will be seen that the literature—contrary to what it appears on the surface—is not without points of comparison in other Christian Cycles —that it does not stand exactly alone, even if its consanguinities, though declared by Official Religion, are not entirely before the face of the world but within the Sanctuaries of Secret Fraternities. To suggest this is not to say that these stories of old are a defined part or abstract of any Mysteries of Initiation : they are like a byway winding through a secret woodland to a postern giving upon the Chancel of some great and primeval Abbey. They are, on the surface, of Secret Churches rather than Secret Tribunals and Crypts haunted by Adepts.

Those who have concerned themselves with the subject of alleged hidden knowledge will know that occult claims have been put forth under all manners of guises. This has arisen to some extent naturally enough in the course of the ages and under the special atmosphere of motives peculiar to different nations. It has come about also through the institution of multiples of convention on the part of those who have become in later times the Custodians of Mysteries—whether actual or putative—such Wardens having been inspired by a twofold purpose, firstly, to preserve their witness in the world and, secondly, to see that the knowledge was, so far as possible, kept away from the world. This is equivalent to saying that the paramount Law of Silence has of necessity a permanent competitor in the Law of the Sign. We may take the readiest illustration in the Rituals of Craft Masonry. They contain the whole marrow of *bourgeoisie*, but they contain also a shadow of Great Mysteries. The unknown persons or assembly which conceived the Closing of the Lodge according to the Third Degree had a set of moral feelings in common with those of all retired masters in the craft of joinery and a language like a journeyman carpenter ; but this notwithstanding the breath of the Adepts had passed over them, and they spoke of the Word and its Quest as none had spoken previously. That Closing gives expression to a loss of the ages in terms of symbolism which can be voiced by the least literate occupant of the Master's Chair. And yet so far from making it commonised and a thing of no moment, its deep significance has shone through all the clouds on the minds of those who were prepared.[1]

The Grail literature is open—*mutatis mutandis*—to a parallel criticism, and the result is also the same. Whatever disappointment may await in fine the pursuit of the present inquiry, partly on account of the uncouth presentation of living symbolism to the mind of the early romancist, partly by reason of the inherent defect of Romance as a vehicle of symbolism, there is enough evidence to shew that a very strange leaven was working in the mass of the texts. Let me add in respect of it that the quality of this leaven can be appreciated scarcely by those who are unacquainted (1) with the inward phases of the life of Christian Sanctity during the Middle Ages, after which period the voices sound uncertain and the consciousness of experience more remote, and (2) with the interior working of those Concealed Orders of which the Masonic experiment is a part only, and elementary at that. The most important lights are therefore either in very old books or in the catholic motive which characterises Secret Rituals that, whether old or not, have never entered into the knowledge of the outside world.

The testimony is of two kinds invariably—first of all, to the existence of a Great Experiment and the success with which, under given circumstances, it can be carried to its term ; and, secondly, to a great failure in respect of the external world. The one is reflected by the achieved Quest of the Holy Grail, and the other by the removal of the Grail. In respect of the one it is as if a Great Mystery had been communicated at a given time in the external places, but as if also such communication had afterwards been suspended, the secret had as if died. In respect of the other, it is as if a House of Doctrine had been voided. Did these statements exhaust the content of the alternatives, the testimony might be that of a sect ; but we shall see at the proper time after what manner they conform to external doctrine, even if the keepers of that doctrine should themselves be unable to penetrate the law of the union.

Now, the great literatures and the great individual books come into the hands of the mystic—as into other hands innumerable—and he interprets them after his own manner, imparting to them that light which, at least intellectually, abides in himself. I make this formal statement because I realise that it is perilous for my position and because it enables me to add that though literatures may be clay in our hands, it must not be imagined that those who in the first place put a shape of their own kind on the material which they had ingarnered were invariably conscious that it might bear that other seal and impression which is set upon it by our own minds. So also it is too much to suppose that within the external sense of texts there was

---

[1] It is the memorial of another Mythos put on record by those who had heard some rumours concerning it and nothing more. There came a time when the Mythos was brought forth with its veils removed *ex hypothesi* in Royal Arches and High Grades ; but this again was on the part of those who had vague suspicions only of that which was hidden in the symbols put into their hands.

underwritten, beyond debate, the one inward significance which in some of them we seem to trace indubitably. The Baron de la Motte Fouqué once wrote a beautiful and stately story in which a correspondent discovered a complete and subtle allegory ; and the author, who planned when he wrote it no sub-surface meaning, did not less sincerely confess to the additional sense, explaining in reply that true art in literature is true upon all the planes.[1] There are certain Romances which need not be enumerated here but would be found to connect after this manner with mystical science—that is to say, in a non-intentional way—and it is beautiful to discern thus that there is a deep below their deep, though we may never press the interpretation into a formal scheme. The books of the Holy Grail are not exactly of this kind. A text which says that certain Secret Words were once imparted under very wonderful and exceptional circumstances is assuredly obtruding a meaning behind meaning ; while another which affirms that a certain imagined personage was ordained secretly by a similar intervention, and was made thereby the first Bishop of Christendom, either manifests an ulterior motive or there is no such motive in the world. And further, when the two Great Quests of the whole literature are written partly in the form of confessed similitude, it is not unreasonable to infer that there is a hidden meaning throughout ; while, in fine, as their undisguised intention is to exhibit an Arch-Natural Mass, the Graces and the Mysteries of which can be experienced and seen by some who are of perfect life, then the interpretation which illustrates this intention by the mystical side of Eucharistic Doctrine, in or beyond the Church, offers a true construction, and its valid criticism is *vere dignum et justum est, æquum et salutare.* I will pour three cups to the health and coronation of him who shall discover the hypothetical proto-Perceval of primeval folk-lore ; yet on the present subject let him and all other Brethren in the holy places of research keep silence, unless God graces them with agreement. The unknown writers of the PERLESVAUS and the QUEST OF GALAHAD hinted at the Great Experiment as those who knew something of their theme and bore true witness on its term.

We know also in our own hearts that eternity is the one thing which signifies ultimately and that great literature should confess to no narrower horizon. It may happen that a beginning is made by proposing a lesser object, but it is exalted afterwards ; and this was the case with the Grail books, which were given the Early Legends of Perceval according to the Office of Nature, but afterwards the Legend of Galahad according to the Law of Grace.

There is no question in the mind of Theosophical Israel that Israel will recover its inheritance on a day of the Lord to come, and it is said that then and thereafter will Mercy be on all sides. We pass now to the witness of another literature, the earliest available records of

---

[1] My reference is to THE MAGIC RING : A KNIGHTLY ROMANCE. As regards the supposed Allegory, its discovery is narrated, I think, in a preface to one of the editions.

which are in Greek of the Byzantine epoch, in Arabic and Syriac of a later period, while it assumed the vesture of Latin in or about the tenth century and passed into the vernaculars of England, France and Germany in its latest and final developments. It may be said almost that a time came when the wonder and rumour of Alchemy was in all men's ears; but its Secret School was dedicated to experimental operations performed on material things, and is nothing as such to our purpose. The Mysteries, authentic or otherwise, of metallic transmutation and the Elixir of Physical Life are, speaking fantastically and yet with a purpose in view, analogous to those folk-lore elements— Magic Cups and Cauldrons, Dishes, Spears and Swords—which may have filled a world of Myth before the Great Christian Hallow reigned in the Kingdom of Romance. As certain folk-lore Myths were acquired *ex hypothesi* and brought into the purpose of the Grail, so there came a day when the cloud of records and experiments in the work of Hermetic Adepts was taken over, so to speak, and adapted to another object: it is this Mystery which became the next witness in the world after that of the Grail and Kabbalism. The first voice on the subject is that of Heinrich Khunrath, as I have shewn forth at some length elsewhere,[1] and the second is Jacob Böhme, both at the end of the sixteenth century, according to whom, writing on the Stone of the Philosophers, it is to be understood that the Stone is Christ. It follows that " the Great Work " of so-called Hermeticism was not in metals but in the soul of man.

While the physical alchemists were trying to make gold they brought to birth the beginnings of Chemistry, finding out this and that, to their great astonishment, though the discoveries were far enough in all cases from their proposed term. Under the pretence of a new translation of certain Scripture Psalms, Khunrath produced a mystical understanding of the whole Hermetic subject, veiling his deeper meanings in a marvellous series of copperplates shewing Christ immanent and transcendent at the heart of the whole cosmos. On his side, Jacob Böhme produced before German Alchemists, standing agaze about him, the revelation that not only the Stone is Christ but that the Way of Attainment in Alchemy is the Way of the Second Birth. He said otherwise that of the physical praxis he knew—and probably cared —nothing, but that hereof is truth in the art and that whosoever sets forth on the Great Work except by and through Life in Christ had and would have always the pains and costs for his one reward. Khunrath said also derisively that the cost of the Great Work is less than thirty thalers, as if the Way of the Christhood could be purchased for this price, as well as sold by Judas to his own destruction. The real significance of these amazing statements must have distracted many laboratory workers in those maniacal days of the *Magnum Opus* fever. As regards meanings, it must have been held inevitably that, given the Second Birth, it would be easy to transmute metals, and they

[1] THE SECRET TRADITION IN ALCHEMY : ITS DEVELOPMENTS AND RECORDS, 1926.

may have gone to work accordingly, producing fictitious regenerations and so finding fresh avenues through realms of failure.

However this may be, after these there arose other witnesses, though few and far between, who made use of the old alchemical terminology—which abounds in Böhme as well as in Khunrath—not only to explain the universe but high things of mystical experience in the soul of man. I do not claim to know how far they went at their best ; but two things are certain : (1) that like those who were, in a sense, their progenitors, the material alchemists, they were an unincorporated sodality who recognised one another, because they spoke the same language, and could distinguish at the same time those who were born to the Mystery from those who aped election, the *souffleurs*, the bellows-blowers, the impostors ; (2) that their peculiar THEOSOPHIA had no doctrine of loss but one of attainment only, being the possession and enjoyment of the Mystical Stone—that is to say, the Inward Christ. The Grail might be taken from the world and the Word might be lost to Israel ; but there remained always the state of the *haut prince*, the state of Galahad, consequent on the Mass at Sarras, praying to be dissolved in Christ. There is of course an implied loss, being the Absence of the Stone, the unespoused state of soul ; but there is no commentary hereon in the alchemical texts. Now, I have said that those who can be recognised as belonging to the spiritual work, a few Rosicrucian writers included,[1] used the same terminology as their ancestors ; and it remains for this reason that we have to interpret them for ourselves, according to our own lights, a task which must be attempted in the few pages that follow. It has to be understood further that here is an excursion into the most cryptic of all literature, about which no one can speak dogmatically, though some have attempted it in the past.

That which the text-books have agreed from time immemorial to term a Stone is that also which is described in Gospel Books as a Stone not made with hands and the conversion performed thereby is that which one of the Adepts recommends to one of his disciples when he exclaims : *Transmutemini, transmutemini de lapidibus mortuis in lapides vivos philosophicos.*[2] The possession of the Stone is, in other words, the possession of the Tingeing Christ. It is most obvious and outside contradiction that either this communication and possession is set forth in the Churches under the sacramentalism of the Holy Eucharist or the Mass and the Lord's Supper are a sacrifice and memorial apart from all meaning. Behind them are shadowed forth the Liturgies and the Ritual of the Grail, as a high and secret rendering of the same subject

---

[1] Among those who may be quoted in this connection is he who was termed Sapiens by the Brothers of R ∴ C ∴, according to Eugenius Philalethes in his ANIMA MAGICA ABSCONDITA. For him the Stone and Treasure of Philosophers was not only the True Medicine but the Way of Truth, the Life that was Light of men, wherein we may behold the Light. This Medicine is found indeed, but never except in Heaven, while the place in which it is found is " within thyself." WORKS OF THOMAS VAUGHAN, pp. 99–104.

[2] THE BROTHERHOOD OF THE ROSY CROSS, p. 297.

in other pictorial terms,[1] as if the sense of certain insufficiencies and of the way in which they might be rectified were in the hands of hidden Masters.   That which in this case lies behind the symbols and physical pictures of Bread and Wine, behind that Priesthood which is according to the Order of Melchisedech, was expressed by the Spiritual Alchemists under the guise of transmutation.

I suppose indeed that there is no labyrinth which it is quite so difficult to thread as that of the *Theatrum Chemicum*.   Expositors of the subject have gone astray over the generic purpose of the art, because some have believed it to have been (1) the transmutation of metals and that only, while others have interpreted it as (2) a veiled method of delineating the states and stages of the soul's attainment on its way through the world within, and besides this nothing.[2]   We have on our part to realise that a second school arose, as stated, at a comparatively late period, and placed a new construction on the old claims and language of the alchemical adepts and their literature.

I propose to tabulate certain points of terminology which are common to both schools.   By the significance of these terms we shall see to what extent the symbolism of Higher Alchemy is in conformity with mystical symbolism and in correspondence also with that Mass of the Holy Spirit which was said once at Sarras.   It should be realised, however, that there is nothing so hard and thankless as to elucidate one symbolism according to the forms of another, and this notwithstanding the identity which may emerge as the term of each.

Both schools indifferently tell us that the whole Art is contained, manifested and set forth by means of a single Vessel which, amidst all manner of minor variations, is described with colourable uniformity throughout the multitude of texts.   This statement constitutes a certain key of understanding ; but as on the one hand the alchemists veil their *vas insigne* by reference, in spite of their assurance, to many pretended vessels, so has the key itself a certain aspect of subterfuge, since the alleged unity, on the mystical side, is in respect only of the term final of the process in the union-state of the Recipient.   This unity is the last reduction of a triad because—according to these aspects of Hermetic Theosophy—man in the course of his progress is at first three—body, soul and spirit—that is, when he sets out on the Great Quest ; he is two at a certain stage, or when the soul has conceived Christ, for the Spirit has then descended and the body is for the time being as something which has been left behind ; but he is in fine one, that is to say, when the man has died and risen in Christ.

The black state of the alchemical matter, on which the process of the Art is engaged, is our unconverted natural manhood.   The white state

---

[1] I am referring of course to that which obviously was said and done in the Mass of the Grail at Corbenic and in the Mass of the Five Changes, celebrated at the Grail Castle in the presence of King Arthur on the testimony of the HIGH HISTORY.

[2] This is Mrs. Atwood's thesis, though not so expressed.   We may compare, at its value, the ethical interpretation of General E. H. Hitchcock in REMARKS ON ALCHEMY AND THE ALCHEMISTS, 1857.

of the Stone is the work of the Second Birth ; and the red state, desired as the term of the Art, is that of the soul's transmutation and the attainment of that unity in which there is no distinction between the soul and the Christ Spirit.

The Mercury of the Sages is that which must be fixed and volatilised : naturally it is fluidic and wandering ; but except under this name, or by some analogous substitute, it has never been described literally. Because it is within and is we ourselves in our inward being, it has been said frequently to be nearer than hands and feet. The Sulphur of the Philosophers is an inward substance through which some souls are saved, as by an inward burning fire. The Salt of the Philosophers is a transmuting principle which is with us through all our days in a state of misdirection, and its true application is the Great Work accomplished. In the last resource therefore the physician heals himself ; but I am speaking here of that which the Spiritual Hermetists have termed the Medicine.

The ostensible object—which was material in the alternative School— was the attainment of a certain Stone or Powder, being that of Projection, and the affirmation is that this Powder, when added to a base metal, performs the wonder of transmutation into pure silver or gold, better than those of the mines. The Stone transmutes what is base, but in its own elements it has undergone transmutation itself, from what is base to what is perfect. In another form it prolongs life and renews youth in the " adept philosopher and lover of learning." In this case it is termed an Elixir ; but this and the Transmuting Powder are identified by the Spiritual Alchemists. If there is one thing which appears more clearly than another in some Books of the Philosophers, it is that the Stone of Alchemy is not a stone at all and that the Elixir of Alchemy is not a brew or an essence which can be poured out from ewers or basins.[1]

It must be affirmed further that—in the spiritual sense—there is an unity in the trinity of the Stone or Powder, the so-called Metal and the Vase. The Vessel is also the Alchemist, for none of the instruments, the materials, the fires, the producer and the thing produced are external to the one subject. At the same time the inward man is distinguished from the outward man ; we may say that one is the Alchemist and the other the Vessel ; and that in this sense the Art is termed both physical and spiritual. But the symbolism is many times enfolded ; and from another point of view the gross matter which is placed within the Vessel is the untransmuted life of reason, motive, concupiscence, self-interest and all that which constitutes the intelligent creature on the normal plane of manifestation. Hereof is the natural man enclosed in an animal body, as the metal is placed in the vessel, and from this point of view the Alchemist is he who is sometimes termed arrogantly the super-man. But because there is only one Vessel it must be understood that herein the Stone is confected and the

---

[1] Appendix I, Note 26.

base metal is converted. The Alchemist is himself finally the Stone, and because many zealous aspirants to the Art have not understood this they have failed in the Great Work on the spiritual side.

The schedule which now follows may elucidate this hard subject somewhat more fully, if not indeed more plainly : There are (1) the natural, external man, whose equivalent is the one Vessel ; (2) the body of desire which answers to the gross matter ; (3) the aspiration, the consciousness, the will of the supernatural life ; (4) the process of the will working on the body of desire within the external Vessel ; (5) the psychic and transcendental conversion thus effected ; (6) the reaction of the purified body of desire on the essential will, so that the one supports the other, the will is again exalted, and therefrom follows this further change—that the spirit of a man puts on a new quality of life, becoming an instrument which is at once feeding and itself fed ; (7) herein is the symbol of the Stone and the Great Elixir ; (8) the spirit is nourished from above by the analogies of Eucharistic ministry—that is to say, the Dove descends from Heaven carrying the Arch-Natural Host to renew the virtues of the Stone ; (9) the spirit nourishes the soul, as by Bread and Wine—that is, the Bread is taken from the Grail ; (10) the soul effects the higher conversion in the body of desire ; (11) it comes about thus that the essence which dissolves everything is still contained in a Vessel, or alternatively that God abides in man.

From another point of view the gross matter is said to be clay by those who speak more openly in order that they may be understood the less, as if they also were singing in their strange chorus :

> " Let us be open as the day,
>   That we may deeper hide ourselves."

It is more often described as metallic, because on the surface of all the literature there is the declared Mystery of Metals, and the concealed purpose is to shew that in the roots and essence there is a certain similarity or analogy on both sides of the alchemical work. The process of the Art is without haste or violence by the mediation of a graduated fire, and the seat of this fire is in the soul. It is a mystery of the soul's love, and for this reason she is called " undaunted daughter of desire." The sense of the gradation is that love is in liberation from the impetuosity and violence of passion, and has become a constant and incorruptible flame. That. which the fire consumes is certain materials or elements which are called *recrementa*, the grosser parts, the superfluities ; and it should be observed that there are two purgations, of which the first is the gross and the second the subtle. The first answers to the normal process of conversion, by which there is such a separation of components seemingly external that what remains is as a new creature, and may be said to be re-born. The second is an exalted conversion, by which that which has been purified is so raised that it enters into a new region, or a certain heaven comes down and abides therein.[1]

It follows from these elucidations that the higher and indrawn understanding of the Eucharist and of Alchemy on its mystical side is concerned with the same subject, that is to say, with man and his conversion : the implicits are therefore the same, and of these things Alchemy was a witness in the world after the epoch of the Holy Grail.

But though it might seem therefore within reason and truth to testify that the *panis vivus et vitalis* is even as the Transmuting Stone and that the Chalice of the New and Eternal Testament is like the Renewing Elixir, such testimony is subject to the reserve of my previous indication. The closer the analogies between distinct systems of symbolism, the more urgent is that prudence which counsels us not to confound them by an interchangeable use. The Priest as Priest neither dealt in the symbolism of Alchemy nor assumed its external offices, while the Alchemist as Alchemist did not celebrate Mass. It is true notwithstanding that all Christian Mysticism came out of the Mass-Book, and it is true that it returns therein. But the Mass-Book in the first instance came out of the heart mystical which had unfolded in Christendom. The nucleus of truth in the Missal is : *Dominus prope est*. The Mass shews that the Great Work is in the first sense a work of the hands of man, because it is he, officiating as a Priest in his own Temple, who offers the Sacrifice which he has dedicated ; but the Elements of that Sacrifice are taken over *ex hypothesi* by an intervention of another order of things, and that which follows is transfusion.

Re-expressing all this in a closer summary, the apparatus of Mystical Alchemy is, comparatively speaking, simple. The First Matter is myrionymous and is yet one, corresponding to the unity of the natural mind and the unlimited complexity of motives, desires, passions and distractions—on all of which the work of wisdom must operate. The Vessel is also one, for this is the normal man, complete in his own degree. The process has the seal of Nature's directness : it is like the gradual but increasing maintenance of a slow fire. The initial work is a change in the substance of mind, aspiration and desire, which is the first conversion, or transmutation in the elementary sense. But it is identical, even to the end, with the term proposed by the Eucharist, which is the modification of the noumenal man by the communication of Divine Substance. Here is the *lapis qui non lapis, lapis tingens, lapis angularis, lapis qui multiplicatur, lapis per quem justus ædificabit domum Domini, et jam valde ædificatur et terram possidebit per omnia,* &c. When it is said that the Stone is multiplied, even to a thousandfold, we know that this is true of all seed which is sown upon good soil.

So therefore the Stone transmutes and the Higher Eucharist trans_

---

[1] There is nothing in the records to intimate that the Spiritual Alchemists were acquainted with that most rare of all mystical experience in which the whole inward being is transformed at once in God.

mutes also ; the philosophical elements on the physical side go to the
making of the Stone, which is also physical, and the sacramental
elements to the generation of a new life in the soul. He who says *Lapis
Philosophorum* says also : My beloved to me and I to him. Christ is
therefore the Stone, and the Stone in adept humanity is the Union
realised, while the Great Secret is that Christ must be found within, and
manifested from within outwardly.[1]

Now, it seems to me that it has not served less than an useful purpose
to establish after a new manner the intimate resemblance between the
deeper understanding of one part of the Secret Tradition and the fuller
interpretation of one Sacrament of the Church. We are not dealing
in either case with the question of attainment. The analogy would
remain if Spiritual Alchemy and Christian Sacramentalism abode in the
intellectual order as theorems only which have been never carried into
experience. And further it is not affirmed that the Hermetic Symbolism has attained a grade of perfection. When Christian Symbolism
took over the old Legends and created out of them the literature of the
Holy Grail, the work was not done perfectly, and it is the same with
alchemical books. It remains that the Doctrine and Practice of
Mysticism offered a Divine Experience, to those who entered the
pathway of the Mystics, as a foretaste in this life of the union which is
consummated in eternity, or of that end, beyond which there is nothing
whatever that is conceivable. We know from the old book that " it
hath not entered into the heart of man," but the heart which has put
away the things of sense may at least conceive it by representations
and types. This is the great tradition of that which the early alchemists
term Truth in the Art ; the experience is representation after its own
kind rather than felicity, but the representation is of that grade which
begins in ecstasy and ends in absorption. Let no man say therefore
that he loses himself in experiences of this order, for perchance it is
then only that he finds himself, even in that way which suggests that
after many paths of activity he is at length coming into his own.

The alchemical maxim which might be inscribed on the gate of the
palais espiriteus or any Castle of the Grail would be :

> " *Est in Mercurio quicquid quærunt sapientes.*"

The Eucharistic maxim which might be written over the laboratory
of the alchemist, in addition to *Laborare est orare*, is :

> " *Et antiquum documentum*
> *Novo cedat ritui :*
> *Præstet fides supplementum*
> *Sensuum defectui.*"

The maxim which might be written over the Temples of the Official
Churches is *Corporis Mysterium*—that the mystery of the body might
lead them more fully into the higher mystery of the soul. And in fine

---

[1] The manifestation, speaking essentially, is from subliminal to normal consciousness.

the maxim which might and would be inscribed over the one Temple of the truly Catholic Religion when the faiths of this Western world have been united in the higher consciousness—that is assuredly *Mysterium Fidei*—the Mystery which endures for ever and for ever passes into experience.

Within the domain of the Secret Tradition the Initiations are many and so are the schools of thought, but those which are True Schools and those which are High Orders issue from one root. *Est una sola res ;* and they whose heart of contemplation is fixed upon this one thing may differ but can be never far apart. Personally I do not believe— and this has the ring of a commonplace—that they will be found to differ widely. I know not what systems of the æons may intervene between that which is imperishable within us and the union wherein the universe will repose in fine at the centre. But I know that the great systems—aye even the great processes—of the times that are gone, as of those which now encompass us, do not pass away, because that which was from the beginning is now and ever shall be—is one motive, one aspiration, one term of thought remaining, as if in the stillness of an everlasting present. In reality we understand one another, and our terms are terms over which our collective dedications are united world without end.

VI

ANALOGIES OF QUEST IN MASONRY

IT should be understood that I am speaking at the present moment only of the Craft Degrees. I have every reason to know that the High Grades do not deserve the unqualified condemnation with which they have been set aside by writers like Ragon and by certain expositors of the German school of Masonic thought. Several of them are Great Rites which shadow forth important mystic teaching —at however far a distance—and without some of them I regard the Craft Degrees as offering, at once without and within, an unfinished experience. Those, however, who are familiar with the Craft Rituals will be in a position to realise to what extent they can be said to embody an ethical doctrine, except as side-issues of their Mystery. There is, of course, a very plain inculcation of certain obvious virtues ; but it is all so slight, and it is all so obvious, that to speak of it as an ethical system seems to magnify the subject out of all due proportion. On the other hand, we do find certain provinces of knowledge recommended to the study of the Candidate at one stage of his advancement. We find also certain illustrations of a great Mystery of Building, certain references to a Secret which has been lost, with a Legend concerning the immolation of a Master of Knowledge who took away with him that Secret, and except under very deep veils, outside all Craft Masonry, it has not been recovered since. As I have quoted Ragon in a connection which was necessarily unfavourable, let me cite him now a little tentatively, but in a different sense. He has said—at its value—that when we find in Masonry, and in some other secret ways of the past, a reference to Building—whether of Temples, Palaces, or Towns—what is intended is that there was a manifestation of Doctrine : in other words, there was an ordered communication of Mysteries. As to the great majority of instances, I believe in this as little as I believe that Troy Town was a Solar Mythos ; but in respect of Craft Masonry it is the one suggestive note in Ragon's great wild of speculation and discursion on the Degrees, high and otherwise, of the Fraternity.[1] It is postulated in the speculation that those who transformed the Building Guild did not intend to put forward an historical thesis. The change which took place presupposes such a spiritualisation of the Traditional Temple that it passes into the world of symbolism, becoming itself a House of Doctrine. If, apart from the *Theosophia* of Mystical Death and Rebirth, we are to seek anywhere for another clue, it is in the amazing inference which follows from the Craft Legend concerning the stultification of the imagined House of Doctrine before its erection was finished. Those who are familiar with the Rituals will understand exactly what I mean, and I give this as a key by which anyone who is properly qualified, and who chooses, may possibly open one of the Emblematic Secret Sanctuaries.[2] We know that the Master was asked One Little Question, and that for One Little Answer which he declined to make the Traditional Founder of Doctrine came to an end of violence ; the Mysteries which he reserved perished in his person ; and although it has never been noticed so far by any Masonic writer in the living world, it follows therefrom that the Great Symbolical Temple was not finished according to the original plans. It is for this reason that symbolically, if not actually, the True Temple still remains to be erected. Meanwhile, in Masonry, as in other institutions, we rest content as we can with certain conventional proxies in which we suppose, by a precarious hypothesis, which may have, however, a profound meaning imbedded, that some analogy inheres. It is understood that two Kings who represented at one time the Royal Houses of Official Grace and Nature knew the canonical answer to the Question, supposing that this had been put under the due warrants ; but it is to be inferred that it was the verbal formula and not the ground-plan of the Mystic Building. In any case it remained *Sacramentum Regis*, the Secret of the King, and it follows, still speaking symbolically, that all Masonry derives not from a Lodge of Masters but from that of an inferior grade—the so-called Fellow Craft, namely. The missing formula was a Word of Life, and the *locum tenens*, by a contradistinctive analogy, is a Word of Death. It is for this reason that the whole corporate Fraternity undertakes a Quest[3] which is in undesigned

---

[1] We can hold the concept loosely and look for light therein.
[2] It is to be remembered that all representation is by way of substitution.
[3] We must understand in this connection a Quest for the Life of Spiritual Things.

correspondence with that of the Round Table ; but they move in the opposite direction to that in which the Mysteries repose.[1] It is the most mystical of all inquests, for it is the history of our human life.[2] But there is an Orient from on high which in fine rises on the soul ; the soul turns in that light and moves thenceforward in the true and one direction.

It is possible to express what follows from these facts in terms of comparative simplicity ; for even as Moses came down from the Mountain of God with a veil upon the face of him, so have I been speaking thus far to the mixed assembly of my readers under the veil of a self-imposed reservation, because these things are not to be discussed in public without changing the voice. Let me say now more openly, if not more clearly, that the ideal of the True Temple is in our hearts, and it is there that we build it. We do this daily by all the aspirations of our nature ; but for want of the lost designs we have not been able to externalise it. No doubt we have failed to lead the Life which entitles us to know of the Doctrine ; but we feel that it is implied and latent in all the roots of our being ; and we seem to die with it on our lips. It speaks in our dreams, but it uses an unknown language ; and if heart utters it to heart, it is only in oracles. Yet we have conceived enough regarding it to be aware—as intimated above—that the Spiritual Temple is a House not made with hands. And so neither Masonry nor any other of the greater Instituted Mysteries has designed a rebuilding of material Holy Places. The Rites of Initiation may deal—as they do certainly—in Parables and in Allegories ; they may present—and they do also—their particular forms of thought in the guise of a Legend of yesterday ; but they are really the Legends of to-morrow, the expressed heart of expectation and not a retrospective review. But if this be the case—as it seems indeed beyond challenge—what part have we otherwise in Masonry, seeing that we have come out of Jewry as others came out of Egypt ?[3] If this, I say, be the case, what manner of House was that which was planned of old in wisdom and was afterwards finished as it best could be, because treason fell upon the Keeper, because, in the absence of preparation and title, there had been an attempt to take the Kingdom of the Rites by violence ? Let us seek our first illustrative answer from an episode of the Law which was once promulgated in Israel. Moses the prophet came down in his glory from Mount Sinai bringing with him the Tables of the Law ; but he found his rebellious people unqualified for the high knowledge, and before the face of them he broke those Tables. Afterwards he gave them indeed certain commandments, but we are told on high traditional authority that they were the shadows of the others only—the code of unruly children,

---

[1] The journey is undertaken westward, instead of to the due east, and hence they return with Substitutes.

[2] We die with Substitutes in our hands in place of Realities in our hearts.

[3] There is one Masonic Grade which speaks of a plan to rebuild the House of God in Zion, but it means obviously after another manner.

not of the elected truly.[1] The world was not worthy. And the next example is that which we know already—that the Grail was taken away and that something was missing thereafter from the House of Quest ; that again the world was not worthy. The three stories are therefore one story, and the same thing is everywhere. It is so much everywhere that the knowledge which remained with Moses was not withdrawn utterly by him—according to another Legend of Israel— when he went up the mountain in fine, when no man living followed him, when he did not return evermore. It has been held always in Jewry that there were certain Elders who received a Secret Deposit[2] and transmitted it in their turn in secret, so that it was perpetuated from generation to generation till it became known to the world at large, but only in an imperfect form, about the middle period of the Christian centuries. The original ZOHAR is reported by a paradox to have been a sufficient load for twelve camels, and the extant ZOHAR is on its own shewing a fragment or a substitute. The correspondence in Grail literature is the disparting of the Hallows among certain Holy Hermits and the removal of the Sacred Vessel to that place of which Perceval should know surely and with all speed.[3]

That which was made void, according to the Craft Legend, was a non-Christian House of Doctrine. The step beyond this is to shew that there is a Parallel in Masonry concerning Christian Doctrine ; but it is found in High Degrees and in those which are militantly Christian. We must set aside those which were concerned in the past with an imagined Legend of Templar Vengeance. It is an old story in the High Grades that the murder of Jacques de Molai was destined to be avenged heavily, and one section of criticism has concluded that this was effected ultimately by the decapitation of Louis XVI ; but this is Romance of Faërie. There are traces, however, of another secret plan, and one more deeply laid, though it was actuated by far different motives than inhere in the idea of vengeance. It is not illustrated by any Legend of murder or by anything that, remotely or approximately, can suggest a *vendetta*. But in one Masonic Grade which by the hypothesis, is the last transformation of the Templars, the fact is shewn forth by the silent eloquence of symbolism. As in the Craft Degrees we learn how the vital secret was taken away, so here the Rite sets before us a picture of all Christendom, personified by the flower of its Chivalry, standing guard, amidst the adjuncts of pomp and ceremony, over a Vacant Sepulchre—the Shrine from which a God has departed. Could anything signify more profoundly the bereavement and widowhood of the Christian House of Doctrine ? Could anything indicate more pregnantly the presence of a sub-surface design among the old Knights Templar, supposing that this Grade were really, at some far distance, descended therefrom ? Would it not seem like a challenge by way of evasion, saying to the modern

---

[1] See THE HOLY KABBALAH, pp. 306–311.   [2] *Ib.*, p. 17.
[3] Potvin, *Op. cit.*, I, p. 346 ; HIGH HISTORY, Branch XXXV, Title 26.

world : " Do you suppose, in your fondness, that about those Hallows of the past our intention was ever centralised except to conceal it ? "

There is obviously no answer hereto in the realm of figurative pageants ; but our next step takes us to a Grade which is, comparatively speaking, obscure, though it is still worked in England. It is one the position and claim of which is a little difficult to determine, whether as to origin or history. On the surface its similarity to the Eighteenth Degree of Rose Croix has caused many persons to repudiate it as a mere copy. The better view may be, however, to infer that both Rites originated from a common prototype—with apologies to past Grail scholarships for trespassing in their most cherished preserves. I may mention here that there are not only several variants of the Eighteenth Degree incorporated by other systems, but there have been also Rosicrucian Grades current from time to time in Masonry which have very slight correspondence—beyond the Rose Croix name—with the Masonically most important memorial of the Ancient and Accepted Scottish Rite. This question apart, the particular Chivalrous and Masonic Order is rendered of consequence to our present purpose because it gives the counterpart by alternative of that intimation which is conveyed in the analogous Templar Grade. The latter represents a particular state of an assumed case at the period of the Crusades, the former at an epoch which—on account of several historical confusions, having an appearance of design—is scarcely possible to determine. In any event it dissolves at a certain stage into yet another Degree, and between the successive points of the two Rituals the Candidate is brought to a period when all earthly Houses of Doctrine have given place to the Spiritual House of Eternal Wisdom. As a preliminary to this, the externalised House of Doctrine, represented by the Holy Sepulchre, is made subject to a simple visitation, with the result that it is found empty ; and those who look therein are told in a veiled manner that in such a place it is useless to go in quest of Lost Secrets, because the Divine Warden thereof has risen and gone away. As the Candidate and this of necessity—is left always in the position of Satan after his lectures at Salamanca, that is to say, with the shadow instead of the substance, so here the Chivalry of the Sepulchre has to be content with what it has—with a rumour of the Resurrection constructed into glad tidings, though it remains that the Place of the Hallows is now an empty Place.

Our last step takes us again to the literature of the Holy Grail, which depicts a House of Doctrine, like the Temples, Towns and Palaces of which we have been speaking previously. It shews how that House was in the first place visited by sin or sorrow ; how secondly it was made void, the secret things thereto belonging being transferred therefrom. Symbolism has sometimes a way of sparing nothing ; and probably the makers of the Legend intended only—as some expressly say—to illustrate how the Realm of Logres had become unworthy of the most holy things ; but in two cases the House of the Doctrine is involved in the common ruin.

The question which supervenes now is one which may occur spontaneously to those who have followed this account. Is it intended to suggest—shall I say ?—that the Secret of Masonry is anti-Jewish and anti-Christian, or, to put it better, that the interests which took over the Building Guild and made up Emblematic Freemasonry had either never entered into those Holy Places of the past or had come forth therefrom ? The answer is a decisive negative. It follows from all the Traditional Histories, all the Symbolism, or that part at least which is other than accidental, and in fine from all the Rituals of Masonry, that those who set forth the widowhood of the House of Doctrine spoke not from without it but from within ; that they looked for the return of that which, for the time, had been taken away ; that when they speak to us of what was lost to Jewry, they were never more assured of the wisdom which once dwelt in Israel ; that when they mourn over the Holy Sepulchre, they were never more certain that what has been removed is alive ; and as all the Degrees end in a substituted restoration[1] it is also certain that thither where the truth and beauty had been taken they looked also to go. In other words, it is the intimation of the Secret Schools that somewhere in time and the world there is that which can confer upon the Candidate a real as well as a symbolical experience. And this is the identical message of the Grail literature. It speaks too as if from within the official House of Christian Doctrine concerning that which once inhered therein and is now in the state of withdrawal or profound latency ; it offers all honour and devotion to the Substituted Sanctuary which remains, as Masonry offers it in the higher understanding both to Jew and Christian. Here therefore is no enemy setting to at the work of destruction, but here rather are the rumours and voices as if of Unknown Superiors, like a power—which makes for righteousness—between the seat of Peter and the seat of the chief Patriarch, as if something were guiding and consoling all the Keepers of the Keys, but dissuading them at the same time from opening certain doors till that which has been lost is at length restored to the Sanctuaries.[2] It is in this sense only that we shall ever get to understand the Inner Mystery of the Holy Grail, the Mystery of the Craft Degrees, and of the great, disordered cohort of things from near and far—reflections, rumours, replicæ and supposititious descents from older Mysteries—which make up the cloud of witnesses in the High Degrees. The work, not indeed of the same hands but of many at the same work, is therefore everywhere, the traces of the same high intention, the evidence—not less strong because it is not declared

---

[1] The Word is always restored : that which was lost according to the record of the Master Grade is recovered in the Royal Arch ; a Christian alternative finding is symbolised in the Eighteenth Degree of Rose Croix ; and its rigid analogy is in Templar Masonry.

[2] It is to be expected but not affirmed that the Rites may then take the Closing in all their Grades and Degrees, because they will have served their purpose and done their work. It would not be useful to add that Church Rites are included.

openly—of Seekers, who are also our Brothers, sharing in the Quests of our humanity and shaping them, at proper seasons, to the true ends.

I conclude therefore (1) that Masonry is referred herein to its true place and is saved otherwise from the category of vain observances which are consecrated only by good intention, because it leads us back, after many travellings, to the one subject ; (2) that it is an index-finger pointing to other Rites, to greater and exalted Ceremonies, which—somewhat shadowy, somewhat dubious, yet distinguishable as to their purpose—remain among the records of the past, not without suggestions that, even at this day, the Mysteries have not died utterly.[1]

I have made it plain already that in so far as there is mystic purpose or Hidden Doctrine in the Grail literature it is often like an echo from afar—a rumour, a legend which had fallen into the hands of romancers. It is as if Sir Walter Montbéliard, the patron of Robert de Borron, being by the hypothesis a Templar, had told a strange story to the poet of things which he also had heard from afar concerning the Sons of the Valley ; it is as if the mythical Kyot de Provence, having seen a transcript from Toledo, had compared it with some Templar Records belonging to the House of Anjou. These are not the directions of research, but they stand for more likely ways ; and I put forward as so many materials of assistance, so many traces of the same implicits perpetuated through several centuries—(1) the Sacramental Mystery of Alchemy as corresponding to the Eucharistic Mystery of the Holy Grail ; (2) the mystical pageant of Kabbalism as analogical to the Grail pageant ; (3) certain quests in Masonry as synonymous—outside all derivation—with the Grail Quest. The conclusion is that from the middle of the twelfth century, and so forward, there has been always a witness in the world that the greatest and the highest among the holy things have been represented by a certain substitution within the Official Churches and in other Sanctuaries of Holy Rites. Meanwhile, the Churches have not been made void utterly ; they are still " those holy fields " ; but they bear the same relation to the Sacred Mystery behind them that the visible Sinai and Horeb, Tabor and Carmel, Gethesame and Calvary, bear to the Church within. Remember that the highest office in so sense makes void the second best among any offices that are inferior—at least till SHILOH comes. The Supernatural Grail is without prejudice to the Instituted Sacrament, even as the transliterations and complexities of Kabbalistic interpretation reduce nothing in the literal word ; while Masonry itself does not less represent an active power at work, within its own measures, because it has only substitutes to offer in respect of great things unrealised, and pictures in place of reality. It is the common disability of Rites. I speak in my humility as one who has tarried also at Eleusis, contemplating its

---

[1] It should be understood, in such case, that they are not of Vegetation Gods, that they do not deal in astral workings and that Miss Weston's Occult Schools, as she found or heard of them between 1909 and 1920, have no part therein.

Elysian Fields, and I have not found more therein. So also the PERLESVAUS and the QUESTE have put into our mouths the so-called living flesh of God Incarnate in place of the Living Spirit.[1]

VII

THE SECRET CHURCH OF ECKARTSHAUSEN

A TIME came when the bare possibility of speaking more openly led to more open speaking, and so at the end of the eighteenth century and in the first flush of the age which followed thereafter we have two or three text-books wherein are put forward some express intimations on our subject which, if they can be taken literally, are the most pregnant that have transpired in the world. I will give account of two only, which were at once independent and concurrent, namely, Eckartshausen's CLOUD UPON THE SANCTUARY and CHARACTERISTICS OF THE INTERIOR CHURCH attributed to the Russian Lopuhin but first published in French. The dates of these works are respectively 1800 and 1801.

Those who are acquainted with the literature of the Mystical Life will not be unfamiliar with the conception of a Holy Assembly in the hands of which the guidance of the Christian Church is held occasionally to have rested during the ages of Christendom. It is not, by the claim put forward, more especially a corporate union than the life of humanity at large on this earth is a corporate union also. It may not have occurred of necessity to my colleagues in thought; but they will understand what is meant when I say that the hypothetical Holy Assembly should be described perhaps as the sodality of a consciousness in common, and as I have spoken already of a consciousness behind the Church as of a region now untrodden, it will be realised that on the present supposition this region is not vacant. As we have inferred further from the researches of the present Eleventh Book that there are records of a Secret Tradition in Christian Times, so in the Doctrine of the Holy Assembly we find a late, sporadic but unusually definite witness which is saying the same thing after a new manner. I believe that the mode in which this claim has been advanced, though in one sense it is the most moderate of all, may possibly tend towards a certain confusion because two streams of influence are identified therein—one being the holy, exalted and saving mind of the official Church, at its own highest in the manifest, and the other that of the Hidden School itself as this is presented in the claim. The inference, moreover, seems to be that the Holy Assembly is a kind of head in concealment, and this I reject because of the misconception which it tends to induce of necessity. If we could suppose for a moment that

[1] Compare the GRAND SAINT GRAAL, on Joseph the II enthroned by Christ at Sarras.

man is the last development and issue from the anthropoid ape—much as one might agree to regard the story of the princess who came out of the water as a little chronicle of fact—that point—and whatever that point might be—at which the animal consciousness passed into the human consciousness would represent the analogical kind of transition by which the members of the mystical body enter—if they do enter—into the consciousness of the Holy Assembly. But the human being is not leading the anthropoid ape, nor are Werner's Sons of the Valley, who devised symbolical Masonry in his radiant dream, ruling the Craft from a specific, unseen centre. The worst of all illustrations would be, in like manner, to say that the Visible Church is the body and the Secret Church is the head. The Visible Church has been described figuratively as the mystical body of Christ, and the Real Presence in the Eucharist is *ex hypothesi* the mystical communication in perpetuity of Christ's life to that body ; but this is on the understanding that the body is the incorporation of souls in sanctity. In respect of the Holy Assembly a similar description may obtain, but also on the understanding that it is a generic union of illuminated spirits in Christ—making use of the term spirit in that sense which attributes to man the possession of a higher soul—meaning the soul in dedication. The head is Christ in both cases indifferently, but in the case of the Secret Church that Divine Union, which here is of faith or imputation, has been established there under the sun of consciousness.

Perhaps, within the more familiar forms of expression, the idea of the Secret Church corresponds most closely with that which is understood by a School of the Prophets, though the term describes an advanced spiritual state by one only of the gifts which belong thereto. The gift itself has little connection with the external meaning of prophecy : it is not especially the power of seeing forward, but rather of sight within. In subjects of this kind, as in other subjects, the greater includes the lesser, it being of minor importance, for example, to discern the Coming of Christ in a glass of vision than to realise, either before or after, the deep significance of that Advent. So also the interpretation of Doctrine is not manifested so much by the exhibition of meaning behind meaning as of truth under-standing truth.

The root fact at the back of what may appear a dream is the actuality of an experiment which has existed always in the world, which has never changed, which has been pursued unceasingly by a few, the rumours of which are everywhere, which has many literatures, and all these literatures are veils. When the German poet Werner produced his wonderful Legend concerning the Sons of the Valley as the guiding hand behind the old Order of the Temple ; when he told how it was withdrawn at last, so that the Knightly Brethren were left to their fate in the power of the French King and the miserable Pontiff ; he—Werner—was dreaming of this Experiment and those who pursued it. In after days he struck out this hypothesis and all element of life from his two strange plays ; but apart from any Templar hypothesis, he knew that he was on the right track, in the light of which knowledge he took the path of Lancelot and died as a Priest of the Latin Church, having sung Mass for I know not how many moons. When Eckartshausen, who had been born in the Sanctuary and was filled with the Spirit of the Sanctuary, made an end of composing little books of popular devotion which took Germany and France by storm, he saw that the Great Experiment and its Great Tradition were in truth the Secret of the Sanctuary and the heritage thereof. People who did not understand him said : " This is Deism "[1]—but it was the Higher Mystery of the Eucharist in the Adyta of a conceived Holy Assembly, and he it was—as I have hinted—who, on the intellectual side, drew nearest of all to the heart of truth within.

The scheme of his interpretation of those Mysteries of Compassion which summarise God's Providence towards man for the fulfilment of our return into union may be divided into a part of preamble and a part of definition. The preamble announces the conditions by which an entrance is hypothetically possible into the Communion of Saints. The requisite faculty is the interior sense of the transcendental world, and the opening of this sense is the beginning of Regeneration, understood as the eradication of that virus which entered into man at the Fall. Rebirth has three stages—that of the intelligence, that of the heart and will, but that in fine which—seeing that it embraces the entire being—is called corporeal rebirth, because the beast is also saved together with the man, and the Great Quintessence by which the soul is converted transmutes the body as well. It is held to follow herefrom that union with God is possible in this life in the opening of the world within us by a triple gradation through the moral, meta-physical and plenary worlds, wherein is the Kingdom of the Spirit. This is the process of Regeneration expressed in other terms. So far as regards the preamble ; but the dogmatic part affirms : (1) that an Advanced School has existed from the beginning of our history, deriving directly from Christ, as He in Whom there dwells substantially the whole plenitude of God ; (2) that this is the enlightened Community of the Interior Church, disseminated throughout the world and governed by one Spirit therein ; (3) that it is the most hidden of all Sodalities ; (4) that the Outer School, which is the visible Church, is founded thereon and gives, by its Symbols and Ceremonies, an external utterance to that truth which abides in the Hidden Sanctuary ; (5) that the work of the Interior Church has been the building of a Spiritual Temple of Regenerated Souls ; (6) that it possesses a direct knowledge of those means by which man is restored to his first estate ; (7) that the External Church became a necessity owing to the weakness of man ; (8) that a time arrived when its outward worship fell away from the service within ; (9) that the Church which was founded in Abraham was raised to perfection in Christ ; (10) that the Inmost Sanctuary is without change

[1] THE CLOUD UPON THE SANCTUARY, by Councillor Karl von Eckartshausen, translated by Madame de Steiger and introduced by myself. Third edition, 1909, p. xiii.

or shadow of vicissitude ; (11) that it is the union of those who have received the light and share in the Communion of Saints ; (12) that it unites the science of the old External Covenant with that of the New and Interior Covenant ; (13) that it has three degrees corresponding to the stages of Regeneration ; (14) that therein repose the Mysteries of all True Knowledge ; (15) that it resembles no secret society, for all external forms have passed utterly away ; (16) that the path thereto is Wisdom and the way is Love ; (17) that although the Inner Sanctuary has been separated from the earthly Temple, they are destined for reunion ; (18) that the Way which is Wisdom and Love is also Christ ; (19) that the Mystery of the Incarnation is the deep Mystery of Reunion with God ; (20) that man in his first estate was the Temple of Divinity, and God in His wisdom has projected the rebuilding of this Temple ; (21) that the plans of His scheme are in the Holy Mysteries and constitute the Secret of Regeneration, which is the Royal and Sacerdotal Science ; (22) that man approximates to Regeneration, and does in fine attain it, by the discernment of the Body and Blood of Christ,[1] or, as I have expressed it myself continually throughout this work, by the Mystery of the Eucharist.

The same testimony was given independently at the same time by the Chevalier Lopuhin in his little tract on the CHARACTERISTICS OF THE INTERIOR CHURCH.[2] He defined the higher spiritual mind as that of consciousness in Grace only, by which those who participate therein become that which Christ is by His nature. Here also the Great Work is that of Regeneration, which is accomplished in Christ, and the Church within has the keys of the process. The testimony is also identical as to the sanctity and indefectible character of the external Church, which is the means of entrance into the Church of Christ unseen. The way, again, is Love, as the essence of the Body of Christ ; by Regeneration that Body is reborn in us ; and so the whole process—though in neither case is the truth stated expressly—becomes the Arch-Natural Mystery of the Eucharist.

There are errors of expression in both these works, and, as I have said, there is a certain confusion ; they are not to be taken by themselves or in connection simply with one another ; but it will be evident that, after their own manner, they bear the same testimony as other Schools of Tradition in Christian Times and as the higher literature of the Grail.

It will be seen that in the mind of Eckartshausen the Office of the Secret Church is that of Divine Communication ; but it should be understood that such Communication attained, and this only, gives entrance to the Inward Church. It abides behind the Sacraments, and yet it is their source. So far as its Office is typified symbolically it can have no more efficient and unspotted outward signs than the Bread and Wine of the Mass. It is in this sense that it connects more

---

[1] Eckartshausen, *Op. cit.*, pp. 59, 72, 73, 74 ; and INTRODUCTION, p. XXXIII.
[2] I. V. Lopuhin (Lopukhin), translated from the French by D. H. S. Nicholson and introduced by myself, 1912.

especially with the Eucharist than with any other observance in the
wide world of Rites and Liturgies. Christian Temples are oriented to
shew that there is a light behind, and our Churches with open doors are
the thresholds of that other Church which is not entered by doors
because it has not been built with hands. There is another sense in
which the so-called Secret Church is the Manifest Church glorified and
installed in the Spiritual Kingdom, even as the latter is installed and
set over the kingdom of the beautiful world. It is therefore the withdrawn spirit of the outward Holy Assembly, and it would seem
unreasonable for those who acknowledge the visible body to deny that
which transcends it. But to speak of a spirit which thus transcends a
body is to say that—because the lesser is contained by the greater—
the latter is until now not exactly without the former or apart therefrom ; while its mode of manifestation, in so far as it can be said to
manifest, is not otherwise than from within. There is no separate
incorporation. It has no ambassadors or *chargés d'affaires* at any Court
of the Hierarchies, nor does it send out visible physicians and healers,
for it has no conventional offices either in the interests of things above
or even of those below. If some have spoken of it as leading the Official
Church, there is here an imperfection of expression, because it is speaking
after a formal manner concerning modes which are apart from all whatsoever that we understand by convention. Without in any sense
representing and much less exhausting the process, it draws rather than
leads ; and if I may attempt one further definition, as a synthesis of
all these statements—echoing and reflecting all—the Secret Church is
the integration of believers in the higher consciousness.

VIII

SUMMARY

BUT now in conclusion generally as to all the Schools of
Symbolism, successive or coincident : it follows from the
considerations which have been developed in what approaches
an exhaustive manner that we are confronted by two theses,
from the first of which it results that the Mystery of Divine Attainment
is of that order which passes into experience, while dubiously and
illusively its traces are met with even in the modern world, though it
does not say " Come quickly " to the majority of Aspirants. From the
second it ensues that the Great Secret—at least so far as its specific
declaration and visible existence are concerned—has passed into
abeyance in the external Sanctuaries. I can scarcely conceive of a
clearer issue established by way of contrast. Several accredited
scholars have recognised the evidences of Secret Doctrine in the Grail
literature, more especially in respect of the Eucharist, but some of them

have been disposed to account for its presence by a familiarity with obscure Apocryphal Gospels. This is a source in Legend, and of sources in experiences of Sanctity or of perpetuated Secret Doctrine they knew little enough. In particular they did not dream that such perpetuation could have taken place except in Schools of Heresy. They appreciated the concealment of Sects which carried their lives in danger, but not the concealment of the Sanctuary. There is, however, that Vision of the Third Heaven, about which—in the typology of the subject—it is not lawful to speak, the reason being that it exceeds expression except by way of similitude, and this tends to erroneous apprehension. The Secret School towards which I look and of which I recognise the existence did not differ, so far as terms are concerned, in respect of Doctrine from the external ways of salvation, but it opened out an infinite realm which lies behind the manifest life of teaching—that realm which was in the mind of St. Augustine when he said, as we have seen, that the definition of Three Persons subsisting in one God was not an expression which satisfied the intellect, but that some kind of formulation is necessary. This School did not come forward with improvements on Doctrine, with proposals to reduce Doctrine, or with new opinions on the Eucharist. It carried the implicits of religious teaching to their final issue : the implicits were catholic and the issue also was catholic ; but the language-symbols dissolved or were left behind in approaching thereunto.

So it remains to this day, while we in our spiritual isolation are conscious of loss everywhere.

The Great Rites are celebrated, the High Offices continue, the moving Liturgical Formulæ are recited from day to day and year after year : we pass hurriedly through crowded streets and over the quiet country-sides ; we pause by solitary seas. The veiled voices signify the Presence, yet the Master is taken away, and we know not where they have laid Him. The Great Legends tell us that He has been assumed into Heaven because of the evil times, or that He is in a place of Hiddenness, or that He is not seen so openly. Prohibited, spoliated and extirpated with fire and sword, the memory of the dead sects of Southern France can offer us at their highest only the lips of the noble lady Esclairmonde communicating the *osculum fraternitatis—consolamentum* of all things saddest—through the flames of the *auto-da-fé*. One Masonic Chivalry consents to protect us from the insidious attacks of the infidel if we visit the Holy Fields, but it is confessed that the Sepulchre is empty and we know that the worst danger is from the infidel who is within. A later and more obscure Chivalry, with a vainer office of observance, keeps Ritual Guard over the shadow of a Sacred Legend, we asking the daughters of Zion whether there is any greater desolation. It pledges us to maintain the Sepulchre when it is agreed that the Master is not there, and we continue to say with our lips : *Et unam sanctam catholicam et apostolicam ecclesiam*, with a certain unconscious relief that the word *Credo* stands far away in the symbol. Saddest and proudest of all, next to the immortal ZOHAR, the great Legends of Masonry tell us that until that which from time immemorial has been lost in the secret places is at length restored to the Mysteries, the true temple can be built only in the heart. The Kabbalistic Sages are also waiting for the Word, that there may be mercy on every side, and the stress and terror of the centuries is because Adonai has been substituted for Jehovah in the true form thereof. It is only the higher side of Alchemy which, without faltering, has continued to point the Path of Attainment, speaking of no change, no substitution therein—telling us of the one Matter, the one Vessel, the one Way of Perfection, yet also saying that except the Divine Guidance lead us in the Path of Illumination, no man shall acquire the most hidden of all secrets without a Master, which is another mode of expressing the same thing. I suppose that there is no more unvarying witness continued through the ages, amidst all which we have felt, as we still feel, that only a small change in the axis of inclination would transform the world of greatest inhibition into that of the greatest grace. It is as if we were in the position of Perceval, according to the HIGH HISTORY—as if we had failed only on account of " one little question." But we do not know what it is, or rather we know it only in its external and substituted forms. We go on, therefore, sadly enough and slowly, yet in a sense we are haunted men, with a voice saying ever and again in our ears : " Ask, and ye shall receive " ; search your heart, for the true Question is within and the answer thereof.

A sad and strange enchantment has fallen even over the animal world, and all the gentle creatures with kind eyes are waiting with us for the close of the Adventurous Times, the term of Enchantment in Logres, and the unspelling Quest. Of these three things, two are of the Order of Mercy and one is of the High Order of the Union. All this is not to say that the High Offices fail, that the great conventions are abrogated, that the glorious sense of chivalry towards our Second Mother in those Sodalities which are external—but yet in that order are some intellectual and some also spiritual—that this sense is not of the highest counsel. But a time comes when the " glory to God in the highest," having been declared sufficiently without, is expressed more perfectly within, and we know in fine that this glory is to be revealed.

The same story of loss is therefore everywhere, but it is never told twice in the same way. Now it is a despoiled Sanctuary ; now a withdrawn Sacramental Mystery ; now the abandonment of a Great Military and Religious Order ; now the age-long frustration of the greatest building plan which was ever conceived ; now the Lost Word of Kabbalism ; now the vacancy of the most holy of all Sepulchres. But the Sanctuary is sacred, the King is to return, the Order of Chivalry has not really died ; at some undeclared time, and under some unknown circumstances, the Word which gives the key to some Treasure-House of the Building Plan will be restored in full, and meanwhile the Quest is continued for ever. The True Word will be restored also to Israel ;

and so from age to age goes on the great story of divine expectation. Meanwhile also the Christian Mystics say : " Take no thought for the morrow, because it is here and now " ; and to this Grand Antiphon the Responsion of the Hermetic Mystery is : " Even so, in the place of Wisdom there is still the Stone of the Wise ".

BOOK XII

THE SECRET OF THE HOLY GRAIL

THE ARGUMENT

I. Later Intimations of Scholarship.—A Retrospective Glance on the Results of previous Critical Studies—Albert Pauphilet on the Quest of Galahad—Galahad as a Minister of God—A Gate of Understanding opened in this Manner—Étienne Gilson on the Mystery of Grace in the Quest—Cistercian Mysticism and the Ecstasy of Love—The Beatific Vision—Grace and the Holy Spirit—Summary of this Thesis. II. A Further Review of the Quests.—Recurrence to the Grail as a Reliquary—The Grail as the Grace of the Holy Spirit—Consequences of this View on the Removal of the Grail—A Call to proceed further—Consideration of the Quests in Search of their present Message to the World—Judgment on the Parzival—Position of the later Titurel—The Epistle of Prester John—Decision in respect of the Albrecht Poem—Views of Miss Weston on the Conte as pure Romance—The Borron Perceval—Age-long Vigil of the Keepers—Grail Ecstasy and the Voice of the Holy Spirit—Intimations of the Perlesvaus—Masses of the Grail—An implied Sequel to the Perlesvaus—The Grail removed from the Castle but not from the World itself—Inward Message of the Story—The Galahad Quest—A Personal History and a Parable of the Soul—Of Parable and Allegory—Fatalities Attached to the Round Table and the Kinghood of Arthur—The Quest as an outward and inward Story—Intermingling of these Elements—The Grail Message begins in the Sanctuary and returns thereto—The Birth of Galahad—The Last Scene at Corbenic—The Scene in the Spiritual City—The Dilucid Contemplation of the Grail—Characteristics of the Experience implied—Of that which was seen by the Maimed King—Galahad and the World of Ascension—The Divine in the Soul and the Divine in the Universe—That this is the Secret of the Grail. III. A Preliminary Excursus concerning the Great Experiment.—A Definition of the Grail Quest—Testimony of the Admirable Ruysbroeck—Testimony of the Galahad Quest—Term of the Great Experiment—The Witness of all Churches and all Religions—A Note on the Secret Orders—Inward Doctrine of Religion—The Communication of Divine Substance—Tradition in the East and the West—The Unity of Witness—Questions of the Path—The Rule of Sanctity—Catholic Doctrine and the Church Mystical—Religious Experiment of the Quest—Counsels of Perfection—Qualifications of Galahad—Grace and the Sanctified State—The Condition of *Virgo Intacta*—Sanctity and the State of Union—The Attainment of Galahad—The Vision of Nasciens—The Quest as a Tale of Eternity—The Gate of the Eucharist—The Secret Temple of the Soul. IV. The Secret School.—The Grail and Secret Doctrine—A School of Christian Mystics—The School and the Church—The Mass and Beatific Vision—The Inward Secret Church and the Mass therein—The Church and the Eucharist—The Rumour in Romance—An Experiment which is always in the World—The Secret of the Sacrament—The Path which leads to the

Union—How it leads behind the Church—Other Aspects which environed the Grail Literature—State of the External Church—The Ferments at work in the Western Branch—Transubstantiation and Communion in one Kind—The Voice of Debate and the Voice of Silence—Personalities of the Hidden School—The efficacious Grail—Mysteries of Sanctity—The Dominant Church and its Voided Claims—The Term of Quest and the Term of Union—The Grail Witnesses—Secrets behind the Altar and the Sacrifice—The Mass of St. Thomas Aquinas—The Secret Church and the Holy Assembly—Of a Mass behind a Mass—A Dream of Chivalry Spiritualised—Tradition and its Many Voices—The Church in Widowhood and Desolation—The World of Loss and the World of Attainment—Christian Witnesses of the State beyond the Vision—Testimony of Hierotheos on the Christ-life in the Soul—Pseudo-Dionysius on All-perfect Agnosia—A Ladder of Paradox—The Way of Negation and the Way to God—The Latin Church and the Mystics—The Areopagite and John the Scot—The Franciscan Movement and other later Developments—Dionysius and Theosis—The Catholic Church and the Mystics—Ruysbroeck and Gerson—The Abbot Joachim—Innocent III and the Papal Empire—Of those who led the Life and found the Doctrine. V. The Conclusion of this Holy Quest.—Of Mystical Transmission from the Past—Of Masses heard in the Heart—Of an unexplored World behind Rite and Symbol—Depth and Wonder of the Mass—Keywords of the Mystery—Lights and Incense of the Outer Sanctuary—Mystical Loss of Logres—The Path of Dereliction and the Path of Heaven—The Pageant of the Eucharist—The Veil of Consecrating Words—Of those who are Called and Chosen—Shadows of Secret Memorials—Antecedents of the Cup Legend —Of a Sanctuary within the Sanctuary—The Spirit imparted to the Soul—Dissolution of Doctrine in Experience—The limits of Expression—The Divine Unimaged Vision—Exotics of the one Subject—The fact of the Great Experiment—The Churches as Witnesses—A Question of the Stewards —The Pearl of Great Price—The World of Quest and the World of Attainment—The End of these Pleadings. VI. Epilogue.—The Grail and its Temple of Images—The Masses of the Perlesvaus—The Inner Chapel of the Grail—The End of Sacramental Marvels—Messages of Many Voices—How the Quest goes on.

THE SECRET OF THE HOLY GRAIL

I

LATER INTIMATIONS OF SCHOLARSHIP

IT has to be confessed that we have come forth from a prolonged study of the Grail Critical Apparatus with empty hands : The explanations of purpose and intention, of meanings behind the Legend, the suggested origins have fallen to pieces in their examination. In the majority of cases they are anything but idle inventions, and a few had so much in their favour that they held the field for years ; but it has not proved in the end that they cover the ground. They have been abandoned by others before myself, sometimes for reasons which seem sufficient in themselves, sometimes on the basis of considerations which have called to be expressed differently or enforced by others. On the one hand, the Templar hypothesis was never justified evidentially and might have slept to this day if Wolfram had not called his Grail Knights *Templeisen* and clothed them after the manner of the Templar Chivalry. If such imitation proves anything, then certain Masonic High Grades are warranted to the same extent and within the same limits, seeing that they claim descent from the Templars ; that they have been called for generations by the old historical name ; that they wear the identical habit ; that they meet in Preceptories and Priories, and are governed by a Grand Master. On the other hand, *pace* Dr. J. D. Bruce and the implication behind his suggestion that the Tuatha de Danaan Talismans were never heard of in writing till Keating produced a HISTORY OF IRELAND in the seventeenth century,[1] I do not suppose that their antiquity is seriously at issue ; and in any case it is not to be questioned that there are folk-lore elements in the wonder-stories of the Grail. But the fact remains that they do not account for the Grail, being its accidents, not of its essence. Miss Weston discovered this after forty years of expatiation on folk-lore subjects ; but unfortunately her Ritual alternative offers no help in turn. Finally, the sects have failed us, though there was good reason to turn in their direction for light,

---

[1] It was completed *circa* 1625 and was written in the Irish tongue. The English version mentioned in a previous note was the work of Dermod O'Connor. I have heard also of another translation which appeared at New York about 1865.

having regard to the claims put forward by two historicity texts
of the Grail literature and reflected into the Quests as their developments, actual or assumed.　On the surface therefore it looks as though
the whole subject has been landed in a *cul de sac* and will have to be
left therein.　I am proposing, however, to try one journey more,
hoping to escape Miss Weston's refuge by way of appeal to Bishop
Butler, who said in his ANALOGY OF RELIGION that we must rest content
with probabilities when we are denied certitude.

That excellent lady—whose reasonable panegyric will be found in
my Appendix II—had made her last contribution to the Grail subject
when M. Albert Pauphilet produced at Paris in 1921 his ÉTUDES
SUR LA QUESTE DEL SAINT GRAAL—otherwise L'ÉVANGILE DE GALAAD.[1]
The question, for him, is no longer that of the Perceval Cycle, " Who
is served of the Grail ? " (and its variants), but *qu'est-ce que la Quête
du Graal ?* It is answered in notable ways.　(1) " It is more than a
convenient framework for stories of adventure :　Knightly prowess,
love and women have no place of honour here ;　and the great heroes
of Romance—Lancelot, Gawain, etc.—are put to shame or defeated.
(2) We are no longer in the romantic world."[2]　The Grail itself
is *la romanesque manifestation de Dieu*, while the Quest thereof
is the search after God, " under the veil of allegory " and *sous
l'apparence chevaleresque*. It is also a presentation of Christian Life
" as observed or dreamed by a mind of the thirteenth century."[3]
(3) As regards Galahad, he is God's own minister after more than one
manner.　" Other Saints are engrossed exclusively with the business
of their own salvation " ;　but he seems charged with a mission which
passes far beyond his personal concern.　*Éternel croisé, il marche au
milieu des prodiges, escorté du vol des anges.*　In a word, he is the personified Imitation of Christ, *un modèle de vertu Chrétienne assez parfait pour
reproduire la terrestre de Jesus*—the Eternal Pattern.[4]

Such is the thesis in brief and broad outline ;　but as my readers
must not presuppose M. Pauphilet's unconditional approval of his
graphic picture, it is desirable to quote the last paragraph of his second
Study.　" In this our day the inspiration and the form of such a work "
—meaning the QUESTE of Galahad—" are alike remote from us.　This
is no moment for explaining the world by Mysticism or recalling the
import of mediæval allegories.　We have other views, moreover, on
the medley of the sacred and profane in literature than prevailed in
the thirteenth century.　No second spring is possible therefore for this
book, which came to be misconstrued so speedily in its own day.
Incomparably less human than any TRISTRAM, it will never become
popular again.　It is reserved for the admiration of those alone who, by
virtue of learning, are qualified to sympathise with forgotten ways of
thought and to discern, *même dans des œuvres pirimiés*, some aspects of
that Art which is eternal."

[1] *Op. cit.*, pp. 3–11.　　　　　　　　[2] *Ib.*, p. 17.
[3] *Op. cit.*, pp. 24, 26.　　　　　　　[4] *Ib.*, p. 155.

I am inclined to speculate whether M. Pauphilet is making an astute concession to his age in France, that he may secure the sympathetic fraction which he separates from the *profanum vulgus* as initiable, if not initiated ; but it happens, in any case, that there are those in England, and they are not few but many, who not only have ears to hear, when such new views are promulgated and such a gate opens. They are likely, I think, to listen with all their souls, and perhaps even will call on the stars to hearken.

If they turn from this outline sketch to the author's own STUDIES, they may question—on the one hand—whether (1) the attributes of the Grail are described correctly as those of God Himself ;[1] and—on the other—whether (2) he is right in proposing a Cistercian origin for the Galahad Quest.[2] Personally I do not see eye to eye with M. Pauphilet on the second point, partly because I remember that the political Antichrist, *sub nomine* Innocent III, entrusted the preaching of the Albigensian Crusade to that Monastic Order, thus blotting all its scutcheon ; and otherwise (1) because he or they who produced the QUESTE and represented the Second Joseph, First Bishop of Christendom, coming down from Heaven to say Mass at Corbenic and Sarras would be certainly acquainted with the Arch-heretical claim of the GRAND SAINT GRAAL, which no Cistercian would have tolerated ;[3] (2) because one of its fatal preachments, placed in a Hermit's mouth, propounds the unorthodox thesis that human beings were created with immortal souls, that they might fill the thrones left vacant by fallen angels. That is doctrinal fable and not good Theology.[4]

For the rest, M. Pauphilet, as suggested, is like one who opens a gate. He is a scholar of the Grail subject, and one of his STUDIES establishes the text of the QUESTE with reference to the available MSS. Moreover, in 1923 he edited the QUESTE itself on the basis of this research. He is important therefore, not only for his standpoint respecting the Legend of Galahad but because he speaks with a certain authority. It is to be hoped that my old casual acquaintance Alfred Nutt, with whom I talked in early days about LE GRAND PERCEFOREST, that Dr. J. D. Bruce and Miss Weston will not hear on their intellectual thrones in some Elysium of scholarship the far-off echo of Pauphilet's voice on this to them tabooed subject, the praise of Galahad and *le caractère exclusivement chrétien du Graal*. For us, however, it is one more piece of evidence that " the old order changeth " and that to-day's criticism of literature, like to-day's science, revokes the findings of yesterday. It is good to be alive when such things happen in our motley Arcadia. It is also a call to proceed and find, if that be possible, what strange things may lie beyond the gate of these ÉTUDES.

We have not to go further at the start than that beloved review which is devoted to all the letter and a modicum, on rare occasions,

---

[1] ÉTUDES, p. 24.   [2] *Ib.*, p. 139.
[3] See Sommer's edition of the QUESTE in *Op. cit.*, Vol. VI, pp. 189, 190, 197, 198.
[4] It happens to be merely fantastic, with little attaching thereto.

of the spirit of Romance—the ROMANIA of 1925. We can read M. Étienne Gilson on *la mystique de la grâce dans la Queste del Saint Graal*. He is working from Pauphilet's edition of the text and admits the latter's contention that romantic themes are used therein to express a Christian conception of man and the universe ;[1] but he is far from accepting the suggestion that the Grail is God, which he reads, like myself, into the affirmation that the attributes of the Grail are Divine Attributes. Perhaps, however, there is a sense after all in which this statement is true, though it is not in the extreme sense. The Grail for M. Gilson is Grace, and this is a gift from God but is not God Himself. Grace is defined as Love, " the Love given us by God to call us back to Him ; " and the canonical maxim which belongs hereto is : *Charitas ex Deo est*,[2] the counter maxim notwithstanding, on the same authority, which affirms a little later that *Deus charitas est*.[3] This may be left to the theologians, so far as the New Testament sources are concerned, though a few figurative hairs could be tendered for splitting on my own part, were space and time provided.

I am wondering, however, what M. Gilson understands by the Grail : it must be surely the traditional content which empowers the Vessel, while it seems obvious that for Robert de Borron and the GRAND SAINT GRAAL, the Precious Blood was not a mere Passion Relic but a living thing, and that with which it was alive was the Real Presence. Even the Talismanic Stone of Wolfram had this Presence within it—of course, *ex hypothesi*—because of the Sacred Host brought down from Heaven to renew its powers from year to year. The PARZIVAL forgets to tell us whether Angels carried the old one back to a Place of Reservation beyond the skies. It looks in any case as if there were something to be said for Pauphilet's alleged implicit, following the Catholic Doctrine that Christ Jesus—who is God, *ex hypothesi*—abides in the Altar Tabernacle under the elements of Hallowed Bread and Wine. We must remember also that for Robert de Borron the abiding Presence in the Grail was the Voice of the Holy Spirit.

This is by the way only ; but it belongs to the logic of the debate and clears the issues. M. Gilson affirms that the central theme of the Galahad Romance is Grace, and that it is moved thereby towards those ecstasies of love which are the Supreme Crown of Grace in Cistercian Mysticism.[4] The allocation may pass ; but it happens that neither then nor subsequently were those Divine activities pursued in one only House of Religion, in one Monastic Order. M. Gilson says that " there are two ways of attaining God for a Cistercian Mystic, in this world by ecstasy and in the other by the Beatific Vision."[5] He adds that the Vision is attained in and through Love for the Augustinians and Cistercians, but by intelligence for the Thomists. He might remember at the same time that the Path of Love is mystically a Path of Contemplation and that it is the Angel of the Schools who

---

[1] M. Gilson agrees also that the QUESTE is of Cistercian origin.
[2] 1 Ep. St. John iv, 27, Vulgate version.
[3] *Ib.*, iv, 16.   [4] *Op. cit.*, p. 323.   [5] *Ib.*, p. 345.

has given us the great definition on this subject, namely, that Contemplation is Love. The question may be left at this point, having been discussed in some other writings of mine, where it has been shewn that the state of Vision is not the state of Union, from which it follows that Thomists, as well as Cistercians, fell short of the true mystical term in their records of experience.[1]

M. Gilson explains further that the Grace of the Grail is the Grace of the Holy Spirit, leading to the knowledge of God, and the Life of God in the soul, not by way of knowledge but by that of feeling—otherwise, the Way of Love. It is certified that the operation of Grace is seen best in Galahad—of course within the measures of Romance. He is its " perfect incarnation ", and as such he is a symbol of our Lord, Who is the *plénitude de la grâce du Saint-Esprit et son distribution parmi les hommes*. Galahad is not merely on the Quest,[2] he is also the Guide of the Knights and goes before them on the way—a manifest type of the Saint and Captain of Souls. As to the Quest of the Grail, " it is the search after the secrets of God, unknown in the absence of Grace and by those who know inexpressible," because they are attained in ecstasy.[3] It follows that the Arthurian Chivalry pursuing the Quest of the Grail were pledged to a Spiritual Work, otherwise the Quest of the Divine, " as seen by the soul, without the aid of bodily sense."[4] Galahad, Perceval and Bors " attain the Supreme Ecstasy

---

[1] See THE WAY OF DIVINE UNION, 1915, and especially LAMPS OF WESTERN MYSTICISM, 1924.

[2] It might be said truly that Galahad is the Quest itself—at once the Path and End. By virtue of that which was within him, he fulfilled the Quest.

[3] The author regards the Mysterious Bed in the Ship of Solomon, which haunts the sea in the GRAND SAINT GRAAL, as a symbol of the mystic ecstasy. It must be confessed that I do not find the evidence, though the suggestion itself is intriguing. The original and admitted object of the Ship and its building was that it might convey to Galahad the foreknowledge of his ancestor concerning the coming of the High Prince in the fullness of far-off times. It was also or became a symbol of Faith, and those who did not possess that Theological Virtue in an eminent degree entered the Ship at their peril. As regards the Bed, no one slept thereon, till Perceval and Bors, sailing towards Sarras with the Grail and Galahad, reminded him that, according to a certain scroll preserved on board, the last Knightly Descendant of Solomon was to repose thereon (Sommer's edition of the QUESTE, *Op. cit.*, pp. 161, 193). Galahad followed the counsel *et dort grant pièce*. He did not awake in fact till the Ship reached Sarras, but as to all that happened in his sleep the text is silent. It follows that M. Gilson's view is a matter of simple inference. He would say no doubt that such a Bed could not have been prepared and that such a rest could not have been taken thereon without a signal object in view. It stands at this, but I think personally that the true mystical ecstasy of Galahad was reserved for the Mass at Sarras.

[4] The words of the QUESTE are, however : *Et il*—that is Galahad—*se traist avant et regarde devant* (variant : *dedens*) *le saint vaissel. Et si tost come il i ot . . . regardé, si commencha a trambler moult durement, si tost comme la mortels char commencha a regarder les espiritels choses.*—Sommer, *Op. cit.*, VI, p. 197. Cf. Pauphilet : LA QUESTE DEL SAINT GRAAL, pp. 276, 277. The passage is represented in the condensed version of Malory by the crucial sentence only : " And then he began to tremble right hard when the deadly flesh began to behold the spiritual things".—MORTE DARTHUR, Bk. XVII, cap. 22. The point is that, according to the alleged Cistercian author of the QUESTE, the " bodily sense " did begin to see, and M. Gilson is to all appearance at issue with his source. This notwithstanding, it is indubitable that he is right, thus making the QUESTE wrong, at least to all appearance, in like manner. But the explanation is that Galahad's experiences opened in the physical by the contemplation of a physical object, which began to exhibit a Real Presence within it, belonging to another order. The flesh trembled therefore, and then for the time being, as it were, " passed in music out of sight ". But it is obvious that the whole experience was of a time-moment only, like the proverbial twinkling of an eye.

at last, but have visions and partial illuminations to prepare the way ".[1] Lancelot, on the other hand, got no further than the revelations of a dream-state.

In summary of all the thesis, (1) the supreme prize reserved to those who are victorious in the Quest is an open vision of the Divine Secrets ; (2) the Quest of the Grail does not cease to be a Romance of Grace because it is a Quest of Ecstasy ; (3) it cannot be the one in very truth without being also the other, since ecstasy is the final efflorescence of the life of Grace in the Christian Soul ; (4) the simple faithful who follow the strait way of salvation and perfect Mystics who enjoy already the Presence of God are alike nourished by the Grail ; (5) but the ecstatic is seated at the Table of God, while the others rest content with the broken meats of the Festival ; (6) from its lowest manifestations to the Highest, it is one and the same life which works in all ; (7) to identify ecstasy therefore as the end proposed by the Quest is to set for their attainment before the Knights of the Round Table the Life of Grace in its perfect state.[2] It is not surprising that many died therein and that all but twelve failed. The Round Table broke about the Quest and Logres drowned in blood.

Remembering my own original book on the Grail subject,[3] for long years out of print and less or more incorporated herewith ; it is a little like coming..into my own to read this interpretation of the QUESTE in the desirable pages of ROMANIA, and to realise how at least one other than myself—and knowing nothing of my excursions—has found that the High Mystery of the soul in the Blessed Vision and of the soul in the Union has once at least been drawn into Romance. Here then, and again in brief outline, is some part of that which lies beyond the gate opened—so to speak—by M. Albert Pauphilet. I say again that it is a call to go forward : it is another sign-post on the road.

II

A FURTHER REVIEW OF THE QUESTS

THE studies which have passed under review in the previous section offer their pregnant suggestions on the Path of Quest and on that which may be understood mystically as the finding of the Grail ; but they leave the last and most vital problem of the whole literature not only unsolved but untouched. It seems handed back to us in fact underscored. If the Precious Blood of Christ Jesus, in its literal pouring out, can—as orthodox dogma

---

[1] There is no authority in the text for saying that Perceval and Bors saw or experienced anything except a Bishop, encompassed by Angels, reciting a Mass of the " Glorious Mother of God ". They did not look within the Grail like Galahad, and they did not receive the Host, which was offered to him alone.

[2] ROMANIA, Vol. LI, pp. 342, 343.

[3] THE HIDDEN CHURCH OF THE HOLY GRAIL, 1909.

affirms— cleanse the whole world from sin, there is no question that a Reliquary containing some part or modicum thereof, is the greatest Palladium in the Christian Treasury of Relics,[1] though the difficulties which it offers to literal Theological Doctrine might baffle all the Doctors and all the Casuists. Now, when it is said to have been removed because the world was not worthy to possess the Vessel of singular devotion, the issue is clear and simple. Yet those who define the Grail as the Grace of the Holy Spirit do so at their peril, in view of those texts which certify that in fine it was taken away.[2] On the authority of the CONTE and the QUESTE, the Comforter has gone back into Heaven. On the authority of the DIDOT-MODENA PERCEVAL, He has one Shrine in Northumbria, and two of all humanity may worship there. On that of the PERLESVAUS the Divine Presence is hidden in an isle unknown, far across the sunlit sea. There is also the testimony of Albrecht which certifies on this hypothesis that the Abiding Spirit is leading in perpetuity the Romanised Nestorian Church of Prester John. It has to be remembered that the QUESTE—so called *par excellence*— does not stand alone and that its various competitors must be taken into account, for which reason it has been desirable to make these otherwise preposterous enumerations. But if it stood alone, if it were the one and only Quest, the root difficulty would remain, namely, that the Grace of the Holy Spirit ascended to Heaven with Galahad and has come nevermore to earth.[3] It follows that MM. Pauphilet and Gilson are in the position of Sebastian Evans, who forgot unaccountably that to remove the Papal Interdict from Logres was in fact to restore the Grail and not take it away, as the PERLESVAUS, his authority, does. It follows also that, having dwelt for a few moments in the sunlight of their suggestive intimations, we are called to go further and, in the first place, to glance again at the Quests in search of their message, if any, for us at the present day. We are concerned no longer with questions of dates and developments, so a beginning may be made with a text which has been regarded very long and very often as among the most significant of all.

If we take Wolfram's PARZIVAL at the highest of all the valuations which ever have been put thereon, what is the message which it offers to the ages continued thereafter ? The victory of self-endeavour, if you will ; the personal values of heroic purpose and self-government

[1] Of course on the hypothesis that sanctity resides in Relics or a certain consecration which justified the Roman Persuasion in their contribution to Pagan Idolatry when it was decreed that no building unprovided with a Relic should be hallowed for Church purposes or used as such.

[2] It happens that they can cite textual justification from which there is no appeal. Not alone does the Voice of the Holy Spirit speak from the Grail in the Metrical Romance of Borron, but the QUESTE implies in formal and literal words that the Grail is the Grace of the Holy Spirit (Sommer, *Op. cit.*, VI, pp. 13, *etc.*).

[3] The position is that Christ promised to send down the Comforter, in accordance with which the Holy Spirit came into the world at Pentecost ; that this Spirit was the Guiding Voice which span the ever-expanding mesh of doctrine, according to the claim of the Church. Against this we have the authority of the QUESTE that it was removed from the world and therefore also from Rome ; that we owe this ultra-heretical thesis—*ex hypothesi*—to that Cistercian source which was concerned at the same time in preaching the Albigensian Crusade.

to attain their end : add all the others at need, as contributed by many panegyrics. But the world of letters, not to speak of the world's history, is full of these examples, and the machinery of the Grail Mystery is not needed to enforce them. Apart therefrom, how are the Talisman and its winner left when the story ends ? It is (1) a writing oracle which appoints successive Wardens and maintains the Chivalry by selections drawn from all quarters. (2) It gives wives to the Grail Kings. (3) It preserves the appearance of youth. (4) It produces that inexhaustible larder on which I have dwelt previously in words of comedy. But it remains *in futuro* that which it was in the past, even from the beginning, a family affair or the heirloom of a self-contained petty principality, which *vi et armis* keeps its gates and walls against all uninvited comers. What message to the world at large lies within these measures, that a Stone should be brought from Heaven by Angels—or fall, mayhap, to earth from the crown of Lucifer ? There is nothing that belongs to eternity ; there is no record of religious observance within the Castle of Montsalvatch ; *Philosophia, Theosophia, Verbum Mysticum*, Secrets of the Vision and the End : there is none of these in the Oracle. And so far as Wolfram is concerned, this kind of thing may go on for ever, as tabulated, unless an individual *Templeise* may chance to fall in battle, worsted by some warrior without. It happened on one occasion, but only once.[1]

There is an independent direction, however, in which it looks as if another story might emerge from the PARZIVAL ; for it is difficult to remember Feirfeis and the Grail Maiden whom he took back as his second wife to the Land of Prester John without concluding that much yet remains to be said in respect of both. Now, this also occurred obviously to the poets who made up the later TITUREL ; while to them as to myself it may have seemed that the Grail hidden in the family repository of Montsalvatch, with no obvious occupation henceforward for Warden or *Templeisen*, lacked something in respect of finality. So they took the whole cohort and their Talisman into that far Cathay, whither the original Grail Bearer had gone before. The plea put forward—borrowed from the French Cycles—was that the Western world had proved unworthy to possess the priceless treasure, however out of view. There were great activities in consequence, and thereafter followed a reign of ten years for Parzival, whose story ends in death, and he is succeeded, as we saw, by the Son of Feirfeis, having regard doubtless to the claims of the Mother who bore him. In this manner the Talisman is removed from a Sanctuary somewhere in the visible Pyrenees into a fabulous region—a Myth into a World of Myth. It has also changed its nature, reverting from a Stone of Destiny to the Chalice or Dish of French Legend, while the problem of its dubious orthodoxy has been cleared up once and for all ; for its Sanctuary is a magnified St. Peter's and the Palace of Prester

---

[1] See Wolfram's PARZIVAL, Book VII. There is a recurrence to the subject in Book IX.

John seems an exaggerated Vatican. It is all, if possible, more Popish than the Pope himself and more Latin than the Roman Hierarchy. So also the super-ecclesiastical potentate has overlord titles which would have satisfied Innocent III, and a warlike disposition which preached the " Gospel " with a sword in the spirit of Albigensian Crusades. Albrecht and his *coadjutores* in the work of the later TITUREL did not realise that the " spoofery " of the Prester John Epistle to Western Popes and Potentates was in all probability a skit on the Italian Papacy and its bids for universal dominion at a period when it was more than usually " drunk with the blood of the saints ".[1]

It may be submitted in all seriousness that the belated sequel which passes under the name of Albrecht has no message to deliver at this day—or any other—to justify and much less to exalt the Grail, whether regarded as a Stone in the Crown of Lucifer or as a Reliquary of " the Blessed Blood of our Lord Jesus Christ, blessed mote it be ", as the Caxton colophon puts it. In truth, some readers of DER JÜNGERE TITUREL, might be disposed to exclaim as they read, in the words of the same text : " Therefore, on all sinful souls, blessed Lord, have Thou mercy," realising the sense of utter frustration which underlies the crude reverberations of the final lines. The new law of Grail succession has been declared, apart utterly from Quests and Questions : the veneration of the Grail is to continue through ages and ages in its own Shrine and Sanctuary, while Wardens follow one another, while Prester Johns on their jewelled throne contemplate their magnificence and proclaim it, demand and obtain their tributes and doubtless wage their wars. I have rendered to folk-lore the things that are folk-lore's and to the Grail the things of the Grail : not these are they. It is the story of the Grail in another kind of decadence than that of the Venusberg or the Sone de Nausay : it is the Grail in dullness.[2]

I suppose that if there or here, in France or otherwise, the excellent Eugène Aroux finds his readers still,[3] and if Mrs. Cooper-Oakley, his English disciple, still finds a few to turn her suggestive leaves, they may object that my critical apparatus " pumps out with a ruthless ingenuity," not indeed " atom by atom " but explanatory thesis after explanatory thesis, concerning the great Mythos, and leaves " vacuity " alone, like Browning's critic. And now it may seem that I am taking the Grail texts and presently may leave no Grail, all my testimony in preceding pages notwithstanding. Let it rest on the knees of the gods for the time being, seeing that we must glance once again at the CONTE DEL GRAAL, with the same purpose in view—whether it has a

---

[1] I do not know whether Dr. Sebastian Evans was himself under the obedience of the Latin Church ; but those who would care to inspect a half-hearted attempt at excusing the Albigensian Crusade may be referred to IN QUEST OF THE HOLY GRAIL. It is the thinnest coat of whitewash which was ever applied to anything.

[2] It does not follow that the story itself is dull, and I would that Sebastian Evans were alive at this day to render it in his talismanic version of Archaic English, under the auspices of a Grail Text Society.

[3] I have spared all reference to DIU CRÔNE in the German Cycle and its story of the Dead-Alive. No maker of wildest hypothesis could look for messages in that quarter of Dreamland.

message which signifies, on or beneath its surface, from the Grail *qua* Grail standpoint, in spite of its motley growth and authorship. I have spoken freely about it already on general lines ; and Miss Weston, who lived with it for longer years than I, shall offer her own witness, in the course of a single paragraph. " To Chrétien the story was Romance, pure and simple. There was still a certain element of awe connected with Grail and Grail Feast, but of the real meaning and origin of the incidents he had, I am convinced, no idea whatever . . . We have here passed completely and entirely into the Land of Romance : the doors of the Temple are closed behind us. It is the story of Perceval le Gallois . . . which fills the stage, and with the Story of Perceval there comes upon the scene a crowd of folk-themes, absolutely foreign to the Grail itself."[1] That is the considered judgment of her own final and most ambitious message to the world of scholarship, written when she believed that she had found " the Secret of the Grail." As regards Chrétien, I am in complete accord, on the understanding that her " real meaning ", rooted in Pagan Myth, is about as far from the living point within the circle of true research as the dedications of Roman legionaries were likely to have been removed from Ruysbroeck's ADORNMENT OF THE SPIRITUAL MARRIAGE, or other still contemplations in the heights above the activities of the logical mind. It remains to point out that the continuation of pseudo-Wauchier is in like case, with its partial restoration of Nature—through the half-fledged offices of Monseigneur Gawain—and its utter absence of Perceval, the acknowledged hero of the story. So also is Wauchier himself, with his Light-o'-Love Seeker of the Grail, who neglects his Sister, betrays his Sweetheart and obtains his reward from the Lady of the Chess-Board Castle, on the threshold of completing the Quest. He does complete it, to all intents and purposes, for he asks the Question, which is the sole condition of attainment according to Chrétien's plan ; but he does not heal the King, as that plan provided also, though before he breaks off Wauchier had an available moment, and let the moment slip, when the Question should have performed its work.[2] Finally, Manessier is out of court altogether, so far as any spiritual or even a moral lesson is concerned (1) because he is the exponent only of a commonplace Vengeance Legend, (2) the consummation of which, and this only, makes whole the Fisher King, thus stultifying Chrétien, as well as the Grail story on its Perceval side. There remains Gerbert de Montreuil, and I have said enough already to shew that his prolonged fragment breathes a different atmosphere and reveals a higher purpose ; but it is a fragment only and does not disclose the whole mind of Gerbert as to beginning or end.[3]

---

[1] FROM RITUAL TO ROMANCE, pp. 152, 153.

[2] Immediately prior to the moment when the Grail Keeper exclaims *Sires, soiés de ma maison.*

[3] There is of course no question that he followed Chrétien, while it seems arguable still that either he was unacquainted with or ignored the two Wauchiers ; in which case his asserted virginity of Perceval means that he interpreted innocently the youth's relations with Blanchefleur on the night of their first meeting.

I proceed in the next place to the Perceval Quest which passes under the name of Robert de Borron. It is characterised by a simple directness and unity of theme which renders it conspicuously attractive as a Quest in brief ; and as regards its occasional stultifications of the Borron and Merlin texts from which it derives, it should be realised that they are of the letter, so to speak, and do not affect the unity of spirit which prevails throughout the trilogy. They may be accounted for readily enough by that favoured device of the past, the existence once upon a time of texts now lost. It was usually invoked then for the benefit of some orphan speculation in search of a foster father. There is no axe to grind in the present case, it being wholly indifferent to my own object whether certain contradictions can be taken out of the way or must be referred to the carelessness of those who produced continuations and sequels at that period. I incline to think on my own part that the author of the DIDOT-MODENA PERCEVAL had variant prose versions of Borron's poems and that he worked on these, instead of on extant texts.[1]

The unity of theme to which I have referred above belongs in part to its links with antecedent branches of the Trilogy, in part to the comparative absence of irrelevant episodes.[2] The spirit of secrecy concerning the House of the Grail is maintained throughout. It will be remembered that the EARLY MERLIN indicates an abode in Northumbria, while the DIDOT-MODENA PERCEVAL—on the authority of a Most Holy Voice—mentions the Isles of Ireland. In any case, it lay beyond all finding, except by Merlin and the one Warden in succession who was called thereto. The Grail itself sends forth no message in the text, save that only which imposed the Quest on Perceval at the Royal Court. It cannot be said therefore that the Search and Finding of the Grail ascribed to Borron has anything to tell us at this day, unless and until we turn to explore in thought those wells of deep experience which were attained once upon a time in ecstatic contemplation of some Hallowed Object. We may speculate then concerning the inward worlds which might have opened to Blaise and Perceval in their age-long Vigil of the Grail—as if it were a Golden Monstrance uplifted on a High Altar in a very Secret Shrine. Some of us would call it Paradise, some the Blessed Vision and some Nirvana. I can say only that the last words of the text bear witness that there was no further story concerning the Grail, meaning on the surface that its rumours ceased in the outer world, but perhaps also for the Heaven-appointed Keeper and the Hermit Priest : they knew within and without, from its first beginning in time unto its eternal end, the true story of the Holy Grail.

---

[1] We can account in this manner for things outside the Borron Cycle, and among them for the GRAND SAINT GRAIL appointing Alain as the next Keeper after Joseph II.

[2] The story of the stag and basset is irrelevant enough in one sense ; but it is so prominent in Wauchier's continuation of the CONTE that it could not well be omitted in an alternative Perceval Quest. As critical opinion has decreed that the Borron Quest is late in the literature, it follows that the Wauchier episode is decisive evidence thereof,

This is like that " new star in Serpentarius," in which the first Brethren of the Rosy Cross saw bright and shining Mysteries ; but there is no evidence before us. We might picture alternatively the Priest and the Keeper listening to the Still Small Voice of the Holy Spirit, speaking from the Grail continually to their inward ears ; and it would be like a Mass of the Comforter communicating, at " the Sacring of the Mass," a Food of Souls, the Words—for us ineffable— behind the Secret Words,[1] and secrets of the Centre which have " never been spoken or spell'd " in any Church on earth. Let us leave it at this, because such dreams are golden and, for the rest, we do not know.

There are yet two Quests to follow, and one of them witnesses over and and over that it was written in the Latin tongue by the First Bishop of Christendom and the " First Priest who Sacrificed the Body of our Lord "—at Sarras, namely, after he had been consecrated and enthroned by Christ. This is " an the Latin lie not " concerning the long tale and its source. We may look in such case for great tidings, even for living messages. It happens, however, that the PERLESVAUS is not a Quest of the Grail, and more than this, that it is a record of Quest failure. The woe on the world of Logres arose solely from the fact that Perceval asked nothing when he paid his first and only visit to the Grail Castle, whether in the official capacity—so to speak—of a Knight on Quest or as a casual errant caller—of course until that time when he himself became the Heir of the Grail. The mind of the story is obviously shewing that the Grail is not won by search. It is reserved to a House of the Elect, an Elect Family, as if to an Adept Company, a Secret Order or Hidden Church. Now, the PERLESVAUS implies a Quest, but in so doing it excludes all Quest-stories which end in attain- ment, it being understood that the GALAHAD excludes itself. It is not therefore a sequel to the DIDOT-MODENA PERCEVAL, the Wolfram PARZIVAL, to Manessier or to Gerbert. Among Perceval texts there remain only the poem of Chrétien and its continuation by Wauchier de Denain ; but it is not less certain that it does not arise from these. As regards the allegation that the Grail is not won by seeking in the mind of the PERLESVAUS, the fact is underscored by the institution of a Gawain Quest which is doomed to end in failure.

I am shewing elsewhere that the Masses of the HIGH HISTORY are Grail Masses and that its Hermit-Priests are all in the Secret of the House.[2] It is to be noted, however, that Perceval is not a participant of any Arch-Natural Sacrifice. These are witnessed by Arthur and others, but not by him. It is to be noted further that the Grail Castle fell into his hands by the right of conquest on the surface side of things ; but he was also the Heir thereof and of all its Hallows. In witness hereto the Grail came back when he took possession of his own. But the succession was not priestly, and Perceval never said Mass. A link is created here with the DIDOT-MODENA PERCEVAL, in which story of the Quest attained Blaise is the Priest-in-Charge at the end

<hr>

[1] Appendix I, Note 27.   [2] Appendix I, Note 28.

of all, while Merlin is Prophet and Perceval is Grail King. There is also an analogy with the Metrical Romance of JOSEPH, in which there is no Mass because there is no Priest. Joseph is instituted Keeper of the Grail, deriving from Christ Himself ; but he is appointed and not ordained ; and this is a ready argument for refusing to recognise the Secret Words imparted at the time of the gift as Words of Consecration. They do not appear as such in any of the events that follow, for the Grail is always an oracle and never a Sacrificial Vessel in the Borron Cycle.

It is to be noted here as a point of criticism which applies to all the literature that the idea of the Grail Reliquary serving as a Chalice stultifies the whole doctrinal claim as regards the Mass.[1] It is essential to the sacrificial nature of the great ceremonial that the Elements of the Sacrifice are consumed or at least reserved thereto ; whereas a Reliquary containing *ex hypothesi* the Precious Blood is an impossible matter of sacrifice, because it must be kept and not consumed. It is likely enough that here is one ground for the hostility of the Church to Grail literature as a whole. We should remember also that in the LONGER PROSE PERCEVAL the Grail does not go about as it does in the Galahad QUESTE, though an Arch-Natural Mass is celebrated once outside the Grail Castle.

It is celebrated within and, as it may be, other Services, from Saturday to Monday in every week of the year. He who will ask the Question and heal thereby the Grail King, shall enter the Chapel of the Grail and hear the Mass therein. But this is not done in the Keeper's lifetime, nor yet after, for then the need has passed. We know, however, that Arthur saw the Grail much later and was present at the Mass. Moreover, Monseigneur Gawain was with him : he saw also and heard, being shriven after this manner for his trance of silence and adoration when he was called to heal the Keeper.

The PERLESVAUS is like a great procession of pictures in the master-craft of glass that is richly stained and a wealth of colour, with Sanctuary Lamps burning at every window. But we know the heads of the story, above all of the ship which took Perceval to an island of the sea, where he was welcomed by men with " beards and hair whiter than driven snow, albeit they seemed young of visage "—as might be sons of the Valley or Keepers of the Mystical Heredom and the hills of isles about. We know also of Masses said therein, in a Holy Chapel. Thither the Grail was taken at the close of all and thither Perceval followed to receive another Kingship and its diadem. The former Grail Castle, that Holy House in the Hiddenness, waited well and patiently through the days and the years till all the manor wasted and fell into decay. But there is an Epilogue to this story which has not been " drawn into Romance " ; for it was allotted to Perceval that he should approve himself in the work of his new royalty. It must be

[1] It will be remembered, on the occasion of the Grail Mass at Sarras, after the consecration of Joseph II, that there was another Vessel on the Altar, admittedly containing Wine.

agreed therefore that a tale which does not finish can offer only an incomplete message. Furthermore, the last Title says paradoxically that "here endeth the story of the Most Holy Grail," whereas it should have added "and here again begins," seeing that there was more to follow. It does not say, and is notable, that the Grail was taken away but only that it "shall appear herein no more," referring to the former Castle of the Hallows. It is somewhere in the lands or in the islands; and those—if any—who at this day are like Perceval may doubtless find the Grail. It seems to me that this is the message, for which reason—and on many other accounts—there is one thing only nearer to my heart than the PERLESVAUS and its High History.

And this is the Galahad Quest, which in the deep spiritual sense is eminently a personal history and a parable of the soul on its way through the world to God. It is parable rather than allegory, but with occasional allegorical excursions, which on account of their utter crudity come perilously near to making shipwreck of the whole story. Monseigneur Gawain, Bors, Perceval, even Galahad himself are schooled like children in the lowest forms, while their doctrinal teachers, their unknown Masters, Hermits, Recluses and so forth may have sailed over strange seas in mysterious ships, may dwell in immemorial Abbeys or keep their fasts and watches in the shadow of the Holy Grail; but their expatiations are like dry wood and their expository interpretations as lead for dullness.[1] Malory saved the QUESTE when he heaved them over among the rubbish, leaving the great parable to teach its own lesson. It is that of the Christ Life, from Birth to Death, from Death to Resurrection in the Soul, and then unto the Soul's Ascension into the ecstasy of Union. This is the message of that which has been called by scholarship—all unconsciously—the QUESTE, as if *par excellence*. They knew not what they said; but it is such in very truth. The exhaustive process of my criticism in the present section has led up to this: it is *aut* GALAHAD, *aut nihil* in respect of the Grail and its finding.

The great prize has been thrown open, as if to all comers. The Grail is not only going about as a veridic rumour through the world of Logres but it is shewn under its proper veils even in the King's Palace. By the hypothesis concerning it, the King's Palace is a place of highest dedication to "high erected thought" and action, "seated in a heart of courtesy". But the seeds of its own destruction have been sown therein. It is foredoomed from the beginning by the adultery of Arthur, committed on the body of his half-sister, though he knew not what he did. He became in this manner the father of Mordred, by whom the High Chivalry of the Round Table was destroyed finally in the last great battle of the West. Mordred also knew not what he did, for it does not appear in any text that Arthur and he ever saw one another in their true relation of father and son. It follows that a very simple sin of sense became pregnant

[1] Appendix I, Note 29.

with fatality for what looks like the greatest scheme conceived in the mind of Romance. I speak of a world of myth, the significance of which may be somewhere in the world of fact, if a star would lead us to find its right direction. As such, it would be a reading of history, a construction placed upon events and a lesson drawn therefrom. But if no such events are found, it is alternatively the shewing of a vision, a lesson on high aspiration defrauded and stultified by the sense-life—otherwise, the world and flesh.

But there was not alone the foredoom of the Mordred episode : there was the fatality of the passion of Lancelot. Arthur was unfaithful from the beginning to his high election, and Guinevere proved unfaithful to the great place assigned her in the Holy House of Chivalry. Part of the intention may be, by possibility, to indicate that Arthur was handicapped *ab origine* by the forbidden passion of his conception. So also Lancelot was handicapped by the vigilance of his nurture in the Faërie of the Lady of the Lake, in virtue of which he came forth at length to face the world and Court devoid of warning or experience. It was another working of doom, by which even the Lady of the Lake contributed unawares to the downfall of the Round Table. So also the course of later events contributed yet further, all through the Table's history. The membership thereof became a prize for valour and not a prize for virtue. It fell away from its high intent by the attraction of Adventurous Times, into sex indulgence as into Times of Enchantment, into endless Knight-Errantries for the sake of errantry and murderous joustings for the sake of the glory of jousting. Galahad alone was the great intent, the high erected thought and the clean heart of courtesy ; did he ever joust for the sake of jousting, except on that one day which followed his Knighting, when all men tried their skill ? Did he ever kill for valour, to give his evidence thereof ?

Year after year, through all his years of Quest, he went about, putting an end to Adventurous Times, which were also Times of Enchantment in the terms of the Great Parable, much as might have fared a Catharist Apostle, commissioned from his Church of the Spirit, ever reforming the misbelief of Christendom, writhing under the yoke of Rome. This is only a casual illustration on the historical plane, and it has been agreed already that the Grail and its literature are not to be explained by reference to the Sects of Southern France. But if the QUESTE, as I have intimated, is above all things a personal history and representative as such of the Christ-Life in the soul of man, then Adventurous Times and their Enchantments are indicative of the states and stages of the soul's experience on its way of return to God, and there should be no need to dwell upon their material nature. They are of course the outward preoccupations and the manifold sense-illusions which must be dispossessed of their engrossing power by those who seek Reality. It is indubitable, however, that there is an outward as well as an inward or personal meaning of the Quest ; and it is desirable to say that, in the story itself, not only do the two meanings co-exist but interpenetrate each other, a fact which would make the work of their disentanglement a very arduous task, were it possible to attempt it here. I am of necessity concerned only in this Twelfth Book with an indication of the Grail Secret, as I understand it, and as the subject is left when all the other theses have been tested and found wanting. A volume of exposition would be needed to go further, and it might prove a failure, because the matter placed in our hands is neither metaphysical solely, nor only of external appeal, but a confusing combination of both, while the vehicle is that of Romance, which there and here obtrudes its own elements.

As regards their message, we must remember that it begins in the Sanctuary and that behind the QUESTE there lies the problem of the Birth of Galahad. It is like a Sanctuary Mystery. Because it is such obviously, a thing pre-arranged and a sacrificial act on the part of the Grail Maiden, it involved no fatality for Galahad, as their own births proved for Arthur and Mordred. It is never mentioned in the QUESTE ; but had the story been told therein, and not in the LANCELOT, I should have felt that it required to be understood mystically, recalling that the soul is born into the flesh of this world through fleshly intercourse, but that some souls are subsequently born again, not after the will of man or the blood of man, but of the Spirit of God. There is no call to pursue this subject, because the Great Prose LANCELOT is not a story of the soul, nor is it under any circumstances to be regarded as the Book of any Sanctuary, though I shall not readily divorce my mind from the feeling that the Birth of Galahad is a theme which in its final understanding does not belong to Romance.[1]

The PERLESVAUS, at least on the surface, ends as it began, among the images, though its *exitus in mysterium*, all pageants notwithstanding of sun-blazed voyage and venture, may suggest a recession which seems analogous to the withdrawal of the Grail and Galahad. But the key is given—as one might say, almost openly—in the QUESTE *par excellence*, which is the crown of the Quest Cycle, and we can see its whole *processus :* (1) The miracles and marvels of Times of Enchantment and Times Adventurous, Times above all of Quest, when the Grail went about, when the Grail healed and hurt, when the Lance was broken on the Keeper, when Knights fell on one another, bewrayed and foiled in Quest, when many died therein. (2) The last scene at Corbenic, when Transubstantiation made its last stand and produced the mournful disillusion of its plenary manifestation, an ensanguined figure bearing the sigils of the Passion, after which the House was voided, the Apostolate scattered, the Keeper disinherited, while the Grail went voyaging on its homeward way, " far in the unapparent ". (3) The last scene in the Spiritual City, when Galahad " received " his

---

[1] In the purely literal sense, it has been treated as negligible from the QUESTE standpoint, because the great parable is not of marrying, of giving in marriage, or of births according to the flesh, howsoever encompassed.

" Saviour ", when Galahad only saw the hidden things in a world beyond the vision, and nothing is said of the " seeing ", because it lies outside the world of words and as much beyond the psychic eyes as beyond the eyes of flesh. (4) Thereafter Galahad claimed or exercised his now inalienable right, being that of Ascension, which in highest Christian Theosophy is to return with Christ to the Father, far past dilucid contemplation, into the Mystery of Union.

On the day of his final departure the PERLESVAUS Perceval was visited, as we know, in the Grail Castle by voyagers from afar and clothed as if to celebrate Mass. But no Mass was said. He left the Castle in their mystical ship and was seen no more. The Grail had gone before him, thither where he was called to follow. He had distributed the other Hallows, and the outward Holy Place was dismembered. These things were left to the world without, in place of the Great Palladium. Perceval was withdrawn, as if into another Sanctuary where there is celebrated only the Mass of Union. It does not shew the five changes of the manifesting Grail. So also, and we know also, at the end of all Galahad beheld no outward sacramental marvels. He saw no doubt in the perfection of his prepared state that which *le Roi Mehaigné* surprised against the Law and the Order. This is the dilucid contemplation, in which state Ruysbroeck sailed the uncharted sea of Godhood—*vastissimum Divinitatis pelagus*. It is the state also in which St. Bonaventura beheld the deeps within the outward and expressed word : *sub cortice litteræ apertæ occultata mystica et profunda intelligentia,*—the illumination of Doctrine by a light shining from within it.

From the Spiritual Palace at Sarras, the soul of Galahad carried the Vision which is he into the World of Ascension, and this, like all things else that belong to reality in experience, is an exploration—further, deeper, higher—of our own world within. Here is the end of the Valid Mysteries, howsoever denominated ; and hereof is that which is descried at the term of the Great Quest—the Vision that is He, " and after this the Union." We think and speak in pictures, while the distinctions which experience attains cannot be conveyed in words, save only at a far distance by a certain change in these. But he who can apprehend the one will apprehend also the other, while he who misconceives the other will scarcely grasp the one. In my oft-quoted witness of the old THEOSOPHIA, Galahad bore the Divine within him to the Divine in the universe—the realm within which lies beyond distinctions. And this is the Secret of the Grail. We have known it under other vestures of language before we found that it had been drawn also into Romance. The testimony of the QUESTE is full of imperfections and calls for re-statement everywhere ; but if I speak the truth as I see it, under all the aspects and in all the directions, so also does the witness of all the Masters, from him who is called Dionysius to St. John of the Cross and those who came after him in their several schools of discipline.

III

A PRELIMINARY EXCURSUS CONCERNING THE GREAT EXPERIMENT

THE Quest of the Holy Grail is for the wonder of all sacredness, " there where no sinner can be "—until he has ceased from sin. The provisional manifestation is in the LONGER PROSE PERCEVAL,[1] while the full disclosure—not as to what it is but as to what it is about—is in the Romance of Galahad. If, after the HAUT PRINCE had given his final message, " Remember of this unstable world," he had been asked what he had seen and what led him to exercise his high prerogative and call to be dissolved,[2] he might have answered : *visi sunt oculi mei salutare suum ;* yet he would have said in his heart : " Eye hath not seen ". But it has been divined and foretasted by those who have gone before the cohorts of election in the life that is within and have spoken with tongues of fire concerning that which they have seen in the vista. One approximation has told us that it is the (realised) " eternal intercourse of the Father and the Son, wherein we are enveloped lovingly by the Holy Spirit in that love which is eternal." Now this is not of doctrine but experience put forth in consecrated symbols. And him who said this the wondering plaudits of an after-age termed the admirable Ruysbroeck. He knew little Latin and less Greek, and, speaking from his own root, he had not read the authorities ; but he had stood upon that shore where the waves of the Divine Sea baptise the pilgrim, or in that undeclared sphere which is *Kether*, the Crown of Kabbalism, whence those who can look further discern that there is *Ain Soph Aour*, the Limitless Light. They can realise also the truth of that High Theosophical axiom which affirms that *linea media ascendit usque ad Ain Soph*. It is the Path of the Mind's ascent to the altitude of its own being.

The equivalent hereof is that which was said by Jesus Christ to the Men of the Quest : " My Knights and my Servants and my true Children, which have come out of deadly life into spiritual life, I will now no longer hide me from you, but ye shall see now a part of my secrets and of my hidden things ".[3] And in the measure of that time

---

[1] *Li Graalx s'aparut el secré de la messe, en V manières que l'an ne doit mie dire ; quar, les secrées chosses del seremant ne doit nus dire an apert, se cil à qui Dex an a donée (la puissance). Lis rois Artus vit toutes les muances ; la dariane si fu el calice.*—Potvin, *Op. cit.*, I, p. 250. " The Graal appeared at the sacring of the Mass, in five several manners that none ought not to tell openly but he unto whom God hath given it. King Arthur beheld all the changes, the last whereof was the change into a Chalice."—HIGH HISTORY, Branch XXII, Title 3. It is to be observed that the mutations were those of the Vessel and not of its content.

[2] We have seen that the message of Galahad was that of a Son to his Father ; but it is peculiar to the text followed by Malory, or is alternatively his own addition. The Vulgate text gives only the first part of the greeting : *Puis dist à bohort (biaus très dous ami), salues moi mon père lancelot quant vous le verrois.*—Sommer, *Op. cit.*, VI, p. 197. Pauphilet's codex agrees, being a collation of many manuscripts. The WELSH QUEST cuts out the message entirely.

[3] Malory's MORTE DARTHUR, Bk. XVII, *cap.* 22. Cf. Sommer, *Op. cit.*, VI, p. 190.

they knew as they were known in full, that is, by participation in and correspondence with the Divine Knowledge. Meat indeed : it is in this sense that Christ gave to Galahad " the high meat " : and " then he received his Saviour ". Vavassour or Graduate of the Classes, or unknown Master of Sentences, he who wrote thus might have exhausted all the language of the Schools, or he might also have known little Latin and less Greek, if any ; but in either case he said only of the Communicants : " They thought it so sweet that it was marvellous to tell."[1] And of Galahad he said later that "he received it right gladly and meekly ".[2] But yes ; and that is fuller and stronger than all the eloquence of the authentic Master of Sentences. It is the voice of Ruysbroeck, in a simpler manner of language, saying the same thing : " And he tastes and sees, out of all bounds, after God's own manner, the riches which are in God's own self, in the unity of the living deep, wherein He has fruition of Himself, according to the mode of His uncreated essence ". Here is the Great Term of the Great Experiment followed by the Mystic Schools ; and it is bodied forth by the Grail Legend in its own words and symbols, as in a shadow-light of earthly human language. And there are some of us who have put forth all powers of mind and all our hearts of yearning in the hope to go further ; but we have been given at our best and highest the changes and counter-changes of other approximations which are also remote from the Term. The Experiment has been made, within their several measures, by all Churches of all Religions, for which reason I have said elsewhere that the skilled craftsman does not quarrel with his tools. All the rough ashlars are possible ; the ascent to Eternal Life can be made on any ladder, assuming that it is fixed in the height : there is no need to go in search of something that is new and strange. Those also who can receive this assurance will understand, I think, that even the Church of one's childhood—assuming that it is a Church and not a latitudinarian chapel of ease or a narrow and voided sect—may contain for him the raw materials of his work ; and these he will be able to adapt as an efficient artist. There is neither compulsion nor restraint ; but the changes in official religion, the too easy transitions from one to another kind, taking the Sanctuaries as one takes High Grades in Masonry, offer a note of weakness rather than a pledge of sincerity or of the true motive which would impel the soul on its quest.

There are undeniably many helpers of the soul in the course of its progress and among these are possibly two or three of the so-called Secret Orders, meaning those which contain the counterparts of authentic Catholic Tradition.[3] They offer no royal road, seeing that there is none of these ; but they do or may shorten some of the pre-liminaries, awaking and unfolding the implicits of a man's own

[1] This was at Corbenic, when Twelve who had fulfilled the Quest were fed in the body substantially and supersubstantially in the soul of each.
[2] This was at Sarras, where we have seen that One of Three was fed by himself alone.
[3] They may be counted on the fingers of one hand, and even then it may prove an exaggerated estimate.

consciousness, which is the setting of a Prepared Postulant on the lineal path. There are of course some who enter within them having no special call, and these see very little of that which lies beyond their official workings, just as there are many who have been born or brought within the Church, considered as the Body of Christ Mystical, but have never entered into that life of the Christhood which is communicated from Christ the Spirit. They remain as children of this world and its pieties, participating according to their degree of so much grace and salvation as is possible within their individual modes. There are others who out of all time have received the High Election, and for them the subject is often found resident and undivided in that state of external religious life into which it has pleased God to call them.

The Inward Doctrine of the Religions and the Schools equally is that of the communication of Divine Substance. I speak of it as inward in both cases, though it is obvious that official Churches have no instituted reservation or conscious concealment on any point of Doctrine or practice ; but the language of the heights is not the language of the plains, while that which is heard in the nooks, byways and corners, among brakes and thickets, is not the voice of the rushing waters and the open sea. That is true of it in the uttermost which was said long ago by Paracelsus : *nihil tam occultum erit quod non revelabitur*. But as there are few with ears to hear, it remains a voice in the wilderness crying in an unknown tongue. We know only that, according to Highest *Theosophia*, the Divine Substance is communicated *ex hypothesi* in the Eucharist—normally in a symbolical manner, but, essentially and vitally in cases here and there, according to true testimonies. It is as if the Elements were at times Consecrated normally, at the speculative value of the work and intent of an Official Priesthood ; but at times by other words, more secret and more efficient arch-naturally. But these are a work of reception and not uttered with lips. It is, I think, in the notable examples, because *signum* has withdrawn into *signatum*, or in other language because communicants have passed behind the symbols.[1] Then do Enchantments terminate which are the swoon of the sensitive life in respect of the individual : he enters into real knowledge—the soul's knowledge before that supervened which is termed mystically the fall into matter.

The Great Experiment is therefore one of Emblematic Reintegration in the Secret Knowledge before the Fall ;[2] and when or if the Holy Grail is identified with the Stone in the Crown of Lucifer, that which is indicated thereby is (1) the perpetuation of this Secret Knowledge and (2) that under all circumstances there is a way back whence we came. So also close those Times of Adventure which—among other

---

[1] In variant words, they have passed unawares or otherwise behind the Veils of Doctrine, or more actually are in that state of experience where Doctrines cease from troubling and the Symbols are at rest.

[2] I have said " emblematic " because the " Fall " is itself figurative of an æonian diversion from true ends of being.

things and manifold—are the life of external activity governed by the spirit of the world ; and this is accomplished by taking the Great Secret into the heart of the heart, as if the Blessed Sacrament, truly and virtually, into the inmost being.

Of such is the Office of the Quests ; but it should be understood that it is not of my concern to postulate these realisations as present in a plenary sense to the minds of the old *scriptores*, who wrote the greatest of the books : they spoke of things which they knew up to a certain point. Without reference or intention, they said—as it befell —what others had said before them of the same Mysteries, and the testimony continued through the centuries. The story of the assumption of Galahad draws into Romance the hypothesis of the Church Catholic concerning the term of all attainment manifested : in both cases it is exemplified by the Eucharist.[1] But the Church is not of Rome, as such, protesting against the Greek Orthodoxy, nor is it of any surviving Bethel preaching against the abuses of Roman Doctrine. The Catholic Church is the eternal spirit of Religion within and behind the Churches—the Christ, the Guide, the Comforter, leading those who can follow unconditionally into all Truth. As regards the Eucharist, I mean to say that this is, by the hypothesis, the symbolical channel of Divine Communion ; and the devotion which was shewn by the Saints to the Sacrament of the Altar was the witness of their dedication thereto, of their belief in its living reality, and was not like a particular, sentimental disposition in pious minds to the Precious Blood or the Heart of Jesus. Concerning these exercises there is no call to pronounce here; but among the misjudgments on spiritual life under Roman rule has been the frittering of spiritual powers in popular devotions. If the Great Mysteries of and behind the Churches are insufficient to command the dedication of the whole world, then the world is left best under interdict, just as no pictures at all are better than those which are bad in art, and no books than those which are poor and trivial.

We have been trending here in directions which will call for more full consideration presently. I have mentioned Secret Orders—not without an implied animus—and I cannot affirm too early that any Secret Tradition—either in the East or in the West—has been always an open secret in respect of the root-principles concerning the Way, the Truth and the Life.[2] It is the experience therein which is for ever secret and incommunicable to those who have not shared it. We are only beginning, and that by very slow stages, to enter into our inheritance; and still in respect of the larger part we are seeking far and wide for the figurative Treasures of Basra. It is desirable therefore to remember that the great subjects of preoccupation are all at our very doors. One reason, of which we shall hear again in another connection, is because among the wise of the ages, in whatsoever regions of the world, I do not think that there has been ever any real difference of

---

[1] Figuratively, that is to say, in ten thousand cases, and once behind the symbols.
[2] The occult associations—and they are many—which claim to convey secrets, as such or as if such, traffic in bogus wares.

opinion about the true object of research. The modes and forms of the
Quest have varied, and that widely ; but to a single point have all the
ways converged. Therein is no change or shadow of vicissitude. We
may hear of shorter roads, and we might say at first sight that such
a suggestion must be true indubitably ; but in one sense it is rather a
convention of language and in another it is a commonplace which tends
to confuse the issues. It is a convention of language, because the Great
Quests are not pursued in time or place, and it would be just as true to
say that in a journey from the circumference to the centre all roads
are the same length, supposing that they are straight roads. It is a
commonplace, because if anyone should enter the by-ways or return on
his path and restart, it is obvious that he must look to be delayed.
Furthermore, it may be true that all paths lead ultimately to the
centre, and that if we descend into hell there may be still a way back
to the light : yet in any house of right reason the issues are too clear
to consider such extrinsic possibilities.

There is one thing more, however, in this connection ; and I bear
my witness concerning it with a mind convinced but an anxious and
trembling heart. It is true that there is one short road, but it is
within us—you even and even me, all expectations contradicting and
all contra-judgments notwithstanding. It is not travelled but over-
leaped. It is not a road at all, as if that which is higher within us
drove that which is lower till it should be crushed out of all being in
the path of a cross beyond all weight for bearing. There is something
realised in the stillness beyond our world of images ; and that which
is immortal within us, " the supernal part which does not leave the
Supernals " takes possession of our henceforth undivided being ; takes
seat upon the " intellectual throne " ; and translates therefrom all life
in the terms of eternity. The appetites are transformed and the
ambitions, *sub specie æternitatis*.[1] We abide in another mode, under
another aspect. The ordeals are over, the temptations dead and done :
we are at the beginning of life in the unity.[2]

On this and on any consideration, we have to lay down one irrevoc-
able law, that he who has resolved—setting all things else aside—
to enter the Path of Quest must look for his progress in proportion as he
pursues holiness for its own end—holiness being the unremitted
direction of mind and thought and heart to the Divine End. He who in
the imputed Secret Orders dreams of the adeptship which is claimed by
some as communicable to those who can receive and who does not say
SANCTITAS in his heart till his lips are cleansed, and then does not say
it with his lips, is not so much far from the goal as without having
conceived regarding it.

Now, it is precisely this word SANCTITAS which takes us back a
little unintentionally, to the claim of the Churches, and raises the

---

[1] Appendix I, Note 30.
[2] There are only the vaguest hints extant on this *pansophia* of highest practical
experience. It may be worth while to mention THEOLOGIA ESOTERICA—in reality,
THEOLOGIA EXOTICA—which I contributed to THE QUEST of Jan., 1928.

question whether we are to interpret it according to the mind thereof
or another mind. My answer is that I doubt if the Great Experiment
was ever pursued to its term in Christian Times on the part of any
person who had once been incorporated by their mystical body but
subsequently had set himself unconditionally aside therefrom. Even
Jacob Böhme, who was hunted, deafened and silenced for overlong by
the post-Lutheran rabble about him, did not explicitly come out of
the raving Görlitz sects. When the Quest of the Holy Grail was in fine
achieved, there were some, as we know, who were translated, but
others became monks and hermits : they were incorporated, that is to
say, by the official annals of sanctity. I am dealing here with what I
regard as a question of fact, not with antecedent grounds ; and the
fact is that the Church has the Eucharist—namely, *Signum Magnum*.[1]
It may have hampered and hindered Christian Mysticism by the
restriction of its own consciousness so especially to the letter which
killeth ; it may, on the historical side, have answered too often and
faithfully to that picture of the King of Castle Mortal who sold God
for money ; it may in this sense have told the wrong story, though the
figurative elements placed in its hands were right and true elements.
But—speaking as a *doctor dubitantium*—I know that the Church
Mystical on the highest throne of its consciousness does not differ
otherwise than *per accidentia* from formal Catholic Doctrine, understood essentially. It can say with its heart of knowledge what the
ordinary churchman says with believing lips : the *Symbolum* radiates,
for its meaning wells up from within. It is as if a shell had opened
and an embodied life had come forth, a life embodied in experience.
In another form of symbolism, the meaning has unfolded itself, like a
flower from the bud. The Christian Mystic can recite therefore his
Credo in unum Deum by clause and by clause, including *in unam
sanctam catholicam et apostolicam ecclesiam*, and there is neither heresy
in the construction nor any casuistry of an *arrière pensée*.[2] It has
seemed worth while to make this plain, because the Holy Grail is the
Catholic Quest drawn into Romance.

It may be inferred that at this stage there can be no need to exhibit
in formal words after what manner the Quest of the Holy Grail became
in the later texts a deeper religious experiment and thus justified
the titles from which it began in that story of Robert de Borron
which is the earliest extant History. Anyone who has proceeded so
far in the present inquisition as to have reached these lines—even
if he be unfamiliar otherwise with the old treasury of books—must
be aware that the Quest was ruled throughout by the dogmatic
Counsels of Perfection. They ruled in fact so strongly as to have
entered that state when two of them were implied only, meaning that
they were taken for granted : (1) Voluntary Poverty, for the Knights-
Errant possessed nothing, and whatever came into their hands was

---

[1] Over *signatum* it has been bewrayed for centuries.
[2] On the score of sincerity, it must be indicated that these statements postulate
implicitly a *noumenon* behind *Symbolum*.

distributed there and then ; (2) Entire Obedience, in dedication to the proposed term, and all the ships of the world burnt with fire behind them : otherwise there followed complete *avortement*, as that of Gawain in the Great Quest ; (3) Perpetual Chastity, as the only Counsel which stands forth declared—and in this connection it will be remembered that Bors returned to Logres. The zeal of these Counsels does not appear—as I have said—to guarantee election utterly : they are rather tests of merit. It has been said also that there are cases of partial success apart from fulfilment in the absolute degree. Gawain received signal favours in the PERLESVAUS, yet it is admitted that he was wanting in purity, and hence he could make no response when the Questionable Mystery appeared once in his presence.[1] The external vision was his, but not the attainment.[2] The King also beheld an Arch-Natural Mass on the manifested side thereof ; but Perceval alone possessed the plenary qualifications in this text. On the other hand, in the story of stories there was one who surpassed him, but not so utterly that they were otherwise than classed together as Companions of the Quest. The distinction seems to have been that Galahad had dissolved temptation, as one more than human. Perceval overcame temptation but was not beyond its reach, as if he carried within him the latent desires of the body :[3] it came about therefore that after beholding the Grail he required the final experience of a Hermit's life before he entered into the true inheritance of those Thrones which are above. By some of my fellowship in research it has been said most truly, though they do not understand Galahad, that the *haut prince* was just as fit for the Quest at its beginning as he was at its end. Now, that is exactly the sign of perfect vocation—of election as well as calling : the criterion of those who are meant for Heaven is that they might ascend thither at any moment. Another test of Galahad was that he knew really from the beginning the whole Mystery by the Tradition thereof.[4] He who returned to the House belonged

---

[1] Potvin, *Op. cit.*, I, pp. 88, 89 ; HIGH HISTORY, Branch VI, Titles 19, 20.

[2] *Atant ez-vos II damoiseles qui issent d'une chapele et tient l'une en ces mains le sentime Graal, et l'autre la lance de quoi la lance (pointe) seigne dedanz.* " Thereon, lo you, two Damsels that issue forth of a Chapel, whereof the one holdeth in her hands the Most Holy Grail, and the other the Lance whereof the point bleedeth thereinto."—*Ib.*

[3] Sommer, *Op. cit.*, Vol. VI, pp. 75–79. The only English translation is that of Dr. W. W. Comfort : THE QUEST OF THE HOLY GRAIL : see *cap.* VI, pp. 84–88.

[4] The illustrations are casual in the text, but prominent here and there. A few may be cited in their order, beginning from the moment when Galahad has taken, as instructed, the Siege Perilous at the Round Table. (1) His greeting to all who abide in the Holy Hostel—obviously the Castle of Corbenic—especially his uncle King Pelles and his grandsire the Rich Fisher King. This may be compared with what has been derived otherwise in my text from the prose LANCELOT. Galahad came from the House Mystical of the Holy Grail and that he knew the way thereto is shewn by his added undertaking to visit those who abode in it as soon as he could. (Sommer, *Op. cit.*, VI, p. 8.) (2) In answer to the King's greeting, he says that he was bound to come—*Je sui venus et je le devoie faire*—Camelot and the Royal Court being the starting-point of that Quest which was about to begin (*ib.*, p. 10). A little later he exhibits (3) foreknowledge of the fact that the Sword fixed in a certain Stone (*perron*) was destined for him and that no others could remove it (*ib.*, pp. 10, 11). As this enumeration must end, I will add only (4) that at the first stage of the Quest Galahad started without a shield, as one who knew well concerning the Shield of Evalach which had been kept through the centuries in view of his advent and which was presently to be conferred upon him in a miraculous manner (*ib.*, pp. 20–26).

thereto and may have been born therein.[1] I am enumerating here the
general implicits of the subject which should be latent at least in the
minds of those who are addressed : they do not constitute a question
put forward for sifting with a view to a settlement, but of fitness and
power to see—of the *verus certusque intuitus animi*, in some degree
and proportion. This being agreed by those who can suffer the ruling,
it will be obvious that the religious experiment about which I begin
to speak can depend only from two express conditions : (1) the manifest
attainment of a sanctified state in the Questing Knights, and (2) the
descent of a peculiar Grace upon them, which may be described alternatively as a manifestation of Grace from within. I enumerate both
points, though it is obvious that one of them has, in another form,
passed already through review ; but in dealing with a very difficult
subject it is necessary to look at it in more than a single light, and I
wish to make it clear that the specifics of the sanctified state—by which
I mean the Counsels of Perfection—are not things that are determined
in the given case by a trend of thought and emotion at a given period,
and are not therefore to be dismissed as a presentation of ascetic life or
as the definition of canons which have passed now into desuetude.
The same experiment always demands the same conditions for its
success, and to set aside these is really to renounce that, or in this
instance it is to reject the Experiment as one of the old ecstasies which
never came to a term. On the contrary, the Experiment of Sanctity
is always approximating to a term, and the measure of success is the
measure of zeal in its pursuit. I propose therefore to look a little
closer at one of the Counsels of Perfection. The essential point regarding the condition of *virgo intacta*—not in respect of the simple physical
fact, which has no inherent sanctity, but in respect of its conscious
acceptance at what cost soever—is that there neither was nor can be a
more perfect symbol of the prepared matter of the work.[2] It is the
analogy in utter transcendence of that old adage : *Mens sana in
corpore sano*, and its nearest expression is : *Anima immaculata in
corpore dedicato, ex hoc nunc et usque*, etc. In other words, the Banns
of Marriage in the Higher Degrees cannot be proclaimed till the con-
tracting parties are warranted in their respective orders to have that
proportion and likeness, apart from which no union could be effected.
The consummated grade of sanctity is an intimate state of union, and
the nearest analogy thereto is found in human marriage :[3] as the latter
presupposes in the Sacramental Order an antecedent or nominal

---

[1] Appendix I, Note 31.

[2] The word " symbol " is used here expressly ; and in this connection there may be
added, as regards what is called liturgically "the unspotted sacrifice," that in the wide
world of symbolism there is nothing to compare with the Eucharist as a figurative
but plenary representation of the Mystical Path and Term. It will be observed that
this affirmation is not in competition with what is said above on the *virgo intacta* state,
which belongs to the inward preparation of those who would travel the Path and reach
its end.

[3] The use of the word " analogy " should not be overlooked : in the deep mystical
sense the state of *virgo intacta* or that of matrimonial union is not a sex question, though
sex may intervene to promote or mar the utter dedication at issue.

purity, and has for its object the consecration of intercourse which in its absence is of the animal kind, so the antecedent condition in high spiritual grades—or the life of perfect dedication—is in correspondence with the state of *virgo intacta*. I need not say that because these things are analogical so the discourse concerning them partakes of the language of symbolism or that the state itself is mystical. Entire Obedience involves no earthly master ; Voluntary Poverty is of all possibility in a palace and the Law would not deny it at the head-quarters of an American Trust ; as Regards Chastity, that is guaranteed to those who receive and maintain the Sacrament of Marriage worthily. It is to be noticed that this Sacrament differs from Baptism, which is administered once and for all, while Marriage, in the effects thereof, is administered in continuity as an abiding presence and a grace abound-ing, so long as its covenants are observed. On the other hand, the perpetuity of Spiritual Chastity in the life within does not mean of necessity that man or woman has never known flesh in the physical order. Galahad in the story had the outward signs as well as the Inward Grace. His Quest is a parable throughout, but allegorical motive obtrudes too often into the expressed matter, which is either an error of art or an awkward explanatory device to indicate that the given text has a second meaning everywhere.

The term which is proposed in the QUESTE, as the consideration thereof, will be given best in the words of the QUESTE itself. " Now at the year's end and the self day after Galahad had borne the crown of gold, he arose up early and his fellows, and came to the palace, and saw tofore them the Holy Vessel, and a man kneeling on his knees in likeness of a Bishop, that had about him a great Fellowship of Angels, as it had been Jesu Christ Himself ; and then he arose and began a Mass of our Lady. And when he came to the Sacrament of the Mass and had done, anon he called Galahad and said to him : Come forth, the servant of Jesu Christ, and thou shalt see that thou hast much desired to see. And then he began to tremble right hard, when the deadly flesh began to behold the spiritual things. Then he held up his hands toward Heaven and said : Lord, I thank Thee, for now I see that that hath been my desire many a day. Now, Blessed Lord, would I not longer live, if it might please Thee, Lord. And therewith the good man took our Lord's Body between his hands and proffered It to Galahad ; and he received It right gladly and meekly. . . . And there-with he kneeled down tofore the Table and made his prayers ; and then suddenly his soul departed to Jesus Christ and a great multitude of Angels bare his soul up to Heaven ", etc. . . .[1]

In this citation the most important point for our purpose rests neither in that which it expresses nor in that which it conceals. It is assumed and realised that such a term is always hidden because it

---

[1] At this point the account of Malory—Book XVII, *cap*. 22—follows the French text without abbreviation. Sommer, *Op. cit.*, p. 197. Cf. Dr. Comfort's translation, pp. 223, 224.

exceeds expression always, and is the closer veiled whenever it is announced the most. But here was the consummation of all. But here was that more open seeing than was granted at Corbenic and that wherein all the outward offices of things arch-natural were set aside utterly. There was no vision of Transubstantiation Metamorphoses, and as evidence that this was of concert and not of chance, there is the same report to make concerning the PERLESVAUS : when the Questing Knight comes to his own therein no signs and wonders are connected with the Holy Grail.[1] As regards the Vision itself of Galahad and that which he saw, we may remember the words of Nasciens after his attempt to penetrate the Secrets within the New Ark of the Covenant. " Et Nasciens dist que il l'en descouverroit tant comme nule mortieus langue em porroit descouvrir, ne deveroit. Je ai, dist-il, veut la coum-menchaille dou grant hardiment, l'ocoison des grans savoirs, le fondement des grans religions, le dessevrement des grans felonnies, la demou-stranche des grans mierveilles, la mervelle de totes les altrez mervelles, la fin des bontés et des gentilleces vraies."[2] This extract from the GRAND SAINT GRAAL is thus rendered in the halting measures of Lovelich :

> " ' I have scin,' quod the sire Nasciens,
>   Of alle manere of wykkednesse the defens ;
>   Of alle boldnesse I have sene the begynneng,
>   Of all wittes the fowndyng.
>   I have sein the begynneng of Religeown
>   And of alle bowntes, bothe al & som,
>   And the poyntes of alle gentrye,
>   And a merveil of alle merveilles certcinlye.' "[3]

Other masters have expressed the same wonder in other terms, which are the same—as, for example : quædam prælibatio æternæ vitæ, gustus et suavitas spiritualis, mentis in Deum suspensa elevatio, etc.

The qualifications of Galahad and Perceval in the Great Quest are not therefore things which are the fashion of a period, like some aspects of what is termed the ascetic mind ; but they obtain from Aleph to Tau, through all grades of expression. Those who speak of the ethical superiority of the PARZIVAL are saying that which, in all moderation and tenderness, signifies that they are still learning the elements of true discipline.

---

[1] When Perceval had overcome the King of Castle Mortal, and when " he who sold God for money " had destroyed himself, it is said in all simplicity that " the Grail presented itself again in the Chapel "—that of the Grail Castle—" and the Lance whereof the point bleedeth, and the Sword wherewith St. John was beheaded that Messire Gawain won, and the other Holy Relics whereof was right great plenty."—HIGH HISTORY, Branch XVIII, Title 36. Cf. Potvin, Op. cit., I, pp. 216, 217. I have noted elsewhere that when King Arthur was at the Grail Castle, on pilgrimage, and saw the Hermit Priests begin the Grail Service, " most holy and most glorious," at which also the Sacred Vessel appeared " in five several manners," it does not seem that Perceval himself was present, but the King only and Monseigneur Gawain.—Potvin, Op. cit., p. 250 ; HIGH HISTORY, Branch XXII, Title 3.

[2] See Hucher : LE SAINT GRAAL, Vol. II, p. 308, and compare Sommer, Op. cit., I, pp. 79, 80.

[3] F. J. Furnivall : THE HISTORY OF THE HOLY GRAIL. Englisht about 1450 A.D., by Henry Lonelich (or Lovelich), Skynner. Early English Text Society, Extra Series, No. XXIV, Vol. I, p. 217.

I have now dealt with the indispensable warrants of the state, and the mode of Grace manifested belongs to the same category : it was a revelation to and within the Spiritual Flowers of Christian Knighthood through the Eucharist—the form of symbolism made use of for this purpose being that of Transubstantiation. I have no design to cover the deeps of disillusion which open on this subject ; but here again we must as our research proceeds approach it from various standpoints ; and, for the rest, it must be obvious that of all men I at least should have no call imposed on me to speak of the Holy Grail were it not for its connection with the Great Emblematic Sacrament. It is the passage of the putative Reliquary into the Chalice of the Eucharist, the pro-gressive exaltation of its cultus and the consequent transfiguration of the Quest which have substituted insensibly a Tale of Eternity for a mediæval Legend of the Precious Blood : in place of the Abbey of Fécamp, we have Corbenic and the *Palais Espiriteux* shining in the high distance, and where once there abode only the suggestion of some relative and rather trivial devotion, we have the presence of that Great Sign behind which there lies the Beginning and the End of all things.

The Romance-writers, seeking in their symbolism a reduction to the evidence of the senses, selected and exaggerated the least desirable side of Eucharistic Dogma ; but it serves no purpose to dispute with them on that score, seeing that—for the skilled craftsman—any material will serve in the purposes of the Great Work. The only point which stands out for our consideration is that—following the sense of all Doctrine and the testimony of all experience—the gate by which Faith presses most readily into Realisation was for them, as for others at the period, the gate of that Sacrament from which all others depend—of that Sacrament the Institution of which was the last act of Christ Mystical and the term of His Ministry : thereafter He suffered only until He rose in glory. When therefore the makers of Grail Books designed to shew after what manner, and under what circumstances, those who were still in flesh could behold the " Spiritual Things " and have opened for them that door of understanding which, according to the Keepers of the Old Law, was not opened for Moses, they had no choice in the matter ; and it is for this reason that they represent the Bread of Life and the Chalice of the Everlasting Testament as being lifted up, not only in the secret places of Logres, but even in the *palais esperiteux* of such a city as Sarras.

Hereof are certain mystical aspects of the Great Quest, and it seems to follow that the Secret Temple of the Soul was dreamed of, if not entered by those who dwelt in the World of Romance as by those in the World of Higher Religion. The Masters of both Schools were saying the same thing at the same period, seeing that during the twelfth and thirteenth centuries, which moved and had their being under the wonderful ægis of the scholastic mind, there began to arise over the intellectual horizon of Europe the light of another experience than that of Spiritual Truth realised intellectually : this was the experience of the Mystical Life, which opened—shall we say ?—with the names of Bonaventura, Hugh and Richard of St. Victor, and closed for the period in question with that of Ruysbroeck. It is understood that there were great antecedent names and great also to come.

IV

THE SECRET SCHOOL

SETTING aside its sacramental part, the literature as literature is Celtic on the surface and Celtic also in atmosphere; but these are the vesture and the environment in which the spirit of its Mystery reposes. The Grail itself is in the root a Reliquary Legend. This Legend was taken over or invented and was connected with rumours of Secret Doctrine concerning the Eucharist and the Priesthood. It passed into Romance or was put forward therein, and it incorporated certain folk-lore elements which seemed adaptable to its purpose : they are naturally its hindrance. In the hands of the Northern French writers, it removed from the Celtic environment as it drew towards its term. We cannot explain therefore the French Cycles and much less the German Grail literature by means of the Celtic Church. On the external side it looks as if it came out of cells and stalls and scriptoria ; but in the last resource it cannot be explained by Rome. We have searched also the findings of qualified research on the Catharist Mystery ; but it is not to be explained thereby. The Secret Doctrine reflected into the literature abode in a Secret School : it was a School of Christian Mystics and was of necessity Catholic at heart.[1] The Doctrine concerning it is that there were High Princes of the Spirit whose experiences surpass not only those of devout souls but of many of its great saints. Their time was not " about half an hour " but an experience as if in perpetuity. The School would have said that the way of the Church, in thesis apart from practice, was a true way and not a good one only ; but it would have added also that the heights are still the heights. It comes about therefore that any message of Secret Words and Super-Apostolical Succession can be only a shadow of reality until its life is attained within : yet that shadow is a sacred reflection. The claim concerning them is like a word written against the Churches, but those who are satisfied with the literal sense of sacred things are not defrauded thereby and can receive ministry therein. Yet the second sense remains, and it is brought from very far away, because it draws from the Sanctuary of the soul. The Mystery which the School explored corresponded in figurative language to a Mass of the Beatific

---

[1] Catholic in the sense of Rome at the highest point of Roman Catholic experience in the way of the Mystic Life ; but Catholic also in a sense unacknowledged by Rome and officially beyond its purview.

Vision. It is obvious that this was celebrated by the Hermit in the GRAND SAINT GRAAL. The Prologue to this Book is the nearest that we are likely to get on the pictured side of the Mystery. The Mass of the Grail is recoverable in the quest of consciousness ; but it is understood that it takes place only in a Secret Church and that Church is within. When the Priest enters the Sanctuary he returns into himself by contemplation and approaches the Altar which is within. He says : *Introibo*. When he utters the words which are Spirit and Life, the Christ Mystical communicates to him in the heart ; or, in alternative symbolism, he is raised into the Third Heaven and enjoys the dilucid contemplation. Like St. Augustine, discoursing of the Holy Trinity, I do not put it in this way as one who is satisfied with the expression : only we must have some expression.[1]

As the Supreme Mystery of the Christian Church, the Eucharist is said to have been compared with the last Ceremony of Initiation, constituting the final enlightenment of the Neophyte. There may be some exaggeration in the statement ; but those who were the original Stewards of the Christian Mystery had in many cases received the Mysteries of the Gentiles and may have adapted some of their procedure. The rumour which came into Romance—and this in the natural manner, because Official Religion, its variants and competitive substitutes permeated Romance everywhere—centred about the Eucharist, and in the minds of external piety was translated into memorials of the Divine Body and the Precious Blood. It would be idle to suggest that any Higher School of Religion was concerned with the veneration of Relics ; but there would be a desire to behold behind the Eucharist that which was held in the symbolism to abide and repose therein. Beyond all knowledge of the outside world, founded on faith and teaching, there is another knowledge ; but it dwells in hidden places of the mind : it has, however, its correspondences in Eucharistic terms, one of which is called the Communication of Christ. In the deeper speculation behind the EPICLESIS Clause, it is described otherwise as a Descent of the Comforter within. He who has performed the one rigorously scientific experiment and has opened the inward Holy Place does enter and that which takes place answers to the Celebration of a Mass :[2] it is not as such the work of an Official Priesthood, though it does not set it aside or compete therewith. Herein is an experiment which I believe to be performed even now in the world, because the great ventures of experience do not pass into desuetude. The Grail Romances in their proper understanding—but chiefly because of their implicits—recall this great subject, testifying after many ways. The Grail is like a guide of the distressed in the Lesser Chronicles : they shadow forth that which is implied inwardly by the Hidden Voice of Christ and the Holy Spirit. Their Secret Words were

---

[1] Remember Schiller in his WALLENSTEIN : " But still the heart needs a language."
[2] Because the experiment is on the subject of that communication which has been mentioned above in the text. The Christ is personal only in the sense of Indwelling Divinity.

Words of Power, because that which rules above rules also below. As such the Lesser Chronicles did not derive from Fécamp, which put forward only the wonder side of Transubstantiation. But the GRAND SAINT GRAAL, which cuts short the discourse between Christ and Joseph in the Tower and so suppresses all reference to the divulgation of Secret Words, can derive no more than a reflection from this source and suffers inevitably from the insufficiency of its doctrinal terms, above all on the picture side. On the spiritual side there is no suggestion that sacramentally the Arch-Natural Body of Christ is communicated to our earthly part and the Divine Life to the human spiritual part. The PERLESVAUS hints at a Secret of the Sacrament which was held in utter reserve, telling us by inference that it was the revelation of Christ in His own Person, behind which there is another Mystery. Curiously enough perhaps, it is only in the texts of Transubstantiation that we find, approximately or remotely, the suggestion of these deeper aspects.[1] The CONTE DEL GRAAL has not heard of them ; the DIDOT-MODENA PERCEVAL is aware of an undeclared Mystery, but has no licence to speak ; the German PARZIVAL suggests an office of concealed mercy amidst suffering, and hereof is Heinrich a shadow. Yet all of them, in their several manners, are haunted from far away : Joseph II began in Priesthood and the Perceval of Manessier ends therein, as if he too discerned that those who attained the Great Mystery were made Priests thereby. I think also that the Fish in the Metrical Joseph has curious sacramental intimations : it is a sign of spiritual sustenance, of Christ's Presence among His faithful, and hence of the Eucharist. Recurring to the GRAND SAINT GRAAL, it only duplicates one part of a canonical miracle. The Catholic master-key is provided most surely by the Galahad Quest, where, long after the Magical Marriage of High Art and Nature has taken place in Transubstantiation, the Questing Knight bows his head, utters his *consummatum est*, and is dissolved. I conclude that the Christian and Grail Mystery of the Mass was a veil which at need could be parted by warranted hands and that behind it there was found the Path which leads to the Union. The knowledge of that Path arose within the Church but led behind it, the Church remaining a gate by which man may enter into attainment. The Quests of the Grail worked towards a knowledge of the Path.

I speak of course as I find, and it is such a finding that it imposes words of witness, not only in Hidden Temples when the Great Rites are held but in the thoroughfares of life, or in books which all may read and a few will cherish in their hearts. If I have said *Introibo* within me through the days and the years ; the *Vere dignum et justum ;* and the *Supplices rogamus ac petimus*, remembering *hæc dona, hæc munera, hæc sancta sacrificia illibata*, it is because of the GALAHAD and the PERLESVAUS, in part for what they are in themselves and in the

---

[1] Possibly because the Master who said that " He who eateth my Flesh and drinketh my Blood," *etc.*, said also that " the Flesh profiteth nothing," and thus opened a world of possibility concerning Spirit and Life in the Word.

greater part for where they have led me, from Romance into Ritual and from Ritual into that not undiscoverable realm which lies beyond and is called the Mystery of Faith.

But we have reached now a stage where it is necessary to glance at other aspects which environed the Grail literatures, though in relation to those which were considered previously.

It is wholesome to remember, among many other points that might be enumerated : (1) That before 1000 A.D. Claudius, Archbishop of Turin, characterised the censure pronounced on his anti-papal writings as the voice of the members of Satan ; (2) that Arnulph, Bishop of Orléans, at the Council of Rheims,[1] pointed to the Roman Pontiff, saying : '' Who is that seated upon a high throne and radiant with purple and gold ? . . If he thus follow uncharitableness . . ., he must be Antichrist sitting in the Temple of God '' ; (3) that Everard, Bishop of Salzburg, said much later : '' He who is *servus servorum Dei* desires to be Lord of lords ; he profanes, he pillages, he defrauds, he murders, and he is the lost man who is called Antichrist '' ; (4) that Cardinal Benno, speaking of Sylvester II,[2] said that by God's permission he rose from the abyss ; (5) that the same Pope was described at the Council of Brixen as the false monk and the prince of abomination. These were the accusations of Prelates, and with them may be compared the opinion of Figueiras the Troubadour, who described Rome as an immoral and faithless city, having its seat fixed in the depths of hell ; that of Petrarch, who called Avignon the Western Babylon, and—like a comparison by way of antithesis to the Rich Fisherman—exclaimed : '' Here reigns a proud race of Fishermen who are poor no longer '' ; and that of the same poet, who described the Papal Court as a people who follow the example of Judas Iscariot—in other words, selling God for money, like the King of Castle Mortal. So also St. Bridget termed Rome the Whirlpool of Hell and the House of Mammon, wherein the devil barters the patrimony of Christ.[3]

These are judgments on life and its conduct, on passion and policy, on the spirit of the world in the Holy Place and its centre : they are not impeachments of Doctrine and much less of that world of intimation and Experience which lies behind Doctrine. It is evident that on the side of government, apart or not from teaching, the yoke of Rome was no longer easy or its burden light. It is conceivable, from this point of view, and were other things equal, that the Grail symbolism of a bereft Castle or Temple might be an appeal against the Church as that which had become unfaithful to itself, a protest against the power of Lucifer which had invaded the Sanctuary. The admission of these facts does not derogate of necessity from the claim that the Church had all the means. Even in new definitions and altered practice there might by supposition be a guiding hand.

---

[1] Such a Council was held in 1119, under Calixtus II.
[2] He reigned from A.D. 999 to 1003. I am not quoting chronologically.
[3] St. Bridget died in 1373.

During the evolution of the Grail literature it will be remembered that two unhappy ferments were at work in the Western Branch : (1) the denial of the Chalice to the laity ; (2) the various doctrinal tendencies which resulted in the definition of Transubstantiation. From this point of view the wound of the Latin Church would be that it misconstrued the *Mysterium Fidei ;* that it had in fact five wounds corresponding to the five changes of the Grail.[1] Among these the last only seemed to be a Chalice, for it is said that there was none at that time, perhaps because *Dominus qui non pars est sed totum* is not contained in a Chalice, though the Lord is *Pars hæreditatis meæ et calicis mei.* Obviously the Latin Church cannot be accused of having failed to discern after its own manner the Body of the Lord, but that discernment was apart unfortunately from the life which its own Scriptures tell them is resident symbolically in the Blood. On the basis of Transubstantiation it might be difficult to reject the Roman plea, that he who receives the Body receives also the Blood, because that which is communicated *ex hypothesi* in the Eucharist is the Living Christ made flesh. On another basis, the implicit of such symbolism looks rather in the opposite sense, namely, that the Elements are twofold to shew how the flesh of itself profits nothing, while the Spirit and the Truth are the communication of Divine Life. By those who regard Transubstantiation as the burden of the Church which defined it, there is a disposition to condemn the Latin Eucharist as a dismembered Sacrament ; by those who look upon the Observance as a mere memorial, all subtleties notwithstanding, there is a feeling that the remembrance is broken and that the isolated Sign does not signify fully. On the other hand, that view which belongs more especially to the Mystics, namely, that the Covenant of Christ to His followers concerns what I have called so frequently the communication of Divine Substance does not of necessity affirm that the accidents of such communication are of vital consequence : if therefore transposition or substitution of external signs need not occasion a shadow of vicissitude in the Mystery which is imparted, it would follow that the Official Church was perhaps more astute than otherwise when it denied the Chalice to the laity. For the rest, and to extinguish these questions, those who speak of Christ's Spiritual Presence say well, but the Mystery of Abiding Redemption is the perpetuity of the Incarnation among those to whom Christ came in flesh.

If it is not to be said that at the epoch of the Grail literature the highest minds had grown weary of the Vatican and all its ways, it can be affirmed at least that there were both competitive and uncompetitive streams of tendency which pursued their paths openly and in secret towards another term. I think that Southern France stands out obviously under the first designation ; but there were those also who raised no voice of debate and pursued their secret way towards the realisation of Divine Ends. They may have had no remedies to offer

[1] See Book VI, sect. 1.

on the practical side of things, and they were too wise to denounce abuses which they were powerless to rectify—even as I who write, supposing that I had attained the term of the Great Experiment, should not for such reason be qualified to purify the commercial houses of exchange. That term belongs to a region about which it is idle to speak in connection with schemes of amelioration or the raising of the masses. So far as those who have prosecuted or do now follow it have led or lead to-day the life of the world, it is implied in their calling that they should do what to do is given them ; yet in respect of the Experiment itself, if those who attain can lead others in the way, they do not come with helping hands for the furtherance and welfare of the body politic.

Some of them were Bishops and Priests in their days and generations, some active in the world and some withdrawn in far-off priories or leading a Hermit's life. A few would not have passed muster as orthodox in the clamour of doctrinal debate, supposing that they had frequented the Schools. A few among these few were heard therein, some at earlier and some at later dates than those of the Grail literature. Within the limits of that period, there were those who left records behind them, and they shew in a plenary sense that the writers were familiar alike with Path and Term. They knew also the void in the heart of the age and the deadly sickness of the outer Church. These old witnesses, whose remains are with us, like golden sheaves of testimony, are indubitably but signposts pointing to many others, their graduating pupils and their silent followers, abiding in many places and helping to produce a still but not ineffective spirit of the time. It is from out this stream of tendency that there came, as I believe, the voices of the Grail Books. They were not of Bêrnard, him above all, of the impassioned Bonaventura, or of Victorines, any more than of Cistercians. They were of poets in the stream and of a few who wrote in prose. They had heard the other voices, and some may have lived among those who loved and honoured them. Some of them spoke as from a great distance, amidst the distraction of outward things and all the sorcery of sense. For others at their best and highest, the efficacious Grail—that which is Life and Grace—came not out of their literal or figurative fasts, their watches and their prayers, but out of their hearts of ardour. They proposed Secret Words and a Super-Apostolical Priesthood to body forth the accredited fact of their Leaders' lonely state apart from all that raged about them, shaping its own ends in the name of Religion. They knew that other but not dissimilar Quests were pursued around them, many and strange. They dreamed of Mysteries of Sanctity which as yet they had not fathomed ; it may even be that the story of Prester John expressed that dream after a manner of parable in their yearning minds.[1] When they left the House of Doctrine empty in respect of its chief Hallow, the PERLESVAUS

[1] It is meant only that the derision of that great hoax had possibly a purpose behind it.

and the QUESTE testified only in their picture-form to the great inhibition of the time. In other language, sounded on every side, the dominant Church in arms had made void its claims and Sacraments. This condemnation is written in great letters on many signposts of the period and is heard in all its voices, those above all which rang through Southern France. But the records of those who spoke otherwise than in Romance perished in the red Thermopylæ of Toulouse and Montségur. There is only a vestige left to speak of the life-experiment behind the white cord of all those lost legions. But it is just sufficient to indicate its analogies with that living catholic research which has been pursued everywhere and of that Mystery to which St. Augustine alluded when he said that Christianity had been always in the world, to which the New Testament itself testified when speaking of the Lamb slain from the foundation of the cosmic order. The Catharist may have connected it only with primitive Christ Doctrine, as this was understood by him ; but it follows that those who look on the experiment as something which became Christian at a certain date are in error over the elements of the subject, to which there belongs in a superlative sense the *locus communis* of the ecclesiastical test : *quod semper, quod ubique, quod ab omnibus.* We should remember that things which concur with one another do of necessity find one another at some point of their extension : so also the one Quest adopts many veils, but without diminution of identity. It has been disguised frequently under the old formula concerning Words of Power ; but though this is an obvious illustration it carries a suggestion of fatality, because in no case did the sign survive the idea—and so lapse into superstition—more often or with greater facility. In its proper understanding the term of Quest corresponds with the conception of an union between the consciousness of the soul and the Word of God, the *verbum caro factum,* declaring itself in the world and in the heart of man. Robert de Borron, an emissary *ex hypothesi,* pictured it as Secret Words of Christ, leaving it seemingly an open question whether they were Eucharistic or not.[1] Those or he who converted his work into prose knew otherwise or concluded that they could have no other office, and so allocated them accordingly, but hardly with an eye on the kind of Mass which was proffered to Simon de Montfort in Joinville's story, if only he came to see. The author of the GRAND SAINT GRAAL, having other intimations, including those which were incorporated in his Prologue, put forward his thesis in the guise of another Sacerdotal Mystery and followed those who had preceded him in developing a Conversion Legend. But the Companions whom he brought from Sarras, where the Evangelical Sodality received their titles in the Ordination of Joseph II, came over, it may be, in his dream, to convert the Papal Saracens of the twelfth century and not the Druids of old. Wolfram von Eschenbach represented the Secret Custodians as an autonomous Chivalry after the model of the Knights Templar, bringing into it

---

[1] We have ascertained the state of the JOSEPH text in an Appendix note to Book IV.

materials from oriental sources and proclaiming that the Grail story, the oldest story of all, was written in the starry heavens, as no one doubts that it is who has contemplated the celestial sphere from a Darien peak of unity. Other Traditions had already presented Joseph of Arimathæa as the Grand Master of an Instituted Knighthood. The authors of the PERLESVAUS and the Galahad QUESTE connected their whole subject with Eucharistic Transubstantiation as the most approximate gate through which they might draw others to follow those things which issue in mystery. But when this symbolism had served its purpose they were glad enough to present its dissolution, as I have shewn. They might have chosen other material; but it has been in no sense my design to suggest that they had overcome all burdens of their period by an excess of wisdom : the glass through which they looked was clouded and scoriated enough; their task was difficult enough ; and in leading towards their peculiar Doctrine as they did it may even be that the more intolerable aspect of Transubstantiation had not occurred to them. It is sufficient for our purpose that they discerned something of the secrets which lay beyond the Altar and the Sacrifice, and which had not been found by Rome. To do this they must have travelled far.

Did they know in the mind's contemplation—a few perchance—outreaching from afar, or—it may be—near at hand, something about a state of being which opens on the infinite ? And because of that which in sacred hypothesis was communicated through the observance of the Eucharist, did they picture it as attained by the help of Secret Words used in Consecrating the Elements ? Did certain others—who also knew—picture it as attained in ordination by Christ Himself ? I question whether they would have dwelt upon an EPICLESIS Clause, were there such in any Celtic literature ; but I am certain in any case that they did not dream of a pan-Britannic Church. Nothing could be less in correspondence with such an ambition than their conception of a Mystery of Grace which could at no time have been expected to prevail in public. But seeing that the Mass went on for ever in the lands and islands, had they found it by way of the Mass, as happened once, it would seem to the Angel of the Schools ? In a state apart and beyond all declaration, did they dream of a Hidden Union and represent it to themselves and others as something beheld inwardly by the help of the Unspotted Sacrifice celebrated according to an Arch-Natural Mode ? In such case the Grail indeed is a Sacred Legend of the Eucharist, and as behind its Castle of Souls there was a Hidden Paradise, so, like a Grail which is behind the Holy Grail, there was conceived an inward or transcendent sense of the entire Mystery.

Herein assuredly is the Quest for that which is real, wherein Enchantments dissolve and the Times of Adventure are also set over. The Enchantments are in the natural world and so again are the Adventures; but the Unspelling Quest is in the world of soul. The witness of this

Doctrine, in one or other of its forms and under many veils, has been always in the world. In its realisation the Shekinah is restored to the Sanctuary : when it is overshadowed there is a Cloud upon the Sanctuary. It is the story of the individual man passing into the concealment of the interior and secret life, but carrying with him his warrants and his high insignia. In a word, it is that Doctrine the realisation of which in the consciousness has been called, under all reserves and for want of a better term, the Secret Church, even the Holy Assembly.[1]

The presence of this so-called Secret Church is like that of angels unawares. In the outer courts there are those who are prepared for Regeneration and in the *Adyta* are those who have attained it : these are the Holy Assembly. It is the place of those who, after the birth of flesh, which is the birth of the will of man, have come to be born of God. It is in the persons of those who are regenerate that the gates of hell cannot prevail against this Church, or utterly against its working substitutes. The place of the Holy Assembly is called Eden and Paradise : it is that whence man came and whither he returns. It is also that unapparent realm of being from which the Spirit and the Bride say " Come " ; or it is the place of the Waters of Life, with power to take freely. It is like the still, small voice : it is heard only in the midst of the heart's silence, and there is no written word to tell us how its Rite is celebrated ; but it is like a Priesthood within the Priesthood and a Mass behind the Mass. Its work upon things without is a work of harmony, wherein is neither haste nor violence. There are no admissions—at least of the ceremonial kind—to the Holy Assembly : it is as if in the last resource a Candidate inducts himself. There is no Sodality, no Institution, no Order which throughout the Christian centuries has worked in such silence. It is for this reason that it remains an implicit in mystical literature rather than a formal revelation : it is not a revelation but an inherence ; when it is not an inherence, it is an attainment vaguely adumbrated. It is neither an interference nor a guidance actually : it is described better as an influence. It does not come down : more correctly it draws up ; but it also inheres. It is the place of those who have become transmuted and tingeing stones.

[1] In so far as it has passed into expression, the idea of the Communion of Saints in the Sanctuary of the Secret Church is that of an union in still consciousness fixed on the abiding God, realised within. It is not the union one with another in psychic consciousness of *Frater Ex Millibus Electus* and *Frater Vix Unus Ex Millibus* under seals of the Rosy Cross in a state of absorbed contemplation, and remembering the Golden Doctrine that IMMANUEL, GOD IS WITH US. The reason is that we meet at the figurative and mystical centre by a participation in God-consciousness and not otherwise. The deep inward state in which such realisation takes place alone is not a travelling in the so-called spirit vision, when Z∴ Y∴ X∴ and W∴ V∴ may haply encounter each other in a mutual psychic act. The mystical centre is not, in other terminology, a dream-medium which is and has been a realm of meeting from time immemorial, all the wide world over. Experiences of this kind would lead nowhere, even if prolonged for ever. The true meetings are not in time and place and not in the external personalities. When those who have dwelt at the centre return therefrom to take up their part in manifestation, it is then that they know one another in the authentic sense, wherever they meet abroad.

The inspired poets and the great prose writers sat in their stalls and scriptoria during the High Adventurous Times, while the rumour of the Holy Grail moved through the world of literature. They dreamed of a Chivalry Spiritualised and a Church of the Holy Spirit. So came into being the PERLESVAUS, the QUEST OF GALAHAD, perhaps even the PARZIVAL of Wolfram. Whether in the normal consciousness I know not, or in the super-consciousness I know not—God knoweth—that dream of theirs was of a concealed Sanctuary behind the official Chancel and the visible Altar. This is the sense in which I understand my own and the other allusions to a Secret Church and its traces, wheresoever discovered. But, as before, I am not speaking of formal institutions, of esoteric brotherhoods, or incorporations of any kind: it is a question of inward realisation, turned in a particular direction and of a growth therein. For the rest, a man need not leave the external Church if he enters that of the Spirit. It is not on record that Ruysbroeck ceased to say Mass because he had been in those heights and across those seas of which we hear in his ADORNMENT OF THE SPIRITUAL MARRIAGE. At the same time his language is not exactly that of the Official Church in its earliest or latest Encyclical ; it is not like that of St. Irenæus thundering forth against heresy or a modern Pope denouncing the spirit of Modernism. So also a lay member of any one among the Churches whose instruction has scarcely exceeded some Catechism of Christian Doctrine need not be less a Christian than he who has' studied SUMMA. But again there are degrees of consciousness in the Mystery of Faith.[1]

The Secret Tradition in Christian Times is like the rumour of a Secret Sanctuary, and the Tradition has many voices. The voice at its highest of so-called Spiritual Alchemy, succeeding that of the Grail at a long distance, is like the voice of the Grail itself under another veil of symbolism ; and it is witnessed that in those days many earnest persons beheld the Vessel of Singular Devotion. The voice of the Rosy Cross says that in places withdrawn He, being dead, yet testifieth. The voice of St. John on Patmos says that he was given a book to eat and that in his mouth it was sweet but in his belly it was bitter, because thenceforward he was in travail with the Secret Doctrine. The voice of Masonry created a pregnant Legend to commemorate a great loss, and testified that the Quest would never end till the Speculative Masons recovered that which was once among them. The voice of the Rosy Cross said that, having found the body of the Master, the Brethren again closed the Sepulchre and set seals thereon, though they also looked for a great Resurrection. On these accounts and all others I have written this book as the record of a Great Initiation. Meanwhile, the Churches are not made void utterly, but they are in widowhood and desolation, holding the letter of the Word. We are not deceived by their distractions ; and yet it is certain also that Divine reflections

---

[1] And the Mass of an Angel of the Schools is something more in the spirit thereof than that of an average Parish Priest, who has no eyes beyond the letter.

abide with them. Chrétien may have drawn from an episodic Romance of Adventure in the possession of a Count of Flanders. Master Blihis, great maker of fables, may have recited things with or without consequence concerning Quests and Findings. Neither theirs nor others that could be cited are Books containing the Secret Words of the Eucharist or texts of the Secret Ordination. The Legends of Welsh Saints may tell us of Sacred Hosts coming down from Heaven ; but the EPICLESIS Clause—again, if the Welsh had it in their Mass—is not the Lost Word which we seek like the Mason. Other stories, for all that I know, may recount Consecrations by Christ, and the inventions may be famous indeed , but they are likely to want that atmosphere which fills the Chronicles-in-Chief of the Holy Grail with meanings and suggestions of meaning. Therefore I hear and listen with all my ears while the voices of many Traditions say the same things differently. The Holy Sepulchre is empty ; the Tomb of Christian Rosy Cross is hidden in the House of the Holy Spirit ; the Word of Masonry is lost more desperately the more often it is found in the Arch and the High Grades ; the Zelator of Alchemy looks in vain for a Master. The Traditional Book of the Grail, by whatever name of convention we may choose to term it—LIBER GRADALIS or SANCTUM GRAAL—remains beyond external finding, like the Grail itself.[1] But beyond this world of loss there lies a world of attainment and the Grail is found therein, perchance—as well it may be—by some among you who listen and— not, as I pray, impossibly—by me who bears this witness, but assuredly by many to come, as there were many in the past behind us, who raise their lamps and lanterns to light our clouded ways.

Within the Christian centuries, the first witness of the unity, of the state beyond the Vision, which is that of *anima transformata in Deo* was he who is called Hierotheos, on the hypothesis that the text which passes under this name is antecedent to pseudo-Dionysius and was or may have been the work of that master to whom the latter appealed. He testifies concerning the Second Birth of the Soul, to its experience of Mystical Death, the Resurrection therefrom and in fine the Soul's Ascension, when the Mind of Soul is united with the Universal Essence.[2] It is notable and pregnant that at such an early date—whatever the date was, fourth or fifth century—the epochs of the Christ Life in Nazareth were adapted thus to the story of the Christ Life in the individual soul. The self-styled Areopagite follows—or precedes as the case may be—and does not adopt the formulary of this symbolism. Dionysius is he for whom an all-perfect *Agnosia* " is a knowledge of Him Who is above all known things ".[3] He is the expositor of a Secret and Mystical Theology which is to be distinguished from another that is evident and known.[4] The *Agnosia* which knows is of course a contradiction in terms, and the Dionysian Jacob's Ladder is an ascent

---

[1] Appendix I, Note 32.
[2] It will economise space if I refer at this point to my WAY OF DIVINE UNION, 1915, pp. 170–172.
[3] Letter I to Gaius Therapeutes. [4] Waite, *Op. cit.*, p. 6.

into attainment on the rungs of paradox. God is not so much light as darkness, were it lawful to conceive Him as either ; but the kind of darkness is greater light than any light of earth or mind. He is approached by the way of negation rather than an affirmative way, and His quest is in a cloud of unknowing. We are not concerned, however, with portents on the Path of Attainment but with the Term itself. It is an union in the highest part of soul with That Which is unknown by mind, but above the mind is known.[1] The Latin Church, which could not dispense with Dionysius because of his ECCLESIASTICAL HIERARCHY, has put up as it could with his MYSTICAL THEOLOGY, and being in that position has had to maintain its orthodoxy. He himself, who knew that the path which he proposed to travel was in pure theism, set off by invoking the Holy Trinity, which Christianity might never have dreamed of, so far as his text itself is concerned. He who borrowed from Proclus knew well where his source was. In the seventh century there is St. Maximus, who wrote Greek SCHOLIA on Dionysius and affirmed that the soul is united with the Unknown Divinity by the suspension of all cognition.[2] John the Scot follows in the ninth century. I have shewn elsewhere that as regards the return of man's spirit to God it is for Erigena a path of seven stages, the last of which is the absorption of the soul in Deity.[3] He was not a witness of experience, his great dedications being those of realisation in the logical mind. We are brought to the threshold of the Grail period when we glance at Hugh of St. Victor and his successor Richard of the same monastic house, for they belong to the twelfth century. The first tells us that to ascend unto God is to enter into oneself and to transcend oneself. Richard says of the soul : *Ascendat per semetipsum super semetipsum*, being the clearest intimation possible that the knowledge of God is attained in exploration of the world within us.

At once by necessity and purpose, this is a bald sketch and passes through a field which I have travelled already in the past. It would demand a special study to exhibit the influence of Dionysius on later Christian Mysticism, through the translation into Latin of his writings by John the Scot, and that of Erigena Johannes in many directions. There arose in this manner an unincorporated school of experience which was with the Church and was of it in the deeper sense, but was following indubitably a course in which the Church and its Offices had the least possible part, always excepting the great symbolical sacrifice and living memorial of the Holy Mass. Its chief developments were subsequent to the Grail period, towards the close of which St. Bernard, St. Francis of Assisi and St. Bonaventura are illustrious signposts but are not of the School itself, though the Franciscan movement had later developments which were in an occasional proximity thereto, while later still the so-called BOOK OF THE MAN FROM FRANKFURT, Nicholas

---

[1] TRACT ON MYSTICAL THEOLOGY, Cap. I.
[2] Migne's edition of Dionysius, Vol. II, col. 422,
[3] WAY OF DIVINE UNION, p. 166.

of Basle and Rulman Merswin were of its spirit at the root thereof.
There is an excellent estimate of Erigena by Dr. F. W. Bussell,[1] which
exhibits the kind of influence that he would exercise, his Theophany
in respect of the universe, his unbending monism, his deification—
Theosis—of the soul, its absolute resumption into God. At the Grail
period itself the New Apocalypse of Joachim and his followers is a
pregnant sign of the times ; but to this I have referred elsewhere. My
position is that the Latin Church has tolerated its Mystics as it best
could when they were of the Dionysian type, and when there was no
excuse or opportunity for dealing with them in a summary fashion ; that
it condemned and persecuted them when it might and dared ; but
that it had no use for any, or if any, for those only who were characterised by dreams and visions, who suffered from stigmatic and other
pathological conditions, who had marriages with the personal Christ,
more especially when the nuptials were made evident—so to speak—
psychically by rings or crowns and by choirs of angels for witnesses.
The pseudo-miraculous side was the side which appealed and that only,
because Rome was dedicated above all to the phenomenal aspect of
things ; and (1) to rigid and literal dogma, literally and rigidly understood, in the teeth of St. Augustine on the Trinity and in the teeth of
the Apostles' Creed in its titular designation as *Symbolum ;* (2) to the
multiplication of dogma, as if the Mystery of Faith could be exhibited
more intelligibly by ever increasing broidery on the veils thereof.
How should Rome take into its heart the *Agnosia* of Dionysius and the
Theosis of John the Scot ? But the one is a plain statement on the
bankruptcy of the logical understanding when confronted by the
issues of Reality, from which it follows that the Way to Reality is in
another mode of mind ; and the other is that to which the Mysteries of
valid experience have borne their witness in all ages, and without break
or interruption through all the Christian centuries. In the face of the
rack and the faggot it may have camouflaged its authentic findings, but
ever are the findings there : the *Theosis* of experience is as much in
Ruysbroeck, all his concessions notwithstanding to the regnant
dogmatism which affirms separation for ever ; and it is almost as much
in Gerson, who accuses Ruysbroeck of Pantheism. It does not come
into mystical records as a favoured point of view, but because the
faithful annals of experience could bear no other witness.

Robert de Borron may have written already his JOSEPH—thus
starting Grail literature on its historicity side—when Clement III
encouraged the Calabrian Abbot Joachim to continue his apocalyptic
writings, *anno* 1188, and Frederic II was his patron when Joachim
died in 1200. A few years later the QUESTE crowned the French annals
of the Grail. Here is one of the spiritual aspects in which the Legend
grew up and flourished, and about it also surged the material terror
and unrest of the times. The year 1198 ushered in the consolidation
of Papal Monarchy, as it is called, under the auspices of Innocent III.

[1] RELIGIOUS THOUGHT AND HERESY IN THE MIDDLE AGES, 1918, pp. 672–679.

But it was an Empire more than a Monarchy in the dream of theory and less or more substantially in the world of fact. " The temporal sword of St. Peter stretched far beyond Italy and Germany to the limits of Christendom, and the spiritual relationship in its political interpretation implied the vassalage of Europe to the See of Rome."[1]　But it happened that the policy of Innocent in his relations with England and his duel with King John " alienated the heart of a nation for ever from its allegiance to the Papacy."[2]　It was the days of Interdict ; but no sentence pronounced in Rome and no Kingly submission was destined to make England a fief of the Papacy.　The Interdict passed in fine, and MAGNA CHARTA followed, when " the Pope stood side by side with John and his tyranny ".[3] So was there sown successfully and ineradicably the seed of an " antipapal spirit preceding the Reformation."　And the Tree of the Grail Legend was putting forth branches and flowers.　Was the spirit not rife already in England during the reign of Henry II ?　And if in England, at that distance from the centre, we have only to look at Rome during the pontificate of Innocent III, at France and Germany. The story repeats itself in many places and times.　Very often also it was the spirit of Christ, as understood by earnest Christians, which was set against the spirit of Rome.　It was of those who believed in the doctrine so much and so well that they denounced the lives and ambitions which gave the lie to doctrine.　It was of those who resented doctrinal accretions.　It was of those who chose the peace and recollection of the inward way, who " let the legions thunder past and plunged in thought again ".　It was of those who adored Masses and bowed to sacred Relics.　It was of those who compared the pattern of the gospel with the pattern of Rome.　It was of those who led the life that they might know the true doctrine.　It was of those who by leading the life had passed behind the doctrine.　Not least of all and possibly more than all, it was of those who said unto themselves : " The end is everywhere " ; that the Spirit of God has left the Church because of the evil therein.　So it came about that the Grail was taken away.　But before it ascended to Heaven, he who wrote the QUESTE saw to it that the real meaning should emerge.　In the authentic state of attainment, and with a valid sign of the union in the Sacred Host between his lips, the Grail went up with Galahad.　And it is thus in other stories, even in the medley of the CONTE.　It is with the Perceval of the Didot-Modena text in a most secret place of the Hiddenness ; it is with him of the PERLESVAUS, who went over a great sea.　In other words, it is still in the heart of the elect, cf those who have led the life and found the Doctrine in the Path of Union.　This is the Secret of the Grail.

[1] Mary I. M. Bull : A SHORT HISTORY OF THE PAPACY, 1921, p. 161.
[2] Ib., p. 162.
[3] Ib.　Cf. Matthew Paris.　" The Sovereign Pontiff who ought to be the source of sanctity, the mirror of piety, the guardian of Justice, the defender of truth, protects such a man.　Why does he take his part ?　To engulf the riches of England in the coffers of Rome's avarice."

And now to move one step forward, being the last point to which I can take the subject : The place of the Cup in this extension of the symbolism under the light of all its analogies, corresponds to the place of Spiritual Life ; to the rest of knowledge ; to the receptacle of the Graces which are above and to the channel of their communication to things which are below ; but this is the equivalent *ex hypothesi* of the Arch-Natural Eucharist. In a word, it is the world not manifested, and this is the world of Adeptship, attained by Sanctity. In so far therefore as it can be said in the open day, hereof is the message of the Secret Tradition in Christian Times on the subject of the Grail Mystery. So also, under a certain transfiguration, does the Grail still appear in the Hidden Sanctuaries.

V

THE CONCLUSION OF THIS HOLY QUEST

THERE is the transmission of records from the past, and while the worship of the heart expresses its unfailing thankfulness for the wealth of our inheritance, it knows too well also that there is a long tale of loss, of vanished and irrecoverable treasure. We meet ever and continually with casual intimations which offer evidence of these things unseen and never to be seen henceforward. It is a second kind of transmission, at once vague and haunting but a food of thought, a food of speculation ; and there is a not unwarranted feeling that the faculty of imagining within us does cast from time to time some quality of light thereon. But there is also, as it seems to me, a third and very real transmission, being that of a memory of things which have never passed into writing. It is obviously the most vague of all, and the most distorted of all obviously ; yet it possesses a certain office and bears a certain witness. It is represented chiefly by a deep awareness within us of meaning underlying meaning, of sense behind the sense on the external side of records. It is as if upon rare occasions the embodied mind to-day were in communion with minds of the past and in touch with that which lay unexpressed behind their written word. It is not all among us who have access to such wells of memory, and not all who possess the gift that can exercise it with wise caution.

When Thomas de Quincey certified that the Ancient Mysteries were the great imposture of the classical world, he made evident that he had no such gift ; but on the other hand a thousand reveries concerning Eleusis and Samothrace, Thebes and Memphis are testimonies of the gift run wild in regions of all extravagance. It calls to be checked on every side by that which can be known otherwise, by the voice of texts and monuments. The post-Platonists proclaiming the sacred truth of the Mysteries might open a world which would call to be explored in this connection with anxious care. It would tell us that the Orgies of Demeter and Persephone may be those of Seed-Time and Harvest, but that they are those of the soul as well. The Death and Resurrection of the God may have their hidden meanings illustrated by the decay and growth of vegetation ; but the Mystical Death and Figurative Resurrection of the soul is their real subject, is that which matters and is that also on which there is a wealth of record outside the Instituted Mysteries.

If I say with French Freemasonry that I also believe in the Resurrection of Hiram, it is because of Plato and the Successors, because also of the long line of Christian Mystics. If I say : Christ is Arisen : Amen : He is Arisen, on every Easter Morning, it is not that the flesh profiteth, though the Spirit has ever its body in all worlds of manifestation. It is because of the Risen Spirit, which unfolds the Law and the Prophets on all the ways to Emmaus and in all the upper rooms in which the mind contemplates and waits expectant on coming revelations.

The records of deep experience are with us from time immemorial ; but there are also unwritten testimonies, as if from the beginning of things, which have passed by word of mouth and have been cherished in the hearts of hearers. And no one shall say with truth that they have not filtered down through the ages, are no part of our spiritual heredity, shrined in subconscious memory and awakened in flashes therefrom. They bring us strange messages beneath the surface sense of Instituted Mysteries. They speak of bournes beyond the " perilous seas " and open the hidden word behind the song of nightingales.[1] They are also a voice which is not a voice but another manner of meaning in age-old lore of folk. They may speak even within Masonic Rituals, and we know too in this manner that the Books of the Dead are that which scholarship claims, yet a faith which is older than Egypt tells us also that they are Books of the Living Soul.

When we hear therefore of Secret Words pronounced at the Sacrament of the Grail, we think of that Mass which we have heard far away in the heart, but otherwise never on earth. There are others before us who may have contemplated thereon more deeply ; and we make our spiritual communion, that we may be joined with their Blessed Company. If he who spoke of Secret Words communicated by Christ to Joseph had Mass-Words in his mind, he is one of us : he has heard in his heart like us and has left a memorial behind him, lest we forget. If he who spoke of a High Priestly Succession which did not come from the Apostles but straight from the Grand Master, we—or a few among us—may recall that pregnant Invocation which is found in one of the Mystery-Books : Give unto us, O Lord, that Priesthood which comes not by the laying-on of hands. Do we not stand here as if on the threshold of that Secret Church about which Eckartshausen wrote ?

[1] Appendix I, Note 33.

Some later makers of Grail texts could only translate such intimations in terms of Transubstantiation on its most crudest side ; but the Galahad Quest finds a way through at long last into another region.

There is thus an unexplored world behind the age-old world of Rite and Symbol ; and because the vague reflections hereof are to be found therein, it is to be observed also that the literature of the Holy Grail is an eloquent witness to the depth and wonder of the Catholic Mass.[1] It is *par excellence* that Rite and Practice through which we can pass most easily behind the modes of symbol. And yet after all the worlds of language have been taxed, if not exhausted, I conceive that we have approximated only towards those wonders, sounding here and there with short lines and floating plummets their immeasurable deeps. The Keywords of the whole Mystery are *Sacramentum Mirabile*. It is *mirabile* indeed and *sacramentum* in all truth ; and some intimations concerning it are found not only in the great testimonies of the great doctors but there and here even in little books of popular devotion, dark sayings of Paracelsus in DE CŒNA DOMINI and disquisitions like that of the learned Dr. Ralph Cudworth on THE LORD'S SUPPER. It happens that a chance word or sentence in their pages opens suddenly, outside all expectation, some gate that we have passed without thinking. Hereof therefore are gleanings from a Catholic Sacramentary, giving further sidelights on the most Catholic of all experiments, the Quest of the Grail. We open such gates successively and at least look down the vistas which expand therefrom ; we travel one or other of the paths and come to Chapels by the way ; we recite our *Introibo* and yet in the end are baffled : we do not go in, except among the lights and incense of an outer Sanctuary. For this reason we feel a divine and loving envy when we hear what Galahad saw after the material visions, when there was no longer any Doctrine of Transubstantiation made sensible, but only *les esperitueus choses*. So also the gracious and piteous Legend haunts us for ever ; and we are aware that we have dwelt overlong in Logres and know the loss thereof.

Is it part of that path of dereliction which leads perchance in fine to the Path of Heaven ? I know at least that we are led forward strangely ; that all our sanity of criticism notwithstanding, and all the schools of scandal which have done their deadliest in the past to open the gates of hell in the Fold of Christ, we may take our hearts of unbelief, on a day marked red in the rubrics, into an unknown wayside Church, and the burden of heart and head will fall away for the time being when a humble Priest utters the *Hic est enim* or in the silent Presence of That which is within the Tabernacle, with the red lamp before it. The wayside Church becomes a Church of the Spirit. It may be that some of us revisit and are given other messages, whatever Sigils of foreign Mysteries are marked upon us. But having regard to the interdictions of the life of sense the great majority,

---

[1] Appendix I, Note 34.

when they receive anything, know only a substituted participation in the Life of the Union.

The Grail Mystery is a declared Pageant of the Eucharist, and in virtue of affirmed powers set forth under the veil of Consecrating Words, it comes before us in the terms and modes of a Higher Mystery. We have only to remember a few passages in the GRAND SAINT GRAAL, in the PERLESVAUS and in the Quest of Galahad to understand the imputed distinction as (1) the communication in the Eucharist of the whole knowledge of the universe from *Aleph* to *Tau ;* (2) the communication of the Abiding Christ in the dissolution of the veils of Bread and Wine ; (3) the communication experimentally of that secret process by which the soul passes under Divine Guidance from the offices of this world to Heaven, the keynote being that the soul is taken when it asks as into the Great Transcendence. Here is the implied Question of the Galahad Legend as distinguished from the Perceval Question. There are those who are called in a sense but are not chosen, like Monseigneur Gawain. There are those who draw near to the Great Mystery but have not given up all things for it, and of these is Lancelot. There is the great cohort, like the apocalyptic multitude which no man can number—called, elected and redeemed in the lesser ways, by the Offices of the External Church—and of these is the Great Chivalry of the Round Table. There are those who go up into the Mountain of the Lord and return again, like Bors : they have received the Last Degrees ; but their office is in this world. In fine, there are those who follow at a certain distance in the steep path, and of these is the transmuted Perceval of the Galahad Legend. It is in this sense that, exalted above all and more than all things rarefied into a great and high quintessence, the History of the Holy Grail becomes the Soul's History, moving through a profound symbolism of inward being, wherein we follow as we can ; but the vistas are prolonged for ever, and it seems well that there is neither a beginning to the story nor a descried ending.

We find also the shadows and tokens of secret memorials which have not been declared in the external, and by the strange things which are hinted, we seem to see that the Temple of the Grail in Corbenic is not otherwise than as the three tabernacles which it was proposed to build on Mount Tabor. Among indications of this kind there are two only that I can mention. As in the Prologue to the GRAND SAINT GRAAL, we have heard that the anonymous but not unknown Hermit met on a memorable occasion with one who recognised him by certain signs which he carried, giving thus the seeming token of some Instituted Mystery in which both shared : as in the LONGER PROSE PERCEVAL we have seen that there is an account of five changes in the Grail which took place at the Altar, being five transfigurations, the last of which assumed the seeming of a Chalice, but at the same time, instead of a Chalice, there was some undeclared Mystery : so the general as well as the particular elements of the Legend in its highest form offer a

Mystery the nature of which is recognised by the mystic through certain signs that it carries on its person ; yet it is declared in part only and that which remains, namely, the greater part, is not more than suggested. It is that, I believe, which was seen by the maimed King when he looked into the Sacred Cup and beheld the secret of all things, the beginning even and the end. In this sense the five changes of the Grail are analogous—as proposed previously—to the five natures of man, as these in their turn correspond to the four aspects of the Cosmos and that which rules all things, within and from without the Cosmos. I conclude therefore that the antecedents of the Cup Legend are (1) *Calix meus quam inebrians est ;* (2) the Cup which does not pass away ; (3) the *Vas insigne electionis.* The antecedent of the Grail question is : Ask, and ye shall receive. The antecedent of the Enchantment of Britain is the swoon of the sensitive life, and that of the Adventurous Times is : I bring not peace, but a sword ; I come to cast fire upon the earth, and what will I but that it should be enkindled ? The closing of these times is taken when the High Priest turns at the altar, saying *Pax Dei tecum.* But this is the peace which passes understanding and it supervenes upon the *Mors osculi*—the mystic Thomas Vaughan's " Death of the Kiss "—after which it is exclaimed truly : " Blessed are the dead which die in the Lord from henceforth and for ever." It follows therefore that the formula of the Supernatural Grail is : *Panem cœlestem accipiam ;* and that of the Natural Grail is : *Panem nostrum quotidianum da nobis hodie ;* and the middle term : " Man doth not live by bread alone." I should add : These three are one ; but this is in virtue of great and high transmutations which cannot be discussed here. So, after all the offices of scholarship—pursued with that patience which may wear out worlds of obstacles—it proves that there is something left over ; that this something carries on its surface the aspects of mystical life ; that hereof is our heritage ; and that we can enter and take possession.

The Books of the Holy Grail tell us of a Sanctuary within the Sanctuary of Christendom, wherein there are reserved Great Sacraments, High Symbols, Relics that are of all most holy and would be so accounted in all the external ways ; but of these things we have heard otherwise in certain Secret Schools. It follows therefore that we can lift up our eyes because there is a Morning Light which we go to meet with exultation, *portantes manipulos nostros.* We shall find the paths more easy because of our precursors, who have cleared the tangled ways and have set up landmarks and beacons, by which perchance we shall be led more straightly into our own, though in their clearing and surveying they did not all know that they were working for us.

When it is affirmed by Doctors of the Church that the Eucharist is the necessity of spiritual life, we keep our heart of recollection, awaiting that day when our daily bread shall become itself the Eucharist, no longer a mere material substitute provided in our material toil and under the offices of which we die. If the body is communicated to the body, it is because the Spirit is imparted to the soul. *Spiritus ipse Christi animæ infunditur*, and this is the illustration of ecstasy. But in these days—as I have hinted—it works chiefly through the efficacy of a symbol, and this is why we cannot say in our hearts : *A carne nostro caro Christi ineffabile modo sentitur*, meaning *Anima sponsæ ad plenissimam in Christum transformationem sublimatur*. Hence, whether it is St. John of the Cross speaking of the Ascent of Mount Carmel or Ruysbroeck of the Hidden Stone, the discourse is always addressed to Israel in the wilderness, not in the Land of Promise. Hence also our glass of vision remains clouded, like the Sanctuary ; and even the books of the mystics subsist under the law of an interdict and are expressed in the language thereof. Those of the Holy Grail are written—as if from very far away—in terms of Transubstantiation, presented thaumaturgically under all the veils of grossness, instead of the terms of the *Epiclesis* in the language of those who have been ordained with the Holy Oils of the Comforter. In other books the metaphysics of the Lover and the Beloved have been rendered in a tongue of the flesh, forgetting that it bears the same relation to the illusory correspondence of human unions that the Figurative Bread of the Eucharist bears to material nutriment. The true analogy is in the contradistinction between the elements of bodies and minds. The high analogy in literature is the Supper at the Second Table in the poem of Robert de Borron. That was a spiritual repast, where there was neither eating nor drinking. For this reason the Symbolic Fish upon the table conveyed to the Warden the title of Rich Fisher ; and it is in this sense—that is to say, for the same reason—that the saints become Fishers of Men. We shall re-express the experience of the mystical life in terms that will make all things new when we understand fully what is implied by the secret words : *Co-opertus et absconditus sponsus*.

The dissolution of Doctrine in experience is the last word on the Mystery in the Galahad Quest ; and this is also at need the last word of the present contribution to the understanding of Grail literature. It is the experience of St. Thomas Aquinas in his state of *contemplatio dilucida*, when on a certain immemorial morning he said his Mass, as he had said it before so often, but for this once in the noumenal part of his being. We may never meet with historical traces of a Secret Company which had high Eucharistic Doctrine and a plenary Apostolical Succession outside the pale of Rome. But we should not consult in vain the records of mystical experience between 1150 and 1225. The Albigensian message to Simon de Montfort, is a great portent of things outside all knowledge among sects of Southern France ; but it may be that there are no records to cast their light thereon. There are the records, however, of that deep experience to which I have recurred so frequently : they are in a great world of thought emerging from the cloud and light of the Middle Ages into that other light of the Renaissance ; and they may prove to be enough at need. We can rest content therefore with a Mass of the High Privities, as of a great symbolism leading into valid knowledge. And beyond the Blessed Vision of Dante and the Vision of the Face of Shekinah there is the absorption of the end in God.

It is obvious that this is the limit beyond which expression suffers complete paralysis. If I say with Elias Ashmole that of what is beyond I know enough to hold my tongue but not enough to speak,[1] even then it is indubitable that my narrow measures are exceeded : " I know not, God knoweth ". It is useless in any case to pursue the evidential questions further than they have been taken up to this point. There is nothing left unstated that is in any sense possible to adduce : those of my own Tradition will understand what remains over and what is indeed involved. I submit no claims : the day has passed long since when one man could be so much as desired to believe on the authority of another, when things so vital are implicated. I invite no verdict. I care utterly nothing for any impression which the considerations of this book may produce in academies of external thought ; and in the words of one who has preceded me carrying no warrants but those of his own intimations, I shall not be " the less convinced or the more discouraged ". When all the debates are over and all the canons of criticism are at length exhausted, it remains that the Quest of Galahad took that High Prince through Veils of Transubstantiation unto the Divine Unimaged Vision : I know that the Sanctuary is made void for him who has so achieved, that the curtains are parted and that it is given him to depart thence, for there is nothing left to detain him. It is of course to be understood that he might have been taken through other veils of Doctrine and of Practice, but it so happens that the Mass is of all things greatest in the time-immemorial and world-conterminous range of Sacred Rites and Doctrines.

Here then are certain exotics of the one subject offered to those who are concerned with the Grail literature as belonging to the term thereof. They will know that the imperfections of our human life are attenuated by the turning of our intellectual part towards the Blessed Zion and that, next after leading the all-hallowed life, the making of holy books to formulate the aspirations of our better self in its best moments may be counted in a man towards righteousness and help himself, as others, on the Path of Quest. It is well indeed for him whose life is dedicated to the Quest, but at least amidst the stress and terror of these our wayward times, in the heart and the inmost heart, let us keep its memory green.

(1) Faith is the implicits of the mind passing into expression formally, and knowledge is the same implicits certified by experience. It is in this sense that God recompenses those who seek Him out. The Mystery of the Holy Grail is like the sun of a great implicit rising

---

[1] Ashmole was speaking of the Hermetic Mystery in the Preface to his THEATRUM CHEMICUM BRITANNICUM.

in the zones of consciousness. If therefore from one point of view we are dealing with great speculations, from another we are concerned with great certainties. And Galahad did not falter.

(2) There is nothing in the world which has less to do with a process or other conventions and artifices than the ascent of a soul to light. Thus, the Quest has no formulæ.

(3) The mistake which man has made has been to go in search of his soul, which does not need finding but exploring only, entering by a certain door which is always open within him. All the doors of Corbenic were open when Lancelot came thereto, even that Sanctuary into which he could look from afar but wherein he could not enter. The chief door is inscribed : *Sapida notitia de Deo*. It is understood, however, that before the door is reached there are gates which are well guarded. So at an hour of midnight, when the moon shone clear, Lancelot paused at the postern, which opened towards the sea, and saw how two lions guarded it.

(4) It is true also that the gates are not opened easily by which the King of Glory comes in : yet we know that the King comes. The key of these gates is called *Voluntas inflammata*. This will works on the hither side, but there is another which works on the farther, and this is named *Beneplacitum termino carens*. When the gates open by the concurrence of these two powers, the King of Salem comes forth carrying Bread and Wine. Of the communication which then follows it is said : *Gustari potest quod explicari nequit*. Galahad and his fellows did taste and saw that the Lord is sweet.

(5) For the Proselytes of the Gate which is external and the Postulants at the Pronaos of the Temple, the Crucifixion took place on Calvary. For the Adepts and the Epopts, the question is not whether this is true on the plane of history but in what manner it signifies, seeing that the great event of all human history began at the foundation of the world, as it still takes place daily in the souls of those for whom the one thing needful is to know when Christ shall arise within them. It is then that those on the Quest can say with Sir Bors : " But God was ever my comfort ".

(6) All that we forget is immaterial if that which we remember is vital, as for example the High Prince of Quest, who said : " Therefore I wit well when my body is dead, my soul shall be in great joy to see the Blessed Trinity every day, and the majesty of our Lord Jesu Christ " —in other words *Contemplatio perfectissima et altissima Dei*. But there is a height beyond this height.

(7) The first condition of interior progress is detachment from the lesser responsibilities, which are external to our proper interests and distract from those high and onerous burdens which we have to carry on our road upward, until such time as even the road itself—and the burdens thereto belonging—shall assume and transport us. From the greatest even to the least the missions of Knight-Errantry were followed in detachment, and those who went on the Quest carried no

impedimenta. So also is the great silence ordained about those who would hear the *interior Dei locutio altissimi.*

(8) The generation of God is outward and thus into the estate of man; but the regeneration of man is inward and so into the Divine Union. The great clerks wrote the Adventures of the Grail in great books; but there was no rehearsal of the Last Branch, the first Rubric of which would read : *De felicissima animæ cum Deo unione.*

(9) Most conventions of man concern questions of procedure, and it is so with the things which are above, for we must either proceed or perish. Monseigneur Gawain turned back, and hence he was smitten of the old wound that Lancelot gave him; but no Knight who achieved the Quest died in arms, unless in Holy War.

(10) In the declared knowledge which behind it has the hidden knowledge, blood is the symbol of life, and this being so it can be understood after what manner the Precious Blood profiteth and the Reliquary thereof. The other name of this Reliquary is the Hidden Church. It has not been built with hands. Such are the offices of its mercy that *in examine mortis* even Gawain received his Saviour.

(11) The root from which springs the great tree of Mysticism is the old theological doctrine that God is the centre of the heart. He is by alternative the soul's centre. This is the ground of the union : *per charitatem justi uniuntur cum Deo.* Gawain entreated Lancelot to " praye some prayer more or lesse for my soule ; " King Arthur as he drifted in the dark barge said to Bedivere : " And yf thou here neuer more of me praye for my soule ; " but Perceval and Galahad knew that their reward was with them : they asked for no offerings, and no one wearied Heaven.

(12) In the soul's conversion there is no office of time, and this is why the greatest changes are always out of expectation. The Grail came like Angels—unawares. The *castissimus et purissimus amplexus* and the *felix osculum* are given as in the dark and suddenly. There is further nothing in the wide world so swift and so silent as the *illapsus Christi in centrum animæ.* So also it is said of Galahad that " sodenely his soule departed."

(13) The consideration of eternity arises from that of the Holy Grail, as from all literature at its highest, and if I have set it as the term of my own researches, in this respect, it is rather because it has imposed itself than because I have sought it out.

The remembrance of the one thing needful is starred over all so-called secret literatures. Their maxim is not so much that God encompasses as that God is within ; and in virtue hereof those who created them could say in their hearts what on rare occasions they said also with their lips : *Absque nube pro nobis.* I affirm on the authority of research ; on other—which is higher—authority ; on that which I have seen of the Mysteries ; and on the high intimations which are communicated to those who seek, that the Great Experiment subsists, that those exist who have pursued it, and that behind imperishable

records—good and just and holy—are found manifold traces of veiled
Masters. The term of quest therein is the term of the Grail Quest, and
its sacramental pageant of procedure sets forth the same process. The
Path of Instituted Mysteries was never the only path, but once it may
have been one of the nearest, because the mind was trained therein, firstly,
in the sense of possibility and, secondly, in the direction of consciousness,
so that it might be overflowed by the fulfilled experiment. It was
carried on in the Secret Schools ; but at this day—in so far as any
survive—the great Instituted Rites are like the Rich King Fisherman,
either wounded or in a condition of languishment, and it is either for
the same reason, namely, that few are prepared to come forward and
ask the indispensable Question, or the consciousness of the Great
Experiment has closed down upon the Wardens of the Rites, and they
stand guard over its memorials only. It has been pursued also in
Official Churches, and they are permanent witnesses to its roct-matter
in the world. But they live in the outward sense, among the clouds
and images : they communicate the *Signum* only and not *Signatum ;*
while as to this last there seems no one now to look in the deep places
for its hidden virtue. The key which we must take in our hands is that
God is everywhere and that He recompenses those who seek Him out.
But those who are on the Quest of the Veiled Masters may save their
pains of seeking them in the Master's Chair of a Craft Lodge or in the
pulpit of a popular preacher : in other words they will do well to
dispense with the notion of any corporate fellowship as a *sine qua non*.
The truly Veiled Master is in the heart of each one of us, and the path to
his throne is like the path to a Secret Church. Some say that the Pearl
without Price is here, some that it is there, some that it has been taken
into hiding, and some that it is withdrawn into Heaven ; but its true
place is with him who can testify truly : *Nunc dimittis, Domine, servum
tuum secundum verbum tuum in pace,* on the one valid ground, namely :
quoniam vidit oculus meus salutare tuum. He also has seen the Grail.

If I have not spoken my whole mind on the faded aspects and
memorials of the Secret Tradition which do now repose in some of the
Instituted Sanctuaries, it is because I am conscious of difficulties which
cannot as yet be taken out of the way, while there are also many
covenants. If therefore some voice in the cloud of listeners should
intervene and say : But again, where are they—the Stewards ?—I
should answer, as I could answer only : I have brought back from a
long journey those few typical memorials which have been interwoven
here and in other books of my making, for the encouragement of men and
women of my kinship, that where I have sought to go they may enter
also in their time, supposing that they are called in truth. If they see at
the end only the trail of the garments of some who elude them at a distant
angle of the vista, they may at least confess with me that Titans have
passed before and have cast their shadows behind. To whatever such
quest might lead in one case or another, be it understood that in
assuming the Legends of the Holy Grail as a sacred and beautiful

opportunity to speak of the Mystical Eucharist and the other Divine Emblems connected with and arising therefrom, I have put forward no personal claim. If I have dwelt in the secret places it has not been to return and testify that no others can enter ; and I least of all am an authorised spokesman of Stewards behind the Veil. But that which it has been given me to do I have done faithfully, within the measure of my mind. I have classified and marshalled the evidence in Christian Mysticism, in Jewish Theosophy, in records of Spiritual Alchemy, in the Rosy Cross, and here at this long last I have borne my witness now that the Grail literature tells also the same story at the highest point of its development. Beyond these memorials, if indeed anywhere, I should look to the East, in the direction of that pure catholic Gnosticism which lies like a Pearl of great Price within the glistening shell of many creeds and systems, which is not of Marcion or Valentinus, of Cerinthus and all their cohorts, but is the deep Mystery of Experience in immemorial wells whence issues no strife of sects.

We know that in its higher grades the spirit of imagination moves through a world not manifest, and this is the World of Mystery. It is that also in which many are initiated who are called but not chosen utterly ; yet it is that in which the Epopt is enthroned at last—that world in which the Grail Castle, Corbenic or Mont Salvatch, the Most Holy Temple and Secret Sanctuary are attainable at a certain point, that point being out of time and place. It is the World of Quest which is also the World of Attainment. There in fine, at the striking of a mystical hour within the holy soul, takes place that translation in which the soul ascends, carrying its Holy Grail. It is there that the Offices of all the High Degrees meet in the term of their unity, and the great systems, at which height we realise vitally what we realise now intellectually—that the perfect transmutation of Alchemy, the passage from Kingdom to Crown in the Kabbalistic Tree of Life, the journey through Hades to Elysium and in Dante as their last spokesman, and finally the Quest of Galahad, are the various aspects and symbolical presentations of one subject. At this stage of the interpretation I shall not need to indicate that in the definitive adjustment even the high symbols are pretexts only : they are tokens " lest we forget " ; the reason being that neither Chalice nor Paten really imparts anything. They are among the great conventions and figurations to which the soul confesses on the upward path of its progress. That which imparts or draws down is the will of the soul to receive through any and all channels, and it chooses these or those on which to fix the high intent of consecrated will. The soul which has opened up the heights of as yet unexplored consciousness within it partakes as itself a great vessel of election, while another which is still under seals may receive nothing.

Independently of corporate connections, the Mystical Quest is the highest of all Adventures, the mirror of all Knighthood, all Institutes of Chivalry. And this Quest, symbolised after another manner, is that of the Holy Grail. The old witnesses spoke of that which they knew, though some of them knew only in part and saw through a glass darkly. We are full of " sad and strange experience," and we have not come to our rest ; but it may happen that we are in a better position to understand some of the old books than they were understood by any when first drawn into language. Better even than they who wrote them in their far past do some of us know now after what manner their highest things go forth into Mystery ; but of the gate they knew and of the way also. Chivalry is a Mystery of Idealism and the Grail a Mystery of Transfiguration ; but when it was said to be removed from this world owing to a faithless time, it was not taken further away : some deeper veils were drawn.

And now to make an end of these pleadings : I have sought to give good account of the Holy Grail, as it was in the mind of the past and as it is to-day in our own, that I could lead up to what it might become, that is to say, how it could be realised in life as well as in high literature, because in other respects some things which are conceivable in the ideal order are those also which are ; and God redeems the future as well as the past. Dilated in the shadows of the mind, as within cloud and moonlight, the Grail appears even now, and that suddenly. It abides in the memory for those who would live in its light, and it is elevated into light for those who can so keep it in a high spirit of recollection that it becomes their guide and palladium. For myself it is in virtue of many related dedications that I have allocated a great experiment in literature to a great consanguineous experiment in mystical life. I have not so much demonstrated the value of a pure hypothesis as elucidated after what manner those who are concerned with the one subject do from all points return at length thereto. As a seeker after the High Mysteries, I testify at this last that whosoever shall in any vesture offer me daily bread, I will say to him : " But what of the *panis vivus et vitalis ?* What of the Supersubstantial Bread ? " And if there be anyone who deals therein, under what rules soever of any Houses of Exchange, I will have him know that if he sells in the open market, even I am a buyer. So therefore the author of this book gives thanks that he has written concerning the Romance-Pageants and Sanctity as of the Catholic and Eternal Secrets of Religion. *Quod erat demonstrandum :* it is written for those alone who in the silence of the heart and in a sacred suspension of the senses have heard the Voice of the Grail, or look at least to hear on a day to come.

In the great desolation of Logres I hear also the penitent Knight Lancelot singing his twelve-month Mass. So also till he turns at the Altar, saying : *Ite, Missa est,* because the King Himself is coming in the morning tide, I will respect all the findings of scholarship concerning Quests which are not of the Grail and Cups which contain no Sacrament ; but I am on the Quest of the Grail and, Master of True Life, after all the long debate, it is not so far to Thee. And even Gwalchmai saw it.

VI

EPILOGUE

I HAVE lived in this Temple of Images for long years of my literary life, and if I have left it from time to time, because there are other Sanctuaries, it has been ever to return at call and dwell among its Shrines and Hallows. I know also that many are on the Quest like me, looking for deeper meanings in all the ways of art ; and I as a father of the chapel, because I have been on this kind of craft and business many decades longer than all or most about me.

We have examined all the texts and have travelled thereafter the paths of comparison and contrast respecting the findings of research.[1] We know that the Celtic hypothesis concerning the origin of the Legend has been attenuated of recent years and is still losing ground. We know that the German version of the Mythos was contaminated with that of the Venusberg, so that it " bent and sank down in search of a shameful pasturage ". We know that another canon of criticism has sought to connect the Grail Vessel and the Lesser Hallows with the Mass of the Orthodox Church and has produced some intriguing analogies which lead us nowhere, though it is very certain that in a high symbolical sense there is a Mass-Book behind the Grail. We have found, moreover, that for those who know the texts and something also of the Instituted Mysteries there are aspects of the Grail which suggest rather strongly a veiled story of Initiation—that is to say, the admission of a Candidate into some circle of hidden knowledge. We have found finally that in such case the successful seeker of the Mystery was admitted rather within the penetralia of a Secret Church. He did not participate in a State Mystery like that which was maintained at Eleusis ; he did not share in a cultus of Vegetation Gods ; he did not enter—among things lesser compared with greater things—a Temple of Ceremonial Observance like the Eighteenth Degree of Rose Croix in High Grades of Modern Freemasonry.

If there is any text which issued from a Hidden School, Sect or Church in Christendom, it would seem to be that story of PERLESVAUS which Sebastian Evans, its translator, called the HIGH HISTORY. There is ever a Mass in the morning to follow its tales of wonder—a Holy Mass heard in some Holy Chapel, the fairest ever seen. It intimates to those who have ears that behind Official Churches and Sanctuaries there is another Holy of Holies, and that behind Masses of the Living, Masses of the Dead, Masses of Corpus Christi, Masses of High Days Holy and Masses of Ferias there is a Mass of the Holy Spirit, a Mass of the Ascended Christ and that more than laying on of hands ordains to Priesthood. Here are great awakenings and to great possibilities for those who feel that *Mysterium Fidei*, the whole Mystery of Faith, is not

[1] Appendix I, Note 35.

contained within the Ordinary of the Mass, whether that of Rome or Sarum, with all their variants for a Mass of Our Lady or a Mass of all the Saints. Wheresoever it is said, in ways within or without, it gives unto those who can receive the Bread of Heaven, even Wine of the Spirit. I think that such a Mass is on record in such Latin as is not found in classical dictionaries or in any LEXICON INFIMÆ LATINITATIS. Assuredly its secret tongue is heard only within, and in rough paragraphs, after my own poor manner, I have here and otherwhere "drawn it into Romance", the Romance of echoes and reflections, of types and images, spoken here on earth. It is written in the hearts of some who hold the story dear and "tell nought thereof to ill-understanding folk". It says to those who have ears : "Hear ye the History of the Most Holy Vessel that is called Grail".

All sacred symbols serve at need to open figurative gates and everlasting portals on the world's verge of emblems ; and therefore *sanctum mirabile* can be said of each in definition. But that of the Holy Vessel, as it seems to me, is the "Master Key" of all the Holy Treasures. It gives entrance into a Master Hall and afterwards into an Inner Chapel, where *Gloria in Excelsis Deo* is chanted world without end. There is always more to follow of chants and stories.

Now the Books of the Soul are books with the meanings in them for us and for ours. Some were written within and without by those who made them, but some without only. In the last resource we give them our own meanings in either case. It is fair work and square, such as is required for the building of Spiritual Houses and such as the Overseers thereof have orders to receive. It is in this way also and only that we make them ours and live therein as in Temples.

The later Grail texts are full of Transubstantiation marvels, and these are ice-cold baths of disillusion for the spiritual mind. But it seems to me that they were the work of people who were not afraid of their symbols and who offer a path behind them to those who can take it. The first Bishop of Christendom may elevate a Host in his Arch-Natural Mass, and it may seem as a Divine Child or a Crucified Man. But at the end of the Great Quest, when Galahad attained his whole intent and hope, I have said that he beheld no outward sacramental marvels. So also Perceval at the end of the HIGH HISTORY was drawn over radiant seas to another Sanctuary where there was celebrated, I think, only a Mass of Union.

I hear new voices also after my own manner, and they are like unto Choirs of Sanctity, Golden Tongues of Tradition, saying the same thing everywhere, even from the beginning of things. There are some to keep in the heart and scarcely tell to any. They are of Enoch and walks with God, of him who was King of Salem and brought forth Bread and Wine. No savour has the sweetness thereof and no lamp the light. It rests on our knees, and we read the Book of the Grail under green leaves in sunlight. It is always a new book, full of new meanings. But there are days of open audition when it may happen that we cease from reading, for the PERLESVAUS and GALAHAD read themselves over and over, speaking with golden tongues. And all the world about us is like that upper room in Jerusalem when the Spirit came down, to sanctify Fishers of Men, making them Rich Fishers. We begin to learn in the heart and begin in the heart to know why Pelles the King became the King-Hermit ; and why, " after a brief space ", it was given that Perceval should know right well the Abiding-Place of the Grail. It is certain also that when it is said, " Here endeth the story of the Most Holy Grail ", this appertains only to one version, one manner of testimony. It begins ever and again after another manner, and ever there is " the Benison of our Lord to all that hear and honour it ".

But the best kind of hearing is always and only within, and the honour is in life and works. There comes a day when the Secret Words are told, but not with lips and voices. There comes a day when Mass is said in the heart and after such a manner as when the Lord and Master ordained the Second Joseph. This is how the tales go on and Holy Houses are built, as it is said, " in the lands and the islands ". And the transfigured Lancelot sings his twelve-month Mass in many a Hermit's hold, in crowded cities, even in the King's Palace. There is also a Holy House in a very Holy Hiddenness, which waits well and patiently through the days and the years for some who shall come in, shall ask the test question and shall not go out thereafter, unless it is on great service. It follows that there are Books of Romance to come for those who are on the Quest of the Grail ; but there are also things beyond telling, which are not drawn into Romance. I am looking for another Mass-Book, even I.

APPENDICES

APPENDIX I

ADDITIONAL NOTES AND EXTENSIONS

I

THE BERNE PERCEVAL

(See Book I, § 3, p. 29.)

IT is to be understood that my knowledge of this text is derived from A. Rochat's UEBER EINEN BISHER UNBEKANNTEN PERCHEVAL LI GALLOIS, published at Zurich so far back as 1855 and embodying selections from a Berne MS., together with a general summary. It is a kind of Grail story in miniature, so to speak, and the complete contents can be given in a few words. I have mentioned elsewhere the thirteen introductory lines, replacing those with which Wauchier de Denain opens his sequel to the CONTE. Perceval is introduced in this manner, and it is said in the words of Wauchier (I, 21, 930) that he has been without food and drink for the space of two days. As in the Montpellier and several other manuscripts, he encounters a huntsman, with a pack of hounds, who will not return his salute and explains the reason. Perceval has been at the Court of the Rich Fisher but refused to ask concerning the Lance and Grail. Had he done otherwise, " this Kingdom " would have been set free, and those who are now in great sorrow would have been restored to joy. He is warned to take another path than that which he is travelling, or he will proceed at his peril. To approach the Horn which hangs at a certain portal will spell disaster, and he will not escape without battle. Perceval replies proudly that he will continue if it means death. This episode introduces Perceval's adventure at the Castle of the Horn ; and the story continues, with one omission and a trivial variation, to the end of Wauchier's section. This has been epitomised already, and there is no call to recapitulate. The version ends with an extract by way of summary from the historicity account of Robert de Borron. (1) Brons is the Fisher King who married a sister of Joseph of Arimathea and became the father of Alain le Gros. (2) As a reward for his services, Pilate gave Joseph the Body of Christ, and when it was taken down from the Cross he collected the Precious Blood in the same Vessel that Jesus used for His Sacrament on Maundy Thursday. As in the DIDOT-MODENA PERCEVAL, Brons dies on the third day after Perceval's arrival at the Grail Castle, and is succeeded by Perceval. It will be observed that the Berne MS. presupposes the Quest according to the Lesser Chronicles of the Holy Grail, being that—in other words—which passes under the name of Borron. In no other text does the Fisher King die on the third day after the Quest has been accomplished ; in no other is the Father of Alain le Gros the Grail King in the days of Quest ; and in no other is there any allusion to the Vessel in which Christ made His Sacrament.

II

CONCERNING WALTER MAP

(I, § 3, p. 30.)

WALTER MAP figures expressly in various Manuscripts as author of the Galahad QUESTE. It was he who *pour l'amor del roy Henri son seignor . . . fist l'estore translater du latin en François*. But he had also a hand in the GRAND SAINT GRAAL, according to MS. 2455 in the BIBLIOTHÈQUE NATIONALE—cited by Hucher—the mendacious ascription stating that this text was translated from the Latin by Robert de Borron, A L'AYDE DE MAISTRE GAUTIER MAP. The vast LANCELOT and the *terminus ad quem* of all Arthurian Romance, the MORT ARTUS, passed also under his name. The GRAND SAINT GRAAL stultifies the Metrical Romance of Borron, although it is based thereon, and it is utterly certain that the latter neither translated it into Romance, nor had any part in its authorship. As regards Walter Map, when he contrived, amidst his manifold activities, to find time for writing, the medium which he chose was Latin, as DE NUGIS CURIALIUM and a sheaf of metrical compositions testify. Those who are acquainted with these are likely to reject with no uncertain voice the probability of his composing Arthurian stories, though Nutt's argument—borrowed from Birch-Hirschfeld—that time would have failed him is not *per se* convincing : the event has too often belied this hypothesis, while it is of proverbial experience that time fails the idle rather than those who work, part of whose secret is how to make time. This notwithstanding, the Map authorship of the LANCELOT and the QUESTE is on a par with the Latin originals from which he translated : personally I shall believe in the one when I can find the others. Skeat, however, in his day, influenced by the Dutch editor of the ROMAN VAN LANCELOT, took the opposite view in both respects, and even appears to have imagined a Map Latin original for Chrétien's share in the CONTE DEL GRAAL. For Malory also, in the case of the LANCELOT, there was no other name to quote, no other author able to invent and write it, " with a talent so prodigious, except Walter Map, to whom alone . . . it has been ascribed " On the score of sentiment, I could wish that these representations possessed some ground in fact ; and I am therefore in full sympathy with Mr. G. M. Harper, who in 1893 endeavoured to restore Map to his traditional throne in the Arthurian past, on the ground that " it is a great satisfaction to have in the Cycle at least one author about whose life and character we possess some outside knowledge ". Unfortunately he could produce only suggestive considerations in place of evidence : (1) The Archdeacon of Oxford's long sojourn in France, his intellectual eminence, and the fact that he was born just when and where he was, " make possible his having been able to know all the Legends and Romances upon which the QUESTE DEL SAINT GRAAL is based " ; (2) if he kept account of them all, " he might quickly and easily have strung them together in his old age ". It may be possible indeed ; but there and there only the matter is likely to remain.

III

HARDYNG'S CHRONICLE

(I, § 3, p. 32.)

It proves on examination that there are variants enough and to spare in this notable metrical version of the Galahad Quest. We must remember, however, that John Hardyng was born in 1378 and that his Chronicle did not apparently reach its conclusion till 1465, he being then at the age of eighty-seven. It is a mere summary account, extending from *Cap*. LXXVI to *Cap*. LXXVIII inclusive. Manifestly all the decadent versions of the Grail Quest might have been before him, as well as the " true story " passing under the name of Map. He felt at liberty, in any case, to produce manifold inventions on his own part, as the following epitome will shew. Galahad, Son of Lancelot and the daughter of Pelles, King of Venedose (North Wales), was fifteen years old when he reached Arthur's Court. He came " clene armed at Meate and obeyed the Kyng, the Quene also and estates." He took his seat in the Siege Perilous of the Round Table, which none but Joseph, who made it, had ever occupied. The authority is Mewyn, whose book testifies further that Galahad was destined to achieve the Grail. He was served by the Knights Companions, they recognising the advent of him who had been foretold by Merlin. In the course of the supper, the Sacred Vessel came, " fluttering thrice through the Hall with a great noise " and then passing away. But it was not till the next morning that Galahad and the Round Table vowed the Quest of the Grail for a full year, " never spending two nights in the same place." The King bewails their departure, as in the chief text. Galahad proceeded to Avalon, where he found a White Shield with a Cross of " gowlys " (gules), as well as a Spear and Sword. He found also a writing, according to which Joseph had lost the Shield and no one should bear it unharmed save he alone who should " ye doughteous Siege achieve." There was similar testimony concerning the Sword, which Vacyan (Nasciens) left behind at his death. After four years of questing Galahad found the Sacred Vessel in Wales. Thence he travelled to the Holy Land, where he was made King of Sarras and Duke of Arboryk, next to Egypt. His Companions were Bors and Perceval. He founded also a Knightly Order of the Seynt Graal, consisting of twelve Brethren, pledged to live chastely and to maintain the Christian Faith. At the end of long years, Perceval and Bors came to King Arthur at Caerleon on a certain Whitsunday, bringing the heart of Galahad encased with gold. He who had achieved the Grail prayed on his death-bed that the heart might be buried at Glastonbury. It was so done accordingly and here ends the Hardyng Quest—a thing without spirit or life ; but it remains for one of Miss Weston's Secret Orders to trace their lineage back to the Grail Knights of Sarras, perhaps even with the Hardyng Galahad emerging as a Vegetation God. The Chronicle was edited in 1812 by H. Ellis.

IV

THE GRAIL TEMPLE IN THE LATER TITUREL

(II, § 6, p. 78.)

IT cannot be said that the Grail Castle is described by Wolfram. We depend on a mere sketch, as the edifice appeared to Parzival when he paid his first visit. It was encompassed by a moat, approached over a draw-bridge and had the aspect of a fortress flanked by turrets of massive strength. There was a great hall which could accommodate four hundred Knights at the banquet which followed his arrival, besides innumerable servitors and the long Procession of the Grail. For the rest, we are left to construct at our will the vast dormitories involved, the armouries, store-rooms, etc., knowing only that the sleeping apartment allotted to Parzival was one of an ornate character. Of a Chapel dedicated and reserved to the Sacred Talisman we hear nothing. Altogether there seems little to warrant the magical transportation of such a " Burg " from the Pyrenees to the Realm of Prester John. Albrecht, however, not only transports but transforms. The Castle becomes a Temple built by Titurel at Salvaterra, between Navarre and Arragon, and it competes successfully with the heavy magnifi-cence of the Priest-King's own environment, as described in his spurious letter. It has been compared with the Sophia in Byzantium and is said to have imitated its grandeur ; but the TITUREL itself affirms that the pattern followed was that of the Church of the Holy Sepulchre in Jerusalem. In any case, it is to be questioned whether such bewildering splendour has ever been seen on earth. The mind reels in the attempted contemplation of its Choirs, its Chapels, its Cupolas, its many-coloured marbles, its mosaics, arabesques and sculpturing of old myths, not to speak of its wealth in precious metals and treasures of jewels, in which " burning rubies " seem to have pre-dominated. The light of the natural world entered through windows where glass was replaced by beryls, with pictures graved thereon, their outlines inlaid with stones of price. It may be added that the deeds of the *Templeisen* were represented on the walls without. After such bedizened manner does the belated TITUREL, *sub nomine* Albrecht, justify the removal of a mediæval Keep on Montsalvatch to the borders of the Fabled Paradise.

V

THE LAND OF SOULS

(II, § 6, p. 78.)

A CERTAIN section of Grail criticism has dwelt from time to time on the Other-World nature of the Quest ; but there is only one text which will tolerate this interpretation, and then only after the Quest has finished and the Hallow-in-Chief has been removed. This is the PERLESVAUS, in which Perceval voyages at the long last to what might pass for a Land of the Departed, following the description given on the occasion of the first visit. We have seen that in this text the Grail Sanctuary itself is termed the

Castle of Souls and also Eden : it is not, however, in any hereafter, hither or further, while in fine it is emptied of its Hallows and left to decay. In DIU CRÔNE the Castle is a place of the dead but not that of the departed ; and the Question must be asked therein before they can go in peace. In the Galahad Quest the Land of the Departed is Heaven, whither Galahad is transported at his own prayer, and the Grail is with him. The Castle of Corbenic is made void utterly, as in the PERLESVAUS. There is no world to come suggested by the conclusion of Manessier to the CONTE DEL GRAAL, nor do I think that Gerbert's substitute ending can be construed after this manner. Mont Salvatch most certainly carries no such suggestion. There remains only the DIDOT-MODENA PERCEVAL, in which the Castle is a Hidden House of this world and will suffer no such reading. I conclude that the notion is arbitrary throughout, unless it be in the PERLESVAUS ; but this answers badly enough to such a construction, for Perceval is appointed the Ruler of a Secret Island and is to answer for his dealings therein. In any case there is not one of the Romances in which the Grail Castle answers to another world of folk-lore Faërie.

VI

PRELIMINARY MATTERS OF THE CONTE DEL GRAAL

(III, § 2, p. 107.)

IN Potvin's edition of the CONTE DEL GRAAL, and therefore in the Mons, as in other manuscripts, the contribution of Chrétien de Troyes does not begin till line 1283, that which preceded being (1) an ÉLUCIDATION DE L'HYSTOIRE DU GRAAL, as it is termed in the prose version printed at Paris in 1530 ; and (2) an opening of the Perceval story, familiar to scholarship as the BLIOCADRANS PROLOGUE. Both are characterised as spurious by Dr. Bruce (Op. cit., II, p. 85), and he affirms further (Ib., p. 86) that Chrétien's genuine Prologue is that of the Montpellier among other MSS., and consists of 68 lines containing the praises of Count Philip of Flanders, who had lent him a book embodying the Grail story and had imposed on him the task of putting it into rhyme. Readers of the spurious Prologue will probably agree with Bruce that " it is a perfectly commonplace account of how Bliocadrans, Perceval's father, was slain in a tournament and of how his wife . . . moved to the Waste Forest . . ., to bring up there in seclusion and security . . . her only child, to whom she had given birth a few days after Bliocadrans' departure for the fatal tournament ", etc. Bruce states further that it exists to explain " how Perceval and his widowed Mother came to be living in the Waste Forest ", as they are found when Chrétien begins his story. It fulfils this office completely, for which reason I have used it with little comment in the analysis of Chrétien's poem. No interest attaches to the invention from any extrinsic point of view. It is otherwise with the ELUCIDATION, which is at least comparable for enigmatic obscurity to Campbell's primitive version of the LAY OF THE GREAT FOOL, and on this account seems to have been regarded occasionally as of considerable antiquity. Nutt, for example, suggests that it embodies a genuine tradition (Op. cit., p. 8). It is, however, not only post-Chrétien but also post-pseudo-

Wauchier, if it is not later than Wauchier de Denain himself. Bruce proposes that it is apparently an introduction to a planned Grail compilation, arranged in seven branches ; but it is this explicitly on his own shewing and seems designed to borrow from the CONTE DEL GRAAL, while adding many variations not to be found therein. It can be summarised shortly as follows :

(1) The Secret of the Grail may be told by no man, either in prose or rhyme. (2) There were certain wells in the Land of Logres, and when wayfarers sought refreshment there issued two damsels from each of them, one bearing a golden cup and the other a gold or silver dish, holding meats, pasties and bread. (3) After this manner they gave their fair and joyous service. (4) But the evil and craven Amangons, who was apparently King of Logres or of some Principality on its threshold, ravished one of the Maidens and took away her golden cup : her companions henceforward served invisibly. (5) They were not, however, to be spared for long thereby, seeing that the King's men, having discovered the damsels, enforced and robbed them after the same manner. (6) Not only therefore did all their service cease but the rich Land of Logres was destroyed, the Kingdom was laid waste, the green things withered, the meadows wilted, the waters failed and the Court of the Rich Fisher could be found no longer. (7) The Companions of the Round Table came in the time of King Arthur and swore to destroy the kindred of those who had wrought this doom and woe. (8) What they found, however, were damsels with their armed Knights, being descendants of those whom Amangons and his Caitiffs had misused. (9) For some obscure reason, they did battle with these Knights. (10) It happened that Monseigneur Gawain encountered and overcame a certain Blihos Bliheris and sent him to Arthur's Court. (11) He was a great teller of stories and, moreover, gave good counsel, namely, that the Companions of the Round Table should go in search of the Rich Fisher, for joy would follow thereon and Logres would be restored. (12) The advice was taken, notwithstanding the fact that the Rich Fisher was skilled in the Black Art, " insomuch that a hundred times changed he his semblance in such sort that whoso should have seen him in one guise should not know him again when he shewed him as another man." (Evans, IN QUEST OF THE HOLY GRAIL, p. 105.) (13) The first who fulfilled the Quest was the young Knight Perceval li Gallois, who asked " whereof the Grail served," and also of the Silver Cross, but nothing concerning the Bleeding Lance and the Broken Sword. (14) Monseigneur Gawain was the second who found the Court and sojourned in joy thereat. (15) The custom of the Palace was this, that thrice daily for three hours there was great lamentation, with offerings of incense and burning of candles about a certain Bier, while a stream of blood ran from the Lance into a Vessel and thence into a silver channel. (16) Thereafter the Hall was filled, and he who had been seen previously clothed as a fisherman—to which the account has not referred— entered in kingly attire, and with a jewelled crown of gold. (17) When all were seated at tables, there was wine poured in great cups ; the bread was set and the Grail, without servitor or seneschal, came through a certain door and provided rich messes on golden dishes. (18) This was followed by " the great miracle of all, whereunto is none other to be compared " ; but of this there is no description. (19) It is affirmed that the Court was found seven times by seven Wardens ; and in stories to follow it is said that each of them will tell of his finding. (20) The promised recital is thus seven and yet one, a chronicle in seven branches ; but they are enumerated upside-down thus. (21) The

seventh and most pleasing is of the Lance which Longis used to pierce the King of Holy Majesty. (22) The sixth is of great toil and travail. (23) The fifth recounts the rage and loss of Huden. (24) The fourth is said darkly to be of Heaven, otherwise of the Bold Knight Mors del Calan, who came first to Glamorgan. (25) The third concerns a warrior who filled with fear the heart of Castrars ; but also of Pecorins—Son of Amangons—who had ever a wound in his forehead. (26) The second has not as yet been told in verse : it is about the sorrow of Lancelot, " there where he lost his virtue." (27) The last— otherwise, the first—is the excellent Adventure of the Shield. (28) We hear also of a Good Knight who shall thrice find the Court of the Rich Fisher, in connection with whom he who is bearing witness promises to reveal the Mystery of the Wells, " whereunto they served," why also the Grail served, with the Mystery of the Bleeding Lance and why the Broken Sword was on the Bier. Whether this business and that of the Good Knight was extrinsic to the Seven Quests must be left uncertain. (29) The finding of the Court and the Grail repeopled the Land, set the waters flowing and clad the fields and woods with verdure. (30) But later on there came forth from the wells no longer those who were cooks but a caitiff set, who built cities and strong-holds, a Castle of Maidens for damsels, the Perilous Bridge and the Rich Castle Orguelleous. (31) They made war on the Round Table, riding through all the Land. (32) King Arthur strove with them and conquered in the space of four years. (33) It is testified that he who made the Book of these Branches desires that those who read shall shew forth to others whereunto the Grail served, lest the good things of that service be hidden.

It will be observed that these seven inverted Branches or Grades of Quest and Finding offer nothing descriptive as regards their subject-matter. To state, for example, that the Seventh=First Quest is concerned with the Lance of Longinus may mean that it embodies an apocryphal Legend ; but it would be nonsensical to suggest that it could be sought apart from the other Hallows, seeing that they are in one place, unless it is intended that the so-called Warden's task is to bring that Hallow to the Castle before he can see the Grail, as happened to Gawain in respect of the Sword with which the Baptist was beheaded. It is observable also that five of the seven Wardens remain anonymous.

The Branches in any case correspond to no extant Quest and are precisely like casual jottings on a plan half-formed in a writer's mind. As such I have said that they give evidence of intended derivations from Chrétien and pseudo-Wauchier, of course on the hypothesis that the ELUCIDATION is later than these sections of the CONTE. It is indifferent to myself whether Bruce is correct or not in his judgment on this point, and we may never know certainly. At the value of a personal feeling under such circumstances, it seems to me that the story of the Wells and their Maidens with golden cups and dishes has an antique flavour. But it is worthless for Grail purposes, so the speculation matters nothing. Miss Weston thought in her fatuity that the golden cups signified the maidenhood of which the bearers were robbed, forgetting that the Fay Women of the Wells carried also gold or silver dishes. She was beginning to develop a touch of the sex-complex when she travelled laboriously from Ritual to Romance and took many wrong turnings.

VII

EPISODES AND MEANINGS

(III, § 3, p. 120.)

An ordered Allegory—as that, for example of Bunyan—shapes all its episodes towards the end in view and that which belongs thereto. There is nothing idle or extrinsic. No allegory of this kind will be found in Grail literature, even in those texts where the Quest Heroes pass from time to time through realms of similitude. This is a point of fact which calls to be recognised by those who would read a specific significance into the literature, and it is obvious that it is one of the chief difficulties which characterise the attempt. There are adventures also for the sake of adventure, because the latter is sufficient to itself. It must be recognised further in the same connection that certain texts or branches should be set aside utterly from any enterprise of experimental interpretation. THE CONTE DEL GRAAL is an instance, though we may add a mental memorandum that Gerbert's contribution suggests a purpose : it is, however, an interpolation as it stands, with a beginning which is not of his making and a conclusion that he does not reach. So far as he went, he tried to give something of moral object to Chrétien, who started the story and had none on his own part, as also possibly to the two poets who continued the work and were themselves in like case. He went to work by ignoring the two latter, so far as the sex-life of Perceval was concerned. Alternatively we have part of Gerbert's poem only, which took up the Grail theme where it was left by Chrétien and justified presumably in conclusion his reference to the Swan Knight and his lineage, as will be found further on in my text. I have passed over Perceval's doings at the Castle of the Horn seeing that they lead nowhere. There are a few other omissions, including those of " hard encounters " mentioned in my text ; but things which move in any " strange glass of vision " are worth including, and for these I have sought to account.

VIII

GERBERT DE MONTREUIL

(III, § 5, p. 130.)

UNTIL 1922 the ordinary student, not domiciled in Paris, had to rest content like myself with the summary and extracts of Gerbert's contribution to the CONTE which appear in the sixth volume of Potvin's PERCEVAL DE GALLOIS, OU LE CONTE DU GRAAL. Presumably he was satisfied—in most cases—with the monograph of some two hundred pages and with the selections mentioned, being (1) the Marriage of Perceval ; (2) the account of his combat with a Knight of the Dragon ; and (3) the story of Joseph of Arimathæa and King Mordrains of Sarras, derived from the GRAND SAINT GRAAL. In the year under notice Miss Mary Williams published the first volume of her GERBERT DE MONTREUIL : LA CONTINUATION DE PERCEVAL, being No. 28 of LES CLASSIQUES FRANÇAIS DU MOYEN AGE, under the general direction of Mario Roques, editor of ROMANIA. A second volume was announced for 1923, but its appearance was delayed during two years, when the third and last was promised in the course of 1926 : unfortunately, it is not even now attainable. I conclude that the CLASSIQUES FRANÇAIS find the same difficulty over ways and means which have been met with so obviously by the Early English Text Society, not to speak of *La Société des Anciens Textes Français*, about the fortunes of which we know little in England. Hindrance is suggested by the fact that the reissue of certain out-of-print items has been long desirable, but remains to this day apparently impracticable. Miss Williams reminds us that Gerbert's so-called interpolation is known by two MSS. of the BIBLIOTHÈQUE NATIONALE, in both of which—as Potvin told us more than sixty years since—it appears between the last unfinished line (34, 934) of Wauchier de Denain and the first of Manessier's completion. The lady to whom, when her task is done, we shall owe the complete text has promised us critical notes thereon ; but they are reserved apparently for her third volume, and there is nothing meanwhile to detain us in her preliminary words, which are concerned with bare points of fact.

The episode of the Knight of the Dragon, who is overcome by Perceval, and to whom he preaches at great and wearisome length the practice of confession and repentance, leads up directly to the Mordrains Episode, a story which contains also a reference to Philosofine, who is the Mother of Perceval—as we have heard otherwise—in this laborious history. It is to be noted that Perceval conceives a desire to heal Mordrains, but leaves a certain Abbey without doing so, and nothing further is found concerning this particular maimed King, who can be restored only by a true and sinless Knight, in whose arms Mordrains will die. This is ignored by Manessier, though he mentions the earlier history of Evalach, before his baptism. Joseph is represented as Keeper of the Grail by Gerbert when the former reaches Britain ; Philosofine carries the Sacred Dish, while another Lady, whose name does not transpire, is the Guardian of the Bleeding Lance. We are able now to check the excellent analysis which Alfred Nutt gave us so long ago and that also of Bruce, which is much inferior.

IX

MAJOR POINTS OF THE BORRON TEXT

(IV, § 1, p. 145.)

It is indispensable that the problem of The Secret Words communicated in the Tower to Joseph by Christ Himself should be placed in the clearest light that is possible under all the circumstances. It has been said in my text that either they have been ignored by most scholarship of the past or identified with the institution of a forced analogy between the Mass Altar and the Holy Sepulchre, the Corporal and the Winding-sheet, the Chalice and the Grail Reliquary, the Paten and the Stone rolled before the Tomb of Christ. This description occupies ll. 901 to 913 of the JOSEPH poem. Still speaking in the person of Christ, the account goes on to certify that all those who shall behold the Grail and are numbered among believers will have joy eternal and satisfaction of heart therein. This, it will be observed, is an independent proposition, and the question of the analogy is at an end. The promise of everlasting beatitude reaches also its term and a third consideration arises, to the effect that those who can memorise certain words shall have influence in their day and credit in the sight of God, shall not be deprived of their rights, suffer misjudgment or incur defeat in battle, if their cause be just. In modern parlance, they will have every opportunity of making the best of both worlds. That there may be no mistake in the matter, I will give again the original words.

> Cil qui ces paroles pourrunt
> Apenre et qui les retenrunt,
> As genz serunt vertueus,
> A Dieu assez plus gratieus ;
> Ne pourrunt estre forjugié
> En court, ne de leur droit trichié,
> N'en court de bataille venchu,
> Se bien ont leur droit retenu—ll. 921–928.

It is at this point that Robert de Borron bears witness on his own part to the fact of a great book, written by great clerks, in the absence of which he would not have dared to speak of these high matters. When the time came later on for Joseph to relinquish his Office in favour of Brons, the Voice of the Grail directed him to communicate the " Holy Words " to his successor. The account of their communication to himself was put for the first time into modern French by Paulin Paris in 1868 as follows : *Ceux qui pourront apprendre et retenir certaines paroles que je te dirai auront plus de pouvoir sur les gens, et plus de crédit près de Dieu* (ROMANS DE LA TABLE RONDE, Vol. I, p. 132). This version must be set aside, however, decisively, not only because it does not represent the original but because it proceeds to discourse of other subjects and does not commit into Joseph's charge any verbal formula which must be learnt by him or others. It follows that *ces paroles* of l. 921 are an allusion to something that has been said previously, and that to which they refer is—on the surface—the Blessed Vision, with all that follows therefrom for those who are worthy thereof. It seems thus indubitable that, as the text stands, the alleged Words have no reference to the Mass, but to the ecstasy of a personal experience and to the promised companionship of Christ.

> Tout cil qui ten veissel verrunt
> En ma compeignie serunt—ll. 916, 917.

The Vision of the Grail is thus the Vision of Christ, the Blessed Vision desired by all the Saints and that which Galahad attained at the term of Quest. But it is pointed out by Nutt among others (*Op. cit.*, p. 73) that the unique JOSEPH text is " an abridged and garbled form of the copy followed by the GRAND SAINT GRAAL." It seems to me that we are justified therefore in contrasting the poem of Robert de Borron, as it now stands, with the later prose version, which is drawn obviously from yet another codex. On reference thereto, it proves that Paulin Paris, who claimed to be rendering the Metrical Romance into modern French prose, had recourse at this point— to say nothing of others—to the old rendering in prose, which I have called the LESSER HOLY GRAIL, in comparison with LESTOIRE of the Vulgate Series. After the passage corresponding to ll. 921–928 of the Metrical Account, Robert de Borron—as rendered—continues thus on his own part. *Lors li aprant Jhésu-Crist tex paroles que jà nus conter ne retraire ne porroit, se il*

bien feire lo voloit (Hucher, *Op. cit.*, Vol. I, p. 227), and so onward concerning
the great book and that which is written therein, namely, *li secrez que l'en
tient au grant sacrement que l'an feit sor lou Graal, c'est a dire sor lou caalice,*
etc. It follows that Christ made a secret communication to Joseph, that it
was a verbal formula and that it was said over the Chalice. The words are
described later on (*Ib.*, pp. 272, 273) as *iceles saintimes paroles que l'en tient
as secrez del Graal.* Cf. the poem at ll. 3332–3336. It appears also (Hucher,
Op. cit., I, p. 274) that Joseph had put the Secret Words into writing and
was thus able, when the time came, to communicate them accurately to his
successor Brons, as he had received them from Christ. Now, seeing that
there were no words to memorise respecting the Vision of the Grail, but an
unforgettable promise, I conclude that the Metrical Account is imperfect and
that I am justified throughout the text in speaking of the Secret Words as
communicated by Christ to Joseph. It will be seen as my work proceeds
that there are other difficulties about them, and they will be dealt with
when they arise. I pass now to the second of the Major Points in the first
historicity text of the Holy Grail.

When the pure of heart and act were nourished in a spiritual sense at the
Grail Table of Joseph, they were nourished also physically. The point is
that Joseph consulted the Grail because the people were without their daily
bread, or in danger of want. It looks as if Robert de Borron had heard
something of the Grail as a Feeding Vessel and placed his mystical interpretation thereupon. It is to be observed, however, that the Service of the Table
has no visible relation to a Church Mass, sacramental as it is after its own
manner. The Elements of the Observance are the Precious Blood, contained in its Reliquary, and a Figurative Fish, laid no doubt upon a Dish.
We have therefore the correspondence of the Paschal Dish and the Cup of
the Eucharist. There is no Bread, but this is represented by the Fish. Now
there is nothing eaten at the Table of Joseph, and yet it is connected
expressly with the Table of the Last Supper. So also Christ reveals to
Joseph the Eucharistic correspondence of the Grail Vessel. On the one hand
therefore we have the higher side of the Mass and on the other of the Feeding
Vessel. That which takes place at the Table is a Spiritual Communion, and
it opens the Path of Ecstasy. It is comparable to the pregnant, if momentary,
experience of a much later text, in which the Knights of the Round Table
behold one another as if in a transfigured state, when the Grail passes
through the Banqueting Hall of the King. We are able now to account for
the Dish or Platter which is carried in most of the Grail Processions. Though
it is not said that anything is laid thereon, it is a memorial of the Fish
Talisman at the Second Table, as instituted by Joseph of Arimathæa and
answers of course to the Paten among Eucharistic Vessels.

Among things which seem quite certain in the antiquities of table dishes,
there must be registered the fact that a Grail has no correspondence with a
vessel containing liquid, except the juices coming from rich meats. When
therefore Robert de Borron likened his Grail to a Chalice, on the pretended
authority of Christ, there was a similitude in the material nature of things,
though it does not happen to be less arbitrary than some other of his analogies
between things belonging to the Eucharist and those of the Holy Sepulchre.
It is to be noted otherwise that the Borron Cycle is that of the Chalice—
Gresal and so forth notwithstanding ; and a Covered Chalice is a possibility
because of the *Ciborium*, a chalice-like receptacle for Hosts, though I do not

know that there is any record of Eucharistic Wine being placed in such a vessel.

The Vulgate Cycle is that of the Dish in which Christ " ate the Lamb on Sher-Thursday " with His Disciples, and unless Jewish antiquities of the Christian period can tell us of a covered Paschal Dish, it is impossible that such an object could serve as a Reliquary. Notwithstanding the GRAND SAINT GRAAL, a search through the other Vulgate texts tends to suggest that the Reliquary side of the Grail Legend had almost passed from the minds of those anonymous or pseudonymous writers who gave us the later Merlins, the LANCELOT and the GALAHAD QUEST. It will be found that their concern throughout is the Body of God, as in the PERLESVAUS also, for the manifestation of a wonder side in the Eucharist, and doubtless reflecting also the growing feeling towards Communion in one kind. There is no indication at Corbenic that Reception was ever in the Element of Wine, though on one occasion there is a wavering shadow of the Intincted Host practice.

X

THE EARLY MERLIN

(IV, § 3, p. 155.)

IT calls to be noted and remembered (1) that Robert de Borron's Metrical Romance of JOSEPH passes without a break of any kind from its original subject, leaving everything at a loose end, to the early history of that Prophet whose record, inferentially and otherwise, he claims to have ; (2) that a vestige only remains of his Merlin poem ; (3) that the fidelity of its prose version to the lost original can be inferred only from its fidelity to the extant fragment ; (4) that, as a point of simple fact, we have no evidence before us whether the over-remaining part of the Borron text is (a) missing as lost or (b) non-existent, because its author never finished. We do not know therefore how far the EARLY MERLIN continuation represents the mind of Borron, or whether the maker of the prose rendering wrote also the addendum to the metrical JOSEPH. It follows that the pious TROUVÈRE of Hucher's characterisation may have had far other things in view than are accredited to his Prophet in the story which stands now under the name of Borron. He may never have intended that Arthur, the King who was to come, should be begotten in adultery by Uther Pendragon, with the aid of the arts of Merlin, as it may have been far also from his thought to borrow the Perceval of Chrétien for his Quest Hero.

There were two Merlins according to Giraldus Cambrensis : (1) Ambrosius, in the time of King Vortigern. He was begotten by an incubus demon and was found at Cærmadin=City of Merlin. According to the Cambrian Biography, he flourished about the middle of the fifth century and was not only a celebrated poet but well skilled in mathematics and was the reputed architect of Stonehenge. He is said also to have constructed a house or ship of glass, in which he went to sea, accompanied by the nine Cylveirdd bards. They were not heard of subsequently. It was one of the three disappearances from the Isle of Britain. This Merddin was himself one of the three chief

Christian bards of Britain, the others being Merddin Wyllt and Taliesin. According to another tradition, the Prophet and Magician was the offspring of a Welsh nun, who was a King's daughter. He was born at Caermarthen and was made King of West Wales by Vortigern.

(2) The alternative or second Merlin was born in Scotland and was named Celidonius, from the Celidonian Wood in which he prophesied. He was also called Sylvester, because when engaged in conflict he beheld a monster in the air and went mad, the result being that he sought shelter in a forest and there passed his remaining days. He belonged to the time of Arthur and is said to have prophesied more fully and explicitly than the other. His works were found by Giraldus at Nefyn after long research. According to another account he fought at Caerleon under the Arthurian banner in A.D. 542, and had the misfortune to kill his own nephew accidentally. It was this which drove him mad. He fled into the woods of Scotland, but returned subsequently to North Wales, and was buried in the Isle of Bardsey. We know already that according to one of his Legends the mother of Merlin became a saintly nun.

XI

THE ROUND TABLE

(IV, § 3, p. 158.)

It is matter of common knowledge among Arthurian students that the first reference to the Round Table is found in Wace's BRUT, the conclusion of which belongs to the year 1155. It is not mentioned by Geoffrey of Monmouth or by those who preceded him, like Nennius, and from whom in part he drew. The account of Wace is as follows :

> Por les nobles barons qu'il ot
> Dont cascuns mieldre estre quidot . . .
> Fist Artus la Roonde Table.
> Dont Breton dient mainte fable.
> Illoc seoient li vassal
> Tuit chievalment et tot ingal . . .
> Nus d'als ne sa pooient vanter
> Qu'il seist plus halt de son per.
>
> (XI, ll. 9994–1002.)

It will be seen (1) that the purpose in view was nothing more strange and great than to prevent disputes over precedence, which in those days might end in speedy slaughter ; (2) that the Round Table was founded by Arthur and none other than he. The hand of Merlin, the connection with Uther Pendagron as institutor instead of Arthur, with all the spiritual significance, its place in a series of three miraculous tables, the marvel of the Siege Perilous—so on and so forward—are the work of Robert de Borron, if we are right in assuming that the prose continuation of his poem represents its completed form.

XII

THE DIDOT AND MODENA TEXTS

(IV, § 4, p. 160.)

IT is my intention throughout to avoid, so far as may be possible, any debate on purely textual questions, as things outside the province of my work in hand. Miss J. L. Weston has and deserves the credit due to her pains in editing the Modena PERCEVAL and in transcribing it for the press. For these reasons and others, she is entitled unquestionably to her personal feelings on the superiority of the Modena over the Firmin-Didot codex. She reflects indeed from others who had adopted this view before she entered the field on the particular subject. We shall see in a brief space the grounds upon which it is based, and they may be left to speak for themselves. At the moment I am concerned with affirming that in the Modena MS. we are on a different and lower level than that of the Didot alternative. This is settled once and for all by the Chess-Board episode and the recompense required by Perceval when and if it was carried to a successful issue. About this there is no debate possible. The proposal came to nothing at the end ; but the intent was present and reduces the Perceval of the Borron trilogy to the status of him who is Wauchier's hero in the CONTE DEL GRAAL. It seems clear also that the moving spirit of the trilogy is represented better by the highest of all directions imposed on Perceval respecting his Grail Quest than by the nebulous discourse between Alain and his Son about what shall happen when the lad has grown up. It is admitted, however, that a variant of opinion may be offered on this score, though it would be unlikely to leave me less assured on my own part.

The points adduced by Miss Weston in favour of the Modena MS. are (1) that it is the earlier of the two Codices and belongs presumably to the latter part of the thirteenth century (LEGEND OF SIR PERCEVAL, Vol. II, p. 6) ; (2) that it is of " extreme interest and value for critical purposes " (p. 8) ; and (3) that it is undoubtedly superior (p. 1). I have searched up and down Miss Weston's prolonged study on the subject without finding further evidence and hope that I have missed nothing. She becomes immersed more and more deeply in affirmations and speculations of anonymous occult schools, and is thus carried far away from the comparative textual value of this and that manuscript. There is no space or need here for transferring the inquiry to antecedent or subsequent opinions of continental scholarship. So much later as 1923, Dr. Bruce, for once in a way, if not entirely for her reasons, concurs with Miss Weston's judgment.

XIII

THE CONSECRATION FORMULA

(V, § 1, p. 172.)

I HAVE suggested that the Words of Eucharistic Consecration used by Joseph II as First Bishop of Christendom are of no interest except for Liturgical History. For the benefit of my readers I give them as printed in

Sommer's edition of the text, s.v. LESTOIRE DEL SAINT GRAAL, p. 40[*]
*Laiens fist Josephe le premier sacrement qui onques fust fais a cel peuple mais
il lot moult tost acompli. Car il ni dist fors que le parole* (variant, *celes paroles*)
seulement que Jhesus dist a ses disciples, quant il sist a la chaine (*cène*) *: Tenes
et mangies, cest li vrais cors qui pour vous et por maintes gens sera liures a
tourment. Et autre tel dist il del vin : Tenes et si* (en) *beues tout car cest li
sans de ma novele loy li miens meismes qui por vos fu espandus en remissions de
vos pecies.* We may compare herewith the Latin of the Roman Ordinary.
Qui (id est, *Dominus noster Jesus Christus*) *pridie quam pateretur, accepit
panem in sanctas, ac venerabiles manus suas : et elevatis oculis in cælum ad
te Deum Patrem suum omnipotentem, tibi gratias agens, bene* ✠ *dixit, fregit,
deditque discipulis suis, dicens : Accipite, et manducate ex hoc omnes. Hoc
est enim Corpus meum. Simili modo postquam cœnatum est, accipiens et hunc
præclarum Calicem in sanctas, ac venerabiles manus suas : item tibi gratias
agens, bene* ✠ *dixit, deditque discipulis suis, dicens : Accipite, et bibite ex eo
omnes. Hic est enim Calix Sanguinis mei, novi et æterni Testamenti :
mysterium fidei : qui pro vobis et pro multis effundetur in remissionem peccatorum.* (It will be observed only that the pregnant interpolation of the words
Mysterium Fidei between the canonical words of Institution was unknown
to the First Bishop of Christendom, who had been just ordained, anointed
and enthroned by Christ in *propria persona.*) *Hæc quotiescumque feceritis, in
mei memoriam facietis.* Supposing by a bare and perilous speculation, that
the Formula of Joseph II was derived from a Mass Book of the Celtic Church,
it does not appear that we are serious losers by the absence of that Sacramentary.

XIV

HOW LANCELOT WENT TO COURT

(V, § 5, p. 201.)

THE Lady of the Lake who carried off Lancelot was she who enchanted
Merlin by arts learned from himself, and her name was Vivien, commemorated as such by Tennyson in THE IDYLLS OF THE KING, following the
VULGATE MERLIN, as represented in Malory's MORTE ARTHUR. She has
learned how to produce a river at will, and the lake into which she plunges
with her infant charge is obviously a work of enchantment. In the HUTH
MERLIN it is the Prophet's apparent creation in order to conceal the house
which he has erected magically at her desire ; but she is known there under
another name. It is obvious that the pseudo-Robert de Borron Cycle is at
variance with the alternative texts ; but even the Vulgate Cycle embodies
contradictory elements. The LANCELOT, for example, begins by traducing
Merlin (1) as a Prophet who owed all his knowledge to the evil one (*qui sot
toute la sapience qui des dyables peut deschendre*, Sommer, *Op. cit.*, III, p. 19) ;
and (2) was treacherous and disloyal by nature, like his father before him
(*il fu de la Nature son peire dechenaus et des-loiaus*, p. 21), a black picture
which is in the teeth of the VULGATE MERLIN. On the other hand, Tennyson
misused or ignored his authorities in respect of the Lady of the Lake, whom
he terms a harlot. I have pictured her love and fidelity in respect of
Lancelot and his cousins, and have mentioned her exposition of the Laws of

Chivalry as the time drew near for Lancelot to leave her and enter the Life of Knighthood. When the day came that they drew towards Camelot, he was clothed in white and silver armour and mounted on a great white horse ; a large retinue accompanied him, she herself included, on a white palfry and vested in white samite, furred with ermine. The procession was met by Arthur and many of his Knights in a wood near the city ; and I suppose that a young squire and postulant for the high Order of Chivalry was never before or after brought to Court in such regal guise.

<h2 style="text-align:center">XV</h2>

<h2 style="text-align:center">PRESTER JOHN</h2>

(VII, § 4, p. 287.)

ALL that it is needful to know on the Prester John mystification was collected by the Rev. S. Baring-Gould in his CURIOUS MYTHS OF THE MIDDLE AGES, published originally in 1867. The earliest reference which he found to the Kingdom of the fabulous so-called Nestorian Christian Potentate was in the CHRONICLE of Otto of Freisinger, under the date 1145. Baring-Gould's volumes are probably still available in popular editions, and I will offer therefore, for the convenience of readers, only a few specimens from the famous Epistle, said to have been addressed by the " King of Kings and Lord of Lords " to various Christian Princes, but especially to Manuel Comnenius, Emperor of Constantinople (1143–1180). The other self-assumed titles of him who was " Priest of the Almighty Power of God and the Might of our Lord Jesus Christ ", are (1) our Exaltedness, (2) our Majesty, (3) our Magnificence, (4) our Supereminence, etc. He, Presbyter Joannes, is said, moreover, to surpass all under Heaven in virtue, as well as in riches and in power. His rule extends over the three Indies and beyond, trending in another direction " towards deserted Babylon, near the Tower of Babel ". He is served by seventy-two provinces—not otherwise specified—and their seventy-two Kings pay him tribute. The Amazons and Brahmins are, moreover, among his subjects. While Seven Kings wait upon him monthly, in turn " with sixty-two Dukes, two hundred and fifty-six Counts and Marquises ", those who sit at table with him are twelve Archbishops on his right and twenty Bishops on his left, " besides the Patriarch of St. Thomas, the Sarmatian Protopope and the Archpope of Susa ". Albrecht drew liberally from this letter in his own much later account of Prester John, as the Grail *Templeisen* and their leader found him in *propria persona*, at home in the far East. There is said to be a fountain some three-days' journey from Paradise —but in or near his Kingdom—and he who drinks thrice therefrom " will be as a man of thirty years so long as he lives ". There is also an account of certain small stones called *Nudiosi*, which are found in the neighbourhood of this fountain and prevent the sight from waxing feeble or restore when it is lost. In the particular codex of the Epistle addressed *ex hypothesi* to the Emperor of Constantinople, his designs on Europe are indicated when he speaks of gifts which will be made to his expected son, namely, (1) " the great city of Rome ", together with (2) all Italy, (3) Germany, (4) the two Gauls, (5) Britain and Scotland, (6) Spain, (7) " all the lands as far as the icy sea ". It was not a pleasant prospect for the easy believing world of the West at that period, more especially as his armies included man-eating giants, forty ells high, among whom were Gog and Magog. It serves, however, to shew that he who was Priest and King besides being King of Kings, was not to be regarded as in any wise a Prince of Peace. But we are told that when he went forth to war it was with " Fourteen golden and bejewelled Crosses " before him, instead of Banners.

XVI

FURTHER CONCERNING PRESTER JOHN
(VII, § 4, p. 287.)

THE expatiations of Julius Bartolocci will be found in his BIBLIOTHECA MAGNA RABBINICA, Vol. I, pp. 125 et seq., published at Rome in 1675. His actual subject is a tract by Eldad Haddani, otherwise Danita of the tribe of Dan, which was circulated in Spain, anno 1283, concerning the Ten Tribes whom the Jews at that time believed to inhabit a region beyond the Mythical River Sabbathion, where they were held in captivity, lest they should break the Sabbath. Numerous authorities are cited for the existence of this river, chief among whom is Eldad. His tract is examined in the course of thirty folio pages, to make evident that the Jews are prone to accept fables, though their unbelieving hearts rejected the way of salvation. It happens that Sabbathion flows with stones and sand instead of water : for six days in the week it pours on without ceasing, but is still on the Day of Rest, when, however, it burns with fire, so that none can approach it. The tract, which is a tale of wonder, is presented at considerable length in Hebrew, as well as in Latin, and we are made acquainted in this manner with the story of the Lost Tribes as they flourished in the vague region termed Ethiopia, presumably at the end of the thirteenth century. Thereafter the task of Bartolocci is to shew that Justus iste, cujus nomen ELDAD de Tribu Dan—as he describes himself—is a false witness of the first magnitude. It is not a difficult task, and the Second Book of Kings gives valuable help at need ; but the Cistercian Hebraist is dull at best and interminable, while Eldad's Romance of the Tribes seems rather a diverting invention. An examination of authorities on the subject of the River of Stones brings Bartolocci at length to a certain Abraham Peritzul, otherwise Abraham ben Mordochai, born at Ferrara in 1525. He wrote an ITINERARIUM MUNDI and has a late and ridiculous allusion to Prester John, with no other object in view than to shew that there were Jews in his kingdom, as in all the wide world over. They were obviously and especially there, on the other side of the river of stone, as it happens to have been one of the boundaries of that monarch's kingdom. Bartolocci falls foul of the tract and to shew that it errs on the locality of Prester John's rule he quotes the pretended Epistle and its fabulæ fere inauditæ, which he proceeds to dismember at length. As regards Abraham Peritzul, he has already expended some ten previous columns upon him in the same volume.

XVII

THE INVOCATION OF THE HOLY SPIRIT

(IX, § 3, p. 349.)

THE career of the Greek EPICLESIS Clause is one of the most interesting in the story of Liturgical Formulæ. It should be understood in this connection that there was not a method of Consecration which prevailed everywhere during the earlier days of the Church. The Latin Rite held, with certain variations, to the Canonical Words of Institution ; but there are traces of instances when it was performed by the recitation of an *Oratio Dominica*— pι ˑ ˑˑˑˑably the *Pater noster*—over the Elements, thus, by the hypothesis, converting the daily bread into the Heavenly Manna. By the hypothesis also, the EPICLESIS Clause brought down upon the Elements the Presence as well as the Influence of the Holy Spirit, and it must be admitted that this contains, ritually speaking, a most high suggestion. At the Council of Florence the Latins required the Greeks to expunge the EPICLESIS, with all forms of Invocation, and there can be no doubt that they were doctrinally and technically correct, within the agreed convention of the subject, because it seems to have been admitted on both sides that the Words of Institution produced a valid Eucharist. But the principle of Invocation endowed the Officiating Priest with an express and personal part in the Mystery of Consecrating, in the absence of which it is difficult in the logic of things to distinguish the ground on which the title of the Priesthood rests. If the Words of Institution recited over the Elements produce an authentic Eucharist *ex opere operato*, the Layman can say his own Mass. On the other hand, the power *ex hypothesi* to call down the Holy Spirit is an exclusively sacerdotal power and sets the Priest apart from the Laity. The Clause remains to this day in the Greek Church, in the Mosarabic as in other Rites, and for those who lay stress on its efficacy that Church and those Liturgies have therefore a valid Priesthood, while there is no true Mass being said in the Western World except in the Greek Church. Figuratively speaking, the Grail has been removed to the realm of Prester John. It happens, however, that the present *rapprochement* between the Orthodox and Anglican Rites has stultified the whole position. Patriarchs, Archimandrites and so forth countenance Celebrations where no EPICLESIS Clause is recited over the Elements. The words are with them therefore, but not the life thereof.

If it be said that on these considerations the Churches are impeached collectively, the conclusion may seem irresistible, and the question must be left at that for those who can deal with it. They are with us, however, and all substitutions notwithstanding in Rite and practice, there is a sense in which they offer at least a reflection of life everlasting projected on the perishable plane, and it is within them as a rule that the first work of Regeneration takes place. They prepare the ground and till the earth of humanity : they fertilise that earth after various manners, as for example by the laws of moral conduct at their value, by the spirit of the great literatures and by such sacramental consecrations as they can and do impart amidst all the confusions between *signum* and *signatum*. After these manners they sow with open hands some seeds of secret life. But the earth is hard and the earth is also unresponsive ; the seed will germinate in many directions, but it is raised above ground in comparatively few cases, and it is then only that the individual enters into the manifested life of religion. It is a question thereafter of the particular quality of the earth and the environment of the life. It is only on rare occasions that it springs up into the high light and the clear air.

The hidden life of the soul is well known to the Doctors of the soul ; but the Church—in whatsoever attenuated sense—has also its hidden life, wherein it communicates with Divine things in the higher consciousness. Official Doctrine is, however, in the same position as normal consciousness : it covers part of the field only. There is hence on both sides a certain aware- ness of the incommensurate, and assuredly it is for this reason that the Churches are desolate ; but such desolation is on account of that which is in hiding rather than of that which is withdrawn. The Offices are not abrogated and the Sacraments are not without their ministration up to a certain point. Perhaps indeed the desolation is not less especially in ourselves, so that it is we individually and collectively who have helped to make void the House of Doctrine. In any case, the Official Church, understood in its widest sense, can act only up to the extent of its consciousness, while the side on which it has derogated has been that of policy and conduct. We can account in this manner for that which we term its abuses and the long story of its failures. There remains notwithstanding the Spirit within its Doctrine, being the treasure which it was instituted to preserve. If it has added some things or many to the jewel-house which are of secondary and dubious value, our part is still to await with patience its awakening in the higher mind. The Greek Rite has slept over-long and the Roman Rite has had nightmares ; but the Happy Prince, who is a true Son of the House, may arrive one of these days and ask the Unspelling Question. Meanwhile, the individual man must be appraised at his highest only, so far as that highest has moved towards manifestation, and it is the same with the Churches. The lower standards are deceptive, and it is for this reason that conduct—as we under- stand it conventionally—is comparatively of less importance than dedication of mind : it is that which maintains the world and not that which renews it. There is also the parlous witness *à rebours* of all those unhappy sects which exist for the dissemination of a contracted symbolism under the guise of pure doctrine, thinking that the situation can be ameliorated by taking in their fairyland. The undue multiplication of symbols tends to attenuate their force by spreading it over too large a surface ; but it is not to be compared with the dismemberment of symbolism, which produces paralysis : the loss of so many limbs causes the body to decay and puts an end to the Office of the Wardens.

XVIII

THE CULTUS OF THE BLESSED VIRGIN

(X, § 2, p. 395.)

IT calls to be remembered that no sect which does not pay high honour to the Blessed Mary as Mother of God could have furnished the matter of the Grail to the World of Romance. The same must be said concerning Trini- tarian Doctrine, the Sacrifice of the Mass and last but not least the Practice of Confession. It is obvious that these Doctrines and this Practice are those of Rome, whence it follows that Grail literature on the surface does not reflect, e.g., from those of Southern France, so far as we know respecting them. It is certain none the less that the thesis on Joseph II as " the first Priest that sacrificed the Body of our Lord ", sets aside the Christian Apostolate and stands for another Succession, even as the alternative Cycle of Grail literature represents an alleged communication from Christ to one who was no Apostle and places Joseph of Arimathæa in a position which is superior even to that of the Beloved Disciple. Now we know that the theses concerning the First Bishop of Christendom and concerning the Secret of the Grail are root-matter of two Grail Cycles and recur expressly, as well as by implication, in the texts of those Cycles, thus forestalling a possible objection that they are casual or idle inventions of makers of Romance. On the contrary they have every appearance of a set purpose and demand explanation as such. On the other hand, the fountain text of the Secret Words transmits on the Lord's part an instruction to Peter and the other Apostles, based on the revelation to Joseph. It is Joseph, be it noted, who is thus empowered to speak as from the highest seat of authority.

XIX

THE GRAIL AND THE KNIGHTS TEMPLAR

(X, § 2, p. 395.)

It is perhaps desirable to note at its value that at a date when Grail criticism was being brought rather laboriously to birth, namely, in 1844, Jacques Matter, at the close of his HISTOIRE CRITIQUE DU GNOSTICISME— published at Strasbourg in three volumes—took up the subject of the Knights Templar, after having made himself acquainted previously, as he tells us, with all that was extant on both sides of the question. His investigations left him in doubt (III, 321 et seq.) whether (1) certain Templars were not in undesirable relations with the Mahommedans ; (2) whether their theistic leanings did not produce an undue antipathy to the Priesthood, Institution, and Practices of the Church ; and (3) approximated their views to sectarian Christology of the period. He was of opinion further that the Ceremonial of Reception into the Order varied with ascertained or manifested dispositions of Candidates, and in such a manner that those who resisted unorthodox suggestions were left to lag behind, while others were advanced rapidly and had the freedom of the Chapters General, which were held in secret. He believed, moreover, that the Ceremonial did involve an Act of Abjuration, but that it was a denial of Jesus Christ as God and as Redeemer, not a profession of Atheism. It involved also outrages offered to the Cross and led to the omission of the words *Hoc est corpus meum* (presumably also *Hic est enim Calix sanguinis mei*, etc.) from the Canon of the Templar Mass. As regards the alleged Templar idol, Baphomet, Matter argues that it was an image of the One Father in God, which was worshipped—as the depositions of the Templar Trial affirm—under the title of Allah, the Mahommedan name of God. Finally, the scholar of Gnosticism seems to have accepted as a fact the alleged Absolution given on various occasions by Grand Masters and Preceptors. The formula as cited at the Trial of the Order in Spain is most unexceptional on the surface : " I pray God to pardon you your sins, as He pardoned those of St. Mary Magdalene and of the Penitent Thief on the Cross ". It has the air of a pious aspiration, which the laity might use continually. It happens unfortunately, however, that the formulæ of the Roman Mass are equally conditional, being (1) *Misereatur vestri Omnipotens Deus, et dimissis peccatis vestris, perducat vos ad vitam æternam ;* and (2) *Indulgentiam, absolutionem et remissionem peccatorum nostrorum tribuat nobis omnipotens et misericors Dominus.*

His admissions, dispositions or suspicions notwithstanding, Matter ends by throwing open the whole subject to further debate. The HISTOIRE, however, marked an epoch and doubtless influenced the fashion of less responsible thought, on this as on other subjects ; and it continued prospecting the realm of Faërie Speculation for long subsequently. It looked back and had a mind to go further than Abbé Grégoire in his HISTOIRE DES SECTES RELIGIEUSES, according to whom Our Saviour placed His disciples under the authority of Saint John, who never quitted the East, and from whom certain sacred teachings were handed on to his successors, the Johannine Christians, leading after many centuries to the Institution of the Knights Templar. This has been cited previously.

In this manner there was discovered a chain of evidence, passing backwards, through Spain and the Templars, to Saint John the Divine, and so to the Essenes, behind whom there was the further East, India in the minds of not a few being the asylum-in-chief of all Veridic Mysteries. Simrock himself suffered from a complex of this kind, regarding the Essenes as repositories of a Secret Doctrine, confided by Jesus to His disciples and by them communicated to Templar Priests, voided Eucharists apparently notwithstanding. There was no authority to cite in Simrock's day and nothing has emerged since.

XX

THE CASTLE OF MONTSÉGUR

(X, § 3, p. 398.)

A TWENTIETH-CENTURY Search for the Holy Grail was announced in the EVENING STANDARD on September 3, 1931, under circumstances which seemed at the moment rather attractive and even promising than otherwise. The announcement was that the Holy Grail is believed to be hidden in a ruined Castle in the South of France, namely, in or beneath the historic ruins of the Château de Montségur, near Foix. It signifies little that the long communication on the subject despatched from Marseilles to the Central News, under date of the previous day, was full of typical errors concerning the Grail subject, and perhaps less than little that it cited " a French poet " —not otherwise identified—according to whom the Sacred Vessel " is in the Foix Department at Montségur, last shelter of the Albigenses ". The notable points of fact were (1) that M. Arnaud, a French engineer, " in charge of hydro-electric development in the Ariège department of the Midi," happens to have made a life study of the Albigenses or Catharist heretics ; (2) that, whether or not he had read the French poet, he believed the Holy Grail to have been hidden by the Catharists somewhere in the vaults beneath Montségur ; from which it follows (3) that his studies had led him to find a rather surprising connection between the Church of the Holy Spirit and the Traditional Reliquary of the Precious Blood, possibly through the writings of Eugène Aroux. Having regard to the *Sacro Catino* at Genoa, the Holy Ampulla once preserved in the Church of St. Maximin du Var and the Grail Chalice at Toledo, not to speak of what was found, some twelve years ago, in " the women's quarter " at Glastonbury, one is not perhaps anxious to increase the objects which are still competing for recognition ; but the report spoke also of other " important treasures " which are supposed to be hidden in the vaults that Montségur must undoubtedly have possessed in common with other historic castles, whether ruined or not. In the course of making his investigations on the spot, the account goes on to tell us that M. Arnaud discovered a thick stone wall, behind certain rocks, and that in his opinion it masks the entrance to the actual subterranean passages. It was said, in conclusion, that the work of clearing the ruins and effecting an entrance would be long and difficult but that M. Arnaud felt confident respecting his theories on the Catharists and that he was justified in pursuing the task.

So far as the press of the outside world is concerned, the subject might have remained at this point ; but my friend Mr. Frank Ashton-Gwatkin, who —in addition to his knowledge of Grail literature, his interest therein and in the Sects and Legends of Southern France—is familiar with the whole Foix and Carcassonne district, paid a visit to Montségur and became personally acquainted with M. Arnaud in the midst of his operations. He learned in this manner (1) that the existence of subsurface passages and vaults beneath Montségur was a matter of common knowledge ; (2) that the entrance was not masked by a stone wall but by masses of concrete, through which M. Arnaud was seeking to blast his way ; (3) that he believed himself to have penetrated already within a short distance of his objective and hoped to reach it before the winter snows put an end to his work for a period : (4) that in the event of his success there was nothing before him to warrant an expectation that he might find a Grail ; (5) that he was hoping rather to meet with the BIBLE CATHARE, basis of Catharist Doctrine, otherwise an esoteric version of the Fourth Gospel—not to be identified presumably with the text of that Gospel found in the Provençal New Testament preserved at the *Bibliothèque Municipale* of Lyons.

Mr. Ashton-Gwatkin found M. Arnaud living at a small farmhouse in the village of Montségur, " a man who has fallen under the spell of the Castle " and who believes that his expected discoveries of " its historical and religious secrets " will be a prelude to " the realisation of the Albigensian ideal, the Church of the Holy Spirit." But it happens unfortunately that many moons have passed and that when heard of last M. Arnaud had not reached his objective. Seeing that, with its " labyrinth of subterranean galleries and vaults ", as old report has it, " the Castle extended as far below ground as above ", I am sufficiently in sympathy to regard it as incredible that they will prove to contain nothing, if ever an entrance is found. Perhaps against all hope, I am hoping therefore still that the zealous endeavours of one who at this day looks for a Catharist Church of the Paraclete to rise up from its ashes, may not fail ultimately of his reward. But if he does, he has set an example which may bear its fruit later. I owe also to the kindness of Mr. Ashton-Gwatkin the following very graphic descriptive account, which—with his permission—may fitly close this notice.

" The Castle of Montségur stands on the summit of the Pic de Montségur, one of the Northernmost peaks of the Pyrénées. The Pic forms a kind of pivot or axle-pin to a circular table-land known as the Pays d'Olmès. The most important town of this region is Lavelanet, a centre of the ' shoddy ' industry, known in France as ' renaissance '. Beyond Montségur rises the higher mountain of St. Barthélémy, draped with pine-forests, and when I saw it—April, 1932—covered with snow. The Pays d'Olmès, in olden times, must have been a self-contained region, accessible only with some difficulty from the cities of the plain of Languedoc, the kind of place where ancient faiths, customs, languages and loyalties lingered long after they had disappeared elsewhere. The Pic de Montségur is to this table-land as the Eiffel Tower is to Paris. It is visible from every point, the most conspicuous feature in the landscape, sheering straight up and down, a natural fortress, a natural sanctuary, not unlike the Puy de Dôme, as it rises behind Clermont Ferrand, only the landscape is much wilder and more savage, and the rock is not the cone of a volcano, but a huge pointed bastion of limestone. The Castle ruins on the summit are dwarfed by the tremendous height and depth of the precipice upon which they are built."

XXI

ST. JOHN THE DIVINE

(X, § 3, p. 407.)

WHEN Origen denied in all truth and sincerity that Christian Doctrine was a secret system he made haste to determine the subsistence of an esoteric part which was not declared to the multitude, and he justified it not only by a reference to the more arcane side of Pythagorean Teaching but by the secrecy attaching to all the Mysteries. The question arises therefore whether the *disciplina arcani*, which is referred usually to the Eucharist, because to all else it must be foreign, may not be imbedded in that Tradition of St. John the Divine concerning which we have traces certainly. There may be set aside without hesitation the obvious objection that the Fourth Gospel has no Eucharistic Memorial, as also its inference, that for St. John less than for other Evangelists did the flesh profit anything. The great contention of the Gospel is that the Word became flesh, and if it fails to recite the High Office and Ceremonial of the Last Supper, it announces in the words of the Master (1) that this is a " meat which endureth unto everlasting life " ; (2) that Christ is " the living bread which came down from heaven " ; and (3) that " he that eateth thereof shall live for ever ". In other terms, the Doctrine concerning the Communication of Divine Substance is taught more explicitly by St. John than by the rest of the Evangelists.

The Traditions concerning the Beloved Disciple are numerous in the Christian Church, and on the thaumaturgic side they issue from the evasive intimation of his Gospel that he was to remain on earth until the Second Coming of the Saviour. From his ordeal of martyrdom he came forth therefore alive, according to his Legend, and so he remained, in the opinion of St. Augustine, resting as one asleep in his grave at Ephesus. St. Cyril also testifies that he never died. But it is Ephrem, I believe, who offers an explicit account of St. John's interment by his own will at the hands of his disciples, after giving them certain last instructions on the Mysteries of Faith. The grave was dug in his presence; he entered therein; it was sealed by the disciples, who returned as commanded on the day following, opened the sepulchre and found only the grave-clothes. This story represents an alternative Legend of St. John's Translation to Heaven in the flesh of his body. From the place where he had rested so briefly an oil or manna was collected and was used for healing diseases.

That which did actually survive was the Tradition of his Secret Knowledge, the implicit of which is that he who reposed on the breast of his Master did not arise and go forth without an intimate participation in the Mysteries of the Sacred Heart. Again, the Tradition has many forms; and seeing that St. Isidore of Seville in the sixth century tells how St. John not only broke and re-joined certain precious stones but transmuted the branches of a tree into golden boughs and changed pebbles into jewels, reconverting both at the end; seeing also that Adam de St. Victor commemorated one of these miracles in a prose of his period:

> " Cum gemmarum partes fractas
> Solidasset," &c.,

it is not surprising that alchemists who had heard of these things adopted the belief that he was a great master of metallic transmutation—by which I speak of the material side and not of any spiritual work.

There is no need to say that this is fantasy of its period, and it is cited only as such. The legends and inventions—but it should be understood that there are many others — are mere rumours, and so being are less even than intimations, concerning a traditional influence exercised by St. John, of which—as I have said—there are traces otherwise. But it has proved impossible in the past for researches into a concealed side of Christian Doctrine to be actuated by other expectations than the discovery of obscure heresy; and it is important that we on our part should make it yet more plain to ourselves that there is rarely anything to our purpose in devious ways of doctrinal thought, nor do those who pursue such paths under the Banner of the Grail and its Quest tend to carry antecedent warrants in the likelihood of things. When I have spoken of the Johannine Tradition in previous sections it must not be understood as referring to a specific external community, such as that which has been described in the past as Johannine Christians. The information concerning them, and reproduced by one writer from another, is based upon exceedingly imperfect research; but among some of my readers, who have not entered these paths, it may remain in some vague sense. It supposed an obscure sect which can be separated at once from all that we ourselves should understand by a connection with the Disciple whom Jesus loved. Their Patriarchs or Pontiffs are said to have assumed the title of Christ, even as Parzival, with a higher warrant, took that of *Presbyter Johannes;* but the Christ of their spurious Legend is neither King nor Lord, and with an irony all unconscious he is disqualified from the beginning by their own tinkered gospel, which substitutes simple illegitimacy for the virginal and supernatural conception of the Holy Canon.

Virus of this kind suggests inoculation from sources like the SEPHER TOLDOSH JESHU rather than from any Christian—as, for example, a Gnostic—sect.

It must be confessed that the traditional sources concerning St. John are chiefly the apocryphal texts, and they lie, one and all, under the suspicion of heresy. Leucius—sometimes called pseudo-Luke—who is said to have been a disciple of Marcion, wrote, among other apocrypha, the ACTS OF JOHN, the particulars of which claim to be drawn from the apostle himself. Now there is, I suppose, no question that *fabulatores famosi* of this kind were not unlike Master Blihis ; if for some things they depended on their invention, they drew much more from floating tradition, and it is obvious on every consideration that round no evangelist and no apostle were Legends so likely to collect as the apocalyptic seer of Patmos. We shall therefore deal cautiously with the criticism which suggests that fathers of the Church like Tertullian drew their mythical accounts of St. John from heretical texts, for it is equally and more likely that the two schools drew from a source in common. The perpetual virginity of St. John, which entitled his body to translation or assumption, on the ground that virginity is not subject to death, is a case in point. The Catholic Church did not derive the counsels of perfection from Encratites or Manichees, and St. Jerome, who tells this story, would not owe it to pseudo-Luke, though Abdias—a very different narrator—in all probability did.

We hear otherwise of an unbroken chain of Tradition hallowed by age, an Esoteric Oral Tradition, revealing " the sacred law of primeval times ", intimations concerning which are to be found in the Johannine Apocalypse. Some have referred it to antecedents of the Anti-Christ Myth, to which allusions are supposed in one of St. Paul's Epistles ; but there is a wider horizon within which the whole subject calls to be regarded anew. Several of the speculative directions in which light has been sought thereon are difficult and—so long as we do not exaggerate the evidential possibilities— unnecessary to set aside. The Essenian consanguinities suggest themselves in connection with that which could have been only a contemplative school, the repository of mystical experience which in early times lay behind external Christianity. Thebaid Solitaries, so called Penitents of the Desert, Sons of the Resurrection, Children of the Valley, Eckartshausen, Lopouhin, and too many others for simple recitation here are offered to the mind in their order as possible channels of Tradition from age into age. We can say only in our restraint that as there were so many sects with variations in doctrine it is not unreasonable to suppose that there may have been one or more in seclusion having differences by way of extension concerning that Spiritual Practice which is called the Science of the Saints.

Speaking generally of the Johannine Traditions, these represent the Apostle as a Saint of Contemplation who transmitted directly from Christ ; and as it is clear by his own Gospel that he regarded the Eucharist, interpreted after a spiritual manner, as a condition of Divine Vision, we shall be prepared for the fact that there is an Eucharistic Tradition concerning him. It is said that on the threshold of Translation he took bread, blessed, broke it and gave to his disciples, exactly after the manner of his Master, but what he asked with uplifted eyes was that each of the brethren might be worthy of the Eucharist of the Lord and that, in such case, his portion might be also with theirs. It does not signify that, according to orthodox canons, this comes from a dubious source in doctrine ; the Eucharistic connection was not devised by that source, and—though it scarcely signifies for my purpose —I suppose—and it is interesting to note—that herein is the first recorded instance of communion in one kind.

The last asylum of St. John was Ephesus, which was a great house of theosophical speculations, and though the pivot and centre of the Fourth Gospel is that the Word was made flesh, that composite and wonderful text bears all the marks of being written in a Gnostic atmosphere. From that which it was intended to denounce, it has been thought to derive something in the higher part of the old eclectic dream, and as the personal influence of the writer must have been great, so also it is reasonable to think that it did not pass with him utterly away. The notion that he communicated something, and that this something remained, is so recurring, and amidst so many divided interests, that it is hard to reject it as a fiction ; it is hard even to say that no Knight Templar sojourning in the East did never, in late centuries, hear strange tidings. Apart from this last, too curious dream, it will be seen that here is slender ground on which to affirm that the Secret Tradition connected more closely with the Church side of Christianity at a Johannine point of contact ; but it is good to remember that not only has the last word not been said on the subject, but that we have listened here and there only to a strange rumour. I conclude that he who reported the deepest and most sacramental words which are on record from the mouth of Christ : " My flesh is meat indeed and my blood is drink indeed " is our first historical witness to the Eucharistic side of a Tradition in Christian Times.

There are strange indications of sources behind the Fourth Gospel. Behind the memorials of the Gnosis there are indications also of a stage when there was no separation as yet between orthodox and heretical schools, but rather an union as if in direct experience and as if Mysteries were celebrated at a certain point of which there was the Presence of the Master. But the Presence of the Master was the term of experience in the Grail. With these words I leave the Johannine Tradition, its possible perpetuation within or behind the Church and its possible Westward transition as a quest so far unfinished for want of materials.

XXII

THE ANTI-ROMAN QUESTION

(X, § 3, p. 408.)

HAVING regard to the enormous machinery which was put in operation to determine the Enchantments of Britain, " the desolation which fell upon Logres " and the Adventurous Times, it is natural to look about for a causation in proportion thereto—for example, some event in history ; but nothing emerges in response except a possible conspiracy or rebellion in matters of Religion. Let us approach the subject therefore apart from Southern France and begin tentatively by assuming that, for what purpose soever, the literature concealed in part but in part also put forward an attack upon the Roman Church. The first observation to make in this connection is that those who were concerned with the movement out of which the impeachment originated must apparently have accepted the Sacraments and the body of Ecclesiastical Procedure, or the outward meaning of all extant texts is not less than mendacity. This is to be admitted *pro forma*, as there would be otherwise no working agreement possible.

Now, seeing that in one case the Keeper of the Grail is supposed to have fallen from righteousness and that—obscurely enough as regards logic in the scheme—he could only look for healing outside his own House of Doctrine, one might be disposed to conclude at first sight that the Grail Church may stand for Christianity and the Rich Fisherman for its central seat of authority. He is the Keeper of the Divine Mysteries, the possessor of the valid forms ; but he and his environment have been laid waste by the spirit of the world. Alternatively there might be involved a confession of apparent failure in respect of God's work in the world. From either point of view the literature would be concerned with the amelioration of the Latin Church by recalling it, let us say, to its higher part. The position, however, becomes involved curiously, and that at once, for the presence of the Hallows may preserve the King alive, but otherwise they cannot help him. No recitation of the putative all-powerful words can ever relieve his sickness, and the House of God is therefore—as it long remains—in mourning. Here also intervenes for our further confusion the difficulty of the unasked Question— of that Question which seems exclusive in symbolism. What purpose, in this connection, could it serve the Hereditary Keeper of the Grail that an apparent stranger should visit him and ask the meaning of the Vessel and its Pageant ? We remember the Question in Masonry, which is one of violence, doing outrage to the Law and the order and voiding the erection of a True Temple. There it is simple in symbolism and almost transparent in meaning ; but here is a Question which is necessary in some utterly mystical manner, belonging to the law and the order, and one by which the Warden is restored : it is less intelligible on this hypothesis than are many darker corners of thought. However this may be, it follows that there is a heavy cloud on the Sanctuary, and if the symbolism belongs by possibility simply to the Official Church, it has the Words of Life, but is still, after some manner, inhibited : it must be challenged before it can speak and it must communicate before it can be healed. The Quests are so far external that they involve transit from place to place, as a Pageant passes through a Temple ; but the Question is an intellectual research. The heroes of research offer no light on the subject, because Perceval at his highest does not ask in the end and the Romance of Galahad confesses to no Question. The DIDOT-MODENA PERCEVAL leaves the new Keeper, with all to him belonging, in final seclusion, where the evidence of things not seen is put away from the eyes of all, and it is impossible therefore that the Hidden Sanctuary should represent an Official Church. To express it in another way, the Son of the Doctrine was received into the House of the Doctrine and had the Great Secret imparted to him. Faintly and far away the DIDOT-MODENA PERCEVAL shews how the æonian Keeper has waited in the Castle of the Soul till the natural man, who is the scion of his House, comes in and asks the Question of the Union. The natural man understands nothing and does not ask till he is driven ; but he is driven at last. As faintly and still farther away, the CONTE DEL GRAAL recites the same symbolical story, with many variations ; but as it reaches no term till a later period in time, when it is simply a reflection of other texts, and has hence no independent implicits, there is no call to examine it in this connection. It may be noted, however, that the Prologue, which is regarded as its latest part, tells of things that exceed experience—that is to say, evidence—of sins against sacred life and of return to the House of the Father, as aspiration returns to its source. But it is difficult to connect it with any Sanctuary Doctrine. The German PARZIVAL bears witness that the House is always in the world, but here assuredly it does not symbolise the Institutes of External Religion. It has, moreover, a strange sacramental side, which seems to indicate that the Office of the Eucharist is to "give us this day our Daily Bread," for the fulfilment of which it comes down from Heaven direct. To conclude hereon, it is obvious from the beginning that the Keepers of Mont Salvatch were a Secret Order of Chivalry, after the manner of the Templars. Albrecht's TITUREL recites the building of the Spiritual House in beauty as a Palace of Art ; but for the rest it represents the exaltation and aggrandisement of a pseudo-Roman Orthodoxy and has nothing to do therefore with a Mystery of Knowledge in the custody of a Hidden Church. The LONGER PROSE PERCEVAL lifts up a different corner of the veil, telling how one Keeper died unhealed and how the last Warden of the Mysteries was taken away, the Hallows were scattered, except the Holy Grail, which passed into the Hiddenness. There remains only the great and paramount Quest, which is that of Galahad, and it tells how the final Inheritor was removed once and for all, together with the Holy Things, as if the House of Doctrine were itself nothing and the Term of Research everything. The Great Quest was written with the highest sanctity as its actuating motive, and we can do no otherwise than accept it as representing the Grail literature in its plenary evolution. It forms, with the PERLESVAUS, the consummation of the Cycle. These Quests are Mirrors of Spiritual Chivalry, Mirrors of Perfection, Pageants of the Mystical Life, and it does not matter what was the state of the Legend prior to their appearance. They are either the teaching of the Militant Church spiritualised or of a concealed Religious Mystery in comparison with which our knowledge of Eleusis is plenary. In any case these texts offer in Romance form a presentation of the Soul's Comedy.

So far therefore from the Grail Sanctuary representing the Latin or any other External Church, we find that the Mystery of a Sanctuary within is written through all the Romances, though it is mainly in the words of the Outer Temple, and the savour of the external incense is more noticeable in some texts than in others.

In this light we shall find the DIDOT-MODENA PERCEVAL a little wanting in meaning and the CONTE DEL GRAAL too composite to reflect a living light of intention. As regards the German Cycle, it tells of a Knightly Conclave which is fed for ever. The PERLESVAUS empties the House of Doctrine and leaves it as a vacant sign before the face of the world. The Galahad Quest says that the world was not worthy, and leaves not only the old Temple but the dispossessed Keeper, not to speak of her who bore the Holy Grail in succession to Elaine.

Above all things, we are not dealing in the Grail literature with an Anglican conspiracy for the furtherance of any independence in matters of Religion : the scheme of the whole Mystery seems opposed to such a supposition. Nor is it feasible to affirm that the Grail writers were at work on a similar plan under a common agreement, as if all were imbued by a pan-Britannic fever. There are few consecutive documents which offer so little trace of a concerted effort, despite the late experiment of the Vulgate grouping. Some writers manifest a very high purpose and some no purpose at all, beyond the true intent which is all for our delight in story-telling. Otherwise than by simple predilection, we shall never understand why these chose for their subject a Mystery like that of the Grail. But the rumours and implicits run through all the texts, as an echo perpetuated, and in their several degrees the stories are plain concerning them. Even the CONTE DEL GRAAL enshrines them after its own manner, in spite of a piece-meal Tradition. Apart from this text, the DIDOT-MODENA PERCEVAL tells a plain story by interning the Warden-in-chief, with the Hallows, in that place which it never names ; but it knows nothing of a House made void. The German PARZIVAL tells a plain story by leaving the Great Chivalry in the great Temple, all things completed and all things as they were at the beginning. Again there is nothing made void. The removal of the Mystery in the TITUREL and the transport of the Sacred House cannot signify more than a change of imputed location and a further withdrawal for a defined reason. The LONGER PROSE PERCEVAL tells a plain story, but it leaves the voided Castle as a public sign to the nations, taking the Keeper and the Hallows into a great distance, so far beyond all identification that it might not be in time or place. The QUEST OF GALAHAD, in fine, tells a plain story also of the voided House and its vacated offices, but it has byways of allusion from which the infinite opens.

Now, the Mystery which covers the Sanctuary is never drawn away in the Lesser Chronicles. We know only that the weight of many centuries presses heavily upon the Keeper. We may infer that the Hermit, Blaise, was taken at length into the Choirs of Heaven, according to the promise of Merlin, and is therefore in *la joie perdurable*. But we know not of any messenger who has relieved Perceval : it follows that, in eternal virginity and in utter loneliness, he is waiting till the world shall be worthy. His place is not known ; he does not come out therefrom ; and there is none that goes in.

But in the PERLESVAUS there is another version of the Legend, which indicates surely, although by implication only, that the DIDOT-MODENA PERCEVAL is not the whole story ; and therein it proves that Perceval is taken away, for the Red Cross Ship carries him, as the dark barge bears King Arthur. This story stands utterly apart and is very difficult to interpret, since all things fail therein. The Grail King dies, the Question is not asked, the Hallows are parted from one another, the Castle of Souls and the Gate of Paradise are left in desolation, as if a sign of wrath to the centuries, while the hands of Perceval are empty as he passes into the unseen. We learn only that he goes through a golden distance and knows that which awaits him.

I have said that there are wars and rumours of wars about Corbenic in the Galahad Quest ; yet is it mostly found by grace or special licence, while it is a House of terrors and of marvels. Under these reserves, it is also a House of many visitations, nor is it therefore so utterly unknown as is that of the Lesser Chronicles. Its building is described at large, as is that of the Temple in Albrecht's TITUREL ; and if its location remains a problem we are not without some materials for reconstructing the broad environment.

Let us now imagine for a moment that the Welsh or another Celtic Church was making through the medium of the Romances a last bid for

recognition. If the prevalence of the Roman Rite constituted the Enchantment and Desolation ; if the Question of the Wardens of the Mystery, on the
Mystery itself manifested, may have signified the illumination of the elect
respecting the faith once delivered to the Celtic Saints and now in danger of
extinction ; we should have then a design adequate to the machinery and
should be able to understand the magnitude of the claim in conjunction
with many follies in the form of its expression ; for it seems difficult to say
that, by example, the Sanctuary in Wales had a wise Church built about it.
It was chaotic rather than in confusion, and in the matter of its working was
almost a prolonged abuse. The suggestion is otherwise fantastic ; but
British Christianity generally, and its desire for independence, centralised, let
us say, in the Crown at the period of Henry II, may be held to account for
a certain complexion discerned sometimes in the literature in relation to
Rome and to explain why, this notwithstanding, it seems otherwise so
Catholic at heart. The speculation had a certain presumption in its favour
through decades of the near past, because a section of scholarship was
inclined thereto ; but a study of the texts must, I think, dispose of it once
and for all.

The short recension, comprised in the Lesser Chronicles, tells how a
Warranted Company came Westward ; how it abode for many centuries in a
Veiled Sanctuary ; how the Quest for this Sanctuary was instituted ; how
it failed in the first instance but was achieved subsequently ; how the
Secrets of the Sanctuary were learnt ; how he who learned them remained
within the Sanctuary, and there is no story afterwards. The Metrical
Romance of Borron and the LESSER HOLY GRAIL are not a Legend concerning the conversion of England but only prolegomena thereto. They leave
the real intention doubtful, outside the bare fact that something would
be brought into Britain which was and is unknown to the Church at large ;
for the canonical Apostles were not present when his great mission was
imposed on Joseph by Christ. There is nothing on the mere surface to
shew that any Priesthood followed the possession of the Grail Vessel or
the knowledge of the Secret Words. Yet these are Eucharistic : according
to the LESSER HOLY GRAIL they are a Formula of Consecration ; whence it
would seem that their possession ordained Joseph, because it is obvious
that at need he could recite the Words effectually. For the rest, it is
certain that Joseph and his Company carried no official Priests Westward.
A lacuna in symbolical time follows, and then comes the EARLY MERLIN,
shewing that the Secret Sanctuary is somewhere in Britain, that a firebrand
Prophet is going about in the land, bearing the ambassadorial warrant of the
Grail, and is bent upon fulfilling prophecy by instituting a Third Table for
the completion of the Grail Trinity. There are no claims put forward
regarding the Sanctuary, and the same statement holds for the DIDOT-
MODENA PERCEVAL.

It remains that the Lesser Chronicles intimate generally the existence of
a particular Eucharistic knowledge, but not of a Church demanding recognition thereon. As secrecy is the primary seal, it is obvious that the Grail
Church is not an Official Church in Britain, nor do the texts contain any
counter-picture, object, or character which might by possibility correspond
to the Roman Obedience apart from that notion of Enchantment which,
in the absence of any warrant, it is arbitrary to explain along these lines.
For example, it would be madness to suggest that Moses, who was interned

in secrecy, represents the Latin Church in apostasy or rejection. It is obvious, in fine, that Robert de Borron was acquainted with no Tradition which connected Joseph of Arimathæa with Glastonbury or even with Britain. In the poem, he remains where he was or returns to Syria, as Moses the Law-giver went up the holy mountain.

The Vulgate Cycle bears the same witness, but the evidence of Transubstantiation and other matters of doctrine suggest that the major texts are typically and militantly Roman. The GRAND SAINT GRAAL tells how the same Company, strangely extended, arrived in Britain and there established, in the person of Joseph II, the beginnings of a Supreme Orthodoxy, so that nothing which came after in the name of the Gospel could abide in competition therewith. The VULGATE MERLIN, reflecting the Borron text, tells how the Prophet and Enchanter Merlin carried a strange warrant to connect his work with the Mystery of the Holy Grail ; how he possessed from the beginning of his symbol the power to promise Blaise that he should be united with the Secret Assembly ; how the Castle of the Grail, though not altogether hidden from the world, was encompassed with perils and difficulties, which notwithstanding there were wars or the rumour of wars about it. The GRAND SAINT GRAAL narrates the conversion of Britain by those who carried the License of Super-Apostolical Succession, the design of which may have been pan-Britannic, or conceivably the implicit of a plan of campaign against papal claims over Britain. It is at least the Legend *par excellence* which, if any, would be regarded as devised in this interest ; and it would stand alone as such among the Anglo-Norman texts. The colonisation, whatever its design, conquered all Britain in all publicity. When however the later MERLIN texts enter the field, everything has passed into seclusion, and the Prophet's personation of the character of Messenger does not carry public knowledge concerning the Grail further than an echoing rumour. Outside the sacro-saintly character of ordinary Church-practice, the texts offer no ecclesiastical element but the implications which are resident in the notion of Adventurous Times and the preparation at the Royal Court for the Quest of the Sacred Vessel, the term of which is to break up the Round Table. The intermediate prose LANCELOT follows the MERLIN texts, working for the same end, and we are already at a far distance from the letter and spirit of the GRAND SAINT GRAAL. In the LONGER PROSE PERCEVAL the term is to strip the Sanctuary, but it remains a consecrated although a deserted place, and those who enter therein become thereafter men of holy lives and saints of the Official Church. The QUEST OF GALAHAD offers in the term thereof the instance of a Keeper who is dispossessed—as we have seen—without any intimation of his end. It may be said that he is treated with something almost approaching contumely. There is an apparent equivalent of an expulsion of the profane in that command for those to withdraw who are not in the Quest of the Grail. But behind this and behind the unnamed yet acknowledged Warrant of the Knights from Gaul, Ireland and Denmark, there is some Mystery concealed deeply. The latter took away from their high experience the memory of a glorious vision which could well serve as the basis of a Tradition thereafter in various parts of the world ; but they had not received communication of the Last Secrets. The Hidden Life of the Holy Grail during the Arthurian period seems next after one the most wonderful of all Hidden Lives. What could King Pelles, with whom the Grail had abode for years, and it may be for centuries, whose Daughter also had borne it through all the Secret Rites from her childhood, what could he learn from the Quest ?

I conclude therefore as regards the Vulgate Chronicles that they may offer in one text, which is the latest of all, a certain aggrandisement of British Ecclesiastical Tradition by the incorporation of a claim which belonged in its root-matter to a different concern entirely ; but the remaining Branches have little part in the scheme. The Grail Church is held in secrecy and mystery, and when the Quest of Galahad certifies that a certain Joseph, not otherwise particularised, was the first Bishop of Christendom, there seems no longer any consequence involved of the ecclesiastical order.

In the German Cycle the Grail had nothing to do with any Conversion Legend and nothing to do with Britain : that country is not entered in the PARZIVAL. The assumption of a particular affinity with the aspirations or ambitions of the House of Anjou is an irresistible inference from that portion which contains the Angevin elements ; but it is accidental and not essential to the design of the poem, and is not its inspiration but its burden. The work is to be judged wholly by other standards.

It must be agreed, I think, from this brief and literal schedule that, except by a bare and utterly speculative possibility in a single sporadic instance, we are not dealing in the Grail literature with a formal conspiracy for the furtherance of revolution in matters of Religion.

XXIII

THE SUMERIAN GRAIL

(XI, § 2, p. 428.)

IT seems long since a new thesis on the origin of the Grail Myth has been proffered in English circles of research ; and it happens that the last contribution to this involved but talismanic problem is made in the course of an investigation which has far other objects in view. It seems to me therefore that I may deserve well of my readers if I remove the proposition from a setting in which it is likely to be buried, so far as they are concerned. Dr. L. A. Waddell, who is ex-professor of Tibetan at London University, and has been described as the foremost living authority on Lhasa and its Mysteries, has published not so long ago a monumental work on the genesis of civilisation about 3380 B.C. in the Homeland of the Aryan and Nordic Race, identified with the Sumerians, "whose vast city-ruins in Mesopotamia . . . began to be unearthed some fifty years ago, and whose treasures now enrich" the national museums of Europe and America.[1] Dr. Waddell's contribution to the general subject centres in his affirmed discovery that "the Sumerians were Aryans in physical type, culture, religion, language and writing." The evidence for these things, which are at issue with the views and conclusions of previous "leading Assyriologists," is to be sought not alone in the work under notice but in the earlier theses of the same author on the Phœnician origin of Britons, Scots and Anglo-Saxons ; on Indo-Sumerian seals ; and on the Aryan origin of the alphabet. At this

[1] THE MAKERS OF CIVILISATION IN RACE AND HISTORY, by L. A. Waddell, LL.B., C.B., C.I.E., etc.

point, having stated the case, the debate must be left to scholarship of the kind involved, remembering that Dr. Waddell carries many titles to consideration in his own sphere. Perhaps I should add that he seems more and not less dogmatic than the most convinced in the cohort of particular experts. He is armed at all points, though I hazard an opinion that there must be many vulnerable places in his array of fantastic etymologies.

And now as to the Holy Grail : he decrees that its original is still extant, being a Sumerian " fetish stone-bowl," described as a war-trophy. It belonged to the first Sumerian King, Dur or Tur, to whose memory it was dedicated subsequently by his great-grandson, King Udu of Kish City, " the fourth Imperial King of the First Aryan Dynasty." He placed upon it " the oldest known historical inscription in the world," being a genealogy of the said Kings. What is the connection, however, with the Palladium of Arthurian Quest ? Dr. Waddell says that " it is now disclosed as the actual material original of the famous Holy Grail of King Arthur." But it is more even than this, for it is also a magical Cauldron " captured from the weirds at the Well of Urd . . . by Her-Thor, as detailed in the Nordic Eddas." It was captured by Dur or Tur from the aboriginal Chaldean Serpent-Worshippers, when he destroyed the degrading Dragon-Cult of the ancient world and substituted the Sun-Cult, characterised as a bland form of worship. Udu himself was termed " the King of the Precious Stone " and " King of the Hidden Vessel." It is called hidden because he buried it under the foundations of a tower " in the oldest Sun Temple in Mesopotamia." It was broken when so entombed, and it remained in concealment till it was " unearthed in a fragmentary condition, but with its inscription practically intact, by the Pennsylvanian University Expedition " —at a date which I do not find specified in the story. In any case, one of the fragments is now in Dr. Waddell's possession.

So far as I am able to gather, the line of evidence for this bizarre discovery is that King Arthur connects etymologically with Tur, the first Sumerian King, as he does also with Thor ; that the second Sumerian King—Gan, Gun or Kan—connects with and is " the historical original of Sir Gawain, described as the chief champion Knight-Errant " of Arthurian Legends ; and that the Grail was taken into concealment as Udu's Bowl was hidden. Dr. Waddell might have added that King Udu was a Priest as well as a Monarch and that his concealment of the Fetish Bowl might suggest a further Grail analogy, because the German Romance Cycle represents the Sacred Vessel as carried away into the Land of Prester John, and that this Priest-King and his successors became its Custodians. It is a mad world, my masters—is this world of scholarship ; for Arthur being also Thor is likewise Odin and St. George, while Gawain is St. Michael, Cain and Nimrod. There is of course no Quest of the Grail in this very new version ; it does not feed the hungry or give drink to the thirsty ; it does not produce oracles ; there is no mystery concerning a Wounded King whose healing depends on the asking of a certain Question. In a word, this last speculation on origins explains nothing connected late or early with the Holy Grail itself, or any branch of its old Romance-literature. It seems unlikely therefore that it will attract attention at the hands of textual scholars. The shewing of such a vision might be left at this point ; but it happened that, very soon after, Dr. Waddell produced yet another volume. It is entitled THE BRITISH EDDA (1930), otherwise " the great epic poem of the Ancient Britons on the exploits of King Thor, Arthur or Adam and his Knights in establishing civilisation, reforming Eden and capturing the Holy Grail." The epic in question is referred to *circa* B.C. 3380-3350 and is really the collection of Sagas known to scholarship as the Icelandic Edda, of which a new version is offered. Not only does Arthur emerge as Adam in addition to his other personalities but is called the first King of Troy, and Guinevere is identified with Eve. The Grail is a Magic Bowl and Witches' Cauldron, the Palladium of a Serpent-Cult which prevailed in Eden till Arthur broke it up.

XXIV

GRAIL HALLOWS AND TAROT TALISMANS

(XI, § 2, p. 432.)

To re-state the fact that the canonical Hallows of the Grail Legend are the Cup, the Lance, the Dish and the Sword may well seem inexcusable at this stage : the least versed of my readers will regard it as a weary reiteration ; for he and they are in plenary possession of all that need be said upon the subject. I must specify the bare fact, this notwithstanding, because of what follows hereafter. And it may seem to arise from the repetition if I recall further to their minds—and my own memory—one experience which comes to us all occasionally, and startles us when it does come, revealing the fund of unobservance to which we must confess too often. When any of us have been studying exhaustively—as we think—a given subject, and are surfeited by our familiarity therewith, it may happen that we alight unawares on something which had escaped us utterly. It may be through the random remark of a stranger, through an apparently detached sentence in some forgotten or unknown book, but a light of sudden intimation flashes, and we see the whole thing under a new aspect. On the surface this illustrates the difficulty with which we notice things that are ever so little outside our special groove ; but there are times when it seems to have a deeper root, and we realise in our hearts that anything may serve as a pretext to open another horizon : " a flower, a leaf, the ocean " may touch and kindle " the electric chain wherewith we are darkly bound." So falls " the spark from heaven." It happens also that a horizon may open for a moment in this manner, but we find no path therein : there was an experience of this kind on my own part when I first heard of the so-called Lance among the Sacramental Instruments of the Byzantine Mass ; but it led nowhere. I am wondering now how many critical works have been written on the Holy Grail and yet it has occurred to no one that its Hallows, under a slight modification, may be somewhere else in the world than in old books of Romance. They are to be found as a fact in the most unexpected of all places, and seem to have existed there as if from time immemorial. They are in the antecedents of our playing-cards—that is to say, in the old Talismans of the Tarot, the divinatory use of which has been long in fashion with Occult Sects of Miss Weston's type. These are things which, in a sense, are of world-wide knowledge, which have interested numerous people, which constitute even now, as they may have constituted for generations and centuries, a prolific form of divination and the vagrant art of fortune-telling. We know nothing concerning their origin and of their distribution little enough. It is to be hoped that I am least disposed of anyone to assume the antiquity of doubtful documents or to pre-date Traditions on the basis of their uncertain origin. I leave to those to whom it may concern the history of our playing-cards and their precursors, this so-called BOOK OF THOTH ; nor do I need to recite, even shortly, what has been assumed regarding it by certain Occult Orders. The measures on the side of speculation are pressed down and running over with every sort of folly and extravagance. There is, however, another kind of learning which has confined itself to the archæology of the subject, with sober and valuable results. I shall not be challenged by these if I say that there are traces of Tarot cards in the fourteenth century, prior to which they are not of necessity non-existent because, like the Grail itself, they are lost to sight.

Archæology is, however, its own term, so that usually there is nothing beyond it ; and therefore, having so far distinguished between two schools, I must say that there is yet another side which might rivet attention generally if it were possible to speak fully concerning it. I record in the first place (1) that the correspondence of certain Tarot symbols with those of the Holy Grail stands rather in the light of a discovery without a consequence which I can pretend to develop here ; and (2) that the reason will be evident, I think, because this side which I have mentioned reposes in certain secret records now existing in Europe. In these the Talismans of the Tarot have been pressed into the service of a complex, constructed system of symbolism with results that are very curious. It might or might not be useless to speak about the system in public, supposing that this were possible, but I think that there are considerations involved which would be almost an unknown language to people who have not had their training in a particular realm of thought. " Those who know " regard the results as important, yet those who see the importance have not in most cases any idea of the term. As I must now say that this term belongs under one of its aspects to the domain of occultism, it should be understood that my strictures on wild Tarot speculations ought to carry a certain weight because those speculations are of the occult order. If any of my readers should wish to look a little further into a strange and problematical subject, they may be recommended to consult one book called LE TAROT DES BOHÉMIENS, issued long since by the French Philosophical Martinists. I can tell them for their consolation that from root to branch it has been termed a tissue of errors, because this school has not the "true reading," while specific alternative readings in other academies are also wrong. Except in purely archæological aspects, the inquirer can, however, get nothing better than the content of this work, and if he misses the major sacraments he will find a limited quantity of fortune-telling rubbish therein which is altogether diverting and may be mastered with a little trouble.

It must be explained that the old sheaf of oracles consists of seventy-eight cards, of which fifty-six are the equivalents of ordinary playing-cards, plus four knights ; and the remaining twenty-two are pictorial keys, the symbolical nature of which is seen on their surface, though it must be understood that hereon all of them are conventional and many are grotesque, as if they were coarse allegories. The keys have been allocated by interpretation in various reveries to the letters of the Hebrew alphabet, and herefrom as a root many instituted analogies with Kabbalism have been devised by the divergent groups which have devoted their attention to the pictures. Some

Sephirotic attributions that have been obtained in this way are especially remarkable. I offer my assurance, as one who has more to lose than to gain by making the statement, that certain secret systems have developed their interpretations to an unexpected point by the allocation of these cards according to a method which is not known outside them.

Having made this explanation, my next point is to state that the four palmary symbols of the Tarot are—

1. The Cup, corresponding to Hearts in the common signs of cards.
2. The Wand, corresponding to Diamonds in the common signs of cards.
3. The Sword, corresponding to Spades in the common signs of cards.
4. The Pentacle, corresponding to Clubs in the common signs of cards.

The Wand is alternately a sceptre in the Tarot descriptions, but its proper alternative in the symbolism is a spear or lance, the misnamed Diamond in the modern suit being obviously the head of the weapon. In respect of the Pentacle that which is depicted under this name answers to a Dish, having usually the outline of a four-leaved shamrock, or alternatively of a circle. In either case the emblem is misdescribed also under the term pentacle, which must have five angles or flanges. With these modifications, which are in no sense of an arbitrary kind, the Tarot suits are actually the Grail Hallows.

When Miss Weston thought it worth while to discover these analogies in FROM RITUAL TO ROMANCE, and decided to forget that I had preceded her in my HIDDEN CHURCH OF THE HOLY GRAIL, she quotes Mr. W. B. Yeats on present-day magical operations with the help of Tarot Cards and resolves that " the ultimate object of Magic in all ages was, and is, to obtain control of the sources of Life." Those who use Grimoires and Alberts in backways and by-streets might be astonished at the news. There is no need to add that her Fertility complex comes again into play, and she prefers to think that the Tarot bits and pieces were used " to predict the rise and fall of the waters " rather than to foretell personal futures.

XXV

THE GRAIL QUESTION

(XI, § 3, p. 438.)

Qui on en servoit? Such is the Question in Chrétien. *De quoi li Graus sert* is the variant of the DIDOT-MODENA PERCEVAL. " Unto whom one serveth of the Grail " is the proffered form in the PERLESVAUS. But in the LANCELOT that Knight of high election exclaimed unprompted : " O Jesu, what does this mean ? " And here is not the only but perhaps the clearest form of an issue behind the Question. It is like a test of merit belonging to a Rite of Initiation, a very simple but inalienable condition on which alone a House of many Hallows was permitted to unveil its treasures, or a Hidden Church to admit a catechumen within its sacred precincts. I am not suggesting that this is the meaning of the literature, of its pageants and its long succession of tales ; but here is one of the ways in which it might become intelligible. My point at the moment is that the vital consequence of the Question in all the

Perceval Quests has been missed throughout by criticism. It was even proposed by Birch-Hirschfeld that it was an idle invention of Chrétien, instead of the pivot round which all events revolve.

Among these there is the temporal rejection of Perceval because he failed to stand the test, and there is the second chance accorded in which he made good ultimately. The DIDOT-MODENA PERCEVAL and the CONTE DEL GRAAL are concerned with these. In DIU CRÔNE Perceval is given no second chance, and there is substituted another Candidate who fulfils the test. The Perceval of the PERLESVAUS fails once and for ever, the result being (1) That the King is stricken and (2) That he dies unhealed. The House of Hallows is left in this manner without a Keeper and yet in the absence, at least for a brief moment, of all manifest detriment. The Grail is there and the other Talismans ; but it does not appear who guards them unless it is certain holy Hermits who pass in and out of the story. For short or for long, this régime continues till the House is taken by the King of Castle Mortal—him " who sold God for money," though in what manner does not emerge in the Romance. The Hallows are then removed by unseen powers. It is relieved by Perceval, who enters thus into possession by right of heirship as well as by conquest, whereupon those Hallows are restored which had passed into the hiddenness. He is Keeper henceforth *de facto* but not by appointment, as in all other cases of the Perceval Quest.

It is to be noted in this connection that Monseigneur Gawain in DIU CRÔNE does not become the Keeper though he performs the task. His mission is to dissolve an enchantment, and the Grail removes automatically, as if with the Ghosts of the Dead-Alive, while the hero returns to Court. In the PARZIVAL the Questing Knight is called to the Kinghood before he has fulfilled the Quest—a contradiction in terms offered to the chief succession of French texts—and thereafter only he asks the vital Question, which heals the suffering King. It is as if the woe of the House has become intolerable, not only to him who endures and those about who witness but to the Grail itself. It is only in this text that the Lord of the Castle is pictured in such dire extremity. In the DIDOT-MODENA PERCEVAL he is merely stricken with years ; he is in languishment only in Chrétien and the PERLESVAUS ; he cannot get away from his body in the poem of Heinrich, but it is not shewn that the body is itself in anguish.

The Quest of Galahad is a Quest without a Question and does not concern us here. It calls to be observed, however, that there is a direct inter-relation between all the Quests, which from this point of view are divisible into four groups : (1) Perceval variants, in which the Question is asked at last, namely, the CONTE DEL GRAAL, DIDOT-MODENA PERCEVAL and the German PARZIVAL ; (2) DIU CRÔNE, which certifies to the permanent disqualification of Perceval ; (3) the PERLESVAUS, which exhibits in plenary form that he was not disqualified but must and did come into that which was his very own, *ab origine ;* (4) The Galahad Quest, in which the Question has passed out of mind, and in which Perceval pursues the task to its last end at Sarras, but counts second of the three heroes in the great emprize, though their comparative positions and values emerge nowhere explicitly, so far as expression is concerned.

As the clearest example of the Question in the whole French Cycle is that of the LANCELOT, which is not a Quest Story, so in the German branch it is found in DIU CRÔNE, almost word for word : " What does it mean ? " But the Quest of Heinrich is a Quest that does not matter. In Wolfram the formula reads : " Uncle, what is it tortures thee ? " All stories, however, agree fundamentally on another point, that the House of the Holy Grail is a House of Sorrow. It can be healed only by help coming from without, which must be yet, in most cases, at the hands of one who is a Scion of the House.

The next point which arises for consideration is the consequence to the outer world of the Quest in its final achievement. There is an end of certain Adventurous Times and there is—as a kind of alternative in other texts—an end of all Enchantments or of a reign of desolation and dread. The last is heard of more especially, and with certain particulars, in the LONGER PROSE PERCEVAL. In the Quest of Galahad there is no such term attained, for that which befalls is the destruction of the Kingdom of Logres, though it is a matter of inference only, and the Morte Arthur is still far away when the Grail is removed to Heaven. So also Enchantments continue and Adventures marshal until there seems no end of either. Finally, the dispensation general belongs to Logres in the French texts, and nowhere else ; while the woe of the House belongs to the House only in the PARZIVAL, having no reaction on the world without.

What it all means has exercised successive speculations for nearly one hundred years. If there is any concerted intent providing a definite purpose to Grail literature, its geographical limit lies within a narrow compass. The point is mentioned here on the hypothesis that the *mise-en-scène* signifies something in the normal logic of the theme. There was something at work in Britain and something in Germany, in the latter case deriving possibly from Southern France, at that point where the Pyrenees separate France and Spain. What was going on in these places during the fourth and first quarters of the twelfth and thirteenth centuries, if the Metrical Romance of Robert de Borron and the GRAND SAINT GRAAL are not to be counted as merely Conversion Myths, and if the PARZIVAL is to rank higher than a Knightly Story centred about a Feeding Dish ?

By the hypothesis of the Lesser and Greater Chronicles, that which came into Britain belonged to no recognised Apostolate, but it began a work of conversion. It succeeded up to a certain point, and then there is a leap through the centuries to Arthurian days, the environment and atmosphere of which are the twelfth century and later, though the events are supposed to be much earlier. If we are dealing here with one of the Traditional Histories which are familiar in Rites of Initiation or with the claims of some Christian Sect, the one or the other was in evidence, at or near the period which saw the evolution of Grail literature, and its Holy Houses or Temples were in more than one place of the world. They were in the land of Vortigern, according to a Merlin text ; in the Isles of Ireland, according to the DIDOT-MODENA PERCEVAL ; for the LANCELOT and the QUESTE, at Corbenic on the Welsh sea-coast, possibly identical with *Terre foraine* of the GRAND SAINT GRAAL : and in the Pyrenees, according to Wolfram. They had been in the hands of successive Custodians from the beginnings of Christianity in the West, according to the Northern French Cycles, and from any date which we may allocate to the first King of the Grail in the German Branch.

The Keepers are of one family : but the blood-bond between them may be understood in the sense of spiritual affinity if we are in the presence of a History of Initiation or of a sect with a past behind it. The Keepers are those who possess and guard the Mystery, who are in full fruition thereof ; and the Candidate for Initiation, or the Novice, called to possess the Mystery in his turn, belongs to the House, in the sense of that affinity which I have mentioned. The rumour of the Grail—that is to say, of the Mystery—goes about in all the texts, but not the Grail itself, except in the Galahad and Perlesvaus. It is otherwise a jealous Talisman, reserved to the House only, except in the fantastic text of Heinrich ; and the Quest of Galahad, which, on the surface, throws it open to competition, takes care that only those who are warranted by highest titles shall achieve the end, Galahad himself being a Son of the Mystery in the highest sense.

XXVI

THE LAPIS EXILIS

(XI, § 5, p. 456.)

According to Wolfram von Eschenbach, the Grail was a Crown of Desire understood on the material plane ; but it would respond also to the title which was allocated by Heinrich to his independent version of the Legend, because assuredly it was a Crown of Adventure, and in more than one sense. In the Parzival it was borne aloft on a green cushion by the Maid who was chosen for the Office, and this suggests that the object was, speaking comparatively, small, or in any case portable. There is nothing in the whole poem to make us connect it with a jewel in the conventional sense, and it is nowhere actually described : it is simply that object of wonder to which the name of Grail is given. Metaphorically it was light as wool, as we have seen, in the hands of its licensed bearer, but an unprepared person could not move it from the place of its repose. This is rather, however, a question of Magic than of variation in specific gravity. *Ex hypothesi*, it was large enough on one specific occasion to hold a considerable inscription on its surface— that is to say, when the King's healing was promised as the reward of the mystic Question. At the same time its figurative dimensions were restricted by the counter-fact that it could and did repose in the nest of a bird which tradition describes as about the size of an eagle. Indeed, the stone which renewed the phœnix recalls the *Lapis Aquilæ*, which, according to another tradition, was sought by the eagle and used to assist the hatching of its eggs.

This enumeration is made to preface some reflections upon the Latin term which Wolfram applied to his talisman. What he wrote—or his scribe rather —we have to divine as we can from the choice of impossibilities which are offered by extant manuscripts, and that which has received most countenance among the guesswork readings is *Lapis exilis*, meaning the slender stone. The *scholia* of lexicographers on the second of these words indicate some difference of opinion among the learned on the question of its philology—*de etymo mire se torquent viri docti*—and as an additional quota of confusion one of them has placed the significance of slender upon the word exile as it is used in English. I do not know of such an adjective in our language and still less of one bearing such interpretation ; but this apart it would seem that the slender stone connecting with the conception of the Grail is even more discon- certing than any philological difficulty. Further, the word *exilis* suffers the meaning of leanness, and this in connection with a stone of plenty, which paints in the PARZIVAL an eternal larder, *à parte ante et à parte post*, is not less than hopeless. It may be said that Wolfram's intention was to specify by *Lapis exilis* that his talisman was least among stones in dimension yet great in its efficacy, even as the Scriptures tell us that the mustard seed is least among grains and yet becomes a great tree. There is a certain plausibility in this; and students of another School will know that *Lapis Exilis* is a term which corresponds wholly to the Great Talisman of metallic transmutation, for no adept experienced any difficulty when he carried the Powder of Projection—which was in fact the Stone—in his wallet or even his girdle : yet this also was great in its efficacy, as there is no need to insist. It happens further that in a tract entitled ROSARIUM PHILOSOPHORUM—citing Arnoldus de Villanova—the Stone is characterised dogmatically as *Lapis Exilis*. The correspondence, however, is to little purpose, for the true description of the Grail Stone in the German Legend would be *è cœlo veniens*. But it is understood obviously that this does not enter the lists as a construction of chaotic readings found in the manuscripts. A possible interpretation, preserving the verbal similarity with a reasonable consonance in the root-idea of the subject, would be *Lapis Exilii*=the Stone of Exile, or *Lapis Exsulis*=the Exile's Stone. The correspondence is here two-fold, for there is the exile of Lucifer, who, if the jewel was once in his crown, lost it on expulsion from Heaven ; and there is also the exile of humanity, which is *ex hypothesi* a derivation from the Fall of the Angels. It was given to men as a Palladium, perhaps even as a gage of their final exaltation to the thrones vacated above.

However this may be—and it is a speculative suggestion only—there are deeper analogies in certain Scripture symbolism. I speak of that other Stone which followed the people of Israel during forty years in the wilderness, and the interpretation of which is given by St. Paul. " Our fathers . . . did all eat the same spiritual meat ; and did all drink the same spiritual drink : for they drank of that Spiritual Rock which followed them : and that Rock was Christ." It will be inferred that the root-idea of the story is based upon the natural fact that torrents or streams may flow through rocky ground ; but the Masters in Israel knew of deeper meanings, or divined them at least in their subtlety, seeing that their whole concern was with a Spiritual Pilgrimage. It is said in the Zoharic Tract entitled THE FAITHFUL SHEPHERD that a Stone or Rock is given, and yet another Stone, the Name of which is Tetragrammaton, otherwise the Divine Name of four letters, which is read by us as Jehovah. Now, this is a reference to the Prophecy of Daniel, according to which the Stone that struck the statue became like a mountain and filled the whole earth. It is applied to Messias and his Kingdom by the Preface to the ZOHAR, which says further that the Israelites, during their exile in Egypt, had lost the Mystery of the Holy Name. When, however, Moses appeared, he recalled this Name to their minds. It follows herefrom that we are dealing with another Legend of the Lost Word ; and of course if Christ was the Rock or Stone which supplied sustenance to the Jews, we can understand in a vague manner not only the correspondence between the Grail and the Mystic Stone but also the manner—otherwise so discounselling—in which the Great Quest and the PARZIVAL ascribe to their Great Palladium, whether Stone or Cup, a marvellous power of nourishment. The allusion is therefore to the Corner Stone, which is Christ and which became the Head of the Building. It is the old Talmudic and Kabbalistic

Tradition that the *Lapis Fundamentalis* was set in the Temple of Jerusalem under the Ark of the Covenant, even as the Rock of Calvary, according to another Legend, is called the Centre of the World. All these Stones in the final exhaustion of symbolism are one Stone, which does not differ from that White Cube which the Elect receive in the Apocalypse, together with the New and Secret Name written therein. This Stone, in any figurative material form, might be the least possible in cubic measurement—that is to say, in the correspondence between things without and within—even as that which is given, strangely inscribed, to the Recipient in one of the most deeply symbolic of Masonic High Grades.

Analogies are subtle and analogies are also precarious ; but those which have been traced here are at least more in consonance with the spirit of Grail literature than some others which have been cited, namely, (1) the Sacred Stone, called the Mother of the Gods, which is mentioned by Ovid and of which Arnobius tells us that it was small and could be carried easily by a single man ; (2) the Roman *Lapis Manalis*, which brought rain in drought, as it might have brought food in famine ; (3) the *Bœtilus* or Oracular Stone, which gave oracles to its bearer, speaking with a still, small voice.

XXVII

THE SECRET WORDS

(XII, § 2, p. 490.)

MISS FISHER presents an entirely unacceptable explanation of the Secret Words affirmed by Robert de Borron to have been communicated by Christ to Joseph of Arimathæa. There is nothing less secret in the world than the so-called *Secreta* of the ORDO MISSÆ, the SUSCIPE SANCTA TRINITAS HANC OBLATIONEM, etc. It was very possible for her to have looked further and to have intrigued us at least by proposing that the Secret Words were unfolded from that daring and pregnant MYSTERIUM FIDEI which the ORDO MISSÆ interpolates between those words of Christ which constitute the Formula of Institution in respect of the Element of Wine. We might have remained dubious but must have confessed to a great suggestion and have planned perhaps a search for any Mass-Book scholarship may have offered by way of apologetics respecting the point of fact. It is to be observed further that Miss Fisher passes over in what is possibly a significant silence the whole problem concerning that First Priest and First Bishop of Christendom who consecrated " the Body of Our Lord." For the rest, it would serve, I conceive, no purpose to challenge her on the whole subject of her Mystic Vision, whether found in the Grail literature or in Dante ; to tell her, I mean, that the state of vision, from its *prima materia* in second sight and clairvoyance to the state of " dilucid contemplation," is not the term of Mysticism, because the images have passed therein and that which has been attained is unity, beyond the seeing and the seen.

XXVIII

PERLESVAUS PRIESTS AND HERMITS

(XII, § 2, p. 490.)

It is scarcely possible to take out a full list, but it would seem that most if not all Hermits, Monks and Priests who appear in the Grail Quests belong directly or indirectly to the business of the Grail, whatever it may prove to be. They are of that ilk or orthodoxy, and it may even be that there is no real allusion—unless in terms of hostile allegory—to the Roman domination. The first Hermit encountered in the PERLESVAUS Celebrates an Arch-Natural Mass and thereafter discourses of the Grail to King Arthur. The second Hermit, who entertains Gawain, is in the service of King Fisherman. The third Hermit is King Pelles of the Grail himself. There are those who say Mass in Castles where harbour is given to Knights, but they are heard of and not seen. The fourth Hermit has knowledge of the Grail and of Perceval's failure to ask the vital Question. The fifth is healing the wounds of Perceval and knows well concerning his lineage. The first Priest mentioned as such is seen at the gateway of the Grail Castle. There is also another Hermit, who has knowledge concerning the Sword of St. John the Baptist and is therefore in touch with the Grail and its Hallows. This Hermit is also a Priest and says Mass. Priests are mentioned again in connection with a certain city, its Church and various Hallows. There is a Castle of Inquest at the entrance to the Land of King Fisherman, and Gawain on a visit thereto meets Priests and Knights of the Grail. A Priest who keeps the Castle of Tintagel seems evidently to know the whole business, even from the birth of King Arthur. There is the Priest of a Waste Castle who has strange learning concerning the genealogy of Monseigneur Gawain. There are, moreover, three Hermits who give hostel on one occasion to Lancelot, and these belong to the Mystery, as does he also who tells of Joseus and of the world's end by fire. In fine there are those twelve who watch over the twelve graves of Alain le Gros and his brothers.

XXIX

PERLESVAUS ALLEGORIES

(XII, § 2, p. 492.)

It calls to be remembered also that the PERLESVAUS in common with the Galahad QUESTE selects certain episodes from among its long sequence of events and unfolds their allegorical meaning. They are like casual examples plucked from their contexts to indicate that if these are to be understood according to an inward sense, so can and should be regarded the whole woof of pictured adventure. There is no clue to guide us ; but if such be the case it may and perhaps must follow, as we have seen already, that Logres is not Britain of necessity ; that Arthur would be known better under another name ; that—if it might work otherwise—his kingdom could be Provence and Languedoc, while he himself would emerge as a Count of Toulouse in the fire of Albigensian warfare rather than as Lord of the Round Table at Caerleon, or wheresoever his Chivalry happened to be called together. We may remember in this connection that the PERLESVAUS in its opening leaves represents Arthur as fallen into a supine state, a state of " slothful will ", as when the Count of Toulouse failed in his championship of the Albigensian cause, seeking to make terms with Rome and the Crusade leaders.

It is to be observed further that in the Cycle of Northern France, the Grail history begins with a Conversion Legend ; but when centuries have elapsed, and when there are no heathens left, either in France or Britain, we find that the PERLESVAUS Perceval is still engaged in putting forward the New against the Old Law. The stronghold of the Old Law and its champions are in evidence over against the Court of King Arthur. It is certain therefore that the alleged Old Law is not that of Israel. The text becomes intelligible at once if such Law signifies the persecuting Roman domination and if the New Law signifies the Dispensation of the Holy Spirit, which is that of Albigenses and Cathari. The PERLESVAUS is the only text which pictures misbelievers abiding, so to speak, at the heart and centre of Christendom or, in other words, is so stultifying on the surface and perhaps so pregnant with meaning inwardly. It would be difficult, however, to lay out the allegorical scheme consistently with events of the outer world. We dare not say that the King of Castle Mortal represents Papal Rome, for the Papacy did not die. But—other things equal—he might personify Simon de Montfort, who died assuredly in the course of his evil warfare.

Recurring now to the declared allegories of certain episodes, there is no space here to exhibit their unfolded meanings ; but it may be stated that these do not involve peculiarly Roman doctrine. They are of course Christian always in the root-matter but otherwise what is called undenominational in the parlance of the present day. Now, if allegory is permitted to transpire there and here, nor this only but is insisted on here and there, it signifies logically that the whole design is allegorical. When the Grail provides a banquet, the inward meaning can be taken as spiritual food of souls. All inward meanings are and must be spiritual, because such are the unfolded allegories in the text itself. The personalities of the Quest texts are figurative, from Arthur the King to the least among the Knights. As such, they may be a combination of historical characters and personified principles. It does not signify that the canons of allegory are broken in this manner : the Grail Romances are not perfect examples of literary art. The King of Castle Mortal may be Simon de Montfort, while Perceval may stand for all and any who are seeking the truth in Christ, as held by the Sects of Southern France. The Holy Grail may be the Albigensian Secret. It may be true also that Wolfram represents the sectarian ideal in his PARZIVAL, and it will be valuable from this point of view because the date of his poem is nearer to that of the utter destruction of Southern France. If there is a sub-surface meaning of this kind in any of the texts, I should be inclined to place the PERLESVAUS as paramount in this respect, and not alone because it is one of the two which insists on allegory behind some of its episodes.

The allegories in themselves are negligible, arbitrary at once and puerile : they read almost as if any kind of meaning would serve to illustrate the fact that a second meaning was everywhere, but to be kept in the background, being too dangerous to disclose openly. Let us glance at three examples.

(1) The Questing Beast is our Lord, and the twelve hounds ever clamant within her are the Jews—twelve presumably because of the twelve tribes. It will be observed that this is a stultifying allegory, seeing that the Beast is female. (2) The two Priests, of whom one kissed and worshipped the Cross, while the other beat it with a rod, were equally men of faith. The one worshipped because of the Redemption, while the other scourged because of the Saviour's sufferings on the Rood. It happens, however, that this explanation makes the whole episode an impertinence : there is no excuse for its appearance in the text, and there is no allegory in its alleged meaning. (3) The Knight with the Burning Dragon on his shield which ultimately burnt the bearer signifies that worshipful men do battle with the devil and, for the rest, that one devil torments another in the world to come. This also is a tale of little meaning, though the fight was strong.

Two things remain to be said : (1) The interpretations may be good, bad or indifferent—perhaps mostly bad ; they help or spoil the episodes, and spoil perhaps mostly ; but the significant fact is that they are there and that they stand out as portents, hinting at an intention which prevails throughout. (2) There is a last event on which Perceval looks for light and does not receive it, being that of the Turning Castle with archers of copper who shoot bolts at all comers. It is said to be the devil's fortress and that in truth he has no other. The Hermit who is explaining meanings tells Perceval that its destruction would not have taken place till the end of the world, if he had failed therein. This is obviously no explanation ; but there would be a bare possibility that the author's hands were held. If the Castle answers to Spiritual Rome, obviously the fact must be concealed, in which case the interpretation which does not interpret emerges as of all most consequent and the excuse for raising the question in respect of all. It shews that ready explanations at their value are available for things trivial but as to one that matters that which is said serves only to darken counsel and to deepen mystery.

Supposing that the Grail literature is throughout a woven veil of allegory, it will follow that its main materials are prominent embroideries of the veil and that they are not to be understood as they appear on the surface. Its knightly deeds belong to no earthly prowess and its Chivalry is not of this world, an affirmation, however, which is not to be regarded as in the sense of those who say that the Chivalry of Romance is fictitious, fabulous and corresponds to nothing that ever prevailed in mundane Courts and Kingdoms. The Galahad Quest and the PERLESVAUS live and move and have their being in a realm of figurative seeming. The Grail is not a Reliquary of the Precious Blood, except in so far as the latter is an outward sign of something far more Divine within. The misbelief by which Logres is encompassed and which prevails also within it is not a contrast created between pagan and Christian but between good and bad belief within the Christian pale itself. The stressful Adventurous Times and baleful Enchantments are no workings of common sorcery, of war and rumours of war : they belong to another order. The House of the Holy Grail is not a feudal Castle, though it is described as such, or a magical Castle, though also so described : it is rather a House of Doctrine. The Sacramental Wonders shew forth other Mysteries than those that obtain outwardly. The Question of the Perceval Cycle is a challenge offered to the Keepers of a Great Secret and a title to participate therein. The Grail Mass may be a deep intimation of something which lies behind

the Mystery of Consecrated Bread and Wine offered sacrificially ; but it is not
a witness of Eucharistic Transubstantiation, though it appears to be such in a
plenary sense on the open face of things. The Secret Words are not a Mass
Formula : they are one of the keys to the mastery of all the hidden meanings ;
while another is contained in the claim on Super-Apostolical Succession.
The Grail is a Christ-Mystery, as this was not understood in the Church
Regnant of the Western World. So formulated, one looks naturally for an
explanation to the historical sects of the period and more especially to
Southern France. But the first question is whether there was anything at
work in Britain which could be held to serve the purpose of interpretation.
Now, much has been made of the friction between Rome and Henry II and
of the alleged dream of a pan-Britannic Church. But it must be remembered
that such was the power of the Papal Pontiff that the King in question had
to do public penance for his share in the death of Thomas à Becket. It must
be remembered also that when the Glastonbury Legends of Joseph of
Arimathæa were manufactured he was provided with Blood Relics which set
aside Grail pretensions and seem indeed as if invented for this purpose. The
Church of Britain could do well enough with Joseph but not with his Secret
Words, and not with a Second Joseph who was first Bishop of Christendom
and first also who ever said Mass in this Christian world of ours. It could not
do with these things, the obvious fact notwithstanding that Joseph II
converted Britain, according to the Myth, while his Pontificate established
the British Church.

It may be advanced of course that the proposed thesis concerning a veil
of allegory would call on us to recognise that Logres was not Britain but
otherwhere in the world and most possibly in Southern France. It must be
realised, however, that the supposed veil adopted the personalities and
localities of Arthurian Romance and that the most suspicious of all the Grail
Texts, after the Metrical Romance of Robert de Borron and the GRAND SAINT
GRAAL, is the PERLESVAUS, which seems content with a literal Britain and
has its centre-in-chief at Glastonbury. Moreover it seems difficult, if not
indeed impossible, to work out a scheme of interpretation with Logres in
Southern France, though it would be valuable if this could be done, because
then we could incorporate the PARZIVAL more readily into the general scheme,
with its supposititious Grail Castle in the Pyrenees, and the Spanish peninsula—full of mystery and portent—linked conveniently with Provence and
Gascony by the Grand Passes.

XXX

THE VIA BREVIS

(XII, § 3, p. 500.)

THOSE who attain this Secret Way have said therefore their *Introibo*, have
passed and gone in. He who comes forth, as one who re-enters the manifest,
can be pictured only as bearing Bread and Wine, like Melchisedech. And
this is the finding of the Grail. It is the state in which Mary conceived in her
heart before she conceived in her body. There are no manifestoes issued of
or about the state, or we should be in a better position to judge regarding it ;
and it has not had its documents extracted, or we should not have had the

Grail Romances extant in their present form. But things have transpired concerning it and are met with in many records, at times in expected places, at others where none would look. It gives to those who can receive it a full answer to the question : " Art thou He that is to come, or do we look for another ? "

So far as there has been any hypothesis put forward on the subject, the speculation has gone utterly astray, because it has assumed that the research is dealing with some corporate and organised body and not with the course of experience in higher consciousness. Now, if there is no such experience, the claim of all the Churches and all the Holy Assemblies, open or hidden, is at once voided.

XXXI

OF EXILE AND RETURN

(XII, § 3, p. 503.)

THE Galahad Quest illustrates the familiar Exile and Return Formula, of which we heard so much in the days of Alfred Nutt : they have passed, it would seem, with him. The hero in this case is native from the beginning to the Holy House and is born therein. But his is a Tale of the Sanctuary in a secret place of the world about us, while behind this Quest there is another Formula, also of Exile and Return. The soul of Galahad is native to the Heaven above us and in fine goes back thereto. The hero of the DIDOT-MODENA PERCEVAL is native to the House according to the line of descent, but he is not born therein, like Galahad, and does not know of his lineage from the beginning, though at the end he comes into his own and abides therein. The story is not one of Exile and Return : it is that of an undisputed succession fulfilled at last. Of Perceval in the CONTE DEL GRAAL there is little need to speak, for his somewhat composite personality in the hands of successive reciters has no settled purpose in view. The PERLESVAUS has nothing to tell us concerning its hero's own genealogy or that of the Grail Keeper, except by vague allusion to the past ; for all things are presupposed in respect of his early history. We have seen that the story is not a Quest but, as the English translator terms it, a High History—following the old French. Perceval does not succeed to the Keepership by right of Quest fulfilled but otherwise by right of warfare, with genealogy in the background, though not as such unrecognised. The Parzival of Wolfram once more is a Son of the House, but as in the DIDOT-MODENA PERCEVAL he is not born therein. He is called thereto before he has performed the prescribed work of Quest, before he has asked the Question of the Mystery and before he has healed the King. It is to be noted also that he does not enter into sole possession of the Talisman, for henceforth there is a triple Keepership. The Grail is not removed, and it is not said to be reserved in deeper hiddenness. The logical dilemma of the French Cycle is that the Grail is the only Relic which is kept in concealment throughout and is at times the only one which is withdrawn further. That of Wolfram is the seemingly purposeless character of the whole scheme : the Grail is a Family Oracle and an inexhaustible licensed victualler.

XXXII

THE LOST BOOK

(XII, § 4, p. 517.)

WHEN considering the claim of the Celtic Church to recognition as a possible guiding and shaping spirit of the Grail literature, we have seen that one speculation regarding it was the existence, less or more in concealment, of a particular book—as it might be—a Liturgy of some kind, preferably a Book of the Mass. I have no definite concern in the hypothesis ; but the affirmation of one or more primordial texts is met with so often in the Romances that it might almost seem simpler to presume it as matter of fact, and thus it becomes desirable to ascertain what evidence, if any, can otherwise be gleaned about it, not forgetting, however, all that has been advanced previously on creative invention.

We must set aside in the first place those texts which depend from one another, whether the earlier examples are extant or not. The illusory QUEST of Kyot—priceless as its discovery would be—is not a term of our research. We must detach further those obviously fabulous Chronicles by the pretence of which it is supposed that the several Quests and Histories were perpetuated for the enlightenment of posterity. No one is wondering seriously whether the Knightly Adventures of the Round Table were reduced into great memorials by the scribes of King Arthur's Court, for which assurance we have the evidence of the HUTH MERLIN—among several deponents. There are other sources which may be equally putative, but it is these which raise the question, and I proceed to their enumeration as follows : (1) That which contained the greatest secret of the world, a minute volume which would lie in the hollow of a Hermit's hand—in a word, the text presupposed by the Prologue to the GRAND SAINT GRAAL ; (2) that which is ascribed to Master Blihis—the *fabulator famosus*—by the *Elucidation* prefixed to the CONTE DEL GRAAL ; (3) that which is called the Great Book by Robert de Borron, containing the Great Secret to which the term Grail is referred, a book of many Histories, written by many clerks, and by him communicated in part to his patron, Walter Montbéliard ; (4) that which the Count of Flanders gave to Chrétien de Troyes with instructions to retell it, being the best story ever recited in Royal Court ; (5) that which the Hermit Blaise codified with the help of the Secret Records kept by the Wardens of the Grail ; (6) that which the author of the LONGER PROSE PERCEVAL refers to the saintly man whom he calls Josephus ; (7) that which the Jew Flegitanis transcribed from time-immemorial Chronicles of the Starry Heavens.

The palmary problem for our solution is, whether in the last understanding a Mystery Book or a Mass Book, these cryptic texts can be regarded as " seven and yet one, like shadows in a dream "—or rather, as many inventions concerning one document. If we summarise the results which were obtained from them, we can express them by their chief examples thus : (1) From the prototype of the GRAND SAINT GRAAL came the Super-Apostolical Succession, the Ordination of Joseph II, the Dogma of Transubstantiation manifested arch-naturally, and the building of Corbenic as a Castle of Perils and Wonders girt about the Holy Grail ; (2) from the prototype of the *Elucidation* we have the Indicible Secret of the Grail, the seven discoveries of its Sanctuary, the account of the Rich Fisherman's skill in necromancy and his protean transformations by magical art ; (3) from the prototype of Robert de Borron we have the Secret Words, by him or subsequently referred to Eucharistic Consecration ; (4) from the prototype of Chrétien we have the History of Perceval le Gallois, so far as it was taken by him ; (5) from the putative Chronicle of Blaise and his scribes, succeedant and concurrent, we have all that which belongs to the History of Merlin, the foundation of the Round Table and the Siege Perilous ; (6) from the affirmed prototype of the LONGER PROSE PERCEVAL we have Perceval's Later History, his great and final achievements—unlike all else in the literature, more sad, more beautiful, more strange than anything told otherwise concerning him ; (7) from the alleged prototype of Kyot, we have the Grail presented as a Stone and with an ascribed Antecedent History which is the antithesis of all other Histories. Had I set up these varying versions in the form of seven propositions on the Gates of Salerno or Salamanca and offered to maintain their identity in a thesis against all comers, I suppose that I could have made out a case with the help of scholastic casuistry and the rest of the dialectical subtleties ; but in the absence of all motive, and detached as regards the result, I can say only that the Quests and the Histories as we have them never issued from a single Quest or a single History. We may believe, if we please, that the Book of the Count of Flanders was really the QUEST of Kyot, reducing the sources to six ; and a certain ingenuity—with courage towards precarious positions—may help one to further eliminations ; but the root-difficulty will remain, namely, that the Quests, as we have them, exclude one another and so also do some of the Histories. It follows that there were many prototypes, or alternatively that there were many inventions in respect of the sources. As to those of the Perceval Legends, we can say no longer—having regard to the latest findings of scholarship—that there was a non-Grail folk-lore Myth which accounts for their root-matter, though not for their particular renderings and not for their individual Grail elements ; but there is at least a talismanic Early History presupposed by the PERLESVAUS. One general source of Borron was transparently the EVANGELIUM NICODEMI, complicated by later Joseph Legends, including possibly the Tradition of Fécamp ; but more than all there is the shadow of another hypothetical source, about which he had heard at a distance and of which I shall speak at the close. The QUEST OF GALAHAD lays no claim on a prototype, but it reflects extant manuscripts of the Vulgate Cycle. For the rest, its own story was of all importance : it cared little for antecedents, and it was only by sporadic precaution, outside its normal lines, that it registers at the close after what manner it claimed to be reduced into writing. Except in so far as it echoes some rumours—and it does so indubitably—which Robert de Borron had drawn into Romance, the authentic prototypes of this text are in the Annals of Sanctity. As regards Galahad himself, his Romance is a great invention derived from the prose LANCELOT. The LONGER PROSE PERCEVAL is an invention after another manner : there is nothing to warrant us in attaching any credit to the imputed Josephus source, but the book drew from many places and transmuted that which it drew with a shaping spirit : it is an important text for those rumours to which I have referred darkly. It works, like the QUEST OF GALAHAD, in a broad region of similitude, and its pretended source is connected intimately with the Second Joseph of the Vulgate Cycle.

We are now in a position to deal with the further ascription which is so general in the literature and was once accepted rather widely—namely, that of a Latin source. It will be noted that this is a simple debate on language, and it leaves the unity or multiplicity of prototypes an open question. It is worth mentioning, because it enters into the history of the criticism of Grail literature. There is no need to say that it is repudiated now by scholarship, and the first person to reject it was Robert Southey in his Preface to the edition of Sir Thomas Malory's MORTE D'ARTHUR which passes under his name, though he had no hand in the editing of the text itself. " I do not believe," he says, " that any of these Romances ever existed in Latin,—by whom, or for whom, could they have been written in that language ? " For the Romances as Romances, for MELIADUS DE LEONNOIS, GYRON LE COURTOIS, and so forth, the question has one answer only, the fact notwithstanding that the Prologue to GUIRON draws all the prose tales of the Round Table from what it terms the Latin BOOK OF THE HOLY GRAIL. There is one answer also for any version of the Grail Legend, as we now know it. Even for that period, the Comte de Tressan committed a serious absurdity when he affirmed that the whole literature of Arthurian Chivalry, derived by the Bretons from the ancient and fabulous Chronicles of Melkin and Tezelin, was written in Latin by Rusticien de Pise, who was simply a very late compiler and translator into the Italian tongue and was concerned, as such, chiefly with the Tristram Cycle. At the same time it is possible to take too extreme a view. In his Preface to another work, PALMERIN OF ENGLAND, Southey remarks that " every reader of Romances knows how commonly they were represented as translations from old manuscripts," and that such an ascription, " instead of proving that a given work was translated, affords some evidence that it is original " The inference is worded too strongly and is scarcely serious as it stands, but the fact itself is certain ; and indeed the Grail Romances belong to a class of literature which was prone to false explanations in respect both of authorship and language. Still, there is something to be said for the middle ground suggested, now long ago, on the authority of Paulin Paris : that while it is idle to talk of Romances in the Latin Language, there is nothing impossible in the suggestion that the Sacramental Legend of Joseph of Arimathæa and his Sacred Vessel may have existed in Latin. From his point of view it was a Gradual, and he even goes so far as to speculate (1) that it was preserved at Glastonbury ; (2) that it was not used by the monks because it involved schism with Rome ; and (3) that, like the Jew of Toledo's transcript, it was forgotten for three centuries, being recalled at last by the quarrel between Henry II and the Pope. This is of course fantasy, but the bare supposition of such a Latin Legend would account in the natural manner for an ascription which is singularly consistent, while it would not pretend to represent an imagined lost prototype of the whole complex literature.

In this connection we might do worse than take warning by one lesson from the literature of Alchemy. The early Latin writers on this subject were in the habit of citing authorities who were regarded at times as mythical because they could not be identified ; all the same many existed in manuscript : they might have been found by those who took the pains ; and some are familiar to students at this day by the edition of Berthelot. In matters of this kind we do not know what a day may bring forth, and from all standpoints the existence of a pious Legend—orthodox or heretical,

Roman or Breton—concerning Joseph and his Hallow would be priceless rather than valuable. Unfortunately, the Quest of the Holy Grail in respect of its missing texts is after the manner of a yet greater enterprise, for there are many who follow it and few that come to the term of a new discovery.[1] There are authorities now in England to whom the possibility of such a text would not be unacceptable, though criticism dwells rightly upon the fact that there is no mention of the Holy Vessel in the earliest legendary records of the Evangelisation of Britain by Joseph.[2] We have heard already of one Latin memorial among the Archives of Fécamp, but of its date we know nothing, and its Conversion Legend does not belong to these islands.

Having thus determined, as I think, the question of a single prototype accounting for all the literature, we have to realise that everything remains respecting the Mystery of Origin and rumours thereupon—claims on behalf of the Celtic Church and Sacramental Legends incorporated from Latin Christianity into the great body of Romances. But I speak here of things which are approximate and explicable in an atmosphere of Myth married to a definite world of Doctrine. There is nothing in these to explain (1) the report of a Secret Sanctuary in all texts without any exception whatever ; for even the foolish CROWN OF ALL ADVENTURES allocates its House of Ghosts to the loneliest of all roads ; (2) the Secret Words of Consecration ; (3) the Arch-Natural Mass celebrated in three of the texts ; (4) the supposititious Hidden Priesthood ; (5) the claim on a Holy and Hidden Knowledge ; (6) the removal of this Knowledge from concealment to further concealment, because the world was not worthy. These are the rumours to which I have alluded previously, and I have attached to them this name, because there is nothing more obvious in the whole Cycle of Literature than the fact that those who wrote of them did not—for the most part—know what they said. Now, it is a canon of reasonable criticism that writers who make use of materials which they do not understand are not the inventors thereof. It may have never entered into the heart of Robert de Borron that his Secret Words reduced the ordinary Eucharist to something approaching a semblance ; to the putative Walter Map that his first Bishop of Christendom reduced the Christian Apostolate to an inferior place ; to any one of the romancers that his Secret Sanctuary was the claim of an orthodoxy in transcendence ; to the authors in particular of the LONGER PROSE PERCEVAL and the QUEST OF GALAHAD that their implied House of the Hallows came perilously near to a taking of the heart out of Christendom. So little did these things occur to them that their materials are mismanaged rather seriously in consequence. From the first Bishop of Christendom, the Second Joseph of the GRAND SAINT GRAAL, we find that the custody of the Sacred Vessel passed into the hands of a layman, and we are offered the picture of a Priest anointed by Christ who does not even baptise, a Hermit on one occasion being obtained to administer this simplest of all the Sacraments. And yet the First Bishop of Christendom had ordained many and enthroned some at Sarras. There is a similar crux in the LESSER HOLY GRAIL and its companion poem. One would have thought that the possession of the Secret Words would be reserved to those bearing the Seal of the Priesthood ; but it is not suggested that Joseph of Arimathæa was either ordained by Christ or by any Bishop of the Church ;

---

[1] St. Matthew vii, 14.
[2] I should include Dr. J. Armitage Robinson, Dean of Wells. Cp. Two GLASTONBURY LEGENDS, 1926.

his successor, Brons, was simply a disciple saved out of rejected Jerusalem ; while Perceval, the *tiers hons*, was a Knight of King Arthur's Court. Of two things therefore one : either the makers of Romance who brought in these elements knew not what they said, reflecting at a far distance that which they had heard, or the claims are not those which they appear on the surface : beneath them there is a deeper concealment. There was something behind the Eucharistic aspect of the Mysterious Formula and something behind the Ordination in Transcendence : there was in fine a more Secret Service than that of a Roman Mass.

If it is necessary to posit the existence of a single primordial Book, then the SANCTUM GRAAL, LIBER GRADALIS, or MISSA DE CORPORE CHRISTI contained these elements, and it contained nothing or little of the diverse matter in the literature. It was not a Liturgy connected with the veneration of a Relic ; it did not recite the Legend of Joseph or account in what manner soever for the Conversion of Britain. It was a Rite as of an Order of Melchisedech and it communicated the arch-natural sacrament *ex hypothesi*. The Prologue to the GRAND SAINT GRAAL has what one would be inclined to call a rumour of this Mass, after which there supervened an ecstasy, as a foretaste of the Divine Rapture.   The term thereof was the Vision which is He ; and the motive of the Dilucid Experience is evaded—consciously or not, but I say, in truth unconsciously—by the substitute of reflections upon difficulties concerning the Trinity.   No Grail writer had ever seen this Book, but the rumour of it was about in the world.   It was held in reserve, not in a monastery at Glastonbury, but by a Secret School of Christians whose position in respect of current orthodoxy was that of the apex to the base of any perfect triangle—its completion and not its destruction. There was more of the rumour abroad than might have been expected antecedently, as if a Church of St. John the Divine were planted somewhere in the West, but not in the open day.   There was more of the rumour, and some makers of texts had heard more than others. We know that in the Prologue to the GRAND SAINT GRAAL there is what might be taken as a reference to this Company, the members of which were sealed, so that they could recognise one another by something which they bore upon their persons.   When, in the QUEST OF GALAHAD, the Nine Strange Knights came from the East and the West and the North and the South to sit down, or to kneel rather, at the Table of the Grail, they entered without challenge ; they took their proper places and were saluted and welcomed, because they also bore the seal of the Secret Order.   King Pelles went out because he was not on the Quest, because his part was done, because he had attained and seen, for which reason he departed as one who says : *Nunc dimittis Servum tuum, Domine, secundum verbum tuum in pace : quia viderunt oculi mei*—elsewhere or earlier—*salutare tuum*.   The minstrels and romancers knew little enough of these Mysteries, for the most part, and on the basis of the rumours of the book they superposed what they had heard otherwise—the Legend of Joseph, the Cultus of the Precious Blood, Clouds of Fables, Multiples of Relics—*hoc genus omne*.   But it is to be noted in fine that the withdrawal into deeper concealment referred more especially to the Company as a Hidden School, which would be sought and not found, unless God led the Seeker.   And perhaps those who came into contact by accident did not always ask the Question : Who administers the Mysteries ?   Yet if they were elected they were brought in subsequently.

It will be observed that in this last speculation the existence of those rumours which were incorporated does not in a strict sense involve the existence of any Book to account for their comparative prevalence.

XXXIII

GIFTS OF UNDERSTANDING

(XII, § 5, p. 522.)

I HAVE indicated in other places that it is we who give meanings to Nature and that she speaks to us with our own voice. So also that which we learn about her is not only that which she reveals to research of mind but is a discovery of mind therein. We are therefore the standard of comparison and the touchstone of Truth. The standard varies from age to age, because of the growth of mind. It is for this reason that the authentic knowledge of Nature is greater far than it was in remote ages or a hundred years ago. We may not dream as yet of that which remains to be found by mind at the highest—highest, that is to say, in comparison with that which it is to-day— because the Absolute is always before us, seeing that there is no end of knowing. We give our meanings also to old books—I am speaking of great old books—and if we have a true canon of criticism concerning them we are liberated from the old folly which was presupposed for so long, namely, that they are the records of the meanings of those who wrote them, as if by some law of necessity. It is encouraging in a few unquestioned cases to know the fact; but it is of more living importance that they are ours than that they are also theirs—supposing that they are ours at the highest of our highest part of mind. Now, that which the Grail books can give to us here " in the foremost files of time " is likely to be of more living importance than at any epoch of the past.

XXXIV

THE GRAIL AND THE SACRAMENT

(XII, § 5, p. 523.)

IT has been said by a certain school of interpretation, but it has failed so far to satisfy the other schools in respect of its titles, that the Grail Vessel is that which contains the universe. There is unfortunately a recurring disposition to put forward suppositions on the basis of research in other fields, and without specific acquaintance with the particular field covered by the speculation which is taken thus lightly in hand. The statement in question is not true in the sense that is intended, because far Eastern symbolism is not to be identified with that which prevails in the West. It is true, how- ever, and exhaustive in its accuracy from another standpoint, as also in a dual manner : (1) because those who receive the Eucharist, not in the sense of an outward symbol and the Official Doctrine concerning it but according to the highest grade and manner of reception, do or may behold the beginning and the end ; and (2) because man in this manner enters into the conscious- ness of himself as being actually that Vessel of Reflection which testifies of everything without to the *centrum concentratum* within. In such sense we may pray all of us that a time will come when man shall reflect in his universal glass of vision that truth which is within the universe and not only its external impressions. When this comes to pass it can be said of him, as it was said once of Perceval: *Et li seintimes Gréax ne s'aperra plus çà dedanz ; mes vos sauroiz bien trusqu'a brief terme là ou il iere ;* " And the Most Holy Grail shall appear no more herein ; but in a brief space shall you know well the place where it shall be ".

The age which saw the production of the Grail literature was, in all the public places, far from this goal like ourselves. The communication of Him Who is *Alpha* and *Omega*, Who brings with Him the knowledge of the beginning and the end, took place in the symbol, not in the life essential ; and the first-hand revelation of Mysteries was therefore wanting. That which Doctrine and ordinary Devotional Practice contrived to impress upon men's memories and to impose on their faith offered an exercise to their intelligence, but in the activity intelligence was baffled. The Sword of the Spirit broke upon the Ineffable Mystery of the Kingdom of Heaven, as the Sword of Perceval broke upon the gate of entrance to the Earthly Paradise. The Hermit-Priest who tells his wonderful story at the inception of the GRAND SAINT GRAAL is in labour with the problem of the Trinity, and when his praying and longing have carried him to the Third Heaven, it is this secret of the Eternal Sanctity which is unveiled before the eyes of his soul. Many noble and learned clerks—Hermits and Anchoresses innumerable—did not toil less hard but without reaping so high a reward. They also who wrote of these wonders in the best sense thereof had their own limitations, and keenly defined enough. It is thus that I account personally for the gross material side of the Grail wonders : to say that they may have come over from folk-lore is a statement of possible fact simply and does not explain their toleration side by side therewith, as a part of the Mystery of Faith. Yet there was also a superincession of the old Pagan Myths and the recognised implicits of Eucharistic Doctrine, namely, that the Inward Spiritual Nourishment may have, as Tradition testifies, a reflex action by which it contributes to physical welfare. He, in other words, who communicates in the higher state in those symbols of Bread and Wine, by which in sacramental hypothesis the Divine is conveyed, as if from without, to the man within, may receive some part and reflection in his external nature of that Grace which is realised on the inward side of his being. It is in this sense that the body as well as the soul can testify at the Altar Rails that it is good to be here. A very curious point is developed in this connection by the mystical theologian Gorres, who affirms—at its fantastic value—that in ordinary nourishment he who eats being superior to that which is eaten assimilates the elements which he receives ; but the transmuted food of the Eucharist is more potent than he who partakes, and instead of being assimilated by him, it is a nutriment which assimilates the man and raises him to a higher sphere. Because of the solidarity between body, soul and spirit, it is to be said therefore that the *salus, honor, virtus quoque* which awaken in our higher part have also their operation without. The food-giving powers are not therefore a counterpart of the *epulum ex oblatis* but a *reductio ad fabulam* of the spiritual truth that Grace sustains Nature, and a guarantee in perpetuity that the Quest of the Kingdom of God will never fail for want of Sacred Taverns carrying a full licence at all points of the way. The Dish of Plenty is therefore a simulacrum of *manna abscondita*, and the Priest who says Mass in his

Chapel, with zeal and recollection, not apart from illumination, turning at the due time to utter his *Sursum corda* in the living sense, is doing more in the fellowship of humanity than all the corporal works of mercy, pressed down and overflowing. He will be inspired assuredly in his season so to organise the higher charity that his people shall be fitly prepared to receive on their part, he offering and dispensing freely with open and venerable hands.

In respect further of the Manna itself, the PERLESVAUS, figuratively speaking, gets nearest of all to the Mystery when it indicates the exaltation of the Recipient by five in the five manifested changes. The text indeed is like a prolonged *Hosannah* or a *Gloria in Excelsis* chanted from scene to scene in a great Cycle of Romance. The same note runs through all the Legends, and its last echo is heard faintly in the late Lohengrin Romance. In this Swan Story the chain of one of the swans was made into two Chalices and, Mass being said therein, the bird was restored to his proper human form. This is like an Eucharistic allegory concerning the deligation of the body by Divine Substance communicated to the soul and putting a period to the Enchantments and Sorceries of the five senses.

I conclude therefore, with pseudo-Dionysius, that the Eucharist in its true understanding is the first of Divine Mysteries ; with the PARAPHRASE of St. Maximus, that it is the consummation of all other Sacraments ; leaving over the Official Doctrine of the Latin Church, that it operates by intrinsic efficacity, *ex opere operato*, in virtue of its Institution by Christ.

XXXV

A LAST RETROSPECT

(XII, § 6, p. 533.)

As an illustration of the fact that the Grail Cycles were not successive or variant memorials of Independent Temples, Chapters or Lodges of an incorporated Secret School, we may take the late editing which produced the Vulgate Series. There is no question that it followed a plan and had thus a fixed purpose in view. But that object emerges as the glorification of Lancelot. It is he who is the chief figure, from the moment when the Round Table began to shine in the light of fame and honour to the end of all, after it is broken and destroyed, he among the few surviving and making his good end in Priesthood, an example to the sad remanent of the Great Chivalry. *Pace* the testimony of King Pelles to his deflowered Daughter, there is no manifest reason or real necessity in the scheme of things that Lancelot should beget Galahad, except unawares to magnify his own status. Perceval, *e.g.*, could have brought him forth in the chastity of lawful marriage.

The fact to which I have adverted is exemplified further by the many points which are left in doubt there and here in the chief texts, an intolerable position in the case of ordered memorials going forth into the world. A few instances may be drawn together into a series, beginning with the Borron Cycle. (I) The notable point that the Secret Words pronounced over the Chalice were never used, so far as records are concerned, though the Daily Grail Service, held at the Hour of Tierce according to the Metrical JOSEPH, suggests that this Service was a Mass. In such case, they were uttered secretly at the Consecration of the Elements. The inference is strong, but the need is open witness. (2) The fact that Petrus, who had a conspicuous part in the general programme, disappears completely—Mission and Brief and all. (3) The conspiracy of silence as to the kind of Enchantments which befell Britain, paralleled by the same reservation in the Vulgate Series respecting Adventurous Times. (4) The introduction of a Fish Symbolism, under circumstances which suggest importance; but the Symbolism passes away and is forgotten.

I have spoken already of the Vulgate Cycle in connection with Lancelot. The intent of the general scheme emerges with a certain clearness in his respect ; yet we must remember that the long sequence of texts is designed also to bring about the destruction of the Marvellous Lion (Arthur), his Court, his Chivalry, and almost Logres itself. But it is invalidated according to the logic of things by a complete absence of all cause and reason. We are left to make our own explanations and persuade ourselves thereon.

The Grail regarded as a literature represents a very curious development of symbolism, an extension and growth in meaning. Surveyed synthetically, we may say and think that the Galahad Path of Quest and the term attained therein were implied from the beginning in the ecstasy which fell upon communicants at the Second Table, according to Robert de Borron, and in that of the Hermit Priest Nasciens, midwise during his Mass of the Presanctified on a Good Friday, according to the Prologue of the GRAND SAINT GRAAL. But this is not to say that it was ever dreamed of by Chrétien and succeeding poets of the CONTE DEL GRAAL, though it may be held that Gerbert de Montreuil would have served this Mass worthily, and that Wolfram would have uttered a DEO GRATIAS, when he remembered that the Grail of his making was renewed from year to year by a Host which came from Heaven. Albrecht, in fine, might have realised on his knees that there are more things in the Roman Rite than Rome itself has dreamed, save in the Angel of the Schools. We also on our own part may begin to see after what manner the imagined Secret Words were a Guiding Voice on the Mystery of Divine Substance communicated to the soul, while the Super-Apostolical Succession was the Ordination and the Priesthood of those who know the Great Attainment behind the Veils of Bread and Wine. So falls into its place and into its high order the seeming medley of the symbolism, and we divine more fully why the Grail went about in some of the Quests and why the Grail Castle was—as it is indeed—in many places of the world ; how the Grail came into the City of Sarras and wrought its wonders ; how it went back thereto and ascended to Heaven therefrom. The great things must bear their witness in the unbelieving world, because those who are capable of election may be found everywhere.

As regards the Keepers of the Grail, in the Quests that really signify, they are those who hand on the Mystery, so that the Grail Temple is like a House of Initiation. But it receives only those who are of the true legitimacy— who are prepared and qualified. Having communicated, they repair to their reward above or remain in the Temple—fundamentally, it matters little— except in the Galahad Quest, which is silent on the life of King Pelles after the Palladium left Corbenic. It passed, as we may dream, in a Hiddenness behind the Hiddenness, where the Grail Castle dissolves into the Earthly Paradise.

APPENDIX II

A BRIEF METHODISED BIBLIOGRAPHY OF THE HOLY GRAIL IN LITERATURE AND CRITICISM

PART I

THE TEXTS

IT is desirable that the limitations of these sections should be made plain from the beginning. A complete Bibliography of the Holy Grail in literature and criticism should include, so far as the texts are concerned, a sufficient study of the chief manuscripts ; while in respect of critical works it should embrace a survey of continental periodical literature—chiefly French and German—wherein contributions of importance to the subject-general are and will remain imbedded. For he study of the manuscripts there has been no opportunity in my own case, and it would exceed, moreover, the scope of my present purpose : it is a work which remains to be done, and so far back as 1888, speaking of the CONTE DEL GRAAL, MR. DAVID NUTT indicated the need of collating all codices in order to arrive at conclusions respecting the growth of the work. For the rest, DR. J. D. BRUCE has appended to his EVOLUTION OF ARTHURIAN ROMANCE an almost exhaustive analysis of the printed literature, to which readers may be referred, premising only that it is methodised so roughly as to be little better than a chaos. I have confined myself, on my own part, to the Bibliography of the texts themselves ; to the most important of the critical works ; and to a few characteristic essays towards interpretation, because these—whatever their value—will be of interest to those whom I address, if only as counsels of caution.

A. LE CONTE DEL GRAAL.—I. *Le Poème de* CHRÉTIEN DE TROYES *et de ses continuateurs d'après le manuscrit de* MONS, being vols. 2 to 6 of PERCEVAL LE GALLOIS, *ou le Conte du Graal. Vide infra* for the first volume, containing the Romance in prose. This is so far the only printed edition of the complete work, all unquestioned continuations included, and it was produced under the auspices of C. POTVIN for the *Société des Bibliophiles Belges.* It appeared from 1866 to 1871, and copies are exceedingly rare. The text is that of a manuscript in the *Bibliothèque Communale de* MONS, and *qua* text it is considered unfavourably by scholarship. The equipment of the editor has been regarded also as insufficient, but the pains which made the poem available deserve our highest thanks, and the gift has been priceless. It may be useful to repeat that the work of CHRÉTIEN is held now to have ended at line 9,198 ; that of the anonymous poet who is known as pseudo-WAUCHIER at line 21,917 ; and that of WAUCHIER DE DENAIN at line 34,934 ; while the conclusion of MANESSIER extends the work to 45,379 lines, outside which there is the alternative version of GERBERT, which exceeds 15,000. The *excursus* which M. POTVIN appended to his last volume is still pleasant reading but represents no special research and at need is almost negligible. It seems to look favourably on the dream of a Latin primordial Grail text ; it affirms that the CONTE was called the *Bible du Démon* by Gallic monks of old and that LANCELOT OF THE LAKE was placed on the Index by Innocent III.

II. CRESTIENS VON TROYES : CONTE DEL GRAAL, PERCEVAUS LI GALOIS. *Abdruck der Handschrift Paris, français, 794, mit Ammerkungen und Glossar,* edited by G. BAIST. This appeared in 1909 and again in 1912, the original issue being withdrawn, owing to its numerous errors. The text edited is superior to that of Mons.

III. *Ueber einen bisher unbekannten* PERCHEVAL LI GALLOIS, by ALFRED ROCHAT, Zurich, 1855. It is chiefly to this work that we owe our knowledge of the Berne PERCEVAL, of which a full account is given, including considerable extracts. The codex is important for textual purposes, but its concluding part only is of moment to ourselves, as an attempt to complete the Quest of Perceval practically within the limits of WAUCHIER'S extension, which it does, in a summary manner, by recounting how the hero becomes Keeper of the Grail. The version follows the historical matter of the Borron Cycle. The Fisher King is Brons ; he is the Father of Alain le Gros ; and his wife is sister to Joseph of Arimathæa. It will be noted that this is the succession of the DIDOT-MODENA PERCEVAL, the Keepership not passing to Alain. An introductory study deals with the Grail Legend and opposes SAN MARTE'S view that the PEREDUR MABINOGI is earlier than the work of CHRÉTIEN.

IV. *Trèsplaisante et Recréative Hystoire du très preulx et vaillant chevallier* PERCEVAL LE GALLOYS, . . . *lequel acheva les adventures du Sainct Graal,* etc., Paris, 1530. This is the prose version of the CONTE DEL GRAAL and some of its chapter-headings are given among the marginal notes of Potvin's text of the poem. It includes, in certain copies, the important *Elucidation,* which was long thought to exist only in this form. The object which actuated the edition is stated very simply—namely, to produce a work which had long become archaic in an available version. As such, it might appeal to some readers who would be hindered by the difficulties of the original ; but it is to be found only in a few great libraries. In 1918 M. GUILLAUME APOLLINAIRE edited a cheap and partial reprint in the *Nouvelle Bibliothèque Bleue.* The Adventures of Monseigneur Gawain are omitted and the spelling is modernised. While the edition is critically worthless in all respects, it might serve a certain purpose for the general reader. Recently DR. MARY WILLIAMS has undertaken to edit the GERBERT continuation for *Les Classiques Français du Moyen Age.* There are two known MSS.

B. THE CYCLE OF ROBERT DE BORRON, which may be called also the LESSER CHRONICLES OF THE HOLY GRAIL, though there is no collection of manuscripts which has been classified previously under this descriptive title.

I. LE ROMAN DU SAINT GRAAL, *publié pour la première fois d'après un manuscrit de la Bibliothèque Royale, par* FRANCISQUE MICHEL, Bordeaux, 1841. The manuscript in question was considered unique at the time and the poem of ROBERT DE BORRON which is now under notice consists of 3514 lines. There is a lacuna between lines 2752 and 2753, being at and about that point when destruction overwhelms the false Moses in the prose version, which supplies thus what is missing. The Metrical Romance was reprinted in the *Dictionnaire des Légendes,* being part of the *Troisième . . . Encyclopédie*

Théologique of the ABBÉ MIGNE, now out of print and scarce. It was included by DR. FURNIVALL in his edition of the SEYNT GRAAL or the SANK RYAL, printed for the Roxburghe Club, 2 vols., 1861–1863. An edition of BORRON has been printed by Professor W. A. NITZE in *Les Classiques Français du Moyen Age.*

It seems desirable to couple with this text certain archaic English versions of the Joseph Legends : (1) the alliterative poem of JOSEPH OF ARAMATHIE, otherwise, the ROMANCE OF THE SEINT GRAAL, known only by the Vernon MS. at Oxford which belongs to the middle of the fourteenth century. It is a summary of the GRAND SAINT GRAAL, beginning with the release of Joseph from the Tower and ending with the departure from Sarras. It is imperfect at the inception and, of course, breaks off far from the term. (2) The LIFE OF JOSEPH OF ARMATHY, printed by Wynkyn de Worde and corresponding to the account given by CAPGRAVE in his NOVA LEGENDA ANGLIÆ. It claims to be founded on a book discovered by the Emperor Theodosius at Jerusalem. It is evident, however, that its real source is the GRAND SAINT GRAAL, though the account of JOSEPH's imprisonment follows the Apocryphal Gospel of Nicodemus and there is no reference to the Holy Vessel. (3) The LYFE OF JOSEPH OF ARMATHIA, believed to have been written about the year 1502 and first printed in 1520. The authorship is entirely unknown and so are manuscripts prior to publication. It is, of course, much too late to possess any historical importance but is exceedingly curious, and in spite of rude verse and chaotic manner is not without a certain pictorial sense and vividness. In place of the Sacred Vessel of Reception there are two cruets substituted in which the Blood of Christ was collected by Joseph. These fragments are all included by the REV. W. W. SKEAT in his JOSEPH OF ARIMATHIE, published by the Early English Text Society in 1871.

II. LE PETIT SAINT GRAAL, *ou Joseph d'Arimathie,* otherwise the LESSER HOLY GRAIL, is known by a number of MSS., one of which is called Cange : it belongs to the thirteenth century and is preserved in the *Bibliothèque Nationale* at Paris. Two codices, together with a version in modern French, are included in the first volume of LE SAINT GRAAL, published by EUGÈNE HUCHER, 3 vols., Paris, 1874. This text was regarded by the editor as ROBERT DE BORRON's original work, from which the metrical version was composed later on by an unknown hand.

III. THE EARLY PROSE MERLIN. We have seen that the Metrical Romance of Joseph concludes at line 3514, after which the unique MS. proceeds, without any break, to the Life of Merlin, reaching an abrupt term at line 4018, all being missing thereafter. The complete prose version forms the first part of the VULGATE and the second of the HUTH MERLIN, bibliographical particulars of which are given later. It follows from one, and apparently one only, of the EARLY MERLIN codices that ROBERT DE BORRON proposed as his next branch to take the life of Alain, and in so stating he or his personator uses some of the words which occur in the colophon of his JOSEPH poem. It appears further that the Alain branch was intended to shew how the problematical and ever unexplained Enchantments fell upon Britain.

IV. PERCEVAL, OU LA QUÊTE DU SAINT GRAAL, *par* ROBERT DE BORRON, otherwise, the DIDOT PERCEVAL, because—as explained elsewhere already— it was once in the collection of M. Firmin Didot. This text is included in the first volume of Hucher's compilation, with a summary prefixed thereto.

The date borne by the MS. is 1301. Critical opinion is perhaps divided equally, or was at least in the past, on the question whether this LESSER PROSE PERCEVAL does or does not represent the third part of a Metrical Trilogy composed by ROBERT DE BORRON. THE name of GASTON PARIS can be ranged on the affirmative side and on the negative that of MR. ALFRED NUTT. The negative view has prevailed of later days. The Modena codex of this Romance was discovered subsequently and was printed by Miss Weston in the second volume of her LEGEND OF SIR PERCEVAL, 1909 : it is much preferred by scholarship. I have spoken of the work throughout as the DIDOT-MODENA PERCEVAL.

C. THE VULGATE CHRONICLES OF THE HOLY GRAIL, so-called in the accepted classification of a particular sequence of texts.

I. LE SAINT GRAAL OU JOSEPH D'ARIMATHIE, called also LE GRAND SAINT GRAAL, LESTOIRE and, otherwise, THE BOOK OF THE HOLY GRAIL. There are several manuscripts, among which may be mentioned that of the Bibliothèque de la Ville de Mans, which is referred to the middle of the thirteenth century. Other texts are at Cambridge and at the British Museum. It was first edited by FURNIVALL (Op. cit.) from the MSS. preserved in England, and subsequently by HUCHER, forming Vols. 2 and 3 of his collection, as described previously. DR. FURNIVALL included also the English rendering called THE SAINT GRAAL or SANK RYAL, known by a single MS. attributed to the middle of the fifteenth century. The work is in conventional verse of exceedingly poor quality, the author being HENRY LOVELICH or LONELICH, described as a skinner, but of whom no particulars are forthcoming. It is a rendering by way of summary extending to nearly 24,000 lines, with several extensive lacunæ. Outside the testimony of its existence to the interest in Grail literature, as illustrated by the pains of translation at length so great, it has no importance for our subject. How-ever, it was edited again by the same scholar (1874–78) for the Early English Text Society, but after more than fifty years remains incomplete, no titles and no satisfactory introduction to the text having been produced. Finally the LESTOIRE DEL SAINT GRAAL was edited by DR. H. OSKAR SOMMER at Washington in 1909, under the auspices of the Carnegie Institution, as Volume I of the VULGATE VERSION OF THE ARTHURIAN ROMANCES. Under any circumstances this would constitute the foremost edition of the text and is that alone under which it is available readily to students, the earlier editions being long out of print and very difficult to obtain.

II. LESTOIRE DE MERLIN, otherwise, LE ROMAN DE MERLIN and the EARLY HISTORY OF KING ARTHUR. The most recent French text is that of DR. SOMMER in the second volume of his VULGATE VERSION OF THE ARTHURIAN ROMANCES, 1908, based on Add. MSS. 10292 in the British Museum. The prose version of ROBERT DE BORRON's substantially lost poem is brought to its term in this edition at p. 88, with the words Ensi fu artus esleus a roy & tint la terre & le regne de logres lonc tans en pais. DR. SOMMER had edited the same text, with a valuable introduction, so far back as 1894. The reader may compare with both and is likely to use at his pleasure the important MERLIN, or the EARLY HISTORY OF KING ARTHUR, edited for the Early English Text Society by MR. HENRY B. WHEATLEY, 1865–1899, which during this modest period of thirty-four years has certainly produced a satisfactory edition of the anonymous rendering of the VULGATE MERLIN in an unique MS. of the University Library,

Cambridge. The text is allocated to A.D. 1450–1460, and as a translation it is fairly representative of the French original. A metrical version was edited also from an Auchinleck MS. by PROF. E. KOELLING in his ARTHUR UND MERLIN, Leipsic, 1890.

III. LE LIVRE DE LANCELOT DEL LAC, edited from Add. MS. 10293 in the British Museum and published by DR. SOMMER in Vols. III–V of his Vulgate Series as above described, 1910–1912. The LANCELOT appeared originally at Paris in three folio volumes, *anno* 1488, and as there were other editions it is desirable to mention that of 1533, which bears the imprint of Philip le Noir, because great stress has been laid thereon. In his *Study on the Sources* of MALORY'S MORTE DARTHUR, DR. SOMMER has taken as his basis the edition of 1513, but without expressing preference. It appears from this text (1) that Galahad was acquainted with his paternity even from his childhood and (2) that he was sent to the Abbey of White Nuns by King Pelles, his grandfather. The omission of these details by MALORY enhances the mystery of the story. Another early edition was that of 1494 and it is described by Southey in his Introduction to THE BYRTH, LYF AND ACTES OF KYNG ARTHUR, etc., 2 vols., 1817. This is MALORY'S MORTE DARTHUR. In 1929 MISS LUCY ALLEN PATON published SIR LANCELOT OF THE LAKE, translated from a manuscript in the *Bibliothèque Nationale*, with an Introduction and Notes. Having regard to the "huge body of material" comprised in the original, her preface explains that she has presented only those parts which are "fundamental for an understanding of the Legend", giving summaries of the incidents that connect them in the French text.

IV. LES AVENTURES OU LA QUESTE DEL SAINT GRAAL, the head and crown of the Legend, is, in the early printed texts, either incorporated with the prose LANCELOT, as in the edition of 1513, already mentioned, or with the GRAND SAINT GRAAL, as in the Paris edition of 1516, also described by SOUTHEY and called : L'HYSTOIRE DU SAINCT *Greaal, qui est le premier livre de la Table Ronde . . . Ensemble* LA QUESTE *dudict sainct Greaal, ffaicte par Lancelot, Galaad, Boors et Perceval qui est le dernier livre de la Table Ronde,* etc. The French QUESTE was edited for the first time by F. J. Furnivall, M.A., in 1864, for the Roxburghe Club. In DR. SOMMER's Vulgate Series LES AVENTURES OU LA QUESTE DEL SAINT GRAAL, 1913, comprises the sixth volume, together with LE MORT LE ROI ARTUS.

V. Everyone is aware that the great prose QUEST was rendered almost bodily into the MORTE DARTHUR, first printed by CAXTON in the year 1485, as the colophon of his last book sets forth. The full title is worth reproducing from the edition of ROBERT SOUTHEY, as follows : THE BYRTH, LYF, AND ACTES OF KYNG ARTHUR ; *of his Noble Knyghtes of the Rounde Table, theyr merveyllous enquestes and adventures, thachyeuyng of the* SANC GREAL ; *and in the end* LE MORTE DARTHUR, *with the Dolourous Deth and departyng out of thys worlde of them all.* DR. SOMMER faithfully reprinted the Caxton Malory in 1889—91, 3 vols., with introductions and studies on the sources. This is the definitive version, and as regards other editions, abridgments and modern productions they are too numerous for mention.

VI. M. ALBERT PAUPHILET edited LA QUESTE DEL SAINT GRAAL in 1923 for LES CLASSIQUES FRANÇAIS DU MOYEN AGE, a critical text with an Introduction which demands attention : it includes an enumeration of all known manuscripts and distinguishes in the long list three only which present particular versions, namely, *Bibliothèque Nationale*, 123 ; *ibid.*, 343 ; and *ib.*, 112.

VII. In 1926 Dr. W. W. Comfort, President of Haverford College, Pennsylvania, translated the *Queste* into English for the first time unabridged. It must be said regretfully that half the enchantment is lost in the modern vesture, which compares most dismally with that of Malory, nor are matters mended by the interminable moral and theological discourses now at last made available to ordinary readers : they are of course important for the student who is seeking to know the whole mind of the author ; but to such it is likely that they will be more welcome in the original French. I offer my homage to the genius and prudence of Malory.

VIII. The Welsh Quest, i.e. Y Seint Greal, *being the Adventures of King Arthur's Knights of the Round Table, in the Quest of the Holy Greal, and on other occasions.* Edited with a Translation and Glossary, by the Rev. Robert Williams, M.A., London, 1876. This is the first volume of Selections from the Hengwrt MSS., the second appearing in 1892 and containing the Gests of Charlemagne, with other texts outside our particular subject. The Welsh Quest is entitled simply The Holy Greal and is divided into two parts, of which the first concerns Galahad and his peers, the second being a recension of The Longer Prose Perceval to which I shall recur below.

D. Other Texts of the Grail Literature.—I. The Longer Prose Perceval. This text constitutes the first volume of Potvin's Conte du Graal *sub voce* Perceval le Gallois, like the Conte itself, otherwise, Le Roman en Prose. Of its translation by Dr. Sebastian Evans, under its proper title of The High History of the Holy Graal, I have said sufficient to indicate the gratitude which is due to a new creation of literature from those who are in the grace of literature. The original is known usually as the Perlesvaus in textual criticism. The date of composition is referred by its first editor to the end of the twelfth century, while later authorities have assigned it to a period a little prior to 1225. Dr. Bruce, however, has found reasons for deciding approximately on that date. The supposed unique manuscript by which it was known at first has been allocated broadly to the thirteenth century and is preserved in the *Bibliothèque de Bourgogne* at Brussels. The second of the Hengwrt Grail texts is a Welsh version of the Longer Prose Perceval and is a brief recension which abounds in mistranslations, though it supplies fortunately a missing portion of the French manuscript which would otherwise be lost, had the Bourgogne MS. proved unique, as Potvin believed. It may be added that the Berne MS., to which allusion has been made in several places of my text, contains two Perlesvaus fragments, some account of which has been given by Potvin and Dr. Evans. It should be understood further that since the edition of Potvin appeared in 1866 other codices have come to light, but it has not been suggested that they offer important variations. The Perlesvaus is said to have been printed in 1521, but I have failed to find particulars. It was announced a few years since that Professor W. A. Nitze is editing one of the recently discovered texts for the Carnegie Trustees.

II. The Huth Merlin, i.e. Merlin, *Roman en prose du XIIIe siècle, publié avec la mise en prose du poème de Merlin de Robert de Borron, d'après le manuscrit appartenant à* M. Alfred H. Huth, *par* Gaston Paris *et* Jacob Ulrich, 2 vols., Paris, 1886. The position and content of this Romance

have been dealt with so fully in the text that although much would remain
to be said in a complete analysis, it will be sufficient for my purpose to
enumerate three salient points : (*a*) the unique portion—which is the great
bulk of the story—is believed to have been composed after the LANCELOT ;
(*b*) it is perhaps for this reason that it shares responsibility for the unfavourable portraiture of Monseigneur Gawain which characterises much of the
Vulgate Cycle ; (*c*) in some undetermined way the death of a Lady who killed
herself over the body of a Knight, slain by Balyn in self-defence, is said by
Merlin to involve the latter in dealing " the stroke most dolorous that ever
man stroke, except the stroke of our Lord ". The mystery of this maiming
is never elucidated.

III. LES PROPHECIES DE MERLIN, edited from MS. 593 in the *Bibliothèque
Municipale de Rennes,* by LUCY ALLEN PATON, 2 vols., 1926, 1927, published
by the Modern Language Association of America. There are several early
editions of the so-called PROPHECIES, the original being that of 1498. Miss
PATON's admirable work has been noticed at length in Book V, sect. 3.

IV. We have seen that Sir Tristram went in search of the Grail according
to some of the French Romances dedicated to his adventures, including that
of the pseudo-Robert de Borron Cycle. Those who are disposed to go further
into this side issue may consult E. LOSETH's extended and excellent analysis
of the ROMAN DE TRISTAN, which forms *Fascicule* 82 of the *Bibliothèque de
l'École des Hautes Études,* Paris, 1890-91. He will there find Galahad
among the other Peers of the Quest ; but we have seen that he is no longer
more than a shadow of the Perfect Knight. An early but undated edition
of the Tristram story was printed at Paris for Anthoine Vérard and entitled
Histoire du très-vaillant, noble et excellent Chevalier TRISTRAN, *fils du Roi
Meliadus de Leonnois* (*redigée par* LUCE, *Chevalier, Seigneur du Chateau de
Gast*). 2 tomes in fol., Goth. Vérard is described as a *libraire demourant
près le pont nostre dame à lenseigne Saint Jehan levangeliste ou au
palais au premier pillier devant la chappelle ou on chante la Messe de
Messeigneurs de Parlement.* SOUTHEY said long ago that the characters
in the story " are in many instances discordant with themselves ; and the
fault, so frequent in such books, of degrading one hero to enhance the fame
of another, is carried here to great excess." Gawain is a case in point ; but
Southey was not in a position to appreciate the unintended dishonour fixed
upon Galahad, the hero of the Holy Quest, by reducing him to the common
herd of Chivalry on its truculent side.

V. SONE DE NAUSAY. This Northern French Poem of 21,321 lines was
edited at Tubingen in 1899 by MORITZ GOLDSCHMID and forms the 216th
publication *der Litterarischen Vereins in Stuttgart.* If another SEBASTIAN
EVANS were to be raised among us, I tend to think that the SONE after all
would make rather a talismanic story in English vesture, though of course
it has none of the great intimations which are found by the elect in the
PERLESVAUS.

VI. THE GRAIL IN ITALY. We have seen on the best authority that
" the story of the Holy Grail took no root in Italian soil " ; but it is obvious
that there will be Grail references at least in certain Italian versions of French
Arthurian texts. As regards manuscripts, e.g., the LANCILOTTO PANCIATI-
CHIANO, recourse must be had to the work of PROF. GARDNER, which is cited
frequently in my text, Book VI, § 7. The following printed texts demand a
brief notice. (1) IL TRISTANO RICCARDIANO, printed at Bologna, 1896, from

an incomplete MS. prior to the end of the thirteenth century and based broadly on the French text utilised by Malory in Book IX of the MORTE D'ARTHUR. There are no Grail references, though the Questing Beast of the Galahad QUESTE and the PERLESVAUS appears at one point. (2) IL TAVOLA RITONDA O L'ISTORIA DI TRISTANO, edited by F. L. POLIDORI, 2 vols., Bologna, 1864, 1865, based on three MSS., respectively *circa* 1350, 1391 and 1462. The text is concerned also with Lancelot *e di molti altri cavalieri*. It contains the Tristram debased version of the Galahad QUESTE and has been mentioned briefly in my text at the point already noted. (3) The French PERCEFOREST of 1528 and 1531, which is certainly not earlier and may be later than the middle of the fourteenth century, could scarcely be included under any circumstances with canonical Grail texts, and I have written already about it. It should be noted that an abridged rendering appeared in Italian at Venice in 1556–1558 as *La dilettevole historia del valorosissimo* PARSEFORESTO *Re della gran Brettagna, con i gran fatti del valente* GADIFFERO RE DI SCOTIA, *vero essempio di Cavalleria.* (4) *L'illustra et famosa historia di* LANCILOTTO DEL LAGO, Venice, 1558, 1559, is a version of the French LANCELOT of 1533, which includes the Galahad QUESTE and the MORT ARTUS.

VII. THE SPANISH AND PORTUGUESE CYCLES. Among the more popular historians of Spanish literature in the past, it was customary to dismiss the texts of Romantic Chivalry with the citation of a few typical examples, such as PALMERIN OF ENGLAND and DON BELIANIS OF GREECE, with AMADIS OF GAUL as inspiration and source of all and usually claimed as Spanish, though unquestionably of Portuguese origin. The fact of an Arthurian Cycle in either of these countries was thus hidden from general knowledge until comparatively recent times. DR. BRUCE gave a few bibliographical pages for a starting-point of instruction, but it remained—as we have seen—for MR. W. J. ENTWISTLE to embody the researches of years in a considerable volume which is and will be likely to remain our expert source of reference. Information was available, however, from anterior directions to those who sought, and the list which follows is drawn from all quarters, it being understood that, as previously, I am concerned with Spanish and Portuguese Arthurian texts so far only as they belong to the matter of the Grail. (1) EL BALADRO DEL SABIO MERLIN CON SUS PROFICIAS, printed at Burgos in 1498, of which there is a single extant copy in a private library at Madrid. The analysis of contents furnished to Gaston Paris shewed it to comprise: (a) the EARLY PROSE MERLIN of Robert de Borron; (b) the continuation of the HUTH MERLIN, so far as the recital of the Marriage of Arthur and Guinevere, or a few pages further; and (c) three final chapters which are unknown in the extant Merlin texts but are thought to be derived from the lost CONTE DU BRAIT of the so-called Hélie de Borron. See the Introduction of Gaston Paris to the HUTH MERLIN, I, pp. LXXII *et seq.*, and an extended appendix which contains not only substantial extracts but a full table of chapters. See also A. BONILLA Y SAN MARTIN'S BALADRO DEL SABIO MERLIN. (2) MERLIN Y DEMANDA DEL SANTO GRIAL, Seville, 1500. But of this text we have seen that no copy is extant. It is mentioned by LEANDRO FERNANDEZ DE MORATIN in his ORIGINES DEL TEATRO ESPAÑOL, Madrid, 1830. I suggest, however, that it may have been reprinted in (3) LA DEMANDA DEL SANTO GRIAL, *con los marvillosos fechos de Lancarote y de Galas su hijo*, Toledo, 1515. This is now in the British Museum, but was once in the collection of Heber, who had heard of no other copy. It is divided into two parts, being respectively the ROMANCE OF MERLIN and a version of the QUEST of Galahad. The first part corresponds to the Burgos EL BALADRO, as we know this by the analysis of its contents, though that of Toledo is much longer and is divided into numbered paragraphs, or short sections, instead of into forty chapters. But the reference to EL BALADRO in the LIBROS DE CABALLERIAS by Pascual de Gayangos, Madrid, 1857, seems to shew that these chapters were subdivided into sections or paragraphs. It remains to say that the first part is in correspondence with the HUTH MERLIN, while the second appears to represent the pseudo-Robert de Borron lost QUESTE attached thereto. It is identical in this case, or at least approximately, with (4) EL HISTORIA DOS CAVALLEIROS DA MESA REDONDA E DA DEMANDA DO SANTO GRIAL, which is the Portuguese QUEST of Galahad, partly printed from a Viennese manuscript by CARL VON REINHARDSTOELLNER in *Handschrift* No. 2594 *der K. K. Hofbibliothek zu Wien*, 1887. The points concerning it are (*a*) that it is attributed to Robert de Borron, following the recurring claim of the French Cycle to which it belongs ; (*b*) that it is the debased pseudo-Borron Quest to which I have referred otherwise, the existence of which was gleaned from various sources by GASTON PARIS : HUTH MERLIN, Vol. I, pp. l–lxii, *s.v.* LA QUETE DU SAINT GRAAL, in the fifth section. (*c*) To complete this enumeration, it is desirable to cite LA ESTORIA DEL NOBLE VESPASIANO, Toledo, *circa* 1486 or 1490, containing the Emperor's healing by the Veronica Face-Cloth, thus connecting with the Metrical Romance of Robert de Borron. It was edited at Lisbon in 1905 by F. M. Esteves Pereira. There is a Spanish version referred to 1499 under the same title. A LIBRO DE JOSEP ABARAMATIA, allocated tentatively to 1469 or 1470, was printed at Chicago in 1924 by K. PIETSCH in his SPANISH GRAIL FRAGMENTS. The collection included part of the GRAND SAINT GRAAL and the Spanish DEMANDA.

VIII. THE DUTCH LANCELOT. Seeing that the extant text of this compilation exceeds 90,000 lines, it will be understood that the task of editing and carrying it through the press was not likely to be attempted on more than a single occasion, the heroic scholar being DR. W. J. A. JONCKBLOET. He published the ROMAN VAN LANCELOT in two mammoth quarto volumes at Gravenhage, respectively in 1846 and 1849, with elaborate introductions. The MORIEN section was edited subsequently by M. T. WINKEL, and was translated into English by MISS JESSIE L. WESTON, forming No. IV of " Arthurian Romances unrepresented in Malory's MORTE DARTHUR ". The few to whom it is accessible assign a place of some importance to the vast poem, as a reflection in part of materials which are not otherwise extant. It may be added that there was also a German LANZELET, by ULRICH VON ZATZIKHOFEN, whose work has been ascribed to the end of the twelfth or the beginning of the thirteenth century : in this case he preceded WOLFRAM, which view more recent criticism is, however, inclined to question.

E. THE GERMAN CYCLE. As the French Legends of the Holy Grail are reducible in the last resource to the QUEST of Galahad, so are those of Germany eclipsed by the great epic with which we are now so well acquainted and which follows here in my list.

I. The PARZIVAL of Wolfram von Eschenbach was written some time within the period which intervened between 1200 and 1215, the poet dying, as it is believed, about 1220, while towards the close of his life he was occupied with another long composition, this time on the Life of William of

Orange. I conceive that in respect of the German Cycle there will be no occasion to enumerate early printed editions, so I will name only (1) the critical text based on various manuscripts, by KARL LACHMANN, the latest issue of which appeared at Berlin in 1891 ; (2) the text edited by KARL BARTSCH and published in *Deutsche Classiker des Mittelalters*, vols. IX–XI, 1875–1879 ; (3) the metrical rendering in modern German, published from 1839 to 1841 by A. SCHULZ, under the name of SAN MARTE ; (4) the competitive version of SIMROCK, 1842 ; (5) that of DR. BOTTICHER in rhymeless measures ; (6) the translation into English of PARZIVAL : A KNIGHTLY EPIC, by MISS JESSIE L. WESTON, 2 vols., London, 1894, being unquestionably in the worst verse of the nineteenth century and a recurring proclamation of " the banns of marriage between M and N ". (7) Finally, MR. E. MARTIN published an independent version in 1903.

II. The poem of HEINRICH VON DEM TÜRLIN, entitled DIU CRÔNE. Of this text there was a serviceable edition published at Stuttgart in 1852, under the editorship of G. H. F. SCHOLL, who prefixed a full introduction. The work forms the twenty-seventh volume of the *Bibliothek des Litterarischen Vereins*. It was edited again in 1879.

III. The TITUREL of Albrecht, i.e. DER JÜNGERE TITUREL, was edited in 1842 for the *Bibliothek der Deutschen National Litteratur* by K. A. Hahn. It was edited also by E. Droyran in 1872 under the title *Der Tempel des Heiligen Graal*. Notwithstanding these issues scholarship of a slightly later period lamented the absence of a critical text, a deficiency which has not been supplied even to this day.

F. WELSH AND ENGLISH LEGENDS, being texts that were once regarded as anterior to those of the Grail but are now accepted as derivations from Chrétien.

I. PEREDUR THE SON OF EVRAWC, first printed, with the Welsh original, a translation and notes in the MABINOGION, by Lady Charlotte E. Guest, 3 vols., 1849. A second edition, without the Welsh text and with abridged notes, appeared in 1877. The collection has since been reissued in many forms. The edition of Mr. Alfred Nutt, published in 1902 with notes by the editor, has still an appeal to scholars. The MABINOGION have been translated also into French and German.

II. THE ROMANCE OF SYR PERCYVELLE OF GALLES, included in THE THORNTON ROMANCES, edited by J. O. Halliwell, and published by the Camden Society in 1844. The manuscript is preserved in the Library of Lincoln Cathedral, and Robert Thornton, its scribe, is thought to have compiled the collection about 1440. The year mentioned is speculative in two ways : (1) because the Thornton volume can only be dated approximately, and (2) because the poem with which we are concerned has been regarded as a transcript from an unknown original. By the evidence of language and style it is thought, alternately, to be about the period of its transcription. SYR PERCYVELLE is a rhymed poem of 2228 lines.

While this work was passing through the press, Professor W. A. Nitze, in connection with Professor T. A. Jenkins, has issued his long-promised text of the PERLESVAUS, not, however, under the auspices of the Carnegie Trust but under those of the University of Chicago Press. It is entitled LE HAUT LIVRE DU GRAAL : PERLESVAUS. A second volume of criticism and commentary is promised at a future date.

PART II

SOME CRITICAL WORKS

It should be understood that the editors of the various texts mentioned in Part I have prefixed or appended thereto introductory matter, sometimes of a less or more elaborate kind, and that they are therefore, within their measures, to be regarded as critical editions in this sense. To these introductions I do not propose to refer in the present section, nor do I lay any claim either to analyses of contents or exhaustive bibliographical enumeration. The List which follows will be of service for those who would carry their studies further, more especially along textual lines, and it has no higher pretension. As it adopts, within certain limits, a chronological arrangement, it will help to indicate the growth of the criticism, where this has not been provided at length in the preceding text.

JOSEPH GORRES : LOHENGRIN, *ein alt Deutsche Godicht*, etc., 1831.

The introduction is sympathetic and interesting as an early study of the Grail literature. The text is a Vatican MS. It may be mentioned that, according to GORRES, Mont Salvatch or Munsalvaesche stands in Salvatierra, in Arragon, at the entrance into Spain, close to the Valley of Roncesvalles.

LE ROUX DE LINCY : *Analyse critique et littéraire du* ROMAN DE GARIN, etc., 1835 ; and *Essai historique et littéraire sur l'abbaye de* FÉCAMP, 1840.

This author also was a student of the subject, and his later work remains our chief authority for the Fécamp Legend.

PAULIN PARIS : LES MANUSCRITS FRANÇOIS *de la Bibliothèque du Roi*, 7 vols., 1836–48 ; and LES ROMANS DE LA TABLE RONDE, 5 vols., 1868–1877.

In the first work there is contained what I believe to be the earliest account of unprinted Grail texts. The second has modernised versions of (1) THE METRICAL JOSEPH, (2) THE GRAND SAINT GRAAL, (3) THE EARLY PROSE MERLIN, (4) THE VULGATE MERLIN, and (5) THE ROMANCE OF LANCELOT OF THE LAKE. The long introduction is still of interest and indeed of a certain value. Paulin Paris considered that THE METRICAL JOSEPH was founded on a Breton Gospel-Legend and that the original Grail text was a Latin Gradual, views which remain, unfortunately, in the same speculative position that they occupied in 1868.

FRANCISQUE MICHEL and THOMAS WRIGHT : VIE DE MERLIN, *attribuée à* GEOFFROY DE MONMOUTH, 1837.

The elaborate Introduction remains serviceable for Merlin literature and for allusions to the Prophet in other Poems and Romances.

SAN MARTE, i.e., ALBERT SCHULZ : DER MYTHUS VON HEILIGEN GRAAL, 1837, regarded at one time as the best survey of the subject ; the PARZIVAL of WOLFRAM VON ESCHENBACH, in modern German, 1836–1842 ; DIE ARTHUR-SAGE *und die Mährchen des* ROTHEN BUCHS VON HERGEST, 1841 ; an *Essay on the* INFLUENCE OF WELSH TRADITION *upon the Literature of Germany, France and Scandinavia*, 1841, a most interesting and noteworthy study, which I know only in its translated form :

under the auspices of the Chevalier, afterwards Baron Bunsen, it was awarded the Prize of the Abergavenny Cymreigyddion Society, at the Eisteddvod of 1840 ; DIE SAGEN VON MERLIN, 1853 ; with other works and numerous contributions to periodical literature. San Marte considered : (1) that the *Lapis Exilis* of Wolfram was the Stone of the Lord, which was at the beginning of all things with God ; (2) that the passage of the Grail to the Kingdom of Prester John was itself a suggestion of Heresy, Asia being filled with numerous Christian Sects ; (3) that Wolfram depicted a Christian Brotherhood, or Kingdom of the Faithful, apart from Pope and Priesthood ; (4) that the Grail was not a Christian Relic ; and (5) that WOLFRAM's Provençal KYOT may have been GUIOT DE PROVINS, that monk of Clairvaux who wrote the BIBLE GUIOT and had himself visited Jerusalem.

KARL SIMROCK : The PARZIVAL of WOLFRAM VON ESCHENBACH, translated into modern German, 1842, immediately after the completion of SAN MARTE's enterprise and traversing his most important views ; PARZIVAL UND TITUREL, 1857.

This writer maintained, as we have seen : (1) that the original Grail Legend was connected with St. John the Baptist, whose head was enshrined at Constantinople and was used to preserve the life of a dying Emperor in the eleventh century ; (2) that the Templar connections of the PARZIVAL are merely an imitative reflection ; (3) that the *Templeisen* were the Knights of San Salvador de Mont Real—founded in 1120 ; and (4) that the Grail and its veneration suggest the Gnostic body called Christians of St. John.

T. H. DE LA VILLEMARQUÉ : CONTES POPULAIRES DES ANCIENS BRETONS, *précédés d'un essai sur l'origine des épopées chevaleresques de la Table Ronde*, 1842, extended and reissued in 1861 as LES ROMANS DE LA TABLE RONDE *et les contes des anciens Bretons ;* BARZAZ-BREIZ : *Chants populaires de la Bretagne*, 2 vols., 1846, this being the enlarged fourth edition ; MYRDHINN *ou l'Enchanteur Merlin*, 1861, also a new edition. I have not met with the early issues of the last two works.

It has been explained in Book X that the Marquis de la Villemarqué was unfortunately a *fausseur* of his period and became well known and denounced as such. In the last work Merlin is treated as a mythological, historical, legendary and romantic character. It is entertaining but largely fantastic, and at the present day it is obviously difficult to accept anything advanced by this writer without careful verification. He considered that a Pagan Tradition was received from the Bards and, in conjunction with a particular presentation of the Eucharistic Mystery, was passed on to the Romance writers of Northern France. The Grail is Celtic, and the word signifies a Basin.

M. FAURIEL : HISTOIRE DE LA POÉSIE PROVENÇALE, 3 vols., 1845.

This work has been curiously neglected on the part of Grail scholarship but remains to this day of singular interest as a collection and study of materials, while it is not without a certain importance in respect of the views expressed on the literature of the Holy Grail. It has been dealt with sufficiently for my purpose in the text of Book X.

REICHEL : STUDIEN ZU PARZIVAL, 1856.

This work was written in opposition to SAN MARTE, and it denied that the Theology of the twelfth century should be applied to the interpretation of Wolfram's poem.

Louis Moland : Origines littéraires de la France, 1862.

(1) The old history, the high history, was contained in a Latin book ; (2) it embodied that chivalrous ideal which it was sought to realise in the Temple ; (3) this was connected with another ideal, namely, that of communion apart ; (4) the vast cycle of literature which arose is to be regarded as a systematic allegory ; (5) but folk-lore intervened and a strange admixture followed ; (6) it is doubtful whether the texts of the Holy Grail can rank as orthodox ; (7) beneath the veil of allegory there are *tendances suspectes ;* (8) the errors diffused among the Templars may have been reflected into works which represent their principles.

S. Baring-Gould : Curious Myths of the Middle Ages, 1867, and several subsequent editions.

At the period of its publication the essay on the *Sangreal*, contained herein, provided a certain knowledge in a popular form ; but at this day it is without office or appeal. The chief authority is Villemarqué, whose inventive proclivities had not transpired at the time in England.

F. G. Bergmann : The San Greal, 1870. The tract is translated from the French, a point which is not specified, either in the title or elsewhere. So far as I have been able to trace, it is the first account in English of Albrecht's Younger Titurel. The two sources of all Grail Romances are the Quest of Kyot de Provence and a History of the Talisman written in Latin by Walter Map. It happens that both originating texts are matters of pure imagination.

Gustav Oppert : Der Presbyter Johannes *in Sage und Geschichte*, 1870. An interesting summary of the known facts and inventions concerning the mythical Prester John, but not otherwise belonging to Grail literature.

Zarncke : *Zur Geschichte der* Gralsage, 1876.

So far from being Provençal or Celtic, the Grail literature has its source in the Legends concerning Joseph of Arimathæa. The Metrical Romance of Robert de Borron is the earliest text in point of time and Chrétien drew therefrom, but also from the Quest of Galahad, which itself was preceded by some form of the Grand Saint Graal. In the light of later knowledge, this is an impossible hypothesis. As regards Kyot, he was an invention of Wolfram.

A. Birch-Hirschfeld : Die Sage vom Gral, 1877 ; *Über die den provenzalischen* Troubadours *des XII und XIII Jahrunderts*, 1878 ; *Geschichte der* Franzosischen literatur, 1900. The first work created a strong impression and exercised great influence for a considerable period. It maintains that the poem of Robert de Borron preceded the Quest of Chrétien, who drew, moreover, from Borron's Perceval Quest, on which Wauchier also depended. The Perlesvaus drew from the Quest of Galahad and from the Grand Saint Graal. The Grail is not Celtic, while as to the sources of Borron they were the Vindicta Salvatoris and the Gesta Pilati. His Sacred Vessel is one of Sacramental Grace. There is a powerful defence of the Lesser Prose Perceval, and Borron ingarnered Breton Legends therein. The source of Wolfram was Chrétien and he only.

E. MARTIN : The decisive findings of BIRCH-HIRSCHFELD were opposed by this writer in a German *Journal of Archæology*, 1878, and in ZUR GRALSAGE, 1880. He maintained the Celtic origin of the Legend, the possibility of a Latin version, the unlikelihood that the PERCEVAL attributed to BORRON belongs to his trilogy, and that the derivation of WOLFRAM was from a source other than CHRÉTIEN.

C. DOMANIG : PARZIVAL-STUDIEN, in two parts, 1878–1880. A defence of WOLFRAM as an adherent of the Catholic Faith.

G. BOTTICHER : DIE WOLFRAM LITERATUR SEIT LACHMANN, 1880 ; DAS HOHELIED VOM RITTERTUM, *eine Beleuchtung des* PARZIVAL *nach* WOLFRAMS *eigenen Andeutungen*, 1886.

The first is a consideration of the argument for and against the indebtedness of WOLFRAM to no source other than that of CHRÉTIEN and tends to the conclusion that another is probable. The second accuses WOLFRAM of incoherence in Book IX of THE PARZIVAL. It was answered by A. B. FAUST, but the controversy is of no importance at the present day.

J. VAN SANTEN : *Zur Beurtheilung* WOLFRAM VON ESCHENBACH, 1882.

A hostile criticism of the poet's ethical position, founded, however, not on the limitations of the PARZIVAL but on WOLFRAM'S general concessions to the morality of his time.

W. HERTZ : *Sage vom* PARZIVAL *und dem* GRAL, 1882.

The motive of the Legends must be sought from their beginning in the anti-Papal spirit of the British Church, within which it was, for this and other reasons, developed.

PAUL STEINBACH : *Über dem Einfluss des* CRESTIEN DE TROIÉS *auf die altenglische Literatur*, 1885.

An exhaustive study of the debt due to CHRÉTIEN and Breton Tradition by the Thornton SYR PERCYVELLE.

M. GASTER : *Jewish Sources of and Parallels to the Early English Metrical Legends of* KING ARTHUR AND MERLIN, 1887.

The contention is that the commerce between women and demons has its authority in the TALMUD, to which I might add that the legendary orgies of the medieval Black Sabbath have some of their roots therein. It may be questioned whether comparisons of this kind serve any real purpose.

GASTON PARIS : *La Littérature française au moyen-age*, 1888 ; HISTOIRE LITTÉRAIRE DE LA FRANCE, Vol. XXX, 1888.

I cite two instances only from the long record of this excellent and charming scholar. It is impossible in a brief note to speak of his whole achievement. It is to be observed that in his opinion, as independently in my own, the beginning and the end of Gerbert's alternative sequel to the CONTE DEL GRAAL may have suffered alteration.

ALFRED NUTT : *Studies on the* LEGEND OF THE HOLY GRAIL, 1888.

The sub-title adds : " With special Reference to the Hypothesis of its Celtic Origin ". It was this work which paved a way for the criticism of the Grail literature in England, and it may be said otherwise that it marked an epoch in the subject. MR. NUTT did more than anyone in this country to promote an acceptance of the Celtic source in Legend ; but he had the gift of treating all competitive and counter-views with moderation and fairness. He regarded the Metrical Romance of ROBERT DE BORRON as the starting-point of Christian transformation. In later years he shewed a certain disposition to accept the possibility of Templar influence on the development of the literature. MR. NUTT made many contributions to ROMANIA and other periodical publications; and in 1902 he issued a pamphlet on the LEGENDS OF THE HOLY GRAIL which offered a serviceable summary.

SIR JOHN RHYS: STUDIES IN THE ARTHURIAN LEGEND, 1891.

A development at length of Welsh analogies with the Grail Mythos and an authoritative theory at its period of Celtic origin. It is still of considerable interest at this day, though the points of view have changed. The work is tinctured otherwise with the old dream of solar symbology at the root of many of the stories. There is a suggestion that Celtic Vessels and Cauldrons more especially may have had " a spiritual or intellectual significance "—p. 326—but it is added " as for instance in connection with the notion of poetry ".

RICHARD HEINZEL: *Über die französischen* GRALROMANE, 1891.

An elaborate and careful examination. The LONGER PROSE PERCEVAL is said to depend from GERBERT, and the priority of the QUESTE is rejected. The journey of Joseph and his Companions in the Metrical Romance of BORRON is held to be modelled on the wanderings of the Children of Israel in the Wilderness. It is said also—pp. 102 *et seq.*— that there are many resemblances between the Old Testament's Ark of the Covenant and the Grail in that poem. It will be remembered that in the GRAND SAINT GRAAL an Ark is built by Divine Command to contain the Sacred Vessel.

G. M. HARPER: THE LEGEND OF THE HOLY GRAIL, 1893.

Though it can be scarcely regarded as a work of original research, there is here an useful resumption of results obtained by scholarship, shewing also an acquaintance with the chief texts of the literature. The Grail, as typifying the Eucharist, was the beginning, middle and end of all the Cycles. " It is as if a Divine hand had been holding the hands of all the writers of these books ". There is no need to add that the writer's main, if not exclusive interest, was in the Christian aspect of his subject.

MISS JESSIE L. WESTON: There has been mentioned already that English translation of the PARZIVAL, with which this lady began her literary life so far back as 1894, and a word has been said also of the ill-starred metrical form which made the attempt unreadable. Since the period of its publication Miss Weston wrote: (1) THE LEGEND OF GAWAIN, 1897; (2) THE LEGEND OF SIR LANCELOT DU LAC, 1900; (3) THE THREE DAYS' TOURNAMENT, 1902; (4) THE LEGEND OF PERCEVAL, 2 vols., 1906, 1909. The last is of particular importance and prints the MODENA PERCEVAL for the first time in the original French, a signal contribution to the textual side. MISS WESTON translated also certain Arthurian texts not included in the great collection of MALORY, and among them may be mentioned (5) The Episode of MORIEN, 1901, derived from the DUTCH LANCELOT, and (6) SIR GAWAIN AT THE GRAIL CASTLE, 1903, being extracts from the CONTE DEL GRAAL, DIU CRÔNE by HEINRICH and the prose LANCELOT. The others are not exactly of our concern. She contributed in 1913 a monograph entitled (7) THE

QUEST OF THE HOLY GRAIL, to a series edited by MR. G. R. S. MEAD ; and her last production, called (8) FROM RITUAL TO ROMANCE, appeared in 1920 : it has been a subject of considerable reference in Book XI, *sect.* 2.

There is no question that among English writers MISS WESTON was for a period of years, or after the death of ALFRED NUTT, our best-known scholar in respect of the literature of the Holy Grail. In the LEGEND OF SIR LANCELOT she dwelt upon the necessity of collating the numerous manuscripts of this vast Romance with a view to the production of a sound text : whether or not Sommer's subsequent edition in the VULGATE VERSION OF ARTHURIAN TEXTS corresponds to this requirement, it is not likely to be supplanted in English-speaking countries for a very long time to come. In the LEGEND OF PERCEVAL she made a valuable study of the CONTE DEL GRAAL. So far as I am aware, she was the first English writer to point out the reference to Fécamp in WAUCHIER, though the place of that Abbey in the Reliquary-History of the Precious Blood has been known to students since the collection of documents included by LEROUX DE LINCY in his account of that ancient religious foundation.

EDWARD WECHSSLER : *Über die verschiedenen Redaktionen des* ROBERT DE BORON *zugeschriebenen* GRAAL-LANCELOT-CYKLUS, 1895 ; DIE SAGE VOM HEILIGEN GRAL, 1898.

The earlier work accepts the ascription of the Vulgate LANCELOT, QUEST and MORT ARTUS to WALTER MAP. It endeavours to shew— p. 135—that Galahad was the original Grail hero, which, however, later criticism has either set aside or ignored. As regards the Grail in WOLFRAM, *Stein*=Stone ; but this in the poet's understanding meant a Vessel in reality : here is affirmation *in excelsis*. There is finally a study of the *amour courtois* and its career in Provençal poetry : it was coloured deeply by Mysticism. The later volume is a monograph on the pseudo-ROBERT DE BORRON Grail Cycle which has won wide acceptance, e.g. by E. BRUGGER and ELLA VETTERMANN. It is held that a reconstructed LANCELOT formed part of the Cycle, which consisted originally of six divisions or branches. WECHSSLER maintained otherwise (1) that the DIDOT PERCEVAL represents a prose rendering of a poem by BORRON ; (2) that the missing branches concerning Alain, Petrus and Moses mentioned by the poet were produced subsequently, though now no longer extant.

DR. WENDELIN FOERSTER—who projected a complete edition of the works of CHRÉTIEN DE TROYES—published several texts, including (1) EREC UND ENID, 1896 ; (2) CLIGES, 1901 ; (3) YVAIN, 1902.

As regards the CONTE DEL GRAAL, he considered that its confessed prototype, the book belonging to COUNT PHILIP OF FLANDERS, was not a Quest of the Sacred Vessel but a prose account of the Palladium.

W. HERTZ : PARZIVAL VON WOLFRAM VON ESCHENBACH, 1898.

This is a second edition, and I do not know whether it varies from the first, which has not come my way. The first allusion to a Vessel which received and conserved the Blood flowing from the side of Christ on the Cross is found in a Greek work ascribed to GERMANOS, Archbishop of Constantinople, *ob.* 733. The authorship remains in doubt and the text has been referred otherwise to the ninth or tenth century. The

Reliquary is identified by analogy with the Cup of the Eucharist in the course of explaining allegorically the *instrumenta* of the Greek Mass. It is notable also that the Priest and Deacon are held to represent Joseph of Arimathæa and Nicodemus. See MIGNE: PATROLOGIA GRÆCA, Vol. 98, cols. 383 *et seq.*, where the Greek text is accompanied by a Latin version. The work of HERTZ includes a study of the Thornton SYR PERCYVELLE, which is regarded as approaching most nearly of all extant texts to the original Perceval Saga. This hypothesis was adopted and extended by GASTON PARIS. It is to be noted that HERTZ cites a Breton oral story, the written version of which is due to Emile Souvestre under the title of PERONNIK L'IDIOTE. While on the one hand it is connected with the Perceval Myth, it has been suggested on the other (1) that Souvestre manipulated the oral story and (2) that Peronnik is only a variant of another tale of faërie known as the JOURNEY FOR THE WATER OF LIFE. It is impossible to gather up all these alleged derivations from an alleged original source. They have one feature in common, being the absence of the Grail in all : it happens, however, that we are in search of the Grail. HERTZ also translated the PARZIVAL into modern German, and the rendering went through several editions.

DR. SEBASTIAN EVANS : IN QUEST OF THE HOLY GRAIL, 1898.

An amazing dream, which identifies Pope Innocent III with the Rich Fisherman, the Emperor with the King of Castle Mortal, St. Dominic with Perceval, the Interdict of 1208 with the Languishment and Enchantments of Britain, and the Question which should have been asked, but was not, with an omission on the part of St. Dominic to secure the exemption of the Cistercians from certain effects of the Interdict. Lancelot is the elder Simon de Montfort ; Gawain is Fulke of Marseilles ; Alain le Gros is Alanus de Insulis, the Universal Doctor ; Yglais, the mother of Perceval, is Holy Church. The Grail is of course the Eucharist, which was denied to Logres. The speculation is founded on the PERLESVAUS, so that no distraction is caused by the presence of Blanchefleur ; but as all French texts of Quest speak of the removal or internment of the Sacred Vessel, it is a pity that the ingenuity which has woven this wonderful web should have passed over such a point in silence. However, it is obvious that the fact of such removal stultifies the whole thesis, whence it follows that DR. EVANS has not succeeded in enlisting more conviction than, I suppose, did DR. VERCOUTRE ; but he has gifts in literature, gifts of entertainment and gifts of subtlety which are wanting to his French *confrère*.

PAUL HAGEN : DER GRAAL, 1900.

PHILIP OF POITIERS, afterwards Bishop of Durham, was the real author of the PARZIVAL sources. He accompanied Richard Cœur de Lion on his return from Palestine, a journey which followed approximately that of Trevrezent in the story of Wolfram. Philip was attached also and deeply to the House of Anjou, to which Richard I belonged. It is to be feared that this engaging hypothesis is the flimsiest stuff of dream. Hagen also maintains that the Grail was conceived originally as a Stone and derived from the Eastern worship of holy BÆTYLI and other Talismanic Stones, of which the lore is endless.

Dr. A. T. Vercoutre : *Origine et Genèse de la Légende du Saint Graal*, 1901.

This tract claims to offer the solution of a literary problem. The Legend of the Grail is based upon an error of translation. The supposed Vessel, or *Vas*, is the Celtic *Vasso*, and the Romances commemorate in reality the Gaulish Temple of Puy de Dome, mentioned by Gregory of Tours. It was originally Gaulish and dedicated to Lug, but became Roman subsequently, and was then sacred to Mercury. It was a place of Initiation and as such hidden from the world, like the Grail. The Temple was excavated in 1873. This appears to be a frantic hypothesis.

W. A. Nitze : *The Old French Grail Romance*, Perlesvaus, 1902.

Published as a dissertation of John Hopkins University. The Grail in the Perlesvaus probably represents the Chalice of the Mass as regards only the Vessel itself and not its contents. The text occupies in this respect an intermediate position between the Joseph of Robert de Borron—which confuses the " Service " of the Grail with the Sacrifice of the Mass—and the Grand Saint Graal, in which the Grail is placed on an Altar, but the Mass itself is celebrated with a Chalice containing Bread and Wine. The Question concerning the Grail— *cui on en servoit*—was originally the means by which the hero identifies himself, but in the Perlesvaus has become a charm which cures disease. It may be asked by Gawain and Lancelot as well as by Perceval. This is rather an obscure thesis, more especially as the healing of the Grail King is the purpose-in-chief of every Grail Quest. In Modern Philology, Vol. I. pp. 247 *et seq.*, Nitze accepted the Legend of a Latin original of the Grail Myth, but qualified his view in the same periodical, Vol. XVII, pp. 162 *et seq.*, and also in Studies in Philology, Vol. XV, p. 12. I have dealt otherwise with his hypothesis that the Grail Legend sprang from a cultus of the Vegetation Spirit. Nitze attempted further to determine more fully the relation of the Perlesvaus to Chrétien and his continuators. It is agreed by him that we have no certain knowledge as to the original form of Gerbert's poem.

C. Macdonald : *Origin of the* Legend of the Holy Grail, 1903.

This is unfortunately an introduction only to a large projected work ; but the death of the author intervened. There is an interesting account of early Apocryphal and later Traditions concerning Joseph, Nicodemus, Pilate, Veronica, etc. The intention was—at the term of a full inquiry into such documentary sources—to consider whether the Grail Tradition at its core was known under another form before it was adapted to Christian Symbolism, " having been borrowed from a system of which it was a legitimate and undoubted growth and which presented many points in common with the Hagiology and Ritual of both Eastern and Western Churches ".

W. Staerck : Über den Ursprung der Gral-Legende, 1903.

The lore of the Earthly Paradise is a study in itself, and it is one which would open with an examination of Eastern Sources, proceeding thence to the great storehouse of the Talmuds and Sepher Ha Zohar. Irish and Welsh Legends of Lands and Islands of the Blest would offer their Western analogies, but would take us rather to the pictured story of life beyond the grave than to the antenatal Home of Souls. We have seen that, according to the Perlesvaus, the Grail Castle was in immediate proximity to the Earthly Paradise and was encompassed, moreover, by " a right fair and plenteous river " which came therefrom—POTVIN, *Op. cit.*, p. 249 ; EVANS, HIGH HISTORY, Branch XXII, Title 1. We are told indeed that as regards the Castle itself one of its names was Eden—*ib.*, p. 249 ; *ib.*, Title 2. Here is the sole connection, instituted or implied between Paradise and the Grail Mythos ; but STAERCK devotes his volume to establish the Grail and its literature as variants of the Paradise Legend. It is rich as a collection of these, but they offer nothing material respecting the source of the Grail itself.

DOROTHY KEMPE : LEGEND OF THE HOLY GRAIL, 1905.

This pamphlet was written to accompany the HISTORY OF THE HOLY GRAIL of LOVELICH or LONELICH. The Prospectus of the Early English Text Society describes it as a capital summary. It is a reflection of immediately previous English authorities and devoid therefore of any personal value.

L. E. ISELIN : DER MORGENLÄNDISCHE URSPRUNG DER GRALLEGENDE, 1909.

WOLFRAM is followed in regarding the Grail as a Stone, and analogies depending herefrom are found in the Scriptural Sagas of a Syriac BOOK OF THE CAVERN OF TREASURES, which is referred to the fifth or sixth century A.D. We hear that Melchisedec guarded the tomb of Adam through the centuries and was maintained by arch-natural food, like Joseph in the Tower.

G. BAIST : PARZIVAL UND DER GRAL, 1909.

We have seen that the PERLESVAUS connects with the GRAND SAINT GRAAL by its untiring references to Josephus, otherwise Joseph, and that it describes him once as *li premiers prestres qui sacrefiast le cors Notre Seignor*—POTVIN, *Op. cit.*, I, p. 113 ; EVANS, *Op. cit.*, Branch IX, Title 8 : " the first Priest who sacrificed the body of Our Lord ". He was therefore Joseph II, who was consecrated at Sarras by Christ Himself, not only as Priest but Bishop. The pretended authority of the PERLESVAUS is not, however, the GRAND SAINT GRAAL but a book written by the own hand of Joseph II, and it was produced, unaccountably enough, in the Latin tongue. The affirmations are : (1) *Josephus nos dist, par l'escriture qui le nos recorde de quoi cist estoires fu traite de latin en roumanz*, etc.—POTVIN, *ib.*, p. 306 : EVANS, Branch XXXIV, Title 9 : " Joseph telleth us in the scripture he recordeth for us, whereof this history was drawn out of Latin into Romance ", etc. (2) *Li latins de coi cist estoires fust traite an romanz fu pris an l'ille d'Avalon, en une seinte messon de religion*, etc. ; POTVIN, *ib.*, p. 348 ; EVANS, *ib.*, Branch XXXV, Title 28 : " The Latin from which this history was drawn into Romance was taken in the Isle of Avalon, in a holy house of religion ", etc. If words mean anything, it follows that the PERLESVAUS was written down in French of its period by one unknown who had the Latin original before him. It appears, however, by the last words of the story that it had been rendered once previously—*une seule foiz*—in Romance ; but *cil qui avant cestui fust fez est si anciens qu'a grant poine an peust l'an choissir la lestre*—" the book that was made before this is so ancient that only with great pains may one make out the letter "—assuredly one too many for the encouragement of a belief in either, more especially when the alleged original author must be placed among the most mythical characters of all the Grail Cycles. BAIST, however, believes in the Latin book and also that it was written *circa* 1191, or about the time that the bodies of Arthur and Guinevere were said to have been discovered at that Sanctuary of Great Inventions. The hypothesis is based on suppositions, not on evidence, and all that can be said of the PERLESVAUS claim is that it betrays itself by selecting such an author as the first Bishop of Christendom, according to the GRAND SAINT GRAAL. For the rest, PROF. BAIST holds (1) that CHRÉTIEN's claim on a book behind him is matter of fact ; (2) that it was actually given him by COUNT PHILIP OF ALSACE ; (3) that it was devoid of wonder elements ; and (4) that the Grail Procession beheld by Perceval had no other object in view than to shew that, proverbs notwithstanding, silence is not invariably golden. It remained for Germany of 1909 to represent the first and greatest poet of the CONTE as producing some ten thousand lines and proposing to go further for the illustration of a complete futility. There is no need to say that the speculation seems to have been still-born.

ROSE J. PEEBLES : THE LEGEND OF LONGINUS, 1911.
Published as Monograph Series IX of Bryn Mawr College. According to one version, the Grail received the Blood which flowed from the side of Christ when He was pierced by the Lance of Longinus and hence, as Miss Peebles tells us, it was natural that CHRÉTIEN should include it in his Grail Procession. It happens, however, that there is no evidence before us as to how the poet regarded his Radiant Vessel : above all there is nothing to shew that it was a Relic of the Passion for him. The monograph has many points of interest ; and in respect of the Grail being borne by a Maiden Miss Peebles shews that women were permitted in the East to carry the Eucharist, a custom which passed on to Brittany and Ireland (p. 209). It is maintained also that similarities, real and alleged, between Grail Rites and Agrarian Cults are without prejudice to the presence *ab origine* of Christian elements in the former. The Church at its beginning was encompassed by non-Christian Mysteries and its Rites reflected these.

PHILIP STEFAN BARTO : TANNHÄUSER AND THE MOUNTAIN OF VENUS, 1916.
PROFESSOR BARTO's sub-title describes his work as " a Study in the Legend of the Germanic Paradise ". It has been a subject of continual reference in Book VII, sect. 5, and it remains only to bear witness in the present place to its value and interest.

LISETTE ANDREWS FISHER : THE MYSTIC VISION IN THE GRAIL LEGEND *and in the Divine Comedy*, 1917.
Published at New York as one of the Columbia Studies in English and Comparative Literature. The chief points of these two suggestive monographs have been subjects of previous reference in Book X and Appendix I. The Celtic " vessel of increase and plenty " became the symbol of Transubstantiation—meaning presumably that it was a folklore prototype (p. 55). The Celtic origin is here assumed tacitly.

ALBERT PAUPHILET : *Études sur la* QUESTE DEL SAINT GRAAL *attribuée à* GAUTIER MAP, 1921. In this case also M. Pauphilet's work has been studied in the Critical Apparatus of Book XII. In contributions to ROMANIA he regards the QUESTE as " a forest of allegories " (*Op. cit.*, XXXVI, p. 605), and maintains that this text and the ESTOIRE, or GRAND SAINT GRAAL, are by different authors, *pace* MISS WESTON and others, who held the contrary view. Quite independently of official authorities, it would seem difficult for a discerning reader to suppose that they were of one source.

WOLFGANG GOLTHER : PARZIVAL UND DER GRAL, 1925.

The KYOT DE PROVENCE fable is rejected definitely in this work, and the fact is notable as the considered opinion of a recent German criticism. The words are : *Wolfram und Kyot sind eben eins*, p. 139. For the problematical *lapis exili, lapis exilli* and so forth of WOLFRAM, GOLTHER suggests *lapis elixis*, p. 207. There is no question that the old emendation : *lapis exilis,* demands consideration and should at least appeal to those who have a lingering notion that the German Grail Stone connects with the Stone of Alchemy. *Lapis exilis* is the description applied thereto by a great Master of the subject, Arnold of Villanova, on the hypothesis that it is small in compass, though great in transmuting power and, I believe, heavy in weight. It has been said also that the Grail could be carried with ease by a Saintly Maid, though no sinner could lift it.

JAMES DOUGLAS BRUCE : THE EVOLUTION OF ARTHURIAN ROMANCE, *from the Beginnings down to the Year* 1300, 2 vols., 1923. Printed and published at Göttingen, the John Hopkins Press of Baltimore acting as distributors in America.

DR. BRUCE was Professor of English Language and Literature in the University of Tennessee, and he did not live to correct the proofs of his second volume. It is explained in the Preface that the work is a development of Six Lectures on Arthurian Romance delivered to " Graduate students of the Modern Language Departments of the John Hopkins University in December, 1912," and " repeated in the Summer School of the University of Pennsylvania in 1915." Having been the subject of frequent citation in my text on points of fact and points of critical opinion, it must be enough in the present place to say that the great undertaking of more than one thousand pages in large octavo is methodised, like its Bibliography, in a rough and far from satisfactory manner as follows : (1) Studies on Early Traditions concerning Arthur ; on the origin of Arthurian Lays and Romances ; on Chrétien and his Successors ; and on the Merlin, Tristram and Lancelot Cycles. (2) Studies on the Holy Grail, with special reference to the Christian, Celtic, Ritual and other theories of its origin. (3) The beginnings of the Prose Romances and studies of the several Cycles into which they fall, together with a section on late inventions, like the memorable PALA-MÈDE, the compilation of RUSTICIANO DA PISA and the PROPHECIES of Merlin. (4) A sheaf of Discussions, mostly shrewd and notable, among which may be mentioned (*a*) the MABINOGION Controversy ; (*b*) the relation of ROBERT DE BORRON to the DIDOT-MODENA PERCEVAL ; and (*c*) the Origin of the VULGATE CYCLE. (5) Analyses of Portuguese, Spanish, Italian, German and Dutch versions of Arthurian Romances. As ALBRECHT'S DER JÜNGERE TITUREL is cited as belonging probably to the third quarter of the thirteenth century, 1250–1275, it is incredible that it should be dismissed in a few lines, with no word of description. By the hypothesis of his title, Dr. Bruce includes works antedating and down to the year 1300.

ARTHUR MACHEN : THE SECRET OF THE SANGRAAL, forming part of a volume entitled THE SHINING PYRAMID, 1925, pp. 70-126.

This enchanting essay by my familiar friend of more than forty years, has been quoted in Book IX, sect. 3. The point of view may be summarised as follows in the author's own words, without pretending that justice is done to the theme. (1) " The stimulation of fertility, animal or vegetable, has nothing in the world to do with the Graal Romances of the twelfth and thirteenth centuries " (p. 75). (2) " It is undoubtedly futile to make the story of the Sangraal a purely pagan Legend into which Christian Symbolism intruded at a late period . . . The Sangraal is essentially and chiefly a high, mystic, sacramental and Christian Legend " (p. 95). (3) " The general position that the ' Graal Church ' symbolises the Celtic Church is, I think, probable in a very high degree " (p. 122).

WILLIAM J. ENTWISTLE : *The* ARTHURIAN LEGEND *in the Literature of the Spanish Peninsula*, 1925.

An excellent and informed account of Spanish, Catalan and Portuguese Arthurian Romances to which—and to DR. J. D. BRUCE—I am indebted largely for my brief study in Book VI, sect. 7. Among the more popular historians of Spanish literature, it was customary to pass over the texts of Romantic Chivalry with the citation of a few typical examples, such as AMADIS OF GAUL, PALMERIN OF ENGLAND and DON BELIANIS OF GREECE, representing the native literature. Of Arthurian translations in Spanish they knew nothing. The same observation, with more excuse, applied also to Portugal. An excellent case in point will be found in the HISTORY OF SPANISH AND PORTUGUESE LITERATURE, by FREDERICK BOUTERWEK. It was translated from the German by THOMASINA ROSS and published at London in 2 vols., *anno* 1823. MR. ENTWISTLE has done good service in putting an end to this.

EDMUND G. GARDNER : THE ARTHURIAN LEGEND IN ITALIAN LITERATURE, 1930.

This is the sole study of the subject which counts as such, at least in the English language ; and for many years to come, if not indeed permanently, it will be regarded as our plenary source of information. There is a graceful acknowledgment of PROF. GARDNER'S debt to Italian scholars who have preceded him ; but they are practically unknown to many or most here. It is obvious that I owe nearly everything to his work in respect of materials for my summarised references, in Book VI, sect. 7, to the vestiges, such as they are, of the Holy Grail in Italy. But I have given no idea of the extent and excellence of PROF. GARDNER'S comprehensive study. I have been concerned throughout, however, with Arthurian matter and the *matière de Bretagne* only in so far as they connect with the Holy Grail or shed some light thereon.

PART III

PHASES OF INTERPRETATION

THE few works which will be included in this section lie outside the ordinary range of scholarship, and for this reason—whatever their merits or defects—

I have placed them under a sub-title which is designed to mark their particular distinction of motive.

I. EUGÈNE AROUX : (1) DANTE, *Hérétique, Révolutionnaire, et Socialiste : Révélations d'un Catholique sur le Moyen Age*, 1854 ; (2) LA COMÉDIE DE DANTE, *Traduite en vers selon la lettre et commentée selon l'esprit . . .*, 2 vols., 1856 ; (3) LES MYSTÈRES DE LA CHEVALERIE *et de l'Amour Platonique au Moyen Age*, 1858.

There are others, but these will suffice, and I have dealt with the author's standpoint adequately in the text of the present work. As instances of criticism moving under heavy spells of sorcery, as phenomena of reverie in research, I know few things so profoundly entertaining. The section entitled LA MASSÉNIE DU SAINT GRAAL in the third work deserves and would receive a crown in any Academy of Fantasy.

II. F. NAEF : OPINIONS RELIGIEUSES DES TEMPLIERS, 1890.

The Grail is the symbol of Mystical Wisdom and of the Communion between God and man. It is affirmed that the Templars possessed a Secret Doctrine which did not perish with them, if they indeed perished : it passed afterwards through Masonry and is still embedded therein. The position of the Johannine Sect is considered in the same connection. On our own part, we have appreciated already and have set aside these interesting views.

III. EMILE BURNOUF : LE VASE SACRÉ *et ce qu'il contient*, 1896.

The Legend of the Holy Grail contains certain essential elements belonging to that universal cultus which prevailed among the Aryan peoples, and these elements are identical with those of India, Persia and Greece. The Romances are not important for the Religious History of the Sacred Vessel : for that in its Christian aspects we must have recourse to the Liturgies and Ceremonies of the Catholic Church. We have reached a diametrically opposed conclusion. The thesis proceeds to affirm that the Grail Legend goes back through Christian Times and thence through the great Faiths of the East, even to the Vedic Hymns, wherein its explanation is found—otherwise, in that Vase which contains *Agni* under the appearance of *Soma*. I have dealt otherwise with the value of these and other kindred imaginings.

IV. ISABEL COOPER-OAKLEY : *Traces of a* HIDDEN TRADITION *in Masonry and Mediæval Mysticism*, 1900.

MRS. COOPER-OAKLEY wrote other volumes and articles in periodical literature dealing with the same subject and its connections. Her chief authorities are GABRIELE ROSSETTI and EUGÈNE AROUX. This is more especially in respect of her views on Masonic subjects, but unfortunately neither of these writers was familiar therewith at first hand, seeing that they were not Masons. As regards the literature of the Holy Grail, a considerable acquaintance is shewn with the German Cycle, though the writer prefers to depend on her somewhat doubtful precursors rather than on her own impressions. In this way she reflects, for example, the opinions of Burnouf as expressed in LE VASE SACRÉ. She has written some interesting papers, but they do not carry us further than the non-evidential preoccupations of those whom she cites. She is right on the fact that—authentic or not—there is assuredly a Tradition in Emblematic Freemasonry and a Tradition of another order in the literature of the Holy Grail ; but on the nature of both she is of necessity far from the goal because those are far whom she follows.

V. A. L. CLEATHER and BASIL CRUMP : PARSIFAL, LOHENGRIN AND THE LEGEND OF THE HOLY GRAIL, 1904.

We have here a summary of Wagner's two Operatic Dramas from the standpoint of Wagner himself ; or, as the sub-title says, " described and interpreted " in accordance with his own writings. The Grail in Wagner is, however, like the Arthurian Chronicles in Tennyson, a high and uplifting ceremonial, but not more faithful to the matter of the German Cycle than is the English poet to Malory whom he chiefly followed. In their account of the Sacramental Legend, apart from Wagner, Miss Cleather and her collaborator have been guided in part by anterior critics of the literature, like NUTT and SIMROCK, whose views they have combined with those of MRS. COOPER-OAKLEY and her sources. It is said that, according to Tradition, the abode of the Holy Grail is on a lofty mountain of India—being presumably a reference to the realm of Prester John. It came also originally from the East, probably from the Himalayas, a reflection of modern Theosophy, which is suggested throughout the pages. The Grail connects, moreover, with Johannine Tradition and the Templar Chivalry.

VI. LOTUS PERALTE : L'ESOTÉRISME DE PARSIFAL, 1914.

A pseudonymous translation of Wagner's Opera with a long introduction on its alleged meaning, which is read also into the Celtic root-matter. It is heavy fantasia, so far as Grail literature is concerned, and the writer might never have heard of WOLFRAM. Korridwen= Ceridwen is called a White Fay who purchases and desires the Lucid Dwarf Kerik-Gwon, Watcher of the Great Cauldron and its stew containing the six herbs of human sciences. There is a reference to an old Celtic collection called Myvyrian—presumably the MYVYRIAN ARCHÆOLOGY—which says that the wicked cannot touch the Per= Basin=Ceridwen's Cauldron, sans qu'il éclate. The book represents French reverie at its poorest.

VII. INTERMEDIARIUS : CHRISTLICHE, THEOLOGIE, COSMOSOFIE NACH DEM ZEICHEN DES HEILIGEN GRAAL, Stuttgart, 1914.

The Preface explains that the work appears under the nom de plume because the author regards himself solely as a trustee for the spiritual teaching vouchsafed to himself and by him handed on in its pages to mankind. The source of the teaching does not emerge in the thesis, so it must be left an open question whether we are confronted by a particular German example of automatic script or by a personal revelation of another and undetermined sort. There is neither need nor opportunity to sketch the theosophical reveries on the Divine Triad, the nine-fold Hierarchy, the Fall of Angels and of Man, the Realm of Nature, the Coming of Christ, the Mystery of Redemption and the work of the Church on earth. As regards the Holy Grail, it seems to be brought arbitrarily into the scheme of things on the gratuitously alleged ground that Joseph of Arimathæa was " a student of the Old Law " as well as a follower of the New, and for this reason became closely connected with " a new centre of the Holy Spirit on earth." Moreover, Grail literature is divided into branches which prove conclusively that the author does not know the texts. It is said, for example, that Perceval became King of the Grail, and that among the other seekers Galahad alone attained, ignoring Gawain in DIU CRÔNE and Bors in the great QUESTE. For the rest, the Sacred Reliquary, containing the Heart's Blood of Christ, passed ultimately into the hiddenness because the world proved unworthy, yet "those who can fulfil the conditions" will find the way thereto. The revelation may be left at this point.

VIII. VICTOR EMILE MICHELET: LE SECRET DE LA CHEVALERIE, 1928.

There are mistakes and misreferences everywhere, a few of which will be noted among other citations. Aroux is the obvious inspiration, as if at long last his theses were to have a second birth in France; in this case, the present experiment proves a miscarriage. M. Michelet maintains resolutely that there is a secret at the heart of Chivalry, but is compelled to confess at the end that he has failed to find it: it has been guarded too well. Unfortunately, he has failed further to furnish even presumptive evidence for its existence in a state of hiddenness. The Templars had also a secret but we are left to determine whether it was peculiar to themselves or was that which underlay the whole chivalrous scheme. For the rest, an opportunity is offered us to contemplate the fact that Louis Moland, a contemporary of Paulin Paris, suspected an esoteric side of Knightly Romance. He seems to have been content, however, with registering the bare impression. M. Michelet is content also on his own part to make us the beneficiaries of many statements which remain unprofitable in our hands for want of authorities. Evidence is required by example for the dogmatic affirmation (1) that the Orders of Chivalry planned to build some earthly city on the pattern of the Heavenly City (p. 44); (2) that the Templar Grand Masters "held the place of God" in respect of the body-general of the Knighthood (p. 45); (3) that Innocent III boasted of being affiliated to the Temple (ib.); (4) that Philip the Fair and his nephew sought in vain to join the Templars—à devenir confrères du Temple (p. 46); (5) that the Chivalry in question initiated Saracen Knights (p. 60); and (6) that the Secretary of one Grand Master was a Mussulman (ib.). Having regard to the slender dimensions of the work, considerable space is devoted to the Holy Grail, but the account is a tissue of errors. (1) The original texts do not say that the Table of Joseph of Arimathæa was square (p. 24), and much less that it had the power of elongation "in proportion to the number of worthy persons who were granted a seat thereat." (2) Joseph did not erect a Château Aventureux to lodge the Grail. (3) Galahad is represented nowhere as placing the Holy Grail on the Arthurian Round Table. (4) Galahad, Gawain and Perceval were not riding together on a bank of a river or lake when they found a Sword in a rock which the first alone could draw therefrom. Parisian occultists and their connections are proverbially and phenomenally inexact, and M. Michelet appears to deserve the palm among them.

INDEX

Library of the Mystic Arts
A LIBRARY OF ANCIENT AND MODERN CLASSICS

1. THE STUDY AND PRACTICE OF YOGA by Harvey Day. A practical manual on Yoga postures and exercises which are within the capabilities of any individual. It shows how this ancient science helps to induce clear thinking, control weight and aid in preserving a youthful appearance and physique. Illustrated.
$3.75

2. YOGA—The Method of Re-Integration by Alain Danielou. Yoga as defined in the Hindu Scriptures with an appendix of Sanskrit text. Processes by which the subconscious may be controlled are treated at length. These processes can lead to unusual attainments both spiritually and intellectually. Illustrated. $3.75

3. THE ORIGINS OF CHRISTIANITY by F. C. Coneybeare. This absorbing volume takes a bold course away from the traditional and conventional story of Jesus; Paul's decisive role is made clear. $6.00

4. EGYPTIAN MAGIC by Sir Wallis Budge. The Egyptian priest made darkness as well as light his realm; his power was exercised by names, spells, enchantments, amulets, pictures and ceremonies accompanied by potent words to be spoken in a certain manner. Illustrated. $5.00

5. MAGIC AND MYSTERY IN TIBET by Alexandra David-Neel. "Precisely the person to explore Tibet . . . absolutely fearless. Her accounts of Tibetan religious ceremonies and beliefs are the fullest and best we have."—The New Yorker. Illustrated. $6.00

6. THE PARTING OF THE WAY—Lao Tzu and the Taoist Movement by Holmes Welch. There is entertaining exposition on the search for the Isles of the Blest; Chinese Yoga; alchemy; the Dionysian Rites for the Salvation of Souls; sexual orgies; church states defended by Taoist armies; cult of drunkenness. $5.00

7. A PICTORIAL ANTHOLOGY OF WITCH-CRAFT, MAGIC AND ALCHEMY by Emile Grillot de Givry. "A unique volume," says Pastoral Psychology magazine, "written with a rare appreciation of the psychological and emotional needs which account for mankind's preoccupation with demons, witches, magicians. An unusual source book." 376 illustrations, 7¼" x 10". $10.00

8. DOWN THERE by Joris-Karl Huysmans. DOWN THERE will interest, repel, disgust, fascinate or horrify. This classic of satanism is a horrifying account of Durtal, a hero whose exploits are based on two of the super-villains of all time. One, the Abbé Boullan who founded with his nun-mistress the Society for the Reparation of Souls, which had as its chief activity the obscene and profane medication of ailing nuns.

Later as an exorcist his patients were again distressed nuns, his treatment supernatural sexual intercourse with Christ and others, including himself. Huysmans interweaves Boullan's career with that of Marshal Gilles de Rais, arch-satanist companion, mentor and protector of Jeanne d'Arc.

Huysmans himself paid an awful price both physically and mentally for his investigations into occultism and satanism. Though a devout Catholic, he protected himself with bizarre rites against "fluidic fisticuffs" and other eerie sensations which troubled him.

Presented as a novel, this book can also serve as a reference on satanism. Huysmans made excellent use of the documents on sorcery, alchemy and satanism as well as of conversations he had had with people intimately acquainted with occult practices. $5.00

9. THE SACRED FIRE—The Story of Sex in Religion by B. Z. Goldberg. The sexual symbolism underlying expressions of faith from prehistoric farmers to present-day evangelists is examined in the light of wide anthropological, historical and sociological evidence. Illustrated. $7.50

10. JESUS by Charles Guignebert, late Professor in the History of Christianity at the Sorbonne. He impartially sums up the results of a century and a half of Biblical criticism and the result has the effect of a blockbuster. $7.50

11. POLTERGEISTS by Sir Sacheverell Sitwell. The noisy and prankish ghosts you read about in newspapers are Mr. Sitwell's subject. He leaves little doubt that poltergeists exist and that no purely natural explanation can account for them. $5.75

12. WORTH LIVING FOR by Eva Bartok. This is the autobiography of the famous Hungarian film star. It is an eloquent testimonial to the spiritual fulfillment to be found in Subud. The climax of the book is Eva Bartok's meetings with Pak Subuh, the Indonesian founder of Subud. $3.50

13. CONCERNING SUBUD, The Story Of A New Spiritual Force by John G. Bennett. Since 1920 Bennett has been known as a writer and speaker for Gurdjieff's system. Here is the story of Pak Subuh's spiritual ministry since 1923. $3.95

14. THE JEWISH WORLD IN THE TIME OF JESUS by Charles Guignebert. The Old Testament closes hundreds of years before Jesus, the New is written long after his death. What, then, do most of us know about his Jewish world? Nothing! Now here is that world—its Essenes, gnostics, magicians, angels and demons, hermetic books and Messiahs. $6.00

15. THE TRAINING OF THE ZEN BUDDHIST MONK by Daisetz Teitaro Suzuki. The clearest introduction to Zen that one could hope for, by the dean of the interpreters to the Western world. 27 illustrations. $5.00

16. THE SELECTED WRITINGS OF THE MARQUIS DE SADE. Now available, the famed controversial works only researchers could see on the restricted shelves. Selected and translated with an introduction by Leonard de Saint-Yves. $4.95

17. AN ENCYCLOPAEDIA OF OCCULTISM by Lewis Spence. A Compendium of Information on the Occult Sciences, Occult Personalities, Psychic Science, Demonology, Magic, Spiritism, Mysticism and Metaphysics. More than 2500 entries and articles. 488 double-column pages size 8 x 10″. Alphabetically arranged with an eleven-page Master Index. Deluxe Edition, bound in buckram and elephant-hide and boxed. $15.00

18. THE PICTORIAL KEY TO THE TAROT by Arthur Edward Waite. Being fragments of a secret tradition under the veil of divination. With 78 plates in full color, illustrating the Greater and Lesser Arcana, from designs by Pamela Colman Smith. $7.50

19. SEVENTY-EIGHT TAROT CARDS IN FULL COLOR. Created by Pamela Colman Smith and Arthur Edward Waite. $5.00

21. COSMIC CONSCIOUSNESS by R. M. Bucke, M.D. One of the great classics of mystical experience. written sixty years ago but still ahead of its time. Neither supernatural nor supranormal, cosmic consciousness is the emergence of a new human faculty which is placing the people of the next epoch as far above us as we are above the simple consciousness of animals. $5.95

22. THE HOLY KABBALAH by A. E. Waite with an introduction by Kenneth Rexroth. A study of the secret tradition in Israel as unfolded by Sons of the Doctrine for the benefit and consolation of the Elect dispersed through the lands and ages of The Greater Exile. 672 pages, 6⅛″ x 9¼″. $10.00

23. THE HAUNTED MIND by Nandor Fodor. From his practice as a psychoanalyst and psychic researcher, Dr. Fodor has selected some 20 cases as the most interesting. They include mediumship, levitation, communication after death. $5.00

24. THE BOOK OF THE DEAD—The Hieroglyphic Transcript of the Papyrus of ANI, the Translation into English and An Introduction by E. A. Wallis Budge, Late Keeper of the Egyptian and Assyrian Antiquities in The British Museum. The Book Of The Dead is the great collection of texts which the ancient Egyptian scribes composed for the benefit of the dead—spells and incantations, hymns and litanies, magical formulae and names, words of power and prayers, cut or painted on walls of pyramids and tombs, and painted on coffins and sarcophagi and rolls of papyri. 15 pages of plates. Complete hieroglyphic reproductions with the transcriptions. 736 pages, 6⅛″ x 9¼″. $12.50

25. THE VAMPIRE: His Kith and Kin by Montague Summers, author of THE HISTORY OF WITCHCRAFT and THE GEOGRAPHY OF WITCHCRAFT. The fascination of this theme has deep roots in human history. "Vampire" comes from a Slavonic word and this belief has had a peculiar intensity among the Slavonic peoples. "The fuller knowledge of these horrors reached western Europe in detail during the Eighteenth Century." $6.00

26. FRAGMENTS OF A FAITH FORGOTTEN —The Gnostics: A Contribution to the Study of the Origins of Christianity by G. R. S. Mead. Until recently, almost all we knew about the Gnostics we were told by the Church Fathers who had burned the Gnostic literature. Gnosticism found in G. R. S. Mead a true and disinterested scholar; he made available to the English-speaking world his translations of Gnostic texts which had survived in Coptic in Ethiopia and in Egypt. FRAGMENTS OF A FAITH FORGOTTEN is an anthology of these Gnostic texts together with Mead's explanations. The Introduction by Kenneth Rexroth is correctly called "A Primer of Gnosticism." 704 pages, 6⅛″ x 9¼″. $10.00

27. THE SIDDUR: The Traditional Jewish Prayer Book. An entirely new translation by Dr. David de Sola Pool, Rabbi Emeritus of the Spanish and Portuguese Synagogue of New York City. Translation approved by the Rabbinical Council of America. English and Hebrew on facing pages. A deluxe edition, 7¼ x 10¼ inches, approximately 900 pages, three-piece library binding, sturdy, printed slipcase. $17.50

28. CAGLIOSTRO by W. R. H. Trowbridge. Cagliostro figures as one of the great pioneers in every serious account of hypnotism and telepathy, magic and alchemy, precognition and spiritualism, psychic healing and modern mysticism. Yet the simplest facts about his life and his teachings remain bitterly disputed now, two hundred years after he was born. Savant or scoundrel! Here is the true role of this splendid, tragic figure! $6.50

29. AMULETS AND TALISMANS by E. A. Wallis Budge. The original texts with translations and descriptions of a long series of Egyptian, Sumerian, Assyrian, Hebrew, Christian, Gnostic and Muslim Amulets and Talismans and Magical Figures, with chapters on the Evil Eye, the origin of the Amulet, the Pentagon, the Swastika, the Cross (Pagan and Christian), the properties of Stones, Rings, Divination, Numbers, the Kabbalah, Ancient Astrology. 22 pages of plates. 300 illustrations. 592 pages, 6⅛″ x 9¼″. $10.00

30. SCIENCE AND PSYCHICAL PHENOMENA and APPARITIONS by G. N. M. Tyrrell. These two famous classics of psychical research are now bound together in one volume. They are the best introduction to the subject. $7.50

31. THE BOOK OF CEREMONIAL MAGIC by A. E. Waite. Readers have met the distinguished author before; he wrote THE HOLY KABBALAH and THE PICTORIAL KEY TO THE TAROT. The present book is a complete Grimoire. Part I, the Literature of Ceremonial Magic, provides the key passages from the principal texts of the 14th, 15th and 16th centuries. Part II contains the complete Grimoire, the best source of magical procedure extant. 9 plates and 94 line drawings. 6⅛″ x 9¼″. $10.00

33. OSIRIS: The Egyptian Religion of Resurrection by E. A. Wallis Budge. Frazer's Golden Bough has made us familiar with a god who dies each year that he and his worshippers may live anew. Attis, Adonis,

Osiris are the great examples. Sir Wallis Budge gives us the definitive study of Osiris in depth. Much of it is startling indeed. Egyptian religion in its cruelty, its cannibalism, its bloodthirstiness, its general coloring, is African through and through. Osiris himself is both the father and the slain. It is his son Horus, the living and victorious Savior, who, "when his arm grew strong," triumphs over Osiris' brother and slayer, Set, and Osiris is resurrected as god-man. 896 pages, 6⅛" x 9¼". 14 pages of plates, 212 illustrations, and hundreds of hieroglyphic reproductions and transcriptions. $15.00

34. HUMAN PERSONALITY AND ITS SURVIVAL OF BODILY DEATH by F. W. H. Myers,
Foreword by Aldous Huxley. Myers made two outstanding contributions: (1) His theory of telepathy as one of the basic laws of life; (2) his conception of "subliminal," which today we call the unconscious, as the greater portion of human personality. William James wrote: "Frederic Myers will always be remembered in psychology as the pioneer who staked out a vast tract of mental wilderness and planted the flag of genuine science on it." Gardner Murphy says: "Myers is the great central classic of psychical research." Aldous Huxley finds Myers' account of the unconscious more comprehensive and truer to the data of experience than Freud's.

One reason this great book has been neglected is the arrangement of material in the original two-volume HUMAN PERSONALITY. The majority of the illustrative examples were placed in the appendices at the end of each volume. One not only had to sift through a voluminous amount of material, but also had to turn from text to appendix and back again — sometimes **several** times in order to read a single page of text. This new volume of 416 large pages, with its streamlined design, provides the essence of Myers' thought — simpler to get at — yet with its original underpinning still intact. The reader is saved the trouble of turning from text to appendix because in **this** edition all the case material is incorporated within the text. Except for this editing and re-arranging of the material, the words are still Myers' own; no essential idea of his has been omitted. $10.00

35. THE BROTHERHOOD OF THE ROSY CROSS, by Arthur Edward Waite. The author's
account bears very little resemblance to the claims of the Theosophists and latter-day Rosicrucians. To put it more plainly, our author has taken their skins off in the course of establishing the true story. But all this is only to make way for his reverence and love for the real Rosicrucians. The myths and frauds fall away and there emerges the inspiring true history of Rosicrucianism, its original doctrines, their unfolding and changing, what was and what was not its relationship to Freemasonry, a most notable chapter on the great English Rosicrucian Robert Fludd, and a particularly fascinating chapter on the history of the Rosy Cross in Russia.

To be a Rosicrucian meant peril of life and limb in the intolerant societies of the seventeenth and eighteenth centuries. But is it necessary to continue a Secret Tradition in the nineteenth and twentieth centuries? The author thinks it remains necessary. 29 pages of plates. 704 pages, 6⅛" x 9¼". $10.00

36. COLOR PSYCHOLOGY AND COLOR THERAPY, by Faber Birren. Faber Birren makes his
living by prescribing color. He prescribes it to government, to education, to the armed forces, to architecture, to industry and commerce. His work has been acknowledged and recommended by the Council on Industrial Health of the American Medical Association. Birren's color code for safety has become internationally accepted in countries as remote from each other as England, Japan, Italy, Argentina, Uruguay. This book gives his prescriptions and how they are arrived at. $7.50

37. ANCIENT, MEDIEVAL AND MODERN CHRISTIANITY: The Evolution of a Religion,
by Charles Guignebert. The late Professor of the History of Christianity at the Sorbonne here applies the theory of evolution to Christianity itself. The author believes that every religion is born, develops, adapts and transforms itself, grows old and dies. Ancient Christianity was a purely Eastern religion. It was followed by, in effect, another religion full of doctrines and things which would have been strange and incomprehensible to the Apostles. Still another religion emerges in modern Roman Catholicism. Guignebert warms these scientific truths, which may be unpleasant to professing Christians, by his fervent belief that the honest study of religion is "the mother of tolerance and religious peace." 640 pages, 6⅛" x 9¼". $7.50